Managerial Communication
Eighth Edition

Managerial
Communication
Eighth Edition

Sara Miller McCune founded SAGE Publishing in 1965 to support the dissemination of usable knowledge and educate a global community. SAGE publishes more than 1000 journals and over 600 new books each year, spanning a wide range of subject areas. Our growing selection of library products includes archives, data, case studies and video. SAGE remains majority owned by our founder and after her lifetime will become owned by a charitable trust that secures the company's continued independence.

Los Angeles | London | New Delhi | Singapore | Washington DC | Melbourne

Managerial Communication

Strategies and Applications

Eighth Edition

Jennifer R. Veltsos

Geraldine E. Hynes

Los Angeles | London | New Delhi
Singapore | Washington DC | Melbourne

FOR INFORMATION:

SAGE Publications, Inc.
2455 Teller Road
Thousand Oaks, California 91320
E-mail: order@sagepub.com

SAGE Publications Ltd.
1 Oliver's Yard
55 City Road
London EC1Y 1SP
United Kingdom

SAGE Publications India Pvt. Ltd.
B 1/I 1 Mohan Cooperative Industrial Area
Mathura Road, New Delhi 110 044
India

SAGE Publications Asia-Pacific Pte. Ltd.
18 Cross Street #10-10/11/12
China Square Central
Singapore 048423

Printed in the United States of America

Library of Congress Cataloging-in-Publication Data

Names: Veltsos, Jennifer R., 1973- author. | Hynes, Geraldine E., author.

Title: Managerial communication : strategies and applications / Jennifer R. Veltsos, Geraldine E. Hynes.

Description: Eighth edition. | Thousand Oaks, California : SAGE, [2022] | Includes bibliographical references and index.

Identifiers: LCCN 2020036351 | ISBN 9781544393285 (paperback) | ISBN 9781544393308 (epub) | ISBN 9781544393315 (epub) | ISBN 9781544393292 (pdf)

Subjects: LCSH: Communication in management. | Business communication.

Classification: LCC HD30.3 .V46 2022 | DDC 658.4/5—dc23
LC record available at https://lccn.loc.gov/2020036351

This book is printed on acid-free paper.

Acquisitions Editor: Maggie Stanley
Editorial Assistant: Sam Diaz
Production Editor: Tracy Buyan
Copy Editor: Laureen Gleason
Typesetter: C&M Digitals (P) Ltd.
Indexer: Integra
Cover Designer: Glenn Vogel
Marketing Manager: Jennifer Jones

21 22 23 24 25 10 9 8 7 6 5 4 3 2 1

BRIEF CONTENTS

DETAILED CONTENTS

PART II • COMMUNICATING WITH GROUPS

PART III • WRITING AS A MANAGER

PART V • COMMUNICATING INTERPERSONALLY

PREFACE TO THE EIGHTH EDITION

The roots of this textbook extend back to 1984, when John Wiley and Sons published *Managerial Communication: A Strategic Approach*, by Larry Smeltzer and John Waltman. Their practical, results-oriented examination of managerial communication was groundbreaking at the time. In the preface, they stated the book's objective: "to develop managers who communicate in a creative manner by understanding and strategically applying appropriate concepts." That objective is still valid.

A second edition added Don Leonard as third author in 1991. Gerry Hynes adopted the 1994 edition, authored by Larry Smeltzer and Don Leonard, by then titled *Managerial Communication: Strategies and Applications*. She had been looking for a graduate-level text that presented a balanced approach to workplace communication and that was written for managers and executives.

These strengths drew Gerry to that early edition:

- A strategic approach

- A solid research base

- Comprehensive coverage of contemporary issues

- An even-handed examination of oral and written communication channels

- A focus on managerial rather than entry-level competencies

Gerry came on board as third author with Smeltzer and Leonard for the 2002 edition and obtained sole authorship starting with the 2008 edition. In 2017, she invited Jennifer Veltsos to join her as a second author on the seventh edition. The Hynes-Veltsos team is working remarkably well, and Jennifer has stepped up to the lead author position for the new eighth edition. Our goal continues to be ensuring that the qualities that made the original book unique and successful are still present in this eighth edition. Truth is truth. It does not change with the times. Therefore, our task is to bring timeless communication principles into the contemporary workplace. To meet the needs of today's busy manager/student, we have updated the chapters, describing current business practices, summarizing relevant research, and providing guidelines for strategic managerial communication.

The reality is that an effective contemporary manager must possess a wide range of skills. While being accountable to an executive team and a customer base, a manager must be able to motivate subordinates and cross-functional work groups with diverse backgrounds, interpret complicated rules, foster process improvement, and meet sometimes unclear organizational expectations. Furthermore, today's manager often must use new technology to accomplish these tasks. Because these advanced abilities do not necessarily come from prior work experience, communication education is a vital component in managerial development.

Working together on this textbook is both enjoyable and challenging. The coauthors continue to evaluate the content to reflect the needs and interests of today's business and professional students, to sort out what is important and what is no longer important for them to know and be able to do. After all, effective communication leads to managerial and organizational success. The value of the book's content is not controversial; the key is to keep it fresh.

WHAT'S NEW IN THIS EDITION

Many adopters of the seventh edition of *Managerial Communication: Strategies and Applications* indicated that major strengths are its balanced approach to managerial writing and oral communication, the end-of-chapter cases and exercises that offer opportunities for practice and application of the principles, and the comprehensive instructor supplements. We have retained these strengths in the eighth edition.

Consistent with earlier revisions, we have updated examples and scenarios in every chapter and have added references to relevant, cutting-edge research in managerial communication.

New features include Learning Objectives at the beginning of every chapter and Critical Thinking Questions inserted throughout. In addition, we have connected the content with the unprecedented upheavals in the current business environment that have been triggered by the global COVID-19 pandemic and the resulting economic crisis. Every chapter now ends with real-life cases that demonstrate how contemporary organizations are applying the managerial communication principles presented in the chapter, followed by discussion questions. Students will recognize many companies, people, and events in the news.

A chapter-by-chapter summary of highlights and new content appears next.

CHANGES TO CHAPTERS

Chapter-specific improvements in the eighth edition include the following:

- Chapter 1 ("Communicating in Contemporary Organizations") has an expanded discussion of diversity in the workplace that managers should address using a contingency approach.

- Chapter 2 ("Understanding the Managerial Communication Process") includes a clearer discussion of the strategic communication model, including a new golf ball visual metaphor that more accurately reflects the contextual, situational, and message factors that managers must analyze when communicating at work.

- Chapter 3 ("Communicating With Technology") has been updated to include current applications of social media and collaboration networks as communication media. We continue to emphasize the principles and best practices that apply to both emerging technologies and better-established technologies.

- Chapter 4 ("Managing Meetings and Teams") features a more balanced view of virtual and traditional teams, recognizing that remote work is growing in popularity and by necessity.

- Chapter 5 ("Making Presentations") has an expanded section on virtual speaking and a closer look at the use of facts and opinions as evidence in informative and persuasive presentations.

- Chapter 6 ("Communicating Visually") continues to help managers prepare presentations and visual aids with clear, ethical graphics and design elements.

- Chapter 7 ("Writing in the Workplace") contains updated references and a case study to help readers see how principles of good writing are applied in practice.

- Chapter 8 ("Writing Routine Messages") offers updated guidelines for formatting and designing e-mail, letters, and memos. Strategic uses of internal messages are explored in depth.

- Chapter 9 ("Writing in Special Situations") has been significantly improved to expand our discussion of non-routine messages. In addition to informal and formal reports, we also provide advice on writing a variety of proposals, crisis messages, and apologies.

- Chapter 10 ("Listening") has new sections on listening digitally and listening during a crisis; it also presents strategies for responding to negative messages.

- Chapter 11 ("Communicating Nonverbally") includes a section summarizing new research about interpreting facial expressions. The impact of various workspace designs on communication behavior is also explored.

- Chapter 12 ("Communicating Across Cultures") recognizes the heightened significance of intercultural sensitivity for business success. Strategies are presented for preparing managers to communicate in culturally diverse environments, both abroad and domestically.

- Chapter 13 ("Managing Conflict") adds new emphasis to advice on choosing conflict-resolution approaches and offers guidance on de-escalating destructive conflict.

- Chapter 14 ("Negotiating") offers new guidelines for sustainable negotiation strategies in intercultural contexts. An expanded section on e-negotiations presents advantages and disadvantages of negotiating online, both synchronously and asynchronously.

- Chapter 15 ("Conducting Interviews") presents additional guidelines for employment interviews and performance appraisal interviews. Virtual interviews, which are growing in popularity, are also addressed.

ACKNOWLEDGMENTS

Most important, we wish to acknowledge John Waltman, Larry Smeltzer, and Don Leonard, who pioneered this textbook. They explicated the centrality of communication for managerial success, which we now know is an enormous undertaking. We deeply respect their wisdom and vision.

Many people helped make this edition a reality. Maggie Stanley, our SAGE executive editor, smoothed the way with her perspicacity and dependability. Tracy Buyan, our production editor, was very professional, positive, and constructive as she shepherded this edition through the final crucial stages. Laureen Gleason did a superb job of copyediting the manuscript, strengthening its content, correctness, and clarity. Several reviewers offered valuable insights and suggestions that shaped this edition:

Bill Ackerman, Columbia College

Steven D. Cohen, Johns Hopkins Carey Business School

Laura Dendinger, Wayne State College

Lisa Kleiman, Boise State University

Linda Lopez, Baruch College

Donald Schalk, Alvernia University

Mary Ellen Wells, Alvernia University

—Jennifer R. Veltsos and Geraldine E. Hynes

Thank you, Gerry, for inviting me to work with you on this book. We both know that collaborative writing can be tricky, yet somehow our ideas and voices have meshed perfectly within each chapter. You have been a mentor and friend. Thank you for your grace and generosity.

I am grateful to Johnna S. Horton for her unfailing encouragement and for her unknowing role as a persona for the revision of this book. Whenever I questioned a decision, I would ask, "What would a manager like her need to know?" and the solution would often become clear.

To our mutual surprise, my husband, Christophe, has become a prolific writer. His enthusiasm and passion for communicating ideas with others has become a model of the kind of career I want to have. I thank him and our sons for their patience and support through this unexpected opportunity.

—Jennifer R. Veltsos

A special thanks goes to Dave Fosnough, former Irwin/McGraw-Hill field sales supervisor, who started me down this path in 1993, and to Patricia Quinlin, former SAGE business editor, who turned me in the right direction. I am where I am today because they believed in me.

Thank you, Jennifer, for continuing with me on this journey. The new edition is better than ever with you in the lead. It's an honor to be your collaborator and friend.

I am forever grateful to my husband, Jim, and our family for their unreserved love and support.

Finally, I salute my former students because they understand that improving their managerial communication skills and strategies is a key to success. Their career trajectories validate the contents of this book.

—Geraldine E. Hynes

ABOUT THE AUTHORS

Jennifer R. Veltsos, PhD, is a professor of technical communication at Minnesota State University, Mankato. She has taught undergraduate courses in business communication, technical communication, visual rhetoric and document design, and research methods; at the graduate level, she has taught managerial communication, proposals, and instructional design. From 2017 to 2019, she was the director of the Center for Excellence in Teaching and Learning. She is currently the university's interim associate vice president for undergraduate education.

Geraldine E. Hynes, PhD, is a communication consultant and executive coach for business, government, and nonprofit organizations. Since 2018, she has served as a judge for the annual ClearMark Awards, sponsored by the Center for Plain Language, which recognizes outstanding communication created by North American organizations. Her award-winning research has been published in scholarly journals and books in several countries and languages. She retired from the College of Business Administration at Sam Houston State University in Huntsville, Texas, in 2017, where she taught business and managerial communication at the undergraduate and graduate levels. Gerry is a past president of the Association for Business Communication.

MANAGING IN CONTEMPORARY ORGANIZATIONS

MANAGING IN CONTEMPORARY ORGANIZATIONS

LEARNING OBJECTIVES

By the end of the chapter, you will be able to:

MANA... IN
CONTE...ORARY
OR...ZATIONS

1

COMMUNICATING IN CONTEMPORARY ORGANIZATIONS

LEARNING OBJECTIVES

By the end of this chapter, you will be able to

- Describe the evolution of managerial communication from ancient times to today.

- Define the contingency approach to managerial communication.

- Explain how diversity affects approaches to communication within organizations.

- Discuss the role of effective communication in developing a culture of quality and ethics in the workplace.

As we move deeper into the 21st century, management communication is both challenging and exciting. Organizations are becoming much more complex, and many new forces confront the manager. Greater competitive pressures, shorter product life cycles, increased demands for quality and service, more regulatory constraints, greater concerns for cost containment, heightened awareness of environmental concerns, and renewed emphasis on human rights are just some of the pressures increasing the complexity of the manager's job. But these pressures also make managerial communication exciting. The contemporary manager has a greater opportunity than ever to make a significant difference in the success of the organization and increase the quality of work life for fellow employees. But that requires effective managerial communication skills, which are becoming more complex, making them more difficult to master.

The workplace is much more diverse and complex than it was just a few decades ago, and it requires more sophisticated management communication skills. At the start of the 20th century, heavy manufacturing was the industrial base of Western countries. Products changed little from year to year, and the workforce consisted mainly of white men. But today, products and entire management systems change rapidly, and employees must adapt just as quickly. In addition, work teams are extremely diverse. At Intel, one of the world's largest and highest-valued semiconductor chip makers, it is not uncommon to have a design engineer from Singapore working with a purchasing manager from Ireland and an accountant from California. This means the project manager must have the sophisticated skills required to communicate to a diverse work group in a rapidly changing environment.

Technology helps with this communication challenge, but it also adds new requirements. Advances in telecommunications have created new media for communicating and the ability to work remotely, but best practices are still evolving. We have more opportunities to interact with multiple cultures, which require that we become better cross-cultural communicators. Furthermore, as technical products and services become more complex, we must be able to communicate about more complicated concepts than in the past.

Effective communication is a leading indicator of financial performance. Towers Watson, a global company that provides human capital and management consulting services, conducted research on 651 organizations from a broad range of industries and regions over a 10-year period. They found that companies that communicate effectively are 3.5 times more likely to significantly outperform their industry peers than those that do not communicate effectively. Other key findings include these approaches:

- Managers at the best companies are three times more likely to communicate clearly the behaviors that are expected of employees, instead of being focused on cost.

- Extensive managerial communication improves the likelihood of successful change. Managers at the best companies pay careful attention to their employees, communicate reasons for changes, provide training, and support the employees, instead of using a top-down approach.

- Effective managerial communication increases productivity and financial performance. Managers at the best companies are more than twice as likely to use new social media technologies to facilitate collaboration on work projects.[1]

Communication and its role in the life of an organization will continue to evolve. As a result, we must think about how communication will occur in the future. One way to understand what this will mean for managerial communication behavior is to look at the different stages through which managerial communication has already passed. As you read the following pages and note how managerial communication has changed over time, speculate how it will continue to change during your career. Knowledge of the past will help us prepare for the future.

A BRIEF HISTORY OF MANAGERIAL COMMUNICATION

Managers communicated with employees in markedly different ways in the past than they do today. To best understand these changes, it is helpful to review the eras of management as listed in Table 1-1. We provide an overview of each era, then discuss the management communication strategies and techniques appropriate for that era.

Management Communication in Ancient Times

The earliest known example of managerial communication may be the record keeping procedure developed by Sumerian priests around 5000 BCE.[2] These records, consisting of pictograms scratched or pressed into clay tablets, reflected cross-cultural business transactions, such as payments of beer to workers.[3] Around the same time, Egyptians were developing hieroglyphics, which they wrote on clay, wood, or, most often, papyrus.[4] The Babylonians seem to have adopted cuneiform, the Sumerian form of writing. The Code of Hammurabi, circa 1750 BCE, includes information about wages and terms of contracts.[5] Tablets found in London reveal that the ancient Romans were the first managers, using commercial

TABLE 1-1 ■ Historical Perspective of Managerial Communication		
Era	Characteristics	Communication
Ancient and medieval	Initial efforts to organize commerce	Written records
1900s Scientific management	Clearly defined job duties, time specifications for completing the task, and adherence to rules	One-way communication, heavy reliance on written job instructions and rules
Administrative theory	Emphasis on authority and discipline	Emergence of gangplank theory
1920s Human relations	Importance of relationship between managers and workers	Importance of listening and interpersonal communication skills
1950s Behavioral	Recognition of complexity of organizational behavior and communication	Development of communication theory, beginning to apply theory to organizational practice
1990s Empowerment	Distribution of power to everyone in the organization	Two-way communication; participation of employees
21st century Contingency	Interdependence of jobs, organizations, and people	Application of appropriate communication strategy to the situation

languages to request payments, lend money, and settle legal disputes in the year 57 CE.[6] The first committee may have been organized around 325 BCE, as Alexander the Great organized staff groups.

Venice, Italy, was a major center for merchants and economic exchange during medieval times. Merchants built warehouses and used an inventory system that required periodic reports for the city governing body.[7] These brief examples indicate that since the beginning of commerce, some type of managerial communication has been practiced.

CRITICAL THINKING QUESTIONS

1. Why was written language so important to the development of managerial communication?

2. Other than technology use, what has changed in the way business is conducted? How does studying the evolution of managerial communication help us understand and appreciate contemporary practices?

1900s: Management Efficiency and One-Way Communication

The systematic evolution of managers as communicators began around the turn of the 20th century. The *scientific management* philosophy stressed the scientific study and organization of work. During this era, it was believed that the greatest levels of efficiency could be obtained with extremely precise job instructions and that employees should not second-guess the instructions. This period was characterized by one-way communication at work.

Scientific management was founded by Frederick Taylor, a supervisor at the Philadelphia Midvale Steel Company in the late 1800s. Taylor believed it was possible to document the most efficient and effective procedure for performing a task, which could be written in elaborate job designs and communicated to employees through extensive training. To Taylor, employees were just another element in his formula.[8] Other proponents of scientific management included Frank Gilbreth, who studied motion to make bricklaying more efficient, and Harrington Emerson, who developed 12 principles of efficiency for the railroads. One of his most repeated principles was discipline, which included adherence to rules and strict obedience.[9]

We still see elements of the scientific method today in such businesses as McDonald's, whose founder, Ray Kroc, used scientific management techniques to bring quality, service, cleanliness, and value to the fast-food industry. Every employee has a precise job description, each task is to be completed in a specified period, and there is strict adherence to rules. These procedures allow employees to be trained in a short time and reduce the number of unique conditions to which managers must adapt. Only limited strategic managerial communication is required.[10]

While scientific management was receiving extensive attention in the United States, *administrative theory* was developing in France. Although this approach to management emerged during the same era as scientific management, its focus was quite different. Scientific management was concerned mainly with making processes efficient, but administrative theory focused on broader issues facing all managers.

A key figure in developing this theory was Henri Fayol, who developed 14 principles of management.[11] Two-way communication between the manager and employee is limited; the manager's authority is emphasized. The manager's role is to give orders and maintain discipline; little attention is placed on listening skills. This approach is similar to the military model of the time, in which officers were extremely autocratic—soldiers were not encouraged to provide feedback to them, and the officers seldom listened. It is also comparable to the political system used in totalitarian governments.

Teamwork and participative decision making were not integral to administrative theory. Fayol recognized the traditional organization hierarchy as important in establishing the chain of command. However, he also saw inefficiencies in the system when employees at the same level needed to communicate. Figure 1-1 shows how Employee B would communicate with Employee J according to prevailing thought at the time. The employee would have to send the message up the organization's chain of command to the top; then the message would come down through another chain of command. The implications for inefficiency and ineffectiveness are clear to contemporary managers.

To bypass these problems, Fayol developed what is now famously known as gangplank theory. According to this theory, Employee B would be allowed to communicate directly with Employee J if each had permission from their immediate supervisors to do so and they kept the supervisors apprised of the communication. Figure 1-2 diagrams informal networks and horizontal communication.

FIGURE 1-1   ■   Following the Hierarchy

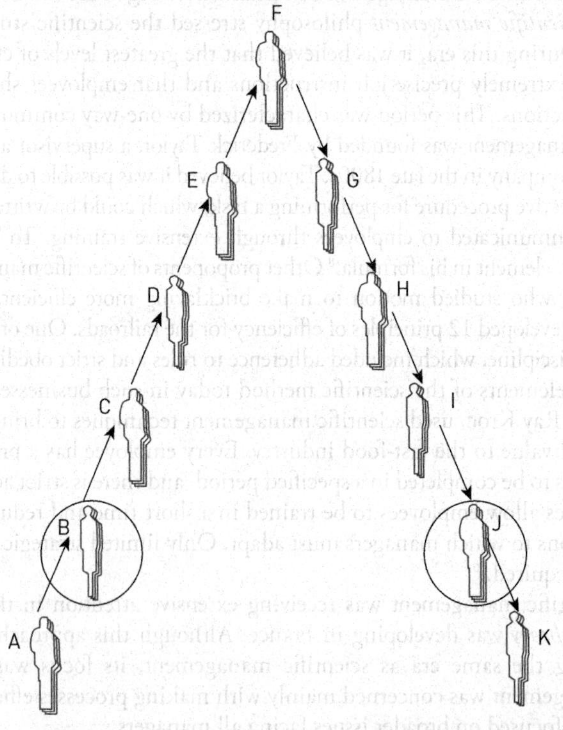

FIGURE 1-2 ■ Gangplank Theory

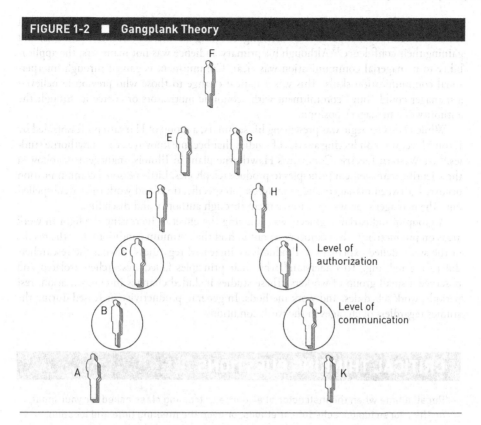

Scientific management and administrative theory attempted to systematize the work environment by establishing a set of elaborate rules and communicating them to employees. Managerial authority was not to be questioned, and deviations from the norm or negotiations were not allowed. Gangplank theory was the first formal recognition of horizontal communication and acknowledged the importance of organizational structure and informal communication networks, which are now taken for granted in most contemporary organizations. As communication practices continued to evolve, autocratic practices began to be replaced by interpersonal communication.

1920s: The Human Relations Approach and the Rise of Interpersonal Communication

While scientific management and administrative theory focused on compliance and efficiency, others were beginning to study the relationships between organizational members. In the human relations approach, managerial communication was the focus of attention, rather than carefully planned procedures. The heart of the human relations approach is that attention to social needs and participation improves morale. In turn, this morale leads to greater compliance with managerial authority.

Dale Carnegie was one of the first writers to link communication skill with managerial effectiveness. In *How to Win Friends and Influence People* (1936), Carnegie argued that gaining compliance from other people depends on interpersonal dynamics of attraction and influence.[12] Influence is possible by listening, showing an interest in others' concerns, and gaining their confidence.[13] Although his primary audience was not managers, the applicability to managerial communication was clear. Commitment is gained through interpersonal communication skills. This was a radical change to those who previously believed a manager could "buy" commitment with economic motivators or coerce it through the authority of a manager's position.

While Dale Carnegie was presenting his seminars, a group of Harvard professors, led by Elton Mayo, was conducting a series of studies that became known as the Hawthorne studies.[14] At Western Electric Company's Hawthorne plant in Illinois, management followed the scientific management principles to produce telephones. Little personal communication occurred between managers and employees; job specifications and work rules were spelled out. The manager's job was to enforce them through authority and discipline.

A group of industrial engineers was studying the effect of increasing the light in work areas on productivity. The engineers set out to find the optimum conditions, but the results of the study defied explanation. Productivity increased regardless of what the researchers did to the lighting. To understand why their principles failed, researchers isolated and observed a small group of workers. These studies included changes in compensation, rest periods, work schedules, and work methods. In general, productivity increased during the studies regardless of changes in the work conditions.

CRITICAL THINKING QUESTIONS

Recall a time when the instructor of a course or training class asked for your input on the course topics, schedule, methods, or even the meeting time and location.

1. How did the ability to voice your opinion influence the amount you learned?

2. How did it affect your interest and motivation?

The researchers finally concluded that the *relationship* between the researchers and the workers accounted for the results. Traditionally, scientific management advocates simply observed workers to identify the most efficient way to organize a job. The Hawthorne researchers had shown personal interest in the workers as they consulted with and kept them informed about changes. The relationship established between the researchers and the employees was quite different from that of the managers and employees in other parts of the plant.

Because the results differed from what was expected, the industrial engineers continued to study working conditions. In what may have been the first use of extensive interviewing in the workplace, the researchers asked thousands of employees about their attitudes toward working conditions, managers, and work in general. The interviews indicated that people who work under similar conditions experience these conditions in different ways and assign different meanings to their experiences.

The research concluded that employees' attitudes depend on the social organization of the group and their positions in these groups. Mayo recommended that managers be friendly in their relationships with workers, listen to workers' concerns, and give them a sense of participation in decisions so that they could meet their social needs.[15] In many respects, both Mayo and Carnegie were similar in their advice, and both were in stark contrast to the scientific management philosophy.

Or were they? Did this human relations approach really differ from the scientific management approach? Some would argue that both Mayo and Carnegie were promoting highly manipulative managerial communication strategies intended only to gain compliance from workers and to promote acceptance of managerial authority.

Although the general orientation of management during this era may have been manipulative, the human relations approach pointed out the importance of interpersonal communication. The legacy of the human relations approach is that managing groups, listening, and interviewing are now all considered integral to managerial communication.

1950s: The Behavioral Approach and Organizational Communication

During the 1950s, managers' behavior, including communication, received extensive attention. Economics, anthropology, psychology, and sociology were all applied to understanding communication on the job. No longer were employees viewed only as tools used to complete a job. Peter Drucker was among the first management gurus to assert that workers should be treated as assets, not as liabilities. He originated the view of the corporation as a human community built on trust and respect for the worker, not just a profit-making machine.[16] Many management theories emerged during this era, such as McGregor's theory X and theory Y, Maslow's hierarchy of needs, Likert's four systems of management, Blake and Mouton's managerial grid, and Herzberg's motivational model. These theories, explained in most comprehensive management textbooks, have valuable information about what is required for effective managerial communication. Unfortunately, the theoretical explanations of managerial behavior became extremely complex—too complex for most managers to understand and apply. Many training programs were developed to help managers apply these theories, but often little benefit resulted.

While theories were being developed about behavior at work, much also was being done in the area of communication theory. For instance, J. L. Austen developed the speech act theory, which maintains that certain communication conventions must be used to be effective, and David Berlo developed a model emphasizing two-way communication.[17] Attention was given to social influences on communication, but unfortunately, the social context of managers was given little or no attention.[18]

The nature of organizational structure also received extensive attention. Organizations of the 1950s and 1960s were recognized as being different from those of the early 1900s. Karl Weick's theory of organizing made it clear that organizations are not stable, static entities; rather, they are continually evolving. Internal and external communication networks are continually evolving, too. Changing types of information and factors such as rumors and informal communication must be considered by managers when communicating.

Forty years earlier, Fayol recognized the importance of communication networks and organizational structure when he presented the gangplank concept. Now, entire organizations and their structure were receiving renewed attention.[19] The nature of managerial and employee behavior, the study of communication, and an analysis of the nature of organizations all had important implications for managers as communicators. However, as mentioned earlier, these studies resulted in a complex body of knowledge that was difficult for managers to use. Out of this behavioral approach, the era of employee empowerment emerged.

1990s: The Empowerment Approach and Participative Communication

Empowerment is power sharing, or the delegation of power or authority to employees in the organization.[20] Since the emergence of the behavioral approach, we have seen a major shift away from the centralization of power. Empowerment encourages employees to participate fully in the organization. In the 1990s, we began to see power being given to others in the organization, so that they could act more freely to accomplish their jobs.

As companies experienced more intense global competition and rapidly developing technology, many top managers believed giving up centralized control would promote faster product development, flexibility, and quality. In a 1989 study, 74 percent of the chief executive officers surveyed reported that they were more participatory, were more consensus oriented, and relied more on communication than on command than in years past. They found less value in being dictatorial, autocratic, or imperial.[21] The chief executive officer's letter to the General Electric stockholders in the 1990 annual report provides an example of the empowerment philosophy. In this letter, the CEO asserted that managers must learn to delegate, facilitate, listen, and trust. He talked about the sharing of ideas to develop one vision for the huge corporation.

Sharing a vision means sharing information. In the traditional organization, the top managers are frequently the only ones who know the financial condition of the company, but in organizations that empower employees, information is shared with everyone. For instance, Springfield Remanufacturing Corp. in Springfield, Missouri, is an employee-owned company where workers on the line know—and are taught to understand—almost everything the president knows about costs and revenues, departmental productivity, and strategic priorities.[22] The empowerment movement can be seen in union–management relations; union members have become more involved in management decisions as management provides more information to them. In fact, information sharing is often part of contract negotiations.[23] Both management and union members can be found on work quality and productivity improvement teams.

You may not be surprised that attempts at empowerment faced many challenges. Caterpillar Inc., the heavy-equipment manufacturer, worked with the United Auto Workers in the 1980s to improve employee relations, including a program that asked shop floor workers to submit ideas for improving operations. However, when the industry met financial troubles in 1991, the employee involvement program became the victim of a bitter battle between the company and the United Auto Workers. An adversarial relationship between union and management returned; accordingly, one-way communication was more frequent than would be expected in an environment of empowerment.[24]

Although efforts to empower employees may run into problems, a number of strategies for empowering employees can be attempted, such as autonomous work groups, self-leadership, work-out groups, and quality circles. But as mentioned in the discussion of the behavioral approach, some of the theories and programs for empowerment can become so complicated that they are difficult to apply and are not suitable for every contemporary organization. As a result, the contingency approach has emerged as a management philosophy that makes sense in the early 21st century.[25]

21st Century: The Contingency Approach to Management Communication

The contingency approach recognizes the importance of matching different situations with varying communication strategies. The most effective and efficient strategy varies from one situation to another and depends on a number of factors. Effective managers see the interdependence of the various aspects of jobs, organizations, and communication. A communication method that is highly effective at one time and place may be ineffective in another situation. The contingency approach recognizes that there is no one best way to communicate.

For example, during a crisis, a manager may tell employees exactly what to do because two-way communication might waste time or employees may not have a holistic view of the organization. But during periods of growth, discussion between the manager and employees may generate new ideas. Each communication strategy—the autocratic approach and the participative approach—is appropriate in different situations.

The contingency approach has grown in popularity recently because of the complexity of organizations. Especially in multinational and multicultural organizations, managers must understand that there is no one best way of communicating; effective communication is contingent on the situation. That is not to say, however, that contemporary organizations are managed chaotically. On the contrary, accountability and oversight systems have been emphasized since the meltdown of multinationals such as Enron, Adelphia, and WorldCom in the early 2000s. The Sarbanes-Oxley Act of 2002 (especially Section 404) stresses the need for business control and auditing processes. The point is that as corporate governance becomes more transparent, information flows more freely and effective managers adapt to the complexities of each situation when communicating.

In summary, each era approaches communication differently but helps us better understand communication within contemporary organizations and the type of communication that may be appropriate in the future. Good ideas can be drawn from the scientific, administrative, human relations, behavioral, and empowerment approaches to communication. For example, without the administrative and human relations orientations, managerial communication might still focus on keeping records, giving orders, and maintaining discipline. Creative analysis is required to ensure that communication strategies adapt to the varying contingencies.

CRITICAL THINKING QUESTIONS

1. What are some of the complexities in today's business environment that make the contingency model appropriate?

2. Think about a message you have received recently from work, school, or another group to which you belong. What might be the contributing factors in the situation that guided the writer's decisions?

FACTORS AFFECTING COMMUNICATION CONTINGENCIES

The nature of communication and a strategic model of managerial communication are presented in Chapter 2. The discussion here presents three contingencies that should be considered when developing a strategy for managerial communication. It is impossible to review all contingencies because every manager faces many unique situations. However, it is possible to review the major current events that may influence a manager's environment. The following sections review diversity, competition and product quality, and ethics as major social and business influences that affect managerial communication.

Diversity

Today, everyone works with more diverse populations than just a few decades ago. Beginning in the 1960s, the United States embraced tolerance and diversity as a strategic mission. However, minimizing cultural bias in the workplace continues to be a challenge for managers. This challenge, which is discussed throughout this text, means managers must not only be able to communicate with a greater variety of audiences but also help their employees see diversity as a corporate asset rather than a liability. Diversity is linked to increased profitability and creativity, stronger governance, and better problem-solving abilities that help organizations be resilient and innovative.[26]

The contemporary manager should be particularly aware of how diversity affects their communication practices. In this section, we consider diversity not only in terms of culture and ethnicity but also gender, sexual orientation and gender identity, people with disabilities, age, and education.

Culture and Ethnicity

The increasing diversity of the U.S. workforce is a reflection of the increasingly diverse population. Things have changed significantly since the early 20th century, and we cannot assume that the typical business professional is white. Data from the Bureau of Labor Statistics show that 17 percent are Hispanic, 13 percent are Black, and 6 percent are Asian.[27] This demographic phenomenon brings a range of interests, languages, and cultures that affects the way business is conducted.

It is also critical for businesses to know the demographic makeup of geographical regions so that they can effectively localize products, services, and marketing. To capture the growing multicultural market, U.S. businesses must offer products and services that appeal to these different regions, and they must adapt advertising and promotional appeals accordingly.

Managers must be aware of regional differences that could influence work values and communication styles to effectively communicate with other managers and employees of all cultural backgrounds. For example, managers in Arizona may have many Hispanic or Latinx employees, but a job transfer to Hawaii may involve managing more Asian employees than before.[28] Executives, such as purchasing managers, must be familiar with cross-cultural communication because of the increase in international business. International purchasing alliances too frequently fail because of poor communication.[29] This may be termed *intercultural business communication*, which is discussed in detail in Chapter 12.

In less than 20 years, the landscape will become even more diverse in terms of race and ethnicity, making effective communication strategies even more important. Managers must be aware of linguistic, cultural, geographical, and even religious differences that could influence their own work values and communication styles as well as those of the people around them.

CRITICAL THINKING QUESTIONS

1. Recall a recent TV commercial or advertisement of one of your favorite products. How does the persuasive message appeal to multicultural audiences?

2. How could it be improved?

Gender

During the early 20th century, women who worked (by choice or by circumstances) often held routine, low-level manufacturing or clerical jobs; their professional options were mostly limited to teaching and nursing. Meanwhile, men had a greater variety of jobs, such as in management and engineering. Overall, men worked mostly with men, and women worked with other women or children.

But today women have greater opportunities and access to most professions. Women represented 40 percent of the U.S. workforce in 1976, and that number grew to 58 percent by 2020, which makes women now the majority of the workforce.[30] Women are also moving into management. In 1983, only about one third of managers were women, but by 2019, according to the U.S. Census Bureau, women filled 51.8 percent of management, professional, and related occupations.[31] Yet in the same year, only 33 companies in the Fortune 500 were led by women.[32] Many organizations have no women in leadership positions. Overall, far more women are employed part-time than men.[33] This "broken rung" of the corporate ladder shows that there is still room to grow.[34]

During the past three decades, much has been written about how men and women communicate differently. Are men more assertive than women? Do women show more social support and sympathy to colleagues? Do men and women provide different types of feedback? Do leadership styles of men and women differ? Do women convey a different nonverbal message with the same gesture? Do men use space differently with other men than with women? Do men and women use different persuasive strategies? In many cases, the answers to these and similar questions are not clear; furthermore, there is evidence that the answers evolve as general social changes occur.

Sexual harassment is an example of a factor that affects communication at work. When some people think of sexual harassment, they think of touching or making physical advances. However, sexual harassment can also be a ribald joke, extensive eye gaze, or even unexpected and unwelcome proximity. Other examples of sexual harassment in the workplace can include changes in work schedules that make it difficult for a worker to arrange childcare or participate in meetings and events.[35] Following the advance of the #MeToo movement in late 2017, organizations began to realize the pervasiveness of sexual harassment and assault in the workplace, and they took action to protect employees through improved reporting procedures and bystander training. An unfortunate consequence has been a "chilling effect" on workplace camaraderie as men are reluctant to interact with women.[36] Addressing the problem will require organizations to revise policies and change cultures to encourage reporting and discussion about the issue. Mentoring relationships and professional networks can also help women address issues of harassment and move into leadership roles in their organizations.[37]

Because of the evolving nature of communication and workplace relationships, definitive answers on gender differences in communication are difficult. But strong arguments for differences have been presented. In her best-selling book, Deborah Tannen makes a case for supporting the differences in communication styles of men and women based on both inherited traits and learned behavior.[38] These differences often cause men and women to experience miscommunication with each other at work. As Sallie Krawcheck, CEO of the financial services firm Ellevest, explains, women in management may be more risk averse than men, often take a longer-term perspective, and are often more relationship oriented. Such gender differences should be considered complementary rather than problematic, because research shows that diversity in work teams leads to better outcomes. (See Chapter 4 for a thorough examination of team communication.) Effective managers must be sensitive to gender differences and make special efforts to adjust their communication based on these differences.[39]

Sexual Orientation and Gender Identity

Although stigma and reporting techniques make statistics difficult to measure, approximately 4.5 percent of the U.S. population identify as lesbian, gay, bisexual, transgender, or questioning (LGBTQ).[40] In 2020, the U.S. Supreme Court ruled that it is illegal to fire employees based on their sexual orientation or gender identity; before this ruling, LGBTQ employees were in a precarious position. Should they present their authentic selves and risk bullying, discrimination, and termination or hide themselves from their coworkers?

According to the United Nations, countries that marginalize LGBTQ employees experience decreased economic output.[41] On a more local scale, employees who are afraid to be themselves experience more stress, more health issues, and lower productivity than other employees. Companies that tolerate bullying, discrimination, or marginalizing behavior are more likely to experience turnover and lose the valuable contributions of this group of employees.[42]

Organizations should review their policies, dress codes, and benefits. Managers should take care to avoid heteronormative language and prying questions about sexual orientation or gender identity. The message to all employees should be "You are welcome and safe here."[43]

People With Disabilities

Approximately 20 percent of the U.S. population live with a physical or mental impairment that limits one or more major life activities. They may struggle to walk, see, hear, lift, concentrate, or learn. They may have weakened immune systems or impaired function in respiratory, circulatory, or neurological systems. Within the U.S. workforce, 19 percent of people with disabilities are employed, compared to 66 percent of those without disabilities. Many people in this group work in service positions, and about one third work part-time.[44] They are underrepresented in management and professional occupations, but they are more likely to be self-employed.

Why is unemployment so high for this group? Employers may have a lack of awareness of disability and accommodation issues, a fear of legal liability, and concern over costs.[45] Stereotypes that portray people with disabilities as unreliable or underperformers may cause unconscious bias during hiring.

As with other forms of diversity, hiring people with disabilities brings valuable perspectives, broadens the pool of talent, and demonstrates corporate social responsibility.[46] To recruit and retain employees with disabilities, managers should ensure that their facilities are accessible, revise human resource policies to remove ableist language, offer flexible work schedules, and restructure jobs and modify the work environment to accommodate a variety of needs and to use principles of ergonomic design.[47]

Age and Generational Differences

People in the United States are living longer, and the average employee is getting older. For the first time in history, five generations are working together. Twenty-nine percent of Baby Boomers (born in 1946–1964) continue to work.[48] Meanwhile, iGen (born in 1996–2012) comprise 5 percent of the total workforce.[49] By 2030, one in five people in the United States will be of retirement age, but it increasingly looks like many won't be retired at all.

These generational shifts can be challenging to managers and employees alike. As more employees report to someone younger, tensions build. Older workers may feel that their experience isn't valued or that they have been passed over for promotions or raises.[50] Younger managers may feel that their decisions are being questioned. Both groups may feel that the skills of the Boomers are outdated.[51] The worker who is 30 years old in 2021 has lived in a much different world from that of the worker who is 60. The 30-year-old, born in 1991, grew up in an era of relative affluence but came of age during the recession of 2008. This worker is an avid techie because personal computers have always been available and tablets and smartphones are ubiquitous. Multicultural social networks are also important to this person. The 60-year-old remembers the wonder of the moonshot and the misery of the Vietnam War. This worker has lived through the 1973 oil crisis, the heady expanse of the 1980s, and the dot-com bubble of the early 2000s. Economic and national securities are major concerns for this person.

Yet there is some evidence that age differences are not as problematic as the generational stereotypes that pit one group against another.[52] Generation gaps are natural, but mutual respect and open lines of communication are the recipe for a productive professional relationship across generations. Managers should help their teams focus on shared goals and values while recognizing individual strengths. Older workers may have a strong work ethic and avoid drama. Younger workers tend to think and act quickly, and they are often willing to try out new ideas and technologies.[53] Respecting each other's strengths and helping others continue to grow will benefit everyone in the workplace. Managers must consider age diversity as a factor that affects their communication contingencies because of its implications for workplace harmony.

Education

In addition to other demographic shifts, the workforce's education is changing dramatically. According to the U.S. Census Bureau, 28 percent of U.S. residents 25 and older have a high school degree, and 22.5 percent have a bachelor's degree or higher.[54] As you move up through the management ranks, there is a good chance that you will manage people who have more experience or knowledge than you do.[55] In the scientific management era, a manager could simply tell an educated employee what to do; however, today managers must listen to the employee and seek assistance with problem solving.

In summary, differences in culture and ethnicity, gender, sexual orientation and gender identity, disabilities, age, and education should be considered when communicating with others. Given the increasingly diverse workforce, today's managers need to develop competencies that will enable effective communication internally with bosses, employees, and coworkers and externally with customers, suppliers, vendors, regulatory agencies, and the public.

Competition and the Drive for Quality

As explained in the previous section, diversity is an important managerial communication contingency. A second is quality, which is a competitive advantage for business. A pioneer of the drive for quality, W. Edwards Deming, pointed out that in order to continuously improve quality, systems must be in place for gathering feedback from the employees and customers. Contemporary managers now accept the idea that business is a globally competitive game and quality is the key to victory. *Competitive advantage* and *quality* are common words in business today. But what do the terms mean?

Competition may be considered the effort of two or more parties acting independently to secure the business of a third party by offering the most attractive terms. In a competitive environment, the organization must produce a product or service in a more efficient and effective manner than its competitors, and the service or product must possess greater value at the same or lower price. Little room exists for errors; defective parts must be minimal, few or no reworked parts can be allowed, few product repairs can be tolerated, and delivery cycles must be short. Continuous efforts are required to find new ways to improve the product or service while reducing costs.

Some of the characteristics an organization needs to gain competitive advantage in today's markets include the ability to do the following:

- Access resources

- Add value

- Develop a good skills base among the workforce

- Attract investment

- Develop nonprice characteristics that appeal to other markets

- Be price competitive

- Be efficient

- Use technology

- Be innovative

As you look over this list of factors, note that most directly rely on management's communication competencies. Today's managers must be able to gather information and ideas, share data, promote solutions, and persuade others to ensure continuous process improvement. Managers must be efficient and effective communicators in a fast-paced, highly competitive environment. When time is limited, managers must be strategic in their communication practices.

Let us look at an example. Toyota is one of the largest automakers in the United States by production, and one of the 15 largest companies in the world in terms of sales and market value.[56] Toyota relies on manufacturing systems, statistical process control, and other proven methods under a continuous improvement strategy to produce high-quality products that consumers demand. All the elements, including management's communication with dealers, suppliers, and employees, contribute to Toyota's reputation for quality.[57]

To enhance their competitiveness, many organizations use cross-functional work teams in which employees learn a variety of tasks and work together. It is almost the direct opposite of the scientific management approach. When cross-functional work teams are used, managers must understand and coordinate a variety of activities. They must be able to communicate from a variety of perspectives.

In some cases, entire organizational cultures must be changed. After struggling in the early 1980s, Ford Motor Company embraced the principles of Total Quality Management and adopted the motto "Quality Is Job One." Here is a simple example of how the organization's quality culture works: A Ford automobile assembly worker believed he had a better way to mount the door mirror. After several discussions with the departmental managers, a better procedure was implemented.[58] In 2003, as Ford celebrated its 100th anniversary, Chairman and Chief Executive Officer Bill Ford said, "Our success always has been driven by our products and our people. . . . We're going to apply fresh thinking and innovative technology to everything we do, from our basic business processes to the products that define who we are as a company."[59] This dedication appears to be paying off: Ford vehicles consistently rank high in J.D. Power quality ratings.

Managers must be able to communicate a real interest in quality, and they must be willing to listen to employees about quality improvements. A corporate culture focused on quality will provide a competitive edge.

Ethics

A third major contingency that managers should consider when communicating is business ethics. The dangers of unethical behavior have been exemplified in recent years by major scandals in the corporate world. In the early 21st century, executives at Adelphia, Arthur Andersen, Enron, WorldCom, Martha Stewart Omnimedia, HealthSouth, and other corporations were charged with major ethics violations—accounting fraud, stock manipulation, obstructing justice, lying, and so on. In many cases, the accused executives were convicted, and in some cases, their companies were even destroyed. In 2016, Wells Fargo admitted that its employees had created hundreds of thousands of fake accounts to meet quotas; a year later, it admitted that employees had also sold customers car insurance that they didn't need, causing some to go into default on their loans and have their cars repossessed.[60] Such events have triggered renewed concern for ethical standards in business.

Ethical dilemmas and temptations face managers at all levels, not just the political leaders and corporate executives who receive the attention of journalists. The top ethical issues in business today include corporate accounting practices, social media and reputation management, workplace relationships (including harassment), health and safety, pay equity, and privacy. Consider the following examples of ethical issues in managerial communication:

- The supervisor of a travel agency was aware his agents could receive large bonuses for booking 100 or more clients each month with an auto rental firm, although clients typically wanted the rental agency selected on the basis of lowest cost. The agents worked on a commission basis. Should the supervisor "warn" his employees, or should they be trusted to use their best judgment?

- The executive in charge of a parts distribution facility told employees to tell phone customers that inventory was in stock, even if it was not. Replenishing the items took only 1 to 2 days; no one was hurt by the delay. Is it ethical for the company to omit this information?

- The project manager for a consulting assignment wondered whether some facts should be left out of a report because the marketing executives paying for the report would look bad if the facts were included. What is the project manager's ethical responsibility?

- A North American manufacturer operating abroad was asked to make cash payments (a bribe) to government officials and was told it was consistent with local customs, despite being illegal in the United States under the Foreign Corrupt Practices Act.[61] Should the manufacturer make such payments?

Answers to these questions are not easy, and in today's atmosphere of cynicism and mistrust, little room for error exists. Chapter 2 discusses the concept of communication climate and points out that trust is essential to developing a positive communication climate. Unfortunately, managers have difficulty developing trust when so many blatant examples of mistrust surface and individual managers face conflicting ethical demands.

No concrete set of ethical rules exists. There is no law to follow. Many behaviors have not been codified, and managers must be sensitive to emerging norms and values. Sensitivity to the nuances of ethical communication is the only way to maintain employee trust.

CRITICAL THINKING QUESTIONS

Examine the code of conduct for a company, profession, or industry you are interested in.

1. How does the code guide the conduct of its members?

2. What are the consequences of violating it (if any)?

3. What do you consider the most important reason that codes of conduct exist?

Because no universal laws exist, what one person or group considers ethical may be unethical to another. The question of taking bribes is a good example; they are quite ethical in one country but unethical and even illegal in another. Organizations are assisting managers with the many ethical quandaries they face when communicating by providing guidelines, seminars, and workshops. A recent survey of 71 U.S.-based global organizations in a range of industries found that employee ethics training is, in fact, commonplace; ethics training not only fosters ethical behavior among employees but also improves organizational performance.[62]

Another strategy many companies use to improve communication ethics is to develop a formal code of ethics. The code clarifies company expectations of employee conduct and makes clear that the company expects its personnel to recognize the ethical dimensions of corporate behavior and communication. A code of conduct may be broad or specific, and most address managerial communication. For instance, the following is taken from International Paper's code of conduct, which is published on the company's website:

> The International Paper Code of Conduct supplies the tools we need as we work together to build our business on a foundation of ethics and integrity. It also serves as a compass that provides guidance in all types of situations. It gives us direction on acting honestly, operating with integrity, treating each other with respect and promoting a culture of openness and accountability wherever we do business around the world.[63]

Another possibility is an ethics committee or an ethics ombudsperson. With this approach, either one executive or a panel of executives is appointed to oversee the organization's ethics and serve as a consultant to managers and employees. This provides an opportunity for a manager to seek advice when confronted with an ethical issue.

THE IMPORTANCE OF STUDYING MANAGERIAL COMMUNICATION

In 2017, the Kansas City Chiefs football team fired head coach John Dorsey, in part because of his poor internal communication style. Sources say that he did not explain important decisions, such as the firing of two successful directors.[64] Employee engagement suffers when employees feel uncertainty, but giving them the information they need helps them become happier and more productive.[65]

A survey by the American Management Association showed that communication, interpersonal skills, collaboration, cultural sensitivity, and diversity are some of the most common topics for employee training.[66] Jennifer Jones, director of the training firm AMA Enterprise, says that communication skills are essential for managers to succeed in their jobs:

> Communication is actually an umbrella term for such core skills as listening, thinking clearly, interpreting organizational concepts, being alert to non-verbal signals as well as dealing with any stress or emotional issues in working with co-workers or supervisors. Indeed, understood correctly communications helps a person understand a situation, resolve differences and build trust. It's essential for a productive workplace to encourage creativity and collaboration in order to solve problems or achieve business objectives.[67]

Furthermore, a recent study showed that managers, particularly those of the Baby Boomer generation, consider interpersonal and oral communication skills when making decisions about promotion. Although written communication did not rate as highly, the researchers suggest that managers consider writing to be a "threshold competency" that all candidates are expected to have.[68]

The Project Management Institute (PMI), headquartered in Pennsylvania, has provided solid evidence for the claim that managerial communication is a critical core competency for business success. In 2013, PMI published an in-depth *Pulse of the Profession* report, "The

High Cost of Low Performance: The Essential Role of Communications." The report was the result of research conducted with more than 1,000 project managers, executives, and business owners involved in large capital projects (at least $250,000) worldwide. PMI's study revealed that $135 million is at risk for every $1 billion spent on a project, and a startling 56 percent is at risk because of ineffective communication with stakeholders. Undoubtedly, effective communication is the most crucial success factor in a complex and competitive business climate. The report concludes that "organizations cannot afford to overlook this key element of project success and long-term profitability."[69]

This introductory chapter presents a historical overview of managerial communication, concluding that the contingency approach is the most appropriate, and it reviews three factors that affect contingencies. But organizational management and the corresponding communication are in constant transition. Not every contingency can be discussed, and managers must remain creative and strategic as they communicate in many unique and challenging situations. Our challenge is to understand management communication and begin to prepare for these changes. This book will help you compose messages that focus on the needs of your readers, explain ideas in a clear and ethical manner, and strengthen your reputation as a good communicator.

SUMMARY

Since ancient and medieval times, managerial communication has changed from an autocratic, one-way practice to a participatory approach that empowers employees to contribute to decisions and solutions. In recent years, the contingency approach has become more widely used as managers realize there is no single best way to communicate. Managers must analyze the contingency factors of each situation and adapt their strategies accordingly.

To better understand managerial situations, several contemporary dynamics affecting communication are presented. Different types of diversity are reviewed: culture and ethnicity, gender, sexual orientation and gender identity, people with disabilities, age, and education. The work population will probably become more diverse in the majority of these attributes.

The drive for competitive advantage through improved product and service quality also affects managerial communication. As a result, everything will occur in shorter time cycles, and less room for error will exist as a result of quality demands.

Ethics is another contemporary dynamic that must be considered. Although management ethics can create difficult communication decisions, organizations provide assistance with training programs and codes of ethics. In addition to these dynamics affecting contemporary communication, trends imply that communication will become more frequent, intense, and intercultural as it grows in importance.

CASES FOR ANALYSIS

Case 1-1

Women in the White House

During Barack Obama's presidency, women on his staff were frustrated about their lack of influence.

They were often outnumbered by men in meetings. They struggled to contribute to the conversation. When they did get a chance to speak, their contributions were often ignored or a man would repeat the idea and get the credit.

To counteract this behavior and make their voices heard, the women used a strategy called amplification. "When a woman made a key point, other women would repeat it, giving credit to its author. This forced the men in the room to recognize the contribution—and denied them the chance to claim the idea as their own."[70]

President Obama soon noticed the technique. He began calling on women more, and the number of women staffers increased as well.

Questions

1. Why might women be reluctant to speak up in meetings?

2. What are the potential consequences of letting one demographic dominate workplace discussions and decisions?

3. What other strategies can people who have been traditionally underrepresented in the workplace use to make their voices heard?

Case 1-2

Ethics and Technology

Chris smiled as he received the analysis packet from his supervisor. He had been working from home for GEH Mortgage Company, analyzing mortgage applications, for the past 3 years. This particular application involved not just a home mortgage but also an entire farmstead, a home and business. Whenever he received an assignment he did not know how to analyze, he would call on his friend Joel, whom he had known since high school, to help him accomplish such tasks. He compensated Joel, usually with a case of beer, when they got together on the weekends. Chris knew he could trust Joel to do a good job on the analysis, because Joel had double majored in finance and accounting at a regional university. Chris would then tailor the analysis according to the way the firm expected reports to be submitted. He quickly e-mailed the application packet to Joel.

Chris was perceived as one of the most dependable analysts in the division because of his past work, much of which had been farmed out to Joel. He had received accolades and raises as a result and was enjoying his successful career with the firm.

Questions

1. The method used by Chris is obviously successful, and the company is satisfied with the results. Is it just good business, or is there an ethical dilemma present?

2. Should Chris confess to his supervisor or just continue the successful deception?

3. What are the privacy issues, given that the information used in these analyses is proprietary and sensitive?

4. Does this activity fit the notion of plagiarism?

5. Do electronic communication and the telecommuting arrangement make Chris's actions more likely than if he were in the office?

Case 1-3

Like Grandfather, Like Granddaughter?

Clarence opened a farm supply store in Montana during the early 1940s. His neighbors in the county were also his customers. Every person who walked into his store felt comfortable. In fact, they would often sit, sip a cup of coffee or shell some peanuts, and solve the world's problems before loading up their purchases. Clarence prided himself on knowing what his customers needed to be successful farmers, and he freely gave them advice about which brand of flea dip would work best on their cattle and which tonic would help a colicky horse. By the time he retired and his son Seth took over, the company had expanded to three stores in three towns and had 14 full-time employees.

As a youth, Seth had attended the state college and earned a degree in agricultural business. When he took over the company in 1975, he eagerly applied what he had learned to the family business. He was convinced that technology was the key to

(Continued)

(Continued)

success, not personal relationships. Over the years, he struggled to convert all his father's old, handwritten records to electronic files. Eventually, he installed a completely computerized information system that tracked inventory, personnel, and accounts. He sometimes boasted about being an entrepreneur, but Clarence snorted at that term. "Just do what's right for your customers, and you'll be doing what's right for yourself," he would retort.

When Seth retired in 2015, his daughter Kathy took over the company, which now had 23 stores with 228 employees in three states and one wholly owned subsidiary of 18 gas stations. Kathy's vision involved offering a broader range of products than farm supplies. She wanted to sell the image of the family farm. Her stores stocked Western clothing; boots, hats, and jewelry; home furnishings; and even CDs featuring country music.

Kathy found herself traveling extensively from the corporate office to the various stores. Finding time to manage everything was a problem, but she had a staff of 12 professionals in the corporate office to assist her. E-mail, laptops, and smartphones helped tremendously.

Questions

1. How have communication practices and expectations differed for Clarence, Seth, and Kathy?

2. How do you think the management behaviors differed for the three owners?

3. What contingency factors might each owner have faced while they managed the company?

Notes

1. Towers Watson, Inc., "Change and Communication ROI: The 10th Anniversary Report," 2013–2014, http://www.towerswatson.com.

2. Robert A. Guisepi, "The History of Ancient Sumeria, Including Its Cities, Kings, and Religions," World-History.org, http://history-world.org/sumeria.htm.

3. "The First Writing: Counting Beer for the Workers," The British Museum, http://cultural institute.britishmuseum.org/asset-viewer/the-first-writing-counting-beer-for-the-work ers/fgF9ioy89DC2Uw?hl=en.

4. "Early Writing," Harry Ransom Center, University of Texas at Austin, http://www.hrc.utexas .edu/educator/modules/gutenberg/books/early.

5. Annunziata Rositani, "Work and Wages in the Code of Hammurabi," *Egitto e Vicino Oriente* 40 (2017): 47–72, https://www.jstor.org/sta ble/26490822.

6. Agence France-Presse, "Hundreds of Roman Tablets Reveal Early London Life," *PRI*, June 1, 2016, https://www.pri.org/stories/2016-06-01/hundreds-roman-writing-tablets-reveal-early-london-life.

7. Claude S. George, *The History of Management Thought* (Englewood Cliffs, NJ: Prentice Hall, 1972), chap. 1–2.

8. Edwin A. Locke, "The Ideas of Frederick E. Taylor," *Academy of Management Journal* (January 1982): 41–44.

9. William F. Muks, "Worker Participation in the Progressive Era: An Assessment by Harrington Emerson," *Academy of Management Review* (January 1982): 101.

10. "McRisky," *BusinessWeek*, October 21, 1991, 114–17.

11. Henri Fayol, *General and Industrial Management* (London: Sir Isaac Pitman and Sons, 1949), 3–13.

12. M. Richetto, "Organizational Communication Theory and Research: An Overview," in *Communication Yearbook 1*, ed. B. D. Rubin (New Brunswick, NJ: Transaction Books, 1977).

13. Dale Carnegie, *How to Win Friends and Influence People* (New York: Simon & Schuster, 1936).

14. F. L. Roethlisberger and W. Dickson, *Management and the Workers* (New York: Wiley & Sons, 1939).

15. E. Mayo, *The Human Problems of an Industrial Civilization* (Boston: Harvard Business School, 1947).

16. John A. Byrne, "The Man Who Invented Management: Why Peter Drucker's Ideas Still Matter," *BusinessWeek*, November 28, 2005, 97–106.

17. J. L. Austen, *How to Do Things With Words* (Oxford: Oxford University Press, 1962); and David K. Berlo, "Human Communication: The Basic Proposition," in *Essay on Communication* (East Lansing, MI: Department of Communication, 1971).

18. Larry R. Smeltzer and Gail F. Thomas, "Managers as Writers: Research in Context," *Journal of Business and Technical Communication* 8, no. 2 (April 1994): 186.

19. K. Weick, *The Social Psychology of Organizing*, 2nd ed. (Reading, MA: Addison-Wesley, 1979).

20. Edwin P. Hollander and Lynn R. Offermann, "Power and Leadership in Organization," *American Psychologist* 45 (February 1990): 179–89.

21. Thomas A. Stewart, "New Ways to Exercise Power," *Fortune*, November 6, 1989, 52–64.

22. John Case, "The Open-Book Managers," *Inc.*, September 1990, 104–105.

23. Stephenie Overman, "The Union Pitch Has Changed," *HR Magazine*, December 1991, 44–46.

24. Donald W. Nauss, "UAW Dispute With Caterpillar Just Crawls Along," *Los Angeles Times*, July 5, 1994, http://articles.latimes.com/1994-07-05/business/fi-11982_1_unfair-labor.

25. Robert L. Rose and Alex Kotlowitz, "Strife Between UAW and Caterpillar Blights Promising Labor Idea," *The Wall Street Journal*, November 23, 1992, 1.

26. Vijay Eswaran, "The Business Case for Diversity in the Workplace Is Now Overwhelming," World Economic Forum, April 29, 2019, https://www.weforum.org/agenda/2019/04/business-case-for-diversity-in-the-workplace.

27. U.S. Department of Labor, Bureau of Labor Statistics, "Labor Force Characteristics by Race and Ethnicity, 2018," October 2019, https://www.bls.gov/opub/reports/race-and-ethnicity/2018/home.htm.

28. U.S. Census Bureau, "Quick Facts: Arizona; Hawaii; United States," July 1, 2019, https://www.census.gov/quickfacts/fact/table/AZ,HI,US/PST045219.

29. Michiel R. Leenders, Harold E. Fearon, and Wilbur B. England, *Purchasing and Materials Management*, 10th ed. (Burr Ridge, IL: Richard D. Irwin, 1993), 480.

30. U.S. Census Bureau, "Table A-1. Employment Status of the Civilian Population by Sex and Age," *Economic News Release*, May 8, 2020, https://www.bls.gov/news.release/empsit.t01.htm.

31. U.S. Census Bureau, "Table 11. Employed Persons by Detailed Occupation, Sex, Race, and Hispanic or Latino Ethnicity," *Labor Force Statistics From the Current Population Survey*, January 22, 2020, https://www.bls.gov/cps/cpsaat11.htm.

32. Claire Zillman, "The Fortune 500 Has More Female CEOs Than Ever Before," *Fortune*, May 16, 2019, https://fortune.com/2019/05/16/fortune-500-female-ceos.

33. U.S. Department of Labor, Bureau of Labor Statistics, "Percent Distribution of Workers Employed Full-Time and Part-Time by Sex, 2016 Annual Averages," *Full-Time/Part-Time Employment, 2016*, https://www.dol.gov/agencies/wb/data/latest-annual-data/

full-and-part-time-employment#Percent-dis
tribution-of-workers-employed-full-time-and-
part-time-by-sex.

34. McKinsey & Company and Lean In, *Women in the Workplace 2019*, https://wiw-report .s3.amazonaws.com/Women_in_the_Work place_2019.pdf.

35. Fatima Goss Graves et al., "Seventeen Million Reasons Low-Wage Workers Need Strong Protections From Harassment," *National Women's Law Center Report*, April 1, 2014, http://www .nwlc.org/sites/default/files/pdfs/final_nwlc_ vancereport2014.pdf.

36. David Boyle and Amanda Cucchiara, "Social Movements and HR: The Impact of #MeToo" (white paper, Cornell University, 2018), https:// digitalcommons.ilr.cornell.edu/cahrswhitepa pers/14.

37. Cindy A. Schipani and Terry Morehead Dworkin, "The Need for Mentors in Promoting Gender Diverse Leadership in the #MeToo Era," *The George Washington Law Review* 87, no. 5 (2019): 1272–98, https://www.gwlr.org/the-need-for- mentors-in-promoting-gender-diverse-lead ership-in-the-metoo-era.

38. Deborah Tannen, *You Just Don't Understand* (New York: Ballantine Books, 1990).

39. Sally Krawcheck, "Diversify Corporate America," *Time*, March 24, 2014, 36–37.

40. Williams Institute, UCLA School of Law, "LGBT Proportion of the Population, United States," *LGBT Demographic Data Interactive*, January 2019, https://williamsinstitute.law.ucla.edu/ visualization/lgbt-stats/?topic=LGBT#density.

41. United Nations Human Rights, "The Price of Exclusion," December 9, 2015, https://youtu.be/ DvSxLHpyFOk.

42. Michaela Krejcova, "The Value of LGBT Equality in the Workplace," GLAAD, February 26, 2015, https://www.glaad.org/blog/value-lgbt-equal ity-workplace.

43. Robert Mitchell, "How to Navigate the Gender Landscape at Work," *The Harvard Gazette*, February 15, 2019, https://news.harvard.edu/ gazette/story/2019/02/lessons-in-how-to- make-the-workplace-inclusive-for-lgbtq- employees.

44. U.S. Department of Labor, Bureau of Labor Statistics, "Persons With a Disability: Labor Force Statistics 2019," *News Release,* February 26, 2020, https://www.bls.gov/news.release/ pdf/disabl.pdf.

45. H. Stephen Kaye, Lita H. Jans, and Erica C. Jones, "Why Don't Employers Hire and Retain Workers With Disabilities?" *Journal of Vocational Rehabilitation,* 21, no. 4 (2011): 526–36, doi: 10.1007/s10926-011-9302-8.

46. Alexis D. Henry et al., "Employer-Recommended Strategies to Increase Opportunities for People with Disabilities," *Journal of Vocational Rehabilitation* 41 (2014): 237–48, doi: 10.3233/JVR- 140716.

47. Kaye et al., "Why Don't Employers?"

48. Richard Fry, "Baby Boomers Are Staying in the Labor Force at Rates Not Seen in Generations for People Their Age," Pew Internet Research Center, July 24, 2019, https://www.pewre search.org/fact-tank/2019/07/24/baby-boom ers-us-labor-force.

49. Catalyst, "Generations-Demographic Trends in Population and Workforce: Quick Take," November 7, 2019, https://www.catalyst.org/ research/generations-demographic-trends- in-population-and-workforce.

50. Associated Press-NORC Center for Public Affairs, "Age Diversity in the Workplace," *2019 Working Longer Study*, https://workinglongerstudy.org/ project/age-diversity-in-the-workplace.

51. Joanne Kaufman, "When You're Older Than the Boss," *New York Times,* March 19, 2017, 5.

52. Eden King, "Generational Differences at Work Are Small. Thinking They're Big Affects Our

Behavior," *Harvard Business Review*, August 1, 2019, https://hbr.org/2019/08/generational-differences-at-work-are-small-thinking-theyre-big-affects-our-behavior.

53. Kaufman, "When You're Older Than the Boss."

54. U.S. Census Bureau, "U.S. Census Bureau Releases New Educational Attainment Data," *Press Release CB20-TPS.09*, March 30, 2020, https://www.census.gov/newsroom/press-releases/2020/educational-attainment.html.

55. Rebecca Knight, "How to Manage People Who Are Smarter Than You," *Harvard Business Review*, August 6, 2015, https://hbr.org/2015/08/how-to-manage-people-who-are-smarter-than-you.

56. Andrea Murphy et al., "Global 2000: The World's Largest Public Companies," *Forbes*, May 13, 2020, https://www.forbes.com/global2000/#3357866f335d.

57. Mary Connelly, "Toyota's Ad Constants: Stress Quality, Seek a Feel-Good Connection," *Automotive News*, October 29, 2007.

58. *Netpiper Auto News*, July 6, 2003, http://www.autoemirates.com/netpiper/news/details.asp?NID=997.

59. "Ford Motor Company's Vision for Next 100 Years," *ORC Newswire*, July 1, 2003, http://www.off-road.com/trucks-4x4/news/ford-motor-companys-vision-for-next-100-years-29941.html.

60. Chris Arnold, "Who Snatched My Car? Wells Fargo Did," *NPR*, August 3, 2017, http://www.npr.org/2017/08/02/541182948/who-snatched-my-car-wells-fargo-did.

61. U.S. Department of Justice, "Foreign Corrupt Practices Act," https://www.justice.gov/criminal-fraud/foreign-corrupt-practices-act.

62. James Weber, "Investigating and Assessing the Quality of Employee Ethics Training Programs Among US-Based Global Organizations," *Journal of Business Ethics* 129 (2015): 27–42, doi: 10.1007/s10551-014-2128-5.

63. International Paper Company, "Company Ethics," http://www.internationalpaper.com/company/ethics.

64. Terez A. Paylor, "Sources: Communication, Management Style Were Factors in Chiefs' Firing of Dorsey," *The Kansas City Star*, June 25, 2017, http://www.kansascity.com/sports/nfl/kansas-city-chiefs/article158155634.html.

65. Preston Lewis, "5 Steps to Creating a Better Employee Experience," *Communication World*, March 2017, 1–3.

66. Jennifer Jones, "Communication Skills Most Needed by Individual Contributors," American Management Association, February 25, 2014, http://www.amanet.org/news/9791.aspx.

67. Ibid.

68. N. Lamar Reinsch and Jonathan A. Gardner, "Do Communication Abilities Affect Promotion Decisions? Some Data From the C-Suite," *Journal of Business and Technical Communication*, 28, no. 1 (2014): 31–57, doi: 10.1177/1050651913502357.

69. Project Management Institute, "The High Cost of Low Performance: The Essential Role of Communications," *PMI's Pulse of the Profession In-Depth Report*, May 2013, 2, https://www.pmi.org/learning/thought-leadership/pulse/essential-role-communications.

70. Juliet Einperin, "White House Women Want to Be in the Room Where It Happens," *Washington Post*, September 13, 2016, https://www.washingtonpost.com/news/powerpost/wp/2016/09/13/white-house-women-are-now-in-the-room-where-it-happens.

UNDERSTANDING THE MANAGERIAL COMMUNICATION PROCESS

Whether working for a hospital, manufacturer, or service firm, more than 75 percent of a manager's time is spent communicating. Considering the amount of information for which a manager has responsibility, this is not surprising. General managers face two fundamental challenges: figuring out what to do as they sort through enormous amounts of information and getting things done through a diverse group of people.[1] Effective communication is the key to planning, leading, organizing, and controlling the resources of the organization to master these challenges.

Communication—the essential process that managers use to plan, lead, organize, and control—is not easy. To understand your message, your employees must be able to perceive and interpret it accurately. The process becomes more complex when communicating to a group of people because of the variety of perceptions and interpretations possible.

At the most general level, the communication process consists of an exchange of messages that are comprised of a set of symbols, such as words or gestures. Understanding the messages depends on a common meaning or frame of reference for those symbols. When sending a message, a manager may have the meaning of the symbols clearly in mind, but if someone receiving the message attributes a different meaning, the message is misunderstood. The process is made even more complicated because the symbols' meanings not only differ between people but also change as the experiences of the people involved change.

In this chapter, we examine those aspects of developing and exchanging symbols that relate to managerial communication, and we analyze the human factors that aid or hinder understanding. Further, we present a model of the strategic approach to communication that managers should follow when developing messages. Finally, we discuss three critical errors that managers must avoid when seeking effective communication.

LEVELS OF MANAGERIAL COMMUNICATION

Managerial communication may occur at five different levels:

1. Intrapersonal

2. Interpersonal

3. Group

4. Organizational

5. Intercultural[2]

One level is not more important than another. Communication may occur at any or all of these levels simultaneously.

Intrapersonal communication focuses on internal cognitive behavior, such as observing, listening, and reading. Most of these activities involve the seeking of information; consequently, this communication level is extremely important for managerial decision making and problem solving because effective decisions require accurate information. Chapter 10 will help you learn techniques to improve your listening skills, and Chapter 11 will help you interpret nonverbal communication.

Interpersonal communication involves two or more people exchanging messages. They may be sharing information, providing feedback, or simply maintaining a social relationship through conversation. Chapters 7, 8, and 9 focus on written communication, and Chapters 13, 14, and 15 address interpersonal communication situations such as conflict management, negotiation, and interviews.

Group communication involves three or more people working toward a shared goal. The most common form of group communication is the meeting, which may be either formal or informal. Chapter 4 will focus on managing meetings and teams, and Chapter 5 will help you learn more about presenting your ideas at work. Chapter 6 describes how visual messages complement or even replace verbal ones.

Organizational communication operates within the networks that link members of a company or other organization. Organizational communication focuses on operations, such as how a group of tasks is linked to complete a job or how policies and procedures guide behavior and decisions. Chapter 3 explains how technology helps organizations communicate with internal and external groups.

Intercultural communication concerns interactions among people of different cultures. Intercultural communication is occurring more frequently because of globalization, improved telecommunications, and transportation.[3] Given the importance of intercultural communication, Chapter 12 is dedicated to this topic.

Communication is a behavior we engage in throughout life and often take for granted. You may reach a managerial position yet never deliberately analyze your communication because it has become such common behavior. However, a lack of strategic decision making can cause communication problems for you as a manager. This chapter describes a strategic approach to communication that will help you analyze situations and compose effective messages.

A STRATEGIC APPROACH

The following discussion analyzes separate elements of a strategic approach to communication. However, these variables do not actually occur separately, nor can they be analyzed separately in the managerial context. They are highly interdependent and affect each other concurrently. For instance, the power of the person sending the message, the intended receiver, the message's purpose, and the organizations involved are all interrelated. Each strategic component is interdependent. Although the following discussion considers each of the components separately, remember that each variable affects the others.

The strategic approach could be compared to a golf ball (see Figure 2-1). The durable outer layer, which we will examine first, is the context in which the communication event occurs. The tightly wound inner layer is the specific situation of sender, receiver, and purpose. The core entails the message content, channel, physical environment, and time.

Layer 1: Contextual Factors

The first layer consists of communication context. Context involves the setting and background factors that influence the message, including constraints on what can and cannot be stated. The organization's communication climate, culture and values, and stakeholder concerns are discussed in the following subsections.

Communication Climate

The communication climate refers to the general attitude about communication within an organization. Past communication, such as whether employees and managers have been trusting and open or closed and defensive, has a cumulative effect.[4] Trust, openness, and communication have a reciprocal relationship. Effective communicating results in trust and openness, which generally improve job performance.[5] In turn, future communication will get easier because of the trust and openness that have developed.

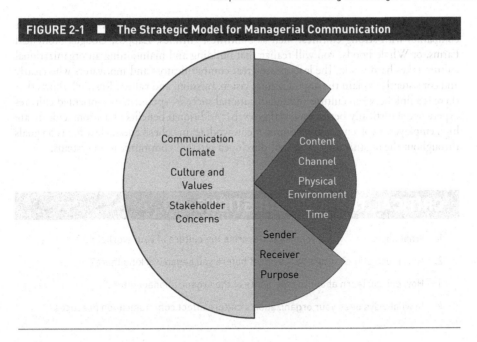

FIGURE 2-1 ■ The Strategic Model for Managerial Communication

Communication Climate

Culture and Values

Stakeholder Concerns

Content

Channel

Physical Environment

Time

Sender

Receiver

Purpose

Major events in an organization's life cycle can affect the communication climate. For example, often when a company is restructuring or a merger is planned, managers reduce the amount of information flowing through the formal channels. The result of this information "vacuum" is employee anxiety and distrust. In such a climate, employees turn to each other, relying on the rumor mill to learn about impending changes and layoffs. Not surprisingly, productivity drops off.

A positive communication climate is fragile. After only one or two critical errors, a positive environment can quickly change to one of distrust and closed communication, making future communication more difficult. This is why the skills and principles discussed in the following chapters are so critical—managers must avoid communication errors that may result in a negative climate.

Culture and Values

Societal and organizational culture form the second factor of the communication context. Culture is the unique set of shared values, beliefs, and behaviors that bind members of nations and organizations together. As Aristotle said, "We are what we repeatedly do." Culture shapes the identity of its members and helps them feel like they belong within the group. It generally remains below the threshold of conscious awareness because it involves taken-for-granted assumptions about how one should perceive, think, and feel. But culture is ubiquitous.

To a large extent, national culture determines how we communicate. In addition to language differences among cultures, many more subtle conventions exist that guide nonverbal behavior, turn-taking, gift-giving practices, and other interpersonal interactions. Chapter 12 discusses more thoroughly how national culture affects business communication.

Organizational culture also affects how managers communicate. If you think about companies with strong cultures, such as Southwest Airlines, Zappos, Google, Stonyfield Farms, or Whole Foods, you will realize that building and maintaining an organizational culture takes hard work. The leaders are great communicators and motivators who clearly and consistently explain the organization's vision, mission, and values. Research shows that there is a link between culture and organizational success—performance-oriented cultures experience statistically better financial growth.[6] Additional benefits of a strong culture are high employee involvement and commitment, work team cohesiveness, clear focus on goals throughout the organization, and well-developed internal communication systems.

CRITICAL THINKING QUESTIONS

1. What adjectives would you use to describe the culture of your workplace?

2. How much of the culture was evident before you began working there?

3. How did you learn about the elements of the organizational culture?

4. In what ways does your organization's culture affect communication practices?

To diagnose the health of your company's culture, look around you during your next meeting or while eating lunch. Listen to the interactions. Watch how the leaders make decisions and disseminate them. For example, in some organizations, e-mail is used for every request, suggestion, and information exchange, whereas in other organizations, face-to-face conversation is the norm.

But an organization's culture affects more than preferences for a particular communication channel. An organization's physical space can affect its culture and encourage or discourage information flow. Office design can consist of closed doors; long, empty hallways; surveillance cameras; and sparse furniture. How many casual conversations are likely to take place among employees who work in such a culture? By contrast, office design can consist of a large, open space free of walls, with lots of seating, music, food, live plants, a waterfall, and employees' work spaces all visible to one another. In such an environment, the organization's cultural values regarding open communication are clear.

CRITICAL THINKING QUESTIONS

1. How does your employer's culture affect your behaviors and decisions at work?

2. What drives the culture? Have you noticed changes over time?

3. Think about how informal communication and rumors circulate through the organization. How accurate are those messages? What is the tone of those messages?

A cultural analysis does not provide definitive answers, but it gives an understanding of generally accepted values. In organizations, these values are manifested in communication practices. For instance, if independence is valued, a persuasive approach rather than a demanding approach may be required. If formality is valued, a formal hardcopy memo rather than a telephone call may be necessary. If extensive technical details are part of the organizational culture, all reports may require technical elaboration. If collaboration is valued, then information flows smoothly and freely among all networked stakeholders.

Stakeholder Concerns

Decisions are not made in a vacuum. Every organization has stakeholders, or people and groups who are affected by its operations. Internal stakeholders include employees and unions, management, and shareholders. External stakeholders include customers, vendors, and government authorities and regulators. Organizations must be aware of the interests of each group and the power they may have to influence decisions.

In recent years, many organizations have gone a step further to develop corporate social responsibility statements. These policies and practices describe how the organization functions as a member of a community, responsible not only to investors and employees but also the public at large.

Effective communicators seek the input of stakeholder groups during project development. Stakeholders can help you identify novel solutions and avoid hidden problems. Failing to secure their cooperation and commitment can interrupt business processes and potentially damage an organization's reputation.

The communication climate, culture and values, and stakeholder concerns will suggest generally accepted patterns of communication. They are depicted as the outer layer of our analysis because these factors are external to the specific situations in which managers communicate. They also tend to be enduring and difficult to change. This layer must be analyzed first as managers develop the communication strategy.

Layer 2: Situational Factors

Once the external context has been analyzed, managers should consider the specific elements of each communication situation: the sender, receiver, and purpose of the message. The relationship of the three variables is circular rather than linear. Each affects the other concurrently; one does not necessarily come before the other. The relationship between the sender and receiver and the purpose of the message—the outcome the sender intends the message to accomplish—will influence the decisions made in third layer of the strategic model.

Sender

The sender is the person, team, or organization who encodes an idea into text, speech, or visual elements. The decisions the sender makes about how to communicate a message are based not only on the external factors of Layer 1 but also on their personal factors, such as age, gender, ethnicity, values, and religious or political beliefs, and their personal and professional experiences. Managers must analyze their own frames of reference and communication preferences to determine how they will affect the outcome of the communication.[7] Thus, self-awareness is critical for effective communication.

For instance, what strategy is best when persuading a work group to accept a new procedure? A manager may have realized he is most comfortable talking with just one person rather than a group, has trouble with grammar but can usually find the right words, is a patient listener, and holds a company position that makes it difficult to place demands on others. Consequently, the manager decides it would be best to meet with employees individually in a face-to-face setting to persuade them to accept the new procedure. The manager thus has strategically analyzed his own frame of reference and his role in the communication situation.

Receiver

The receiver is the person, group, or organization that interprets the message and uses the information to take action, make decisions, or understand concepts. Like the sender, the personal factors of receivers influence the way they interpret messages.

In addition to the personal factors, several characteristics of the receiver require analysis: the relationship between the receiver and the sender, the receiver's relative status, their potential interest in the message, their emotional state, their prior knowledge about the subject of the message, and the impact of the message on their work. Together, these characteristics may cause distortions to the intended message, which are sometimes referred to as *internal noise*. A review of these items indicates the types of strategic communication decisions a manager must make relative to the receiver.

Relationship. Participants in a friendly relationship tolerate error and initial misunderstanding more than do those in a neutral or hostile relationship.[8] Friendly participants need less time and concentration when communicating than is required in a hostile relationship. For instance, suppose a manager discussing a report with a colleague finds a certain table difficult to read. A friendly colleague will be more tolerant and more willing to ask for clarification than will a hostile one who might criticize the report rather than seek clarification or provide constructive criticism.

Status Difference. Status differences may require that certain customs or traditions be integrated into the communication. For example, the sender may need to refer to certain people by their title or honorific to avoid offending the receiver. Also, the sender may need to stand when addressing a person of higher status, but it may be appropriate to sit down with a person of equal or lower status. People of different status levels may easily interpret words and gestures differently.[9] Suppose a manager says, "Can I meet with you for a few minutes?" This simple statement may be a request or a demand, depending on the receiver's status. Obviously, verbal emphasis needs to be adapted to different audiences.

Receiver's Interest. The potential interest level of the receiver in the message affects their level of attention to the message. Senders must assess the receiver's potential interest and make strategic decisions on how to compose the message.[10] If the receiver has low interest, some persuasive elements may be appropriate to get the person's attention, even when the ultimate goal of the message is to inform. A common mistake is to focus on what the sender needs to say rather than what the receiver wants or needs to know. The manager must adapt the nature of the message to fit the interests of the receiver.

Receiver's Emotional State. The receiver's emotional state at the time of communication may affect how the message is received. A receiver upset about something requires a communication strategy different from that used with a relaxed person. Similarly, a receiver who is resistant to an idea requires a different strategy from what would be used with someone who is interested and receptive to the idea. Chapter 8 explains how a direct or indirect organizational pattern can improve the likelihood that the receiver will respond positively.

Receiver's Knowledge. The accuracy of a message is irrelevant if the receiver cannot understand the content. If the receiver does not have sufficient prior knowledge of the situation, or if they do not understand the words or symbols being used, then the message will fail to achieve its purpose. Technical words and examples are appropriate only if everyone involved in the communication transaction understands the terminology; decisions and analyses are understandable only if receivers understand the assumptions and background that support them. Incorrectly assuming the receiver has considerable knowledge may result in a communication breakdown. But assuming too low a level of knowledge may waste time and insult the receiver. A receiver's level of knowledge can be gauged quickly by asking questions and getting feedback. The answer given to an open-ended question on a specific topic is often the best indication of a receiver's level of knowledge. The sender should then adapt the message as necessary.

CRITICAL THINKING QUESTIONS

Think of a communication breakdown you experienced at work between you and a coworker, supervisor, or direct report.

1. Which of the six characteristics of the receiver discussed here can you identify as contributing to the breakdown?

2. What elements of audience analysis will you consider the next time you interact with that person?

Impact on the Receiver's Work. To provide the correct type and amount of information, senders must consider what the receiver will do with the information. How will the information affect the receiver's ability to take action, make decisions, or understand concepts related to their own work?

In addition to the intended receiver, a message may have one or more audiences who also receive the message or may be affected by it. These secondary receivers may be known to the sender (such as when they are included on the cc: line of an e-mail), but they may also be hidden, such as when a report is shared with others, leaked to the public, or archived for future reference. During their strategic analysis, managers should try to imagine who secondary readers might be and how they might interpret the message as well.

In summary, a manager should consider six characteristics of the receiver before communicating, as summarized in Table 2-1: personal relationship, status, interest in the message, emotional state, knowledge, and impact on work. Knowing one's audience is a critical strategy. Next, the manager needs to analyze the purpose of the message for effective communication in critical situations.

TABLE 2-1 ■ Checklist for Analyzing the Receiver
What is the personal relationship of the receiver to the sender?
What is the receiver's relative status?
How interested in the message is the receiver?
What are the receiver's feelings toward the message?
How much does the receiver know about the topic of the message?
What will the receiver do with the information they learn from the message?

Purpose of the Message

The communication goal or purpose often defines the appropriate strategy for a given situation; consequently, effective managers are keenly aware of their communication goals. A manager has four major reasons for choosing to communicate. First, the mere act of communicating with a fellow worker may be enjoyable. Communication does not always have to mean business, although one should not confuse working with socializing. At work, some socializing by managers can boost employee morale and build relationships that make work more efficient and more pleasant.

Second, managers communicate to present information to others. They must share information with their teams, with other groups within the organization, and with clients or vendors. (Chapter 5 addresses presentations in more detail.) Third, managers communicate to gain information that is needed to do their work. Ironically, not all managers distinguish between gaining and presenting information. Many managers tend to do all the talking when they are trying to gain information. Listening, the focus of Chapter 10, is an essential part of effective communication.

Fourth, managers communicate to persuade.[11] Persuasive strategies include the use of data and logical reasoning, emotional appeals to shared values, or references to one's character and credibility. Although each strategy may work independently, the strongest persuasive messages use all three.

The question of goals can become complicated because goals may be combined. For instance, a goal may be to inform a direct report of a new procedure while also persuading them to accept the procedure. In these situations, managers need to identify goals clearly and develop appropriate strategies; otherwise, they may achieve neither goal.

Unless managers analyze their goals, the resulting communication may waste time and effort. By identifying the purpose of the message and analyzing the sender and receiver factors described above, managers can develop strategies to compose effective messages.

Layer 3: Message Factors

We now come to the third layer of the strategic model, which comprises the message itself. When composing a message, managers should consider four elements:

- The specific content of the message
- The message's channel

- The physical environment in which it occurs

- The time the communication occurs

Review the strategic model in Figure 2-1 again. These four elements appear as the central layer because they depend on the contextual factors of climate, culture, and stakeholder concerns and the situational factors of sender, receiver, and purpose of the message. For purposes of discussion, we review each component separately. But again, remember that in reality a manager needs to consider all interrelationships when developing a communication strategy. Neglecting any one component when analyzing a critical situation may result in a communication failure.

Message Content

We can simplify our discussion by classifying the content of a message according to four factors.

First, will the receiver perceive the message as *positive*, *negative*, or *neutral*? When the message is positive, the best strategy is to present the good news immediately; however, with a negative message, it is usually best to present neutral information before the negative news.[12] To determine whether the message is positive or negative, consider the receiver's perspective. What may seem positive to a manager may be negative to the receiver. For example, the manager of an accounting firm was ecstatic as she announced a new contract with a growing firm. But staff members were unhappy with the news because they already felt overworked.

Second, does the message deal with *fact* or *opinion*? Facts are established with data and evidence, but opinion is largely based on assumption. Managers should critically analyze the objective basis of their message because they may feel so sure about their opinion that they will present it as fact. When a manager presents opinions as facts, the receivers may be deceived.

Third, to what extent is the message *important* to the receiver? If the message is important to the manager but not to the receiver, the manager has to use attention-getting techniques and connect the message to the receiver's interests. For instance, an announcement that a staff meeting is to be held at 2:00 p.m. may not capture an employee's interest; however, if the notice states that one of the items on the agenda is a new incentive program, employees are more apt to pay attention.

Fourth, to what extent is the message *controversial*? A controversial message calls for greater explanation of the contextual factors and neutral words that can reduce the emotional response. In these situations, phrases such as "surely you realize," "everyone else believes," "can't you see," or "you have to understand" can make the receiver defensive and create conflict.

Effective managerial communication requires analysis of the content factors summarized in Table 2-2. An effective communicator will consider these factors simultaneously with the sender, receiver, and purpose because they all affect one another when developing a communication strategy.

Channel of the Message

With the advent of sophisticated telecommunications and instant delivery, the question of how the message is to be sent becomes increasingly complicated. Habits further complicate

TABLE 2-2 ■ Checklist for Determining Message Content
Will the receiver consider the message to be negative or positive?
Will the message deal with facts or opinions?
How important will the message be to the receiver?
How controversial will the message be?

channel selection. Managers find ways of communicating that are comfortable for them and continue to use the same methods, even when they are inappropriate. One accounting manager was known for communicating by sticky notes. While these small adhesive papers are handy for commenting on documents, this manager used them to communicate with his direct reports all the time. He would silently approach an employee in her cubicle, attach the sticky note to her monitor, and walk out again. How do you think the employee reacted?

Which channel is appropriate for which message? Written communication (memos, letters, reports) provides the opportunity for permanent records and may be precise and clear; however, it usually does not provide the opportunity for immediate feedback. E-mail is less formal and is often hastily written, but it has the advantages of immediacy, speed, and permanence. Oral communication is often more persuasive than a written message. Texting and phoning can be quick, but they generally provide no permanent record of the conversation. Also, while phone calls allow oral feedback, the participants cannot observe nonverbal behaviors. If body language is important, videoconferencing might be warranted. Because so many factors are involved, it is difficult to declare one channel invariably preferable to another.

The question becomes one of minimizing costs while maximizing communication effectiveness. Should the message be presented to one individual at a time or to a group? While individual communication allows the manager to adapt the message to each person, group communication is quicker and cheaper. The manager needs to decide if individual adaptation is necessary or if the time saved with group communication is more important. Should the message be written, oral, or visual? Should it be formal or informal? Table 2-3 presents some of the options for communication channel. It quickly becomes apparent that there is no single best channel for communication. This is why Chapter 3 presents an extensive discussion of communication channels mediated by some form of technology.

The question of individual versus group is a key to persuasive communication. In some situations, it may be easy to persuade a group of people; however, in other situations, one-on-one communication may be more effective. The manager must strategically analyze all the factors to determine which would be best in a given situation.

Not surprisingly, cost affects all questions regarding channel selection. A letter requires time for drafting and typing. A group meeting requires many individuals to commit their time, and that pooled time can be expensive. These costs need to be balanced with the fact that groups allow for input and feedback from different employees. A telephone call is quick but impermanent. A formal report may be extremely time-consuming to put together, but others may refer to it again later. Thus, managers balance cost and time factors when selecting the appropriate channel for their communication.

TABLE 2-3 ■ Channels of Communication		
	Informal	**Formal**
Oral	Personal conversations	Staff meetings
	Interviews and counseling	Public address system
	Telecommunication	Conferences
	Employee plant tours (orientation)	Directives and training
		Briefings
Written	Bulletin boards	Policy manuals
	Daily news digests	Management newsletters
	E-mail	Intranets
	Blogs	Reports and white papers
	Text messages	Company website
Both oral and written	Face-to-face contact between superior and direct report where written information is exchanged	Company meetings where reports and data are presented
		Performance appraisals
Visual	Video calls	Videos
	Closed-circuit TV	PowerPoint slide decks
	Infographics	Chart talks
	Emoji	
	GIFs	

Physical Environment

The environment in which communication occurs has a clear effect. Just as receiver characteristics may cause internal noise, elements of the physical environment may cause *external noise*. The result is message distortion. Ask four questions when you analyze the environmental factors in strategic communication:

1. Is it a public or private situation?

2. Does it involve a formal or informal setting?

3. What is the physical distance between the sender and the receiver?

4. Is it a familiar or unfamiliar environment?

The answers to each of these questions can significantly affect the communication strategy.

Privacy. Some choices between public and private settings are obvious. For instance, neither the manager nor the direct report would want their annual performance appraisal interview to be conducted in the company cafeteria. But choosing the correct environment for other situations is more difficult. For instance, should a team's performance problem be discussed with each person individually, or should the discussion be held with all members of the team in a public forum? In the past, managers were advised to "praise in public, punish in private." But this simplistic approach to employee feedback can backfire. Singling out direct reports for special attention can result in other employees ostracizing them as the "boss's pet." The outer layer of the strategic model reminds us to consider culture and climate when deciding whether privacy is important as a communication strategy.

Formality. The formality of the setting affects the wording of the message as well as the opportunity for feedback. Thus, while official titles may be appropriate when presenting a formal oral report, they may restrict communication in an informal group discussion. Also, feedback is often more difficult to obtain in a formal setting because questions may seem inappropriate or the questioner may be shy. Finally, people are generally more reserved in their nonverbal behavior in a formal setting, which makes their feedback more difficult to read.

Physical Distance. A third variable to consider is the physical distance between the sender and receiver. Proximity makes messages compelling. In oral communication, physical distance mutes the variations in the voice's tone and loudness and in the participants' gestures and posture. Thus, it is less effective to use these strategies for emphasis when distance is great. In written communication, distance also affects feedback and time. The quality of feedback for a report mailed from Lima, Ohio, to Lima, Peru, may be less timely (and consequently, less useful) than it is for a report exchanged in one building. A manager can expect less comprehensive feedback as distances increase. Distance also makes persuasion more difficult because opposing arguments cannot be answered immediately. A manager may have to decide if it is better to wait until a face-to-face opportunity is available or if the persuasive efforts should occur over a greater distance for the sake of timeliness.

Familiarity. The final factor to consider when discussing environment is its familiarity. This concept needs to be analyzed from the perspective of the sender as well as the receiver. A familiar environment allows the participants to be relaxed, which is important when the information is sensitive or controversial. When communicating in an unfamiliar environment, a manager should anticipate the distractions that may occur. Distractions that we might be accustomed to in our own environment can be unnerving when we encounter them in unfamiliar surroundings. Something as seemingly simple as heavy traffic outside an office window can be a distraction when we are not used to it.

Table 2-4 summarizes the factors that managers must strategically analyze when considering the physical environment of a communication event.

TABLE 2-4 ■ Checklist for Analyzing the Physical Environment
Is the environment public or private?
Is the environment formal or informal?
What is the physical distance between the sender and the receiver?
Is the environment familiar or unfamiliar?

Time

The timing of the message is another important consideration. Messages should be sent at a time when the receiver is most likely to be receptive to its content. It is not appropriate to try to get the attention of someone immediately before an important meeting. Also, it is highly unlikely that a report will receive much attention if it arrives late on a Friday afternoon. As another example, consider the timing of an announcement made at a large urban hospital consisting of several buildings. For several years, landscaping improvements were being installed to improve water runoff. The grounds were beautiful on completion. But as the project was completed, layoffs of hospital staff were announced. It appeared that the landscaping was done at the expense of jobs. Understandably, many employees were bitter about the allocation of funds.

Managers need to consider the amount of time spent in preparing to communicate and the amount of time spent in the process. Consider the time of both managers and receivers to obtain cost and communication efficiency. Thus, while a meeting may at first seem advisable because it allows for questions and feedback, it may not be efficient because of the time required to assemble people. An e-mail or text message may be more efficient in certain situations. If meeting attendees do not receive an agenda well before a meeting, they may be unprepared to participate in the conversation and follow-up will be necessary, requiring even more time. This effort is the type of strategic time decision a manager must make.

Finally, remember that time is power, and time is status. People with busy schedules are perceived as more important than those whom you can approach at any time. While the direct report must make an appointment to see the manager, the manager, who has higher status, can drop in on the employee without notice. Status is also communicated by the amount of time a person is kept waiting.

CRITICAL THINKING QUESTIONS

Think about a situation in which you committed, experienced, or witnessed miscommunication. Analyze the situation using the strategic model presented here.

1. Where did you (or whoever was communicating) go wrong?
2. What could have been done to avoid the miscommunication?

FEEDBACK AND MEASURES OF EFFECTIVENESS

Integral to a strategic management communication approach are feedback and measures of effectiveness. These variables are not included in the strategic model (Figure 2-1) because they are inherent in each variable and cannot be separated. Feedback is important in two ways. First, it should be continually obtained to determine how changing events may affect the overall strategy. For instance, a manager determines that an e-mail about a new procedure was not as clear as he thought because many questions were being asked. Based on this feedback, he quickly calls a meeting to clarify the procedure. In this case, the channel is changed to improve the communication strategy.

Second, feedback may be obtained to determine if the strategy was effective, even though it may be too late to change it. Unfortunately, many managers may avoid this feedback because they believe nothing can be done about it. For example, an advertising agency submits a proposal for an ad campaign. When the contract is given to another agency, the tendency is not to evaluate the effectiveness of the written proposal. After all, nothing can be done about it now. But this is the opportunity to thoroughly evaluate all aspects of the proposal, including such items as an analysis of the receiver, writing style, and timing. Lessons thus learned should be applied to the next proposal. Postmortems, while unpleasant and often avoided, are valuable tools for organizational improvement.

Obtaining feedback and measuring effectiveness may be extremely difficult. In one case, a regional insurance manager was disappointed in sales. She wrote a number of letters, made phone calls, and personally met with her independent sales agents to motivate them, yet sales continued to slide. She contracted with a management consultant to determine how she could improve her motivational strategies. However, it could not be determined if poor sales were the result of communication with the sales agents or the insurance products themselves. Managerial communication is so interrelated with other factors that it is often difficult to determine effectiveness.

CRITICAL THINKING QUESTIONS

Consider a time when you failed to reach your goal, whether in a personal activity or on a work project.

1. Who provided you with feedback?

2. How welcome was the feedback you received from each source?

3. What did you do differently the next time you faced a similar challenge?

CRITICAL ERRORS IN COMMUNICATION

The communication process depends on the personalities of those involved and the environment in which they operate. The strategic model helps managers analyze communication situations and plan their messages to increase their effectiveness. Yet managers still make critical errors caused by problems with the way we interpret the world around us.

Even when people believe they are communicating what is real, they are communicating only their perception of reality, which is filtered by their personal experience, values and beliefs, and even language.[13] These mental filters cause three critical but common errors that inhibit our ability to communicate: the assumption–observation error, the failure-to-discriminate error, and the allness error.[14]

The Assumption–Observation Error

An assumption occurs when people accept something as valid without requiring proof. Every day we act on assumptions. For example, we assume the food in the cafeteria is not toxic (despite our persistent jokes to the contrary), the ceiling in the office will not fall, and numbers being used in a report are valid. In each case, we may not have proof that what we believe is true, but we place our trust in others to be able to continue our day. Assumptions are essential and desirable in analyzing materials, solving problems, and planning. Without them, we would be paralyzed by indecision or lack of information.

When we drop a letter in the mailbox, we assume it will reach its destination in a reasonable time. But is this assumption completely accurate? Evidence suggests the letter may be lost, delayed, or even destroyed. So we take a calculated risk. If the same envelope contains something valuable, we insure the envelope's contents. If it is irreplaceable, we may deliver the item ourselves to ensure its safety.

The assumption–observation error occurs when managers assume their personal observations, experiences, and interpretations of the world around them are accurate and ignore other explanations that are equally or more valid. Consider the following example.

The manager of the quality control department noticed that Andre, a new chemist, was extremely conscientious. Andre remained after work at least a half hour every night to check all the figures. The manager was so impressed with Andre's commitment that she wrote a special commendation letter for his personal file. Later, the manager discovered Andre was really having a lot of difficulty with the tests and was remaining late to correct the many errors he normally made.

To avoid the assumption–observation error, a manager should ask, "What are the facts? What else could be causing this to happen?" Facts and assumptions should be clearly stated. For instance, a fact is "I see we got a shipment of copper," but an assumption is "We must have paid extra for expedited shipping." Expressions such as "in my opinion," "it looks to me as if," and "I am assuming" can differentiate between fact and assumption. Just as these phrases can help managers clarify in their own minds when they are using assumptions, they also give the receivers a clearer understanding of the message.

The Failure to Discriminate

In addition to making assumptions, we also take shortcuts in our thinking. We often look for similarities rather than differences. In its most extreme form, this penchant for similarities leads us to think in stereotypes rather than individual cases.

The failure to discriminate is the failure to perceive and communicate significant differences among individuals or changes in situations. This failure to make clear distinctions can lead us to ignore differences and overemphasize similarities. Diversity in teams can help us overcome this weakness by providing alternate points of view that bring those differences into focus.

One of the consequences of the failure to discriminate is what William Haney called "hardening of the categories." A leading researcher in the field of interpersonal communication and organizational behavior, Haney observed,

Most of us have a penchant for categorizing—for classifying. Show someone something he has never seen before and one of his first questions is likely to be: "What kind is it?" We meet a new person and we are uneasy until we can pigeonhole: What is she? How is she classified? Is she a salesperson, plumber, farmer, teacher, painter? Is she Protestant, Catholic, Jew, atheist? Democrat, Republican, independent? Lower, middle, upper "class"?[15]

This hardening of categories can result in stereotypes because people may apply their preconceived notions of the group to any individual within the group, regardless of their accuracy. One common example concerns managers who are interviewing job applicants. An applicant may have attended a school whose graduates the interviewer categorizes as undesirable. Therefore, the interviewer does not fully listen to the applicant. The hardening of categories can also cause a person to communicate in terms of general categories rather than specifics and thus lose valuable information. For example, "Joyce is a union member" omits the fact that she is the most qualified inspector in the department.

Even more dangerous than the categorization itself is the fact that people are usually not aware they are doing it. Unconscious bias develops from years of societal and parental conditioning to think certain ways or accept some beliefs over others. Unconscious bias makes failure to discriminate an extremely difficult tendency to overcome. However, Haney provided two valuable suggestions.[16] The first is to internalize the premise of uniqueness—to develop a sensitivity to all the differences in the world. No two things, whether snowflakes or siblings, have ever been found to be exactly the same. A second technique is to index evaluations. This means each person, thing, or situation should be indexed according to some unique characteristic. This can soon lead to the conclusion that everything and everyone is unique and, in turn, provides sensitivity to differences.

Polarization is a special form of failure to discriminate that involves "either-or" thinking. Some situations are true dichotomies that can be stated in terms of either-or. An employee is either absent or present. However, we cannot accurately describe many situations in either-or terms: A product is neither good nor bad; a worker moves neither fast nor slow. Polarization occurs when a person ignores gradations and middle ground and focuses on strict either-or terms. Thus, if a person is told the only options are either success or failure, the person may begin to believe that no other possibilities exist. When managers are wary of either-or statements, they can more accurately distinguish the degree of differences between two items and more accurately perceive the world.

Frozen evaluation is another failure to discriminate. It occurs when people disregard changes in persons, places, or things. Because everything in the world changes, evaluations cannot remain static. However, while it is easy to say that change is a major aspect of business, it is often difficult to adapt to that continuous change. Frozen evaluation can result in an inaccurate perception of the world, and management errors may result.

The key to avoiding frozen evaluations is to remember that all things change. The manager who continually asks what has changed about the situation and how that may require them to reevaluate opinions can prevent this common and critical communication error.

Allness and the Process of Abstraction

A third critical error that managers often make is to structure communications as if what they are stating is all there is to know about a subject. The astute person knows that reality is too complex for anyone to know all there is to know about something. As Bertrand Russell stated, "one's certainty varies inversely with one's knowledge." Haney states that allness is the result of two false beliefs: (1) It is possible to know and say everything about something, and (2) what I am saying (or writing or thinking) includes all that is important about the subject.[17]

Normal communication patterns contribute to the problem of allness because people abstract as they speak. Abstracting is the process of focusing on some details and omitting others. But what we choose to include can manipulate receivers of the message, suggesting that our interpretation is the only one and offering no warning that certain information is being left out. Sometimes the more that is omitted, the harder it is to recognize that one has left out anything.

Almost everything we do involves some level of abstraction, so the solution to the allness error is not simply to omit abstraction. Rather, the solution is to be aware of the level of abstraction occurring and phrase the message accordingly: "as far as I know," "according to the information I have," or "this is what I consider to be the critical information." When you are the receiver, overcome the allness error by asking, "What information has been omitted?" or simply "What else?" Table 2-5 summarizes the questions to ask in order to avoid committing three critical errors when communicating.

The foregoing critical errors—assumption–observation, failure to discriminate, and allness—have been discussed largely from the perspective of the intrapersonal and interpersonal levels of communication. However, management communication seldom operates at just the intra- or interpersonal level. Communication becomes more complex as more people become involved and commit their own versions of each error. More is said about group and organizational levels of communication in Chapter 4, which is dedicated to meetings and group dynamics, while Chapter 12 addresses intercultural communication.

TABLE 2-5   ■   How to Avoid Critical Errors

Critical Error	Question to Ask
Assumption–observation	What are the facts?
Failure to discriminate	What labels have I applied to this situation?
Allness	What else is going on?

SUMMARY

Managerial communication occurs at five levels: intrapersonal, interpersonal, group, organizational, and intercultural. Each of these levels is considered in this text.

The strategic model of managerial communication helps managers analyze situations and reduce errors in critical situations. The contingency approach to communication suggests that there are no concrete rules that will serve in every instance, but the strategic model offers several factors managers should review before communicating.

The first layer of the strategic model is the contextual factors of communication climate, culture and values, and stakeholder concerns. These external factors tend to be durable and intractable. The second layer involves the specific situational factors of sender, receiver, and purpose of the message. The third layer is the message itself, which includes content, channel, physical environment, and time. Managers must analyze the variables in each layer to compose messages that are appropriate for each situation. After the message is delivered, managers must also seek feedback and measures of effectiveness to continuously improve their communication skills.

In spite of this preparation, several critical errors in the communication process are caused by our interpretations of reality. The assumption–observation error results when a manager relies on personal observation and experience rather than objective data. The failure to discriminate happens when a manager focuses on similarities and ignores significant differences between people or things. The allness error occurs when a person structures communication as if it states all there is to know about a subject. Managers need to consider all these factors and human foibles when communicating.

CASES FOR ANALYSIS

Case 2-1

Can Temperature Be Sexist?

The negotiation terms of a political debate include time, format, question style, and topic. But in 2018, the debate between New York Governor Andrew Cuomo and challenger Cynthia Nixon included the temperature of the room, too. Nixon argued that the chilly settings were "notoriously sexist" and gave an advantage to Cuomo, who has a reputation for preferring cooler settings.[18]

Was this a ruse, or did Nixon's argument have merit? A 2015 study suggested that temperature recommendations for office spaces are based on metabolic rates of men in the 1960s who wore business suits.[19] Those standards continue today, even though offices are now filled with women, who often have lower metabolic rates and wear lighter clothing than their male counterparts.

Questions

1. How does this standard reflect the failure to discriminate?

2. How might a cold physical environment affect communication and working conditions for employees?

3. What are other situations in which a small group of people assumed that their experience or limited data set applied to other groups when making decisions?

Case 2-2

The Shroud of Technology

Ben knocked on the door of Nancy Kerr, his supervising director.

"Come in," Nancy said, and Ben entered. He was frustrated, and his demeanor reflected it.

"I need to talk to you about Stacey Burton, who works in the office beside mine," Ben said. "Ever since we rearranged the office suite about a month ago, Stacey has been coming by and standing in the door of my office, just to flirt and to chat. It interrupts my work, and I'm uncomfortable with the overt attention, especially flirtatious attention," Ben continued. "I'm also getting deluged with non-work-related e-mails from Stacey."

"Have you asked Stacey to stop?" asked Nancy.

"Well, not really. The interaction could easily be taken as office banter, if you just heard the words. It is the way Stacey gestures and speaks and looks at me that makes it flirting," Ben said. "I'm really not comfortable with initiating a confrontation with Stacey and thought maybe you would be willing to say something instead."

"I'll be happy to—probably today," Nancy replied. "I'll send an e-mail now. Thanks for bringing this to my attention."

Nancy sent an e-mail asking Stacey to come to Nancy's office briefly at 2:00 p.m.

At 1:55, Nancy heard a knock and said, "Come in."

A young man came in and sat down. "Can I help you?" Nancy asked.

"Well, you said you wanted to talk to me. What can I do for you?" he asked.

"I wanted to talk to you?" asked Nancy.

"Yes," the young man replied. "I'm Stacey Burton."

Questions

1. What assumption–observation error might be made in this scenario?

2. To what extent did the use of technology for these message exchanges contribute to the miscommunication between Nancy and Stacey?

3. What gender stereotypes discussed in Chapter 1 apply to this case?

4. How would you, in Nancy's shoes, handle the awkward moment and the ensuing discussion?

Case 2-3

Developing a Brochure

Mitch Finley, a 29-year-old with a degree in finance, began working as a loan officer at a bank 2 years ago. Later, he began consulting for other businesses in financial planning. His career goal has been to start his own business.

Recently, Finley opened The Suite Thing, a development company using one of his original business ideas—the construction of two large hotel-like buildings containing suites (living room, bedroom, kitchen) rather than single rooms.

The hotels are located in two cities that are important regional centers for the oil industry. Instead of renting the suites, he is selling them to large oil companies to meet entertainment and tax-planning needs.

Finley had been using a brochure his architects put together, but he was not pleased with its presentation. He had collected other company brochures that he liked and decided to call an advertising firm to design a new brochure and logo for his company.

In the initial meeting, Finley told the advertising representative he needed a new company logo and a brochure folder that would hold his leaflets. Most important, the logo and kit had to be completed as soon as possible because time was money to him.

The advertising representative (very new on the job) acknowledged that his company could do logo and brochure layouts. The representative then asked Finley a few general questions about his two projects—what they involved, where they were located, and their surroundings. The agency rep said he would return within 1 week with his ideas.

More than 2 weeks later, Finley called the advertising agency and wanted to know if it had developed the materials. The representative came by later that afternoon with his idea. The agency's approach centered on a hard-sell theme of "Beat the Hotel Game with the Suite Thing." Finley, frustrated by the response delay and the inconsistency between the advertising agency's offering and his own image of the project, said, "No, that's not at all what I want." The advertising representative, taken aback, sat in silence for a time before responding in a frustrated voice, "Well, what do you see your project as being?" and reminded him of the time constraints Finley had given. Finley said he did not see hotels as his competitors, and he wanted a brochure and logo that used soft-sell to introduce his idea to top-level executives as an investment.

The next day the advertising representative returned with a more conservative, soft-sell piece. Finley said, "That's *kind of* what I want, but not really."

Finley cannot understand why he did not get what he wanted the first time because "that's their business and they should know how to do it."

Questions

1. What are some possible causes of Finley's communication problem? Of the advertising representative's?

2. Identify how assumptions caused communication problems in this case.

3. What actions would you recommend to the advertising representative to ensure this does not happen again?

4. Do you believe there is a communication deadlock? If so, what should the participants do to resolve it?

(Continued)

(Continued)

Case 2-4

Resigning From the TV Station

Jane Rye is a student of advertising at the local state university and will graduate at the end of the next term. She has a part-time job in the sales department at a local television station. When hired, Rye thought she was very lucky to have a job there, not only for the money but also for the work experience.

Pat Trent, the sales manager who hired her, was Rye's immediate supervisor. Rye was doing a very good job and received considerable support from Trent. In fact, the sales manager had nothing but praise for Rye's work when reporting to top management. Trent often told her direct report that her work was exceptional and that Trent would like to hire her on a permanent basis after graduation to head a new media research department for the station. The job seemed to promise a challenging and rewarding career.

While Rye was flattered by the offer, she was not interested in the position because she found her present job unsatisfying. However, she never told Trent her feelings about the job or the possible appointment. Because Trent had trained Rye and had promoted her to everyone, Rye had become very loyal and grateful to her sales manager. Thus, Rye thought she would betray Trent if she were to refuse the job. After 6 weeks, however, Rye decided to quit and work part-time

at the university, but she did not know how to approach her boss.

Rye, feeling unable to say anything unpleasant to Trent, let time pass until the day she was ready to quit to start her new job. When Rye got to work that day, the sales manager was scheduled to leave town later that morning. Rye was forced to go into Trent's office while two other people were there discussing another matter. Trent asked Rye what she wanted, and Rye replied, "I am resigning." The sales manager was taken completely by surprise, asked Rye why she was resigning, and wondered what was to be done with the project Rye was handling. Rye apologized for such short notice. Rye explained that she was taking a part-time job at the school starting tomorrow. Trent, very disappointed in her direct report, said, "If you had told me sooner, I could have transferred the project to someone else—now I'm in a bind."

Questions

1. Analyze the situation using the strategic model. What factors did Rye fail to consider when planning to share her news with Trent?

2. How should Rye have handled her resignation differently? Why would that have improved the experience?

3. What are some possible long-term repercussions of the way Rye handled her resignation?

Notes

1. A comprehensive guide for managers of diverse workforces is found in Geraldine E. Hynes, *Get Along, Get It Done, Get Ahead: Interpersonal Communication in the Diverse Workplace* (New York: Business Expert Press, 2015). For a list of key managerial skills that 2,115 managers and executives identified, see the results of the American Management Association's "AMA Critical Skills Survey: Workers Need Higher

Level Skills to Succeed in the 21st Century," available online at https://www.amanet.org/articles/ama-critical-skills-survey-workers-need-higher-level-skills-to-succeed-in-the-21st-century.

2. Lee Thayer, *Communication and Communication Systems* (Burr Ridge, IL: Richard D. Irwin, 1968). For a comprehensive review of

communication theories and taxonomies, see Stephen W. Littlejohn and Karen A. Foss, *Encyclopedia of Communication Theory* (Thousand Oaks, CA: Sage, 2009).

3. Cynthia Stohl, "Globalizing Organizational Communication," in *The New Handbook of Organizational Communication: Advances in Theory, Research, and Methods,* eds. Fredric M. Jablin and Linda L. Putnam (Thousand Oaks, CA: Sage, 2001), 323–77.

4. Kendra Reed, Jerry Goolsby, and Michelle Johnston, "Extracting Meaning and Relevance from Work: The Potential Connection Between the Listening Environment and Employee's Organizational Identification and Commitment," *International Journal of Business Communication* 53, no. 3 (2016): 326–42.

5. Two examples of studies confirming a direct relationship between work performance and corporate climate are Michael Riketta, "The Causal Relation between Job Attitudes and Performance: A Meta-Analysis of Panel Studies," *Journal of Applied Psychology* 93 (2008): 472–81; and Malcolm G. Patterson et al., "Validating the Organizational Climate Measure: Links to Managerial Practices, Productivity and Innovation," *Journal of Organizational Behavior*, 26 (2005): 379–408.

6. Shawn Parr, "Culture Eats Strategy for Lunch," *Fast Company*, January 24, 2012, http://www.fastcompany.com/1810674/culture-eats-strategy-for-lunch.

7. John Petit Jr. and Bobby C. Vaught, "Self-Actualization and Interpersonal Capability in Organizations," *Journal of Business Communication* 21, no. 3 (1984): 33–40.

8. Joseph N. Cappella, "Interpersonal Communication: Definitions and Fundamental Questions," in *Handbook of Communication Science,* eds. C. R. Berger and S. H. Chaffee (Newbury Park, CA: Sage, 1987), 184–238.

9. Vanessa M. Strike and Claus Rerup, "Mediated Sensemaking," *Academy of Management Journal* 59, no. 3 (June 2016): 880–905.

10. Kitty O. Locker, "Theoretical Justifications for Using Reader Benefits," *Journal of Business Communication* 19, no. 3 (1982): 51–66.

11. Mohan R. Limaye, "The Syntax of Persuasion: Two Business Letters of Request," *Journal of Business Communication* 20, no. 2 (1983): 17–30.

12. Barbara Shwom and Lisa Gueldenzoph Snyder, *Business Communication: Polishing Your Professional Presence*, 3rd ed. (Hoboken, NJ: Pearson Education, 2016), 189–91.

13. Kenneth Burke, *Language as Symbolic Action: Essays on Life, Literature and Method* (Berkeley: University of California Press, 1966).

14. Much of this discussion is drawn from William V. Haney, *Communication and Interpersonal Relations: Text and Cases,* 6th ed. (Burr Ridge, IL: Irwin Professional Press, 1992).

15. Ibid., 360.

16. Ibid.

17. Ibid.

18. Shane Goldmacher, "Cuomo vs. Nixon Debate? It's Already Heated (Literally)," *New York Times*, August 28, 2018, https://www.nytimes.com/2018/08/28/nyregion/cuomo-nixon-debate-demands-ny.html.

19. Boris Kingma and Wouter van Marken Lichtenbelt, "Energy Consumption in Buildings and Female Thermal Demand," *Nature Climate Change* 5 (2015): 1054–56, https://doi.org/10.1038/nclimate2741.

3

COMMUNICATING WITH TECHNOLOGY

LEARNING OBJECTIVES

By the end of this chapter, you will be able to

- Describe the roles of bandwidth, perceived personal closeness, feedback, and symbolism in technologically mediated communication.

- Explain how technology affects message sensitivity, negativity, complexity, and persuasiveness.

- Select appropriate digital channels and apply best practices for a variety of workplace messages.

If you spend as much time as most managers do creating and responding to e-mail, texting your staff, blogging, participating in webinars and virtual meetings, and compulsively checking your phone at stoplights, you may well assume that developments in technology will determine the future of business communication. Where does a discussion of technologically mediated communication begin? Technology is changing so quickly that it sometimes seems impossible to get a focus on the topic. Forty years ago, a communication theorist stated, "Communication is essentially a social affair . . . but life in the modern world is coming to depend, more and more, upon 'technical' means of communication, telephone and telegraph, radio and printing."[1] That observation was prescient.

Think about how rapidly technology has developed in the past fifty years. Only a couple of generations ago, the communication revolution meant the long-distance telephone. The computer on the *Apollo 11* spacecraft in 1969 had less computing power than a modern pocket calculator. Until the VisiCalc spreadsheet was developed in 1979, few people could imagine the need for a personal computer. Today, you probably carry a personal computer in your pocket: a smartphone that is more powerful than IBM's Deep Blue supercomputer.[2]

Electronic communication channels are an integral part of our work lives. The whole rationale for reliance on technology is increased efficiency and productivity, and recent research does provide some evidence to support this assumption. But technology is not merely a beneficial tool; it's a force that must be constantly reassessed. Technological innovation is not always good merely because it is innovative. It's a thin line to walk, and it requires some creative thinking to stay balanced between technological aptitude and overkill.[3]

Given the speed with which business communication technology changes, it is unrealistic to assume that this chapter will accurately reflect available technology when we wrote it and when you read it. The chapter focuses on *best practices* instead, some time-honored principles for using technology in the workplace. Reading it will help you develop a framework for making strategic decisions in the use of whatever technologically mediated communication tools are available at that time.

CRITICAL THINKING QUESTIONS

1. How often are you interrupted by incoming e-mail, instant messaging, or text messages at work?

2. How does that impact your productivity? How long does it take you to refocus on your work after the interruption?

3. Given that 28 percent of a typical office worker's time is spent being interrupted, to what extent does technology help versus hinder efficiency?

A FRAMEWORK FOR USING TECHNOLOGICALLY MEDIATED COMMUNICATION

With technologically mediated communication, a technological channel transmits the communication. The decision to use a telephone, e-mail, text message, or teleconference can be complicated because of the many variables involved. To understand these variables, refer to the strategic communication model in Chapter 2 and the discussion on strategy. Four concepts help us understand the use of technologically mediated communication: *bandwidth*, *perceived personal closeness*, *feedback*, and the *symbolic interactionist perspective*.[4]

Bandwidth

Communication occurs along five sensory channels: visual, auditory, tactile, gustatory, and olfactory.[5] Bandwidth is the information transmission capacity of the available sensory channels. Face-to-face communication between two people within an arm's length of each other has a wide bandwidth because it can use all five channels. When a manager first meets a job applicant, the two people usually shake hands. They are concurrently sharing visual, auditory, tactile, and olfactory cues, so this communication has a wide bandwidth.

Mediated communication generally omits one or more of the channels. For instance, a videoconference omits tactile and olfactory cues, while the telephone omits tactile, olfactory, and visual cues.

How many messages sent via different channels can the mind comprehend at one time? This theoretical question has plagued communication researchers for centuries, but it remains a relevant question when considering technologically mediated communication. To help understand this question, imagine a Y. The arms of the Y are different communication channels. Assume that each communication message or bit is a ball that approaches our brain—the base of the Y—along an arm of the Y. What happens if both balls approach the intersection of the Y concurrently, but there is room for only one ball? Information jamming will occur. In terms of information theory, selective attention results, so the receiver pays attention to only one of the information bits while ignoring the others. In other words, the mind decides which ball can proceed to the base of the Y. This process is diagrammed in Figure 3-1.

The goal is to have as much information as possible processed in the central nervous system without jamming. How many cues from different sources can be processed simultaneously?[6] The concept of between-channel redundancy (BCR) suggests that we can process more information when it is shared among auditory, olfactory, tactile, gustatory, or visual channels.

Consider meeting a job applicant. When auditory and visual channels transmit identical information, BCR is complete. When the person speaks in an articulate, precise manner and sustains eye contact, the cues complement each other and signal confidence. BCR is mixed or incomplete when different channels transmit conflicting or incongruous

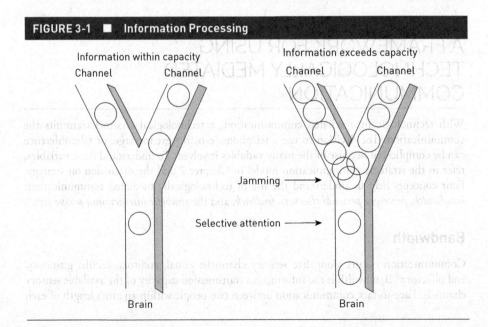

FIGURE 3-1 ■ Information Processing

Information within capacity

Channel   Channel

Information exceeds capacity

Channel   Channel

Jamming →

Selective attention →

Brain   Brain

information. BCR is zero when each channel transmits completely different or contradictory information. Other things being equal, information transfer is theoretically most effective when BCR is complete. Interference is highest when BCR is zero. Information theory has not been able to totally determine what information humans process or how they process it, but we do know that humans can process only a limited amount of information they encounter. Managers must be aware of these limitations and avoid overpowering others with useless cues.

Bandwidth is a factor in the choice of communication technology. Videoconferencing might offer a richer experience, but sharing data and files in real time during a meeting may not be important. Even visual cues may be of little value or even distract from the critical audio message that can be provided with a simple, audio-only teleconference.

On the other hand, managers typically should not choose communication channels with narrow bandwidths for emotional messages. Text messaging an employee that she has been terminated or e-mailing an expression of sympathy for the loss of a loved one are "tech-etiquette" blunders that are becoming all too common. And the broadest bandwidth channel, face-to-face, may be crucial for effectively communicating with key clients, especially in certain cultural contexts, as discussed in Chapter 12.

If circumstances require the use of a narrow bandwidth channel to transmit a sensitive message, managers should do their best to offset the consequences. An example was provided by a major corporation that used e-mail to notify 400 employees of layoffs. While initial reactions to that channel choice for termination notices may be critical, a closer look shows that the company chose e-mail because it was efficient and practical for the mass announcement. In addition, company officials had held a series of meetings (a broad bandwidth channel) during which they explained the method they would use. Employees also could use the company intranet site to find answers to their questions.[7] Thus, managers should consider using multiple channels of varying bandwidth for important, emotional messages.

In addition to the concept of bandwidth, the theory of *electronic propinquity* or perceived personal closeness provides a framework for understanding technologically mediated communication.

Perceived Personal Closeness

Participants in the communication process can feel either attached or removed from each other. Two people in the same room may feel miles apart, whereas those on different continents may feel close to each other. Many factors, such as the history of the two people as communication partners, can affect this feeling of closeness. Of particular concern here is how media affect the feeling of closeness or propinquity.

Much research indicates that electronic media affect the extent to which people feel close to each other. For instance, some people are much more apprehensive about leaving voicemail messages than others and feel uncomfortable even when making a simple call.[8,9] When this apprehension exists, telephone conversations will not help a person feel psychologically close to another. Indeed, the psychological distance could be increased because of the accompanying apprehension. Some suggest it is the inability of the communicator to read nonverbal communication that causes this apprehension.[10] Others, however, may prefer and enjoy some form of technology over face-to-face communication. An example is a person's reliance on a smartphone for friendly interactions. When a person feels warm to the technology, psychological distance may be decreased.

Telecommunications may actually increase a person's sense of closeness. Instant messaging (IM) has become the long-distance communication medium of choice for young adults. More similar to electronic conversations than e-mail, IM conversations often consist of inconsequential small talk, but they also offer opportunities for more substantial social support.[11] A recent study found that texts and instant messages, particularly those with emoticons, can create a sense of playfulness that enhances interpersonal relationships.[12] There are more than 3.2 billion IM accounts worldwide, and the fastest growing sector is business use.[13] Some managers prefer texting coworkers rather than e-mailing or leaving voicemail messages because they ensure quick, brief responses, especially when they are in the field rather than in their offices.

Interestingly, voicemail is becoming obsolete as an interpersonal communication tool. Coca Cola and JP Morgan Chase recently eliminated voicemail from many of their offices to save money on unused technology.[14] While a human voice may seem to convey personal closeness more successfully than text, the number of steps required for dialing in and checking voicemail messages, recording the phone numbers, redialing, and leaving a return message may be more trouble than it is worth. Research shows that employees take longer to reply to voice messages than other types of technology—more than 30 percent of voice messages are not retrieved after three days. By contrast, 90 percent of all text messages are read within a few minutes.[15]

The impact of electronic media on feelings of personal closeness has not yet been adequately determined, but there is some evidence for an inverse relationship between technology use and closeness. Preliminary research on this question indicates that overuse of technology does indeed affect interpersonal relationships. For example, a research team led by Brian Wansink at Cornell University found that children and adults who avoid or are denied eye contact are more likely to suffer from feelings of isolation and to exhibit antisocial traits and other psychological problems. The researchers hypothesize that people who spend more time looking at their mobile devices than at one another suffer impaired emotional intelligence and social facility.[16] Managers need to determine the extent to which perceived personal closeness is important in different situations. Also, to what extent do various types of technology affect this closeness between the sender and receiver? If this question is not addressed, inappropriately used technology designed to enhance managerial communication may be destructive rather than constructive.

In addition to bandwidth and electronic propinquity, we should consider a third factor, *feedback*, when discussing technologically mediated communication.

Feedback

Feedback binds the sender and receiver together so that they truly communicate with each other. Feedback is always present if it is sought. To understand fully the implications of this statement in relationship to mediated communication, it is important to consider both bandwidth and perceived personal closeness.

Mediated communication may reduce channels for obtaining feedback. When using the telephone, we do not see the facial expression of our communication partner. Thus, feedback is reduced. Also, when managers are not totally comfortable with a particular medium, they may ignore potential feedback cues. Consider a conference call involving five people at five locations. Such a call requires a different set of skills than a normal conversation, and the manager may not be totally comfortable with the situation. Not only are different skills required to monitor feedback; the manager's anxiety may also reduce attention to feedback.

Videoconferencing offers an additional channel of feedback, although it is reduced and it is not possible to make eye-to-eye contact. These limitations suggest videoconferencing works better for groups that already know each other. The major advantages of videoconferencing are time savings. A meeting with participants miles apart can be arranged without accounting for travel time or costs, an important consideration for geographically dispersed members of an organization. Meetings via videoconference also tend to be shorter than face-to-face meetings.[17]

The feedback cycle can be dramatically shortened with technology. Document exchange and review has shortened from hours using fax to minutes using e-mail and file-sharing technologies, even when managers are separated geographically. At the same time, the reduced time for feedback can cause problems. According to information theory discussed earlier, we have limited capabilities to process information, so managers may be pressured to decipher information and respond quickly just because the technology allows it. Imagine a manager who receives about 200 e-mails and text messages daily. These media represent speed and responsiveness. But constant interruptions such as text and e-mail alerts may result in stress and overload. Recent research examining the effects of interruption overload and continuous partial attention is alarming. Many people believe they can work on multiple items at once, but only 2 percent of the population can truly multitask.[18] The rest of us make small shifts in attention that slow us down as we repeatedly refocus and reduce productivity by as much as 40 percent.[19] Higher cognitive functions, starting with decision making, can be impaired. Fragmentation of attention also appears to impede creativity.[20] Multitasking, rather than a step toward efficiency, apparently prevents us from focusing on anything in a significant way.[21] Managers need to be aware that continuous availability for feedback may have damaging consequences on their thought processes.

The impression that a manager must respond quickly brings us to our discussion of the fourth concept that helps us understand technologically mediated communication, *symbolic interactionism*.

A Symbolic Interactionist Perspective

Symbolic interactionism is a concept that can be used to explain sociological and psychological phenomena. In the imagery of symbolic interactionism, we view society as a dynamic web of communication. Thus, society and every organization in which managers function constitute an interaction. An interaction is symbolic because people assign meaning to things and events. Over time, many symbols evolve within the organization as members collectively agree on their meaning.[22]

The media that managers choose to use for communication may be based partially on symbolic reasons. Some argue that managerial communication behavior represents ritualistic responses to the need to appear competent, intelligent, legitimate, and rational.[23] For example, a face-to-face medium may symbolize concern or caring. Conversely, the manager who congratulates an employee on 25 years of service with an e-mail message may unintentionally communicate a lack of personal concern. A handwritten note or a special card would symbolize more personal warmth to some people.

CRITICAL THINKING QUESTIONS

1. Pretend that a close coworker has just suffered the loss of a family member. You wish to express your condolences. Which channel will you use: a paper sympathy card sent by mail, an e-mail, a phone call, or a post on the coworker's Facebook page? Why?

2. Which channel do you think the coworker will appreciate the most? Why?

3. What is the symbolic value of each channel?

A comprehensive study of managers and their communication media indicates that channel choice is highly symbolic.[24] Managers interviewed in this study said they choose the face-to-face channel to signal a desire for teamwork, to build trust or goodwill, or to convey informality. Both face-to-face and telephone communication symbolized urgency, showed personal concern, and signaled deference to the receiver who preferred that medium. By contrast, written media were thought to show authority, make a strong impression, and be legitimate and official. Written media were also used to get attention and to comply with protocol. The results of this study indicate that managers should not simply rely on the channel they feel most comfortable with when communicating; they should consider its symbolism.

In summary, managers should consider four factors when deciding on the most effective and efficient use of mediated communication: bandwidth, perceived closeness, feedback, and symbolism. The choice of technology has become rather complicated, and it is difficult to generalize from one situation to another. But certain general conclusions can be stated.

USING THE FRAMEWORK TO MAKE DECISIONS

The framework for technology mediated communication explains why not all technology is appropriate for all types of messages. This section will help you apply the framework for technology mediated communication to decisions about technology by categorizing messages along four continuums: sensitivity, negativity, complexity, and persuasiveness (as illustrated in Figure 3-2).[25]

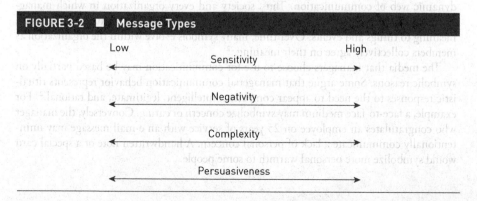

FIGURE 3-2 ■ Message Types

Sensitivity
Low ←——————————————————→ High

Negativity
←——————————————————→

Complexity
←——————————————————→

Persuasiveness
←——————————————————→

Message Sensitivity

A sensitive message is one that evokes an emotional reaction from the receiver. Neutral messages convey information that readers process and respond to intellectually but not emotionally. Receivers will not become upset with neutral messages, but neither will they become ecstatic or pleased.

Sensitive messages should usually be communicated in face-to-face settings to increase the personal element. An extreme example is when a U.S. soldier is killed in battle. A military representative first informs relatives in a personal meeting. Telephone calls are not considered an option. An example at the other end of the sensitivity continuum is that a regular meeting's agenda could be circulated by e-mail, and a meeting reminder could be posted on employees' calendars using Microsoft Outlook. Face-to-face interaction would be an inefficient channel for this routine purpose.

What if it is not possible to communicate a sensitive message face-to-face? Here, the technology with the widest bandwidth should be used. Also, an interactive system with an opportunity for feedback should be used in a supplemental way if possible. Symbolically, this may indicate a high level of concern. For instance, a company with offices in several states was forced to restructure. The grapevine was rampant with concerns about layoffs, loss of benefits, and forced relocations. It was not possible for the CEO to visit all the locations in a timely manner, so she chose to announce the general plan for the restructuring via an interactive video teleconference. All the employees met in various conference rooms and lunchrooms throughout the company. After the CEO announced the restructuring, the telephone lines were opened for questions.

This technology had one distinct advantage, even though it may not have been as personal. It allowed the message to be sent throughout the company concurrently so that all the employees received the same message at the same time, thus controlling rumors and minimizing anxiety. This is an advantage that would not have been possible without the technology.

Message Negativity

Messages extend along a continuum from positive to negative. Positive messages will be received well and often require little feedback. But when sending a negative message, managers should generally think about the receiver's reaction. They should use technology with higher bandwidth and perceived personal closeness and an opportunity for feedback. Consequently, the extent to which a message is negative and the extent to which it is sensitive are highly related. Some of the same generalities exist for the other categories.

Another important consideration exists when communicating negative messages via technology, however. A person receiving bad news via a technological channel may believe the manager was hiding behind the technology rather than facing the receiver directly. Or it may appear that the manager did not want to be responsible for the message.

Technology often depersonalizes communication. Almost everyone has complained to a company about poor service or an incorrect billing. Traditionally, the response to the complaint was an impersonal form letter, which probably increased frustration and even hostility. Today, many complaints are made using social media, which requires organizations to balance high tech with "high touch." Addressing customers by name, expressing empathy, and moving correspondence to private channels can help manage the negativity.[26] Other strategies for softening the blow when sending negative messages are presented in Chapter 8. Managers can successfully influence receivers' reactions to bad news.

CRITICAL THINKING QUESTIONS

Consider a time when you complained to a company about their service or product.

1. How personalized was the company's reply message?

2. If the response was negative and you did not get what you asked for in your complaint, how did it make you feel? Are you a repeat customer? Why or why not?

Message Complexity

Guidelines for using technology are somewhat clearer when considering message complexity. As the complexity of the message increases, managers should attempt to use (a) wider bandwidth, (b) the medium that will add to psychological closeness, (c) the technology that provides for the greatest amount of feedback, and (d) symbolism consistent with the complexity.

Within a single project, messages of varying complexity will exist. Assume seven managers at four locations are a virtual team. A number of viable solutions exist for communicating complex messages without getting everyone together face-to-face. E-mail, cloud file storage, messaging and collaboration apps, and videoconference software are common technologies for team communication. To negotiate responsibilities, a relatively wide bandwidth is used; feedback is provided, and the sophisticated technology symbolizes the seriousness of the task. But tracking the schedule and budget involves less complexity; these messages may use less bandwidth and feedback and little personal closeness.

Research shows the communication of complex, detailed information is not necessarily improved by face-to-face interaction.[27] An explanation of a complex engineering formula, for instance, can be just as effective with audio and graphic communication as when the person doing the explanation is physically present. Managers should carefully consider the situation using the strategic model presented in Chapter 2 and make decisions accordingly.

Message Persuasiveness

Persuasive messages involve an effort to induce a receiver to take a particular action. Persuasion is not an effort to coerce, fool, seduce, or manipulate the receiver. Rather, it is an attempt to get employees to comply with behaviors that will meet the goals of the organization. When thinking of persuasion, salespeople probably come to mind; however, managers frequently use persuasion, influence tactics, or compliance-gaining strategies to affect employees' performance. Efforts to introduce new work procedures, increase teamwork, or change corporate culture require persuasive communication. Suggestions for delivering persuasive business presentations are found in Chapter 5.

The topic of persuasion has been of interest since Aristotle's time. But a leading researcher more recently wrote: "Despite the vast number of pages written and the countless studies undertaken about persuasion, it is difficult to shake the uneasy feeling that we have precious little reliable, socially relevant knowledge about it."[28] Our understanding of persuasion is further complicated when considering technologically mediated communication.

Little research has been conducted in this area; consequently, it is necessary to generalize about what we know from nonmediated communication.

A popular book, *Influence: The New Psychology of Modern Persuasion*, presents three conclusions about persuasion that are particularly pertinent to our discussion.[29] First, managers can more easily persuade those who like them. Second, people are more easily persuaded when they perceive the persuader as an authority. Third, it is easier for managers to persuade others as they get psychologically and physically closer to them.

Few would be surprised to learn that we prefer to say yes to the requests of someone we know and like. In addition, we like people with whom we spend more time, even if we are forced to spend this time together. This research finding is important to our discussion because the quality of the time we spend with people via technology is generally not the same as if the person were physically present. In other words, no matter how much time we spend with people in teleconferences, it cannot fully substitute for personal presence.

CRITICAL THINKING QUESTIONS

Consider a project team you participated in, either at school or at work.

1. Did your team meet in person or virtually?

2. To what extent did you develop positive feelings about the other team members?

3. If you have worked in teams both virtually and face-to-face, compare the intensity of the team spirit you developed in each environment. Which was stronger? Why?

The second principle is not overly surprising, either. We listen and are persuaded by those who appear to be authorities on the topic. But how do managers project authority to people they may not meet in person? Video calls could be used to establish relationships, and collaboration software, e-mail, and other communication technologies can maintain them.

Finally, it is more difficult to say no when looking a person directly in the eye. Even when we like a person or believe she is an authority, it is easier to say no from a distance. Technology seems to buffer the importance of trust that has been built into the communicators' relationship, diminishing its prominence as an element of the environment. When persuasion is the goal of the interaction, it is best to have the person physically present. When physical presence of an authority is not possible, a well-organized presentation by a somewhat less credible source may be a good substitute.

Technology makes communication easier. When considering persuasive managerial communication, however, one principle must always be considered. A person physically present is more persuasive than one who is present only via technologically mediated communication. That is why, despite the recent dramatic increase in online automobile sales, dealers continue to make an effort to lure online shoppers into their showrooms. And a test drive remains the best way to close a sale.

COMMUNICATING WITH TECHNOLOGY AT WORK

So far, this chapter has described the advantages and disadvantages of technology for communication in organizations. Problems with technology include the danger of sensory overload with useless cues (jamming), narrow bandwidth, diminished feelings of personal closeness, and reduced opportunities for feedback. Despite these disadvantages, however, networked organizations are the norm, mostly because they increase productivity. The strategic decision for managers, therefore, is not *whether* to use technological channels but *which* digital channel will best suit the situation and *how* to maximize its capabilities. In the following paragraphs, we will examine the strengths and weaknesses of five communication technologies commonly used in today's workplace—e-mail, electronic messaging, videoconferencing, social media, and collaboration software—and offer guidelines for best practice.

E-mail

More than half of the world's population uses e-mail for personal or business use. An estimated 306 billion e-mails are sent each day worldwide, up from 269 billion in 2017.[30] Employees spend 3 hours or more every day on e-mail and "every few hours" outside of work.[31] Nearly 50 percent of employees avoid e-mail before work, but 25 percent continue to check it on vacations.[32] The e-mail overload problem has grown so large, in fact, that a 2017 French law gives employees the "right to disconnect" from e-mail outside of business hours.[33]

The risk of sensory overload—rather than motivating managers to ignore technological media—has stimulated managers to develop a variety of coping skills. They may use an assistant to sort and redirect the crush of messages. Turning off e-mail notifications eliminates distractions, and checking messages at set times each day can help managers budget their time. Features in most e-mail programs can code and filter messages according to sender or topic. Some companies try to help their managers cope with e-mail overload by enforcing "e-mail-free Fridays" or at least banning the use of the Reply All feature. Internal e-mail policies, such as limiting recipients and using the subject line to code messages by priority and response time, can help audiences manage their inbox.[34] Tony Hsieh, CEO of Zappos, uses a technique he calls "yesterbox" to ignore incoming mail (except urgent messages) and respond only to messages that arrived yesterday.[35]

In response to the problems caused by overreliance on e-mail, best practices have emerged. Here are a few guidelines (see Table 3-1):

- Keep e-mails short so that readers see the entire message on one screen and do not need to scroll. Many recipients will be reading messages on small screens like tablets and phones, and short messages are generally more readable than lengthy ones.

- Place the most important information first. Use emphasis strategies like bold or colored text to help readers find key ideas.

- Be clear and specific about your purpose and topic in the subject line.

TABLE 3-1   ■   Best Practices for E-mail
Keep the message short.
Organize the content to place the most important information at the top of the message.
Use the subject line to summarize the main idea of the message.
Use descriptive file names for attachments.
Do not use e-mail for urgent messages that call for an immediate response.
Do not use e-mail for dialogues.
Push companywide announcements to the intranet.
When deciding what to include in your message, think of e-mail as a public forum.

- When sending attachments, notify the receiver and use logical file names to inform them of the content.

- Do not use e-mail for urgent messages that call for an immediate response. Many business professionals check their e-mail only once or twice per day.

- Do not use e-mail for dialogues. Discussions will be slow and inefficient.[36] Use the Reply All function sparingly.

- Push companywide announcements to the intranet and simply e-mail the link to everyone. Focusing on the company's intranet as a source of routine information will relieve e-mail overload.[37]

- Create an e-mail code of conduct, train all employees on it, and periodically remind employees to follow it. The policy should address issues such as spam, message retention, records management, privacy, and non-work-related use.

Managers also turn to IM and text messaging to avoid the crush of e-mail. That strategy, described earlier in this chapter, cuts e-mail traffic but does not diminish the amount of time spent interacting with technology or the level of resultant anxiety.

Electronic Messaging: IM and Text

Although e-mail remains a staple of workplace communication, more and more organizations are also adopting electronic messaging to transmit business messages. Speed of transmission, message archiving, improved communication efficiency, and ease of implementation are the primary advantages of instant messaging and text messages.

Instant messaging (IM) and text messaging allow users to send short messages directly to one or more people. The two media function similarly for users but differ in their infrastructure. IM requires users to have the same software and to create accounts to communicate with each other. Messages are transmitted using the Internet, and the service is usually free. Text messages, also known as Short Message Service (SMS), need only a phone number to send messages between mobile phones and other handheld devices. Text messages allow users to communicate with different operating systems or software, but because messages travel over cellular networks, there may be a small fee for each message. Software is available to send and receive text messages on computers and IM on phones, so the differences between the two have blurred in recent years.

Texting and IM are fast because the message travels instantaneously, like a live conversation in person or by telephone. By contrast, e-mail is asynchronous, and servers often have a delivery delay, so interaction is not expected to be in real time. The speed of transmission can be so fast, however, that some conversations lose coherence as some parties post new messages while others are still writing, interrupting the conversational flow.[38]

Maintaining accurate records of communication improves employee efficiency and is beneficial during legal proceedings. Referring to transcripts of a conversation allows employees to retain and understand the intent of the conversation. During legal discovery, these archives may protect an organization from false accusations. Most free IM programs have message archiving options. These archives are easy to set up and require significantly less server space than e-mail archives.[39] Instant messaging archives provide the same level of legal documentation as e-mail archives, at a lower cost. Text messages can also be archived, but the process of retrieving them is more difficult, particularly if employees are using personal phones. It can also be difficult to authenticate the identity of the other party in a text conversation because other people may have access to the cell phone.[40]

Electronic messaging greatly improves communication efficiency compared to e-mail and other traditional communication methods. Instant messaging programs allow users to immediately ask clarifying questions, converse at a comfortable pace, and also have a transcript of the conversation for review. Finally, instant messaging programs are very easy to implement because many employees already use them.

There are several disadvantages to electronic messaging that must be identified in order to minimize their impact and protect your organization. Electronic messaging can establish legally binding contracts and expose companies to legal jurisdiction in other states. Other potential problems are accidental overtime, lack of security, structure and informality, and distractions that lower productivity.

The legal elements of a contractual agreement are offer, consideration, and acceptance. E-mail, IM, or text conversations that include these elements can be legally binding even if the specific details of the deal need further negotiation. The following electronic messaging exchange could be considered a legal contract:[41]

Buyer:	How's it going? Hope to see you and the family on the lake Friday.
Supplier:	We should be there.
Buyer:	Could you get me six of those new widgets by the end of the month? Got a project coming up, the boss is pushing hard.
Supplier:	Those systems are pricey.
Buyer:	They would make the job go a lot easier.
Supplier:	No problem. We've got plenty in stock, so I'll deliver them on the 20th.
Buyer:	Great and see you Friday.[42]

Any specific details that are not included would be negotiable, but the supplier could be forced to deliver six widgets to the buyer on the 20th. Breaching a contract can expose a company to legal liability and hurt its reputation. Employees must be educated on safe use of electronic communication, whether e-mail or instant messaging, to protect the organization.

A related disadvantage of electronic messaging is that it can expose companies to legal jurisdiction liability in other states. In 2006, the New York Court of Appeals ruled that a Montana business could be sued in a New York court. The Montana business entered into and later breached a contract using instant messages. Conducting business using instant messages was sufficient contact for New York courts to have jurisdiction over the Montana business. Employees using instant messaging to conduct business with outside parties must understand the legal implications.[43]

Ubiquitous technology can make it difficult for employees to disconnect. In 2019, 86 percent of U.S. adults owned smartphones.[44] As many as 44 percent of employees use them to check e-mail and electronic messages after their workday ends. This kind of work-life blurring and the expectation by managers that employees respond immediately, regardless of the day or time, could create accidental overtime and violate the Fair Labor Standards Act.[45]

Security is a major issue because texting is instantaneous, and it does not allow enough time for virus scanners to check completely for viruses, thus leaving computers unprotected. No matter how fast virus scanners become, they will always be able to protect against e-mails better than SMSes.[46]

Lack of structure and informality are other disadvantages of instant messaging. Unlike e-mails, which are set up in memo format, IM and text messages do not have a set form and usually take on a very casual, conversational writing style. Although slang and shorthand might be commonly used in personal messaging, they do not convey the kind of professional style that managers usually wish to project.

> For example, a synopsis of the classic novel *Pride and Prejudice*, sent as a text message, might look like the following:
>
> TFW you and your 4 sisters want to get married but there are only 2 wealthy guys you'd want.
>
> Although longer, a more professional tone with concrete information would yield something like this:
>
> The Bennet sisters are wanting husbands. They have their sights set on Bingley and Darcy, two new men in town who are handsome and wealthy.

This type of message can be difficult for new users to understand. Perhaps more importantly in business settings, a cryptic text message may lead to serious misunderstandings and costly errors. It may encourage employees to take more care when crafting text messages if you remind them that texts can be archived and are discoverable in a court of law.

Finally, electronic messaging can disrupt workplace productivity. Unlike e-mail, electronic messaging is expected to be instantaneous. A flood of non-urgent or personal text messages can be distracting to busy workers. Because IM and text (as well as e-mail) are often used for personal communication, checking a business message may also lead to checking personal ones, thereby reducing time on task. Texting was designed for recreational "chatting," and it is easy to get involved in personal exchanges that take up valuable work time. Additionally, from a distance, an employee who is typing messages may appear to be off task. Company policies for e-mail should be adapted to manage instant messaging to maintain employee productivity.

Clearly there is great potential for growth in instant messaging by businesses. Many companies are already utilizing instant messaging in their daily operations. Managers cannot ignore the growth of IM communication. Table 3-2 lists some best practices for instant messaging.

A recent study by research company Radicati Group indicated that IM accounts are expected to grow to over 9.3 billion worldwide by 2024.[47] With this increased personal and professional use of instant messaging, companies are responding by providing workers with enterprise-grade IM accounts, which have functionality and security that cannot be attained with public IM accounts, thereby overcoming concerns, especially when they are communicating with customers or business partners.

Billions of dollars in commodities, stocks, bonds, and commercial goods are traded every day using electronic messaging technology. The strong international communication, easy message archiving, high level of efficiency, and easy implementation will lead more organizations to use instant messaging. The contract-formation issues, employee distraction, and legal jurisdiction concerns associated with instant messaging can be easily managed. The productivity and cost-reduction benefits of instant messaging far outweigh the potential negatives to businesses.

After reviewing the advantages and disadvantages, a business can decide whether using electronic messaging will be beneficial to them. Many companies that have already adopted this technology have been increasing their usage of this communication channel, but they are not abandoning e-mail. Instead, they are using IM and texting in tandem with e-mail

TABLE 3-2 ■ Best Practices for Electronic Messaging
Archive all incoming and outgoing messages.
Develop an electronic messaging policy and circulate it among employees.
Do not use text or instant messaging for highly sensitive communication.
Educate employees about the potential legal liability they expose the company to through electronic messaging.
Remember that texts are generally not secure, so limit proprietary information.
Be concise, but be sure your shortcuts (acronyms, abbreviations, jargon) are familiar to all.
Use punctuation for clarity and accuracy.
Avoid emoticons and formatting for emphasis (all caps, multiple exclamation points).
Do not ban electronic messaging, but provide guidance on how to use it.

to send reminders or announcements that need to be communicated immediately.[48] For example, an employee might send an important e-mail to his boss and then send a reminder SMS, letting her know that the e-mail was sent.

Videoconferencing

Communication is essential for geographically dispersed teams and multinational corporations. International phone calls are expensive, as is telepresence equipment; in addition, telepresence requires a fixed location. Services like WebEx, Adobe Connect, Zoom, and Microsoft Teams offer chat functions, document exchange, and screen-sharing functions from any Internet connection in the world without IT support. Most free IM programs have conferencing features that allow team members around the world to collaborate instantly using smartphones and tablets. Thus, videoconferencing improves collaboration without increasing expenses. Some best practices for videoconferencing are shown in Table 3-3. Videoconferencing is an integral tool for virtual teams, as discussed in Chapter 4.

TABLE 3-3 ■ Best Practices for Videoconferencing
Use videoconferencing instead of meetings for simple and quick progress updates, information sharing, and gathering of feedback.
Have a backup communication plan in case some participants have trouble connecting.
Use videoconferences in team-building stages to develop rapport.
Continue to use videoconferences regularly to help remote workers feel visible to the team.
Test audio and video settings prior to every meeting.
Look at the camera when speaking, not at the screen or at your notes.
If possible, mute your microphone when you are not speaking to reduce ambient noise.

Social Media

Social media allows users to create and share content easily and participate in social networks of people with similar interests. Social media accounts allow businesses to interact with their audiences quickly, informally, and in ways that users find useful. Finding their audiences will take some work, though. According to the Pew Research Center, 72 percent of U.S. adults use social media, including 40 percent of those age 65 and older. Nearly 70 percent of them use Facebook and YouTube. Other popular social media are the content-sharing sites Instagram (37 percent) and Pinterest (28 percent), Snapchat (24 percent), the networking site LinkedIn (27 percent), and the microblog site Twitter (22 percent).[49] But just because audiences are using social media does not mean that they want to connect with your organization. Most users are connecting with family and friends. Furthermore, users often have accounts on multiple social networks, and each fulfills a different purpose. Targeted messaging is the way to connect with audiences on social networks. Organizations should use psychographic research on customers to identify the best channels for their messages.[50]

Once your organization has chosen its social networking outlets, provide information that users want or need to know. For example, Merriam-Webster produces dictionaries, a product that may not seem very cutting-edge. Yet the company has had great success using Twitter to participate in conversations about world events, providing "the right information at the right time." For example, when the BBC announced that the next star of its long-running sci-fi series *Dr. Who* would be a woman, many fans complained publicly. Merriam-Webster responded to the outcry on Twitter by noting that "'doctor' has no gender in English," which led to a conversation about the quirks of language.[51] The clothing company M.M.LaFleur uses Facebook to share photos of models, videos of staff, and testimonials by customers. The company also responds directly to comments, whether they are compliments, inquiries, or complaints. Starbucks uses a webpage to crowdsource ideas for new products (https://ideas.starbucks.com). These examples show how the organizations are connecting with audiences and demonstrating social media "reach."[52]

Blogs were the original social media, and they continue to be an important communication tool for businesses. A descendant of diaries and online journals, organizational blogs feature short, concise articles, photos, or videos that are arranged chronologically.[53] A customer-focused blog allows companies to build and maintain relationships with their public, strengthening their brand and positioning in the marketplace.[54] Communication using blogs or similar technology is viewed as more genuine, credible, and "real" compared to the rote and often boring language of mission statements and press releases. Blogs are written in a conversational tone, which external stakeholders view more favorably.[55] Unlike press releases or websites, blogs accept comments and often invite guest authors. Composing posts that connect with readers' interests and responding directly to comments can encourage audiences to remain engaged with the organization, its products, or projects in development.[56] Companies can use blogs to gather new ideas about changes or new products that they should consider offering.[57]

Companies can also take advantage of users' social media to advertise. Many companies operate in niche markets and are constantly looking for new ways to reach their target market. Social media allows individuals to tell a personal story that demonstrates expertise and builds a personal brand. Linking to other accounts, inviting guest bloggers, and responding to comments are ways to take advantage of the relational nature of social media and develop a strong, positive reputation in your industry.[58] Companies can capitalize on this opportunity by sponsoring posts and negotiating product placement, virtually guaranteeing that the people who come to read the blog are in their target market.[59]

Social media offers companies a chance to learn about criticisms, crises, or information much more quickly and respond almost immediately.[60] Previously, corporations relied on press releases, industry trade publications, or time-intensive website upgrades to announce new products or services. Social media provides a means for corporations to communicate with consumers before, during, and after new products are brought to market.

Job search and employee recruitment increasingly use social media. Prospective employees research an organization through its website but look for the most current information on its social media accounts, and hiring managers scan social media to investigate applicants.

Social media also offers challenges in managing external relations. Although maintained by individual employees, social media accounts represent the "voice of the corporation." It is important to ensure that the voice speaking through corporate accounts agrees with the voice speaking in mission statements, press releases, advertisements, websites, and other forms of external communication. Without proper monitoring, it is possible that the company could get a bad reputation.[61] One way to ensure this continuity of voice and avoid legal troubles is to create guidelines that employees must follow when writing for external audiences. Companies must also remember that social media posts are easy to document in screen captures, meaning even deleted posts may linger.

Another risk of using social networks is sharing control of your message. The candy company Skittles was an early adopter of social media and is often considered a role model of successful brand engagement and interaction. Yet the company discovered in 2009 that sharing control can be dangerous. Skittles converted its website into a portal that streamed user messages from Twitter, Facebook, and other social networks. Perhaps not surprisingly, the experiment quickly went awry as some users posted inappropriate and abusive messages. Today, Skittles continues to engage users with tweets, videos, and memes, but it controls its website much more tightly.

Unfortunately, many companies use social media for one-way messaging. A recent study showed that 80 percent of corporate posts on Facebook and Twitter were for informational purposes only. In fact, more than 60 percent of organizations do not reply to customers publicly, although they may be contacting them privately using IM. It appears that most companies use social media to broadcast messages rather than to converse with audiences and cultivate relationships.

Table 3-4 offers a summary of best practices for corporate social media.

TABLE 3-4 ■ Best Practices for Social Media

Select the right network for your message and your audience.
Establish a social media voice and tone that is consistent with other instances of the corporate voice (website, press releases).
Focus on customers' needs rather than your own. Provide content they care about.
Be sure that company-sponsored postings are consistent with the company's brand, mission, and image.
Monitor social media daily to keep abreast of public sentiment and mentions of your brand.
Respond quickly to user comments, whether positive or critical. Switch to private messages to resolve complaints.
Maintain a professional writing style, remembering that posts are permanent records.
Develop a social media disaster plan.

Collaboration Networks

Corporate intranets have evolved into collaboration networks like Slack, Jive, Microsoft Teams, and Facebook for Business. Other firms are using proprietary networks. For example, KPMG's Global Tax Hub connects employees at its member firms around the world and helps them share knowledge and expertise.[62] These internal social networks combine aspects of social media with communication, collaboration, and project management tools to facilitate teamwork and internal messaging. Collaboration networks flatten hierarchies and allow users across an organization to connect and share information. Teams can share calendars, work on shared files, ask questions or crowdsource ideas using IM, and meet by videoconference. As they work, communications are streamlined and project activities are archived, making groups more productive.

Blogs are often used internally as a project coordination tool. A team working on a project can use a blog to share information or provide progress updates. This information can be seen by the team members, managers who wish to check in, or any other individuals within the company who are allowed access. Instead of spending the time to have a meeting with the team to discuss the team's progress on a project, the manager can simply take a look at the group's project blog. The benefit of blogs as a project coordination tool is amplified for teams that include members located in different geographic locations.

Blogs can also be used to share information and collect feedback from stakeholders.[63] If a company is looking for feedback from employees about a new policy, for example, it could start an internal blog about the issue. Previously, a series of meetings, reports, letters, memos, or "town-hall" gatherings may have been necessary. Blogs allow everyone to participate in the discussion at their convenience and keep a permanent record of all the thoughts, comments, and input that can be reviewed and considered at the convenience of the decision maker. Best practices for collaborative networks are summarized in Table 3-5.

In summary, e-mail, electronic messages, videoconferences, social media, and collaboration networks are integral communication. With their use, the hierarchical culture is dissolving. Rank does not matter as much to workers who are on the network and who know what everyone is doing. Today's managers no longer manage information; they manage networks of people. Teams use technology to collaborate, overcoming geographic barriers among team members. In addition to increasing efficiency, technology reduces groupthink, defuses emotional issues, and enhances the creativity of decisions. Clearly, these advantages outweigh the risks and costs of using technology for workplace communication.

TABLE 3-5 ■ Best Practices for Collaborative Networks
Use instead of meetings for simple and quick progress updates, information sharing, and gathering of feedback.
Give the online community time to grow.
Find internal influencers to lead discussions and generate interest.
Set guidelines for information that can and cannot be shared with others in the organization.

CONSIDERATIONS FOR TECHNOLOGY USE

Advances in technology are often celebrated for the ways they allow work to be completed more quickly and accurately, but they also introduce new tasks and responsibilities for managers to consider. This section reviews several ways that communication technology has changed the way managers work. Communication technology allows managers to monitor employee behavior and performance, make decisions based on data and research, revise the design of jobs and organizations, and facilitate collaboration within teams.

Monitoring Technology Use

Surveillance methods are developing hand in hand with innovations in communication technology. These efforts are exemplified by federal law enforcement and national security officials' sweeping regulations that allow surveillance of Internet communications, including encrypted e-mails, social networking websites, and peer-to-peer software. In the United States, phone and broadband networks are already required to have interception capabilities, under a 1994 law called the Communications Assistance to Law Enforcement Act. These capabilities also apply to companies that operate from servers abroad and that conduct international business.

The business sector is following the example of governmental surveillance policies by developing technologies that allow eavesdropping on employees. Electronic monitoring systems allow employers to gather very detailed information about how their employees spend their time at work.[64] Companies monitor employees for many reasons. These include the following:

- Mitigating legal liability

- Reducing the misuse of company resources

- Protecting intellectual property[65]

First, companies monitor in order to prevent lawsuits. Companies can be held liable for any and all communication that uses their computer systems.[66] In fact, a sexual harassment suit was brought against Chevron when an employee sent an offensive e-mail over the company system. This seemingly incidental e-mail ended up costing the company $2.2 million.[67]

Second, companies monitor to catch employees who are misusing the company's resources. For example, employers want to know if an employee is spending valuable work time surfing the Internet, playing computer games, or planning a vacation online.

Third, many companies need to protect intellectual property and trade secrets. Monitoring employees is one way to keep tabs on their property and make sure it is not leaked out to a competitor. All an employee would have to do is accidentally or even purposefully send an e-mail to the wrong person, and it could end up out of the company's control.

Companies now have various ways to monitor employees in the workplace. They may use firewalls to block access to certain Internet sites, router logs to monitor Internet traffic, or keylogging software to record every keystroke ever typed on the worker's computer (even ones that have been deleted). E-mail is routinely backed up and archived. Global positioning systems on employees' badges to allow them to record workers' movements.[68] In addition, 48 percent of employers use video surveillance to watch employees, and of these organizations, 22 percent do not inform workers that they are being taped.[69]

Secret monitoring by employers is widespread and supported by the courts.[70] Perhaps surprisingly, 52 percent of people in the United States consider surveillance to prevent theft and monitor performance to be acceptable.[71] The monitoring of individuals has enabled employers to prevent problems and to reprimand workers who have disobeyed corporate policies. *The New York Times*, Xerox Corp., and First Union Bank have apparently terminated employees after discovering improper use of company-provided Internet.[72] A recent study indicates that 30 percent of employers have terminated employees for inappropriate Internet use, including accessing inappropriate content and excessive personal use, and

24 percent have terminated employees for e-mail misuse, including inappropriate or offensive language and violating confidentiality rules.[73]

Employees should realize that any time spent using technology at work should be limited to work-related activities. Further, any communications being sent or received to a work e-mail address, smartphone, or tablet should be considered appropriate for anyone to read. In 2010, in its first ruling on the privacy rights of employees who send messages on the job, the Supreme Court unanimously agreed that supervisors may read through text messages of direct reports if they suspect that work rules are being violated. Because employers are not required to let employees know when they are monitoring, it is up to the employees to be on their best behavior and to think twice before doing something even slightly inappropriate while on the job.

Decision Making

Managerial decision making may be defined as the process of identifying and solving problems. Decision making requires that managers scan for pertinent information. Most discussions on this topic generally contain two major stages. One is the problem identification stage. Information about relevant conditions is monitored both to determine whether performance is meeting expectations and to diagnose the cause of any shortcomings. The other stage involves solution identification. Alternative actions are considered, and one alternative is selected and implemented. A more thorough explanation of the rational problem-solving process is presented in Chapters 4 and 13. In both stages of the process, the more information available, the greater the probability that effective decisions will be made. And more and more information is available with increased technologies.

Burger King provides an example of the effect of communication technology on decision making. Each Burger King restaurant is networked via computer to a central office where each sale is transmitted and recorded. When one store is running low on a product, even without the store manager placing an order, the central facility is aware of the shortage and can send supplies. Thus, stage one in the decision process, the problem identification stage, may become easier, even automated, with communication technology.

The solution identification stage, however, has become more difficult. Even just a few years ago, locating quality data or research to support decision making was difficult. Much of the data was proprietary information, and public research was usually in print form, requiring users to travel to a library or request a copy to be sent by mail or e-mail. Today, many public and private researchers share reports and data sets online, but as we explain in Chapter 9, a web search engine search often yields results that are not as reliable as professional databases and industry sources. Managers are bombarded with masses of information, and the volume of information makes choosing the best alternative more, not less, challenging. If managers receive large quantities of both relevant and irrelevant information, the important facts and figures may be overlooked and can create problems, because the human mind can process only so much data. As noted earlier in Figure 3-1, a point develops at which the mind blocks out any additional, though valuable, information. As technology allows for rapid acquisition of greater amounts of information, poorer rather than better decisions may result.

As presented in Chapter 2, the manager's challenge is to know where to get information, when and how to present it to others, and how and when to use it. In some ways, information technology makes the decision-making process easier, but in other ways, it becomes more complex.

Job and Organizational Design

Business communication technology allows managers to monitor more closely the standards expected from a job performance. Take a simple example of a sales representative responsible for calling on furniture stores. The objective is to obtain cooperation in setting up a special display within the stores. The standard of performance is to make two calls per day and obtain three displays per 10 calls. The formal agreement is to report the day's activities to the central office at the end of each day. This is done via smartphone, tablet, or laptop. E-mail and text messages are exchanged continuously, including photos of the displays.

Without sophisticated technology, such an intensive and immediate level of interaction among employees and their managers would not have been possible. Interaction via technologically mediated communication allows managers to maintain control over their direct reports and allows employees in the field to stay connected.

Organizational relationships may also change with mediated communication. We generally think of jobs being connected by means of either horizontal or vertical integration. Horizontal communication or integration occurs between people at the same hierarchical level. Managers may meet horizontally to coordinate activities, solve problems, resolve conflicts, or just share information.

Consider this example. The board of directors of a hospital system with eight locations directed the human resources managers to implement a safety training program in each hospital. The managers want to share ideas with each other on the most efficient way to implement the program. Technology makes travel for a meeting unnecessary—a videoconference, satellite downlink, or teleconference would meet the purpose. In this case, technology allows for greater integration at lower expense.

Vertical integration is the coordination among higher and lower levels within the hierarchy. Unfortunately, it often seems that different levels of the organization typically do not communicate well with each other.[74] But as noted when discussing formalization and collaboration networks, mediated communication should assist this process. Managers and employees are more accessible with technology. Distance and time are less troublesome.

This improved vertical and horizontal integration is resulting in dramatically different job and organizational structures. Recent research indicates that in an effort to create competitive advantage, managers' jobs have become more information oriented, while the number of layers of managers has decreased.[75] And technology facilitates this trend toward networked information exchange.

Finally, the increasing use of bots, automated programs that use artificial intelligence to respond to inquiries and perform routine actions, suggests a promising way to engage customers and automate some workplace tasks. Amazon Echo, Microsoft Cortana, Facebook Messenger, and Apple's Siri already use this technology to answer questions and help customers place orders.[76] As technology takes over routine tasks, employees will be able to turn their attention to projects that require critical thinking and strategic planning.

Collaboration

Complex business documents require more than one person to be involved in the writing process. Examples include proposals, reports to regulatory agencies, annual reports to shareholders, policy manuals, operating procedures, newsletters, directives, user manuals, training materials, mission/vision and strategic goal statements, progress reports, and personnel reports. In the past, collaborative writing too often meant one person wrote part of the report and then sent it to another person for revision by e-mail. The second person passed it on to another and so forth. This method is extremely time-consuming, and document version control can be difficult to coordinate.

Collaboration software like wikis, cloud-based productivity applications, file storage, and versioning software allow members of a team to compose documents concurrently, not just sequentially. Using built-in features like comments and chat, members can compare ideas, discuss different viewpoints, and make revisions in real time. As versions of the text are compared, a better product results without bruising egos. Because collaborative writing is becoming so important, it is discussed more extensively in Chapter 7.

CRITICAL THINKING QUESTIONS

Recall a team project you participated in, either at work or at school.

1.   What communication tools did you use to expedite team collaboration?

2.   How well did they work?

3.   What could the team have done better to ensure that everyone's input on the deliverable was maximized?

Group decision support systems (GDSSs) are software and associated processes that have been designed to advance coordination of group projects for unstructured problems. The fundamental goal of a GDSS is to support collaborative work activities, such as idea creation, message exchange, project planning, document creation, copyediting, and joint decision making.[77] GDSSs provide a platform on which groups can collaborate when members are dispersed, working in their separate offices, homes, or client locations. Other systems support face-to-face meetings that occur in one physical setting, such as a conference or boardroom. With these, it is possible to instantaneously display ideas on large screens, vote on individual preferences, compile the anonymous input of ideas and preferences, and electronically exchange ideas between members. GDSS programs include various quantitative analysis techniques. The most sophisticated systems include expert advice in the selecting and arranging of rules to be applied during interpersonal communication.[78]

THE MANAGEMENT CHALLENGE

What does all this mean for managers? It means they must become sensitive to the correct type of communication channel to use in different situations. It means managers must learn to use these new technologies. It means another dimension has been added to managerial communication.

Let us expand on each of these points. Several studies have indicated that a strong correlation exists between a manager's media sensitivity and managerial performance. When a task involved complex information or was highly emotional, for instance, effective managers were more inclined to use communication channels with a broad bandwidth than were ineffective managers.[79] Innovations in communication technology have added a whole new dimension to the manager's job: understanding and selecting the correct communication channel. A corollary to this requirement is that managers must guide their direct reports in the proper, ethical use of the technology. New communication tools are constantly becoming available, requiring strategic decisions. The proliferation of communication technologies in the workplace improves productivity, communication, and collaboration but also introduces risks, such as hacking, accidental information leaks, corporate espionage, and sabotage by disgruntled employees. Information security is becoming a significant concern for managers in all industries. It is clear that business is committed to investing in technology, and companies expect managers to make this investment pay off.

The technology payoff could be increased if managers had a guidebook summarizing when each technology is best used, but such a resource is not possible. Too many contingencies must be considered to say categorically which technology should be used when. This chapter, however, has attempted to raise some of the important questions managers should ask themselves as they choose a channel for their message. Figure 3-3 illustrates the factors that managers should consider when selecting a technology.

As the workplace begins filling with Generation Z, a group who has never lived without smartphones or the Internet, older employees will need to teach them about workplace norms, including the appropriate use of their smartphones for work. Jonah Stillman, the teenage coauthor of *Gen Z @ Work*, explains, "Phones are crucial to our identities and lifestyle. Telling people in my generation to put our phones away is not a solution. Just ask our teachers how it worked for them."[80] His advice, based in part on his work on an advisory board for the educational software Blackboard, is patience and mentoring.

SUMMARY

To understand better how technology affects managerial communication, four concepts are discussed. First, bandwidth is affected because one channel is generally omitted when technologically mediated communication is used. The technology mediating the communication may reduce perceived closeness between individuals. The feedback cycle is much shorter with technology. Finally, various communication channels have different symbolic values.

Not all technology is appropriate for all types of messages, so managers must make decisions by categorizing messages along four continuums. Sensitive messages require greater bandwidth and personal touch than neutral ones. Negative messages require attention to personal connection and feedback. Managers must be careful not to hide behind

FIGURE 3-3 ■ Technology Choice Factors

	Communication Medium					
Message Type	**IM/Text**	**E-mail**	**Collaboration Software**	**Phone**	**Videoconference**	**Face-to-Face Meeting**
Sensitive Content	Poor	Poor	Poor	Good	Excellent	Excellent
Negative Content	Poor	Good	Good	Good	Good	Excellent
Complex Topic	Poor	Good	Good	Excellent	Excellent	Excellent
Routine Content	Excellent	Excellent	Excellent	Good	Poor	Poor
Persuasive Purpose	Poor	Poor	Good	Excellent	Excellent	Excellent
Situational Factors						
Multiple Participants	Poor	Excellent	Excellent	Good	Excellent	Excellent
Diverse Cultures	Poor	Good	Good	Good	Excellent	Excellent
Geographically Dispersed	Good	Excellent	Excellent	Good	Excellent	Poor
Time-Critical	Excellent	Good	Good	Good	Excellent	Good
Difficult to Schedule	Poor	Good	Excellent	Excellent	Excellent	Poor
Cost Is a Factor	Excellent	Excellent	Excellent	Good	Good	Poor
Interactivity Required	Good	Poor	Good	Good	Excellent	Excellent

● Excellent
O Good
O Poor

technology when presenting negative messages. Complex messages require higher bandwidth, feedback, and symbolic channels that emphasize their importance. Persuasive messages are more likely to be accepted when the receiver likes the sender and the sender is perceived as an authority on the subject. In general, persuasion is less effective when the communication is mediated by technology.

Going forward, technology will continue to proliferate, and so will surveillance mechanisms. Managers must decide which digital channel will best suit the situation—e-mail, electronic messaging, videoconferencing, social media, or collaboration software—and how to apply best practices to ensure successful communication. Technology will continue to affect managerial communication in decision making, job and organizational design, and collaborative writing. All these technologies will challenge future managers as they make strategic decisions and as they monitor and guide their employees' technologically mediated communication.

CASES FOR ANALYSIS

Case 3-1

The Adidas Social Media Blunder

Social media has transformed marketing from a one-directional broadcast to an interactive experience between businesses and their customers. User-generated content (UGC) is often seen as more authentic and trustworthy than corporate content. Sponsored blog posts, product placement in Instagram, and Twitter hashtags are common examples of UGC. When done well, UGC can create genuine interactions with customers that increase brand loyalty. But when an organization relinquishes control of its message to others, it must be vigilant about protecting its reputation.

Adidas learned this message in 2019 when it unleashed the #DareToCreate campaign.[81] Users who used the hashtag were rewarded with a response from Adidas saying "This is home. Welcome to the squad." Artificial intelligence inserted the user's Twitter handle into an image of jerseys for the Arsenal (U.K.) football team. But the company did not expect users to troll the company by creating racist and anti-Semitic usernames, which made it appear that the company endorsed the offensive messages.

Questions

1. What should Adidas have done differently to protect its campaign and its reputation?

2. How should the company respond to the social media blunder?

3. What are examples of user-generated content marketing that have worked out well for businesses? How could their strategies be emulated and adapted for other products or services?

Case 3-2

Communicating With Technology on Friday Afternoon

Colleen cheered as she completed the last of her attachments for the report, which had been a last-minute request on a fair-weather Friday. She was eager to begin the weekend, because she had made plans to spend it with her partner, Brian. She saved the interactive PDF file, which linked to 18 ancillary files, and attached all 19 files to her e-mail to her boss.

(Continued)

(Continued)

Colleen pressed Send and logged off. She rushed from her office to catch the 5:15 p.m. uptown bus. If she missed it, she would have to wait about a half-hour for the next one. As she jumped on the bus before the doors closed and grabbed a seat in the back, she opened her purse. She quickly turned off her phone, which had only a small charge left, to preserve the battery. She brushed her hair and put on some lip gloss in preparation for dinner at a nice uptown bistro. Brian had made reservations for outdoor dining on the bistro's balcony overlooking the bustling street below.

At the same moment, Colleen's boss was opening Colleen's e-mail. As he downloaded the files, error messages began popping up. Six of the files had been corrupted in electronic transit. He called Colleen's extension; it went immediately to voicemail. He called her cell phone and heard a familiar message—the recipient was not receiving calls. He e-mailed her, hoping that she would somehow still be available, to no avail. Panic quickly set in—the report had to be delivered at a meeting in 1 hour, and the other four functional area managers would be present.

Questions

1. Do you perceive any possible repercussions from the failure of the electronic transfer of the six files?

2. What would you suggest as a 1-hour plan for Colleen's boss?

3. How could problems like the one in this scenario be avoided (a) by Colleen, (b) by Colleen's boss, or (c) by company policies?

Case 3-3

Reply to All?!

Jamal Wright arrived at the office a bit late on Monday morning, around 9:45. He had been invited to speak at the Miami Chamber of Commerce breakfast as the chief operating officer for

InterWorld Traders, an international shipping service. His topic, ironically, was communication efficiency. His speech was well received, and he was in a good mood as he logged in for the day. As he opened his e-mail, he was instantly struck by the incredible number of internal e-mails he had waiting in his inbox. Normally about 20 messages, today the tally was 21,291! The e-mail messages were from all over the world and were short messages in reply to others' messages. Thousands of them!

Jamal scrolled down the list until he got to the last ones he had read on Friday afternoon. The culprit soon surfaced. It was a message from Sue Knowles, a manager in charge of distribution analysis. Her job focused on the efficiency of logistical matters concerning the shipping of parcels and the organization of the firm's headquarters warehouse. Sue had sent out a call asking for input concerning any efficiency issues that had been noticed in any of the areas within the firm. Unfortunately, the question was open-ended, and her delivery method had created a monster. She had sent the message to all the 546 supervisory- or higher-level managers within the company. She had not used a mail merge process to send the messages; instead, she had listed a group with all the e-mail addresses included in the recipients line of her message. The result was disastrous. As several well-meaning recipients responded with their observations and suggestions, they had unfortunately selected Reply All. Apparently, the recipients were under the impression that only two or three people had received the initial e-mail. Unfortunately, as others also hit Reply All in their responses to the responses, thousands of e-mail messages flooded the firm's servers.

Jamal returned to the more recent messages. They were noticeably aggressive messages, like "Remove me from this e-mail list" and "I wish you people would learn to use e-mail properly!" and "You idiots stop e-mailing me!" There were even some who obviously realized what was going on—they had replied to all saying, "Everyone stop pressing Reply All!"

The tumult of messages was growing greater minute by minute. The company was bogged down in its inability to function by e-mail, and there seemed to be no end in sight.

Questions

1. How could blunders like the one described above be prevented?

2. Considering that this blunder was not prevented, what should Jamal do now?

Case 3-4

Improvements at ServeNow

ServeNow is a grocery store chain that has seven stores in the southeastern United States. ServeNow's strategy is to target smaller towns (under 50,000 population) so that it can become the dominant store in the area. The chain is headquartered in the largest town (population 75,000) in which it has a store. Each store is at least 50 miles from another store within the network.

The owner of the stores, Edward Bushley, has found that it is extremely difficult to monitor store activities because of travel logistics. As a result, the manager of each store has traditionally had a lot of latitude. Many of the pricing and inventory decisions are made at the individual locations. However, most purchasing is made through a central purchasing office in the headquarters city.

But during the past 2 weeks, three managers left ServeNow to start an online grocery brokerage service. This took Bushley by surprise, but being an entrepreneur himself, he understands their desire to start their own business. In addition,

another manager is nearing retirement. Bushley has found that it is extremely difficult to find qualified replacements for these energetic, creative managers.

Bushley had hoped that potential managers would be available among his present employees, but he discovered the company is weak in its succession planning. Current staff members do not seem to have the capabilities or desire to become store managers. It has become obvious that managers have to be found outside of the present staff.

Bushley has retained Solange DePeres, a small-business consultant who specializes in personnel problems. DePeres agreed that no potential managers were on the present staff. The assistant store managers would be able to manage during the transition, but ultimately new personnel would have to be hired. She stated that Bushley would have to hire managers who were not familiar with the stores' operations and simply spend more time with them than he had with the previous managers. In particular, Bushley would have to spend time training them and answering operational questions.

Bushley asks DePeres, "How can I possibly spend more time at the individual stores? It seems that I am already too busy to maintain a balanced lifestyle."

Project

Assume you are the small-business consultant Solange DePeres and make several recommendations to help Bushley stay in touch with his stores and develop his managerial force. Consider especially the technological communication tools on the market. Explain your recommendations.

Notes

1. C. Cherry, *On Human Communication*, 3rd ed. (Cambridge, MA: MIT Press, 1978), 3–5.

2. Tibi Puiu, "Your Smartphone Is Millions of Times More Powerful Than All of NASA's Combined Computing in 1969," *ZME Science*, May 17, 2017, http://www.zmescience.com/research/technology/smartphone-power-compared-to-apollo-432.

3. Benjamin van Loon, "Productivity Is Money," *Profile Magazine*, April–June 2013, http://pro filemagazine.com/2013/productivity-is-money.

4. Selection of these variables is partially based on C. Heeter, "Classifying Mediated Communication Systems," in *Communication Yearbook*, vol. 12, ed. James A. Anderson (Newbury Park, CA: Sage, 1988), 477–86.

5. Felipe Korzenny and Connie Bauer, "Testing the Theory of Electronic Propinquity," *Communication Research* 8, no. 4 (1981): 479–98.

6. For further discussion, see Larry R. Smeltzer and Charles M. Vance, "An Analysis of Graphics Use in Audio-Graphic Teleconferences," *Journal of Business Communication* 26, no. 2 (1989): 123–42.

7. "Radio Shack Uses Email to Fire 400 Employees," *Huntsville Item*, September 1, 2006, 1.

8. N. L. Reinsch et al., "Measuring Telephone Apprehension," *Management Communication Quarterly* 4, no. 2 (1990): 198–221.

9. Ross McCammon, "Pick Up the Damn Phone," *Entrepreneur*, November 2016, 15–16.

10. N. L. Reinsch Jr. and Raymond W. Beswick, "Voice Mail Versus Conventional Channels: A Cost Minimization Analysis of Individuals' Preferences," *Academy of Management Journal* 23, no. 4 (1990): 801–16.

11. Amy Quinn, Bonka Boneva, Robert Kraut, Sara Kiesler, Jonathon Cummings, and Irina Shklovski, "Teenage Communication in the Instant Messaging Era," *Computers, Phones, and the Internet: Domesticating Information Technology*, January 2012, 10.1093/acprof: oso/9780195312805.003.0014.

12. Sara H. Hsieh and Timmy H. Tseng, "Playfulness in Mobile Instant Messaging: Examining the Influence of Emoticons and Text Messaging on Social Interaction," *Computers in Human Behavior* 69 (2017): 405–14, https://doi .org/10.1016/j.chb.2016.12.052

13. The Radicati Group, "Instant Messaging Statistics Report, 2015–2019," March 2015, http://www.radicati.com/wp/wp-content/ uploads/2015/03/Instant-Messaging-Statis tics-Report-2015-2019-Executive-Summary .pdf.

14. Yuki Noguchi, "Businesses Are Hanging Up on Voice Mail to Dial In to Productivity," *All Things Considered*, National Public Radio, June 10, 2015, http://www.npr.org/sections/ alltechconsidered/2015/06/10/412866432/ businesses-are-hanging-up-on-voice-mail- to-dial-in-productivity.

15. ConnectMogul, "Texting Statistics," March 23, 2013, http://connectmogul.com/2013/03/tex ting-statistics.

16. Aviva Musicus, Aner Tal, and Brian Wansink, "Eyes in the Aisles: Why Is Cap'n Crunch Looking Down at My Child?" *Environment and Behavior*, April 2, 2014, doi: 10.1177/0013916514528793.

17. Jon Martin Denstadli, Tom Erik Julsrud, and Randi Johanne Hjorthol, "Videoconferencing as a Mode of Communication: A Comparative Study of the Use of Videoconferencing and Face-to-Face Meetings," *Journal of Business and Technical Communication* 26, no. 1 (2011): 65–91, doi: 10.1177/1050651911421125.

18. Maria Konnikova, "Multitask Masters," *The New Yorker*, May 17, 2014, http://www.newyo rker.com/science/maria-konnikova/multitask- masters.

19. Lisa Quast, "Want to Be More Productive? Stop Multi-Tasking," *Forbes*, February 6, 2017, https://www.forbes.com/sites/lisaq uast/2017/02/06/want-to-be-more-produc tive-stop-multi-tasking/#35034bde55a6.

20. Sharon Begley, "Will the BlackBerry Sink the Presidency?" *Newsweek*, February 16, 2009, 37–38. See also Gail Thomas and Cindy King, "Reconceptualizing Email Overload," *Journal of Business and Technical Communication* 20 (2006): 252–87.

21. Maggie Jackson, *Distracted: The Erosion of Attention and the Coming Dark Age* (Amherst, NY: Prometheus Books, 2008).

22. R. L. Daft and K. E. Weick, "Toward a Model of Organizations as Interpretation Systems," *Academy of Management Review* 9, no. 2 (1984): 284–95.

23. M. S. Feldman and J. G. March, "Information in Organizations as Signal and Symbol," *Administrative Science Quarterly* 26, no. 1 (1981): 171–86.

24. R. L. Daft, R. H. Lengel, and L. K. Trevino, "Message Equivocality, Media Selection, and Manager Performance: Implications for Information Systems," *MIS Quarterly* 11, no. 2 (1987): 355–66.

25. This categorization was largely drawn from Ronald E. Dulek and John S. Fielden, *Principles of Business Communication* (New York: Macmillan, 1990).

26. Jay Baer, "How To Respond When Customers Get Sour on Social Media," *Marketing Land*, February 9, 2018, https://marketingland.com/respond-customers-get-sour-social-media-233605.

27. R. E. Rice, "Evaluating New Media Systems," in *Evaluating the New Information Technologies: New Directions for Program Evaluation,* ed. J. Johnson (San Francisco: Jossey-Bass, 1984), 53–71.

28. Gerald R. Miller, "Persuasion," in *Handbook of Communication Science,* eds. C. Berger and S. Chaffee (Newbury Park, CA: Sage, 1987), 446–83.

29. Robert B. Cialdini, *Influence: The New Psychology of Modern Persuasion* (New York: Quill, 1984).

30. The Radicati Group, "Email Statistics Report 2020–2024,"February 2020, https://www.radicati.com/wp/wp-content/uploads/2020/01/Email_Statistics_Report,_2020-2024_Executive_Summary.pdf.

31. Giselle Abromovich, "If You Think Email Is Dead, Think Again," *Insights from Adobe,* September 2019, https://cmo.adobe.com/articles/2019/9/if-you-think-email-is-dead-think-again.html#gs.61vx5k.

32. Adobe, "Email Usage: Working Age Knowledge Workers (U.S. Trended Results)," September 12, 2019, https://www.slideshare.net/adobe/2019-adobe-email-usage-study.

33. Alanna Petroff and Océane Cornevin, "France Gives Workers 'Right to Disconnect' From Office Email," *CNN Money,* January 2, 2017, http://money.cnn.com/2017/01/02/technology/france-office-email-workers-law/index.html.

34. Christine Comaford, "Email Overload? Do This and Gain 10 Hours per Week," *Forbes,* February 20, 2015, https://www.forbes.com/sites/christinecomaford/2015/02/20/email-overload-do-this-and-gain-10-hours-per-week/#3373dc54671d.

35. Oliver Burkeman, "How to Avoid Email Overload," *The Guardian,* April 15, 2016, https://www.theguardian.com/lifeandstyle/2016/apr/15/how-to-deal-with-email-overload.

36. "Choosing a Communication Channel," *Strategic Communication Management* 16, no. 2 (2012): 38–39.

37. D. Dick, "Designing a Web Site for a Corporate Intranet," *Intercom* 51, no. 2 (2004): 12–13.

38. Jo Mackiewicz and Christopher Lam, "Coherence in Workplace Instant Messages," *Journal of Technical Writing and Communication* 39, no. 4 (2009): 417–31, doi: 10.2190/TW.39.4.e.

39. Nancy Flynn, *Instant Messaging Rules* (New York: AMACOM, 2004), 145–155.

40. Andrew D. Myers, "Texts as Evidence: Electronically Stored Information in Court," http://attorney-myers.com/2014/05/texts-as-evidence.

41. Stephen Yoch, "When 'You've Got Email' Means 'You've Got a Deal!,'" *FCA Contract Insight* 4, no.

1 (March 2010), http://www.finishingcontractors .org/uploads/media/CI_Mar.10.pdf.

42. Ibid.

43. Kenneth Rashbaum, "A Single Instant Message Can Land Your Company in a New York Court: The Deutsche Bank Case," *The Privacy and Data Security Law Journal* 10 (2006): 889–96.

44. Pew Research Center, "Mobile Fact Sheet," June 12, 2019, https://www.pewresearch.org/ internet/fact-sheet/mobile.

45. Bill Carmody, "Contacting Employees After Hours May Come at a Price (Literally)," *Inc.*, June 12, 2015, https://www.inc.com/bill-carmody/contacting-employees-after-hours-may-come-at-a-price-literally.html.

46. Allan Pratt, "Texting Security Concerns— AWTTW," *Tips4TechsBlog*, June 20, 2013, http:// tips4tech.wordpress.com/2013/06/20/texting-security-concerns.

47. The Radicati Group, "Instant Messaging Statistics Report, 2020–2024," February 2020, https://www.radicati.com/wp/wp-content/ uploads/2019/12/Instant-Messaging-Statis tics-Report-2020-2024-Exceutive-Summary .pdf.

48. Deb Shinder, "Instant Messaging: Does It Have a Place in Business Networks?" *TechGenix*, November 2, 2004, http://www.windowsecurity .com/articles/Instant-Messaging-Business-Networks.html.

49. Pew Research Center, "Social Media Fact Sheet," June 12, 2019, https://www.pewre search.org/internet/fact-sheet/social-media.

50. Kevin Popović, "How to Choose Social Media Channels That Best Support Your Strategy," *Communication World*, January 2, 2016, https:// www.iabc.com/how-to-choose-social-media-channels-that-best-support-your-strategy.

51. Merriam-Webster, Twitter post, July 17, 2017, 10:15 a.m., https://twitter.com/merriamweb ster/status/886997710376775681.

52. Elise Veroza Hurley and Amy C. Kimme Hea, "The Rhetoric of Reach: Preparing Students for Technical Communication in the Age of Social Media," *Technical Communication Quarterly* 23 (2014): 55–68, doi: 10.1080/10572252.2014.850854.

53. Jacqueline A. Gilbert, Dorie Clark, and Donald P. Roy, "Blogging: What's All the Fuss?" *SAM Advanced Management Journal* (Autumn 2016): 4–15.

54. S. Baker, "The Inside Story on Company Blogs," *BusinessWeek Online,* February 14, 2006, http://www.businessweek.com/technol ogy/content/feb2006/tc2006014_402499.htm.

55. Pete Blackshaw and Mike Nazzaro, "Consumer-Generated Media (CGM) 101: Word-of-Mouth in the Age of the Web-Fortified Consumer" (white paper, Nielsen BuzzMetrics, spring 2006), http://www.artsmarketing.org/marketing resources/files/Consumer-Generated%20 Media.pdf.

56. Gilbert et al., "Blogging: What's All the Fuss?"

57. Stephen Baker and Heather Green, "Social Media Will Change Your Business," *BusinessWeek Online*, February 20, 2008, http://www.businessweek .com/stories/2008-02-20/social-media-will-change-your-businessbusinessweek-business-news-stock-market-and-financial-advice.

58. Gilbert et al., "Blogging: What's All the Fuss?"

59. Rachel Monroe, "#vanlife, the Bohemian Social Media Movement," *The New Yorker*, April 17, 2017, https://www.newyorker.com/maga zine/2017/04/24/vanlife-the-bohemian-social-media-movement.

60. C. Catalano, "Megaphones to the Internet and the World: The Role of Blogs in Corporate Communication," *International Journal of Strategic Communication* 1, no. 4 (2007): 247–62.

61. Max Totsky, "The 10 Worst Social Media Fails of 2019," *Inc.*, December 24, 2019, https://www .inc.com/max-totsky/social-media-fails-2019 .html.

62. Ceri Hughes and Alex Chapel, "Connect, Communicate, Collaborate and Create: Implementing an Enterprise-Wide Social Collaboration Platform at KPMG," *Business Information Review* 30, no. 3 (2013): 140–43, doi: 10.1177/0266382113507378.

63. Baker, "The Inside Story."

64. H. Joseph Wen, Dana Schwieger, and Pamela Gershuny, "Internet Usage Monitoring in the Workplace: Its Legal Challenges and Implementation Strategies," *Information Systems Management* 24, no. 2 (2007): 185–96.

65. D. Elmuti and H. H. Davis, "Not Worth the Bad Will," *Industrial Management* 48, no. 6 (2006): 26–30.

66. R. L. Wakefield, "Computer Monitoring and Surveillance," *The CPA Journal* 74, no. 7 (2004): 52–55.

67. Ibid.

68. A. D. Moore, "Employee Monitoring and Computer Technology: Evaluative Surveillance v. Privacy," *Business Ethics Quarterly* 10, no. 3 (2000): 697–709.

69. American Management Association, "The Latest on Workplace Monitoring and Surveillance," 2007, http://www.amanet.org/training/articles/the-latest-on-workplace-monitoring-and-surveillance.aspx.

70. G. S. Alder, M. L. Ambrose, and T. W. Noel, "The Effect of Formal Advance Notice and Justification on Internet Monitoring Fairness: Much About Nothing?" *Journal of Leadership and Organizational Studies* 13, no. 1 (2006): 93–108.

71. Lee Rainie and Maeve Duggan, "Privacy and Information Sharing," Pew Research Center, January 24, 2016, http://www.pewinternet.org/2016/01/14/privacy-and-information-sharing.

72. A. M. Everett, Y. Wong, and J. Paynter, "Balancing Employee and Employer Rights: An International Comparison of Email Privacy in the Workplace," *Journal of Individual Employment Rights* 11, no. 4 (2004–2005): 291–310.

73. American Management Association, "The Latest on Workplace Monitoring and Surveillance," April 8, 2019, https://www.amanet.org/articles/the-latest-on-workplace-monitoring-and-surveillance.

74. Gerald M. Goldhaber, *Organizational Communication* (Dubuque, IA: Wm. C. Brown, 1983), 156.

75. Jeffrey Pfeffer, "Producing Sustainable Competitive Advantage Through the Effective Management of People," *The Academy of Management Executive* 19, no. 4 (2005): 95–108.

76. Kurt Wagner, "Bots, Explained," *CNBC*, April 11, 2016, http://www.cnbc.com/2016/04/11/bots-explained.html.

77. Paul Benjamin Lowry, Aaron Curtis, and Michelle Rene Lowry, "Building a Taxonomy and Nomenclature of Collaborative Writing to Improve Interdisciplinary Research and Practice," *Journal of Business Communication* 41, no. 1 (January 2004): 66–99.

78. Marshall Scott Poole and Geraldine DeSanctis, "Understand the Use of Group Decision Support Systems: The Theory of Adaptive Structuration," in *Organizations and Communication Technology,* eds. J. Fulk and C. Steinfield (Newbury Park, CA: Sage, 1990), 173–93; and "Smart Programs Go to Work," *BusinessWeek*, March 2, 1992, 97–105.

79. Gail S. Russ, Richard L. Daft, and Robert H. Lengel, "Media Selection and Managerial Characteristics in Organizational Communications," *Management Communication Quarterly* 4, no. 2 (November 1990): 151–75.

80. Jonah, Stillman, "I'm Not Texting. I'm Taking Notes," *The New York Times,* April 9, 2017, 7.

81. Arvind Hickman, "Arsenal's Adidas Twitter Campaign Hijacked by Racists Is 'Another User-Generated Own Goal,'" *PR Week*, July 3, 2019, https://www.prweek.com/article/1589929/arsenals-adidas-twitter-campaign-hijacked-racists-another-user-generated-own-goal.

COMMUNICATING WITH GROUPS

COMMUNICATING WITH GROUPS

4

MANAGING MEETINGS AND TEAMS

LEARNING OBJECTIVES

By the end of this chapter, you will be able to

- Explain the role of meetings and teams in gathering information, solving problems, making decisions, and coordinating work.

- Evaluate the advantages and disadvantages of teams.

- Plan effective meetings by considering pre-meeting arrangements of whether to meet, who should attend, what the purpose of the meeting will be, which leadership style is appropriate, and where it should take place.

- Consider how relationships, cultural differences, and disruptions affect team dynamics.

- Guide teams through decision making using the rational problem-solving approach, the nominal group technique, and the Delphi technique.

Meetings are an important organizational communication process that continues to be useful for coordination of work functions. The American Management Association concluded that collaboration and team building (which are primarily accomplished during meetings) are among the most critical workforce skills today and will be even more so in the future.[1] In fact, 90 percent of all U.S. businesses and 100 percent of the Fortune 500 companies use some form of group structure. Their need lies in the complexity and interdependence of tasks, which make it difficult for one person to have the knowledge to make decisions and solve problems in today's organizations. The contemporary regulatory environment illustrates this interdependence and the high cost of decisions. Governmental regulations on how and what an industry can do often require that lawyers, industrial relations managers, tax specialists, accountants, and governmental experts discuss ideas before a decision is made.

From a broader perspective, it is easy to see why teams have been adopted as a key personnel configuration in the postmodern business environment. As discussed in Chapter 1, today's workplace is fast paced. The traditional management hierarchy has been replaced by flexible, cooperative, mission-driven managers who expect their direct reports and associates to participate fully in the task or project at hand.

Managing teams—and the meetings that teamwork requires—calls for special skills. Just because a work group is labeled a team doesn't mean it automatically functions as a team. As a team leader, you must use a variety of communication strategies to maximize your team's effectiveness. This chapter describes those key strategic considerations. But first, we briefly review the range of functions that meetings and teams perform.

Managers use meetings for several functions: information sharing, fact finding, problem solving, decision making, and coordinating (see Table 4-1). While a meeting may be labeled team, staff, marketing, committee, ad hoc, or something else, any meeting should allow members to share information, obtain ideas, solve problems, coordinate efforts, make decisions, and build working relationships. A gathering of workers who simply sit and hear the manager make announcements is not a true meeting.

Managers use informational meetings to explain important new decisions or company activities to employees, answer questions, or help them understand how to perform a desired task. The essential aim is to communicate a company point of view and have it accepted by employees. Such meetings succeed when they get the employees to examine, articulate, and align their own interests with the company's.

TABLE 4-1 ■ Functions of Meetings
Share information
Find facts
Solve problems
Make decisions
Coordinate tasks

CRITICAL THINKING QUESTIONS

1. What kinds of teams and groups have you been a part of, either at work or in your personal life?

2. What factors helped your team accomplish its task? What factors made it more difficult?

Managers conduct fact-finding meetings to tap the expertise of several employees and obtain facts for planning and decision making. For example, a sales manager may call in all the sales representatives to find out about such matters as business conditions, competition, customer desires, and complaints. A production manager having trouble with a specific operation might meet with all the key people who have knowledge of a situation.

In a problem-solving and decision-making meeting, team members pool their specialized expertise with the objective of developing a solution. This meeting goes beyond simply finding facts; it seeks to identify the issues and discuss the probable gains and losses resulting from alternate actions.

In coordination meetings, project teams keep each other informed of their progress and plan each stage of their joint efforts. Whatever their purpose, meetings are a way of managerial life; however, managers must use meetings prudently to maximize their benefits and minimize their costs.

An outstanding example of meetings that accomplish the goals described previously was the Katrina Working Group sessions led by the mayor of Houston, Texas, Bill White, following the devastation of Hurricane Katrina in September 2005. Every morning, he presided over a session of community leaders, corporate executives, church leaders, emergency services staff, and elected officials to determine how to serve the thousands of evacuees from New Orleans and other Gulf Coast areas who were seeking shelter in Houston. Forty people sat at long tables arranged in a square in a large room, with dozens of others sitting in rows behind the tables. Mayor White refused to allow speeches or grandstanding. Instead, he asked participants to raise issues and helped them formulate response plans. As a result of the efficient methods that the mayor's team used to handle the crisis, ensuring humanitarian aid to evacuees while maintaining the city's normal functions, Houston reelected Bill White in November 2005 with 91 percent of the vote.[2]

Although face-to-face meetings are most common, companies operating in the global marketplace require their employees to connect and collaborate no matter where they are. A recent Gallup poll showed that 37 percent of employees telecommuted at least one day per week, up from 9 percent in 1995.[3] A survey by Global Workforce Analytics suggests that 56 percent of the U.S. workforce hold jobs that could be partially or fully remote. In 2019, 5 million people worked remotely at least half-time.[4] During the COVID-19 pandemic that started in 2020, that number skyrocketed, and companies like Facebook, Twitter, Nationwide, and Square announced plans to permit remote work permanently.[5]

Although some managers express concern about employee commitment or productivity, studies have shown that remote employees work 5 to 7 hours more per week, on average, than office workers.[6] More remote workers say they are happy in their job and are more likely to stay in their jobs than on-site workers.[7] Furthermore, 77 percent of teleworkers say they are more productive when they work outside of the office. They also report more job satisfaction and better quality of life because the flexibility of telework allows them to sleep more, find time to exercise, and eat healthier.[8]

Telework has benefits for employers, too. Companies that offer the option to work off-site report that it has significantly helped retain employees, reduce absenteeism, and recruit qualified personnel without being restricted by geography. In fact, 36 percent of employees say they would take a pay cut in exchange for the ability to work off-site some of the time.[9] For this model to be successful, flexibility, responsiveness, cost-effectiveness, and rapid response time are imperative. Clearly, managing virtual teams is an important skill for managers.

ADVANTAGES AND DISADVANTAGES OF WORKING IN TEAMS

Whether participating in a team or leading one, managers should be aware of advantages and disadvantages of group work, as summarized in Table 4-2.

TABLE 4-2 ■ Advantages and Disadvantages of Teams	
Advantages	**Disadvantages**
Higher-quality decisions	Low-quality or premature decisions
Increased productivity	Wasted time
Increased commitment, loyalty, retention	Expensive
Fewer communication breakdowns	Overused
Increased motivation	Risk of groupthink

Advantages of Teams

One advantage is that a group decision may be of a higher quality than that made by an individual. But before using a team, you must analyze the nature of the problem. Teams are better at solving problems for which there is no single correct solution or for which solutions are difficult to verify objectively.[10] Such problems require decisions that cannot be programmed. Non-programmed decisions are the result of infrequent situations that require creativity, insight, and the sharing of ideas and perspectives regarding a problem.[11] Groups, especially heterogeneous groups, bring a greater variety of information and a wider choice of solutions.

A second advantage to a team is that when members have had an opportunity for discussion, they are more likely to be committed to the information presented or the decision made. In other words, they become "owners" of the decision. A classic study conducted by Coch and French nearly 75 years ago investigated workers' resistance to technological changes in their jobs. During team or employee meetings, they noted that when workers participated in discussions regarding implementation of the changes, significantly less resistance resulted than that which occurred among workers excluded from participation.[12] Each employee who participated in the meeting had increased ownership of the outcome, and the responsibility felt for making the solution or program work was enhanced.

A more recent study of employee retention factors found similar results. Clear communication about the goals of an organization and the ability to play a part in formulating those goals are two important factors in an employee's intention to stay with an organization.[13]

Another advantage of a team meeting is that it may reduce the chance of communication problems. When a group of people hears the same message at the same time, the possibility of misinterpretation declines. Participants' questions can clarify the message, and each participant has the opportunity to hear the answer and ask additional questions. Feedback is increased and timing is reduced as a barrier to communication.

Finally, teams help managers develop their influence. Qualcomm is a multinational corporation headquartered in San Diego, California. It creates semiconductors, software, and services related to wireless technology and counts Apple as one of its biggest clients. Qualcomm is leading the way to 5G technology. Steve Mollenkopf, CEO since 2014, describes the importance of team decision making. At Qualcomm, managers

lead teams on a project basis, with the teams made up of people from different departments that don't report to you. So you learn how to influence people that don't have to listen to you. . . . Ninety-five percent of the time . . . you go through a process that allows people to reach consensus.[14]

CRITICAL THINKING QUESTIONS

1. Which of the advantages listed here accurately reflect your own experience on teams?

2. How have teammates influenced your own efforts? How do you believe you have influenced others?

Disadvantages of Teams

We have seen that working in teams can improve quality, productivity, creativity, loyalty and commitment, and even retention. But there is a downside. Richard Hall put it well when he noted, "Time spent on meetings is time not spent on other activities."[15] The hourly cost of a meeting includes not only the base pay of each participant but also payroll taxes, fringe benefits, and general overhead. Meeting costs often go unnoticed because they are not budget line items. When one large manufacturing organization recently tallied the costs of a regular meeting of its midlevel managers, it discovered the expense was $15 million per year.[16] Meetings are a hidden cost that can either impede or improve the effectiveness of a work group.

In addition to the high cost, the team may develop low-quality decisions. Pressures to conform, premature decisions, hidden agendas, extensive conflict, disruptive and dominant individuals, lack of planning, and poor leadership can easily reduce effectiveness.[17] Later in the chapter, we detail these factors and techniques for managing them.

A common disadvantage of meetings is their frequent overuse. Organizations often develop a *meeting style* of management in which groups meet for every little thing. Meetings are often held just because "we always have a meeting at this time" or "we want to make sure everyone is on the same page." This phenomenon is so widespread that it even spawned the meme "This meeting should have been an e-mail." Meetings generally are not necessary for routine or repetitive programmed decisions that can be handled by an established procedure. Overuse of meetings may cause employees to find them a nuisance, so they avoid them. Consequently, employees may miss truly important meetings or be unable to distinguish between a critical and a useless meeting.

Another problem is that the weekly team meeting might be a waste of time if members are not required to gather facts before the meeting, make decisions at the meeting, or present information. The manager must analyze each meeting to determine need. Still another often useless meeting pattern finds the manager telling a group about a new event or presenting a progress report without providing an opportunity for questions or interactions. If interaction is not part of the meeting, it may be more efficient to share information through a memo or e-mail.

Groupthink

Groupthink is the tendency of a group to conform to ideas simply because the general sense of the group has moved in a particular direction. Members of the group feel committed to continue in the same line of thought and ignore alternatives. Although the group may be pursuing an incorrect conclusion, the group does not alter direction for fear of creating dissent or offending a group member. It is the extreme form of cohesiveness and is especially likely when a group has a high sense of teamwork and desire for consensus or harmony.

The concept of groupthink was defined in 1972 by Irving Janis, who wrote a book titled *Victims of Groupthink*.[18] Groupthink is especially important because of its potential for disastrous effects. Some say the disaster of the space shuttle *Challenger* was a result of groupthink.[19] The night before the space shuttle's launch in 1986, engineers urged managers to delay because they were worried about failure of the O-rings in the cold weather. Their concerns were overruled, the *Challenger* was launched, and the O-rings failed, causing the deaths of seven astronauts. Subsequent investigations indicated that despite evidence of the potential risks being presented in meetings, the meeting members kept redefining their definitions of risk to downplay the problem. Unfortunately, dissenters and whistleblowers are too often ignored, and many other disasters have been at least partially attributed to groupthink, including the collapses of Enron and WorldCom, the Iraq war, and the housing bubble and stock market crash of 2008.[20]

Based on Janis's concept, Von Bergen and Kirk describe symptoms of groupthink that managers should watch for:[21]

1. The illusion that everyone in the group holds the same viewpoint, with an emphasis on team play

2. The belief that the group can make no mistakes

3. The belief that disagreements are to be avoided, faulty assumptions are not to be questioned, and personal doubts must be suppressed in favor of group harmony

4. The tendency to comfort one another and to ignore or at least discount warnings that an agreed-on plan is either unworkable or highly unlikely to succeed

5. The tendency to direct pressure on any dissenting group member who expresses strong challenges to the consensus opinion of the group

6. The presence of inordinate optimism that predisposes members to take excessive risks

When in a decision-making meeting, the effective manager is alert to groupthink symptoms and takes appropriate action. Or more appropriately, managers take actions to ensure that groupthink does not develop. Three actions help avoid the tendency toward groupthink:

- *Do not make an early decision.* Do not commit early or become locked into a position early in the problem analysis. When managers begin a discussion by saying, "This is what I would like to see" or "This is the best solution . . . but I would like your comments," they are probably preventing an open discussion and setting the stage for an early unanimous decision.

- *Be open to criticism.* This is easy to say but difficult to do. It is natural to defend one's idea, but a wise manager will encourage employees to push back. Criticism of an idea should not be taken as criticism of another's self-worth. When criticism cannot arise within the group, it may be solicited from an outsider who will generally be less susceptible to status and conformity pressures.

- *Use a devil's advocate.* The term *devil's advocate* comes from the Roman Catholic Church. When the church hierarchy was debating whether a person should be sainted, a devil's advocate used to be appointed to present the argument against doing so.[22] Good ideas are often ignored if they lack an advocate. The constructive controversy technique assigns members of the group to advocate for one alternative and to question the others. During the discussion, each idea is presented without interruption, then the rest of the group asks questions and challenges conclusions. At the end of the discussion, group members work together to summarize the pros and cons of each alternative and develop a consensus of the best option.[23]

CRITICAL THINKING QUESTIONS

1. Have you been in a situation in which you witnessed behavior or decisions that may have been illegal, unethical, or simply made you uncomfortable? What did you do about it?

2. What advice would you give to a new employee who experienced a similar situation and came to you for advice?

STRATEGIC CONSIDERATIONS FOR MEETINGS

As we have seen, meetings have advantages as well as disadvantages, and groupthink adds to their complexity. The following discussion of 10 strategic considerations, which are listed in Table 4-3, is provided to assist managers when considering the various contingencies.

Strategic Consideration 1: Should We Meet?

There are good reasons to have a meeting and poor reasons to do so. As we have seen, the best reason is to get everyone's input on a complex problem or task. A poor reason to meet is to show others that one has the power to call people together or to be the center of attention. Another wrong reason is social or recreational—a meeting as an opportunity to get away from the desk, to visit with Bill from accounting about the football game, or to be seen with some influential decision makers. Often, a brief, informal group conversation may

TABLE 4-3 ■ Strategic Considerations for Meetings
1. Should we meet? Determine if the information warrants a meeting or a memo.
2. Who should attend? Identify people who have necessary expertise and who represent areas that will be affected.
3. What will the group do? Plan the agenda and materials.
4. What type of leadership style is appropriate? Determine the level of control required to manage the group's work.
5. What happens during the meeting? Manage participation and disruptions.
6. What was accomplished? Review meeting goals and follow-up.
7. Where should the meeting be held? Choose an appropriate location.
8. How will the group connect? Arrange for appropriate technology requirements.
9. How will the group build trust? Foster team relationships.
10. How will the group accommodate diversity? Recognize and respect cultural differences.

be better than a formal meeting. A good way to handle the former is to hold the meeting with everybody standing up.[24] This strategy ensures involvement, attention to the meeting's purpose, and brevity.

If you have decided to have a meeting, you next must attend to the pre-meeting arrangements.

Strategic Consideration 2: Who Should Attend?

Once you have decided to hold a meeting, you need to select the meeting participants. Among the criteria to consider are (a) how many people to invite, (b) whom the members will represent, (c) the members' functions in the meeting, and (d) their team-ability.

First, choose a manageable group size. There is no ideal group size, but research shows that as a group grows, communication becomes distorted and stress between members increases. Research on work groups suggests the optimum size is generally about five.[25] Smaller groups are often faster and more productive. They are also more agile than large groups. Small groups are able to quickly self-correct when errors in judgment or reasoning occur, whereas large groups tend to propagate those errors as the discussion evolves more slowly.[26] However, small groups may also be dysfunctional, engage in superficial discussion, and avoid controversial subjects.

When the problem is more complex, relatively larger groups—as large as 12 to 13 members—have proved more effective. But the larger the group, the less inclined an individual group member is to participate. If it is not possible to limit the size of the group to five or seven employees, a manager could break the large group into smaller subgroups. The improved decisions or more accurate sharing of information may justify the time and effort required to coordinate several groups. When creating groups, remember the guideline that increasing the size limits the extent to which individuals want to communicate.

Second, when selecting members, an important thing to remember is that the team should reflect the organizational members the problem affects. For instance, if the concern is a departmental one, then members of the department should be involved. If two departments share the problem, team membership obviously should be drawn from both areas. When possible, membership should also include people with authority to follow through on the chosen action with time, personnel, and financial resources. But salience of the meeting's topic should be considered more important than organizational status when selecting participants.

Third, consider participants' potential functions within the team. When scheduling a problem-solving meeting, include people who are familiar with the different aspects of the problem. Also, include people who will actually carry out the solution to ensure implementation of the decision. In short, subject-matter expertise should be a prime criterion for membership in a team or work group.

Finally, consider participants' team-ability. Task knowledge is an insufficient qualification for meeting participation. Ability to work with others may become even more of a concern for cross-functional teams and virtual teams because of the special communication challenges they involve. Members of teams may be too passive, tactful, or constrained to work together in a satisfying manner. They fear alienating one another.[27] On the other hand, members may be too passionate, stubborn, and aggressive. They might be unable to cooperate and compromise in a team setting. Clearly, your group must have the needed team skills to function in a meeting and resolve the problem.[28]

If a manager has difficulty finding employees with team-ability, training may be called for. Teamwork is a skill that can be acquired, not a gift one is born with. Understanding group dynamics comes with study and practice. Parts IV (Understanding Messages) and V (Communicating Interpersonally) of this book offer guidelines for developing some of the process skills required for meeting participation, including collaborating, listening, giving constructive feedback, negotiating, compromising, and other conflict-resolution strategies.

Strategic Consideration 3: Agenda and Materials

The agenda is the script or working paper from which the meeting operates. As one chief executive says, "give me an agenda or else I'm not going to sit there, because if I don't know why we're in the meeting, and you don't know why we're there, then there's no reason for a meeting."[29] Regardless of the type of meeting, the agenda needs to communicate the *what*, *why*, *when*, and *who* (the Ws) of a meeting. Frequently, one or several of the elements of an agenda are omitted, yet each is important. For instance, if time frames for each agenda topic are included, the meeting is less likely to run long and more likely to address all the topics. And if expected outcomes for each topic are specified, the meeting participants are more likely to reach the stated goals. An agenda template is shown in Figure 4-1.

Everyone knows that agendas are important, but half of all business meetings are held with no agenda. Maybe the extra effort of an agenda seems unjustified, or the lack of an agenda may merely reflect a lack of planning. It may also be that agendas are not the common practice in many companies. Agendas are often not needed in small, informal meetings where two or three employees get together or when one obvious topic is the only point for discussion. However, some managers assume agendas are never needed for small meetings. Agendas require planning time—an asset that ineffective managers rarely possess.

FIGURE 4-1 ■ Meeting Announcement and Agenda Template

MEMORANDUM

DATE:

TO:

FROM:

SUBJECT: Meeting Notification and Agenda

DATE:

START TIME: END TIME:

LOCATION:

AGENDA:

Topic	Time	Leader	Expected Outcome
A			
B			
C			
D			
E			

Many managers would rather spend additional time in a poorly conducted meeting than take the time to plan. To prepare the agenda, ask members to suggest topics but include only those that affect the entire team.

What. People first need to know the topic under discussion, so they may understand exactly what is to be discussed. Let the agenda make this clear. A topic listed as "Maintenance" will not communicate as fully as one that reads "Maintenance Status of the Emergency Generator" or "Should We Replace the Emergency Generator?" A more complete description enables participants to gather any special information or prepare questions relevant to the discussion.

Why. People attending a meeting need to know the goal for each agenda item. Identify the purpose of each item as an announcement, a discussion, or a decision, so that members will know when and how to participate. If any preparation is needed, such as reviewing documents or collecting data, note that on the agenda as well.[30] Failure to clarify a group discussion's goal leads to circular talk, and when people do not know why they are attending a meeting, apprehension and frustration arise.

When. Setting the time involves several strategic factors. First, what time of day is best for all the participants? Are there cultural, organizational, or temporal constraints on parts of the day? Some managers grumble that "all times are equally bad" when trying to assemble groups, but time zones, competing activities, and even the after-lunch slump make some meeting times more desirable than others. Enterprise software can often scan multiple calendars to identify availability, and polling applications like Doodle or Rallly allow users to choose from options offered by the meeting organizer.

Second, how long should the meeting last? If a meeting schedule does not allow sufficient time, critical issues may receive superficial coverage. But remember that people value time highly and resent its waste or misuse. Be sure to list both the start time and the end time on your meeting announcement to allow participants to plan their day.

A standard time limit that applies to all meetings is impossible to set. However, some ground rules on length are possible. The most effective meetings last no longer than 1.5 hours. After this long, people need to break to stretch or get fresh air. Short, single goals can be met in less than an hour, and this should be the time span a manager aims for. Individual agenda items should also be assigned a time limit. Too often, meetings go on and on because no one has established definite time parameters.

When applies to the appropriate time to send out the agenda as well. The purpose of the agenda and any supporting material is lost if none of it arrives until the last minute. Neither should one send the materials with so much lead time that the participants forget about it. A useful guideline is that the longer a meeting is (and consequently, the more scheduling and preparation required by the participants), the greater the lead time required for the agenda and supporting materials. But avoid too long a lead time, which could bring about forgetfulness. Generally, participants need 2 or 3 days' notice to prepare for a meeting.

Who. Tell participants who will be at the meeting and who will be presenting topics on the agenda. This knowledge allows the participants to complete their own audience analysis. Knowing who else will be present lets the participants prepare any material or information that others in the meeting may request. A list of participants also forces the meeting manager to think about possible group dynamics. For instance, will a verbally dominant person attempt to control the group? Will the correct mix of expertise be present? Answers to these questions can influence meeting outcomes.

Careful planning is half the battle; the other half is sticking to the plan. Open the meeting by asking the group to review and modify the agenda to include last-minute developments, but otherwise, if others try to introduce new elements during the meeting, refer to the written agenda.[31]

Strategic Consideration 4: Leadership Style

The problems facing organizations are so varied and complex that no one style of leadership suits all situations. Consequently, a manager must be flexible and diagnose the situation to determine the appropriate leadership behavior from one situation to another.

When diagnosing the situation to determine the most effective style, managers need to consider three factors: the group, the objective of the meeting, and the type of leadership behavior with which the manager personally feels most comfortable.[32] Figure 4-2 shows how these three factors operate together.

Each group differs but needs a leader with some degree of interpersonal orientation; therefore, tight control is generally inappropriate. Less control is required when the group is mature and knows the topic, whereas a new or immature group needs a leader who provides more control and direction.

A routine or structured meeting may call for more leader control and task orientation, but a democratic or more laissez-faire approach may be required for a solution to an abstract problem or one requiring a creative solution. A highly emotional task requires less control, while more control may be best for a nonsensitive objective.

Finally, managers must be aware of the type of leadership behavior with which they are personally most comfortable. This awareness helps managers monitor their own behavior

FIGURE 4-2 ■ Determining Leadership Style

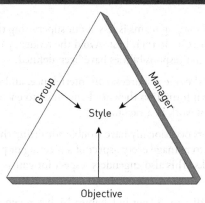

and remain flexible rather than use the same behavior repeatedly. Increasing one's repertoire of management tools is a requirement for today's fast-paced, constantly shifting workplace.

Leading Project Teams

Managing project teams calls for special leadership skills. Among them is the ability to select team members who communicate information freely and honestly. One nontraditional tool for objectively evaluating project team members is social network analysis (SNA).[33] SNA examines relationships and information flow between people. It begins with a survey about whom respondents go to for advice or information, whom they communicate with most frequently, and who their most valued contact in the organization is.

Survey results are analyzed, and "sociograms" are designed that reveal employees' social network and connections. From these sociograms, a project leader can identify people with *centrality*. Centrality is a measure of a person's relative importance based on their location in the social network. Thus, when putting together a project team or when analyzing a dysfunctional team, a manager should consider whether individuals have high degrees of centrality. These people control the flow of information and collaboration, bridging potential communication gaps in the team and in the organization.

Analyzing SNA results helps managers understand the interactive patterns and communication networks that are present in their team and across the organization. SNA is also a tool for determining how best to leverage these connections in order to motivate staff, improve performance, enhance knowledge sharing and learning, and reduce conflict.[34]

CRITICAL THINKING QUESTIONS

Consider a person in your organization who exhibits high centrality.

1. What are some of the ways this person develops a social network?
2. To what extent can you adopt these behaviors to strengthen your own centrality?

The following are some other strategies that will help you maximize your project team's effectiveness:

- *Be a facilitator.* Managing teams is less about supervising than it is about motivating members to do their best. Avoid the tendency to micromanage once the team's objectives and responsibilities have been defined.

- *Support the team.* Provide resources, run interference, and resolve internal conflicts. Give them all the information they need and more to encourage trust. Remember that people cannot work in a vacuum.

- *Delegate.* Managers occasionally have trouble admitting that they cannot do it all. Instead of trying to manage every aspect of a meeting or project, trust members to perform their tasks. This also engenders respect for you as a leader and maintains morale.

- *Seek diversity.* As discussed later in Chapter 13, heterogeneous groups experience more conflict but often produce higher-quality results than homogeneous groups. Stress the importance of collaboration, flexibility, and openness toward unfamiliar viewpoints and work styles.[35]

Strategic Consideration 5: Managing Disruptions

One of the most aggravating behaviors is when a team member continually disrupts the communication flow. This person may be unskilled in group dynamics or may be coming to the meetings with a hidden agenda (that is, private objectives) that conflicts with the stated agenda. Disruptive behavior may include continuous clowning, dominating the conversation, attempting to change directions, or making accusations. These disruptions need resolution; otherwise, teams can quickly deteriorate.

Before the Meeting

A manager can minimize disruptions by taking a preventive point of view. John Jones suggests seven tactics that managers may use ahead of time when they believe a person will disrupt a meeting:[36]

1. Before the meeting, ask for the disrupter's cooperation.

2. Give the person a special task or role in the meeting, such as posting the viewpoints of others.

3. Work out your differences before the meeting (possibly with a third-party facilitator) to present a united front to all other members.

4. Structure the meeting to include frequent discussion of the meeting process itself.

5. Take all the dominator's items off the agenda.

6. Alert the person to the consequences of disruption. For example, say, "I have learned that a number of people are angry with you, and they plan to confront you in the meeting."

7. Arrange for allies to support you in dealing with the disruptive behavior of the individual.

During the Meeting

While prevention is preferred, a manager also needs to have options for controlling disruptive behavior during a meeting. The following are some strategies:

1. When dealing with an emotional conversation, make sure only one person speaks at a time, paraphrase each statement to ensure accuracy before allowing anyone else to speak, and be sure that everyone takes turns. One surprisingly effective technique is to move on to the next agenda item. One can return when tempers cool.[37] You might also stand and move to the flip chart or screen or casually stand near the parties involved. This will help keep control in a nonverbal manner.

2. A less obvious disruptive influence occurs when participants do not get involved in the discussion. One way to ensure that participants become involved is to use the Delphi technique (discussed later). When the participants need to have answers prepared for specific questions before the meeting, ask for these answers during the meeting.

3. Discourage multitasking during meetings. In a study of information workers, 92 percent admitted to multitasking during meetings, usually checking e-mail or working on other projects, and 41 percent said they do it nearly all the time.[38] Distractions like these weaken the quality and efficiency of group discussions.

4. Ask participants to jot down answers on a notepad when sensitive issues are discussed. Ask the participants to submit their written reactions anonymously to you, then read them to the group. Participants thus have an opportunity to present viewpoints in a "safe" manner.

5. Ask questions throughout the meeting to help keep the participants involved. When worded correctly and addressed to the right audience, questions develop a participative climate. Questions have the greatest chance of soliciting participation when they are open-ended, brief, unbiased, easily understood, and immediately pertinent to the topic.

A manager needs to consider four possible alternatives when asking a question.[39] When an *overhead question* is asked, anyone in the group may answer. A good idea is to begin with an overhead question and continue until forced to change. Either domination or nonparticipation by certain individuals may require a *direct question*, simply one that is directed to an individual. With direct questions, keep a balance instead of continually asking a verbal person or an assumed expert.

A *reverse question* is one originally asked by a group member. The leader then directs it back to the person who asked it. Do this when it is apparent that the participant really wants to make a statement but is not quite sure it would be appropriate. A final alternative is the *relay question*, which is asked by a group member and is relayed by the leader to the group: "Mary's question is interesting. What is a good answer?" The relay question gives you an opportunity to keep the communication moving among all the members of the group.

Strategic Consideration 6: Follow-Up

At meeting's end, reanalyze the original goals to ensure you have met them, make appropriate follow-up assignments, and evaluate the meeting process to determine if and how future meetings could be improved. One way to determine if the goal has been met is to review the rational problem-solving process (described later in this chapter) to ensure each step was followed. If the group has defined the problem and has reviewed alternative solutions to this problem, it can be assumed the original objective has been met.

Another easy way to determine if the objective is met is to write out the decision or summarize the discussion in a few sentences. This clear statement allows the participants to review it and make sure they understand it. A summary of the decision reached will bring to the surface any individual misunderstandings or disagreements.

A good idea is to point out differences that exist at the end of the meeting. This recognizes that disagreement is not always bad; also, the disagreements will probably be vital to future discussions. A clear understanding of differences at the end of that meeting should make future meetings go more smoothly and help prevent unnecessary meetings.

Appropriate post-meeting follow-up is also an important component of team management. Before closing the meeting, clearly set out the next steps each member is to take. Also, announce the next meeting, if necessary. Written confirmation of the decisions reached and any future actions to be taken by the participants is a good practice. Such a memo or e-mail serves as a reminder of the results and informs other personnel who are interested but did not attend the meeting.

Stress the positive when writing the follow-up memo, so that the participants can see the fruits of their labor. A follow-up memo or e-mail becomes a record of the meeting, ensures follow-up, and establishes accountability for future action. Some companies have a standard form for the follow-up memo (shown in Figure 4-3) that helps keep it short, simple, and accurate.

In a meeting, much happens that is lost forever. A manager may need to provide more detailed minutes. Minutes are particularly valuable as a starter for future meetings on the same topic. Traditional minutes should capture a summary of the meeting that includes action items, decisions, and open issues.

- *Action items.* Action items are to-dos assigned to meeting participants. Record the task, the person responsible, and the date agreed on to complete the task.

- *Decisions.* All decisions that may affect future choices of the group should be recorded.

FIGURE 4-3 ■ Meeting Follow-Up Memo

Subject of meeting _____

Name of sender _____

Where and when held _____

Present _____

Major conclusions _____

Future actions _____

Next meeting _____

- *Open issues.* New issues raised at the meeting but not resolved there should be recorded, so that they can be carried over to a future meeting.[40]

The minutes should record these three results for each topic on the agenda. In addition, any significant comments about that topic should be recorded. Participants appreciate having their comments displayed in a way that is visible to everyone. Conventional minutes are often distributed to all meeting members. For political or corporate culture reasons, a manager may want to summarize the information for larger distribution and post it to an intranet site.

The final step in the management of a meeting is the evaluation of the meeting itself, an important self-development activity. One extreme form of evaluation is audio recording the meeting and evaluating it step-by-step. This may be especially worthwhile for project teams that meet regularly over extended time periods. In fact, your organization may require this of all project managers when they begin a project with a new team of specialists.

The evaluation sheet in Figure 4-4 represents one tool that can be used to evaluate a meeting.

FIGURE 4-4 ■ Evaluation Sheet

Listed below is a series of statements about a meeting. Circle the number of the scale that best describes the meeting in which you just participated.

1. The objective of the meeting was clearly defined.

| Strongly agree | 5 | 4 | 3 | 2 | 1 | Strongly disagree |

2. A systematic approach was used to solve problems.

| Strongly agree | 5 | 4 | 3 | 2 | 1 | Strongly disagree |

3. All the participants were involved in the meeting.

| Strongly agree | 5 | 4 | 3 | 2 | 1 | Strongly disagree |

4. Disruptions were effectively managed.

| Strongly agree | 5 | 4 | 3 | 2 | 1 | Strongly disagree |

5. An appropriate format was established for the meeting.

| Strongly agree | 5 | 4 | 3 | 2 | 1 | Strongly disagree |

6. Appropriate pre-meeting details (agenda, room, etc.) were arranged.

| Strongly agree | 5 | 4 | 3 | 2 | 1 | Strongly disagree |

7. Time was well managed.

| Strongly agree | 5 | 4 | 3 | 2 | 1 | Strongly disagree |

8. The stated objectives could have been met without a meeting.

| Strongly agree | 5 | 4 | 3 | 2 | 1 | Strongly disagree |

9. The objective of the meeting has been met.

| Strongly agree | 5 | 4 | 3 | 2 | 1 | Strongly disagree |

Strategic Consideration 7: Location

Once the participants have been selected and the agenda and supporting materials have been prepared, meeting leaders should choose an appropriate location. Whether hosting a physical or virtual meeting, managers must consider how the setting and layout can affect the group's work. A few simple guidelines will help make a face-to-face meeting productive:

- Use a room where the chairs and tables can be arranged to meet group needs.

- Match the size of the room with the size of the group. Meetings held in close, cramped rooms with the members jammed together around narrow tables make for an unpleasant conversational climate and hamper decision making. Tension, a prime breeder of conflict, builds in a close and uncomfortable meeting room. At the same time, however, a room seating 45 can be cold and overwhelming to a group of five.

- Check for comfortable chairs, ventilation, and lighting. Remember, though, that soft, overly comfortable chairs can affect concentration and even prolong the meeting.

- Make sure space exists for visual aids if they are to be used. If you know you will be needing equipment, writing materials, and so on, be sure they are available. Keep the audience in mind. Thus, providing place cards may be useful if the participants are strangers.

- Above all, arrange to have the meeting in a meeting room rather than the meeting leader's office. It will create an environment that emphasizes the participants are coming together for specific purposes at a specific time on neutral turf. The atmosphere created is one of urgency and seriousness, which helps keep the meeting on the topic.

Seating Arrangements

After designating the appropriate facility for the meeting, managers should consider which of several possible seating arrangements to use. Depending on the situation, more than one arrangement may be possible; however, a few arrangements should be avoided. The first arrangement to avoid is the long, narrow table that makes it nearly impossible for all participants to see one another. A manager can use eye contact to gain attention or control a participant; consequently, such a seating arrangement works against the manager's attempts to use all the nonverbal techniques available.

A second arrangement to avoid is one that divides up sides. For instance, if two groups are in natural opposition, they should not sit across from each other. Similarly, one should keep two hostile participants apart or in such a position that they cannot easily see each other. As described in Chapter 14, people seated directly across from one another at a table are more likely to feel competitive than cooperative.

Several seating arrangements lend themselves to effective communication in meetings: the table with the leader at one end, the round table or circle, and the *U* shape.[41] When the leader sits at one end of the table, control of the meeting is easier because all communication will tend to flow toward the head person. However, this arrangement loses effectiveness with a group larger than six or seven participants. As groups get larger, sidebar comments tend to increase and eye contact is difficult to maintain.

When the size of the meeting becomes larger than 10 to 12 members, a *U*-shaped arrangement is preferred. The manager sitting in the middle of the *U* can maintain eye contact with all the participants; at the same time, communication among subunits of the group is less likely. A variation is the oval-shaped table. When the president of the United States meets with the Cabinet (most senior appointed officers), for instance, everyone sits at an oval table, with the president at the middle, directly across from the vice president. Other members are seated according to the order of precedence, with higher-ranking officers sitting closer to the center of the table.

The manager using the round table or circle arrangement has less direct control of the group than with other arrangements. Because the manager has a less dominant position, participants tend to address each other rather than the leader. A table is, in a sense, a kind of communication line, as the contour of the table establishes the flow of communication. Thus, the round table is best when seeking a true participative form of decision making and trying to minimize status differences. Figure 4-5 illustrates the different arrangements.

FIGURE 4-5 ■ Seating Arrangements

CRITICAL THINKING QUESTIONS

Think about meetings you have attended for work, school, and as part of your community.

- Where did the meeting take place? What is the significance of that location?
- What effect might the room size, table shape, furniture arrangement, and other environmental factors have on group dynamics during those meetings?

Managers might consider the advice of Dennis Crowley, chief executive of Foursquare, the location-based social networking site, regarding seating. When he conducts regular meetings, he mixes up the arrangement so that everyone sits next to everyone else occasionally. Crowley believes in the importance of his staff getting to know each other, which is reflected in the company's relaxed, open culture.[42]

Location is equally important in virtual meetings, although in a different way. Meeting participants should set up their workspace with a neutral background to minimize distractions. If other members of your household might accidentally wander into view, position yourself in front of a wall. The camera should be located at (or just above) eye level; a stack of books or a box can temporarily raise your computer to the correct height. Although we may not think about lighting in face-to-face meetings, it is essential for a clear image on video. Natural light is best, but a window behind your chair can create a silhouette effect. Lamps placed behind or just to the side of the camera can supplement overhead lighting. Finally, think about sound in the room. Carpet, rugs, curtains, or cloth wall hangings can dampen noises and prevent echoes.

Strategic Consideration 8: Technological Requirements

Whether connecting by videoconference or projecting a document on a screen, meetings often require technological support. Confirm that the room has the equipment you need, including a microphone if the room or group size is large. Although many people believe they can speak loudly, meeting rooms are plagued by background noises like the hum of ventilation, the clicking of keyboards, and the murmur of side conversations. Saying "I don't need a mic" suggests an ableist attitude that everyone can hear equally well, and it requires those who do not to self-identify their disability or miss the conversation.[43]

Teleconferencing, a richer channel than phone, e-mail, or instant messaging, and online videoconferencing tools are proliferating. Among the more popular are Skype, GoToMeeting, WebEx, Adobe Connect, Google Hangout, Zoom, and RingCentral. All are low cost and allow participants to observe nonverbal behaviors, which can help prevent misunderstandings. Most web conferencing software has capabilities for desktop sharing, encrypting, meeting through mobile devices, and even recording. On the other hand, video and audio quality rely on Internet bandwidth, which may be problematic. Mobile hotspots can connect users to the Internet using cell phone service if broadband access is unavailable.

In between meetings, teams need to be able to communicate with each other and share files. Teleworkers report that they use e-mail most often to keep in touch with their coworkers, followed by instant messaging, videoconference, VOIP telephony, and enterprise solutions.[44] Although conventional wisdom says to pick the best tool for the job, the reality is that virtual teams rely on lean, asynchronous media for most of their work.[45] Lean media allow workers to maintain privacy and create boundaries between work and home, which is particularly important when work and home are the same place. Lean media also help accommodate differences in time zones and language.

Managers must ensure that the technology is well supported so that remote employees and virtual teams can develop rapport and meetings can achieve the work goals. They should also regularly check that cross-team communication systems are working. During every virtual meeting, they should address this aspect of the project, discuss productive methods for interaction, and consider the latest technologies for team collaboration.

Strategic Consideration 9: Team Relationships

As described in Chapter 2, the outer layer of the strategic communication model consists of the organization's culture and climate (see Figure 2-1). A trusting, open climate makes it much easier to communicate freely. But when groups and teams "meet" mostly (or only) through technology, the hardware can form a barrier, making it more difficult to establish trust. In organizations where the cultural norm is to communicate exclusively through technological channels, as in a multinational corporation or a workforce of telecommuters, developing relationships among team members becomes even more of a challenge.

Today's cross-functional work teams may never physically be in the same room. Members may work at home, in different offices, even in different parts of the world. Yet in order to accomplish their assignments, they must be able to communicate smoothly and freely. Wise meeting leaders will help their people overcome geographical and technological barriers in order to develop trusting relationships. As you have learned, interpersonal communication builds relationships, relationships build trust, trust builds commitment, and commitment expedites productivity (Figure 4-6). Videoconferencing can be impractical when meeting members are in different time zones. Nevertheless, managers should use videoconferencing early in projects to help their virtual teams develop rapport. Later meetings can use leaner media, but videoconferencing should continue to be used periodically to connect team members, help them feel visible, and respect cultural differences about interpersonal relationships.

Remote workers are not challenged by the work or technological skills as much as they are challenged by lack of social interaction, achieving work-life balance, and gaining access to information and resources that on-site employees have.[46] Remote workers may struggle to make themselves and their work visible to other members of their team.[47] Given cultural attitudes about visibility and socialization, they may find themselves given less responsibility and fewer promotions than their on-site colleagues. Managers should regularly check in with team members and evaluate the telework experience. Remote employees should use self-audits to track invisible work, like maintaining technology, project preparation, research, and thinking about solutions. They should also talk to others on the team about the telework experience and speak up about problems or ideas.[48] Teams should also develop informal communication patterns, such as instant messaging, social media, or a designated channel in collaboration software like Slack or Teams, to mimic the interactions they would have at an office. When new members join a team, time should be spent helping them become acquainted with the individuals and the norms of the team, including how to ask questions.[49]

Understanding that virtual teams will become more productive when members have strong affiliation with each other, managers should encourage relationship building by applying the similarity–attraction principle. Team members will be more attracted to each

FIGURE 4-6 ■ Effects of Interpersonal Communication

interpersonal communication → interpersonal relationships → trust, loyalty, commitment → productivity

other if they perceive that they are similar. In what ways can members of a team who work off-site possibly find similarity? Well, at a minimum, they have similar work values and goals. When virtual teams recognize that they are working toward common objectives with similar payoffs, then they will find it easier to work together. The manager should carefully and consistently communicate these common objectives and provide opportunities for frequent communication among the team members, thereby encouraging relationship development. The result will be increased productivity.

CRITICAL THINKING QUESTIONS

Think about people with whom you regularly interact but who are relationships created by circumstances rather than choice.

1. What behaviors or activities helped you get to know the other person?

2. Are your work relationships limited to the people who hold similar values and beliefs?

3. What strategies can you use to have a strong relationship with someone whom you frequently disagree with?

Strategic Consideration 10: Cultural Differences

As we explained in Chapter 1, workplaces are becoming increasingly more diverse in terms of race and ethnicity, gender, sexual orientation and gender identity, disability, age, and education. The global workplace adds the element of cultural diversity to the mix. Cultural diversity fosters increased creativity, innovation, and flexibility, but it may cause communication difficulties, misunderstandings, decreased cohesion, and increased conflict.[50] Managers must be aware of the cultural differences in their teams and promote cultural training for all members.

Once team members have learned the importance of cultural sensitivity, they can put teammates at ease by respecting the conventions of that culture. Writing styles, for example, vary from culture to culture. A direct, concise e-mail may be standard in the United States, but Japanese recipients may consider it rude and vulgar. In the Japanese culture, a more indirect, lengthy, polite style is preferred. U.S. business writers can show their awareness of these stylistic differences by adding honorifics, such as -*san* or -*sama*, when addressing Japanese teammates, much like people in the United States may address someone as sir or ma'am.[51] When transnational team members are interacting in person rather than in writing, the language barrier among employees may pose a challenge. Sensitive managers should build in more time during teleconferences and perhaps hire translators. Nonverbal behavior, which will be discussed in Chapters 11 and 12 of this book, also varies from culture to culture. For example, direct eye contact is important in U.S. meetings, but in many Eastern cultures, it is considered disrespectful. Therefore, when managers use videoconferencing tools in an attempt to allow their team to see each other's nonverbal cues of posture, facial expression, and voice tone, the risk of misunderstanding remains strong. Managers must decide whether these more expensive methods of communication are worth reducing the assumptions and barriers involved. Again, cultural diversity training can reduce the likelihood of misunderstandings and blunders in communication practice.

In summary, managing effective meetings requires planning about people, purpose, and priorities. The location and technology requirements should support interaction. Relationships and respect among members of the group are equally important as the outcome of the project. Participants in virtual meetings and remote teams face an extra challenge to reach shared understanding, to coordinate perspectives, and to establish a sense of social presence, and these need to be acknowledged and dealt with by management.[52]

GROUP DECISION-MAKING FORMATS

One additional factor needs a meeting leader's attention. Whether a team or work group meets virtually or face-to-face, its leader should identify and follow a formal decision-making plan. This section describes three standard processes for reaching a group decision.

A diagnosis of the environment, task, group, and leader's personal preference will help determine the appropriate decision-making format for the meeting. A formal plan is essential. Do not fall into the trap of believing that once the participants know the goal, everything will automatically fall into place. Both experience and research suggest that group members are haphazard and unorganized in their discussion and decision attempts when managers fail to use organizing formats.[53] The appropriateness of each of decision-making format is determined by the objective of the meeting, the participants in the meeting, and the leader's style preference.

Rational Problem-Solving Process

The rational problem-solving process is a linear model of how groups identify, analyze, and solve challenges. In 1910, John Dewey described the steps that rational individuals use to solve a problem.[54] Most know these as the six stages to problem solving: (1) defining the problem, (2) analyzing the problem, (3) brainstorming the possible solutions, (4) determining the criteria that must be met to eliminate the problem, (5) selecting the best solution, and (6) implementing the solution (see Table 4-4). This process is also an excellent conflict-resolution strategy.

TABLE 4-4 ■ The Rational Problem-Solving Process
1. Define the problem
2. Analyze the problem
3. Brainstorm the possible solutions
4. Determine the criteria that must be met to eliminate the problem
5. Select the best solution
6. Implement the solution

When using this process in a meeting, it is critical to follow the sequence. People tend to begin to discuss solutions or even implementation of a solution before the problem has been precisely defined. However, it is critical to get everyone to agree on the problem being discussed and its scope before addressing solutions. One way of doing this is to write the problem on a flip chart or whiteboard so that everyone can see it. This same procedure can be followed for each step to ensure progress and focus.

Next, the group must spend time analyzing the problem fully. Again, you may meet resistance, especially if the members are intimately familiar with the problem. However, exploring causes, effects, extent, and history of the problem may help the group avoid solutions that address mere symptoms rather than root causes of the problem. Outsiders can be particularly helpful about identifying issues that insiders take for granted.

The third step, brainstorming possible solutions, has received much attention in business literature. Alexander Osborn, an advertising executive, first described brainstorming as a special technique for facilitating the idea-generating portion of the decision process.[55] The objective of brainstorming is to generate ideas rather than evaluate or analyze those ideas. A group can brainstorm successfully and produce a maximum number of ideas by adhering to three rules:

- Ideas are expressed freely without regard to quality. All ideas, no matter how unusual, are recorded.

- Criticism of the ideas produced is not allowed until all ideas have been expressed.

- Elaborations and combinations of previously expressed ideas are encouraged. The major strength of brainstorming is that one idea will create another. The ratio of high-quality ideas to the total number is not high, but often only one creative idea is needed for the solution.

Groups allowed to produce for longer work periods typically generate more ideas under brainstorming instructions than do individuals. Most groups continue to produce indefinitely, whereas individuals taper off.[56]

For consistency and fairness, the group must identify a set of criteria to evaluate the brainstormed options. Upper management sometimes imposes these criteria—or standards—on the group. Other times, the decision-making team may develop its own. Typical criteria are that a solution must be cost-effective, legal, timely, practical, and consistent with the organization's mission and/or values.

To select the best solution, the group compares each option to the list of criteria or standards to determine which idea fulfills the most criteria. Following this process prevents groups from choosing a solution that is favored by someone with authority or someone who dominates the discussion. Rather, the best solution is chosen rationally.

As a final step, the group considers implementation of their solution. In today's business environment, where continuous quality improvement is stressed, it is important to put systems in place that will monitor how well the new solution is working. The monitoring systems can detect weaknesses and shortcomings before they create major damage and wipe out the good work of the problem-solving team.

The Nominal Group Technique

Sometimes face-to-face meetings experience an imbalance of participation among the members. Some people dominate the discussion, and others are relatively silent. Common causes include unequal organizational status, varying interest levels among the group members, and differences in introverted and extroverted personalities. The nominal group technique for decision making can rebalance input in face-to-face and virtual meetings.

When using the nominal group technique (NGT), the meeting leader directs each participant to create a list of ideas, solutions, or advantages and disadvantages for the topic under discussion. After a predetermined time, the participants take turns presenting items from their lists, which are posted so that everyone can see them, either in the room where the group has gathered or in a shared electronic document. The group eliminates duplicate items and asks clarifying questions, with the meeting leader guiding the discussion to ensure that the group does not spend too much time on a single idea. New ideas can be added during the discussion phase, but none can be removed without unanimous consent. Members work alone again to rank items from highest to lowest priority, and then the leader tallies the scores to determine the outcome of the group's decision.[57] When groups follow this procedure, they generate a basis for group discussion that reflects all the participants' views that were individually developed by working alone.

The NGT has several advantages that a manager should consider when planning a meeting. One is that all participants can express their views without intimidation from more powerful or vocal group members. The procedure also ensures that each step in the rational problem-solving process is followed. Finally, it can save time because the meeting participants can generate their initial lists before the meeting. The NGT thus integrates the advantages of both group and individual creativity, whether or not the participants are ever physically together.[58]

The Delphi Technique

The Delphi technique is a unique group problem-solving process that does not require physical proximity of group members. This technique has been beneficial when team members are geographically dispersed or their schedules preclude a common meeting time. It is generally used with an ad hoc meeting of experts and with virtual teams who meet only electronically.

Delphi uses an initial questionnaire that elicits the participants' expert opinions on a topic. Once these opinions have been collected, all group members receive a second questionnaire listing others' contributions, and all are asked to evaluate each idea using several specified criteria. This step is then followed by a third questionnaire that reports the second-round ratings, a mean rating, and any consensus. The participants then revise their earlier ratings, considering the average or consensus. A final questionnaire includes all ratings, the consensus, and remaining problems.

The advantages of the Delphi technique are that it does not require physical proximity and that it controls some of the possible disadvantages of face-to-face group decisions. The most vocal or highest-status person does not have an opportunity to control the group because everyone's comments are pooled. Also, the coordinator can guarantee that the decision-making process does not omit any critical steps or ignore important comments.

In summary, managers should follow a preselected decision-making format to maximize the efficiency of the group meeting. You may wonder which of the three formats described above yields a superior decision. Some research has been done in an attempt to answer that question, but the results indicate that the quality of decisions is generally higher with any of the three—Dewey's rational problem-solving process, the NGT, or the Delphi technique—than when no particular format is followed and the discussion wanders freely.[59] Managers should consider decision-making formats to maximize group effectiveness.

SUMMARY

The team is a common personnel configuration today. Teams develop higher-quality decisions and are often more productive than individuals, but they are also expensive and time-consuming. When not managed properly, dysfunction and groupthink can occur.

To make effective use of meetings, a number of contingencies need to be reviewed. The first consideration is whether a meeting is necessary. If the objective is a programmed decision or if a commitment does not present a special problem, a meeting may not be required.

Once it is clear that a meeting should be conducted, it is important to consider who should attend. Criteria for selecting meeting members include how many to invite, whose interests they represent, their knowledge and authority, and their team-abilities.

Next, a manager must make the pre-meeting arrangements. These involve deciding what should be on the agenda and which additional materials should be attached to the agenda. The situation, group, and objective should suggest the appropriate leadership style. Project team leadership calls for special skills. The physical space should be arranged, including seating options for face-to-face meetings and technology to facilitate interaction and document sharing.

Managers must also consider the human element of meetings. Relationships within team members are crucial for cohesion, and respect for cultural differences must be emphasized. Overlooking any one of these considerations may reduce meeting effectiveness.

This chapter presents three decision-making formats for a meeting: the rational problem-solving approach, the nominal group technique, and the Delphi technique. Each of these approaches has inherent strengths and challenges.

Regardless of the format selected, disruptions can occur during a meeting, but they can be prevented if a manager takes precautions, including talking to potential disrupters ahead of time or planning special activities for them during the meeting. Once a disruption occurs, strategic communication can control it.

Finally, a manager's responsibility as the leader of a meeting includes the post-meeting follow-up. This follow-up may take the form of traditional meeting minutes, a short memo, or an e-mail and an effort to ensure that various commitments have been met. Also, formal evaluation of the meeting helps determine ways a future meeting could be improved.

CASES FOR ANALYSIS

Case 4-1

Shifting to Remote Work at Facebook

In 2019, approximately 5 million U.S. employees worked remotely most of the time. Many employers were skeptical about the productivity of remote workers. After all, "management by walking around" relies on the ability to observe employees in action.

But during the COVID-19 pandemic that began in 2020, when many state governments implemented "stay-at-home" orders across the United States, businesses began to rethink their attitude. Companies ordered their employees to work from home, relying on technology (and employee work ethic) to keep operations running. But is this just a crisis response, or could it signal a lasting shift in the way we work?

A survey by Gartner suggests that 74 percent of businesses may move at least some of their operations to remote work permanently.[60] One of these companies is Facebook, which announced in May 2020 that as many as half of employees would be able to work remotely.[61] CEO Mark Zuckerberg described a cautious approach, starting with senior engineers and then making decisions based on performance reviews. In addition to productivity, Facebook expects the change to increase the diversity of its workforce, now that employees are not required to live near its headquarters in Menlo Park, California. However, Zuckerberg warned that salaries for remote workers would be based on the cost of living in their location rather than in the pricey San Francisco area.

Questions

1. What are the benefits of telework for the organization? For its employees?

2. What challenges might employees face when working outside the office?

3. What concerns might managers have about leading a virtual team?

4. What strategies can managers use to ameliorate some of those challenges and concerns?

5. Think about your employer or industry. Is remote work a feasible option for employees? Why or why not? Would remote work appeal to you if it were available?

Case 4-2

Teams and Technology

Team Green was ecstatic. Their analysis of the firm's latest investment projects had been chosen over the Blue and Red teams yet again, for the sixth time in a row. The competition, the brainchild of CEO Roger Cannon, had been going on for 3 years, once every quarter. The teams were to analyze the projects under consideration and present their analysis and recommendations to the top management and any board members who wanted to attend. Managers and directors were all together for quarterly corporate retreats in remote locations, so the presentations were accomplished via videoconference from the company to the location of the retreat. For the first year and a half, the teams were fairly competitive, but then Team Green had dominated the competition and the reward: time off and 3-day paid vacations at a Destin, Florida, resort.

The members of the other two teams had become disgruntled, and Team Red seemed to have given up, turning in a marginal analysis and a short, minimal presentation. Rather than foster a cooperative and edifying mood, the competition had taken a turn for the worse, creating hostility and suppressing communication among the groups. Roger had noticed the trend away from the analysts debating and negotiating with each other, but he did not want to fail in his rewarding of excellence. The competition, he felt, had greatly enhanced the quality of the firm's capital investment decisions.

Prior to the establishment of the competition, the analysts had been one big group, arguing back and forth about the best way to analyze the firm's projects and about the best decision. Roger wanted to enjoy the benefits of both systems but wondered if that was possible given the current state of affairs.

Questions

1. Was the competition a good idea? What are the benefits and drawbacks?

2. How does the use of videoconferencing technology affect participants' attitudes toward the other teams and teamwork in general?

3. Suppose you are hired as a communication consultant with the task of coming up with a system to reward excellence but avoid hard feelings and discouragement. What would you change?

(Continued)

(Continued)

Case 4-3

The Regional Relationships

Jerry Blaire is the regional manager of a national electronics franchise retail store. This franchise has more than 200 locally owned stores throughout the eastern United States. As the regional manager, Blaire is responsible for an urban area in which there are eight stores plus the remainder of the state, which has another six stores.

The regional manager is the liaison between the manager-owner of the stores and the corporate offices in Boston. Responsibilities include monitoring the individual stores to ensure that the provisions of the franchise agreement are maintained, dealing with any complaints from managers, taking product orders, introducing new products, and managing the regional advertising program.

Blaire has been with this company for 7 years, and before that, he worked with a home entertainment retail store for 3 years after he earned his degree in marketing.

Blaire is responsible for coordinating the advertising campaign for all 14 stores in the region. A major part of the campaign involves store hours, which had traditionally been from 10:00 a.m. to 8:00 p.m., Monday through Saturday. The minimum number of hours required by the national office is 40 per week. However, several of the managers have been pressuring lately to change the store hours, especially those from downtown areas. They maintain that their business is minimal after 6:00 p.m., so they would like to close earlier. Meanwhile, the suburban stores want to stay open later because they do more business in the evening. According to the provisions of the franchise agreement, all the stores in a region must maintain the same store hours.

The problem is getting more attention from the store managers and is a frequent topic of discussion as Blaire makes his visits. Blaire has decided to have a meeting for all the managers so that he can systematically analyze the problem of store hours.

Questions

1. What type of leadership style should Blaire use in this meeting? Why?

2. What meeting format would you recommend?

3. What special problems would you anticipate for this meeting?

4. What preliminary arrangements are particularly important for this meeting?

5. Do you think it is a good idea for Blaire to have a meeting, or should he make this decision about hours himself?

Case 4-4

Keeping the Meeting on the Topic

Waith Manufacturing Company's data-processing department was preparing to implement a new computerized production information system at its new Madison plant. The project was divided into two parts. One consisted of the installation of a new computer network at the plant and the development of new database programs. The second involved hooking the plant's network into the company intranet so that all departments had access to the production reports.

Alonzo Mendoza was the systems analyst responsible for the development and implementation of the project. Janet DeLaura was a lead programmer under Mendoza working on the plant side of the project. Bill Synge was the other lead programmer responsible for the intranet. Mendoza scheduled a series of weekly status meetings with DeLaura and Synge to ensure that the project was moving along as scheduled and to allow for discussion of critical problems. One month before the scheduled implementation of the project, Mendoza called a special meeting to develop the actual series of tasks needed for the final system conversion. During this meeting, Mendoza outlined the major tasks concerning the whole project that had to be done on that last day.

He then solicited input from DeLaura and Synge. DeLaura spoke up immediately and began talking about several new problems that had surfaced on her side of the project. Mendoza interrupted her, saying those problems would be discussed at the regular status meeting, because this meeting had been called to develop final conversion tasks only. DeLaura became irritated and was silent for a few minutes. Synge said he had a few items to add to the conversion list and covered the first two tasks. Then he said the last task covered reminded him of a current problem he had in the interface program. Mendoza replied brusquely that only conversion tasks would be discussed at this meeting. Neither DeLaura nor Synge had much to say during the rest of the meeting.

Questions

1. What would you have done to keep the meeting on the right topic?

2. What technique might Mendoza have used to avoid interfering with the flow of ideas?

3. What might DeLaura and Synge have done to improve communication?

Notes

1. American Management Association, *AMA 2012 Critical Skills Survey*, http://www.amanet.org/uploaded/2012-Critical-Skills-Survey.pdf.

2. Rick Casey, "The Katrina Coffee Klatch," *Houston Chronicle*, September 14, 2005, 1B.

3. Jeffrey M. Jones, "In U.S., Telecommuting for Work Climbs to 37%," Gallup, August 19, 2017, http://www.gallup.com/poll/184649/telecommuting-work-climbs.aspx.

4. Global Workplace Analytics, "Latest Work-at-Home/Telecommuting/Mobile Work/Remote Work Statistics," March 13, 2020, https://globalworkplaceanalytics.com/telecommuting-statistics.

5. Lifeshack, "Remote Work Policy Tracker," accessed June 29, 2020, https://remote.lifeshack.io.

6. Michael Boyer O'Leary, "Telecommuting Can Boost Productivity and Job Performance," *U.S. News and World Report*, March 15, 2013, https://www.usnews.com/opinion/articles/2013/03/15/telecommuting-can-boost-productivity-and-job-performance.

7. OWL Labs, "2019 State of Remote Work Report," September 2019, https://www.owllabs.com/state-of-remote-work/2019.

8. CoSo, "CoSo Cloud Survey Shows Working Remotely Benefits Employers and Employees," February 17, 2017, https://www.cosocloud.com/press-release/connectsolutions-survey-shows-working-remotely-benefits-employers-and-employees.

9. Global Workplace Analytics, "Costs and Benefits: Advantages of Agile Work Strategies for Companies," http://globalworkplaceanalytics.com/resources/costs-benefits.

10. H. Simon, *The New Science of Management Decision* (New York: Harper and Row, 1960).

11. P. S. Goodman, E. Ravlin, and M. Schminke, "Understanding Groups in Organizations," in *Research in Organizational Behavior*, vol. 9, eds. I. B. M. Staw and L. L. Cummings (Greenwich, CT: JAI Press, 1987), 121–73.

12. Lester Coch and John R. P. French Jr., "Overcoming Resistance to Change," *Human Relations* 1, no. 4 (1948): 512–32.

13. Piyali Ghosh et al., "Who Stays With You? Factors Predicting Employees' Intention to Stay," *International Journal of Organizational Analysis* 21, no. 3 (2013): 288–312. doi: 10.1108/IJOA-Sep-2011-0511.

14. David Gelles, "He's Stared Down Activists and Apple, and Is Still in Charge," *New York Times*, February 14, 2020, https://www.nytimes.com/2020/02/12/business/Steve-Mollenkopf-Qualcomm-corner-office.html.

15. Richard H. Hall, *Organizations*, 5th ed. (Englewood Cliffs, NJ: Prentice Hall, 1991), 180.

16. Michael Mankins, Chris Brahm, and Greg Caimi, "Your Scarcest Resource," *Harvard Business Review*, May 2014, https://hbr.org/2014/05/your-scarcest-resource.

17. M. E. Gist, E. A. Locks, and M. S. Taylor, "Organizational Behavior: Group Structure, Process, and Effectiveness," *Journal of Management* 13, no. 2 (1987): 237–57.

18. I. L. Janis, *Victims of Groupthink* (Boston: Houghton Mifflin, 1972).

19. G. Moorhead, R. Ference, and C. P. Neck, "Group Decision Fiascoes Continue: Space Shuttle *Challenger* and a Revised Groupthink Framework," *Human Relations* 44, no. 4 (1991): 539–50.

20. Roland Bénabou, "Groupthink: Collective Delusions in Organizations" (Working paper #14764), National Bureau of Economic Research, March 2009, http://www.nber.org/papers/w14764.

21. C. Von Bergen and R. J. Kirk, "Groupthink: When Too Many Heads Spoil the Decision," *Management Review*, March 1978, 46.

22. Wynne Whyman, "A Question of Leadership: What Can Leaders Do to Avoid Groupthink?" *Leadership in Action* 25, no. 2 (May/June 2005): 13–14.

23. David W. Johnson, "Key to Effective Decision-Making: Constructive Controversy," *Psychology Today*, May 11, 2017, https://www.psychology today.com/blog/constructive-controversy/201705/key-effective-decision-making-constructive-controversy.

24. Robert Towensen, *Up the Organization* (Greenwich, CT: Fawcett, 1970), 171.

25. Knowledge@Wharton, "Is Your Team Too Big? Too Small? What's the Right Number?" June 14, 2006, https://knowledge.wharton.upenn.edu/article/is-your-team-too-big-too-small-whats-the-right-number-2.

26. Michael Hogan, "Collective Behavior Algorithms and Group Size," *Psychology Today*, June 30, 2019, https://www.psychologytoday.com/us/blog/in-one-lifespan/201906/collective-behavior-algorithms-and-group-size.

27. P. Slater, "Contrasting Correlates of Group Size," *Sociometry* 21, no. 1 (1958): 129–39.

28. J. M. Levine and R. Moreland, "Progress in Small Group Research," *Annual Review of Psychology* 41 (1990), 585–634.

29. Adam Bryant, "How to Run a More Effective Meeting," *New York Times Business*, https://www.nytimes.com/guides/business/how-to-run-an-effective-meeting.

30. Roger Schwarz, "How to Design an Agenda for an Effective Meeting," *Harvard Business Review*, March 19, 2015, https://hbr.org/2015/03/how-to-design-an-agenda-for-an-effective-meeting.

31. K. G. Stoneman and A. M. Dickinson, "Individual Performance as a Function of Group Contingencies and Group Size," *Journal of Organizational Behavior Management* 10, no. 1 (1989): 131–50.

32. N. Shawchuck, *Taking a Look at Your Leadership Style* (Downers Grove, IL: Organizational Research Press, 1978).

33. Stephen P. Mead, "Using Social Network Analysis to Visualize Project Teams," *Project Management Journal* 32, no. 4 (2001): 32–38. https://doi.org/10.1177/875697280103200405.

34. Sinead Monaghan, Jonathan Lavelle, and Patrick Gunnigle, "Mapping Networks: Exploring the Utility of Social Network Analysis in Management Research and Practice," *Journal of Business Research* 76 (July 2017): 136–44.

35. Liz Hughes, "Do's and Don'ts of Effective Team Leadership," *WIB, Magazine of the American Business Women's Association,* January–February 2004, 10.

36. John E. Jones, "Dealing with Disruptive Individuals in Meetings," *1980 Annual Handbook for Group Facilitators,* ed. J. William Pfeiffer and John E. Jones (San Diego, CA: University Associates, 1980), 161.

37. D. J. Isenberg, "Group Polarization: A Critical Review and Meta-Analysis," *Journal of Personality and Social Psychology* 50, no. 4 (1986): 1141–51.

38. "Fuze Survey Reveals U.S. Workforce Hampered by Multitasking and Disengagement," January 27, 2014, https://www.fuze.com/blog/fuze-survey-reveals-u-s-workforce-hampered-by-multitasking-and-disengagement.

39. Lawrence N. Loban, "Question: The Answer to Meeting Participation," *Supervision,* January 1972, 11–13.

40. "3M Meeting Network: Articles and Advice," accessed June 12, 2006, http://www.3m.com/meetingnetwork/readingroom/meetingguide_minutes.html.

41. J. R. Hackman and C. G. Morris, "Group Tasks, Group Interaction Process and Group Performance Effectiveness: A Review and Proposed Integration," in *Advances in Experimental Social Psychology,* vol. 8, ed. I. L. Berkowitz (New York: Academic Press, 1975), 1–50.

42. Adam Bryant, "If You Don't Know Your Co-Workers, Mix Up the Chairs," *New York Times,* July 29, 2012, Sunday Business section, 2.

43. Erika A. Hewitt, "What You're Saying When You Say 'I Don't Need a Mic,'" *Worship Lab,* Unitarian Universalist Association, August 31, 2017, https://www.uua.org/worship/lab/what-youre-saying-when-you-say-i-dont-need-mic.

44. Aliah D. Wright, "Study: Teleworkers More Productive—Even When Sick," Society for Human Resource Management, February 13, 2015, https://www.shrm.org/resourcesandtools/hr-topics/technology/pages/teleworkers-more-productive-even-when-sick.aspx.

45. Cynthia P. Ruppel, Baiyun Gong, and Leslie C. Tworoger, "Using Communication Choices as a Boundary-Management Strategy: How Choices of Communication Media Affect the Work-Life Balance of Teleworkers in a Global Virtual Team," *Journal of Business and Technical Communication* 27, no. 4 (2013): 435–71, doi: https://doi.org/10.1177/1050651913490941.

46. Tammy Rice-Bailey, "Remote Technical Communicators: Accessing Audiences and Working on Project Teams," *Technical Communication* 61, no. 2 (2014): 95–109.

47. Kyle P. Vealey, "The Shape of Problems to Come: Troubleshooting Visibility Problems in Remote Technical Communication," *Journal of Technical Writing and Communication* 46, no. 3 (2016): 284–310, doi: 10.1177/0047281616639478.

48. Ibid.

49. Erin Friess, "'Bring the Newbie Into the Fold': Politeness Strategies of Newcomers and Existing Group Members Within Workplace Meetings," *Technical Communication Quarterly* 22, no. 4 (2013): 304–22, doi: 10.1080/10572252.2013.782261.

50. Rathtana V. Chhay and Brian H. Kleiner, "Effective Communication in Virtual Teams," *Industrial Management* 55, no. 4 (2013): 28–30.

51. Ibid.

52. G. R. Berry, "Enhancing Effectiveness on Virtual Teams," *Journal of Business Communication* 48, no. 2 (April 2011): 186–206, doi:10.1177/0021943610397270.

53. David R. Weibold, "Making Meetings More Successful: Plans, Formats, and Procedures

for Group Problem-Solving," *Journal of Business Communication* 16, no. 3 (Summer 1979): 8.

54. John Dewey, *How We Think* (Boston: D. C. Heath, 1910).

55. Alexander F. Osborn, *Applied Imagination* (New York: Scribners, 1957).

56. Marvin E. Shaw, *Group Dynamics*, 3rd ed. (New York: McGraw-Hill, 1981), 57.

57. U.S. Centers for Disease Control, "Gaining Consensus Among Stakeholders Through Nominal Group Technique," *Evaluation Briefs* no. 7 (February 2006), http://asq.org/learn-about-quality/idea-creation-tools/overview/nominal-group.html.

58. Andrè L. Delbecq et al., *Group Techniques for Program Planning* (Glenview, IL: Scott, Foresman, 1975).

59. Robert C. Erffmeyer and Irving M. Lane, "Quality and Acceptance of an Evaluative Task: The Effects of Four Group Decision-Making Formats," *Group and Organizational Studies* 9, no. 4 (December 1984): 509–29.

60. Gartner, "Gartner CFO Survey Reveals 74% Intend to Shift Some Employees to Remote Work Permanently," April 3, 2020, https://www.gartner.com/en/newsroom/press-releases/2020-04-03-gartner-cfo-survey-reveals-74-percent-of-organizations-to-shift-some-employees-to-remote-work-permanently.

61. Kate Conger, "Facebook Starts Planning for Permanent Remote Workers," *New York Times*, May 21, 2020, https://www.nytimes.com/2020/05/21/technology/facebook-remote-work-coronavirus.html.

5

MAKING PRESENTATIONS

Managers today find that presentation skills are important for a multitude of situations. At any time, they might be called on to present a product report, a marketing status report, a persuasive report to convince executives to accept a proposed new product design, a financial report, or an after-dinner speech to honor the winner of a cost-saving campaign.

Results of a recent survey of more than 1,600 business professionals in the United States indicate that managers make presentations on average one to three times per month. Regarding the different organization levels to which they present, about 92 percent reported presenting to persons above their level, 62 percent to below their level, and 81 percent to their same level.[1]

As managers move up the corporate ladder, the likelihood increases that they will need competence in making presentations to external as well as internal audiences.[2] First, as organizations become more complex, managers are often called on to present proposals and make explanations to large groups of employees. Second, products and services also are becoming more complex, so customers, stakeholders, and even the public may require detailed explanations of their function and/or design. Third, managers and executives may find themselves representing the company while speaking to the media about a crisis or special event.

To be effective presenters, managers need to understand key strategies for planning, organizing, and delivering formal presentations that are described in this chapter. After offering general strategies, this chapter describes ways to succeed in four special situations: virtual presentations, media presentations, team presentations, and impromptu presentations. Knowing how to analyze the audience, organize your thoughts, and deliver your message with confidence will not only ensure that you have made your point but will also enhance your professional image.

PLAN YOUR PRESENTATION

When planning a presentation, consider your purpose, length of time to speak, and audience.

Purpose

The first step is to determine your purpose. The purpose of business presentations is generally to inform, convince, or cause action. Some presentations have multiple purposes. For example, when an engineering sales representative presents a product design to a client's engineering management group, he might have two purposes in mind. He will want to inform the audience of the product's technical features, and he will want to persuade the group to order the product.

In some situations, the exact purpose is easy to determine, but in others, the purpose may be complex because the speaker and the audience have different goals. For instance, the audience may want to know the most cost-effective location for a new manufacturing plant. The speaker, however, may want the audience to accept a certain location that has a special need for economic development. The audience wants to be informed, whereas the speaker wants to persuade.

The purpose may also vary within a group. Consider an audience that consists of five people: a vice president, a production superintendent, a director of finance, a marketing manager, and a personnel director. Suppose they were all attending a presentation comparing the relative success of two products introduced in a test market 3 months ago. What is relative success to each audience member? Each will look at the products from a different perspective because of differing functional responsibilities. The marketing manager may think in terms of market share, whereas the finance director may look at only the cost factor. What type of information should the speaker emphasize?

The power and status of the different audience members can also influence the overall purpose. One member's viewpoint may initially differ from that of another member, but the more powerful person can quickly influence the less powerful member. In the previous example, the vice president may simply say that the most important consideration is the expansion of production facilities required by the two new products. Suddenly, the definition of relative success has changed again. Though the goal of informing the audience has remained the same, the audience has shaped the information required to meet this goal.

The best way to ensure clarity of purpose is to write out a purpose statement. Not only does this act force you to think about the purpose; the written statement can then also be presented to an associate or to likely audience members for their reaction. The feedback will help you define the purpose clearly and accurately. Figure 5-1 will help you write out your purpose statement. Just fill in the blanks.

FIGURE 5-1 ■ Your Presentation Purpose

I want to tell you _____

(content)

So you will _____

(purpose)

CRITICAL THINKING QUESTIONS

1. Think of a public service message you recently saw on television or heard on the radio. While the primary purpose may have been to inform, can you identify any other purposes?

2. What do you think the sponsor of the message was trying to accomplish?

Once you have clearly established your purpose, you are ready to consider cost and time to determine what expense can be justified. One 5-minute presentation might involve hundreds of work hours and cost thousands of dollars; another might require a minimum of effort. As with any managerial communication, a manager must make strategic decisions.

Length

Sometimes, managers are assigned a set length of time to speak during a meeting or conference. In such cases, it is crucial to stay within the time limit. When speakers exceed their time limits, the audience becomes less and less receptive to the proposals of the transgressors. All they can think about is escape. That is one reason why TED Talks, presentations about ideas and innovations, are held to a strict 18-minute time limit.[3]

Even when speakers are given some choice on the length of a presentation, most make them too long rather than too short. It is generally difficult to hold adults' attention beyond 20 minutes. John F. Kennedy's inaugural address was only 15 minutes long.[4] Even the Truman Doctrine, which set the course of U.S. foreign policy for a half-century, took just 18 minutes to deliver.[5] One of history's most inspirational public speakers, President Franklin Delano Roosevelt, advised that when presenting, one should "be sincere, be brief, be seated."[6]

To keep your presentation on schedule, one strategy is to put time markers on your slide notes, listing when you want to be at every point. Be sure to time yourself when practicing the presentation, too, making small adjustments to your supporting material if you are not hitting your time markers.[7]

Audience Analysis

At the same time when effective managers analyze their speaking purpose, they begin to analyze the audience. Dr. Mickey Bannon, Director of the Oral Communication Lab at the University of Pittsburgh, explains, "Most audience members are egocentric: they are generally most interested in things that directly affect them or their community. An effective speaker must be able to show their audience why the topic they are speaking on should be important to them."[8]

Many presentations are technically well delivered, but they fail because the speakers do not anticipate audience reaction. In any communication process, people naturally tend to become egocentric. One group of consultants on oral presentations noted that managers often prepare messages that fail to tell the listeners what they want and need to hear but instead focus on the speaker's own interests.[9] The most successful presentations are prepared with a particular audience in mind and are organized to suit their knowledge, attitudes, likes, and dislikes.

Though audience analysis is part of the *pretalk* preparation, a speaker should also be ready to analyze on the spot. During delivery, the presentation may be modified to reflect audience factors not available in advance. For instance, you would need to alter your presentation if you found that a critical decision maker needing special information decided at the last minute to attend the presentation. Nevertheless, when a thorough audience analysis precedes a presentation, few last-minute adjustments should be required.

The Audience Analysis Worksheet at the end of this chapter (Exercise 5-1) not only provides practice in analyzing audiences; it also can guide you when preparing for any business presentation. When the presentation is critical but you know little about the audience, it might be beneficial to ask another stakeholder to complete the worksheet with you.

If you already know the audience well, say, for an internal presentation, a thorough analysis is not necessary. For instance, an internal auditor who gives a quarterly report to a bank's board of directors may not need a separate analysis each quarter. However, a periodic review of the audience may remind the speaker about some of its special characteristics. It may be easy to forget that the interests, technical knowledge, or attitudes differ from one board member to another; thus, a quick audience analysis will help reorient the speaker.

CRITICAL THINKING QUESTIONS

Recall a time when you had to deliver the same message to two different audiences. For example, you might have just had a collision while driving your car, and you now have to tell both your mother and your insurance agent. How would you tailor the message to each listener? Why?

ORGANIZE YOUR PRESENTATION

The second step is organizing the presentation. Every presentation has a beginning, a middle, and an ending. These three main parts are described next. To a great extent, your purpose and audience will determine how you structure your presentation.

Introduction

The most crucial part of a presentation is the introduction. A presentation should begin with a statement that captures the audience's attention. Quite often, a business speaker will begin with humor or trite remarks. Depending on the gravity of your message, these timeworn openings may not be appropriate.

Though common, a speaker should rarely begin with an apology. Beginning with "I know that you do not want to be here," or "I realize that it is late in the day," or "I am not much of a speaker" does little to enhance speaker credibility and may detract from the audience's perception of the meeting. Instead, begin the presentation with a positive statement that enhances your credibility. Strategies for getting the attention of business audiences are listed next:

- *A startling statement.* If our costs continue to increase over the next 5 years at the rate they have in the past 5, we will have to charge more than $250 for our lowest-priced shirt. Today, I will present four strategies for reducing costs in. . . .

- *A hypothetical statement.* What would happen if we could no longer obtain the copper we need to produce XY 115? I am going to show you a viable substitute for that metal.

- *Some historical event or story.* Just 8 years ago this week, we purchased the Bordin division, our first major acquisition. This presentation will review the progress of our purchases.

- *A rhetorical question.* What will the inflation rate be in 2025? Will the global energy problem continue? This presentation will outline the reasons why we need a market projection plan.

- *Reference to some current event.* On Tuesday, February 19, Millville suffered a chemical fire that killed five people and injured 15. To avoid that kind of disaster in our operations, we need to increase our budget for safety training.

- *A quotation.* Sheryl Sandberg, COO of Facebook, said, "People need to feel supported and understood at work."[10] If our company offered comprehensive medical benefits, we would attract more loyal and productive workers.

- *A personal anecdote.* The other day I was talking to one of our longtime customers, when she said the reason she keeps banking here is that nothing ever changes. That got me thinking about our reputation for stability in a chaotic economy. But I also began to wonder whether we've become stagnant.

Any of these strategies will serve as a dynamic, attention-getting opening and set the tone for the rest of the presentation.[11]

The second part of the introduction is to clearly state the purpose (inform, convince, cause action, inspire, introduce, congratulate, and so on) and the topic. Even if your purpose and topic were disclosed on the agenda or by your meeting moderator, it is a good idea to restate them in your introduction to avoid any confusion.

The discussion of listening in Chapter 10 indicates the difficulty of maintaining attention for a long period. By telling your listeners what is to come and why, you encourage them to make an effort. Thus, the third part of the introduction should establish the audience's motivation to listen. The speaker explains the significance of what the audience is about to hear and how it pertains to their interests and needs. A common error is to focus instead on the significance of the content to the *speaker*. While statements such as "I care deeply about this" might increase speaker credibility, they do not always lead to the listeners' agreeing to care, too. The best word to use at this point is "you," as in "After hearing my presentation, *you* will be able to. . . ." Focusing on audience benefits will also help build the speaker's credibility, which is especially critical in persuasive speaking.

In some situations, it may also be appropriate to give the audience some directions regarding interruptions and questions. For instance, you may ask them to jot down their questions and raise them after your remarks are finished. Alternatively, you can ask meeting members for their reactions and maintain a dialogue throughout the presentation. Effective speakers usually stay away from the "I talk; you just listen" syndrome, which risks losing audience interest and goodwill.

One optional subsection of the introduction is the establishment of the speaker's credentials. Obviously, if the audience knows the speaker well, this can be omitted. For external or new audiences, however, it is important that they perceive the speaker as an expert on the topic. Rather than relying on the meeting moderator's introduction to achieve this goal, you might describe the research you've conducted, the extent of your involvement in the topic, your position title, or even an anecdote that will enhance your image.

The final part of the introduction should be a preview of the main points you will cover. Forecasting your main points will clarify the structure of the presentation and help your audience stay on track. You might even enumerate the points so that your audience can "count down" as they listen. This preview acts as a transition between the introduction and the body of your presentation.

Table 5-1 summarizes the parts of a presentation's introduction. Next, we will describe strategies for organizing the body of a presentation. Typically, a business presentation includes three to five main points that support the purpose, with each main point supported by evidence.[12] Because organization is determined by the speaker's purpose, organization of persuasive presentations and organization of informative presentations are discussed in separate sections.

TABLE 5-1 ■ Parts of the Introduction
Attention step
Purpose statement
Motivation to listen
Directions about interruptions and questions (optional)
Speaker credibility (optional)
Preview of main points

Organization of Persuasive Presentations

As mentioned previously, the purpose of a business presentation is generally to inform or to persuade, and the body of your presentation should be organized according to your purpose. This section shows you some basic organizational structures for the body of a persuasive presentation.

Howell and Bormann discuss three classic patterns that provide meaningful strategies for persuasive situations: the problem-solving pattern, the state-the-case-and-prove-it approach, and the psychological–progressive pattern.[13] The first pattern, *problem solving*, is the most common in business presentations and works especially well for uninformed and hostile audiences. With this approach, the speaker leads the audience through a series of steps, beginning with defining the problem, then analyzing the problem (which includes causes and effects), then enumerating and evaluating possible solutions, then, when appropriate, recommending the best solution. This process is also useful in team meetings (Chapter 4) and when managing conflict (Chapter 13).

The second pattern of organization for persuasion, *state the case and prove it*, is relatively simple. It entails the straightforward development of a central thesis or proposition with supporting arguments. Normally, each supporting element begins with a topic sentence followed immediately by evidence/proof for support. The presentation closes with a summary repeating the proposition.

Whereas the problem-solving pattern is an inductive organizational approach, the state-the-case-and-prove-it approach is deductive. It begins with a general conclusion and then justifies it. This second approach is appropriate for organizing discussions of familiar, much-argued topics. It is also used in advocacy, such as courtroom settings.

The third organizational strategy, the *psychological–progressive pattern*, is ideally suited to presentations designed to effect change. It involves five steps: (1) arouse, (2) dissatisfy, (3) gratify, (4) visualize, and (5) act. Applying this pattern, a manager first uses an appropriate attention-getter. Next, the speaker defines a problem and demonstrates its nature and urgency. Then the speaker recommends a solution.

Step 4 in the psychological–progressive pattern is key because the manager helps the audience visualize the recommendation. Demonstrating the solution's implementation—or providing a "free sample"—often will clinch the audience's decision to comply. Finally, the speaker should call for a specific and concrete action. The psychological–progressive pattern is the typical structure of television commercials and sales pitches.

Persuasion Variables

As the preceding discussion indicated, different persuasive approaches are suited to different occasions or circumstances. To be a truly strategic attempt at persuasion, however, your efforts and ultimately your success should be moderated by a number of variables. These variables are categorized under the labels of sender, message, receiver, and context (see Figure 5-2).[14] The strategic communication model discussed in Chapter 2 provides background information about each of these variables. Context is described as a factor in the model's first, outermost layer. Sender and receiver variables are described in the second layer of the model. And message variables appear in the third layer.

Among variables associated with the *sender* of a persuasive message, probably the most significant variable is the speaker's credibility. Dimensions of speaker credibility include competence and trustworthiness; education, occupation, and experience; the

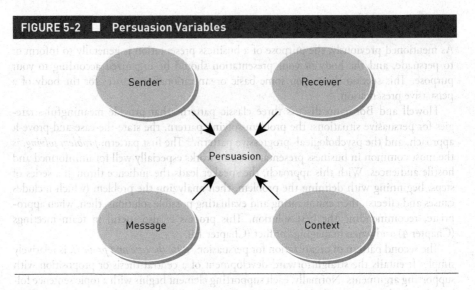

FIGURE 5-2 ■ Persuasion Variables

citation of evidence; likeability; and the degree of similarity between the speaker and the audience. Even physical attractiveness has been linked to persuasiveness in some studies.

A number of *message* variables can contribute to the success of a persuasive effort. The arrangement of the information is one variable. (In addition to the organization patterns described here, the direct and indirect patterns are described in Chapters 8 and 9.) Another factor involves whether a person should be explicit or implicit in stating what is desired. Though most studies indicate that being explicit is generally best, some evidence supports being implicit for audiences that are high status, highly intelligent and educated, and/or familiar with the subject.

Another issue relevant to message content is whether a persuader should ignore or refute opposing arguments. Usually business audiences expect the persuader to identify potential objections and refute them. Finally, the content should include a range of evidence that the audience will consider appropriate.

Among *receiver* variables, the speaker should consider the general persuadability of the audience. Some listeners are open to persuasion, while others resist ideas that threaten their worldview, even when those ideas are based on undisputed facts.[15] Receiver readiness to accept appeals is a complex factor, so persuasive speakers should conduct extensive audience analyses and plan to present appeals that are most likely to move their listeners. Audience demographics, knowledge levels, and attitudes all must be considered when choosing appeals and benefits.

Context variables include primacy/recency effects and persistence effects. There is some evidence that primacy effects are more likely to be found with interesting, controversial, and familiar topics, so begin with the strongest reason when persuading a hostile audience. Recency effects are more common with relatively uninteresting, noncontroversial, and unfamiliar topics, so build toward your strongest reason when persuading an apathetic audience.

CRITICAL THINKING QUESTIONS

A job interview is a high-stakes, persuasive situation. Analyze your communication strategy during your latest job interview by answering these questions about the four persuasion variables.

1. How did you enhance your credibility? (sender)

2. When answering questions, did you use direct or indirect order? Why? (message)

3. In what ways did you adapt your message to the receiver? (receiver)

4. Were you one of the first or last applicants interviewed? How do you think that affected the hiring decision? (context)

The second context variable is the persistence of the persuasive message. Generally, persuasive effects will decline over time, so for maximum effectiveness, persuasive messages should be delivered as close in time as possible to the point of decision or action. Thus, politicians usually spend the bulk of their advertising budget in the week before the election.

Though no one can prescribe a guaranteed plan for persuading people, managers should consider the variables in Figure 5-2 as they develop their persuasive presentations.

Ethical Persuasion

Before turning to the topic of organizing informative presentations, it is appropriate to consider the importance of taking the high road in persuasive speaking. Ethical persuasion calls for the speaker to tell the truth, the whole truth, and nothing but the truth. A persuasive speaker who misleads the listeners, whether deliberately or inadvertently, will lose credibility and lose business.

Dr. Anne Bradstreet Grinols, a business professor retired from Baylor University who specializes in ethics, suggests strategies for ethical persuasion that are based on audience analysis. Using terms from force field analysis, she recommends beginning by identifying the *driving forces* for the audience behind the change in belief or behavior that the speaker is advocating. What do the listeners need to know? What do they care about? Driving forces are good reasons to say yes.

Second, she recommends identifying the *restraining forces* that are roadblocks to the advocated change in belief or behavior. Restraining forces are reasons to say no. What will prevent the listeners from acting? What arguments against the change will listeners find compelling? Grinols recommends that persuasive speakers tell the story that listeners need to hear by emphasizing the benefits of making the advocated change and removing the barriers to making the advocated change. The story, of course, must always be truthful and respectful of the listeners.[16]

Organization of Informative Presentations

In informative-speaking situations, it is best to organize the information in a clear sequence. Clarity may demand that a subject be presented one way as opposed to another, or the subject itself may suggest the best pattern or arrangement. Some arrangement possibilities and examples of appropriate topics for each sequence are listed next:

- *Spatial or geographic.* Description of our new facility's layout
- *Political or economic categories.* Sales of our product line for various social groups
- *Increasing or decreasing importance.* Changes to employees' benefits package
- *Chronological.* History and future of our company
- *Advantages or disadvantages.* Various computer virus protection software on the market
- *Comparison or contrast.* Where we stand among competitors in our industry
- *Structure or function.* New management layer being added to our company

A typical informative-speaking situation is when a manager must explain new work procedures or processes. Giving instructions can be a challenge. The wrong approach is simply listing the steps in the process and ending with "Do you have any questions?" Listeners may hesitate to ask questions for fear of seeming inattentive.

A better strategy for giving instructions is to use *tell–show–do*. First, the manager should explain the steps in the new procedure, contrasting it with the current one. If the task is complex, the manager should cluster the steps into groups or stages. For example, instead of describing a 12-step procedure, the speaker could describe three stages, with four steps per stage. Dividing a body of information into smaller pieces makes it less daunting to listeners.

After telling the audience about the new procedure, the manager should show the audience how to do it, either demonstrating it personally or using a model. More audiences are visual learners than auditory learners, so a demonstration is often very effective.[17] Finally, the manager should let the employees try the new procedure themselves, offering liberal feedback and encouragement as they observe, because positive reinforcement is a powerful motivator for learning.

To summarize, the body of any presentation is the longest and most complex part. It must be carefully organized, and the organizational pattern must help the audience understand the content. Speakers' options for organizing the main points in the body of their presentation are determined by their purpose (informative or persuasive). After the main points have been selected and arranged in a logical sequence, each must be supported and developed by evidence. The most common organizational patterns for the body of persuasive and informative presentations appear in Table 5-2.

TABLE 5-2 ■ Sequencing Options for Main Points	
Persuasive Purpose	**Informative Purpose**
Problem solving	Spatial or geographic
State the case and prove it	Political or economic categories
Psychological–progressive	Increasing or decreasing importance
	Chronological
	Advantages or disadvantages
	Comparison or contrast
	Structure or function

Transitions

Adding transitions is the best way to clarify the organization of the presentation content. A bridge or link must exist between units so that the audience can follow the organizational plan. Sometimes this link may take the form of a simple announcement that a new unit will now be discussed. More helpful to the audience, however, is a transition that explains how the next point will compare with the previous one. A transition that begins with a review of the previous idea and follows with a preview of the next one is sometimes known as a "Janus statement," after Janus, the god in Roman mythology who had two faces, one looking backward and one looking forward. (The use of Janus statements in report writing is described in Chapter 9.) Another device is the repetition of key words or phrases for emphasis. Examples of transitions at four levels of complexity appear in Table 5-3. A skillful speaker will use transitions liberally to keep the audience on track.

TABLE 5-3 ■ Types of Transitions	
Function	**Examples**
Show relationship between ideas	"And," "in addition," "also," "or," "however," "on the other hand," "by comparison," "furthermore"
Enumerate ideas	"First," "to begin," "my second point is," "finally," "in conclusion"
Summarize ideas	"Now that we have discussed its features, let's turn our attention to its benefits"
Emphasize ideas	"If you remember nothing else, please remember this"

Evidence

Whether your purpose is to inform or persuade, your business presentation must include evidence. The type of information and the corresponding research required largely depend on the types of evidence: fact or opinion. Evidence of *fact* is an objective description of something using empirical evidence without interpretation or judgment. A fact can be proven—it is either true or untrue. Evidence of *opinion* is the application of interpretation and judgment rather than truth.

Factual Evidence

Business speakers often are expected to present facts, especially statistics, as evidence for their main points. Audiences respect speakers who "deliver the numbers." However, facts, such as the features of a product, are not persuasive in themselves. More than 3,000 years ago, Aristotle demonstrated how a speaker should apply patterns of logical reasoning—or *topoi*—to help listeners arrive at rational conclusions about the evidence.[18] For example, analogies help audiences understand new concepts by comparing them to familiar ones.

James Fowler, a social scientist at the University of California–San Diego, provided a contemporary example of Aristotelian logical reasoning when he presented the results of his team's research on social networks. They studied Facebook activity and mortality rates and found that people who received many friend requests were far less likely to die over a 2-year period than those who did not. When drawing conclusions about the relationship between health and social networking, he pointed out that this study shows only a correlation, not a causation.[19]

CRITICAL THINKING QUESTIONS

Think of the last time you made a major purchase—a car, a house, a vacation package.

1. What kinds of factual evidence were the most important when making your decision?
2. What patterns of logical reasoning did you apply to the factual evidence?
3. What kinds of opinion evidence were the most important?

Audiences may value logic and rational thought, but a body of recent research in neuroscience and psychology highlights the important role that emotions play in decision making.[20] Thus, in addition to data and statistics, speakers should consider using factual evidence that elicits emotions, such as examples, illustrations, and anecdotes. Examples add concreteness and specificity, helping listeners visualize abstract ideas and relate them to their own experiences. Anecdotes and stories add emotional appeal because they are vivid and personal, helping ensure recall.[21] Business leaders recognize the power of a personal story that highlights their company strategy and motivates employees. For example, when H. James Dallas was CIO of Georgia-Pacific, he told about his first job as a janitor at the Pepperidge Farm plant in Aiken, South Carolina. His plant manager "would tell us how important our jobs were. He explained that if bugs got in, it would cause quality problems, leading to people not buying our products, resulting in the company losing money, and people losing jobs. . . . His actions made me think of myself not as a janitor, but as a key part of our company's success."[22] The take-home point is that business speakers should analyze their audience's expectations and values when selecting the most impactful factual evidence (data, statistics, examples, anecdotes) to support their main points.

Opinions as Evidence

Three types of opinions may be used in a presentation: personal, lay, and expert. Success in using *personal* opinions for support largely depends on the manager's credibility with the audience. A manager uses *lay* opinions when citing the opinions of ordinary people (nonexperts), such as customers, workers, or the public. This source is particularly useful in presentations on marketing or personnel issues.

A manager uses *expert* opinions when citing an authority to provide evidence. This form of evidence works well when the topic is not well understood, objective facts are difficult to find, or the speaker wants to leverage the authority of specialists.

Different presentation strategies require different types of evidence. The state-the-case-and-prove-it and problem-solving patterns call for extensive use of facts. In persuasive presentations, the psychological–progressive pattern generally calls for less factual information and more emotional appeals. Consequently, it places more emphasis on opinion than on empirical information. Opinion is advisable when the manager has a high degree of credibility, and expert opinion is valuable when there is no doubt about the authority of the expert.

Audiences judge evidence, whether facts or opinions, according to its timeliness and its source. Personal opinion is the weakest type of evidence, unless the speaker has high credibility—authority, power, dynamism, trustworthiness, and expertise. Thus, a manager is wise to cite details about the research conducted, including when and from where the evidence was retrieved. In situations where the audience does not know the speaker, the credibility of the evidence becomes important to the speaker's credibility.

Closing

The end of the presentation is relatively easy to prepare yet crucial to the presentation's final impact. It should contain a brief summary of the purpose and the main points covered in their appropriate order. Of course, this summary should match the preview of purpose and main points that were stated in the introduction. Do not present any new information in the closing or leave a question unanswered. Repeat the significance of the message to the audience, as stated in the introduction, to ensure retention. If some action is to be solicited from the audience, make the expectations clear. And leave the audience with a powerful *final thought* or challenge. Whatever the specific nature of the ending, it should strongly and clearly communicate that the speaker is ending. Too often, speakers just trickle off with a shrug and a comment like "Well, that's it; thanks for listening." Your audience is following closely at this point. They will be affected by your final impression as well as your first impression.

Table 5-4 summarizes the parts of a presentation's conclusion.

TABLE 5-4 ■ Parts of the Closing
Purpose statement
Main points
Significance of the message
Call to action (optional)
Final thought or challenge

ANTICIPATE QUESTIONS

Speakers solicit questions after the presentation to allow for appropriate additions and clarifications. In a situation where the group may be inhibited but questions are important to open the dialogue, the speaker may want to ask one member of the audience to be ready with a question to stimulate further questions.

Here are some tips for the question-and-answer (Q&A) period:

- Repeat the question to ensure that it is audible to everyone and that you understand what is being asked.

- Select questions from all areas of the room, not just from one section or person.

- Do not evaluate a question by saying, "That's a good question." Such a response could be inadvertently telling others that their questions are not as good.

- Do not answer with responses such as "as I said earlier," or "well, obviously," or "anyone would know the answer to that." Such responses can be quite demeaning.

- Look at the whole group when answering a question, not just the person who asked it.

- When you have finished, do not ask, "Does that answer your question?" because that makes you seem tentative. If you did not answer their question satisfactorily, they will likely let you know.

- Do not point a finger to call on a questioner. It is a scolding pose and may appear authoritarian. Instead, invite the question by extending an open hand, palm up.

- If you have no answer to a question, admit it. Consider telling the questioner where else they might find an answer.

- Budget sufficient time in your presentation to answer questions.

PREPARE YOUR VISUAL AIDS

Visual aids are a must for all but the most informal business presentations. They represent another way of maintaining audience attention and involvement. Because the spoken word is, at best, limited in communication, and because its sound is transitory, the listener may miss the message, and the opportunity to hear it again may never arise. However, visual support can help overcome these limitations. Additionally, visual aids can clarify complex information. You can successfully use visual aids in the introduction, body, and closing of a presentation.

Criteria

Good visual aids make a positive impression on the audience and justify the time spent in their preparation. An effective aid is one designed to fit the speaker, the audience, and the room. Chapter 6 presents comprehensive guidelines for developing and designing your visual aids. Briefly, four criteria make for an effective visual aid:

1. *Visibility.* Be sure the entire audience can easily see the visual aid.[23]

2. *Clarity.* Make the main points easy to identify and understand. Avoid busy backgrounds and distracting or low-contrast color combinations.[24]

3. *Simplicity.* Avoid design elements that may be distracting or irrelevant to the speaker's message. Textual visual aids should follow the 6 × 6 rule: no more than six lines per graphic and no more than six words per line.

4. *Relevance.* Do not use a graphic, movement, or sound effect for the sake of novelty. Special effects can backfire if used merely to impress.[25]

To accentuate or emphasize content of a visual aid, you might point with a laser pointer or use the build feature of PowerPoint. During a PowerPoint presentation, you can change the cursor from an arrow to a pen by hitting Ctrl+P on the keyboard. Then you can use the cursor to circle or underline data or words on a slide for accentuation. Hitting Ctrl+E changes the cursor to an eraser. Hitting Ctrl+A brings back the arrow.

Along with the criteria of visibility, clarity, simplicity, and relevance, the timing of a visual aid contributes to its effectiveness. Because a visual aid is a graphical message intended to complement the verbal message, both messages should be presented at the same time. An aid should not be visible until it is used, and it should be removed from sight after it has been discussed so that it does not distract the audience. An easy way to hide a PowerPoint slide while you are presenting is to hit B on the keyboard—the screen goes to black. Hitting B again brings back the slide. Similarly, the W key makes the screen go to white.

CRITICAL THINKING QUESTIONS

Recall a business presentation you listened to where the speaker used visual aids.

1. To what extent did you find the visual aids helpful? Distracting? Confusing?

2. What elements of the visual aids had the biggest effect, either positive or negative, on the impression the speaker made on you?

3. What elements of the visual aids had the biggest effect on your retention of the message?

Presentation Software

The criteria for effective visual aids are universal, but a speaker's choice of visual aids will be influenced by the size and type of audience and by the type of equipment provided in the presentation room. This section offers tips for using computer-generated graphics during presentations.

The most common type of visual aid used for business presentations, of course, is computer-generated graphics, such as Microsoft PowerPoint, Apple Keynote, Google Slides, and Prezi. Introduced by three Hungarian media designers in 2009, Prezi is a cloud-based presentation software tool for presenting ideas on a virtual canvas. The product employs a user interface that allows speakers to zoom in and out of their presentation media and navigate through information within a 3-D space. Panning, zooming, and rotating objects can be very effective, but overuse of such visual stimulation may risk inducing motion sickness in the audience.

PowerPoint is currently the standard presentation software. One writer compared delivering a business presentation without PowerPoint slides to serving French fries without ketchup. In busy corporate settings, absent audience members have been known to request copies of the slides, assuming that the visual aids contain all relevant information from the presentation. Indeed, some government and defense organizations use PowerPoint rather than MS Word as a report format.[26] Companies are now incorporating presentation graphics software into their day-to-day internal communications and into their decision-making process.[27]

One alternative to the traditional list of bullet points or text on PowerPoint slides is gaining popularity. The design strategy calls for placing an "assertion" as a complete sentence in the title or headline space at the top of a slide. Then images, equations, or charts that provide evidence supporting the assertion appear in the body of the slide. Callouts with arrows are sometimes added to explain the images (see Figure 5-3). This *assertion–evidence* (AE) design graphically displays relationships between ideas on the slide. Research by Michael Alley and his team at Penn State University shows that audiences understand and retain more information from presentations accompanied by AE-designed slides than from presentations accompanied by traditional bullet-point-designed slides.[28]

FIGURE 5-3 ■ Sample PowerPoint Slide Design

**This sentence headline makes an assertion
on the topic in no more than two lines.**

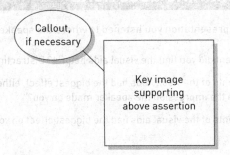

Callout, if necessary

Key image supporting above assertion

If necessary, background or explanatory text
in no more than two lines.

DELIVER YOUR PRESENTATION

Now is the time for the real test: delivering the message. Thorough preparation will allow concentration on a number of elements that require attention during the delivery. A well-prepared speaker will have analyzed the audience and will have an idea of what to expect from the various members. The purpose is clear, the opening statement is ready, the message is organized, the closing is prepared, and visual aids have been created.

Speaking Anxiety

What about stage fright? It might be consoling to know that about 60 percent of all speakers experience anxiety before speaking. Research indicates that even business professionals who are veteran presenters continue to experience low levels of confidence regarding delivering the presentation and high levels of nervousness.[29]

Well-researched strategies for relieving speaking anxiety include systematic desensitization, cognitive restructuring, visualization, and skills training. But in general, being prepared is the most effective strategy for coping with nervousness.[30]

Unfortunately, no matter how well prepared you might be and how many times you have practiced your presentation, some anxiety may remain. A small amount of tension is good because it keeps a speaker alert; when anxiety is so great that it interferes with the presentation's effectiveness, however, several simple techniques may help.

First, consider the value of the presentation and remember that the material is important. Believe that the audience is there to listen and that you have an opportunity to provide a valuable service. Trust yourself and the work you have done to prepare your topic.

CRITICAL THINKING QUESTIONS

Athletes, actors, and musicians know the difference between eustress and distress. It is the difference between helpful stress and harmful stress. Think of a time when you had to perform before an audience. Did the level of your anxiety make you perform better? Or did it work against you?

Second, sit with your eyes closed and take a few deep breaths. With hands relaxed and dangling to the side, rotate your head slowly while you concentrate on an especially pleasing thought (a mountain valley with beautiful flowers; soothing, fluffy clouds floating across the sky; waves breaking on a beach).[31] Deep breathing oxygenates your brain, thus increasing alertness. It also relaxes tense muscles in your throat and neck. As a bonus, increasing the amount of air in your lungs ensures that your voice will project farther. One minute of relaxation can be worth an hour of frantic preparation.

A third way to reduce anxiety is to memorize the first few remarks in the presentation. By the time these memorized comments have been presented, some of the initial anxiety should have subsided.

Fourth, planned bodily activity can help reduce anxiety. Strategic movements during the delivery can be used to control the higher level of energy produced by the anxiety. This movement may take the form of appropriate gestures or of walking across the stage.

Speaker Notes

How can notes be best arranged and used to support a business presentation? Whether you use a manuscript, an outline, 5 × 8-inch (127 × 203-mm) index cards, notes pages in presentation software, or even your computer graphics as cues, good speaker notes will help you channel your efforts toward effective delivery. Notes written clearly and concisely make it easy to maintain eye contact with the audience, unless, of course, you stand with your back to the audience while you read the speech from the screen, which would be unprofessional.

While notes can be a valuable source, they can easily become a psychological crutch. To make sure they do not become so, keep the following *do nots* in mind.

- Do not twist, bend, smooth, roll, or fold hardcopy notes in an aimless way because of nervousness. This behavior does nothing to relieve a speaker's anxiety, and it may increase anxiety in the audience.

- Do not gaze at the notes out of a feeling of insecurity. Looking down to keep from looking at the audience can get to be a bad habit that physically and psychologically separates you from the audience.

- Do not write out your notes (or slides) in full sentences. You will be tempted to read the presentation aloud rather than speak extemporaneously from key points.

- Do not write your notes in a small typeface. You must be able to find keywords and phrases quickly and easily at a glance.

Rehearsing will help you arrange notes for maximum benefit. Managers who are completely familiar with their subject and neglect to use notes may wind up embarrassing themselves, their audience, and their organization. Practicing the presentation helps settle the number of notes required and how detailed they should be. Also, notations can be made for clear transitions or ideas that need to be spoken more slowly, loudly, or clearly. And you will not be tempted to read the presentation out loud. In the United States, a conversational (aka extemporaneous) style is considered the most effective.[32]

Nonverbal Aspects

Several nonverbal aspects of communication need to be considered during the delivery of a presentation, including eye contact, facial expressions, posture, gestures, movement, and vocal style. Speakers are integral parts of the messages they convey, so how they present themselves affects the message directly.

Body Language

As you will see in Chapters 10 and 11, the nonverbal components of communication are an essential part of effective speaking and listening. For instance, just as eye contact is important when listening for the total message, eye contact can be used to complement the delivery of a message. By looking at members of the audience in a random pattern, effective speakers involve the audience in the presentation. Speakers can also use the rest of their faces to show appropriate emotions about the message. A smile, a puzzled frown, a grimace—all complement the verbal message.

Preview Chapter 11 to learn how a speaker's posture, gestures, and body movement may add to the spoken word. Briefly, a forward-leaning posture may emphasize or show involvement, and walking toward the audience may psychologically draw them into the message. A well-timed gesture can reinforce the spoken message, while mindless swaying or pacing will betray nervousness and undermine credibility. In short, body movements have meaning, and they should be used to enhance the message, not distract from it.

Another aspect of nonverbal communication discussed in Chapter 11 that is relevant to making presentations is proximity. Few would question the speaker's need to stand when the audience includes more than seven or eight people, at least to increase visibility; standing also communicates the importance of the topic and occasion. On the other hand, many managerial presentations are delivered to audiences of fewer than seven people in a conference room or via video. Such situations call for managers to use their analysis of the group, the purpose, and themselves to determine whether to stand or sit.

Vocal Style

Other nonverbal aspects important to the delivery of a presentation reside in the quality of your voice. Among the major vocal considerations of nonverbal communication discussed in Chapter 11 are rate, pitch, and volume.

The best speaking rate depends on your material. Generally, speakers should present ideas that are potentially difficult to comprehend at a slower rate than ideas that are easy to understand. Try slowing down to emphasize an important and/or primary point and speaking faster when presenting secondary information. If you are feeling nervous, make a special effort to slow down, because nervousness usually speeds up a speaker's speech rate, and you do not want to seem out of control. Also, out of consideration, you might slow down for an audience that may have difficulty understanding unfamiliar language or technical terminology. Vary your rate to keep the attention of the audience; a voice that never changes speed becomes boring.

Speakers who talk at a constant pitch will also find it difficult to hold the audience's attention. A failure to vary pitch is a habit, commonly known as monotone speaking. Using wide variations in pitch can create emphasis and interest to the message and make the presentation lively and easy to follow. To see how pitch can affect the way audiences might understand a message, read the following sentence aloud three times, raising the pitch on the italicized word each time.

I never said he promoted *her*. (Give him some credit. He has better insight than that.)

I never said *he* promoted her. (I just said she got promoted, not by whom.)

I never *said* he promoted her. (But I might have implied it in a number of ways.)

The third voice quality, volume, ensures that the listeners are able to hear the message. The correct volume depends on group size and the physical surroundings; however, regardless of the situation, changes in volume improve emphasis and add variety. A speaker who is difficult to hear may be perceived as incompetent and shy. Keep in mind one special warning about volume: A speaker does not gain attention or make stronger emphasis merely by being loud. If a microphone is available, use it rather than merely projecting your voice. Background noises like ventilation systems, keyboards, whispering, and other sounds can make it difficult for listeners to hear, particularly those with hearing disabilities.[33]

In summary, research shows that 55 percent of your impression is the result of how you look, 38 percent is the result of how you sound, and just 7 percent is the result of what you say.[34] So if you announce, "I'm delighted to be here today," while your voice shakes and your eyes dart to the door and you fumble with your notes, the audience is more likely to believe that you are *not* delighted to be here.

CRITICAL THINKING QUESTIONS

1. In addition to rate, pitch, and volume, what other aspects of voice affect your impression of a speaker? How about regional accent? Quality or tone?

2. When listening to a speaker's unusual vocal style, do you listen more carefully, or does your attention wander?

3. How do a speaker's disfluencies ("um," "uh," "so," "you know") affect your perception of the speaker? Your reaction to the message?

SPECIAL SITUATIONS FOR PRESENTING IDEAS

Virtual Presentations

In today's global economy, managers may need to use technology to speak to their audiences. For example, managers can announce policy changes, deliver motivational messages to employees who are geographically dispersed, and post presentations on the company's intranet.

Set the stage for your virtual presentation by considering your background. A plain wall, curtain, or bookshelf sets a professional tone. Adjust the lighting to ensure that your face is clearly visible on the screen. Avoid sitting in front of a window, which may create a silhouette effect. Instead, position a light in front as well as overhead. Test your microphone and speakers. If your computer does not include noise canceling, you may need to use earphones to eliminate feedback.

When presenting to remote audiences, speak as though the audience is right there. Look into the camera rather than the screen to simulate eye contact with listeners. Think of the camera as a friendly, trusting person. This approach reduces the likelihood of insincere, stilted, overly dramatic, inappropriate communication styles.

Use the face, hands, and body as in ordinary conversation to keep the presentation as natural as it would be in person. Normal gesturing helps communicate honesty, and it can complement the ideas being expressed. Some caution, however, should be exercised. Excessive facial expressions and sweeping gestures are magnified by the camera and may distract. Keep gestures close to the body and above your waist so that they can be seen in close-up shots.

Occasionally, poor display resolution or Internet connectivity may muddle or eliminate nonverbal cues. Adding to the challenge are conference room screens that are inadequately sized. Presenters can overcome these challenges and give clearer presentations by focusing on the graphics and voiceover.[35] The combination of verbal and nonverbal cues is critical for clear and complete communication with virtual audiences.

Media Presentations

Occasionally managers must appear in televised speaking events, participate in video-conferences and webinars, create public service announcements, and make product marketing presentations to external audiences. In these formal media presentations, it is essential to prepare a script. A script allows for coordinating the audio, visual, time, content, and graphics. In media presentations, the script includes the words, which often appear on a teleprompter, and instructions for production members, enabling them to visualize how to integrate their responsibilities with the overall performance. In other words, a script helps all parties know the sequence—how and when the presentation will begin, move, and conclude.

We have already seen the importance of rehearsing for face-to-face and virtual presentations; practice is even more important for media presentations. For one thing, time limitations are in terms of seconds. In reaction to the tight scheduling, the novice media speaker should resist the tendency to speak rapidly and thus appear nervous.

In addition, practice is called for because of the higher level of refinement required for a media presentation. Familiarity with the teleprompter will reduce stumbling through the message. Audiences expect polished, professional speakers onscreen. Remember that every detail becomes a permanent record that can be shared with anyone.

The speaker's appearance is a factor in preparing for media presentations. The obvious recommendation is to wear what you want others to see you in and what you feel good in, but you'll also want your outfit to be unobtrusive.

Professor Tom Hajduk, management professor at Carnegie Mellon University, developed a communication audit form for evaluating media presentations.[36] The audit provides a useful checklist of the unique delivery requirements for media presentations, as summarized in Table 5-5.

TABLE 5-5 ■ Delivery of Media Presentations		
Vocal Impact	**Nonverbal Impact**	**Visual Image Impact**
Maintain normal volume (do not shout into the microphone)	Avoid white, black, stripes, large patterns, and distracting jewelry	Design clean, uncluttered visuals that can be read in 30 seconds
Use a conversational rate (approximately 110 words per min.)	Maintain eye contact with the camera	Avoid long, bland bulleted lists
Project extra vocal enthusiasm and energy	Stand tall and straight	Label chart columns, rows, and parts to help speed understanding (avoid legends)
Articulate clearly	Use natural but slower chest-high gestures	
Maintain fluency; avoid filled pauses ("uh," "OK," "so")	Move slowly and stay within microphone and camera range	Keep the right side of visuals empty so that the presenter picture-in-picture (PIP) won't mask the visual image
Pause before important points for drama	Use natural facial expressions and head movements	
		Point to visuals on the document camera or draw on computer slides

Team Presentations

When the stakes are high and the situation is complex, a single presenter may not be able to accomplish the task. For example, an architecture firm is bidding on a contract to design a new science complex for a university. The firm sends a team of experts to make a presentation to the planning committee. The team consists of the principal in charge of the project, a design principal or project manager, an interior designer, a laboratory designer, and a mechanical engineer. Each team member will speak about their area of expertise, and each will help achieve the goal, winning the bid. Team presentations allow shared responsibility, but they are difficult to do well. Clearly, presenting as a team requires advanced communication, organization, and planning skills.

Team presentations can be divided into the following three phases: planning, design, and delivery:

1. *Planning.* The team defines its purpose and analyzes the occasion of the presentation, selects a moderator, establishes channels of communication among themselves, and assigns segment speakers.

2. *Design.* Each speaker on the team makes their individual presentation plans, then shares them with the other team members. The team creates appropriate visual aspects (a single slideshow, coordinated outfits, handouts, and demonstrations), rehearses once or twice together, and brainstorms how they will handle the Q&A session.

3. *Delivery.* The team delivers the presentation, with each speaker staying within time limits. Each speaker uses previews or summaries to smooth the seams. The team presentation begins and concludes with the moderator. All team members appear to listen closely to the others when not presenting. After the team's presentation, each member is prepared to answer audience questions according to their individual expertise.

Here is a summary of the characteristics of successful team presentations:[37]

- *Content.* Organized, supported, and relevant to audience
- *Visuals.* Creative, professional, and consistent in design
- *Delivery.* Consistent, polished, and dynamic

Impromptu Speaking

So far, this chapter has focused on strategies for planning, organizing, and delivering prepared presentations. In addition, business professionals frequently are expected to offer a brief statement when they have not had time to prepare. As a manager, you may suddenly be invited to "make a few remarks" or answer an unexpected question during business and quasi-social settings. What should you do? The natural reaction is to blurt out the first idea that pops into your head, then hope that another idea occurs to you so that you can say it as well. This approach is called stream-of-consciousness speaking, and it suffices in ordinary conversations. However, in business settings, managers need to know how to deliver informal, impromptu presentations with style.

CRITICAL THINKING QUESTIONS

Think of a time when someone was suddenly asked to "say a few words" in a meeting or at a special event that you attended.

1. To what extent did you judge the speaker according to what was said, as opposed to how it was said?

2. How well do you recall the speaker's message content? How important is message content compared to speaker delivery style in impromptu settings?

Here are some techniques for making informal presentations and impromptu remarks:

1. *Get mentally ready.* Use nonverbal communication tools (vocal style, body language, appearance) to look and sound confident. Nonverbal communication is discussed in depth in Chapter 11. As you will see, 93 percent of the impression you make is determined by nonverbal elements.

2. *Work the question or subject around to fit your knowledge and interests.* Restate the question as you plan a response. If you cannot talk and think at once, stall for time by asking the person who has called on you to repeat the question. In most impromptu speaking situations, you will be allowed to tailor the subject to suit your expertise.

3. *Begin with a main point.* Your opening sentence should be a generalization or a statement of opinion or belief. In writing, the main point is called the topic sentence or thesis, and it usually appears at the beginning of a paragraph. Similarly, in speaking, you should begin with a broad, sweeping statement.

4. *Support your main point by developing it with facts, statistics, examples, analogies, reasons, illustrations, or personal stories.* Supporting ideas are more specific, concrete, and narrow than main ideas. They help the listeners understand your opening statement.

5. *Come back to your main point.* By restating the main idea, you will reinforce it and aid the listeners' retention.

6. *Stop talking.* A common mistake during impromptu speaking is to speak for too long, repeating yourself or talking in circles. A brief, well-organized comment will make a stronger impression than a long-winded speech consisting of random, scattered thoughts.

Table 5-6 summarizes impromptu presentation techniques. These recommendations will help managers take full advantage of the opportunities presented by digital presentation tools. Such appearances can be challenging but enjoyable experiences that provide a valuable service to your organization while offering a tremendous opportunity for professional development and visibility.

TABLE 5-6 ■ Impromptu Presentation Techniques
1. Get mentally ready. Look confident. Breathe.
2. Work the question or subject around to fit your knowledge and interests. Restate the question as you plan a response.
3. Pick a main point.
4. Support your main point by developing it with facts, examples, analogies, reasons, and so forth.
5. Come back to your main point.
6. Stop talking.

SUMMARY

To ensure an effective presentation, a manager should thoroughly analyze the purpose, time requirements, and audience; complete all necessary preparations; and use appropriate delivery techniques. A thorough analysis of the purpose means the speaker should determine if everyone involved has the same goal for the presentation.

Once the goal has been clearly established, the necessary preparations must be completed. Preparation includes the development of an introduction, a sequence of main points that is appropriate for an informative or persuasive purpose, and a strong closing. The sequence of main points should be determined by the speaker's purpose, and each main point should be supported by evidence. Transitions must be added to bring unity and coherence to the completed presentation plan.

Visual aids help maintain interest and accurately communicate the key ideas. Visibility, clarity, simplicity, relevance, and timing are important to ensure that the visual aids complement the verbal communication.

Both nonverbal and verbal characteristics of the speaker are important for an effective, professional delivery. Eye contact, facial expressions, posture, gestures, and movement all need to be considered. Voice rate, pitch, and volume affect the impact of the presentation.

A speaker should schedule sufficient time for questions and answers at the end of the presentation. When this part of the presentation is well managed, feedback and two-way communication develop.

There are four special presentational situations that more and more managers face today, the first of which is virtual speaking. Most of the rules that apply to a traditional face-to-face speaking situation also apply when the audience is remote. Additional factors to consider are the physical setting, nonverbal behaviors, and speaking to the camera. The second type of special situation, presenting via media, calls for even closer control through a script, rehearsal, and a communication audit.

A third special speaking situation is the team presentation. Together, team members should plan, design, and deliver their message. Successful team presentations are well organized, supported, and relevant to the audience. Visuals are creative, professional, and effective. The team members' delivery style is consistent, polished, and dynamic.

A fourth special speaking situation is the impromptu presentation. When there is no time to prepare remarks, a speaker should use a confident speaking style, begin with a main idea, support it with reasons or explanations, and conclude by restating the main idea.

CASE FOR ANALYSIS

Case 5-1

A Video Message From Arne

Marriott International CEO Arne Sorenson released a 6-minute video to Marriott employees, shareholders, and customers about the COVID-19 crisis on March 19, 2020.

Presentation Transcript (Edited for Length)

Hello, Marriott associates. . . . Because of the profound impact COVID-19 is having on so many of us around the world, this is the most difficult video message we have ever pulled together. Our team was a bit concerned about using a video today because of my new bald look. Let me just say that my new look is exactly what was expected as a result of my medical treatments. I feel good, and my team and I are 100 percent focused on overcoming the common crisis we face. Now, let's talk about that crisis. . . .

In terms of our business, COVID-19 is like nothing we've ever seen before. For a company that's 92 years old—that's borne witness to the Great Depression, World War II, and many other economic and global crises—that's saying something. But here are the facts.

COVID-19 is having a more severe and sudden financial impact on our business than 9/11 and the 2009 financial crisis, combined. . . . In most markets, our business is already running 75 percent below normal levels. . . . The restrictions on travel, gatherings of people, and required social distancing are having an immediate impact by depressing demand for our hotels. . . .

Given these circumstances, we've been forced to take proactive steps to respond to the crisis and are putting into place business contingency plans globally. . . .

We've worked to take controllable costs out of the business. . . . We have paused all new hires, with the exception of a small number of mission-critical positions. We have stopped all hotel initiatives for 2020 and have gone dark on our brand marketing and advertising. . . . Both Mr. Marriott and I will not be taking any salary for the balance of 2020, and my executive team will be taking a 50 percent cut in pay. . . . More details about these actions and what they mean will be shared through local HR teams.

While it's impossible to know how long this crisis will last, I know we, as a global community, will come through the other side. And when we do, our guests will be eager to travel this beautiful world again. When that great day comes, we will be there to welcome them with the warmth and care we are known for the world over. . . . Together we can, and we will overcome this, and we'll thrive once again. Thank you and be well.[38]

Questions

1. Why do you think this video presentation was released by posting it on social media (Twitter, LinkedIn)?

2. What is the effect of Sorenson's opening remarks about his newly bald appearance?

3. Is the speaker's purpose informative or persuasive?

4. Which of the organizational patterns discussed in this chapter (Table 5-2) is used here? How effective is this pattern, considering the topic, purpose, and audience?

5. How does the speaker demonstrate empathy with the audience?

6. What is the speaker's final thought? How appropriate is it, given his topic, purpose, and audience?

EXERCISES

Exercise 5-1

Choose an upcoming formal speaking situation at work, in your community, at a social organization, for a special occasion, or at school. Complete the Audience Analysis Worksheet below as you prepare your remarks.

Audience Analysis Worksheet

1. How many do I expect in the audience?

2. Who are the most powerful or influential members?

3. What is their knowledge of the content area?

    _____ High; may be higher than mine

    _____ About the same as mine

    _____ Less than my knowledge of the subject

    _____ Probably do not have even basic knowledge

    _____ Varies

4. What types of evidence will most impress this group?

    _____ Technical data

    _____ Statistical comparisons

    _____ Cost figures

    _____ Historical information

    _____ Generalizations

    _____ Demonstrations

    _____ Stories and examples

    _____ Opinions of the speaker

5. What is the group's attitude toward the subject?

    _____ Exceptionally positive

    _____ Somewhat positive

    _____ Neutral

    _____ Somewhat negative; reluctant

    _____ Definitely negative

    _____ Group varies; some positive and some negative

6. What is the group's attitude toward me as the presenter?

    _____ See me as credible and knowledgeable

    _____ Neutral; probably do not have an opinion

    _____ See me as having little knowledge and credibility

7. What is the group's attitude toward the organization I represent?

    _____ See the organization as reliable and trustworthy

    _____ Neutral

    _____ Might question its capabilities and reliability

8. What will be the group's disposition at the time of my presentation?

    _____ They will have listened to many other presentations similar to this one; they could be tired.

    _____ They will have been sitting for a long time; they may need a minute to stretch.

    _____ This presentation will be unique, so it should be easy to grab their attention.

    _____ This is an early item on the agenda; they should be fresh.

9. What are the *most important* audience characteristics to consider in the presentation?

Exercise 5-2

Prepare a 5-minute informative presentation for your class on the latest developments in office ergonomics. Begin by analyzing your audience and selecting your topics and their order of presentation. Your discussion should address the following elements:

- How will you introduce your subject so that you grab the audience's attention?

- What will be your three main points?
- What type of supporting information will most impress your audience?
- What should you say in the closing?
- How will you encourage questions at the end of your presentation?
- What would be the best type of visual aids to maintain the audience's attention?

Exercise 5-3

Pick one of the following topics to use in the development of a 5-minute persuasive presentation:

- Lie detectors should (or should not) be used in the hiring process.
- Employers should (or should not) check a candidate's financial record in the hiring process.
- Top executives should (or should not) be held criminally liable for their companies' illegal (or unethical) actions.
- Social responsibility should (or should not) be a major concern of today's corporations.
- Managers should (or should not) be concerned about the personal problems of their employees.

- An international code of ethics should (or should not) be developed.
- Unionization is (or is not) appropriate for today's white-collar workers.

After picking a topic, visualize an audience to whom you would speak on the subject. Of the three persuasive presentation patterns described in this chapter, which would be most appropriate for your presentation? Given the topic you have chosen and the audience you have visualized, what type of evidence would you use to persuade them to accept your point of view?

Exercise 5-4

Pick one of the following scenarios and develop a 5-minute informative presentation that follows the guidelines in this chapter:

- For an audience of graduating seniors in business administration, discuss the topic of appropriate dress for employment interviews at your company.
- For an audience of business executives, discuss the topic of appropriate dress for media interviews.

Notes

1. Mary Marcel, "What's the Best Course? Evidence From Alumni on the Value of Business Presentations," *Journal of Education for Business* 90 (2015): 10–17. doi: 10.1080/08832323.2014.968515.

2. Cheryl Hamilton and Tony L. Kroll, *Communicating for Results: A Guide for Business and the Professions*, 11th ed. (Boston: Cengage Learning, 2018), 304.

3. TED: Ideas Worth Spreading, "Speaking at TED," https://www.ted.com/about/conferences/speaking-at-ted.

4. John F. Kennedy, inaugural address, January 20, 1961, doi: JFKPOF-034-002.

5. Charles Krauthammer, "Make It Snappy: In Praise of Short Papers, Short Speeches, and, Yes, the Sound Bite," *Time*, July 21, 1997, 84.

6. This widely quoted advice is believed to have been given to FDR's son, James, though it was first published posthumously in Paul L. Soper, *Basic Public Speaking*, 2nd ed. (Oxford University Press, 1963), 12.

7. Bill Steele, "Master Any Slide Deck," *TD: Talent Development*, June 2017, 22–23.

8. Mickey Bannon, "Egocentrism," University of Pittsburgh Oral Communication Lab, 2020, https://www.comm.pitt.edu/audience-adaptation.

9. Ernest G. Bormann et al., *Interpersonal Communication in the Modern Organization* (Englewood Cliffs, NJ: Prentice Hall, 1982), 197.

10. Sheryl Sandberg and Adam Grant, *Option B: Facing Adversity, Building Resilience, and Finding Joy* (New York: Alfred A. Knopf, 2017), 20.

11. Steele, "Master Any Slide Deck," 23.

12. Steve Kaye, "It's Showtime! How to Give Effective Presentations," *Supervision*, 78, no. 5 (May 2017): 8–10.

13. William S. Howell and Ernest G. Bormann, *Presentational Speaking for Business and the Professions* (New York: Harper & Row, 1971), 122–30.

14. Daniel J. O'Keefe, *Persuasion Theory and Research*, 2nd ed. (Thousand Oaks, CA: Sage, 2002), 181–264.

15. Michael Shermer, "How to Convince Someone When Facts Fail," *Scientific American*, January 1, 2017, https://www.scientificamerican.com/article/how-to-convince-someone-when-facts-fail.

16. Anne Bradstreet Grinols, "Ethical Persuasion: Taking the High Road in Compelling Communication" (paper presented at the Association for Business Communication Southwestern United States Regional Conference, March 12, 2013).

17. T. J. McCue, "Why Infographics Rule," *Forbes*, January 8, 2013, https://www.forbes.com/sites/tjmccue/2013/01/08/what-is-an-infographic-and-ways-to-make-it-go-viral/#117743e67272. See also Visual Teaching Alliance for the Gifted and Talented, "Why Visual Teaching?" http://visualteachingalliance.com.

18. Lane Cooper, trans., *The Rhetoric of Aristotle* (New York, NY: Appleton-Century-Crofts, Inc., 1932), 9.

19. William R. Hobbs et al., "Online Social Integration Is Associated With Reduced Mortality Risk," *Proceedings of the National Academy of Sciences of the United States of America* 113, no. 46 (November 15, 2016): 12980–84, doi: 10.10;73/pnas.1605554113.

20. Baba Shiv et al., "Investment Behavior and the Negative Side of Emotion," *Psychological Science* 16, no. 6 (2005): 435–39.

21. Steele, "Master Any Slide Deck," 23.

22. H. James Dallas, *Mastering the Challenges of Leading Change: Inspire the People and Succeed Where Others Fail* (Hoboken, NJ: John Wiley & Sons, 2015), 64.

23. Mary Munter and Dave Paradi, *Guide to PowerPoint* (Upper Saddle River, NJ: Pearson Prentice Hall, 2007), 65, 94.

24. Robert P. Sedlack Jr., Barbara L. Shwom, and Karl P. Keller, *Graphics and Visual Communication for Managers* (Mason, OH: Thomson South-Western, 2008), 71.

25. Munter and Paradi, *Guide to PowerPoint*.

26. UNL Office of Research and Economic Development, "Quad Charts Promote Faculty Research to DoD," *Research News*, May 2013, https://research.unl.edu/researchnews/May2013/quad-charts-promote-faculty-research-to-dod.

27. Martin J. Eppler and Friederike Hoffmann, "Does Method Matter? An Experiment on Collaborative Business Model Idea Generation in Teams," *Innovation: Management, Policy & Practice* 14, no. 3 (2012): 388–403.

28. Joanna K. Garner and Michael Alley, "How the Design of Presentation Slides Affects Audience Comprehension: A Case for the Assertion-Evidence Approach," *International Journal of Engineering Education* 29, no. 6 (2013): 1564–79. See also Michael Alley, *The Craft of Scientific Presentations*, 2nd ed. (New York: Springer-Verlag, 2013).

29. Marcel, "What's the Best Course," 14.

30. Sally Quinn and Adam Goody, "An Evaluation of a Course Aimed at Reducing Public Speaking Anxiety Among University Students," *International Journal of Teaching and Learning in Higher Education* 31, no. 3 (2019): 503–11.

31. Amy Jen Su, "How to Calm Your Nerves Before a Big Presentation," *Harvard Business Review*, October 27, 2016, 4.

32. Kaye, "It's Showtime" 10.

33. Erika A. Hewitt, "What You're Saying When You Say 'I Don't Need a Mic,'" *Worship Lab*, Unitarian Universalist Association, August 31, 2017, https://www.uua.org/worship/lab/what-youre-saying-when-you-say-i-dont-need-mic.

34. Albert Mehrabian, *Nonverbal Communication* (New Brunswick, NJ: Aldine Transaction, 2007).

35. Joseph Colannino, "Best Practices for Video Presentations," *Chemical Engineering Progress* 115, no. 11 (November 2019): 49–51.

36. Tom Hajduk, "Communication Audit: TV/Videoconference Presentation," vol. 11.1, Communication Consulting Group, accessed August 11, 2014, http://www.ccg-usa.com.

37. Michael S. Dalis, *Sell Like a Team: The Blueprint for Building Teams That Win Big at High-Stakes Meetings* (New York: McGraw-Hill Education, 2017).

38. Marriott International, Twitter post, March 19, 2020, 7:00 a.m., https://twitter.com/MarriottIntl/status/1240639160148529160.

6

COMMUNICATING VISUALLY

LEARNING OBJECTIVES

By the end of this chapter, you will be able to

- Explain the role of visual elements in workplace documents.

- Apply the design principles for managerial communication to organize the layout of pages or slides, signal relationships in the content, create areas of emphasis, and unify multipage documents.

- Differentiate the role of tables, quantitative charts, and conceptual charts and choose the correct one for given data sets.

- Use graphics to tell accurate, ethical visual stories.

- Make decisions that improve the accessibility of your documents.

Although we may think of writing as the main component of effective communication, visual elements are often the first thing that people see when they open a report, skim a webpage, or look at a slide during a presentation. Visual communication is the use of graphics, color, typography, and layout to communicate with an audience. The visual elements of your documents can reinforce the message in the text, complement the message with additional information, contradict or clash with the text, and set a tone. In the past, composing text, creating graphics, and designing a page layout were often three separate jobs. But today, these jobs are often collapsed into one. Managers and other professional communicators are responsible for constructing reports, presentations, and other documents on their own, and audiences expect visual messages to convey information just as effectively as words.

Visual literacy is the ability to understand and compose visual messages. As children, our earliest "writing" used graphics to communicate ideas. As we grew older, we learned how to integrate words with graphics, and eventually words became our primary means of communicating with others.[1] But visual communication never went away. We are surrounded by advertisements, videos, instructions, infographics, sales brochures, slide decks, and other messages that rely heavily on visual elements to convey their message. Through experience and education, we have learned how to focus our attention and interpret visual cues.

Visual communication can improve a document's usability, present quantitative information accurately and efficiently, and enhance the persuasiveness of your message. When used effectively, visual elements can attract attention, organize information, and establish trust in the message and its author. In this chapter, we will help you use those cues in your own documents to create more powerful, effective, and accurate messages at work. By using the design principles and selecting or creating useful graphics, you can improve the impact of your reports, presentations, and other messages.

DOCUMENT DESIGN

Visual communication might seem intimidating to people who do not consider themselves artists or even very creative. With so many choices at your fingertips, where do you even begin? Visual design principles help you make decisions about color, typography, size, orientation, layout, negative space, and unity quickly and confidently. Design principles are based on common practices by professionals and educators in fields like art, architecture, and graphic design. They are not rules but rather guidelines based on common experience. Your decisions to apply these principles must always be based on the specific characteristics of the audience, purpose, and communication context.

Design Principles for Managerial Communication

The design principles for managerial communication (see Table 6-1) are a collection of design decisions that are commonly used in workplace documents. This list of design principles is not exhaustive. In a recent study, more than 70 design principles were identified by graphic design practitioners and visual rhetoric educators.[2] The most common principles are based on the Gestalt principles of perception: figure/ground contrast, similarity, repetition, balance, symmetry, closure, and continuation. We have adapted these principles, along with a few others, into visual design principles that managers are most likely to need when composing or reviewing workplace documents. The design principles for managerial

TABLE 6-1 ■ Design Principles for Managerial Communication			
Building Blocks	**Relationships**	**Emphasis**	**Unity**
Grid	Similarity	Contrast	Repetition
Alignment	Proximity	Hierarchy	Consistency
Typography		Negative space	
Color			
Conventions			

communication are a starting point to help you become more conscious of the decisions you make and the ones that your word processor, desktop publishing, or presentation software may be making for you.

Building Blocks

The building blocks of document design are grid, alignment, typography, color, and conventions. These elements set the foundation of your document, whether a memo, a report, or a slide deck, and are the easiest to use with little or no experience. Word processor, desktop publishing, and presentation slide software offer a variety of templates that control the building blocks with style sheets, themes, or master slides, but modifying these preset combinations can create a custom look that sets your documents apart from the crowd.

Grid

A grid is an imaginary table that divides the page or screen into columns and rows (see Figure 6-1). The grid helps you decide where to place items by marking areas in which you can place content and areas that are protected. The simplest design uses a single-column grid to organize content, with margins on all sides. A two-column grid places text and graphics into columns of equal or different widths, with margins on the outside edges and a gutter in between the columns. Newspapers, newsletters, and booklets often use grids with multiple columns to arrange content. Electronic slides use a two-row grid, with a narrow row for the headline and a longer row for body text or graphics.

FIGURE 6-1 ■ Sample Grids for Documents and Slides

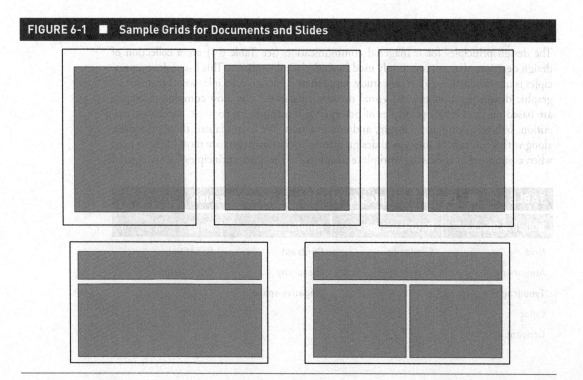

Alignment

Alignment refers to the arrangement of items along an invisible line to create an orderly layout. Without alignment, items might seem random or haphazard, suggesting carelessness in the composition and organization.

Flush-left alignment places words and objects against the left margin. In most text documents, the text and lists will often be aligned along the left margin with a ragged (or uneven) right edge. This alignment is comfortable for many users because we were trained through writing exposure and through reading books and other printed materials to read from left to right.

Flush right, by contrast, aligns text and other objects along an invisible line on the right side of the page or screen. In most cases, flush right should not be used for body text because the ragged left edge makes it difficult for readers to locate the beginning of new lines. (Arabic and Hebrew are examples of languages that do use the flush right alignment.) Because the position is somewhat unexpected, flush-right text may be used for numbers, headlines, callouts, and other items that you want to emphasize.

Centered alignment places text equally on either side of an invisible centerline with ragged left and right sides. Centered text is commonly used for titles, headlines, column labels in tables, promotional text on posters and flyers, and formal invitations. In short line lengths, centered alignment can create a strong impact, but avoid using it for body text because readers may struggle to track new lines.

Justified text combines all three: balancing text on either side of a center line and forcing flush left and flush right margins. To create the justification, the word processor will insert extra spaces between characters or words, resize the characters, or hyphenate the text to force the alignment. These modifications may create inconsistencies in the look of the document, and readers often find hyphenated words difficult to read.

Flush left/ragged right is the default setting in word processing programs, so you may be using this alignment without thinking about it. In other applications, such as desktop publishing or presentation software, you will have much more freedom to manipulate objects on the page or screen. Turn on gridlines to guide your alignment, or create your own guides by drawing lines and removing them when your document is finished. In tables, align text and row labels to the left margin, but align numbers to the right.

Typography

Typography refers to the shape of characters like letters, numbers, and symbols. Through years of experience, we have developed mental models of what letters look like. Their distinctive shapes help us recognize letters even when they are distorted, transposed, or upside down. In fact, our brains are so good at recognizing letters that they rarely read all of them. As we read, our brains are actually looking for patterns of letters and interpreting them as words. For example, when your eye sees two characters with ascenders and a rounded third character, your brain probably interprets the combination as the word *the*. When you notice misspelled words (like *teh*), your brain sends a small alarm because the characters do not fit a usual pattern or because the word doesn't fit into the context of the rest of the sentence. This ability to read characters as words is the Gestalt principle of closure: A collection of letters is interpreted as words because that's what you expect to see. Even when letters are partially obscured, your mind fills in the gap with what it expects to see, and usually the guess is correct.

But typographic choices can interfere with the brain's efficiency. Messages written in ALL CAPS lose the distinctive shapes of the individual characters. Instead, you see blocks of characters that have roughly the same size and shape. Your mind must slow down and look at each character, combine them to create a word, and then string the words together to form sentences. Although this mental processing happens quickly, messages in capital letters require more cognitive work to comprehend and take longer to read. Try it yourself by reading Figure 6-2.

Your word processor, desktop publishing, or presentation software contains dozens of typeface options. A typeface is a style of alphabetic and numeric characters. A font is a group of characters in a particular size and style of the typeface. A professionally designed typeface might consist of several fonts, such as condensed, italic, bold, and so forth. An inexpensive typeface may consist of only one font that is manipulated by the computer to be thicker, thinner, or slanted. Early typefaces in the 16th and 17th centuries simulated the calligraphy of handwritten texts that preceded the printing press. Over time, typographic trends shaped the way documents looked (see Figure 6-3).[3]

FIGURE 6-2 ■ Messages Are Easier to Read in Uppercase and Lowercase Letters Than All Capital Letters

THIS IS AN EXAMPLE OF A MESSAGE IN CAPITAL LETTERS. IT IS PERFECTLY LEGIBLE BUT NOT AS EFFICIENT OR COMFORTABLE FOR READING. IT IS ALSO MORE DIFFICULT TO SPOT ERRORS IN THE MESSAGE. FOR BEST RESULTS, USE CAPITAL LETTERS SPARINGLY TO CREATE EMPHASIS.

FIGURE 6-3 ■ A Brief History of Typeface Styles

Old Style typefaces have graceful curves and a moderate contrast between thick and thin strokes within the letters. Claude Garamond, working in the 16th century, was one of the first typographers to simplify letterforms to be more geometric and less like handwriting. The Adobe Garamond typeface is based on his designs.

Modern typefaces feature geometric shapes with strong contrast between thick and thin strokes in the characters. Modern typefaces evolved during the Enlightenment to reflect the values of logic, rationalism, and science that were popular. Big Caslon, designed by Matthew Carter, is based on the designs of typographer William Caslon from the 18th century.

𝔅lackletter typefaces emerged to attract attention to the growing number of commercial advertisements toward the end of the 19th century. Typefaces like 𝔏ucida 𝔅lackletter imitate the early characters of 15th-century printing presses.

Old Style returned to popularity in the early 20th century. Times New Roman, designed in 1931 for the British newspaper *The Times*, is still one of the most widely used typefaces. Its ongoing popularity is due to its clarity and its ubiquity: It was the default typeface in Microsoft Word until 2010.

Sans serif typefaces, which feature clean, compact, and rounded letter forms, took the world by storm in the mid-20th century as minimalism grew popular in most areas of design. Helvetica, designed in Switzerland in 1957, may be the most widely known example of a sans serif typeface. It appears on signs and documents all over the world, and it is valued for its readability and clarity at a variety of sizes.

Today, typefaces are usually grouped into four categories. Serif typefaces are based on old style or classical letterforms. They feature small projections on the edges of letters. Sans serif typefaces are minimalist designs that end simply, without serifs. Within each of these larger categories are decorative or novelty typefaces, which are useful for attracting attention and creating a tone, and script typefaces that imitate handwriting. Both decorative and script typefaces can be difficult to read, so they should be used sparingly.

As you select typefaces, consider the subtle effect your choice may add to your message. Studies have shown that people ascribe personality traits to typefaces.[4] Using a style with personality traits that conflict with your message won't prevent audiences from understanding your message but may weaken its credibility (and by extension, your own).[5]

Figure 6-4 contains a sample of some common text and decorative typefaces. As you look at the table, notice how much easier the serif and sans serif typefaces are for reading blocks of text. The decorative/novelty and script typefaces are more difficult to read and force you to slow down rather than skim and scan, which is how we normally begin reading. And you might be surprised to learn that all the typefaces in Figure 6-4 are the same size . . . point size, that is. Point size measures the distance from the top of the tallest ascender (think about the letters b, d, f, h, k, l, t) to the bottom of the lowest descender (g, j, p, q). When printers used metal type—or individual characters carved from metal—point sizes were somewhat consistent. Modern digital type, on the other hand, is much more

FIGURE 6-4 ■ Typographic Styles and Relative Sizes		
Serif Classical letterforms with "feet" or small projections on the ends of letters	Bookman Old Style	The quick brown fox jumped over the lazy dog.
	Cambria	The quick brown fox jumped over the lazy dog.
	Garamond	The quick brown fox jumped over the lazy dog.
	Times New Roman	The quick brown fox jumped over the lazy dog.
Sans Serif Modern letterforms without serifs	Arial	The quick brown fox jumped over the lazy dog.
	Calibri	The quick brown fox jumped over the lazy dog.
	Century Gothic	The quick brown fox jumped over the lazy dog.
	Gill Sans	The quick brown fox jumped over the lazy dog.
Decorative and Novelty Ornate or whimsical letterforms Serif or sans serif	American Typewriter	The quick brown fox jumped over the lazy dog.
	Cooper Black	**The quick brown fox jumped over the lazy dog.**
	Impact	**The quick brown fox jumped over the lazy dog.**
	Lucida Blackletter	The quick brown fox jumped over the lazy dog.
Script Imitation of handwritten, calligraphic letterforms	Apple Chancery	The quick brown fox jumped over the lazy dog.
	Brush Script	The quick brown fox jumped over the lazy dog.
	Lucida Handwriting	The quick brown fox jumped over the lazy dog.
	Zapfino	The quick brown fox jumped over the lazy dog.

diverse. Today, point size is a way to estimate the size of your text, but as you can see, it's not absolute. Most text typefaces will be easy to read at 10-, 11-, or 12-point sizes, but trust your own eyes by printing a copy of your document or slides to review yourself before giving it to others.

In general, there is a direct relationship between line length (the width of the page, column, or text box) and the size of your typeface and leading, or the space between the lines of text. Longer line lengths need larger type sizes and wider leading—spacing—between each line of text. Smaller line lengths (such as multicolumn grids) need smaller type sizes and thinner leading.

Informational documents must be legible and easy to read, so use traditional serif or sans serif text typefaces for most purposes. Create similarity by minimizing the total number of typefaces to two or three—one for headings, one for the body text, and perhaps a third for items that need special emphasis. Within that combination, experiment with variations in size, *shape*, **weight**, and color to create contrast and variety that help audiences skim and scan the text or slide. If you do use decorative and script typefaces, apply them sparingly. Their contrast with the text typefaces will create focal points that create visual interest and emphasis. In promotional documents, you can be more whimsical with typographic choices, but legibility is always the benchmark to meet.

Color

One of the most multifaceted design principles is color. Color directs attention to specific elements and organizes content. Spot-color—or a single color in an otherwise black-and-white document—creates an immediate impact and draws the audience's eye before they ever read a word. Adding color to the background of text boxes is another way to create focal points in a text-heavy document. Color can also help you organize your content by emphasizing hierarchies within the information or unifying elements into groups. Subtle shading in alternate rows helps audiences follow a line of numbers across the width of a table. Color-coding data can help audiences spot the connections across multiple data displays.

CRITICAL THINKING QUESTIONS

Some designers think typography should be like a crystal goblet filled with wine: Your focus should be on the contents, not the container.

1. Have you experienced a document in which the tone of the typeface clashed with the content of a message?

2. Did the clash affect your understanding of the message? Did it affect your attitude toward the writer or organization that created the message?

Finally, color can also be used symbolically to send subtle messages about the product or the organization that sells it. For example, green is often used to suggest natural or ecologically friendly products. Blue suggests calmness and responsibility. If you are trying to communicate low prices at your grocery store, green could cue viewers to think about the freshness of the produce and the health benefits of home cooking, but if you are trying to persuade people to invest their money at your bank, blue could suggest trustworthiness.[6] Black, gray, green, and blue are often used for products or services that fulfill practical needs, while red, pink, yellow, and purple are more common for products or services that fulfill symbolic or social needs.[7] Organizations often have custom color palettes that differentiate them from their competition and unite their messages across multiple media. Think about your favorite sports team, for example, and chances are that you picture the colors that appear on the team's uniform, such as black and gold or black and red. By using symbolic colors, you connect your message to a bigger concept or reinforce your role as a member of your organization. In short, color can tell audiences what to look at and suggest what they should think about as they read.

How do you choose one or more colors from the endless options available to you? One place to start is to find out whether your organization has preferences or requirements that you must follow; many organizations have preapproved color palettes as part of their visual identity or design standards. You can also consider whether the topic suggests one or more colors. For example, a presentation for a landscaping business might use green as a main color (connoting grass, plants, and leaves), brown or tan as a secondary color (connoting trees and earth), and a bright yellow or orange for emphasis (inspired by flowers).

Once you pick your main color, you can also use the color wheel to inspire its companions.[8] *Monochromatic* color schemes use variations of a single color. These schemes are useful for low-budget projects. *Analogous* schemes use the adjacent secondary colors to accent the main color and create calm, often soothing combinations. *Complementary* color schemes use colors that lie opposite each other on the color wheel; these colors have the highest contrast, but the effect can be jarring. *Split complementary* schemes use the colors that are adjacent to the complement instead. *Triadic* schemes use hues that are equally spaced around the color wheel. Table 6-2 lists some options for color schemes using green as the main color.

As you experiment with combinations, remember that you do not have to use the pure hue. Your software will allow you to manipulate the saturation and brightness to create interesting, sophisticated combinations. For more information about color palettes and color models for screen, print, and webpages, visit the U.S. government's usability website at https://www.usability.gov/how-to-and-tools/methods/color-basics.html.

TABLE 6-2 ■ Sample Color Schemes Based on a Common Main Color			
Color Scheme	**Accent Color 1**	**Main Color**	**Accent Color 2**
Monochromatic	Dark green	Green	Light green
Analogous	Teal	Green	Chartreuse
Complementary	Red	Green	None
Split complementary	Vermilion	Green	Maroon
Triadic	Orange	Green	Purple

Conventions

When people pick up a document, open a website, or view a slide, they bring with them a collection of past experiences that influences their interpretations of what they see. For example, they expect blue, underlined text to be a hyperlink. They expect a budget to be organized as a table and numbers formatted as currency. And they expect an annual report to be bound as a booklet with thick, glossy paper and professional photos. If you violate those expectations (such as presenting the budget as a narrative or formatting the annual report as a trifold brochure), your audiences may become frustrated and will question your communication competency.

Expectations about design are called conventions. Design conventions are tacit social agreements about graphics and visual communication.[9] For example, in the United States and many other cultures, red signals danger. When red is combined with shapes, complex messages begin to form: A red octagon with the word "stop" directs traffic nearly all over the world. A red circle with a diagonal bar over an icon indicates something is forbidden.

You have probably been using several design conventions for years without realizing it. For example, in books, newspapers, and traditional letter format, each new paragraph begins with a small indent from the margin. In many memos and other workplace documents, however, the first-line indent is eliminated. The full-block format begins each paragraph flush with the left margin, but an extra line of leading or negative space separates each paragraph from the next. The purpose of the indent and the leading is to help readers quickly find the beginning of paragraphs as they skim and scan the document, but you don't have to explain that. Your audience will know—or quickly learn—why they are used.

By adhering to conventions, writers help audiences quickly and easily understand what they are looking at and how to use it. Using conventions correctly can also help you prove that you are an "insider" within a larger group. For example, using jargon is discouraged when writing or talking to the general public because they may not know what the terms mean. But at work, jargon is an acceptable type of shorthand that shows you respect your audience's understanding of the material. Design conventions work the same way. Your organization may expect its employees to use a certain typeface in their documents or to use a preapproved template for slide decks. A visual identity is a set of conventions that creates a consistent look and feel to unify an organization's communications. For example, your organization may require that its logo appear on the cover of every report, sales brochure, and webpage. If your organization has an established color palette, you may be expected to use it when adding spot-color in headings, designing slide masters, or ordering promotional items.

For most users, conventions offer reliable solutions to common design situations. But use them with care. One danger of conventions is that they are based in culture, so elements may have multiple, even conflicting meanings. Red might mean danger in the United States, but in Great Britain, it is the color of tradition and travel (think double-decker buses), and in Russia and China, it is associated with communism.[10] On the U.S. flag, red, white, and blue represent hardiness, purity, and justice, respectively, but on the French Tricolor flag, the same colors represent the monarchy (white) and the city of Paris (blue/red). Symbols, colors, and other design conventions may vary even within the same culture. In the United States, red symbolizes not only danger but also patriotism, love, health, aggression, and speed.

Another potential problem with conventions is the ease with which they can misdirect audiences.[11] For example, tourism maps often mark the locations of sponsors on the street plan. If users expect maps to be neutral and objective representations of the city, they may not realize that other restaurants or shops are also nearby. If a building plan faces south at the top of a map and the user expects that to be north, they may struggle to locate the entrance when they arrive for a meeting. In budgets, deficits are double-coded with red ink and parenthesis marks for emphasis. If you use only a minus sign, users may initially overlook the potentially bad news in the numbers.

The building blocks of document design are elements that you probably use every day. Typography and color are two design principles that may seem most familiar, particularly given the ease and control that word processor, desktop publishing, and presentation software have put at our fingertips. Grid, alignment, and conventions, on the other hand, create the structure of every document we create.

CRITICAL THINKING QUESTIONS

1. What are some design conventions for documents that you use regularly?

2. How did you learn to understand those conventions? Did someone explain them to you?

Relationships

As audiences move through a document, they instinctively try to connect what they are reading with other things they have read and with their own prior knowledge. The grouping strategies of similarity and proximity signal relationships to help readers understand the organization of your content and form mental models of how things work.

When we see objects that look alike, we assume that they *are* alike. The principle of similarity suggests that a fundamental relationship exists between objects, even if that relationship is not obvious. Size, shape, and color are three variables that can be manipulated to suggest that a relationship exists. For example, bulleted points mark the items in a list. The shape of the bullets creates similarity, signaling that the items share a common characteristic, even though the content of the items will be different. Instructions use conventional icons and color to warn users about danger. When the warning in one document looks like icons we see elsewhere, we understand their meaning and pay special attention. The body text of your document or slide deck should be the same style and size from beginning to end. Meanwhile, headings are larger and use a different typeface. By making headings look similar to each other—but different from the body text—you tell audiences visually that the text blocks serve different roles.

Proximity is the relationship of objects in space. When we see objects that are clustered together, we assume they are related to each other in some way (see Figure 6-5). The application of proximity is sometimes called *chunking*. A business card often chunks name and title into one block and contact information into another. Website navigation groups hyperlinks into a column or row, and web ads are often grouped and aligned on the right side of the page. Captions are placed above or below the graphic they describe. Proximity organizes the document to help audiences see connections within the content.

When used intentionally, similarity and proximity help audiences understand relationships. When used carelessly, however, audiences may infer relationships where none exist.

FIGURE 6-5   ■   Showing Relationships Through Proximity and Similarity in Size, Shape, and Color

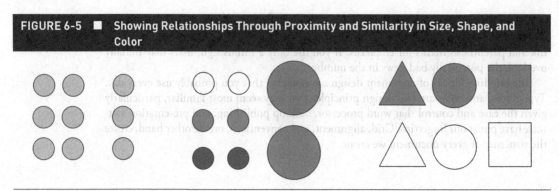

Emphasis

Within your documents, some ideas, facts, or data are more important than others. Which ones they are might be obvious to you, but will your audiences recognize them, too? Emphasis strategies like contrast, hierarchy, and negative space create focal points that help audiences spot the essential ideas and use them to understand your message.

Contrast makes items stand out through differences in size, color, shape, or style. The first type of contrast users see is the figure-ground, or the difference between the background and the items arranged on top of it. In this book, black text is printed on white paper, creating strong contrast and making the text easy to read. But if the black text were printed on red or blue paper, the contrast would weaken and audiences would struggle to see the characters on the page. Other forms of contrast help audiences skim the document and distinguish different sections or elements. For example, the body text may be black, which is comfortable for extended reading, but section headings might be larger and blue. The contrast in color and size helps audiences find the headings and understand that they have a special role to play on the page. As designer Robin Williams explains, "if the elements (type, color, size, line thickness, shape, space, etc.) are not the *same*, then make them **very different**."[12] But contrast works only when it is strong and purposeful. When contrast is weak, it may look accidental and confuse or distract audiences rather than help them.

Hierarchy is the real or implied order of importance. Arrangement and size are the two most common techniques for suggesting hierarchy. Placing items at the top of a page or grouping suggests that is the "starting place" for the design, and thus it must be the most important element. Numbered lists suggest a sequence or rank order, with the first item usually considered the most important one. Bulleted lists do not suggest a sequence, but audiences still perceive the first item to be the most important. Relative size also suggests importance, with larger objects appearing more important than smaller ones. Headings in word processors and slide templates use the principle of hierarchy: The title is the largest text size and footnote text is the smallest, and levels of headings vary by size, color, and shape to suggest their relative importance.

Negative space is the unused portion of the page or screen, such as margins on the outer edges, gutters between columns, and leading between lines of text. Like a soloist in a choir, generous negative space creates emphasis by allowing the focal point to be viewed without competition from other objects. (The term *white space* is also used, but negative space can be any color.)

Emphasis strategies work because they tell audiences, "Look at this!" To be effective, use the emphasis strategies in moderation. When used too often, the strategies lose their effectiveness. After all, when everything is emphasized, nothing stands out from the crowd.

Unity

Unity is the cohesiveness of the visual elements. Unified documents give the sense that everything belongs together and the entire message was carefully composed.

Repetition extends the principle of similarity by reusing design elements across multiple pages, slides, or files. It "teaches" people how to read the document by creating a local set of conventions. For example, sidebars have a light blue background and black sans serif type. Bold type identifies keywords, both to help you spot them on the page and to help you remember them later. As you advance, each page or slide fits in with the whole package.

CRITICAL THINKING QUESTIONS

1. What is an example of design repetition that you have noticed and admired?

2. What design decisions do you make to create unity in your documents?

But repetition does not mean objects must be exactly the same each time they appear. For example, if you are laying a textbox over a graphic on a presentation slide, the location of the box may change to improve its contrast with the background or to avoid covering the focal point of an image, but other elements like shading and typeface would be repeated each time. Color-coding sections of a multipage document can help audiences locate information quickly, particularly if color conventions are used. For example, in a quick-reference guide, green borders and headings can indicate the "getting started" section, and red borders and headings can indicate troubleshooting instructions.

The key to unity is consistency. Contrast suggests difference, so inconsistency in design will attract attention. At best, inconsistency is a distraction. At worst, it can be misleading. A style sheet defines the roles that elements like color, size, and shape will play in your document. The advantages of using styles rather than formatting text and other graphical elements manually are consistency and flexibility. Suppose you write a memo using the default style, which uses Calibri for body text and Cambria for headings. If you change your mind later, you can modify the styles to change the body text to Book Antiqua and headings to Franklin Gothic Demi. In a matter of a few clicks, the typography of the entire document changes. Word processing, desktop publishing, and presentation slide software have style sheets of typefaces and themes of color palettes installed, but you can modify the default template to create your own combinations.

USING GRAPHICS

Graphics are visual representations of data, ideas, and objects. They show relationships, convert concepts into tangible form, render the appearance of physical items, and even decorate the document. Informative graphics convey information needed to understand a topic, whereas decorative graphics evoke a feeling.[13] In her book on document design, Karen Schriver describes five relationships between text and graphics:

- *Redundant.* The text and graphic reinforce each other by providing the same information in visual and verbal modes, or forms.

- *Complementary.* The text and graphic each present some of the information; together they provide a complete message.

- *Supplementary.* Either the text or the graphic presents the message, and the other mode provides supporting information.

- *Juxtaposition.* The text and the graphic present different information.

- *Stage setting.* The text or the graphic sets a tone or forecasts information that will be presented using the other mode.[14]

In this section, you will learn about some of the common graphics that managers use to communicate their work. Data displays allow audiences to quickly and easily use data to understand a situation or make decisions. Data displays—tables and charts—are used to analyze data, to communicate with others, to monitor progress, and to plan for the future.[15] Illustrations are pictures or diagrams that represent ideas, processes, or objects.

Data Displays

The main difference between tables and charts is simple: Tables present data. Charts summarize data. But how do you decide which form is appropriate? Think about how people will use the information (see Table 6-3). When accuracy is needed, present data in a table. Tables organize data into columns and rows. Audiences can locate specific data points, tally multiple data points, or make comparisons within the data set. When the data set is small, audiences can make judgments or estimates fairly easily. But when the data set is large, it can be overwhelming and confusing. When patterns or trends are needed or when the data

TABLE 6-3 ■ Reasons to Choose a Table or Chart to Display Your Data	
Reasons to Use a Table	**Reasons to Use a Chart**
• Precise values are required.	• Precise values are not required.
• Users will look up individual values.	• Users need to know the overall shape of the data.
• Users will compare individual values but not entire sets of values.	• Users need to understand relationships within a data set or among multiple data sets.
• The quantitative data involve more than one unit of measure.	
• Some of the data are text or categorical numbers.	• The data are only quantitative numbers.

set is very large, present data in a chart. Charts create visual summaries of the data using symbols and conventional shapes.

Tables

Tables organize content into columns and rows, making it possible to find individual values or text quickly. Some of the data will be quantitative, and some will be qualitative or categorical. To understand the difference between these types of data, think about numbers that are not intended to be used in calculations, such as your employee identification number, telephone number, or address. Data like these are often included in tables, but they are treated like text.

The main feature of tables is the grid of intersecting lines that creates cells for the data, although you may choose to make some or all gridlines invisible. The goal of table design is to help audiences understand the organization of the data and find the information they need. Minimizing the visual clutter in the table will help you meet this goal. Heavy black gridlines throughout the table create visual clutter and hide the relationships within the rows or columns. In smaller tables, negative space is an effective way to separate rows, columns, and even groups within the data set. In larger tables, though, you may need to offer a little help. Subtle shading in alternating rows (or columns) can help audiences follow the data from one side of the table to the other. If you must use lines, weaken their contrast (for example, using light gray lines on a white background) or reduce their thickness to keep the audience's focus on the data.

In the top row of your table, insert a title that describes the data. (If you have multiple columns, merge the cells so that your title spans the table width.) The body of the table is the section that organizes the quantitative data; use row and column labels to identify their content. Text should align to the left side of cells, but column labels are often centered. Your spreadsheet or word processor can probably rotate text to one side or stack the letters in a vertical column, but these techniques violate the English language convention of reading left to right and may be difficult to read. When space permits, format the text horizontally. Numbers should be aligned to the right to line up integers and decimals. (If some values have decimals and others do not, force the alignment by adding the same number of zero decimal digits to the end of each value.) When quantitative data are tabulated, the totals are usually shown in footer rows at the bottom of the table, but if the totals are the most important data to know, you can insert a line at the top of the table instead.

Tables often use sans serif typefaces because they are legible at small sizes. Use one typeface for all tables. When emphasis is needed, use bold, italics, color, or shading to create contrast with the other text or values in the table. Do not use word processor styles to format the text in your table because they can make formatting difficult and can present problems for audiences with visual impairments.

Place the table following any text that introduces or describes it. (For example, Figure 6-6 follows this explanation.) If your table is small, you may choose to wrap text around it to reduce the total page length. For each table, add a caption that numbers the table and summarizes the data. Within the text, referring to the table by its number will help audiences confirm that they are looking at the correct one.

Charts

Charts present a summary of the data and suggest how the data "look" using conventional patterns, which is particularly useful in very large data sets. The design principles

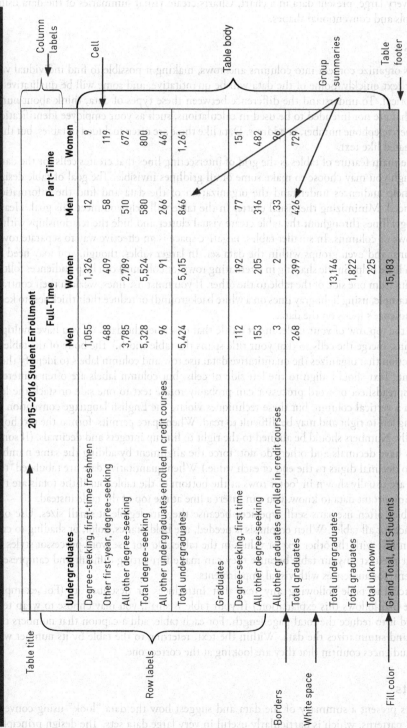

FIGURE 6-6 ■ Elements of Tables

for managerial communication will help you create attractive and usable charts that tell a story about the data, so your decisions must make that story obvious to others who haven't analyzed the data set as thoroughly as you have. The terms *charts* and *graphs* are often used interchangeably. Graphs are displays of mathematical functions, whereas charts may display either mathematical or textual information (such as organizational charts or flowcharts). For the purposes of this discussion, we will use the more inclusive term *charts*.

Quantitative Charts

Quantitative charts show relationships between two or more variables to show similarities and differences in the data set. If audiences need to see a few individual values, you can add textual elements to emphasize them, but if they need to see many precise values, then you should probably use a table.

Charts representing quantitative data usually plot values on a two-dimensional plane; the dimensions are represented by a horizontal *x*-axis and a vertical *y*-axis. The intersection of the axes is the zero-point. Most charts show only one quadrant along these axes, with the zero-point in the bottom left corner of the chart. This layout represents positive numbers, with the measures on each axis increasing as they move up or to the right. If your data set includes negative numbers, you may need to extend an axis below the zero-point to accommodate them.

Scatter charts illustrate the performance of a variable in repeated tests by plotting quantitative values as dots or coordinates on the *x*- and *y*-axis. Scatter charts show the cohesiveness of the data—how closely they group together and whether some data points are outliers. Trend lines (or the line of best fit) suggest a pattern within the data, such as increasing or decreasing from the zero-point.

Line charts illustrate performance over a period of time. By organizing the data chronologically, line charts show how the size or quantity of the variable changes, with the zero-point representing the start of the time period. The shape of the line(s) indicates trends or performance of the variable over the period of time being measured.

Bar charts illustrate total values of variables using the length of horizontal rectangles (or bars). When the data are oriented vertically, it is called a column chart. In either version, the bars can be arranged in any order. Pictographs replace the solid bars with icons that usually resemble the item being measured. Icons are the same size and represent standard quantities, but partial icons may be used to suggest fractions. Another variation of the bar chart is the stem and leaf chart (see Figure 6-7), which

FIGURE 6-7 ■ Example of a Stem and Leaf Chart

Average Life Expectancy of Top 10 GDP Countries

Men	Age	Women
	86	Japan
	85	France
	84	Germany
	83	UK
	82	USA
Japan	81	
	80	
Germany, UK, France	79	Brazil
	78	China
USA	77	
	76	Russia
China	75	
	74	
	73	
	72	
Brazil	71	Indonesia
	70	India
	69	
	68	
India, Indonesia	67	
	66	
Russia	65	

Source: World Health Organization, 2016 data.

shows the frequency and distribution of values in a data set by arranging each value (the leaves) against a vertical axis (the stem).

Pie charts display the relative sizes of two or more categories in data sets. A circle is divided into sectors; the area of each sector represents a fraction of the whole group. Doughnut charts are a variation of the pie chart in which the center of the circle has been removed; the data are represented by sections of the ring. Although commonly used in business, both pie and doughnut charts are problematic because most people cannot accurately judge the size of the fractions, particularly when the chart features more than three or four sectors or when the sectors are similar in size.[16] The problem is worsened when pie charts are "exploded" so that each sector is viewed as a separate shape.

Concept Charts

Concept charts describe abstract ideas, relationships, and processes. Like quantitative charts, concept charts use words, lines, and shapes to organize data and illustrate their structure. But the values in your data set will dictate the form of quantitative charts. You have much more flexibility when designing concept charts.

Organizational charts illustrate hierarchies and relationships of the personnel within an organization. Individuals or positions are arranged in terms of their rank within the organization, with the leader at the top of the page. Lines show relationships between individuals, such as between managers and their direct reports. Work breakdown structures are a variation of organizational charts that illustrate hierarchies of tasks in a project. The project is divided into main components; each component has one or more tasks and often several subtasks below.

Gantt charts illustrate the sequence of activities within a project. Gantt charts help project managers identify the critical path of a project, allocate human and other resources, and estimate time to completion. Each bar in the chart represents a task. The length of the bar represents the task's duration. Overlapping bars indicate concurrent tasks, and arrows indicate dependencies. The bars can be shaded to indicate the progress toward completion.

Critical path charts illustrate the activities of a project by mapping tasks and their durations, dependencies, and milestones. By combining the task information with scheduling data for earliest and latest start and end times, the critical path or minimum amount of time needed for a project becomes visible. PERT charts, which were developed by the U.S. Navy to plan large, complicated projects that contain lots of uncertainty, resemble critical path diagrams but lack the calculation of start/end dates.

Flowcharts illustrate the steps involved in a process. The three main elements of flowcharts are rectangles (activities), diamonds (decisions), and the flow lines that connect them. At decision points, the process branches to describe the possible outcomes. Other symbols include parallelograms to indicate data needed for the process to continue and ovals to mark the beginning and end of the process. Swim lane charts are a variation of flowcharts that organize the tasks or decisions into lanes that represent the person or group responsible for activities within the process. By including these responsibilities, the swim lane chart can identify areas within an organization where delays, problems, or errors occur.

Fishbone charts (or Ishikawa diagrams) illustrate factors that lead to problems in a system. The name refers to the shape of the chart, which resembles the spine, ribs, and head of a fish. A horizontal line divides the page, with the problem (or effect) placed at the right end. The causes and contributing factors splay out from the spine. Fishbone charts are commonly used in troubleshooting and brainstorming.

Successful charts follow conventions about their use and design. Through experience or training, your audiences will have learned how to interpret the graphic, so do not confuse them by violating their expectations. If you are using a chart that audiences may not have encountered before, explain how to read it and summarize the main idea in your text.[17]

CRITICAL THINKING QUESTIONS

1. What types of charts are commonly used in your discipline?

2. Think about bad charts that you have encountered at work, at school, or in other areas of your life. What factors made them difficult to understand?

Creating Ethical Data Displays

Tell a story with your data. A popular saying is "data speak for themselves," but that's not true. Data are shaped by the person who is using them. Choices like the type of chart, the colors used, and the depth (or shallowness) of the data being used will determine what audiences will see and how they interpret it. For example, spreadsheet software can create quick charts, but it is up to the writer to organize the data it uses. In a bar chart, should the largest data point be at the top or the bottom? Flowcharts map out a process, but how much precision is needed to describe the steps? These types of decisions mean you are truly a writer, not just someone reporting facts and figures.

Sort your data to focus on your story. Some common methods of organizing data are by chronology, size, category, or alphabet. Of these choices, alphabetical order is often the least effective. Sort data by alphabet only when the names of the person, object, or organization are the focus of your story. Otherwise, let the data help you choose the order. Is timing the important factor? Organize chronologically to show how past performance led to the current state or to compare data at intervals. Do you need to focus on quantity, such as highest sales, lowest errors, or meeting quotas? Organize your data by size and develop the chart from there (see Figure 6-8). Do you want to compare groups within the data, such as department, age groups, or service providers? Create categories that make the grouping easy to understand.

Be accurate in how you represent the data visually. Inaccurate data displays deceive audiences, particularly those who may not examine charts closely. For example, Figure 6-9 shows two column charts using the same data. At first glance, the chart on the top suggests that there are significantly more women than men enrolled in the training program. But look closer and you will see that the chart has an elevated zero-point. The rationale may have been innocent, saving space by removing the area the two bars have in common. By returning the zero-point, the bottom chart shows that the two groups are nearly the same size. The actual difference—which would be evident in a table—is 1,000 students, or about 7 percent of the total population. To emphasize their similarity and increase

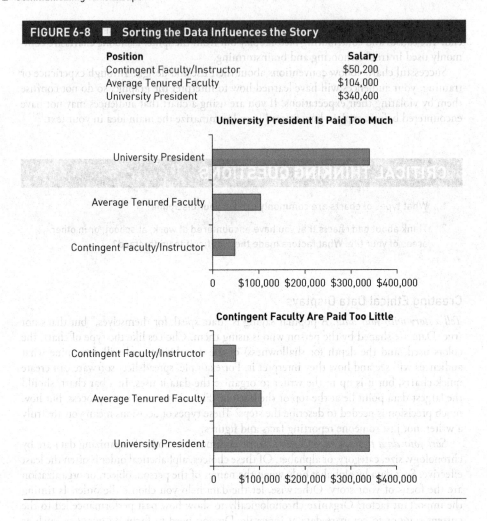

FIGURE 6-8 ■ Sorting the Data Influences the Story

Position	Salary
Contingent Faculty/Instructor	$50,200
Average Tenured Faculty	$104,000
University President	$340,600

University President Is Paid Too Much

Contingent Faculty Are Paid Too Little

specificity, data labels could be added to each column to show their percentages of the total enrollment.

A similar deception occurs when the scale for the axis changes, which may make values seem more similar than they really are. In Figure 6-10, data from two colleges were compared to understand faculty participation in an extracurricular event. Does it look like the faculty in the human performance department had the highest participation? Or was it the English department? Problems with the axes, including the discrepancy shown here, can be introduced by spreadsheet software, so inspect your charts carefully and edit as needed before including them in your documents.

Deception can also be intentional. Some writers may choose data that tell only the story they want audiences to know. For example, a line chart of new housing construction for the last 5 years would be drastically different from one showing 15 years of data. Election results in urban areas are often quite different from those in rural areas, so showing only

FIGURE 6-9 ■ Elevated Zero-Points Distort the Difference in the Data Set

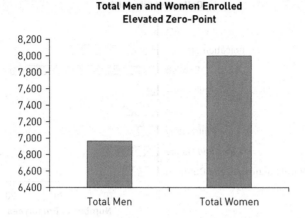

**Total Men and Women Enrolled
Elevated Zero-Point**

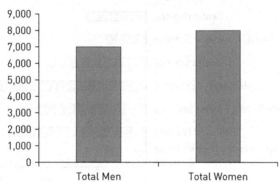

**Total Men and Women Enrolled
Axis Starting at Zero**

state totals rather than totals for individual precincts (usually illustrated with a chart called a heat map) can hide these ideological differences. The chart type can also create deception. When a sample size is small, it can be tempting to display the data as a pie chart to suggest greater significance than the numbers warrant.

Be clear and concise in your table and chart design. Clarity is an essential quality of data displays because it ensures that audiences will be able to comprehend the data.[18] Edward Tufte, a guru of information design, says that minimalism and clarity work together to help audiences understand data displays: "Graphical excellence is that which gives to the viewer the greatest number of ideas in the shortest time with the least ink in the smallest space."[19] Tufte coined the terms *data-ink* and *chartjunk* to describe two common problems with quantitative charts. Data-ink refers to the parts of the graph that represent data; everything else—gridlines, borders, background shading, textures—is non-data-ink. Chartjunk refers to elements that do not help audiences comprehend the data. Three-dimensional designs,

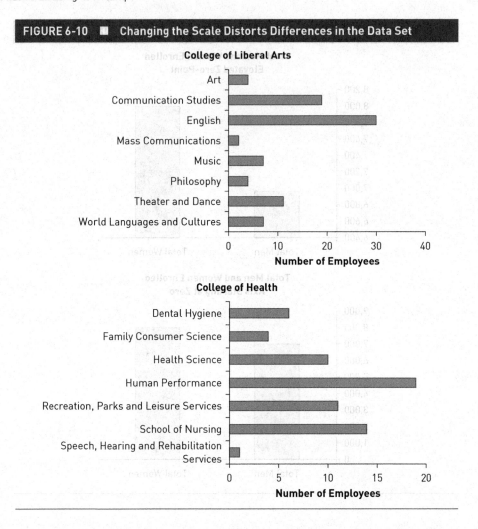

FIGURE 6-10 ■ Changing the Scale Distorts Differences in the Data Set

using graphics to fill bars or sectors, distracting patterns, and decorative graphics are all examples of chartjunk (see Figure 6-11). Simplify the design of your charts to maximize the data-ink. For example, if you add data labels to a bar chart, you can eliminate the gridlines and the *y*-axis. By removing a shaded background, you improve the figure-ground contrast. By using color sparingly, you create emphasis.

Humanize the data when possible. Abstractions like tables and charts suggest a detachment or neutrality by focusing on numbers, but they hide the human stories that often lie beneath them.[20] For example, charts about life expectancy, such as the stem and leaf chart in Figure 6-7, show that women typically live longer than men in countries with the highest GDP, and both sexes live longer in Japan than in any other country. But why? What factors might lengthen or shorten life expectancy in otherwise wealthy countries? Charts describing "displaced persons" tend to focus on migration patterns and numbers, sanitizing the misery of the refugees out of the story. If appropriate for your audience and context,

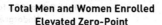

FIGURE 6-11 ■ Chartjunk Impedes Our Ability to Interpret the Data

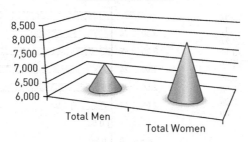

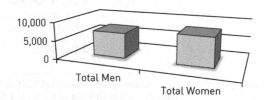

consider humanizing charts with explanations through callouts, sidebars, or narrative in the body text. Icons or illustrations can complement text and charts, but use simple images and avoid cartoon-like clip art that may trivialize the subject matter.

Finally, consider that your story may not need a chart at all. Figure 6-12 shows four ways to report a university's institutional data about the high school grade point average (GPA) for its incoming class of students. The table shows specific values, which could be useful to administrators who must report student demographics for accreditation or other assessment materials. The data are sorted categorically by GPA rank (3.75 and above, 3.5 to 3.74, and so on). Adding a line in the table helps audiences find the groups of students who earned GPAs of 3.0 or higher, suggesting that this difference is part of the story. But does the table help the administrators talk about the new students with faculty, staff, or other stakeholders?

Because the data are presented as fractions of the incoming class, it is tempting to create a pie chart. But other than suggesting that the sizes of the categories are roughly equivalent (most of them, at least), what other information does the pie chart tell you? Can you make decisions or understand patterns based on the pie chart? For example, can you estimate the percentage of students who have a 3.5 or higher GPA using this chart? As you try, notice the extra work the writer has given you by placing the series labels in a legend rather than on the chart itself and leaving the data labels out entirely. The pie chart is less informative than the table.

FIGURE 6-12 ■ Tell a Compelling Data Story With or Without Tables and Charts

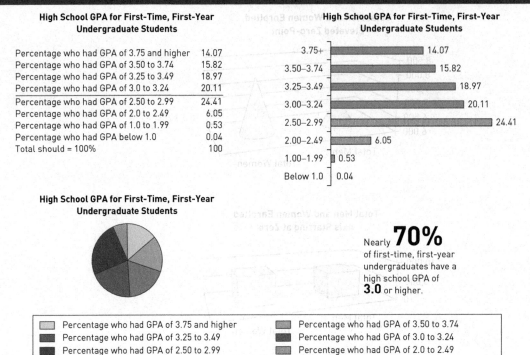

High School GPA for First-Time, First-Year
Undergraduate Students

Percentage who had GPA of 3.75 and higher	14.07
Percentage who had GPA of 3.50 to 3.74	15.82
Percentage who had GPA of 3.25 to 3.49	18.97
Percentage who had GPA of 3.0 to 3.24	20.11
Percentage who had GPA of 2.50 to 2.99	24.41
Percentage who had GPA of 2.0 to 2.49	6.05
Percentage who had GPA of 1.0 to 1.99	0.53
Percentage who had GPA below 1.0	0.04
Total should = 100%	100

High School GPA for First-Time, First-Year
Undergraduate Students

GPA	Percentage
3.75+	14.07
3.50–3.74	15.82
3.25–3.49	18.97
3.00–3.24	20.11
2.50–2.99	24.41
2.00–2.49	6.05
1.00–1.99	0.53
Below 1.0	0.04

High School GPA for First-Time, First-Year
Undergraduate Students

Nearly **70%** of first-time, first-year undergraduates have a high school GPA of **3.0** or higher.

- Percentage who had GPA of 3.75 and higher
- Percentage who had GPA of 3.50 to 3.74
- Percentage who had GPA of 3.25 to 3.49
- Percentage who had GPA of 3.0 to 3.24
- Percentage who had GPA of 2.50 to 2.99
- Percentage who had GPA of 2.0 to 2.49
- Percentage who had GPA of 1.0 to 1.99
- Percentage who had GPA below 1.0

The bar chart makes the sizes of the GPA ranks easier to compare. To minimize the design elements and improve clarity, the gridlines and *y*-axis were removed and the values were added as data labels. We can now see that most of the students had at least a 2.5 GPA, and the size of each rank decreases as the GPA increases. These factors suggest that a normal distribution may exist in the high school population, which was not evident in the table, but why do the numbers drop off precipitously? Why is the university admitting students with low GPAs? Are these questions the narrative, or a distraction from it?

The fourth display removes all doubt. By removing all the other data and using the design principle of contrast in size and type style to emphasize the numbers, the sentence demands your attention and tells the story the writer wants you to remember.

Illustrations

Illustrations show what something looks like. They can help audiences recognize an object or envision the internal components that are usually hidden from view. Unlike tables and charts, illustrations like photographs, line art, and pictographs (or icons) may be used either to represent information or to decorate your website, slide, or promotional material.

Photographs

Photographs are realistic images of physical objects and people, providing visual proof of their appearance. They can also add interest and emotion to otherwise bland documents. Professional photographers use composition techniques to arrange the people or objects in an imaginary frame, creating focal points or areas of emphasis. If you are not using a professional photographer, you can use some of their strategies to take photos for your presentations, reports, or social media.[21]

The rule of thirds is an imaginary 3 × 3 grid within your frame (see Figure 6-13). Photographers recommend placing the most important elements of the photo at the intersections of the cells. Positioning your photo using the rule of thirds usually creates a sense of balance in the image, particularly if you use the rows or columns of the grid to contrast elements in the frame, like sea and sky or natural and human-made objects.

Leading lines within the frame draw the eye toward objects in the foreground or background. Look for naturally occurring lines, such as railroad tracks, table edges, telephone poles, and buildings, to frame your subject. Keep natural lines like the horizon level because that's what people expect to see. (As a last resort, you can also use a photo-editing program to rotate the image later.) When your photo includes people, pay attention to where their eyes are looking. Our brains are wired to notice other humans, so when there are people in a photograph, our eyes turn to them first, before taking in the rest of the scene. And when we see the people in the photograph looking at something, curiosity makes our eyes turn in

FIGURE 6-13 ■ Use the Rule of Thirds to Create Balance and Focal Points in Photographs

Source: Photograph by Jennifer Veltsos, 2011.

that direction, too. Eye lines are the implied leading lines that direct our attention to other parts of the image. To use eye lines to your advantage, place headlines or textboxes in the eye line (see Figure 6-14).

While framing your shot, take a moment to consider the background as well as the focal point of the image. A great shot can be ruined when it lacks sufficient contrast, when it is cluttered, or when something in the background competes for the viewer's attention. When photographing products for sale or promotion, place them on a simple background and light them well from all directions to remove shadows. Position your camera directly above or in front of the object for a clear, accurate view. If the product's shape varies, take multiple perspectives using the same lighting and distance.

Zooming adjusts the length of the lens to focus on objects that are far away from the camera. It can be tempting to zoom in close to your object to eliminate unwanted elements of the scene, but digital cameras use a digital zoom technique that can cause pixelation. (SLR cameras use special lenses to zoom, so the problem is not as pronounced.) Whenever possible, move closer to the subject of the photo rather than using the zoom feature. When you cannot get close, take a photo and crop it later. Cropping removes undesirable portions of the photograph, leaving only the main subject. Given that

---

FIGURE 6-14 ■ Use Leading Lines to Find the Focal Point and Insert Text in Photographs

Eye lines and leading lines suggest optimal placement for text and information.

Strong contrast between the background and the typeface makes the text readable.

Source: © Pexels.com/Donald Tong.

cropping reduces the size of your image, use a high-resolution setting for the original photos. When resizing photos to fit into a layout, control the aspect ratio to avoid distortions in height or width.

Screen captures are photographs of the user interface of electronic devices. Use these composition tips to mark the edges of your screen capture tool or to crop the image to minimize extraneous information.

Line Art

Line art consists of two-dimensional images that represent two- or three-dimensional objects using straight lines, curved lines, and little or no shading. Line art, which may be hand drawn or created using drawing software, allows you to reduce the image to only its most essential features. Photographs are superior when you need a realistic image, but sometimes they contain more details than necessary. Furthermore, photographs can show only what the human eye can see. When you need to focus on parts of an object, expose its internal workings, or show abstract concepts, line art is the solution. Exploded-view diagrams show how components fit together by disassembling an object and aligning the pieces on a diagonal plane. Cutaway diagrams "remove" part of the surface of an object to reveal what lies underneath.

Maps illustrate physical spaces. Geographic maps show land features, like lakes, mountains, cities, and roads. They are usually drawn to scale and use compass directions to indicate orientation. Although many maps are oriented with north at the top of the page, not all follow this convention. Look for a compass rose to help you understand how the directions are arranged. Audiences expect maps to accurately reflect reality, but that is not always the case. Some of the decisions that cartographers or artists make can cause distortions, such as omitting elements, emphasizing others, or changing features. The London Underground map, for example, suggests that the train lines follow straight lines with smooth turns and have stops at nearly regular intervals. In reality, the shape of the rail lines (and the River Thames that runs through the middle of the city) is irregular, and the distances between stations can be misleading.[22]

Pictographs are illustrations that represent real objects, abstract ideas, or processes. Icons resemble the object they represent, like a drawing of a chair. Symbols, on the other hand, are arbitrary or habitual connections between the picture and what it represents. The question mark symbol is often used to represent a question or a place to ask for information. The floppy disk icon continues to signal the command to save a file to a computer hard drive, long after floppy disk drives have fallen from use. Symbols can be powerful ways to communicate with diverse audiences, but it is dangerous to assume that they have the same meaning for all people.[23] Test your documents with users to ensure that the meaning you intend is the one other people are likely to understand.

DESIGNING GRAPHICS FOR ACCESSIBILITY

Some members of your audience may have visual or other impairments that require them to use a screen reader. Designing graphics for accessibility will make it easier for the software to interpret their contents for users. Accessible graphics are useful for everyone, so the guidelines below should become part of your document design repertoire:

- To help audiences using screen-reader software prepare for the explanation they are about to hear, number all figures and write a caption that includes a title and a brief description of the image content.[24] (The caption can also help you create lists of tables and figures in formal reports.)

- In webpages and electronic files, add "alt text" that describes the graphic.[25]
  a. For tables, describe the number of rows and columns and the contents of each.
  b. For charts, describe categories of data and their relative size or shape.
  c. For illustrations, describe the main components and how they fit together. Move left to right, or start at the top of the image and move clockwise around the image.
  d. For photographs, describe the foreground, background, colors, and the orientation of the main components.

- If an illustration is decorative, indicate that in the alt text.

Tables

- If a table spans multiple pages, repeat the column labels on each new page so that audiences do not have to flip pages to understand what the numbers mean. Use the table-formatting options in your word processor or presentation software to turn on the "repeat row headers" feature.[26]

- If your table spans multiple pages, do not allow rows to split across pages. Check the table-formatting options to ensure that the option to "allow row to break across pages" is turned off.

- Do not use tabs, line breaks, or blank rows to create negative space, because screen-reader software will read each one to the user. Instead, adjust the cell padding or margins. To separate groups in the table, manually adjust the height of individual rows to create the extra space you need.

- If you have a simple data set of a few rows and columns, consider avoiding the table altogether and using tab stops to align text instead. (Do not use the spacebar, though. Tabs create alignment using the ruler, which is particularly helpful if you change your typeface style or size later.) Create tab stops in the paragraph formatting option.

- Do not use a table to format a text document into two or more columns. Use the columns feature in your word processor instead.

Charts

Charts present two special challenges for audiences with visual impairments. Screen-reading software cannot interpret charts, which could limit their usefulness. Many charts rely primarily on colors to differentiate categories (bars, lines, sectors). Although colors are easy for many audiences to see, nearly 8 percent of men and 0.5 percent of women are color blind or limited in their ability to differentiate colors.[27] Red-green color blindness is the most common; blue-yellow and total color blindness are rarer. There is a good chance that members of your audience have excellent vision but have color impairments and may struggle to read your chart.

- Supplement the chart with text that summarizes the data. If you know that some people will be using screen readers or other assistance to read the document, consider replacing the chart with a table.[28]

- Use data labels within the chart to identify lines, bars, or sectors directly rather than requiring audiences to repeatedly refer to a legend.

- When choosing color palettes, avoid the following combinations.[29] If your chart does use these colors within a larger palette, do not place lines, bars, sectors, or other shapes using these colors adjacent to each other:
  - Red and green
  - Green and brown
  - Green and gray
  - Green and black
  - Green and blue
  - Blue and purple
  - Blue and gray
  - Light green and yellow

- Limit your color palette to three to four colors with good contrast. Audiences with color impairments can usually differentiate colors by their brightness. If you are using a monochromatic scheme, choose two to three shades with strong contrast to each other. Print a copy in black and white to evaluate the contrast between shades in your palette.[30]

- Do not rely only on color to signal differences in charts. Encode the data using two signals, such as color, subtle texture, shape (pictograms or icons), labels, or callouts. In line charts, use line patterns or icons to differentiate the lines.[31]

- If the chart represents a process or procedure, re-create it as an outline.

COPYRIGHT CONSIDERATIONS FOR GRAPHICS

When writing text, you know that you must cite the sources of any outside information that you use. (Outside information, often called secondary research, is any text that you did not write yourself or data that you did not collect and analyze yourself.) Citations are both a sign of respect to the original author (and to your audiences) and a way of acknowledging copyright. According to U.S. copyright law, works of art and authorship are protected by copyright as soon as they are "fixed in a tangible medium of expression."[32] For our purposes, that means when you save a file to your computer's hard drive, take a photograph with a digital or film camera, or put pen or pencil to paper to sketch a diagram or illustration.

The principle of fair use allows small excerpts of material to be used for the purposes of criticism, news reporting, teaching, research, or parody. If the use of a work is challenged by the copyright holder, courts will look at four factors to determine if infringement has occurred:

How is the item being used? Educational or nonprofit uses are more likely to be protected by fair use than commercial ones.

What is the nature of the copyrighted work? Creative or imaginative works (such as a novel, movie, or song) and unpublished works are more likely to be protected than factual works (such as a technical article or news item).

How much of the item is being used? In general, small portions of a work are more likely to be considered fair use than large ones, but courts look at the unique circumstances to determine fair use. However, if the original the selection is considered the "heart" of a copyrighted work, any use might be a violation.

What is the effect of the use on the potential market for the item? If the use is likely to harm the potential use or sale of the original item by the person who created it, it is unlikely to be considered a fair use.

The determination of a fair use is based on all four factors. As a student, you might find a graphic online that seems like a perfect fit for a course assignment. In many cases, this type of use fits into the fair use doctrine. When you are creating documents at work, though, fair use is less likely to apply, particularly if the documents will be used for commercial purposes, like advertising on a website or in social media. For a complete explanation, visit the U.S. Copyright Office website (www.copyright.gov).

The safest course of action is to create your own graphics, photos, charts, and other graphical elements. If you cannot create them, you may be able to find items licensed under a Creative Commons license that permits use by others.[33] You can also purchase graphics from design bureaus like Getty Images or The Noun Project. Even when you purchase an image, there are often conditions of use that limit how or where you may use the image. For example, you may not be able to use images of people in ways that suggest they endorse specific products. And you will probably have to include a source line that identifies the copyright holder in a caption or a credits page, which is similar to the list of references that you compile for text sources.

SUMMARY

Visual communication helps audiences focus their attention; understand the organization and relationships of components or data; and understand concepts, take action, or make decisions. When used well, visual elements also give documents a professional polish and enhance the persuasiveness of your message. The design principles for managerial communication are guidelines that can help you make decisions about the visual components rather than relying on the default settings and styles in software. The grid and alignment create the page layout into which you insert text, graphics, and data displays. Typography and color help audiences focus on ideas and set a tone that should reinforce your content. Following conventions helps you give audiences what they expect to see. Once these building blocks are in place, you can use similarity and proximity to show relationships and create emphasis with contrast, hierarchy, and negative space. Repetition and consistency create a coherent look and feel that unifies the entire document or presentation.

When audiences need more than text to understand information or data, graphics help them envision the message. Tables list data for precision, and charts summarize data to show patterns or make comparisons. Conceptual charts record systems and processes, which can be useful for understanding how things work together. Line art depicts physical objects, but it can also decorate documents and set the stage for explanations or ideas.

As you work, think about the audience who will read your document or watch your presentation. Who will use it? Where will they be? What experiences or cultural values might affect how they interpret your work? Look for examples of similar materials within your organization to understand the expectations that internal and external audiences might have regarding color, typography, layout, negative space, and the choice of graphical elements (and indeed, the decision to include them in the first place). Look for your organization's style guide to help you make design decisions. And above all, make choices that help audiences locate and understand the information you are sharing with them.

CASES FOR ANALYSIS

Case 6-1

Georgia Chart Misleads the Public

An important part of public health information is tracking infection rates and sharing that information with the public to warn them about dangers and risky behavior. In 2020, during the COVID-19 pandemic, daily news cycles were dominated by data about infections, hospitalizations, and deaths caused by the virus. Amid exhortations to "flatten the curve," the world watched anxiously as the World Health Organization tracked more than 26 million confirmed cases and nearly 865,000 deaths around the world by early September.[34]

In the United States, departments of health in each state were responsible for reporting information that would help governments make policy decisions about health and safety, which often meant "stay-at-home" orders that lasted several weeks or even months. Some states took a conservative

approach, trying to slow the transmission of the virus while building up medical infrastructure and purchasing personal protective equipment. Others opened quickly, believing that the risk was manageable.

Georgia was one of the first states to lift stay-at-home orders. But officials were criticized for their data-collection procedures, and they often struggled to communicate clearly with the public. In late May 2020, the Georgia Department of Health released a column chart that suggested infection rates were declining (see the figure). But observers noticed that the x-axis of the chart was not in chronological order. After critics suggested it was an attempt to mislead the public, the graphic was replaced. "Our mission failed. We apologize. It is fixed," tweeted Candice Broce, a spokeswoman for the governor.[35]

Questions

1. What was the likely cause of the misleading graph?

(Continued)

[Continued]

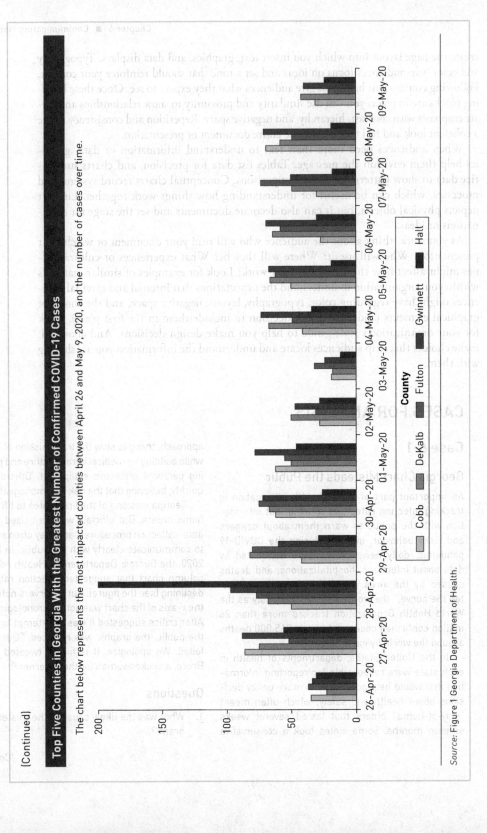

Top Five Counties in Georgia With the Greatest Number of Confirmed COVID-19 Cases

The chart below represents the most impacted counties between April 26 and May 9, 2020, and the number of cases over time.

Source: Figure 1 Georgia Department of Health.

2. What story was the Georgia Department of Health trying to tell readers? What message did the graphic actually tell?

3. Analyze the graph using the advice presented in this chapter. In addition to correcting the x-axis, what other changes would make it more usable?

4. What other misleading or hard-to-read graphs have you seen? Consider the source and the story being told. What caused the problem? How could it be remedied?

Case 6-2

Cleaning Up a Cluttered Slide

The founders of Quantum Clothing were preparing their second annual report for their start-up investors. Like many small businesses, the owners had multiple roles in the company. Trained in apparel design and fashion merchandising, Becca Ridley and Andi Crawford felt somewhat comfortable managing the budget, negotiating with vendors, and working with a marketing agency to promote their collections. Years of presentations in classes and student organizations had prepared them for public speaking. But neither woman felt confident as a writer, so they approached the annual report with trepidation. In particular, they worried that their slides weren't as effective as some of their competitors, but they could not quite explain why.

Analyze the following slide using the design principles for managerial communication and offer suggestions for improvement.

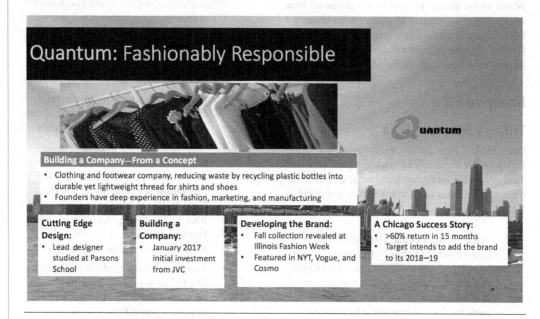

Image credits: Clothing, FreeImages.com/Marcos Oliveira; background, Jennifer Veltsos.

EXERCISES

Exercise 6-1

Identifying the Design Principles for Managerial Communication

A style sheet is a combination of formatting characteristics, such as typefaces, colors, sizes, and layouts, that creates a standardized look. In web design, cascading style sheets—or CSS—modify the look and feel of a webpage while leaving the content unchanged. The website CSS Zen Garden (http://www.csszengarden.com) demonstrates how a CSS works by allowing users to manipulate the site's appearance with a single click.

For our purposes, CSS Zen Garden offers an opportunity to witness the design principles for managerial communication in action. Select two templates and compare their design elements. Which of the design principles are present? How are they used to suggest a mood and create unity? What kinds of businesses would be appropriate for the designs you chose? What kinds of businesses would be inappropriate for the designs?

Exercise 6-2

Telling a Story With Data

Data displays help audiences understand a situation or make decisions by organizing data into an easily readable form. Tables, charts, and illustrations can help you tell a story that is grounded in facts.

1. The Bureau of Labor Statistics of the U.S. Department of Labor (http://www.bls.gov) is a federal agency that collects, analyzes, and disseminates data about employment and the economy in the United States. Look for the most recent information about occupational employment and wages for three cities in your state or for three cities where you would like to live in the future. Create a chart that compares the employment rate for the following industries:

- Architecture and engineering
- Business and financial operations
- Computers and mathematics
- Food preparation and serving related
- Healthcare practitioners
- Legal
- Management
- Office and administrative support
- Sales and related

2. The CIA's *World Factbook* presents an array of international data about people, government, economy, geography, communications, transportation, military, and transnational issues around the world. Use data from the *World Factbook* (https://www.cia.gov/library/publications/the-world-factbook/index.html) to create graphics that answer the following questions:

- Where are the 10 countries with the highest median age?
- What are the energy production and consumption of the 10 largest countries by geographic areas and by population?
- What are the GDP (purchasing power parity) and taxes and other income as a percentage of GDP for the following countries: Belgium, Canada, Denmark, France, Iceland, Italy, Luxembourg, the Netherlands, Norway, Portugal, the United Kingdom, and the United States?
- Select a country in which you would like to live one day or one that is home to a client or business partner of your organization. How does that country compare to the United States on at least two of the following factors? Choose from people, government, economy, geography, communications, transportation, military, or transnational issues.

Notes

1. Robert E. Horn, *Visual Language: Global Communication for the 21st Century* (Bainbridge Island, WA: Macro-Vu, 1988).

2. Miles A. Kimball, "Visual Design Principles: An Empirical Study of Design Lore," *Journal of Technical Writing and Communication* 43, no. 1 (2013): 3–41, doi: 10.2190/TW.43.1.b.

3. Rachel Bonness, "A History of Typography," DesignBySoap.com, https://www.designbysoap.co.uk/a-history-of-typography-infographic.

4. Jo Mackiewicz and Ryan Moeller, "Why People Perceive Typefaces to Have Personalities" (paper presented at the International Professional Communication Conference, January 2004), *IPCC 2004 Proceedings*, doi: 10.1109/IPCC.2004.1375315.

5. Eva R. Brumberger, "The Rhetoric of Typography: The Awareness and Impact of Typeface Appropriateness," *Technical Communication* 50, no. 2 (2003): 224–31.

6. Wouter A. Alberts and Thea M. van der Geest, "Color Matters: Color as Trustworthiness Cue in Web Sites," *Technical Communication*, 58, no. 2 (2011): 149–60.

7. Paul A. Bottomly and John R. Doyle, "The Interactive Effects of Color and Products on Perceptions of Brand Logo Appropriateness," *Marketing Theory* 6, no. 1 (2007): 63–83.

8. "Basic Color Schemes—Intro to Color Theory," TigerColor.com, http://www.tigercolor.com/color-lab/color-theory/color-theory-intro.htm.

9. Charles Kostelnick, "Social and Cultural Aspects of Visual Conventions in Information Design: The Rhetoric of Hierarchy," in *Information Design: Research and Practice*, eds. Alison Black et al. (Abingdon, Oxon, UK: Routledge, 2017), 257–74.

10. Claudia Cortes, "Color in Motion," http://www.mariaclaudiacortes.com/colors/colors.html.

11. Charles Kostelnick and Michael Hassert, *Shaping Information: The Rhetoric of Visual Conventions* (Carbondale: Southern Illinois University Press, 2003).

12. Robin Williams, *The Non-Designer's Design & Type Books, Deluxe Edition* (Berkeley, CA: Peachpit Press, 2008), 13.

13. Christina Rosenquist, "Visual Form, Ethics, and a Typology of Purpose: Teaching Effective Information Design," *Business Communication Quarterly* 75, no. 1 (2012): 45–60, doi: 10.1177/1080569911428670.

14. Karen Schriver, *Dynamics in Document Design: Creating Texts for Readers* (New York: John Wiley & Sons, 1997).

15. Stephen Few, *Show Me the Numbers: Designing Tables and Graphs to Enlighten,* 2nd ed. (Burlingame, CA: Analytics Press, 2012), 10.

16. Walter Hickey, "Pie Charts Are the Worst," *Business Insider,* June 17, 2013, http://www.businessinsider.com/pie-charts-are-the-worst-2013-6.

17. European Environment Agency, "Chart Dos and Don'ts," March 21, 2016, https://www.eea.europa.eu/data-and-maps/daviz/learn-more/chart-dos-and-donts.

18. Charles Kostelnick, "The Visual Rhetoric of Data Displays: The Conundrum of Clarity," *IEEE Transactions on Professional Communication* 50, no. 4 (2007): 280–94, doi: 10.1109/TPC.2007.914869.

19. Edward Tufte, *The Visual Display of Quantitative Information* (Cheshire, CT: Graphics Press, 2001).

20. Sam Dragga and Dan Voss, "Cruel Pies: The Inhumanity of Technical Illustrations," *Technical Communication* 48, no. 3 (2001): 265–74.

21. Digital Camera Magazine, "The 10 Rules of Photo Composition (and Why They Work),"

TechRadar, March 10, 2017, http://www.techra dar.com/how-to/photography-video-capture/ cameras/10-rules-of-photo-composition-and-why-they-work-1320770.

22. Johndan Johnson-Eiola, "Maps, Reality, and Purpose," *Work/Space* (blog), April 25, 2007, http://people.clarkson.edu/~jjohnson//work space/2007/04/maps_reality_and_purpose .html; and Simon Rumble, "Daily Use," comment on EdwardTufte.com, accessed July 6, 2017, https://www.edwardtufte.com/bboard/q-and-a-fetch-msg?msg_id=00005W&topic_ id=1.

23. Wendy Winn, "Increasing Accessibility With a Visual Sign System: A Case Study," *Journal of Technical Writing and Communication* 44, no. 4 (2014): 451–73.

24. "Best Practices for Designing Accessible Views," Tableau.com, https://onlinehelp.tab leau.com/current/pro/desktop/en-us/accessi bility_best_practice.html.

25. "Image Description Guidelines," Diagram Center, http://diagramcenter.org/table-of-contents-2.html.

26. Karen McCall, "Accessible Word Document Design: Tables and Columns," Karlen Communications, 2015, http://www.karlencommunications .com/adobe/TablesAndColumnsOptimizeWord Documents.pdf.

27. National Institutes of Health, National Eye Institute, "Color Blindness," July 3, 2019, https://nei.nih.gov/health/color_blindness/ facts_about.

28. Accessibility and Usability at Penn State, "Charts and Accessibility," http://accessibility .psu.edu/images/charts.

29. Robyn Collinge, "How to Design for Color Blindness, *Usabilla* (blog), January 17, 2017, http://blog.usabilla.com/how-to-design-for-color-blindness.

30. Joshua Johnson, "Tips for Designing for Color-blind Users," *Design Shack*, July 28, 2010, https://designshack.net/articles/accessibility/ tips-for-designing-for-colorblind-users.

31. Accessibility and Usability at Penn State, "Charts and Accessibility."

32. Copyright Law of the United States, 17 U.S.C. § 101, https://www.copyright.gov/ title17/92chap1.html.

33. Curtis Newbold, "You Can Use a Picture If: Guidelines for Image Copyrights," *The Visual Communication Guy* (blog), March 24, 2016, http://thevisualcommunicationguy .com/2016/03/24/you-can-use-a-picture-if-guidelines-for-image-copyrights.

34. World Health Organization, "WHO Coronavirus Disease (COVID-19) Dashboard," accessed September 4, 2020, https://covid19.who.int.

35. Willoughby Mariano and J. Scott Trubey, "'It's Just Cuckoo': State's Latest Data Mishap Causes Critics to Cry Foul," *The Atlanta Journal-Constitution*, May 13, 2020, https://www.ajc .com/news/state--regional-govt--politics/ just-cuckoo-state-latest-data-mishap -causes-critics-cry-foul.

WRITING AS A MANAGER

7

WRITING IN THE WORKPLACE

Conventional wisdom says that managers spend about 80 percent of their time communicating, and the higher managers go in their organizations, the more time they spend communicating. A recent study found that managers spend 25 hours per week reading and another 20 hours per week writing.[1] While much of this communication involves oral, face-to-face interaction, some requires writing e-mails, memos, letters, and reports. All have the potential to play a critical part in the success of the manager and the organization.

Given the time and effort required to put things in writing, readers may wonder why managers would prefer to write a message rather than communicate it orally. Written managerial communication offers several strategic advantages: economy, efficiency, accuracy, and official permanence.

Writing is usually more economical than long-distance phone calls and much more economical than long-distance travel. Writing is efficient because the manager can work independently and use words selectively. The manager can write the message whether or not the receiver is immediately available to receive it, and receivers can read messages at their convenience. Thus, writing avoids the time wasted in telephone tag.

Accuracy is another advantage of writing. Managers have greater control of words and message organization in writing than in oral communication. Accuracy, in turn, often eliminates confusion, ensures clarity, and further contributes to economy and efficiency.

Finally, writing provides an official record that can be retained for recall and review. In our increasingly litigious society, the importance of documentation cannot be overstressed. Managers must understand that all documents generated by their organization are "discoverable." Attorneys can compel their disclosure as part of pretrial procedures. This fact implies that all official records must be accurate and clear—able to stand up to scrutiny. The difference between a legal judgment for or against organizations and their managers is becoming more often a matter of adequate documentation.

Once a manager has decided to capitalize on the benefits of writing as a communication channel, they should consider the unique characteristics of managerial writing.

THE UNIQUE ROLE OF MANAGERIAL WRITING

In recent years, the various fields addressing composition have given much attention to discourse communities. A *discourse community* is a group of people with similar expertise who share values and goals, who agree on what makes up legitimate knowledge, and who communicate with each other, often using specialized language and document genres.[2] These communities may be large or small. Any organization may contain a number of discourse communities, and any manager may be a member of several internal and external communities.

Managers serve in sufficiently common roles and work in sufficiently common contexts to create a unique discourse community. Managers plan the organization's objectives, organize the functions of the organization, lead people in the accomplishment of those objectives, and control activities to make sure they are proceeding in the right direction.

Equally important in defining the discourse community of managerial writers is the context in which they do their work. Context may be the most powerful variable affecting what writers in organizations do and how these writers perceive, interpret, and value their own activity. The following paragraphs examine several aspects of the unique context in which managerial writing occurs.

One of the most critical aspects of the context of managerial writing is the fragmented nature of a manager's workday. Most people think of managers, especially higher-level executives, as having meticulously organized days overseen and protected by assistants. Henry Mintzberg found the opposite to be true. As he and colleagues recorded the activities of a number of managers, he found their days to be filled with interruptions. On average, they had a full half hour of uninterrupted time only once every 4 days.[3] More recently, Gloria Mark observed employees at two high-tech firms and found that the average worker spends only 11 minutes on any given project before being interrupted. IT workers have it worse, getting interrupted every 3 minutes.[4] Most people faced with a writing task like to go somewhere quiet and work in sizable blocks of time. Such a luxury is rarely available to managers.

CRITICAL THINKING QUESTIONS

1. What are some other discourse communities that you have participated in?

2. What norms of behavior do they use?

3. What knowledge do they value?

Another aspect of the managerial writing context is the extent of collaboration and delegation that occurs. As noted earlier, collaboration is becoming more common in business and requires managers who can work well with others. Additionally, managers have the option of delegating some of their more routine writing chores.[5] This delegation, however, presupposes the manager's knowledge of various employees' abilities and willingness to handle the assignment.

The size and culture of the organization are also important elements of the context of managerial communication. Small companies can communicate many things orally, but the larger a company gets, the greater the need to put things in writing for the record. With size also comes a tendency for greater formality in many written documents. With regard to culture, bureaucracies thrive on formality, while more participative organizations lean toward informality.

Authority and politics play a significant role in the context of managerial writing. Max Weber described three types of authority: traditional, charismatic, and legal.[6] How managers communicate messages is greatly influenced by the type of authority they are perceived to have. Also, business organizations must be viewed as political systems.[7] Managers who forget to consider the political forces at work in the company may soon find they no longer work at the company.

In our increasingly litigious society, and given the ever-increasing role of government in business, legal concerns represent another important element of the managerial writing context. Managers are considered legal agents of the organization in many types of writing they do. They must be conscious of such things as libel, slander, privacy, and equal opportunity.

These elements of a manager's work create a discourse community with a unique writing environment (see Table 7-1). Managers must carefully analyze the organizational culture in which they work, they must find the best time and place to write, and they must always remember that writing has an essential role in their job.

A manager who has committed to using the written communication channel and who has considered the unique characteristics of writing in an organizational environment, as described previously, is now ready to begin the writing process. This process consists of three stages: planning, composing, and revising. If the manager follows this process, the resulting document is more likely to be successful in reaching its goal.

TABLE 7-1 ■ Elements of a Manager's Discourse Community
Fragmented workday
Extensive collaboration
Option to delegate
Organization's size and culture
Lines of authority
Political forces
Legal concerns

STAGE 1: PLANNING

Tim Glowa, cofounder of the marketing analytics firm Bug Insights, wanted to create more effective documents that would improve his professional reputation and generate business, so he studied the organization of reports and other documents that he admired. Today, he begins every memo and report with an outline of three main objectives. "You can't just start typing and expect to go somewhere," he says. "That's like going for a walk and not knowing where the destination is."[8]

The planning process for a managerial writer is a lot like the one a journalist is trained to use. The parallel is logical because both might be characterized as professional writers. Both spend a significant amount of time writing at work, and both write for readers who are in a hurry. Thus, both might be expected to determine the five Ws—what, why, who, when, where—and how. The strategic model in Chapter 2 will help you answer these planning questions.

What Is the Main Idea?

The *what* question deals with the nature of the message. A manager should have a fairly clear idea of what needs to be communicated early in the planning stages. Is certain information needed? Is a request being granted or rejected? Do employees need to know about a policy change? Is cooperation needed to implement certain procedures?

Any time readers see a message that seems to bounce from one side of an issue to another, any time readers are forced to wade through a message that rambles on endlessly and incoherently, or any time readers wonder, "What is this person trying to say?" the chances are good that the writer *did not know* exactly what to say or what the purpose was.

Why Is It Important?

The rationale for the message should be just as clear to the reader as it is to the writer. Unfortunately, many miscommunications occur because the sender does not know why a message is being sent or does not bother to share with the reader the reason for the message.

Many corporate policies, procedures, and rules, for example, are imposed on employees without any accompanying justification. Personnel would probably be much more receptive to these directives if they understood why the directives were necessary. Humans are complex creatures who like to deal with cause and effect. When an effect is imposed and the cause is withheld, one likely result is resistance.

Who Is Affected?

Who will receive the message? What is their relationship to you or the organization? Demographic characteristics, such as age, gender, education, political affiliation, and job title, may provide some indication as to how the reader will interpret a message. Within an organizational setting, however, these characteristics fall short of telling us about the writer–reader relationship and about the characteristics of the organization and the department that may be pertinent to successful message transmission.

To engage in a truly thorough reader analysis and to be fully attuned to the reader's likely reception of a message, a writer should consider the following points:

- The relative power position between the writer and the reader
- The communication requirements the organization exerts on the reader and the writer
- The business functions in which the writer and reader work
- The frequency of communication between the writer and the reader
- The reader's reaction to past messages from the writer
- The relative sensitivity of the message

The time spent on reader analysis may vary with the relative importance of the message. For very important messages, a writer may scrutinize all the information available to determine the best wording, the most appropriate organization, the right medium, the best timing, and the best source and destination for the message. However, even routine messages will improve as a result of audience analysis and adaptation.

When Will the Message Be Delivered?

The timing of the message may be affected by its purpose. Many routine messages, such as sales reports, are distributed periodically. No actual decision has to be made as to when they are sent because dates have already been set. Likewise, trivial information is likely to be received in the same way regardless of timing.

For a nonroutine message, however, the decision on when to send it may directly affect how the message is received. For example, the managers of a textile mill had to tell employees they were not going to get a pay raise, even though the company had shown a profit the preceding quarter. Management chose to convey this message just before the employees went on vacation. Not only did this timing likely ruin the vacations of many employees; it probably encouraged a number of them to spend their vacations looking for another job.

On the subject of timing, managers need to keep in mind that it is possible to send messages too early as well as too late. For example, we noted in Chapter 4 that agendas should be sent to participants 2 or 3 days before a meeting. If the agenda and supporting materials are sent too early, the recipients forget the meeting by the time it is scheduled to occur. But if the material is sent too late, participants might not have time to get fully prepared for the meeting.

Where Does It Take Place?

The *where* question should be addressed at both ends of the communication spectrum: Where should the message come from, and where should it be directed to? Should the message come from a manager at a particular level, or should it come from elsewhere, perhaps to carry the additional weight of authority or to take advantage of positive relationships?

At the other end of the spectrum, we may have to decide where the reader should be while receiving the message. To illustrate, some companies have grappled with the problem of newsletter distribution: whether to send it to employees' homes or distribute it at work. Sending it to the homes might get the families interested, but it might also be viewed as an infringement of employee privacy or personal time.

How Will the Message Be Transmitted?

When managers decide to put a message in writing, they are still faced with a number of written media options: letter, memo, report, e-mail, brochure, newsletter, manual, or even bulletin board. The choice of medium is determined at least in part by how personal the message needs to be, how widespread its distribution will be, and how quickly it needs to reach the audience. Many of these factors were reviewed in Chapter 3.

Additionally, managers should remember a guideline that applies to media selection in general. If a manager regularly uses one particular medium, the choice of a different medium might communicate a sense of urgency or importance. For example, if a manager regularly communicates with employees in person, a memo might suggest something unusual and worthy of extra attention.

Though the preceding planning concerns were discussed separately and in a particular order, they are all interdependent and should not be treated in isolation. The good managerial communicator learns to see the interrelationships and to treat the five Ws and H as a decision package.

CRITICAL THINKING QUESTIONS

Think of a situation other than business writing where planning is the key to success. Try to answer the five Ws and H for that situation. Then decide to what extent going through that process will help you reach your goal.

STAGE 2: COMPOSING

The planning stage helps you analyze the situation and prepare to write. The next stage is to compose a message. Words need to be chosen with care and organized in a clear, comprehensive, and coherent fashion. Follow the guidelines described next when selecting words and composing them into sentences and paragraphs. The result is a document written in contemporary style.

Selecting Words

Words are symbols that define the content of a message. Each word carries the potential for contributing to the effectiveness of the message, and each carries the potential for causing misunderstanding. Thus, words should be carefully selected to ensure message effectiveness and avoid misunderstanding.

The U.S. Congress has recognized the importance of "plain language" in government forms, benefits applications, reports, regulations, and other documents. The Plain Writing Act of 2010 mandates that federal employees be trained to write clear, concise, well-organized documents to the public regarding their benefits or services or regarding filing taxes. Documents include (whether in paper or electronic form) letters, publications, forms, notices, and instructions. More than 22 states now have plain-language statutes on their books, notably New York, Connecticut, Pennsylvania, Florida, Minnesota, California, Oregon, and Washington. The governments of Sweden, the United Kingdom, Australia, and Portugal also have plain-language requirements.

The following principles will help writers accomplish their goals.

Principle 1: Choose Words Precisely

While some business documents (e.g., contracts, job offer letters, performance appraisals) may call for high levels of precision, managers would be wise to exercise care in choosing words in all their writing. And as you strive for this precision, remember that words can have both denotative and connotative meanings.

Denotative meanings are objective; they point to; they describe. Dictionary definitions are considered denotative meanings because these definitions are compiled from the common usages associated with a word. Most people agree on the denotative definitions of terms—that is, they agree as long as there are no words similar in sound or appearance to confuse the issue. For example, can you pick out the correct word in each of the following sentences?

- The advertising agency that we just bought should profitably (complement, compliment) our manufacturing and distribution interests.

- My computer printer has operated (continually, continuously) for the last 5 years.

- The manager assured us that he had (appraised, apprised) his superior of the shipping problem.

- The secretary made an (illusion, allusion) to what had taken place in the cafeteria.

- To persuade upper management to take this action, we will need the testimony of an expert who is completely (uninterested, disinterested).

Along the same lines, consider the following excerpts from letters written to a government agency:

- "I am very much annoyed to find that you have branded my son illiterate. This is a dirty lie as I was married a week before he was born."

- "Unless I get my husband's money pretty soon, I will be forced to lead an immortal life."

In business writing, wrong word choices can produce embarrassing humor at best and considerable confusion at worst. Neither is likely to provide a boost to a manager's career.

Connotative meanings, on the other hand, are subjective. They can be different for different people because they are determined largely by a person's previous experiences or associations with a word and its referent.

Though connotations are subjective, people can manipulate the language to bring forth either positive or negative connotations. An expression with intended positive connotations is called a *euphemism*. The words *slim* and *slender* are much more euphemistic than are words such as *skinny* and *scrawny*.

As advertisers and other interested parties try to portray life in the most pleasant way possible, euphemisms have become a part of life in the United States. However, when euphemisms are used in an effort to veil or gloss over major human and environmental tragedies, we must recognize the language abuse and the feeble cover-up. When *collateral damage* is used to describe the deaths of innocent civilians in war, for example, we must wonder at the value assessed to human lives by the people using these descriptions.

Managers as well as people in other careers bear a responsibility to their audiences to use language as accurately as possible. Managers should strive to communicate precisely and honestly and to avoid insulting the reader's intelligence. Additionally, they should try to act as responsibly as they can in using words as control tools and instruments of change.[9]

Principle 2: Use Short Rather Than Long Words

Winston Churchill once said, "Big men use little words, and little men use big words." People who are genuinely confident in their ideas generally feel quite comfortable using simple words that are easy to understand. Short words are usually less confusing than long words. Long words, especially when strung out with several other long words, can produce a communication barrier between writer and reader.

Written business communications should be economical and efficient. Table 7-2 provides alternatives for some of the many longer words used and abused in business writing.

We are not suggesting that the use of any words in the left-hand column will condemn a message to ambiguity and obscurity. The caution here refers to the unnecessary use of long, difficult words. When overused, they tax a reader's understanding—and patience—and create a barrier to effective communication.

Principle 3: Use Concrete Rather Than Abstract Words

In discussing a topic, a writer can choose from a range of words. This range or continuum might be thought of as a ladder that the writer can climb. This ladder (see Figure 7-1) moves from concrete (specific) words on the lowest rungs to the more abstract (general) words on the highest rungs. Concrete words tend to be specific; they create clear pictures in the reader's mind. Abstract words are vague and produce wider, more general interpretations of meanings.

The level of abstraction or concreteness you should use depends on the reader's background, needs, and expectations. Abstract words and phrases can generate mistrust and confusion. They give rise to questions that the text may or may not answer: When? How many? Who? How much? Which one? Notice the differing amount of information in the pairs of expressions in Table 7-3.

TABLE 7-2 ■ Words to Avoid and Acceptable Alternatives

Instead of Writing This	Try Using This
advise	tell
ameliorate	improve
approbation	approval
commence	begin
demonstrate	show
encounter	meet
expectancy	hope
explicate	explain
locality	place
modification	change
perspicacity	sense
subsequent to	after
terminate	end
usage	use
utilize	use

FIGURE 7-1 ■ Abstraction Ladders

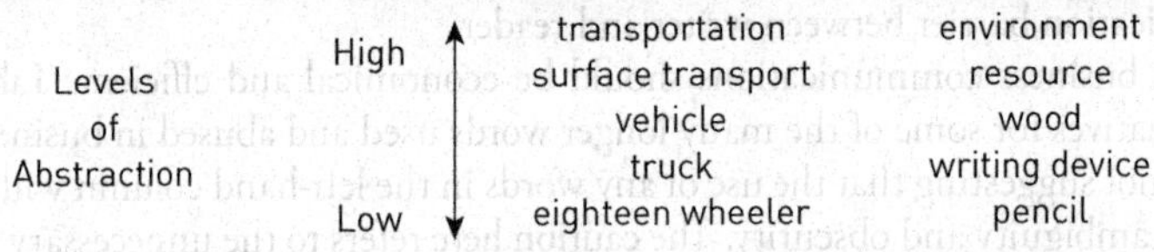

Levels of Abstraction	High ↑ ↓ Low	transportation surface transport vehicle truck eighteen wheeler	environment resource wood writing device pencil

TABLE 7-3 ■ Abstract and Concrete Expressions

Instead of Writing This	Try Using This
a good student	the student earned the highest semester-total grade point in a class of 68 students
in the near future	by Friday, June 19
a significant profit	a 28 percent markup
a noteworthy savings	50 percent off the normal price
at your earliest convenience	by the close of business this Friday

Principle 4: Economize on Words

Concrete words and phrases frequently create sharp, vivid images and stimulate reader interest. Forming concrete phrases may take more time and thought, but such phrases are more efficient and stay with the reader longer than do abstract phrases.[10] Additionally, concrete writing takes less time to read, produces better message comprehension, and is less likely to need rereading than abstract writing.[11]

A practical, bottom-line reason exists to write concisely. Wordiness costs money. Unnecessary words take valuable time to compose and read; they waste paper and resources. Consider the following two versions of a business message:

- Enclosed please find a check in the amount of $82.56. In the event that you find the amount to be neither correct nor valid, subsequent to an examination of your records, please inform us of your findings at your earliest convenience.

- Enclosed is a check for $82.56. If this amount is incorrect, please let us know.

The second version takes 15 words to say the same thing said by the first version in 41 words—a reduction of more than 63 percent.

Why do people in business continue to be wordy when conciseness is easier to understand? One reason is time. Early drafts tend to be wordy as writers develop their thoughts. The scientist Blaise Pascal wrote a 20-page letter to a friend in 1656. In a postscript, he apologized for the letter's length, saying, "I hope you will pardon me for writing such a long letter, but I did not have time to write you a shorter one." Pascal was testifying to the fact that conciseness—economy of word choice—takes time and effort.

Another reason is that untrained business writers often look to the files for a model when faced with a writing assignment on the job. When the files are filled with jargon and wordy expressions and when the novices mimic these writing patterns, the tradition of verbal waste continues.[12] Note in Table 7-4 examples that follow how the wordy/redundant expressions on the left can be replaced by the more economical alternatives on the right.

TABLE 7-4 ■ Wordy Phrases and Concise Alternatives	
Instead of Writing This	**Try Using This**
due to the fact that	because
for the purpose of	for
for the reason that	since; because
in order to	to
in the event that	if
with reference to	about
pursuant to your request	as requested
subsequent to	after

(Continued)

TABLE 7-4 ■ (Continued)

Instead of Writing This	Try Using This
along the lines of	like
true facts	facts
necessary steps required	requirements
basic principles	principles
enclosed herein please find	here is
look forward with anticipation	anticipate
consensus of opinion	consensus
from the point of view of	from
inasmuch as	since; because
in accordance with	as
on the grounds that	because
at a later time	later (or a time)
within a period of 1 year	within 1 year
take into consideration	consider
a check in the amount of	a check for
for which there was no use	useless
that could not be collected	uncollectible
notwithstanding the fact that	although

Some writers believe that complex or formal words sound more professional than simple ones. And finally, some writers use wordy phrases out of habits that developed when they had to write long essays in school. To some teachers, the quantity of words is as important as quality. But writing in the workplace should focus on clear expression of ideas, not word counts.

Though writing concisely is time-consuming at first, it eventually becomes a relatively easy habit. A good example of economy in writing is text messaging. Students and workers alike have learned to extract main ideas from chunks of information and experiences and to communicate these ideas in cryptic messages. As discussed in Chapter 3, texting has replaced e-mail in many organizations as the channel of choice because of its simplicity and immediacy. Living in the era of information overload, readers ask, "What do we need to know? Why do we need to know it?" And texters limit their messages accordingly.

One might argue that economy in writing necessarily causes meaning to be lost. However, Larry Smith and Rachel Fershleiser, founders of the online magazine *SMITH*, have shown that messages can be short on words while deep in meaning. They asked the world to send in six-word memoirs, using Ernest Hemingway's example as a model. According to legend, when asked to write a novel in only six words, Hemingway came up with "For sale: baby shoes, never worn." More than 15,000 people responded to the challenge. Some notable examples posted on *SMITH* include these:

- "My second-grade teacher was right." —Janelle Brown
- "Secret of life: Marry an Italian." —Nora Ephron
- "Took scenic route, got in late." —Will Blythe
- "Became my mother. Please shoot me." —Cynthia Kaplan
- "It's pretty high. You go first." —Alan Eagle[13]

CRITICAL THINKING QUESTIONS

1. Which of the two following statements is more powerful?
   - "Well, please stop me if you've heard this before, but I've been giving this matter a lot of thought, and I'm concerned about whether the solution we're considering is actually going to help us achieve our goals; don't you agree?"
   - "That won't work."

2. If you selected the second statement, what conclusion should you draw about the importance of conciseness?

Principle 5: Avoid Clichés and Jargon

Trite expressions or clichés have an accepted meaning; however, these words yield dull messages that lack creativity. Readers may understand what is written, but the message appears impersonal, because the writer has injected nothing original into it.

Additionally, trite phrases often go out of style quickly, so the writing (and writer) may seem timeworn. Table 7-5 presents some examples of overused phrases to avoid and their alternatives.

The examples in Table 7-5 illustrate a significant shortcoming in the use of these hackneyed phrases. They can have more than one meaning. Furthermore, sometimes they are simply vague, and sometimes their logic can be questioned. These weaknesses are illustrated in the following examples:

"At an early date" or "at your earliest convenience"

Such phrases usually follow a request for information or for a favor of some sort. They are normally used by people who do not want to appear pushy. Such people do not realize two things. One is that the reader's "earliest convenience" may end up being something quite different from what the writer had in mind. The second is that businesspeople deal with deadlines all the time. They are not likely to take offense when asked for something within

TABLE 7-5 ■ Trite Expressions and Alternatives

Instead of Writing This	Try Using This
white as a sheet	pale
not enough bandwidth	busy; working
smart as a whip	intelligent
few and far between	rare
follow in the footsteps of	pursue the same career
run it up the flagpole	try it out; test a solution
in this day and age; nowadays	today
stretches the truth	exaggerates; lies
clean as a whistle	sanitary; clean
for all intents and purposes	in every practical sense; in essence
really down-to-earth	realistic; honest; sincere
as luck would have it	unfortunately; luckily

a range of time if the writer concisely and courteously states the reason for the time range, as in the following example:

"So that we may fill your order as quickly as possible, please send us this information by March 21."

Some readers interpret these two clichés as presumptuous:

"Thanking you in advance" and "permit me to say"

Besides being timeworn, mechanical, and impersonal, the first expression seems to say, "I expect you to comply with my request, but I don't want to have to take the time to thank you later, so I'll do it now." The second expression seems to seek permission, but the writer expresses the idea before getting that permission. The second expression should be dropped, and the first might be replaced by this:

"I appreciate any help you can give me in the matter."

Jargon is the technical language or specified terms that become part of the everyday vocabulary of an organization or discipline. Insiders know what the words mean, but outsiders or customers may not. Jargon includes technical terms, acronyms, and terms used in special ways. When writing to readers outside the organization, managers should avoid using jargon. Rather, they should choose the layperson's version whenever possible to reduce the likelihood that the reader will misunderstand the message.[14] Additionally, some organizations are so large that the people in one functional unit may not understand the jargon of other units. The lists in Table 7-6 illustrate how some jargon used in business might be simplified.

With only one exception, the descriptions on the right are wordier than the jargon on the left. If these wordier versions ensure understanding and prevent inquiries aimed at

TABLE 7-6 ■ Jargon and Simpler Alternatives	
Instead of Writing This	**Try Using This**
TQM	total quality management
accounts receivable	firms or people owing money to the company
amounts payable	amounts owed by the company
HVI bonus	extra pay for selling high-volume machines
maturity date	date that final payment is due
feedstock	raw materials used for manufacturing in the petrochemical industry
duplexing	photocopyist's term meaning copying on both sides of a sheet of paper
FAA	Federal Aviation Administration
abstract	history of the property
per diem	daily
assessed valuation	value of the property for tax purposes
current ratio	ratio of current assets to current liabilities
CRM	customer relations management
ROI	return on investment; expected outcome

clarification, then the extra effort and words used will have been worthwhile. Balancing conciseness with clarity is a decision managers must make when writing.

Acronyms can be particularly troublesome. In some situations, an acronym may be perfectly appropriate, while in other situations, it may cause a problem. For instance, in one division of Exxon, a DHR is the director of human resources, but in other divisions, it is a by-product of the chemical scrubbing process.

Finally, a word of caution about *business-ese*. Expressions and terms can quickly become popular in business circles and then become obsolete just as quickly. A Texas entrepreneur, Ron Sturgeon, captured 1,200 examples of "biz jargon" in his book *Green Weenies and Due Diligence*. Some are funny and colorful ("herding cats," "circling the drain," "mouse milking"), while some are more sober ("dilution," "FTE," "synergy").[15] Sometimes, in a misguided attempt to sound professional, business-ese makes longer words out of short ones, such as *functionality* for "functions" and *objectivality* for "objectives." When deciding whether to use business-ese in your message, be guided by your receiver's expectations, the communication climate, and the cultural context (see Chapter 2).

Principle 6: Use Positive Words That Convey Courtesy

As stated earlier, written communications present stimuli and generate responses. Generally, the more positive the stimuli, the more positive the response. Conversely, the more negative the stimuli, the more negative the response. Behavioral scientists, for example, tell us that employees will live either up or down to the expectations communicated by their managers.[16]

Whether managers are dealing with direct reports, superiors, peers, customers, suppliers, or others, they want their messages to be well received. The positive wording of a request, of information, or even of bad news should increase the probability of a positive or at least neutral reaction by the receiver.

The difference between positive and negative wording is not a matter of content but of emphasis. Negative messages emphasize the least desirable aspects of a situation. As such, they are likely to arouse defensive or antagonistic responses from the reader.

The sender of an effective communication must establish credibility and goodwill with the receiver, and positiveness and courtesy aid the manager in developing these aspects. The following examples illustrate the different impacts that can be generated by positive and negative wordings of messages:

I cannot have the report ready by tomorrow morning.

I can have the report completed by 3:30 p.m. Wednesday.

You should not use Form A to file the weekly sales report.

Form B is the weekly sales report form.

We regret to inform you that we must deny your request for a promotion because you haven't earned enough continuing education credits.

As soon as you earn six more continuing education credits, we can process your request for a promotion.

In each of the alternative statements in the preceding examples, the writer uses positive and concrete words to state what can be done or what has been done rather than what cannot be done or what has not been done.

Let's look at a real-life example. In the hospitality management industry, theft of hotel-room amenities is a major cost of doing business. Guests routinely steal towels, pens, and even furniture from their hotel rooms. Instead of posting warnings or threats, Holiday Inn Express takes a positive approach. A notice placed on the bathroom countertop reads:

Dear Guest,

Due to the popularity of our guest room amenities, our Housekeeping Department now offers these items for sale:

Irons: $40.00

Ironing boards: $30.00

Blow dryer: $30.00

Bath towels: $15.00

Hand towels: $10.00

Each guest room attendant is responsible for maintaining the guest room items. Should you decide to take these articles from your room instead of obtaining them from the Executive Housekeeper, we will assume you approve a corresponding charge to your account. Thank you.

Is that not better than saying, "Don't steal items from the room"?

Although we should not totally avoid negatives, we can minimize them. Some phrases, because they seem discourteous, are likely to irritate readers. Words and phrases like "inexcusable," "you claim that," "your insinuation," "you failed to," and "obviously you overlooked" should be avoided if possible. The next chapter on messages will explain this point further.

Being positive and conveying courtesy in word choice also involves using gender-neutral language. Rarely is it necessary for writers to identify people based on their gender identity.

Today, we use gender-neutral terms to describe jobs. Pronouns and nouns that refer to gender (e.g., *manpower*) are unacceptable. Likewise, expressions that belittle the behavior or qualities of a certain gender should be avoided. Table 7-7 presents unacceptable and acceptable terms.

TABLE 7-7 ■ Terms to Avoid and Acceptable Alternatives

Instead of Writing This	Try Using This
man (when referring to species)	humanity; human beings; humans; people
man (verb)	staff; guard; mind; watch
man hours	work hours
man-made	handmade; artisanal; handcrafted
manpower	employees; staff; workers; workforce
grow to manhood	grow to adulthood; grow up; mature
businessman	business executive; manager
cameraman	camera operator
chairman	chairperson
freshman	first-year student
fireman	firefighter
foreman	supervisor; spokesperson (of a jury)
housewife	stay-at-home partner
lady doctor/lawyer/realtor	doctor/lawyer/realtor
mailman	mail carrier
middleman	intermediary
policeman	police officer
salesman	salesperson
stewardess	flight attendant

On the subject of gender in writing, one particularly thorny problem is the generic or universal pronoun *he*. Until about 30 years ago, the standard practice had been to use *he* in impersonal constructions where all people were to be included: "Each person has his own problems to resolve." Authorities noted that such constructions could make women feel ignored in the business world. Another option was the use of "he or she," "his or her," "s/he," or "his/her." Though not entirely graceful, this option was considered acceptable, even though it sometimes hindered style and readability.

A similar technique was to alternate masculine and feminine pronouns. One paragraph might have used *she* as the generic pronoun, while the next might have used *he*. While this technique avoided the generic *he*, it did not sacrifice style the way *he or she* sometimes did. However, it perpetuated the idea of an exclusively binary nature of gender and excluded gender-nonconforming individuals, so this option has fallen out of favor more recently.

Fortunately, managers have several options available for avoiding such pronoun use altogether. One is the use of plural nouns and pronouns. Instead of writing, "A manager should motivate his employees," one could write, "Managers should motivate their employees."

Another technique is more courteous and inclusive of all users, including transgender and non-binary readers. The singular *they* is the use of plural pronouns for traditionally singular antecedent references, such as *each*, *every*, *everyone*, *everybody*, or *anybody*, or to represent singular language that applies to people generally—for example, "Everyone has their problems to resolve" or "A manager has to navigate regular interruptions in their workday." This technique legitimizes popular use. Many style guides, newspapers, and other sources have adopted the singular *they*, and in 2019, Merriam-Webster's dictionary declared it to be the word of the year.[17]

The last and best suggestion is to replace third-person pronouns (e.g., *he*, *she*, or *they*) with the second person (*you*). The direct address engages the reader by including them in the action. Thus, "If you are going to be late, call your supervisor" is better than "If an employee is going to be late, he or she should call his or her supervisor."

Principle 7: Use a Conversational Style

Sentences communicate effectively when they use everyday language—when the words are those that would be used in face-to-face communication. A conversational style involves writing with words from a person's speaking vocabulary. Usually, the words should not include colloquialisms, slang, or jargon; they should be the language most people would use in conducting everyday business.

The most successful business professional who exemplifies writing in a conversational style is billionaire investor Warren Buffett, chairman of Berkshire Hathaway, Inc. In 2005, the National Commission on Writing honored Buffett's folksy annual report. "No annual report has had a greater impact on American business," said Bob Kerrey, the commission's chair and president of The New School, a university in New York.[18] Other successful executives, such as Bill Gates, openly admire Buffet's style. In an interview with Maria Bartiromo in February 2009, Gates admitted that writing an annual letter about his foundation's activities was Buffett's idea—and Gates "ran a few drafts by him. . . . His advice is very helpful."[19]

A conversational style is particularly important in business letters, because it aids in developing the "you viewpoint." The you viewpoint analyzes the reader's interests or concerns and addresses them in the message. Before writing, the sender identifies who will receive the information; the reader's need for the information; and as much as possible, their knowledge, expertise, interests, culture, and value system. This strategy helps a writer personalize letters, something most readers appreciate in business correspondence.[20]

Even form letters and mass messages can be written with a personal touch if the writer considers typical audiences and their concerns that have to be addressed. These messages can be written in a conversational style, and technology makes it easier than it has ever been to personalize a form letter with fields containing unique details for each receiver.

These first seven principles have focused on the selection of words. Because each word can influence the total message, each word deserves attention. The manager also needs to analyze the combination and organization of words strategically to ensure effective communication. The remaining principles will address the ways in which words might be grouped for best effect.

Organizing Words for Effect

The next four principles discuss organizational guidelines for putting words together to convey a message. Comprehension is largely determined by the extent to which the writer uses these principles.

Principle 8: Keep Sentences Short

We sometimes encounter long-winded sentences in business writing. These seemingly never-ending constructions stem from several possible causes. One cause mentioned earlier is the need to impress. Consider the following example from a government report:

> It is obvious from the difference in elevation with relation to the short depth of the field that the contour is such as to preclude any reasonable development potential for economic utilization.

One would have to study the preceding message long and hard to figure out that the writer was, in fact, saying:

> The field is too steep to plow.

On the other hand, some people write these lengthy, roundabout sentences to avoid appearing forward or pushy, as in the following example:

> During the past 2 weeks, we have been wondering if you have as yet found yourself in a position to give us an indication of whether or not you have been able to come to a decision on our offer.

Most businesspeople who face deadlines daily would not be offended if they were asked a question more to the point:

> Have you decided on the offer we made you 2 weeks ago?

Another possible cause for unnecessarily long sentences is an attempt to say everything in one sentence. Note the confusion created by the following example and the improvement in the alternative version:

> Although 17 people from our department (purchasing) attended the workshop, nine of them, including Jerry Stoves, had no background for the topic of the

workshop (advanced negotiating technique) offered by the Purchasing Association of Chicago.

Last week 17 people from our purchasing department attended a workshop on advanced negotiating techniques. The Purchasing Association of Chicago offered the workshop. Of the 17 who attended, Jerry Stoves and eight others lacked the necessary background.

One way to shorten sentences is to avoid expletive constructions: "It . . . that" and "There is . . ." or "There are. . . ." An expletive has no grammatical antecedent in a sentence, and it often diffuses the focus of the message by displacing or even eliminating people in the sentence. For example, in the sentence "It is thought that interest rates will fall," the word *it* has no antecedent, yet *it* gets the main emphasis. The person who holds this opinion is unknown. A better wording would be "I think that interest rates will fall." Instead of "It is suggested that you rewrite this proposal," say, "Please rewrite the proposal." Generally, "there is" and "there are" constructions merely add length and waste time. Rather than saying, "There are three options from which you can choose," say, "You can choose from three options."

Unnecessarily long sentences require readers to spend too much time trying to understand the message. And the more time and patience required to understand a message, the less likely the reader is to understand the purpose.

Effective writing is easy and quick to read. Studies show that good business sentences are 15 to 20 words long. They also use no more than 10 long (three-or-more-syllable) words in every 100 words.

Effective sentences express one main point. Any connected phrases or clauses should explain that point. When we place two or more important ideas in the same sentence, we reduce the importance of each and often confuse the reader.

Principle 9: Prefer the Active to the Passive Voice

The active voice presents the parts of a sentence in the normal order expected by English-speaking people. The subject of the sentence is the actor, who is acting in a way portrayed by the verb, and the action is directed toward the object. The following sentences illustrate the active voice:

- David Lopez directed the meeting.
- Donna Hebert enforced the policy.
- Ridley Gros promoted the university.

The passive voice reverses the order of the parts so that the subject is being acted on by the object in a way depicted by the verb:

- The meeting was directed by David Lopez.
- The policy was enforced by Donna Hebert.
- The university was promoted by Ridley Gros.

Besides the reversed order and the slight additional length, the passive voice weakens the sentence construction by making the doer of the action the object of the *by* phrase.

Furthermore, the passive voice carries the hazard of luring the writer into longer, more roundabout expressions.[21] For example, instead of writing,

The new president reorganized the administration,

we see

A reorganization of the administration was effected by the new president.

Though managerial writers should favor the active voice in the majority of the sentences they construct, they may occasionally prefer the passive voice. In sensitive or controversial matters, the passive voice is more diplomatic because it de-emphasizes the person doing the action. If the action is routine or if the identity of the actor is not important to the action being described, eliminate the *by* phrase from a passive-voice sentence. Note the following diplomatic transformation:

Active: The director of purchasing has been soliciting bids from unauthorized vendors.

Passive: Bids from unauthorized vendors have been solicited by the director of purchasing.

Passive minus the by *phrase:* Bids from unauthorized vendors have been solicited.

Principle 10: Organize Paragraphs Logically

Paragraphs unite separate thoughts around a single important idea. Alone, sentences might seem illogical or out of context. A paragraph combines sentences to form coherent messages.

Five guidelines can help writers develop effective paragraphs (see Table 7-8). First, present one major idea in a paragraph, along with whatever support is necessary for the development of that idea.[22] This paragraph quality is called *unity*.

Second, determine if a deductive or an inductive pattern is appropriate. Deductive paragraphs present the main idea in the first sentence and the supporting ideas in the sentences that follow. Inductive paragraphs begin with the details or the support and end with the main idea. The deductive pattern is the most commonly used, but the inductive pattern is useful for persuasion.

TABLE 7-8 ■ Developing Effective Paragraphs
1. Present one major idea in a paragraph.
2. Decide whether a deductive or an inductive pattern is appropriate.
3. Use a variety of sentence structures in a paragraph.
4. Structure paragraphs to emphasize important points.
5. Keep paragraphs relatively short.

Third, use a variety of sentence structures in a paragraph. A paragraph that contains all simple sentences can be tedious; interest builds when a combination of sentence structures is used.

Fourth, structure paragraphs to emphasize important points. Emphasis can be accomplished in a variety of ways:

- Repeat key concepts.

- Use attention-getting words, such as action verbs and the personal pronoun *you*.

- Use typographical devices, such as bullet points, text boxes, italics, boldface, or numbers.

Be sure that bulleted lists, repeated phrases, and compound structures are in *parallel* form. Sentence elements that are alike in function should also be alike in construction.[23] Look at the following examples:

Parallel: The company has *a* mission statement and *a* code of ethics.

Not parallel: Citizens are concerned with whether the president *has lied* under oath or *looking* directly into the cameras.

Excellent examples of parallel structure can be found in the words of great orators. Look at this excerpt from the Rev. Dr. Martin Luther King, Jr.'s famous "I Have a Dream" speech: "So let freedom ring from the prodigious hilltops of New Hampshire. Let freedom ring from the mighty mountains of New York. Let freedom ring from the heightening Alleghenies of Pennsylvania. Let freedom ring from the snowcapped Rockies of Colorado." Notice how the repetition and parallel structure of these sentences add rhythm, balance, and a buildup of emotion.

Fifth, keep paragraphs relatively short. Short paragraphs are easy to read and give more emphasis to the information they contain. Readers need visual and mental breaks so that they can assimilate the message; short paragraphs help achieve these breaks. In business letters and short memos, paragraphs usually average four to six lines in length; in reports, they average eight to ten lines. Exceptions, however, will sometimes be justified by the need for emphasis (shorter paragraphs) or by the complexity of the material (longer paragraphs).

These guidelines for composing short, strong, clear messages are followed by prominent leaders in fields other than business. One example is Sir Winston Churchill, the Prime Minister of Britain during World War II. Churchill required his War Cabinet to compose tightly structured memos and reports. "It is slothful not to compress your thoughts," he said. "To do our work, we all have to read a mass of papers. Nearly all of them are far too long. This wastes time." Most important, Churchill believed that "the discipline of setting out the real points concisely will prove an aid to clear thinking." Under harrowing wartime conditions, Churchill's reliance on good writing contributed to his success.[24]

Principle 11: Be Coherent

With coherent writing, sentences flow from one to another easily and smoothly because the relationship between their ideas is clear. This movement from one thought to another is accomplished through transition, which is sometimes described as a bridge that connects thoughts. Transitions may be natural or mechanical.

Natural transition occurs when the content of the thoughts is such that the second flows naturally and smoothly from the first. Note the smooth movement from the first thought to the second in the following opening paragraph to a job application letter:

> Now that the Dillon Pharmaceutical Company is expanding its Western region, won't you need trained and experienced sales representatives to call on accounts in the new territory? With a degree in marketing and 8 successful years in pharmaceutical sales, I believe that I am well qualified to be one of those representatives.

The first sentence introduces the ideas of training and experience, and the second sentence builds on that introduction.

Often, however, a writer cannot rely on the content of thoughts to show a clear connection between them. The writer may have to show that connection with mechanical *transitions*. A writer can (a) repeat key words, to show the reader that the same subject is still being addressed; (b) use pronouns and synonyms, to avoid being too repetitious; or (c) use transition words, which are used to connect thoughts and show a particular type of relationship between them. Table 7-9 lists some frequently used transition words.

In addition to making sure the thoughts within a paragraph flow smoothly, writers should be concerned that this quality of coherence pervades the entire document. More specifically, paragraphs, like sentences, need to be clearly related. Sometimes this relationship is shown through the use of transitional devices, such as those previously discussed. At other times, an entire sentence at the beginning or end of a paragraph will be used to show the relationship of that paragraph to the one that precedes or follows it.

In longer and more complex documents, such as reports, the task of ensuring coherence becomes more involved. For example, a five-page section of a 25-page report may need an introductory paragraph to show what is included in that section. It may also need a concluding paragraph to tie up the section and show how it relates to the larger purpose of the report. A simpler kind of transitional device is a "Janus statement," named for the Roman god with two faces—one looking backward and one looking ahead. The writer can

TABLE 7-9 ■ Frequently Used Transition Words		
but	accordingly	even so
next	again	on the other hand
thus	consequently	furthermore
then	otherwise	in summary
finally	besides	similarly
hence	conversely	as a result
still	to illustrate	in contrast
also	in addition	subsequently
and	however	for example

accomplish both a review and a preview with a Janus statement, such as "Now that we have described *X*, let us turn our attention to *Y*."

A final way to build coherence in long documents is by using headings and subheadings. Chapter 9 addresses report and proposal writing in more detail, including heading use.

Before we leave the subject of coherence, a word of caution may be in order. Though the transitional devices discussed here can show relationships to readers, logical organization of ideas is the foundation of coherent writing. Writers must clearly understand why information is being arranged in a certain way. They must have a logical plan of presentation, for transitional devices cannot show relationships that do not exist.

STAGE 3: REVISING

The third stage, revising and editing, is perhaps the most important to practice. Few writers possess the skill to write clear copy in one sitting.[25] Revising is a service to the reader. Thus, managers should begin Stage 3 by shifting perspective, distancing themselves from the writing, and assuming the role of the reader. The following questions can systematize the revision process and examine the message from the reader's viewpoint:

- What is the purpose of the message?

- Have I included all the information the reader wants or needs to know to understand my message?

- Does my message answer all the reader's questions?

- Is there any information nonessential to the reader that I can delete?

- Have I included reader benefits?

Revising involves (a) reading what has been written for clarity, concreteness, and conversational tone; (b) determining factual accuracy; (c) organizing to ensure coherence;[26] (d) rewording awkward sentences and phrases; and (e) rearranging content and adding illustrations and transitions. Writers should not assume their prose is satisfactory after only one or two drafts. Few people write that well.[27]

The final step is to edit the document for correctness. Running a spell checker and grammar checker will catch most surface errors. However, these devices will not always detect when the wrong word is used if it is spelled correctly, such as *too/two* or *read/red*. Grammar checkers also follow rules and may ignore elements that change the intended meaning. An amusing, well-known case where punctuation significantly changes a sentence's meaning is the following:

A woman, without her man, is nothing.

A woman: without her, man is nothing.[28]

The amount of revising and editing necessary will depend on the individual writer's skill. However, all good writers rewrite. Many have someone else read their work before finalizing it. Other readers can often detect errors or confusing statements that writers miss because writers read into their messages what they want to communicate. For example,

David McCombie, principal of the McCombie Group, uses his partner as a sounding board: "I send anything that's important to my partner and he reads it over. We talk about whether there is a better way to convey an idea, how we can be more succinct."[29]

At the very least, a writer should set aside a draft and let it "cool off" for a while before revising. When e-mailing, a writer can queue messages to be reread rather than composing and immediately clicking the Send button. Hastily sent e-mails can be embarrassingly incomplete or inaccurate.

Though revising and editing may seem time-consuming and tedious, the results are worth the effort. By making the message clearer and easier to understand, revising benefits the reader and reduces the likelihood of requests for later clarification. In the long run, it saves time and money while enhancing the writer's image.

When revising and editing, an easy way to keep your goal in sight is to remember the "seven Cs" of good business writing. Table 7-10 presents these guidelines.

In a recent survey of business writers, 81 percent of respondents agreed with the statement "Poorly written material wastes my time." They identified the characteristics of poorly written documents as too long (65 percent), poorly organized (65 percent), unclear (61 percent), using too much jargon (54 percent), not precise enough (54 percent), and not direct

TABLE 7-10 ■ The Seven Cs of Good Business Writing	
Completeness	Answer all reader questions
	Include the five Ws and H
Conciseness	Shorten or delete wordy expressions
	Avoid repetition
Consideration	Focus on the reader ("you viewpoint")
	Show reader benefits or interests
	Emphasize the positive
Concreteness	Use specific facts and data
	Use active (not passive) voice
	Rely on vivid, image-building words
Clarity	Use short, familiar words
	Avoid jargon
	Follow a logical sequence of points
Courtesy	Be tactful and appreciative
	Avoid discriminatory language
	Respond promptly
Correctness	Maintain accurate writing mechanics
	Avoid wrong-word errors

enough (49 percent).[30] The planning, composing, and revising process described here can help you avoid these problems and compose more effective messages at work.

COLLABORATIVE WRITING

The increased emphasis on teamwork has increased collaborative writing as well. One researcher notes that collaboration has increased by 50 percent in the last two decades, with collaborators contributing informational (knowledge), social (professional connections), and personal (time and effort) resources to projects.[31] In spite of this surge, a study of U.S. employees found that 38 percent of workers want more collaboration at work.[32]

Collaborative writing comes in a number of different guises. Sometimes a supervisor has a staff member research and write a document, after which the supervisor edits it. Sometimes the collaboration comes in the planning of the document, which is composed and revised by an individual. Other times, an individual does the planning and composing of work that is revised collaboratively. Peers often critique one another's work. And there are times when the collaboration pervades the entire writing process from start to finish.[33] Recent research indicates that a typical document cycles through three to five revisions before it is sent to the intended readers.

Advantages of Collaborative Writing

The advantages of collaborative writing are similar to the advantages of group decision making. Documents are more thorough because of the additional minds and perspectives being applied to creating the document. Collaborative writing is also advantageous when the size of the task and/or time limits call for the labor of more than one person, when the scope of the job calls for more than one area of expertise, or when one of the task goals is the melding of divergent opinions.[34] The collaborators are usually more invested in the document and motivated to carry out its directives.

CRITICAL THINKING QUESTIONS

1. Why do you think that businesses typically cycle documents so thoroughly before releasing them?

2. How important is it that business documents generated by a business have a clear and consistent "voice" or style?

Richard Gebhardt notes that the theoretical underpinnings of collaborative writing are "the rhetorical sense of audience; the psychological power of peer influence; the transfer-of-learning principle by which (people) gain insights into their own writing as they comment on the works of others; and the principle of feedback through which (people) sense how well their writing is communicating."[35] Terry Bacon has found that collaborative writing socializes employees in several fundamental ways. It helps acculturate newcomers by teaching writers about the corporation's capabilities and history and by modeling the corporation's values and attitudes in the actions of the experienced members. It also helps break down functional barriers, and it fosters the informal chains of communication and authority through which the corporation accomplishes its work.[36]

Finally and perhaps most important, collaboration can improve writing quality.[37] People can respond to each other's drafts with sharply focused and relevant comments.[38] Recent developments in technology facilitate collaborative writing. As we explained in Chapter 3, today's word processors allow groups to compose, revise, and edit documents synchronously and asynchronously, resulting in better messages while avoiding emotional conflict among collaborators.

Disadvantages of Collaborative Writing

Some disadvantages of collaborative writing are also those associated with group decision making. Some members do not do their fair share. Coordinating schedules for meetings can be complicated and vexing. Personality conflicts can all but stall the group's progress. And some people believe that one person acting alone could probably complete the chore in much less time than it takes a group to do so. Finally, though one person may do a poor job on part of the project, everyone is held responsible for the entire end result.

Respondents in one study noted that the two major costs of collaboration were time and ego. One commented that in collaboration you had to "check your ego at the door"; you had to be "confident in your own abilities and yet able to take criticism."[39]

Another surveyed group of professional writers cited several problems associated with collaborative writing. They spoke of difficulty in resolving style differences; the additional time required to work with a group; the inequitable division of tasks; and the loss of personal satisfaction, ownership, or sense of creativity.[40]

Probably the most serious problem associated with collaborative writing is ineffectively dealing with conflicts that arise. Some people see all conflicts as bad and try to ignore them or sweep them under the carpet. They do not realize that some conflicts are functional and can help the group come to a more creative resolution of its problem.

Guidelines for Effective Collaborative Writing

In their extensive research into the collaborative writing of people in a number of professions, Lisa Ede and Andrea Lunsford came up with the following profile of effective collaborative writers:

> They are flexible; respectful of others; attentive and analytical listeners; able to
> speak and write clearly and articulately; dependable and able to meet deadlines;
> able to designate and share responsibility, to lead and to follow; open to criticism
> but confident in their own abilities; ready to engage in creative conflict.[41]

Generally, this profile depicts people who are able to work with others—people who are going to be in greater demand as collaboration becomes more the norm than the exception.

To achieve successful collaborative writing experiences, make sure the work is divided equitably among group members. Nothing is surer to destroy a person's morale than to begin feeling overworked compared to others in the group.

Second, writing teams should use electronic technology for collaboration; the media appear to buffer emotions while increasing efficiency.

Third, all collaborative writing groups should have a team leader, even though the person may not have any formal authority. The leader should be responsible for coordinating the team's collaborative efforts, shaping the team's vision, and resolving conflicts among individuals and functional departments. The latter task usually requires good interpersonal skills if the leader has no formal authority.[42] Though no one can guarantee that all collaborative writing experiences will be problem free, we are confident that anyone who follows the preceding guidelines will encounter fewer insurmountable problems and will attain greater success in group writing projects.

The most surprising thing about effective collaboration may be that communication is more important than expertise. A series of studies on workplace collaboration suggests three characteristics of effective teams: energy, engagement, and exploration.[43] Members of the team face each other and balance talking and listening, ensuring that no one dominates the conversations. Although the team leader is a hub, members connect directly with each other to discuss the project. Side conversations and "back channels" are encouraged to build team cohesiveness and trust. But team members also feel free to leave the group to collect information, which can help the team avoid groupthink.

SUMMARY

Written managerial communication has several strategic advantages: economy, efficiency, accuracy, and official permanence. Managers are part of discourse communities that shape the way they communicate, and they work in an environment that makes special demands on their documents. Among the aspects of their managerial writing context are the fragmented nature of their time at work, the extent of collaboration and delegation, the size and culture of the organization, the authority and politics they must deal with, and the legal considerations of which they must remain aware as they write.

Once managers recognize these unique aspects, they are ready to write. The writing process consists of three stages: planning, composing, and revising. In the planning stage, the manager identifies what, why, who, when, where, and how. In the composing stage, the writer selects words and arranges them for proper effect, keeping certain strategic concerns in mind. The following principles guide the selection and arrangement of words for message clarity, comprehension, and coherence:

Selecting Words:

1. Choose words precisely.
2. Use short rather than long words.
3. Use concrete rather than abstract words.
4. Economize on words.
5. Avoid clichés and jargon.
6. Use positive words that convey courtesy.
7. Use a conversational style.

Organizing Words for Effect:

8. Keep sentences short.

9. Prefer the active to the passive voice.

10. Organize paragraphs logically.

11. Be coherent.

In the revising stage, the writer examines the message for ways to improve on these 11 principles. Additionally, the manager edits for correctness of expression. Surface errors affect the success of a document in reaching its goals and also can damage the reader–writer relationship.

Collaboration is a fact of modern organizational life. In addition to the advantages of group decision making, it also socializes employees in several ways and can improve the quality of the writing. Good writers are flexible, respectful, attentive, articulate, responsible, and confident people who work well with others. In addition to the disadvantages associated with group decision making (e.g., domination, reluctant contributors), time, potential ego damage, style differences, and conflicts can work against effective collaboration. Guidelines for effective collaboration include dividing the work equitably among members. Conflict should be viewed as potentially constructive. The group's leader should coordinate efforts, shape the team's vision, and resolve conflicts.

CASES FOR ANALYSIS

Case 7-1

The Oracle of Omaha Speaks About Board Members

Warren Buffett, the chairman and CEO of Berkshire Hathaway, published his annual letter to shareholders on February 22, 2020. The letter discussed how Berkshire Hathaway's business fared throughout 2019 and addressed a number of topics, including corporate governance. In the following excerpt, Buffett described the qualities of a good director:

I'd like you to know that almost all of the directors I have met over the years have been decent, likable and intelligent. They dressed well, made good neighbors and were fine citizens. . . . Nevertheless, many of these good souls are people whom I would never have chosen to handle money or business matters. It simply was not their game. They, in turn, would never have asked me for help in removing a tooth, decorating their home or improving their golf swing. Moreover, if I were ever scheduled to appear on *Dancing With the Stars*, I would immediately seek refuge in the Witness Protection Program. We are all duds at one thing or another. For most of us, the list is long. The important point to recognize is that if you are Bobby Fischer, you must play only chess for money.

At Berkshire, we will continue to look for business-savvy directors who are

(Continued)

(Continued)

owner-oriented and arrive with a strong specific interest in our company. Thought and principles, not robot-like "process," will guide their actions. In representing your interests, they will, of course, seek managers whose goals include delighting their customers, cherishing their associates and acting as good citizens of both their communities and our country.[44]

Questions

1. Who are the primary intended receivers of this letter? What secondary audiences did Buffett intend to reach?

2. What is the letter's primary purpose—informative or persuasive? Are there any secondary purposes?

3. How would you describe the tone of this letter? What elements of Buffett's writing contribute to the tone?

4. Why do you think Buffett adopted this writing style for such a widely read document?

5. What are the positive and negative effects on the readers' impression of Berkshire Hathaway?

Case 7-2

Back to School

Because you are known to be a good writer, the director of human resources has asked you to put together a seminar on written communication for employees in your company who need help. The seminar would cover basic principles of written communication, letters, memos, and formal business reports. Managers have complained to the HR director that their employees do not write well. They produce as evidence sloppily proofread e-mails. The employees, on the other hand, are grumbling that having to attend a writing seminar would be like going back to high school, where a fussy old English teacher berates them over minor punctuation concerns.

Questions

1. How would you determine who should attend the seminar?

2. How would you market it so that participants of the seminar would attend willingly, rather than through coercion?

3. How would you organize the seminar? What materials would you use?

4. What topics would you address in the seminar?

Notes

1. Josh Bernoff, "The Sad State of Business Writing," September 6, 2016, https://without-bullshit.com/blog/new-research-on-business-writing-infographic-and-report.

2. John M. Swales, "Reflections on the Concept of Discourse Community," *Concepts and Frameworks in English for Specific Purposes* 69 (2016): 7–19, https://doi.org/10.4000/asp.4763.

3. Henry Mintzberg, *Mintzberg on Management: Inside Our Strange World of Organizations* (New York: Collier Macmillan, 1989), 8.

4. Sharon Begley, "Will the BlackBerry Sink the Presidency?" *Newsweek*, February 16, 2009, 37.

5. Marie Flatley, "A Comparative Analysis of the Written Communication of Managers at Various Organizational Levels in the Private Business

Sector," *Journal of Business Communication* 19, no. 3 (Summer 1982): 40.

6. Max Weber, *The Theory of Social and Economic Organization*, trans. A. M. Henderson and Talcott Parsons and ed. Talcott Parsons (New York: The Free Press, 1947), 324–86.

7. James G. March, "The Business Firm as a Political Coalition," *Journal of Politics* 24 (1980): 662–78.

8. Carolyn O'Hara, "How to Improve Your Business Writing," *Harvard Business Review*, November 20, 2014, https://hbr.org/2014/11/how-to-improve-your-business-writing.

9. Barbara Czarniawska-Joerges and Bernward Joerges, "How to Control Things With Words: Organizational Talk and Control," *Management Communication Quarterly* 2, no. 2 (November 1988): 170–93.

10. Sarah Ellen Ransdell and Ira Fischler, "Effects of Concreteness and Task Context on Recall of Prose Among Bilingual and Monolingual Speakers," *Journal of Memory and Language* 28, no. 3 (June 1989): 278–79.

11. James Suchan and Robert Colucci, "An Analysis of Communication Efficiency Between High-Impact Writing and Bureaucratic Written Communication," *Management Communication Quarterly* 2, no. 4 (May 1989): 454–84.

12. "Weak Writers," *The Wall Street Journal*, June 14, 1985, 1.

13. Larry Smith and Rachel Fershleiser, "Not Quite What I Was Planning: Six-Word Memoirs by Writers Famous and Obscure," 2008, http://www.smithmag.net.

14. Peter Crow, "Plain English: What Counts Besides Readability," *Journal of Business Communication* 25, no. 1 (Winter 1988): 87–95.

15. Ron Sturgeon, *Green Weenies and Due Diligence: Insider Business Jargon* (Lynden, WA: Mike French, 2005).

16. Sterling Livingston, "Pygmalion in Management," *Harvard Business Review*, September–October 1988, 121–30.

17. Merriam-Webster, "Merriam-Webster's Words of the Year 2019," https://www.merriam-webster.com/words-at-play/word-of-the-year/they.

18. Associated Press, "Billionaire Buffett Gets an Award—for Writing," February 4, 2005, https://www.nbcnews.com/id/wbna6913932..

19. Maria Bartiromo, "Facetime: Melinda and Bill Gates on Making a Difference," *BusinessWeek*, February 16, 2009, 21–22.

20. Kitty Locker, "Theoretical Justification for Using Reader Benefits," *Journal of Business Communication* 19, no. 3 (Summer 1982): 51–65.

21. Pamela Layton and Adrian J. Simpson, "Deep Structure in Sentence Comprehension," *Journal of Verbal Learning and Verbal Behavior* 14 (1975): 658–64.

22. Thomas L. Kent, "Paragraph Production and the Given-New Contract," *Journal of Business Communication* 21, no. 4 (Fall 1984): 45–66.

23. For a comprehensive explanation of parallel structure, see Gerald J. Alred, Walter E. Oliu, and Charles T. Brusaw, *The Business Writer's Handbook*, 11th ed. (New York: Bedford/St. Martin's Press, 2015).

24. Erik Larson, *The Splendid and the Vile: A Saga of Churchill, Family, and Defiance During the Blitz* (New York: Penguin, Random House, 2020).

25. Larry Smeltzer and Jeanette Gilsdorf, "How to Use Your Time Efficiently When Writing," *Business Horizons*, November–December 1990, 61–64.

26. Larry Smeltzer and Jeanette Gilsdorf, "Revise Reports Rapidly," *Personnel Journal*, October 1990, 39–44.

27. Jeanne W. Halpern, "What Should We Be Teaching Students in Business Writing?" *Journal of Business Communication* 18, no. 3 (Summer 1981): 39–53.

28. Lynne Truss, *Eats, Shoots and Leaves: The Zero Tolerance Approach to Punctuation* (New York: Gotham Books/Penguin Group USA, 2003).

29. O'Hara, "How to Improve Your Business Writing."

30. Bernoff, "The Sad State of Business Writing."

31. Rob Cross, Reb Rebele, and Adam Grant, "Collaboration Overload," *Harvard Business Review* 94 (January–February 2016): 74–79.

32. Cornerstone OnDemand, "The State of Workplace Productivity Report," August 2012, https://www.cornerstoneondemand.com/sites/default/files/research/csod-rs-state-of-workplace-productivity-report.pdf.

33. Nancy Allen et al., "What Experienced Collaborators Say About Collaborative Writing," *Journal of Business and Technical Communication* 1, no. 2 (September 1987): 70–90.

34. Ibid., 85.

35. R. Gebhardt, "Teamwork and Feedback: Broadening the Base of Collaborative Writing," *College English* 42, no. 1 (September 1980): 69.

36. Terry R. Bacon, "Collaboration in a Pressure Cooker," *The Bulletin*, June 1990, 4–8.

37. A. M. O'Donnell et al., "Effects of Cooperative and Individual Rewriting on an Instruction Writing Task," *Written Communication* 4 (1987): 90–99.

38. Rebecca Burnett, "Benefits of Collaborative Planning in the Business Communication Classroom," *The Bulletin*, June 1990, 10.

39. Allen et al., "What Experienced Collaborators Say," 82–83.

40. Lisa Ede and Andrea Lunsford, *Single Tests/Plural Authors* (Carbondale: Southern Illinois University Press, 1990), 62.

41. Ibid., 66.

42. Bacon, "Collaboration in a Pressure Cooker," 5.

43. Alex (Sandy) Pentland, "The New Science of Building Great Teams," *Harvard Business Review* 90, no. 4 (April 2012): 60–70.

44. Warren E. Buffett, "CEO's Letter," Berkshire Hathaway, February 22, 2020, 13, https://www.berkshirehathaway.com/letters/2019ltr.pdf.

8

WRITING ROUTINE MESSAGES

As Chapter 7 emphasized, written communication is an important part of a manager's job. Studies of business professionals with varying years of experience have consistently found that they spend a significant portion of their time at work writing e-mails, memos, letters, reports, and proposals.[1] Writing is considered a "threshold competency" or a "tool skill"—a necessity for managerial functioning.[2] Paul Glen, author of the award-winning book *Leading Geeks*, observes that "the most important thing you can do to ensure you have a vibrant career for years to come is to learn to write well. . . . Whether you are an executive, project manager or hard-core technologist, writing is the key to your future."[3]

E-mails, letters, and memos are probably the forms of written communication that benefit most from the strategic considerations we discuss in this text. The conciseness of these messages and the relatively detached atmosphere in which managers usually write them can help ensure that the principles of reader adaptation and strategic analysis are used.

Unfortunately, too many managers take routine writing tasks for granted. Perhaps because managers write so many of them, e-mails, letters, and memos frequently can become impersonal, lifeless ways to convey information. Rather than being responses to a specific communication situation, many messages use generic answers that ignore unique situational factors. The result is a disengaged readership—the typical office worker averages 199 unopened e-mails on any given day, according to a recent survey of 2,000 enterprise workers. Further, the survey found that a majority of workers blame excessive e-mails for getting in the way of their work.[4] A clogged inbox is an indication that business writers are not reaching their audience.

Additionally, because e-mails, letters, and memos are such common and relatively informal media, managers often become lax regarding the quality of their messages, dashing them off without revising and editing. "So what?" you might think. "Who cares about surface errors, so long as the message gets across?" In response, a mounting body of research indicates that grammar, mechanics, and sentence-level errors can indeed damage a manager's credibility.[5]

Another potential shortcoming of routine messages is that the language can become choked with stock phrases and clichés that turn the message into a ritual utterance: "as per your request," "reference your letter," "herewith acknowledge receipt," "please do not hesitate to contact me," and so on. Such documents often communicate very little except a negative impression of a stuffy, impersonal author.

This chapter takes a strategic approach to e-mail, letter, and memo writing, emphasizing ways in which a writer can adapt routine correspondence to fit as nearly as possible to the needs of the intended reader. The chapter also offers two general patterns for writing occasions you are likely to face as a manager and specific types you can use for guidance in certain cases. Of course, use these models as a foundation only; as suggested in Chapter 2, each message a manager writes needs to be adapted to fit the audience and the situation.

AUDIENCE ADAPTATION

In many business writing situations, a writer may not know the reader of the message very well, if at all. Yet readers expect that any message they receive will be personal and relevant. To meet this challenge, managers must use the strategic model from Chapter 2 to analyze their audience and compose messages with a "you attitude."

The you attitude is the basis for the organizational strategies this chapter details. Writers who have this attitude prepare messages matching their readers' interests. They do this by putting themselves in the reader's place. A writer with the you attitude begins by asking, "How would I feel if I were this person in this situation? What would I want to read in this message?"

The you attitude requires empathy, the ability to understand another's feelings; we show empathy when we say to a coworker who is having trouble solving a problem, "I know you're having a tough time." Similarly, we show empathy when we write what our audience wants to read. As an example, recent research on the importance of expressing gratitude indicates that workers appreciate written thanks over spoken thanks from their managers. Written thanks require effort and time, which are signs of a manager's empathy. Written thanks also document success, can be shared with others, and can be referred to later when the reader needs an emotional boost.[6]

CRITICAL THINKING QUESTIONS

1. When you are thumbing through a magazine, what makes you stop and read an article?

2. Why does a particular billboard message or TV commercial catch your attention?

3. What is the implied strategy for capturing the attention of the intended reader?

Basis of the You Attitude

Every audience is unique. Just as you would not give the same birthday gift to every member of your family, you should not give the same message to different employee groups. Audiences want to know that you understand their specific needs and concerns, so you must address them personally.

The you attitude, which is reader oriented, grew out of an awareness that most people tend to focus on their own interests. In reading a business message, they want to know what they might gain or how they can minimize a loss. Thus, when communicating in a positive situation, good writers seek to emphasize the positive impact of the news for each stakeholder group. In a negative situation, good writers seek to reduce negative impact by focusing on what the bad news means to each stakeholder group and describing possible benefits.

Anticipating Questions

To be effective, writers should anticipate the questions a reader might have. Thus, as they write, they ask themselves what the reader might be uncertain about and then answer the uncertainties so that no additional correspondence is needed. The five Ws described in Chapter 7 (who, what, when, where, and why) can help writers imagine the audience's questions or concerns.

Stressing Reader Benefits

Busy audiences want to know how your message affects their own work. Arguably, the most likely audience question is "What's in it for me?" A message with the you attitude shows the reader how they benefit. For example, a businessperson trying to collect on a past-due account might explain that the reader needs to pay the account balance to retain credit privileges at the store and a good credit rating. The potential for success in this case is far greater than if the credit manager had stressed only the company's interest by writing of its need to receive payment.

Avoiding Negatives

A writer should avoid negatives and words with negative connotations, such as *unfortunately*, *claim*, *allege*, *problem*, *damage*, and *regret*. These words have a way of jumping off the page and putting the reader on the defensive. A negative word can affect a reader's perceptions so much that the rest of the message is lost. Stressing the positive aspects of the situation, on the other hand, will improve the writer–reader relationship and make it more likely that the writer's goal will be reached.

An easy way to find positive words for a negative message is to say what *will* happen rather than what *will not* happen. So instead of telling a customer, "Unfortunately, we can't meet Friday's delivery deadline," one could say, "Your shipment will arrive on Monday." As described in the previous chapter, Holiday Inn Express uses this strategy well. Instead of warning hotel guests not to steal the towels from the rooms, a card simply announces, "Should you decide to take these articles from your room . . . we will assume you approve a corresponding charge to your account." Note the positive terms in the message: *take*, *approve*. Guests are less likely to be offended or insulted by this announcement.

Here is another example of a negative message couched in positive words. In early 2017, Wells Fargo agreed to pay $110 million to settle a class-action lawsuit related to the creation of up to 2 million sham accounts that customers didn't request or authorize. On April 5, a full-page letter signed by Timothy J. Sloan, the CEO and president of Wells Fargo, appeared in the *Houston Chronicle*. It began with, "Thank you," and listed the "progress" that the corporation had made to "make things right for our customers . . . and ensure we always put our customers' needs first." The letter ended by announcing to readers that the corporation was building "a better bank."[7] The language in this message put a positive spin on bad news.

Diction

The you attitude also influences a message's wording. To demonstrate that the reader's interest is of central concern, use language that makes the reader central as well. Revise sentences to address the reader's concerns and interests. Instead of using *I*, *me*, *mine* or *we*, *us*, *our*, *ours*, use *you*, *your*, *yours*. Thus, rather than saying, "We are sending the samples of the ads we worked up for Reality Industry's new pumps," a sentence with you attitude would say, "You will soon receive three samples of the magazine ads for your new pumps." The revision makes the reader rather than the writer the focus of attention.

Nonverbal Elements and the You Attitude

The you attitude shows itself in a variety of ways, some more obvious than others. One of these ways is metacommunication, the nonverbal cues that enhance or contradict a message. Without reading a word, an individual receiving a message can tell a lot about the sender and the sender's attitude toward the reader.

In hardcopy messages, the stationery chosen for correspondence or paper grade used in printing, smeared or pale print, typos, stains, and incongruent typographic choices and graphics can create static in the communication channel. While the text of the message says that the writer cares, the physical elements of the medium suggest indifference at best. Attention to details suggests professionalism and respect for the reader.

Similarly, the nonverbal elements of softcopy correspondence such as e-mail can make a positive or negative impression on the reader. Concise e-mails limited to one screen in length mean that readers do not have to scroll. Brief paragraphs separated by whitespace, headings, and bold text for questions or action items improve readability. If the message is part of a string of exchanges, delete earlier messages that are no longer relevant and check that the Subject line is still appropriate. Formatting may change when a reader opens an external e-mail, so limit the use of design and formatting elements such as tabs.

ORGANIZATIONAL STRATEGIES

Thus far, we have looked at a variety of ways in which a manager can personalize messages to make them better understood and received by readers. One key element remains: organizational strategy. The suggestions given so far for signaling concern for the reader will fall short if you do not organize the message in a manner that helps your reader understand them. The next section of this chapter describes two basic strategies that, when used properly, can deliver the message effectively, address reader reaction, and promote a positive image of the writer.

Direct Strategy

The direct strategy is used for messages conveying good news or neutral information. Deliver the news as quickly as possible. If the message's main idea is buried in the middle or near the end, the reader loses interest and becomes frustrated at wasting valuable time searching for the main point. This frustration can affect the reader's attitude toward the writer: "Why can't they come right to the point?" Poorly organized messages can weaken and even destroy the positive impact of the message and the reader's goodwill.

Opening

For good news and neutral messages, put the main point first. A brief introduction might be needed to orient the reader, but this introduction should not delay the presentation of the main point. An easy way to remember this principle is the acronym BIF, or big idea first. Begin with a purpose statement that answers the reader's question: "Why is this person writing to me?"

Body

The next step is to provide the necessary supporting details: the reasons for the decision, background or history, specifics about the situation, or the procedures the reader needs to follow. These details promote the writer or the company they represent, especially when the message grants a favor.

Close

A direct message has a positive ending. Among the choices can be an offer to help, a statement of gratitude, or a call for any further action the reader needs to take. Closing with a goodwill statement as simple as "Thanks" leaves a positive impression.

CRITICAL THINKING QUESTIONS

1. In addition to routine business messages, where else have you seen messages organized according to the direct strategy, which puts the big idea first?

2. Consider the effectiveness of this organizational strategy for the nonbusiness messages you've noticed. How did you react?

Indirect Strategy

Unfortunately, not all business messages communicate good news or even neutral information. Requests are denied, proposals are rejected, and job applications are turned down. The readers naturally are not pleased, but effective bad news messages convey negative information while creating minimum resentment. If the reader is desirable as a customer, client, or future employee, using the right organizational pattern should help build goodwill for the company.

A good strategy for negative situations is the indirect one. Using this strategy, a writer leads the reader logically to the bad news and builds goodwill. A comparison between the direct and the indirect approaches is presented in Table 8-1.

Not all indirect messages convey bad news. The persuasive message is a specialized type of indirect message that will be detailed later in the chapter.

Opening

Instead of BIF (big idea first), writers using the indirect strategy should use the BILL formula—big idea a little later. The indirect message begins with a buffer, a neutral or positive statement that clearly relates to the purpose of the message. The beginning might summarize the situation, express appreciation for the business relationship, or offer a compliment.

A good opening begins to let the reader down gently. Ideally, it subtly sets up the explanation that follows in the body of the message. The reader expects things to go their way. When the indirect beginning fails to reinforce that expectation, the stage is set for the denial or bad news to follow.

TABLE 8-1 ■ The Direct Approach Compared to the Indirect Approach

Direct	Indirect
Opening	**Opening**
Main point	Neutral buffer
Body	**Body**
Supporting information	Explanation and negative news
Close	**Close**
Positive statement; action item; goodwill	Goodwill

Body

Next, the message analyzes the circumstances or provides details about the facts that lead to the bad news about to be conveyed. The challenge here is to be convincing. The tone of this part is cooperative. The writer does not have to say, "Let's look at the facts," but the reader should have that feeling. A study of data breach notifications sent to customers by state and federal agencies found that more than 75 percent of the messages followed this indirect strategy—they provided background information before stating the bad news that the readers' personal information had been compromised.[8]

Next, the writer implies or directly expresses the negative information in as positive a tone as possible. Naturally, a writer should not be so subtle in implying the negative news that the reader is left hanging. But any direct statement should be tactful and not blunt. The best approach is to subordinate the actual point where the bad news is stated in the middle of a paragraph rather than the beginning or end.

Close

The next step is important: At the end, the writer should strive to rebuild goodwill. Depending on the situation, several options are available. One is to suggest another course of action open to the reader. In response to claims for goods, for example, the writer might suggest others that are more durable or equally appropriate for the reader's use. Similarly, a letter rejecting a proposal might suggest another outlet for the idea.

Close the indirect message on a positive, friendly note. Often, the effort to build goodwill is enough. Sometimes a little more is necessary. A manager might want to offer services or information. For example, a letter written to an established customer might enclose a catalog and end by looking forward to the reader's next order.

CRITICAL THINKING QUESTIONS

1. In addition to negative business messages, where else have you seen messages organized according to the indirect strategy, or BILL?

2. Consider the effectiveness of this organizational strategy for the nonbusiness messages you've noticed. How did you respond?

Handling Negatives

Given that an indirect message conveys bad news, it is potentially very negative. To minimize the damage to a company's goodwill, good writers generally avoid negative words and keep the overall tone positive. The following three rules hold the key:

- Place negative information at points of low emphasis.

- Avoid *no* or *not* when possible.

- Avoid words with negative connotations.

De-emphasize negative facts by placing them in a subordinate structure (a dependent clause, a parenthetical expression, or a modifier) rather than in a main clause or a standalone sentence. In a paragraph, put negative information into an inconspicuous position. Compare the following two short paragraphs telling a job applicant that the company has no openings:

> We do not anticipate any openings in the Baytown Company anytime soon, since we have been laying off people in your field. You might apply at Rumfield and Company or Bennington, Inc., since they are adding to their staffs.

The writer could easily have softened the negatives by placing them in a less prominent position:

> Please consider applying for one of the engineering positions now open at Rumfield and Company or at Bennington, Inc., rather than at Baytown Company. Currently Baytown's personnel needs are in other areas.

The second suggestion for avoiding negative writing (avoiding *no* and *not*) is easier to follow than it seems. Recall the Holiday Inn Express example described earlier in this chapter, which uses positive words to ask guests not to steal items from the rooms. In the two revisions in the following example, the writer emphasizes what the company *can* do, not what it *cannot* do:

> We cannot fill your order until you tell us what size grill your restaurant currently uses.

> We can fill your order as soon as you let us know your restaurant's grill size.

> Please specify your grill size so that we may fill your order as quickly as possible.

The third suggestion (avoiding words with negative connotations) is one of the most important. Whereas *claim* and *state* might have very similar denotations, their connotations are widely separated. Writing to a person and saying, "You next claim that . . ." makes it sound as if the reader is wrong. Numerous words are likely to irritate or even inflame when they appear in bad news messages. (See examples of such words in the box below.)

allege	argue
failure	mistake
claim	damage
regret	error
careless	broken

SPECIFIC TYPES: DIRECT MESSAGES

The direct and indirect strategies are useful for most writing situations managers face. Nevertheless, because some situations are so frequent (for example, the inquiry) and because some are so sensitive (for example, negative responses to claims), several specialized versions of the direct and indirect patterns have developed. Table 8-2 lists seven specific versions reviewed here.

TABLE 8-2 ■ Types of Direct and Indirect Messages	
Direct	**Indirect**
Inquiries and requests	Negative responses to inquiries and requests
Positive responses to inquiries and requests	Refused claims
Claims	Persuasive messages
Positive responses to claims	

The patterns suggested here are not absolute. After strategic analysis, a manager may determine that a different approach is appropriate. That kind of adaptation is to be encouraged because it helps prevent following a mechanical pattern. First, we look at correspondence using the direct pattern; then we consider correspondence following the indirect. Remember to use a direct approach for good news and neutral, informative messages.

Inquiries and Requests

Perhaps the most common direct correspondence is the inquiry. Managers in all areas of business routinely need information to conduct their affairs. A manager might need to know about the performance of a product; another might want credit information about a client or wish to know about the qualifications of a job applicant. Because most readers see these requests as routine and reasonable, they are likely to respond to them willingly.

If you project yourself into the position of a reader receiving an inquiry, you'll see why the direct approach is so appropriate. You are probably busy with other matters and need to know quickly what is required of you. When you receive an inquiry, you appreciate the writer's efforts to be direct and to let you know from the start what they want.

Opening

Make the inquiry clear from the start. One effective method is to begin with a question that summarizes the writer's objective. For example, an inquiry about a potential employee could begin with "Would you please comment on Mary Keynes's qualifications to become a management intern? We at Infovend are considering her for the position, and she has given your name as a reference." The question beginning the inquiry makes the purpose immediately clear.

Body

In many cases, the next step in the inquiry is an explanation of the inquiry's purpose. In the example just given, you quickly made it clear that you are considering Keynes for a job. The amount of information a writer gives depends on the situation. In an inquiry about a potential employee, you also probably would want to assure the reader that their response will be kept confidential.[9] The body of the inquiry needs to be efficiently organized; it cannot simply be a "fishing expedition" for information. Even after the purpose is clear, the reader usually needs guidance to answer the inquiry satisfactorily. Given as much of the sample letter about Mary Keynes as we have so far, it might be answered in several ways, depending on how the reader projects your needs—or it might not be detailed at all. Thus, the next part of the inquiry should set out the areas requiring information, plus any necessary additional information. Numbering the questions may also help the reader respond.

Close

The close of the inquiry is friendly and builds goodwill. In some cases, it is appropriate to offer similar services. In situations where a purchase might follow, you might ask for a speedy reply.

Let us look at the complete inquiry about Mary Keynes. Note that in this inquiry about a person, you emphasized confidentiality, an advisable practice.

Dear Professor Renton:

Would you please comment on Mary Keynes's qualifications to become a management intern? We at Infovend are considering her for the position, and she has given your name as a reference. Of course, whatever information you give us will be held in confidence.

1. How well does Keynes manage time? Is her work punctual?

2. Did you have a chance to observe her under pressure? If so, does she manage well, or does pressure adversely affect her performance?

3. How well does she relate to her peers? Please comment on her relationship with them: Is she a leader or a follower, gregarious or shy, and so on?

I look forward to receiving your comments on Keynes's qualifications by the end of this month and will appreciate whatever insights you can share with us.

Sincerely,
Tim Inman
Human Resources Manager

Positive Responses to Inquiries and Requests

Inquiries naturally need answers. The favorable response to an inquiry should follow the direct strategy, as the reader will be pleased to receive the requested information or item.

Opening

Begin by identifying the request you are responding to. The opening also makes it clear that the reader's request is being granted:

- I found Mary Keynes, the subject of your June 5 inquiry, to be one of the most promising students I have ever taught.

- As-Best-As Filing Cabinets have all the features you mentioned in your March 4 letter and several more you might be interested in knowing about.

- Here is my response to your September 14 inquiry about our experiences with the M-102 Security System.

You can begin by directly answering the most general of the questions originally asked (as in the first two examples) or by agreeing to respond to the question originally posed (as in the third example).

Body

The way in which you organize the body of the message varies, depending on the original inquiry. For an inquiry that asked one question, the details in response appear in order of importance. If you are responding to a series of questions, normally answer them in the order asked. If the original is really a request (for example, "May we use your facilities for a club meeting?"), the body gives necessary conditions for use.

Not all responses to inquiries are completely good or bad news. Thus, although a manager is willing to answer most questions, some topics are confidential. In these cases, the denial is subordinated and appears after the writer explains why. For example, the response to the inquiry about a company's experiences with the M-102 Security System may withhold some details for security reasons.

Close

The positive response to an inquiry continues to be positive in the close. Note the following closings to the messages whose beginnings we gave earlier:

- If I can provide any other information about Mary, please contact me.

- If you need any other information on how As-Best-As Filing Cabinets can meet your storage needs, please call me.

- I'd be delighted to answer any further questions about our experiences with the M-102 Security System. I think you'll be pleased with the system.

Claims

A third type of direct message is the claim. Dissatisfied customers make claims, or complaints, about problems and request a solution. Customer dissatisfaction leads to a loss of goodwill and revenue, so managers should find out quickly what the problem is and resolve it. Effective claims provide information about the problem and suggest an acceptable remedy.

Opening

Even though the claim deals with something negative, it is written in a direct pattern. From the writer's perspective, directness strengthens the claim. In fact, some readers may interpret indirectness as lack of confidence in the claim being made. Indirectness would thus be a strategic error.

Early in the claim, you should include details about the faulty product, service, or sale. The details to incorporate depend on the situation, but they may include invoice numbers, dates, and the product identification or serial number.

Another good tactic that makes the message convincing is to include the significance of the problem to you or your business. For example, a warehouse manager whose new intercom system failed might write:

> The new intercom system you sent us 2 weeks ago (Invoice #16789) has broken, thus considerably slowing the processing of orders in our company warehouse.

Body

The next step is logical: The facts of the case need detailing. In the intercom example, you discuss how the system broke down and the possible cause. Naturally, you do not need to be an expert analyst, but the more facts you include, the more convincing your argument. If appropriate, you may also wish to detail the damage that resulted.

Of course, detailing the problem requires tact and forbearance. You may feel justified in writing about the problem, but do not attack the person who sold or installed the product or its manufacturer. Name-calling or accusations do little if any good and may create reader resentment, which usually precludes a favorable settlement. Abusive messages are best left unsent.

The next part of the letter states what you want: What will set things right? Unfortunately, some letters end before this point, and the problem remains unresolved. Specify the action or amount of money needed for satisfaction. Occasionally, the settlement can be left up to the reader if the situation is routine.

You may also wish to include a deadline for action on the matter. Naturally, a deadline needs something to back it up. If you make a threat or ultimatum, be sure that you are willing and able to carry it out if the situation is not resolved. Weigh threats carefully. They can be counterproductive.

Close

Once again, avoid negativity in the close. If you threaten to take your business elsewhere, the reader may lose any motivation for cooperation. End by expressing confidence in the good faith of the reader or by expressing intended gratitude for the early resolution of the problem.

Let us look at the rest of the claim about the faulty intercom and see how it illustrates these points:

Dear Mr. Packard:

The new intercom system you sent us 2 weeks ago (Invoice #16789) has broken, thus considerably slowing the processing of orders in our company warehouse.

Although the system worked fine immediately after installation, we began to notice problems with it during stormy weather. When it rained, static garbled many of the messages. Finally, during one heavy downpour, the main transmitter stopped working and began smoking.

We are shipping the transmitter to you via Brown Express. We would like it either repaired or replaced. Your prompt attention will help our warehouse return to normal.

Sincerely,
Patricia Muranka
Purchasing Manager

In this message, the manager detailed the problem her department faced, yet she resisted accusatory language. She set out her experience with the system and provided enough information for the manufacturer to diagnose the problem. The ending is positive yet assertive.

Positive Responses to Claims

The fourth type of direct message is the positive response to a claim. While the use of the direct order is unquestionable, this type still challenges the writer who is aware of the business losses the reader experienced. The challenge here is to rebuild goodwill and, in many cases, restore faith in the product. The reader who does not believe in the product will buy elsewhere next time. Occasionally, especially when dealing with angry customers, you may find yourself responding to a very unpleasant or accusatory letter. It's best to grant the claim while maintaining a professional, unemotional tone.

Opening

Begin the adjustment grant with the good news. The reader also may need a quick reminder to recall the situation. Thus, the letter responding to the claim about the faulty intercom might begin with this:

Your transmitter is now in working order and should arrive in Cedar Rapids by truck in the next few days.

Body

After the good news, the information in the body depends on the situation. Routine cases need little explanation. In many cases, however, the reader needs more. It is usually necessary to explain what went wrong, and it is often a good idea to stress that the problem is corrected and will not recur.

Occasionally, you will need to explain the proper use of the product to a reader who unintentionally misused the product. This explanation needs to be tactful and is most effective when presented impersonally, as in the second example that follows:

- You left the valves open on the unit. As a result, your heater was on constantly and wore out.

- The valves leading out to the unit must be kept tightly closed to reduce the demand on the heating unit.

In the explanatory material and the close, maintain a positive tone. Common courtesy seems to dictate an apology, but it often serves to open old wounds. Instead, look to the future with a confident, positive approach:

You can expect many more years of trouble-free service from your transmitter.

Close

The closing of an adjustment grant is positive. It anticipates continued good relations with the customer and may include information on other products or services the company offers. You build goodwill by discussing the advantages of the product. You also do not blame the electrician's faulty installation, although you have taken steps to protect the equipment in the future. Let's continue the example of the intercom transmitter:

Dear Ms. Muranka:

Your transmitter is now in working order and should arrive in Cedar Rapids by truck in the next few days. Please call your electrician when it arrives, so that the installation will protect the warranty.

You reported that the system had static in it during rainstorms and that it smoked when the system stopped working. I've checked the new patented fusible ground lead and found that it had melted, as it was designed to do, and protected the transmitter and you from electrical shock.

When your electrician installs the transmitter, the unit's grounding should be checked. At present, when it rains, the unit is shorting out because of incomplete grounding.

You might be interested in our new security alarm system that hooks into the existing intercom system. The enclosed pamphlet gives you the details. We will be glad to discuss its installation with you.

Sincerely,
Robert Packard
Customer Service Manager

SPECIFIC TYPES: INDIRECT MESSAGES

The next section describes three specific types of messages that follow the indirect organizational pattern (Table 8-2). By presenting the big idea a little later (BILL), you may soften the blow of bad news or persuade resistant audiences to consider your ideas.

Negative Responses to Inquiries

The first type is negative responses to inquiries. Most managers cannot comply with all the requests they receive. In those situations, the response is best organized according to the indirect plan. Constructing negative responses to inquiries calls for a bad news strategy in which reasons appear first, followed by the refusal.

Opening

The opening should remind the reader of the request. This initial statement should also serve as a neutral buffer. Furthermore, the opening should lead logically into the body.

Suppose, for example, you received a letter from a researcher inquiring into the sample used to determine your company's marketing strategies. Because such questions deal with proprietary information that the company keeps confidential, you must deny the request. However, your message may seem rude if you refuse directly. Therefore your response might begin with one of the following buffers:

- Thank you for your inquiry about our marketing research and strategies.

- The results of your study of research samples should prove interesting.

This introduction gives no false hope for a positive reply, but it does not deny the request yet.

Body

From this beginning, you move into the reasons why the request cannot be granted. Using your analysis of the audience, choose examples or reasoning likely to convince the reader that your decision is the only viable option. In the preceding letter, you could appeal to the reader's own experience as a researcher who has spent hours developing ideas. Similarly, after great expense, your company developed ideas that it applies to its own needs.

Once you have given the reasoning, state the refusal. Occasionally, writers refuse requests so vaguely that the reader still sees hope for the request, so be clear.

Close

Close positively to build goodwill. The close can look to the future, such as a wish for success in the reader's work or a suggestion for some other sources of information the reader could use.

In the letter refusing the request for information on marketing strategies, note that you make no apology for refusing:

Dear Ms. Leeper:

The results of your study of research samples should prove interesting, as most companies protect these data because they are so central to their marketing strategies.

At Flo-Sheen Fabrics, we develop our marketing strategies only after our test market has had a chance to examine our new fabrics. As a researcher, you can surely appreciate the countless hours that go into any marketing campaign. We keep the sample subjects used for our marketing analysis confidential, both to protect their privacy and to help us keep our competitive edge. We do not share the results outside of our organization.

Please be assured that we abide by best practices for selecting our research samples. Best wishes for your project's success.

Sincerely,
Sheila Hebert
Vice President

Refused Claims

A greater challenge than the negative response to an inquiry is the refused claim. In most cases, the person making the claim believes it is justified due to your bad products or services. However, for whatever reason, you have determined that you must reject the claim.

In doing so, you must maintain a positive tone and build goodwill. The key is empathy. Imagine how you would want to be treated in this situation—probably reasonably. The language must be positive and selective. Most likely, the reader will be sensitive to nuances.

Opening

The claim refusal must begin as most negative, indirect messages would: with a buffer. This buffer can refer to the reader's original claim as its subject, or it can be an expression of appreciation—some opening that brings the reader and writer together neutrally.

The effective opening also indicates the line of reasoning to be followed. Take, for example, this opening sentence: "Whitlow Co. does guarantee its sump pumps for 18 months in normal operation under normal circumstances." The reader is reminded of the original claim and is introduced to the line of reasoning in "normal operation" and "normal circumstances."

Body

The body details your findings. This explanation should be objective and convincing, but it should avoid a my-side/your-side dichotomy. One effective tactic is to describe the effort that went into investigating the matter. For example, a negative response to a warranty claim may emphasize the laboratory tests made on the broken part. This detail is useful because it projects a caring image; the decision made is not just some automatic response.

Give the refusal once the reasons are clear. Of course, the refusal should appear at a point of low emphasis. If the refusal is based on company policy, the policy should be clearly explained. But remember that customers generally resent managers "hiding behind" company policy. Use logic whenever possible instead.

Close

Most claim refusals close with an effort at resale. If the customer has been treated fairly in a reasonable manner, you may be able to keep the account. Frequently, it is a good idea to mention an upcoming sale or enclose a recent catalog.

Dear Ms. Clark:

Whitlow Co. does guarantee its sump pumps for 18 months in normal operation under normal circumstances. After your recent letter, we looked closely into the questions you raised.

Our laboratory examined the returned pump and found that the entire unit had been submerged for some time. This submersion was in keeping with the newspaper accounts of heavy flooding in your town last month. Apparently, the area where your unit was located was also inundated. While the pump is designed to take care of normal seepage, it should be mounted at least 18 inches above the basement floor to keep the housing and pump dry.

Although we cannot refund the cost of the sump pump, you might be interested in another model, the SubMerso. Its waterproof housing withstands even prolonged immersion. The enclosed pamphlet details its capacities. We'll be glad to answer any questions you might have about it.

Sincerely,
Lionel Naquin
Customer Service Representative

Persuasive Messages

The indirect strategy is appropriate for persuasive messages as well as negative messages. A manager uses the indirect strategy when trying to persuade others to do things they might not ordinarily wish to do. You might need to write a persuasive letter to convince a reluctant client to pay their bill. Or you might write a persuasive e-mail to gain a coworker's support on a project. Or you might compose a sales letter to potential customers.

Opening

The persuasive message opens by catching the reader's attention. One effective way of doing this is to show the reader that their goals are your goals. The best way to show this identity of goals is to match this message with the reader's interests. At the same time, the opening must be brief. Often, the opening will engage the reader with a question. Thus, a sales letter for a tropical resort hotel might begin with "Ready for a vacation?"

Body

The body follows a *problem, solution, benefits* format. First, it convinces the reader that you understand their problem. Then, it reveals the solution to the problem—the solution that you want the reader to embrace. This part reflects careful strategy, because the reader's possible objections must be anticipated and answered. Then you stress the benefits accruing to the reader as a result of the solution. In the case of a resort hotel's sales letter, the body might consist of a list of features and benefits in vivid detail.

Close

The ending is important. The effective persuasive message does not end after the proposed answer is revealed. The reader's interest must be channeled into action. Otherwise, interest will decline, with nothing accomplished. The action item should be specific: a meeting, an order, a phone call, a payment, an interview, a change in procedure. An action must be prompt and may include a deadline, because delay reduces the probability of action.[10] A resort hotel's sales letter might, therefore, end with an enticing discount offer "for a limited time only."

The following job application letter illustrates the implementation of the indirect persuasive strategy:

Dear Ms. Harris:

Now that Tea Time is about to open its third cafe in Jonesboro, won't you need a highly motivated assistant manager? I have the background and motivation necessary to become your most productive new hire.

As a junior marketing major at State University, I am currently taking marketing courses. I could apply what I learn over the next 2 years to managing your new Tea Time location. The job references listed on the attached résumé will all attest to the fact that I am very energetic and enthusiastic about my work.

Another reason I would make a good assistant manager for you is that I am very interested in pursuing a career with Tea Time after graduation. I would see these 2 years as a testing period to prove myself, and you would have the 2 years to decide whether or not you would be equally interested in me as a member of senior management.

If I have described the kind of person you want at Tea Time, may I have an interview to further discuss the position? I can be reached at 123.555.8403, and I can be available at a time convenient to you.

Sincerely,
Jonna Morris

LETTER FORMAT

Thus far, we have discussed two strategies for organizing routine messages—direct and indirect—and showed how to use them when sending messages to external audiences, such as customers, clients, regulatory agencies, and hiring agents. Typically, these messages are in letter or e-mail format. Good writers know that the appearance of a document can affect the reader's reaction to its content, much the same way a speaker's appearance affects the listeners' response to the message. A word about contemporary letter format is therefore appropriate.

Many routine business messages are sent electronically, either as e-mails or as e-mail attachments. Formatting elements, such as tabs (indents) and centering, can change or even disappear according to the technology used to open the message, so the appearance of a message should be simple, plain, and as easy to read as possible.

A standard contemporary style, whether hard copy or soft copy, is to begin every part of a business letter at the left margin (flush left, ragged right). Standard business letter style calls for single spacing within paragraphs, with double spacing between paragraphs and between elements of the letter to create white space. This line spacing format eliminates the need to indent when you begin a paragraph. Keeping paragraphs short, as discussed in Chapter 7, also builds white space. The persuasive letter in Figure 8-1 exemplifies excellent strategies for both content and format.

FIGURE 8-1 ■ Sample Persuasive Letter

LaSalle Senior Center
1111 N. Wells St., Suite 500, Chicago, IL 60610
312-573-8840 Fax 312-787-1212

Gerry Hynes
3780 Copperfield Dr., Unit 1018
Bryan, TX 77802

Dear Gerry,

As the year moves to an end, I think about two of our seniors who died this year. They were each exceptional in their own way; each had a key role at the LaSalle Senior Center and each benefited from the services we offered just as we benefited from their gifts. They were like many of the seniors we work with, both a client and a volunteer.

Marc Stuart was a regular volunteer at both the Wednesday and Sunday meals. Having management experience, he was inclined to supervise both clients and volunteers. He was part of the fabric of the Senior Center and showed his support by his presence and by his care for other seniors. The Senior Center provided Marc with a place to serve and live out his faith. He told me on several occasions that his first priority was LaSalle Street Church followed by the Senior Center.

Allene Hales was exceptional by any standard. With little formal education, very modest means, and compromised health, she brought people together at the Senior Center and in her community. She knew everyone. And she was always helping others, offering a kind word, sharing money or food. The Senior Center recognized her for her gifts and provided her some real help with day-to-day matters.

Marc and Allene found a home at the Senior Center. They found a place that offered them help, a place where they could serve and a place to belong. Thanks to your support, the LaSalle Senior Center continues to be that place for over 200 local seniors every month.

Please consider making a gift* to help continue our ministry to our neighborhood's older friends.

Sincerely,
Keith Chase-Ziolek
Director

*A generous donor will match the first $5,000 in gifts.

Source: Chase-Ziolek. Reprinted by permission of the author.

Regarding typography, a detailed discussion of the impact of type style in business documents is found in Chapter 6. Serif typefaces like Times New Roman, Garamond, and Cambria create a classic, traditional standard in business. In addition to business letters, paper documents such as newsletters, brochures, and manuals typically use a serif font. Electronic messages often use sans serif typefaces, such as Calibri, Verdana, and Helvetica.

Sans serif fonts are easier to read onscreen and are often used for websites, posted announcements, and signs.

INTERNAL CORRESPONDENCE

The writing strategies described in this chapter apply to internal as well as external correspondence. Memos and e-mail are the formats most frequently used for written messages within an organization.[11] The memo is an efficient, straightforward kind of communication. Often, memos are sent electronically, as e-mails. As described in the previous section, e-mail is becoming more commonly used for routine external communication as well. A hybrid format is a business letter or memo sent as an e-mail attachment, a practice that allows the sender to stabilize design and format elements when the document is opened.

As in the case of external correspondence, the writer needs to be strategic about adapting to the audience when composing internal correspondence. This is especially true when writing to employees at a different level within the organization, when writing to those who possess a less specialized knowledge of the subject, or when the memo deals with sensitive matters. While internal messages are often routine, informal exchanges of information, they should be composed carefully. After all, they are official, permanent records that might be accessed and read by multiple audiences, including external audiences, regardless of the writer's intentions.[12]

Memo Format

Memo formats differ from one another in minor details, but they generally have four standard guide words at the top: *To, From, Subject*, and *Date*. In e-mails, these guide words are automatically provided. The From line offers few problems. However, if needed, a writer can clarify her authority by including her job title after her name. She can add the names of others here as well—assuming she has their agreement.

The Subject line has obvious value in directing the reader's attention. Be specific about your topic and purpose. For instance, "Subject: Request for Vacation Schedules" is more likely to stimulate reader response than the vaguer "Subject: Schedules." Using key words in the Subject line will often aid in the memo's later retrieval from archives and files as well.

Just as with face-to-face interactions, memos sent within an organization typically have a set protocol one should respect. This means paying attention to the format generally used, as well as noting any subtleties related to the recipients of the memo or its copies (cc:).[13] For example, by including the boss in the cc: line, the writer is implying that they enjoy easy access to that boss or that the boss is monitoring the situation. Be sure to copy your immediate supervisor when contacting the supervisor's bosses. In general, copying your supervisor keeps them aware of what is going on. Even when not immediately involved, the supervisor will appreciate knowing about events. However, the proliferation of e-mail copies and Reply All in most organizations is a real problem. Do not flood people with excessive, irrelevant messages.

In printed memos, sign your initials or name on the From line. This authenticates the document, just as a signature does on a letter. Because your name is in the header, there is no need to add it to the end of the memo. In e-mail, a signature with your name and contact information confirms your identity, which can be useful if the message is forwarded to others. However, pithy quotations, images, and similar elements at the bottom of e-mails add clutter and can be annoying distractions to business readers. Remember that short, simple messages have the most impact.

Finally, remember that design elements such as tabs and bullets may not be preserved in e-mails at the receiving end. If your e-mail needs a simple bulleted list, create it using characters on your keyboard, such as the dash or asterisk. If more complex formatting like tables or multilevel lists are needed, create a separate document and send it as an attachment to your e-mail.

E-mail Format

Beyond the standard guide words at the top, e-mail format varies from organization to organization and often from writer to writer. You have probably noticed differences in the following categories:

- Forms of address—greetings and "Dear" lines

- Linguistic novelties—emoticons, jargon, and acronyms

- Punctuation and capitalization

- Spelling—conventional or "text shorthand"

- Endings—signature blocks; security warnings

Rules have emerged for e-mail style or *netiquette*, but they are often ignored. For instance, some writers begin an e-mail with a salutation or "Dear" line, despite the To line at the top. *Dear* was born about a thousand years ago, meaning "honorable, worthy," and took on the sense of "esteemed, valued" and "beloved." Today's e-mails are more likely to begin with the less formal "Good afternoon," "Hello," or just "Hi." Occasionally, managers address multiple audiences as "All" or even "Folks."

Judith Martin, author of *Miss Manners' Guide to Excruciatingly Correct Behavior, Freshly Updated*, suggests that you may begin an e-mail "with almost anything civil. Or even nothing, because an e-mail is like a memo and doesn't require a salutation. But informality is not a euphemism for rudeness or sloppiness."[14]

Just as conventions for e-mail greetings vary from organization to organization, so do conventions for e-mail signoffs. While business letters typically end with "Sincerely," that closing may seem too formal for routine e-mail messages. Instead, you may see "Thank you," "Regards," "Cheers," or "Warm regards." Currently the most popular closing is "Best," which is a streamlined version of "Best wishes," a phrase that goes back centuries.[15] All of these are safe and more succinct than "Have a good day" or "Make it a great day." The popularity of texting as a business communication tool has resulted in internal e-mails becoming briefer and more informal, to the extent that a closing is often omitted. Good advice for e-mail writers, then, is to be courteous as well as concise. Overly formal formatting is as inappropriate as overly casual formatting.

Finally, a word of caution regarding e-mail formats and the overuse of punctuation and capitalization for emphasis. As business writers shift toward texts and tweets for casual exchanges, they should be careful to avoid applying those conventions to routine but official correspondence. In particular, when exclamation points are used merely as a sincerity marker, then multiple exclamation marks are needed to convey emotional intensity. Ending an e-mail with "Thanks!" is becoming the norm, not an enthusiastic shout. Linguists such as Judith Roof at Rice University warn against punctuation inflation as a substitute for expressive capacity.[16]

Memo and E-mail Uses

Memos and e-mails serve a variety of uses within an organization. We have listed the most common in this section. You may see other practices where you work as well.

Communicating to Groups

Not only does the memo or e-mail save time over talking to several coworkers; it also ensures that each person has the same information at the same time.

Fixing Responsibility

A manager who uses memos and e-mails for giving assignments has a written record if questions of responsibility arise later.

Communicating With Opponents

Personal dislikes crop up in any organization from time to time, but memos and e-mails bridge the gaps that may ensue. Recently, texting and Twitter have been added to the list of communication channels used for this purpose. However, it is never appropriate to "flame" a reader with an emotion-packed e-mail, text message, or tweet. Remember the permanency of all messages generated at work, whether paper or electronic. Never write something you could not defend in a meeting or courtroom.

Communicating With the Inaccessible

Memos and e-mails are handy for dealing with people (especially supervisors) who are hard to reach. A series of memos can also be proof of past attempts to contact a boss if problems arise.

Making Announcements

Announcements concerning policy changes, meetings and conferences, new products, and personnel changes are informative, nonsensitive messages and follow the direct order strategy. Other types of notifications include status reports, such as progress and periodic reports. The following informative memo is an example of an announcement:

MEMORANDUM

TO: All Salaried Employees

FROM: Alan Reynolds, Director of Human Resources

DATE: October 3, 2021

SUBJECT: Changes in Payroll Practices

We've made a couple of changes in the payroll procedures to alleviate some of the bottlenecks that have delayed paychecks in the past few months.

1. Paychecks will no longer be mailed out. You will receive your check for the month on the last working day of that month. Direct deposits will still be made to your checking or savings account, provided you use direct deposit for only one account.

2. All travel and expense reimbursements received before the 20th of each month will be included in that monthly paycheck. Requests for reimbursement will no longer be paid by individual checks as in the past. Of course, these expense reimbursements are not taxed.

These changes in payroll should help guarantee timely paychecks.

Requesting Action

The nature of the request-for-action memo dictates its organization. When a manager requests action that typically falls under their jurisdiction, direct order is appropriate, and the memo or e-mail begins with a clear Subject line that includes the writer's purpose and topic. When the requested action may meet with resistance, a less specific Subject line and a more persuasive strategy (indirect order) are appropriate. Whether direct or indirect, these memos and e-mails often require lists of steps and clear terms for successful action. Remember, when requesting behavior change, concrete language is always preferable to vague expressions, such as "please give your attention to this matter" and "reply at your earliest convenience" (see Chapter 7).

Political Uses in Business

Recall from Chapter 7 that managers belong to a discourse community with unique characteristics and uses for their writing. The memo and e-mail are examples of strategic tools for managers that are used for communicating with groups, opponents, and the inaccessible; fixing responsibility; making announcements; and requesting action. In fulfilling these tasks within an organization, these tools may be put to additional strategic uses. Some strategic or political uses are detailed next.

One political device is the copy list. Managers can protect themselves, project their achievements, publicize alliances, establish accountability, and show favor by including—and not including—certain people as cc: recipients.[17]

Another strategic practice is to write a memo or e-mail summarizing a meeting and send it to attendees, other stakeholders, or even "To File." While the message is ostensibly "for the record," its role as a record of the meeting or discussion can affect perceptions and document decisions or conversations. The meeting minutes become the reality and may, for example, prove ownership of an idea or evidence of dissent.

Managers sometimes use memos and e-mails to shape readers' opinions. An announcement of a policy or procedure change that uses positive language and stresses reader benefits may influence employees' willingness to adopt the new system. In summary, managers should remember that anything they put in writing, whether hard copy or soft copy, is permanent, and its circulation is often uncontrollable. Knowing how to write "routine" messages can have an important impact on a manager's effectiveness and image.

SUMMARY

Letters, e-mails, and memos can benefit greatly from strategic considerations. However, they are frequently mere impersonal messages written automatically. One key consideration for audience adaptation in routine messages is the you attitude. Writers with this attitude project themselves into the reader's position and prepare messages to suit that reader.

The you attitude also influences the organization of ideas into the direct or indirect order. Direct order is appropriate for good news and neutral information because it places the big idea first (BIF). Common types of direct messages are inquiries, requests, positive responses to inquiries and requests, claims, and positive responses to claims. The indirect order is appropriate for bad news messages and persuasive messages because it places the big idea a little later (BILL), after some explanation has been provided. Common types of indirect messages are negative responses to inquiries and requests, refused claims, and persuasive messages.

Negatives must be handled carefully in correspondence. A writer should de-emphasize the negative by using subordination, by avoiding terms such as *no* and *not*, and by avoiding negative wording or words with negative connotations.

Memos and e-mails are most frequently used for internal written communication. E-mails and memos are efficient, concise messages that require some strategic considerations in their writing. They have several uses for a manager, including communicating to groups, fixing responsibility, communicating with opponents, communicating with the inaccessible, making announcements, and requesting action. Memos and e-mails are frequently used in office politics.

CASES FOR ANALYSIS

Case 8-1

A Minor Inconvenience

The following bad news message was printed on corporate letterhead stationery and slid under the doors of guest rooms at a hotel in a major U.S. city.

Dear Valued Guest,

Thank you for choosing the [hotel name redacted]. We recognize that you have numerous lodging options, and we are pleased you have decided to stay with us.

This letter is to bring to your attention that on Wednesday, November 21, the water will be turned off throughout the hotel for maintenance repair.

The water will be turned off at 11:00 p.m. and will be turned back on early Thursday morning.

Once the water is restored, you may experience discoloration due to rust when turning on the sink or shower in your room. Please let the water run for a few minutes before using.

The front desk will have available extra bottled water at your request. Should you need anything additional during your stay, please feel free to dial "O" for the hotel operator and let us know how we can help.

We thank you for your patience and understanding and look forward to assisting you in any way possible.

All the best,
General Manager

Questions

1. What is the primary purpose of this message? Are there any secondary purposes?

2. What organizational pattern did the writer use? How appropriate is it?

3. To what extent did the writer show consideration for the audience? Your analysis should address delivery method, message length, content, format, and word choice.

4. If you were a business writing consultant, how would you rate this letter's effectiveness? What suggestions (if any) would you make to help the writer achieve the goal?

Case 8-2

Claim Refusal Letter

You are the sales manager for a furniture manufacturer and have just received a strongly worded claim letter from Hyram Blalock, who owns a large hotel in a nearby city. Blalock has been refurbishing his hotel and had placed a special order with you for 115 headboards to fit specifications he sent.

He ordered headboards an inch and a half narrower than the measurements for conventional king-size beds. He also specified a finish different from that normally used in this grade of headboard. Finally, he wanted his hotel's logo imprinted on each headboard. You completed this order and shipped it to him about a week ago.

He ordered the mattresses directly from a manufacturer that has since gone out of business. The company did, however, deliver his mattresses before going bankrupt, just a week before your headboards arrived. The problem is that all these mattresses were manufactured in the conventional dimensions, rather than the narrower ones for which the headboards were designed.

Blalock is asking you to take back the current shipment and either change the dimensions to fit the conventional mattresses or send a different set (which would, of course, have the finish he specified and his hotel's logo on them).

(Continued)

(Continued)

Obviously, you cannot comply with his request. Write an appropriate strategic claim refusal. The facts are on your side—he ordered the headboards in the size and finish that he received. However, the challenge is to tell him so without lecturing or using negatives. If you do choose to alter the headboards in the original order, be sure to charge him. Most important, you want to keep Blalock as a customer.

Case Note

This case tempts the writer to respond to Blalock with the same kind of letter he sent. Those using the appropriate indirect negative response will avoid lecturing to the reader as they remind him of his role in the problem. The suggested option (remodeling the headboards) is one strategy, but it should not be presented as if the writer feels guilty. If the letter suggests guilt, then the writer can expect more problems.

Case 8-3

Inquiry Letter

You are the assistant human resources manager for an insurance agency whose territory includes your state and three surrounding states. Your company has recently revamped its retirement and employment benefits packages, and you have been assigned the task of communicating these changes to all employees.

Because some of the changes are complex, you will be traveling to four sites in your region to meet with the company's agents and their personnel. You need to arrange hotel accommodations for the personnel at each of the sites, and you will need a meeting room with a screen and equipment for projecting your PowerPoint slideshow. Because the company has had a very good year, management wants the employees to enjoy their stay at the hotels, so you also need to inquire into the recreational and banquet facilities available.

Write a letter of inquiry to the Hotel Beacon in a major city in one of your surrounding states. The letter should elicit the information you will need to decide whether the hotel is the right one for your meeting. Make it clear that you will be looking at other hotels, seeking the best rate for services required.

Case Note

The most common pitfall in this case will be the lack of clear details. The letter is actually more complex than it seems. The temptation for some will be to write a brief letter, which the hotel marketing manager will be unable to answer with proper specifics. In addition to being thorough, the letter should also build goodwill; the writer may be interested in doing more business in the future with the reader.

Case 8-4

Request Refusal Letter

You are the administrative assistant to R. D. Spenser, president of Flo-Sheen Fabrics. Flo-Sheen employs more than 300 people in its mill and corporate offices. Each year, these employees contribute generously to the city's annual fundraising drive. Spenser also has developed a volunteer program that allows some employees to work on charitable projects on company time.

On your desk today, you found a letter that was sent to Spenser from a statewide youth organization requesting permission to conduct a fundraising drive in your plant for a new project it is developing. The organization wants to establish a scholarship fund for its brightest members.

Spenser jotted a note at the bottom of the letter asking you to deny the request. Do so, but build up goodwill. Be positive yet assertive; do not leave the organization wondering if the request is denied.

Case Note

Because the letter should build goodwill, the writer must use tact in denying the request. One option would be holding out the possibility of putting the youth organization on next year's list. But do not leave the reader feeling that another letter might get the results that the first one missed. The letter also needs to explain why the president of the company is not responding.

Case 8-5

Persuasive Memo

You are a district manager at GO, a chain of convenience stores. Recently, a break-in occurred at a store located near downtown Waco. As a result, GO's CEO has invited all district managers to weigh in on the idea of contracting with PhotoCop Inc. to install surveillance camera systems at all stores.

PhotoCop installed a camera system at one GO location, Woodway, on a trial basis. After 2 weeks, the security company reported that crime declined 66 percent at the Woodway location. In addition, PhotoCop conducted a spot survey of customers that indicated a 20 percent increase in the perception that the store is safe.

PhotoCop has now presented the CEO with a proposal to install surveillance systems in all 102 GO convenience stores at a cost of $350,000. Write a persuasive memo to the CEO that explains your opinion about the wisdom of adopting this proposal.

Case Note

This case sharpens critical thinking as well as writing skills. The cost of implementing PhotoCop's plan might require layoffs at GO. On the other hand, failing to install additional security might damage brand recognition and sales at all locations. Writers might want to offer alternatives to PhotoCop's proposal, such as a partial rollout, improved lighting and signage at each store, or less expensive police alert systems.

EXERCISE

Exercise 8-1

As you prepare to revise the following memo, consider purpose, audience, organization, and tone. Change the headings to standard format. Consider using design elements such as bullets, headings, or a word table to clarify the information in the memo's body. Proofread your revised version for surface errors.

Interoffice Correspondence
St. Louis, Missouri

To: Purchasing   **From:**

Date: January 21

Subject: Schedules

Well we had our team meetin just like usual this week. We talked about alot, but I thought I should remind you of a few things that are pressing. Don't forget that we are supposed to send our schedules for the week to Buffi. These should be transmitted by EMail each Monday or Friday if you can get it done early. It'r really helpful to know where you are when we can't find you.

Your vacation schedules should be estimated by now so please give them to me by the end of next week.

cc:

Notes

1. Workfront, "The State of Enterprise Work: 2017–2018, U.S. Edition," 2018, 5, https://www.workfront.com/thank-you/2017-2018-state-enterprise-work-report?nid=26301&fid=7826&t=p2&type=PDF.

2. For a list of the most important managerial skills, see also Graduate Management Admissions Council, "Corporate Recruiters Survey: 2014 Survey Report," 2014, http://www.gmac.com/~/media/Files/gmac/Research/Employment%20Outlook/2014-corporaterecruiters-final-release.pdf.

3. Paul Glen, "The Pen Is Mightier Than the Code," *Computerworld*, December 20, 2010, 30.

4. Workfront, "The State of Enterprise Work," 22.

5. Lucia S. Sigmar and Traci Austin, "The Professional's Guide to Relevant Grammar: The Sequel" (paper presented at the Association for Business Communication–Southwestern U.S. Conference, March 2015).

6. Peter W. Cardon, Janna Wong, and Cole Christie, "Preferences for Written Versus Spoken Expressions of Thanks among American Professionals" (paper presented at the Association for Business Communication–Southwestern U.S. Conference, March 13, 2020).

7. Renae Merle, "What Wells Fargo Dodged by Agreeing to Pay $110 Million to Settle Fake Accounts Lawsuit," *Houston Chronicle*, April 2, 2017, B2; the CEO's letter appeared in the *Houston Chronicle*, April 5, 2017, A7.

8. Jennifer R. Veltsos, "An Analysis of Data Breach Notifications as Negative News," *Business Communication Quarterly* 75, no. 2 (2012): 192–207.

9. "Set Guidelines for Letters of Recommendation Requests," *Volunteer Management Report* 20, no. 1 (November 2015): 4.

10. Jeanette Gilsdorf, "Write Me Your Best Case for . . . ," *Bulletin of the Association for Business Communication* 54, no. 1 (March 1991): 7–12.

11. Gerald Alred, Charles T. Brusaw, and Walter E. Oliu, *The Business Writer's Handbook,* 11th ed. (Boston: Bedford/St. Martin's, 2015), 319.

12. L. M. Sixel, "How You Say It Matters in a Big Way as Companies Get Training on Email," *Houston Chronicle*, July 10, 2014, D1, D6.

13. Alred et al., *The Business Writer's Handbook*; Sixel, "How You Say It."

14. William Safire, "To Whom It May Concern: Here's How to Address E-mail," *Houston Chronicle*, October 22, 2006, E6.

15. Rebecca Greenfield, "No Way to Say Goodbye," *Bloomberg Businessweek*, June 8, 2015, 86.

16. Jennifer Latson, "Why Are Exclamation Points Everywhere?!" *Houston Chronicle*, November 26, 2018, B3.

17. Ifigeneia Machili, Jo Angouri, and Nigel Harwood, "'The Snowball of Emails We Deal With': CCing in Multinational Companies," *Business and Professional Communication Quarterly* 82, no. 1 (2019): 5–37, doi: 10.1177/2329490618815700.

9

WRITING IN SPECIAL SITUATIONS

LEARNING OBJECTIVES

By the end of this chapter, you will be able to

- Describe the work involved in writing in special situations.

- Prepare informal and formal reports that help organizations achieve their objectives.

- Compose proposals that solve workplace problems, plan research, sell products or services, or secure external funding.

- Respond quickly and responsibly to crisis situations, including making apologies when the organization is at fault.

As you have learned, workplace documents often record decisions, direct action, and respond to requests. These kinds of routine situations may require familiar responses and formats. But inevitably unusual situations will occur. Managers will be called on to inform supervisors or stakeholders about their work. They may need to persuade others to try something new. And increasingly they are called on to respond to negative situations.

In general, the stakes are high in special situations. Managers must have the know-how to research business problems, solve them, and communicate the findings to their readers accurately, clearly, and concisely.[1] This chapter describes principles that apply to the most frequent types of business reports. It offers advice about writing effective proposals that will persuade receivers to take action and make decisions based on your recommendations. It also offers advice about how and when to respond in times of reputational and operational crisis.

PREPARING TO WRITE IN SPECIAL SITUATIONS

Although managers may spend considerable time communicating with others, they do not just sit down and write reports one after another. The prewriting process mirrors the "Stage 1: Planning" section on routine documents that is discussed in Chapter 7. This preliminary effort often takes more time than actually writing the report and can intimidate some writers.[2]

As with the other situations discussed in this book, prewriting begins with a strategic analysis using the model in Chapter 2. Consider the external factors that set the context in which you are writing. Reflect on your role as the sender, your relationship to the receiver, what they already know or need to know about the situation, and the purpose you are trying to achieve. Finally, identify the content, channel, physical environment, and appropriate timing of the message.

When it is time to write, special situations like reports, proposals, and crisis communication typically demand particular attention to defining the problem or objective, gathering evidence to investigate the situation, and developing recommendations. The information about planning to write and writing style from Chapter 7 and organizing information and focusing on reader benefits from Chapter 8 also play an important role in writing in special situations.

Define the Problem or Objective

Managers must make sure the process leading up to the report will yield optimum results. Your time is valuable not only to yourself but also to the company. First, determine the purpose of the message. What is the problem that needs to be solved? The problem may be nothing more than an information gap—someone needs data or demographics on sales, for example. The problem may be that a decision needs to be made. Thus, the writer must choose from among several options and recommend a plan of action. Finally, the problem may be an internal or external threat to the organization's reputation or operations. Defining the problem will help you determine the type of document to compose and the evidence you must collect.

CRITICAL THINKING QUESTIONS

1. How does thinking about a report's purpose compare with the prewriting strategies you read about in Chapter 7?

2. When considering a report's audience, how does the "you" attitude (described in Chapter 8) apply?

Collect Evidence

Once the manager has done the problem analysis and determined the information needed for the report, the next step is to gather supporting data. Most of the data needed for business reports are primary data—data the writer collects from interviews, surveys, experiments, and observation. Occasionally, writers draw from secondary research data—material already published. Numerous sources are readily accessible online, but managers should evaluate them for credibility, objectivity, and accuracy. In general, websites that pop up first when you use a search engine such as Google or Bing will provide free information aimed at consumers and the public. Managers researching business topics for reports should consider accessing professional databases and industry sources via search engines such as Biznar for high-quality, valid information.[3]

Develop Recommendations

Once the problem and purpose have been determined and the situation has been analyzed, the final step is to develop solutions or action items. The manager must analyze the need for change and determine the best plan for improvement. For example, productivity in a plant has dropped, and a manager has determined the cause (or causes), such as raw material shortages, equipment malfunctions, abuse of sick leave, or a host of combinations. Now the manager develops solutions and recommendations that consider constraints such as resources and time frames.

After gathering and analyzing the data, the manager transforms the results into a format that will clearly and easily be understood by the report readers. Strategies for presenting data in easy-to-read formats, including tables and graphs, are described in Chapter 6.

BUSINESS REPORTS

Reports are among an organization's most important communication tools. They appear in a variety of forms, carry out a number of functions, and ensure the efficient transfer of data both within an organization and between an organization and its stakeholders. Managerial reports carry verifiable information that addresses some purpose or problem. Business reports must present information objectively and clearly in order to help organizations achieve their objectives.[4]

Typically, managers write reports for one of three reasons. The most common is simply that someone has asked them to. A higher-level manager who sees an area where information is lacking or a problem that needs solving will ask a direct report to fill that gap or solve that problem. A report may also be part of a company's regular business. Thus, writing progress or periodic reports may be one of a manager's regular duties. Finally, a manager may write reports spontaneously, perhaps to fill gaps they identified or to share information with the rest of the staff or to propose changes.

Business reports are often classified according to six elements:

- *Function:* inform, analyze, or recommend action

- *Frequency:* periodic or special

- *Subject matter:* accounting, production, finance, marketing, and so forth

- *Formality:* informal or formal

- *Reader–writer relationship:* internal or external; vertical or lateral

- *Communication medium:* print, digital, or oral[5]

Types of Reports

The most informal routine reports are short and may even resemble forms. The manager simply fills in several blank spaces and, in some cases, provides a brief narrative or description. Examples are the trip report, the expense report, and the attendance report. Memo reports are usually written in response to an internal request for information, smaller projects and events, and routine progress or status reports. These documents are crisp and efficient and suggest a no-nonsense approach. They invariably have some form of headings—*To, From, Subject,* and *Date*—at the top for efficient routing and a quick understanding of purpose. The comments made about Subject lines in Chapter 8 apply here as well. In an indirectly ordered report, the Subject line should not give away the conclusions. Supporting information may be included as attachments.

The letter report is similar to the memo report, with three essential differences: audience, format, and tone. Letter reports are for external audiences, so the formatting includes an inside address, salutation, and complimentary close. A more subtle difference between memo and letter reports is tone. Because the letter report goes to an external reader, it is a tool for building goodwill, and goodwill means increased business. Thus, the letter report stresses reader benefits more than the memo report and is likely to close with a goodwill statement that promises continued cooperation.

Though you may not often write long, formal reports, when the situation arises, you will want the report to look right. Formal reports address large, high-profile, or complex topics, such as a corporate annual report, research or investigations, feasibility studies, and compliance. They are usually formatted as paper documents, even when they are delivered in electronic form, and may be sent to internal or external audiences. In the next sections, we discuss the components that are common to all reports and those that are reserved for formal reports (see Table 9-1).

To determine the appropriate form, a report writer should use any clues given in the initial assignment. It is unwise to prepare a formal report if the original assignment from your manager was to "shoot me an e-mail when you've found the answer." If that same manager indicated the report might be forwarded to top management, you might give it a more formal look.

When you are unsure of what form to use, ask to see examples of similar types of assignments. Many global companies, such as ExxonMobil, Honeywell, and Accenture,

TABLE 9-1 ■ Components of a Report		
Front Matter of Formal Reports	**All Reports**	**Back Matter of Formal Reports**
Title page	Introduction	References
Transmittal document	Body	Bibliography
Table of contents	Summary	Appendixes
List of illustrations	Conclusions	
Executive summary	Recommendations	

have templates or strict formatting guidelines. Precedent is especially relevant with periodic reports, which are expected to look like previous periodic reports.

Recently, some companies and government agencies have begun using graphics software such as Microsoft (MS) PowerPoint as a report format. Considered by some managers to be simpler and more user-friendly than word processing software, such as MS Word, graphics software will produce decks or flipbooks that include more text, data tables, and illustrations than are seen on traditional presentation slides and that can stand alone. Quad charts, used mostly in scientific, government, and technical fields, limit the entire report to a single page divided into quadrants.[6] The space limitations make these new report formats more concise than traditional narrative reports.

Karl Keller, a corporate communication consultant in Chicago, notes that PowerPoint decks "are often used to marshal business arguments, e.g., 'we should do X' rather than reporting business activities in a broader sense. These decks accompany face-to-face or distance meetings with screen sharing."[7] Ulrike Morphett, a business professor at Nanyang Technological University, agrees, adding that for strategy consulting projects, companies in Singapore invariably want PowerPoint decks rather than traditional word-processed reports as the key document deliverable to accompany a presentation. Best practices for PowerPoint report formats have yet to emerge, but they seem to fill the gap between sparse bulleted lists on presentation slides and long, formal, corporate reports.[8]

Components of Reports

Introduction

Every introduction should include the purpose statement and the problem addressed in the report.[9] In many cases, the type of report suggests its purpose. A periodic report will indicate the time period covered by the analysis. An incident report will describe a problem, its causes, and the solution that was established.

Introductions also identify who authorized the report. For example, an informal report may remind the reader of a request for information: "Recently, you asked me to look into the purchase of a new copier." The authorization establishes the chain of responsibility and justifies the time, effort, and resources that went into the preparation of the report.

It is also appropriate to indicate how the writer derived the information. In an informal report, the methodology might be a sentence or two: "I called sales representatives from three manufacturers," or "I examined sales materials supplied by three companies." A statement of methodology is essential in formal reports because readers judge that to evaluate the degree of authority of the contents. If the data were the result of primary research, the writer should describe the methods (sample size, data collection instrument) in sufficient detail to allow the reader to judge the quality of the research. Previously published data and information is called secondary research. Describe the source and include citations to permit readers to follow up on their own if necessary.

A statement of the scope of the report—its focus and what was excluded from consideration—is appropriate as well, although it is often obvious. A statement of limitations details external factors that may have limited the range of exploration in developing the report, such as limited budgets or time. These statements address any inconsistencies between the reader's expectations and the report's content. For example, in the scope statement for a report recommending a new plant site, the writer might note that the report covers only the top four sites and that architectural and engineering details are available elsewhere.

Some introductions include definitions of key terms used throughout the report that are unfamiliar to the reader. On the other hand, if only a few unfamiliar words are used a few times, they should be defined the first time they appear in the text. If many terms need defining, a glossary should be added as an appendix.

Workplace readers are busy, so many reports summarize the conclusions or recommendations in the introduction. This use of the direct order is appropriate for routine reports or in topics that are likely to be well received by readers. In the example on copiers, the writer using direct order might end the first paragraph with her choice of copier. Controversial topics or documents written for resistant audiences should use the indirect order instead to explain your reasons first and persuade them to agree with your conclusions.

The introduction ends with the plan of development, in which the writer tells the reader how the body of the report is organized. This invaluable element signals a major transition and sets the order of the report's ideas firmly in the reader's mind. The plan of development is usually simply written: "This report first . . . then . . . and finally. . . ."

Body

The body of the report details the research and findings that led the writer to the conclusions or recommendations. If readers are unlikely to know the background that led to the current situation, a summary should be included as well. Despite your experience with writing term papers in school, length is not a virtue of business reports. In fact, short business reports are more likely to be read than long ones. When deciding what to include in the body of your report, remember the advice of Elmore Leonard, the prolific, award-winning crime novelist: "Try to leave out the part that readers tend to skip."[10]

Because readers tend to skim and scan documents, headings, lists, charts, and infographics will guide the reader through the contents and structure of the report body. (Review Chapter 6 for advice on document design.) Headings guide the reader through the document, make the structure of the report explicit, and create much-needed white space in text-heavy documents. Write headings with the reader in mind. They should be descriptive of the content to follow but relatively short. Generally, seven words (or fewer) are appropriate for first-level headings, and even fewer than seven are usually needed for lower-level headings. Figure 9-1 demonstrates headings in a three-level hierarchy. Although single words and phrases are typical content headings, a question can serve as a heading. When responding to a request for proposals (RFP), headings should mirror the sections or questions to help readers find the answers and confirm that you have addressed each component. The principles of contrast and consistency are essential for usable headings.

Lists are particularly helpful in cutting down on prose, and their simplicity can improve reader comprehension and retention of the material. To maximize reader comprehension, lists should be constructed in parallel grammatical form. For example, in the report on copiers, the writer might state the following:

My evaluation of the copiers sought to determine four things about each unit:

- Use of energy
- Cost of operation
- Speed of operation
- Frequency of repairs

Writers must be careful not to let the report degenerate into an outline, a series of listed phrases, or a collection of graphics without narrative in an effort to be concise.

FIGURE 9-1 ■ Report Headings Style Sample

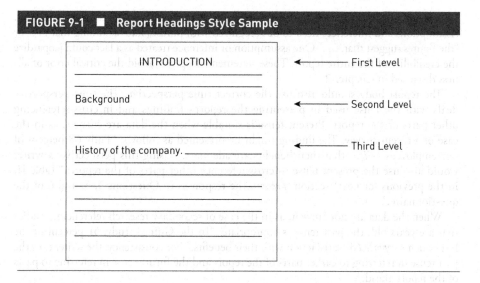

Organization. If the report is informational or nonsensitive, or if readers are likely to be receptive to your ideas, it is written using direct order. Conclusions and recommendations will appear right after the introduction. Persuasive, sensitive, or controversial reports are written using indirect order, with conclusions and recommendations appearing at the very end of the body (but before any back matter). This gives you an opportunity to build your case and win over resistant readers.

The main points in the report's body should be organized in a logical pattern. For example, a chronological pattern would be used to review the events that led to the present situation or the content of a quarterly report. A spatial pattern would be used to describe the appearance of a product or a geographic space. Sequential patterns organize by quantity, such as product sales or population sizes, or by order of steps in a procedure. Topical patterns organize by category, and compare/contrast patterns weigh options based on a set of established criteria.

Criteria-based organizational patterns are especially useful in evaluation and recommendation reports because they permit the reader to understand your thinking and evaluate the options for themselves. For example, a personnel report recommending the selection of a job candidate would be organized by the required characteristics of a new hire. A report recommending the fleet purchase of a particular car might begin with an overview of criteria used, such as safety, comfort, financial considerations, and dependability. Then each of three or four car models under consideration might be described. The report would conclude with a recommendation based on the criteria.

CRITICAL THINKING QUESTIONS

Recall the concepts of BIF (big idea first) and BILL (big idea a little later), also called the "direct strategy" and the "indirect strategy," that were described in Chapter 8 as ways to organize routine messages. When organizing a report by criteria or factors, should you begin with the most important criterion/factor (BIF), or should you work up to it (BILL)?

Writing Style. In all reports, writers need to distinguish between facts and inferences. Assumptions and inferences need to be recognized with phrases like "assuming that . . ." or "the figures suggest that. . . ." One assumption or inference treated as a fact could jeopardize the credibility of the entire report. These statements help you avoid the critical error of all-ness discussed in Chapter 2.

The report body should also use the correct time perspective. The time perspective deals with the tense used in presenting the report's findings and in cross-referencing other parts of the report. Present tense is suitable when the data are current, as in the case of a recent survey. The finding might be presented as follows: "Fully 68 percent of our employees *believe* that their benefits are adequate." Using this perspective, a writer would also use the present tense to cross-reference other parts of the report: "Table II, in the previous (or next) section, *presents* the responses to Questions 4, 5, and 6 of the questionnaire."

When the data are not current, as in the case of secondary research referencing studies that are years old, the past tense is appropriate: "In the Gifford study, 51 percent of the respondents *reported* dissatisfaction with their benefits." For consistency, the writer uses the past tense in referring to earlier parts of the report and the future tense in referring to parts of the report ahead.

Transitions help readers see connections between ideas as you build toward your conclusion. In moving from one major section to another, a writer should summarize the previous section and preview the next to show the change. In long, formal reports, internal summaries warrant their own heading and section. But in routine reports and proposals, a brief sentence may be sufficient to signal the shift and help the reader see the flow of ideas. Think of the Roman god Janus, who has two faces—one looking back and one looking ahead. Thus, a Janus statement consists of a review of the previous section plus a preview of what is to come in the report.

Conclusions

The conclusions section looks back to summarize the research and the findings and suggest what the reader should think about it all. The recommendations section looks ahead to suggest next steps or future actions that the reader should take. Occasionally, the person authorizing the report may want conclusions—that is, the results of the investigation—but not the writer's decision.

The end of a memo report needs planning. If the report uses indirect order, the last paragraph will give the conclusions and recommendations reached. On the other hand, a report using direct order easily ends on the last point. The writer might wish to introduce the last paragraph with a simple transition: "Finally, I evaluated the ease of operation of the copiers. I found. . . ." A summary is an appropriate ending for a report in direct order, because the conclusions and recommendations appeared at the beginning.

The conclusions should not introduce any new material; the report body should support all conclusions. Of course, the recommendations will be new material, but they should logically arise from the conclusions. The evidence should not point in one direction while the conclusions point in the other.

The last paragraph of a letter report is a statement of goodwill. Readers appreciate the writer's personal involvement, and writers appreciate an opportunity to close on a positive note, procuring the likelihood of future business transactions.

Components Unique to Formal Reports

As the report's purpose becomes more formal, front matter appears, automatically lengthening the document. Front matter sets the stage for the document, forecasting the content inside. Very complex or technical documents may also include back matter at the end of a document. Back matter, such as appendixes and glossaries, contains the technical information that helps readers understand the content of the body of the report. Each element appears on a separate page.

Front Matter

The *title page* is the first page for most formal reports. Generally, it consists of four main components: the title, the complete identification of the reader, the complete identification of the writer, and the date. The report title should be a concise description of the report's purpose and topic. Because of their charge of completeness, titles of business reports tend to be longer than titles of other literary works.

The identification of the reader and writer includes each person's name, position, organization, city, state, and (if needed) country. The identifying blocks of information are generally preceded by expressions such as "presented to" or "prepared for" and "prepared by." If the organization and/or location are the same for the reader and writer (internal reports), they may be omitted. These blocks of information should be spaced evenly down the page and laterally centered.

A *transmittal document* is a memo or letter that announces the accompanying report. Generally, it replaces the conversation the writer would have with the reader if the report were being handed over in person. It briefly states the nature of the report and mentions authorization details. This might be accomplished in one sentence, as in "Here is the report on cost-cutting options you requested in your memo of July 10." If other people helped with the research and composition of the report, the writer might wish to acknowledge them in the transmittal message. To keep the transmittal short, do not summarize the report here. That function is served by the executive summary.

Typically, the transmittal closes with a call to action ("After reading the report, please call me.") and a goodwill gesture. It thanks the recipient for the assignment and looks forward to continued service. To some, the idea of thanking someone for giving them work might sound strange. Such skeptics should remember that report-writing assignments present chances to showcase analytical abilities and communication skills—abilities and skills that might be valued when promotional opportunities arise.

The *table of contents* follows the transmittal document. The real value of the table of contents is that it displays all the report sections at a glance and refers the reader to the page number of a section of particular interest. Word processing software has a feature that allows automatic creation of the table of contents using the content of headings and subheadings in the text. If you create the table of contents by hand, be sure the entries use wording identical to that in the text. Also, to connect an entry to its page number, use leader dots (made by alternating periods and spaces on the line, aligned for all the entries). The page numbers should have their digits right aligned.

A *list of illustrations* is an optional feature that is often used in reports with five or more visual aids, such as a technical report. If needed and if there is room, the list begins immediately following the end of the table of contents. Depending on the number and type of illustrations, the list can be subdivided into lists of tables and figures. Like the table of contents, the list of illustrations contains the title of each table and figure and its page number, separated by leader dots.

The final component of formal report front matter is the *executive summary*. Also called the epitome, abstract, brief, digest, or synopsis, it provides a quick overview of the report.[11] Managers are often interested only in a report's highlights. They will use the executive summary as a replacement for the report. The challenge is to shrink the report down to its major facts, analyses, and conclusions, including everything that is key, while keeping it to about one-tenth the length of the report. The easiest way to accomplish this task is to first write the entire report, then go through it and highlight the key statements, generalizations, and topic sentences. Typically, they appear at the beginning of each section and paragraph. Transfer the key statements to a fresh file or page, in the same order in which they appear in the report, and revise for clarity and conciseness.

CRITICAL THINKING QUESTIONS

1. Why is the executive summary so challenging to compose?

2. When composing a report's executive summary, to what extent should you apply the strategies you learned in Chapter 7 for writing concisely?

Back Matter

Back matter is optional. Many formal reports are complete without attachments at the end. However, under certain circumstances, the writer may choose to add one or more of the parts described next.

If secondary research was used in the report and if readers might want to trace back the information to its original sources, then a *references list* is helpful. Sometimes labeled "Works Cited," the references section lists just that. Further, the writer may add a *bibliography* of relevant sources that the reader might find useful. The difference between a references list and a bibliography is that a bibliography identifies all the secondary sources that a writer looked at when composing the report, while a references list identifies only the sources that the writer specifically "referred to" in the report. Thus, the references list for a research report may be shorter than or the same length as the bibliography but not longer than the bibliography.

A standard bibliographic format should be followed for both lists. American Psychological Association (APA) style is the simplest and most popular for business research reports, but other styles may be used by your industry. Style guides for citations are readily available online, and a range of free reference manager software tools, such as Zotero, offer the ability to store and export author, title, and publication fields, making it easy to format citations and reference lists. The key for determining how much information to include in a citation is that the source must be recoverable.

Supplemental material should be added to formal reports as *appendixes*. Examples of such material are tables of financial data, graphs, work samples, pictures, interview transcriptions, survey results, and mock-ups. In short, if the information does not fit into the report proper because it is too lengthy or detailed or would disrupt the continuity, then this information should be presented in appendixes.

Appendix format conventions are as follows: Each table, chart, or other type of information should appear as a separate appendix, numbered and titled, on a separate page. Page numbering from the body should continue through the appendixes. If the report has a table of contents, the appendixes should be included in it.

PROPOSALS

At their essence, proposals offer solutions to problems. Internal proposals request time, staffing, funding, or access to resources to help the organization do its work. External proposals offer products, services, and expertise to solve problems that clients may be facing. Research proposals request resources to conduct empirical studies, design prototypes, or test new product designs. Grant proposals suggest projects that solve problems related to the funding agency's goals and mission.

Proposals are the most persuasive documents that managers typically write. The first step is to identify the problem and its significance to the reader or decision maker. The concept of reader benefits from Chapter 8 is especially important in writing proposals. If the decision maker does not agree with your definition of the problem or its effects, they are unlikely to support your recommendation.

For example, imagine that you are the manager of a medical equipment plant in the Midwest. While reviewing the quarterly production report, you notice that one of the production lines is creating a significant amount of waste product. The line supervisor explains that the equipment is 25 years old. Because it has been maintained regularly, it can probably continue operating for another 20 years of use. But newer machines use technologies that control speed and temperature more accurately and a different design that uses more of the raw materials, reducing waste. You decide to request funding to purchase a newer model.

The decision to replace the equipment may seem straightforward to you, but your supervisor may balk at the cost. After all, the existing machine is paid for and can continue to operate for many years. The new machine might help your facility, but you supervisor has to take a holistic view and allocate resources across multiple facilities. Why should your suggestion take priority over requests from other divisions? Rather than focusing only on the production line, your proposal should connect to broader managerial concerns, such as overhead costs, energy efficiency, and employee safety.

Proposals serve as planning documents and as contracts. If the proposal fails to accurately budget the cost of a project, or you fail to follow through on the plan it described, your credibility may be harmed. At worst, legal action may be taken.

Types of Proposals

Proposals are often categorized by their audience, impetus, or purpose. The audience for internal proposals consists of members of your organization. External proposals are written for prospective clients, vendors, or funding agencies. Solicited proposals respond to requests that define the problem, budget, and objectives. Unsolicited proposals are written on your own initiative.

This section explains the purposes of several common types of proposals. In each, you must define the problem, explain why it is a problem in terms that are meaningful to the decision maker, and suggest a solution. Care must be taken to avoid overselling your idea and delivering less than you promised.

Planning Proposals

Planning proposals solve problems in the workplace that prevent the organization from achieving its goals as effectively or efficiently as possible. Managers often ask for staffing to perform work, funding to purchase equipment, time or space to complete projects, or campaigns to increase sales. They may recommend changes to policies and procedures or request special recognition for employees who have exceeded expectations.

Planning proposals are usually informal, written as an e-mail or memo to your supervisor. Some proposals may be a verbal pitch during a conversation or meeting, but we recommend that you follow up a with a written summary that documents the plan, the terms, and your understanding of the verbal approval in case questions arise later.

Sales Proposals and White Papers

Sales proposals identify problems that other organizations are likely to be encountering and position your company's product, service, or expertise as the solution. Sales proposals are written for external audiences and are usually unsolicited. They may be formatted as formal reports, letters, videos, or business plans.

Writing effective sales proposals requires a thorough analysis of the target audience to identify pain points in their operations and psychological factors that may make them more receptive to your ideas. For example, a cable company wanted to upsell clients on its specialized programming. It analyzed its client base, identified customers who were likely to have family or connections overseas, and sent sales letters promoting international channels with news and entertainment programming from those countries.

White papers are a special form of sales proposal because they resemble traditional research papers. In fact, white papers originated as government research reports and are often used in technical industries to forecast trends or evaluate products. But white papers are also a sales tool. Marketing white papers position a product or service as the ideal solution to a given problem.[12] Like research papers, they open with a problem and a research statement. They include secondary research to support claims about the problem's significance and potential impact. White papers identify criteria for a feasible solution ("what to look for"), then evaluate several options. The style and tone are carefully designed to suggest objectivity. But the problem is aligned directly to the product or service being promoted, and only the vendor's product will perfectly fulfill the evaluation criteria. The white paper concludes with a call to purchase the product or service. These papers often include disclaimers and legal information, such as copyright notices.[13] Successful white papers drive sales while establishing the expertise of the organization.

Research Proposals

When faced with a problem for which no known solution exists, individuals or businesses must conduct primary (original) research. Research proposals describe plans for collecting and analyzing data, developing prototypes, and testing new products.

Research proposals begin with a research question that the study intends to answer or a hypothesis that the study will test. The main component is the methodology, the section that describes the design of the research study: sampling technique, data collection, analysis methods, data storage and security, and procedures that will protect human participants. The scope of the project should clearly explain the work to be done, its limitations, and the benefits and applications of the research findings.

Grant Proposals

Grant proposals seek external funding for a project. When writing a grant proposal, remember that you are promising to do something the funding source finds beneficial. Philanthropic organizations have missions, goals, and constituents. There are always more requests than available monies, so funding agencies set objectives and select projects that help them move forward with their agendas. For example, the Bill and Melinda Gates Foundation is a large philanthropic organization. It receives many proposals, but winning projects must be linked to the Gates Foundation's strategic priorities of global health, global development, sustainable global economic growth, schools and vulnerable children in Washington State, and policy development.[14] Projects that do not fit into one of these categories are not funded.

Funding agencies often have templates for grant applications. These templates help the reviewers locate information and make direct comparisons between proposals. Varying from the template may disqualify your proposal from consideration.

Request for Proposals

Not all proposals are internally motivated. When organizations identify a problem they cannot solve on their own, they often ask experts for help. A request for proposals (RFP) expresses an organization's intent to purchase products or services. (They are also referred to as call for proposals, call for bids, and invitation for bids.) An RFP describes the problem, lists specifications for a solution, defines criteria for evaluation, and sets the project budget and timeline. The organization sends the RFP to businesses with relevant expertise and asks them to submit bids.

For example, the charge of the Louisiana Office of Tourism is to contribute to the economic impact of the state's 64 parishes (counties) by promoting Louisiana's five regions as travel destinations.[15] The Office has marketing and sales specialists on staff, but they rely on advertising agencies to help them identify target markets, compose messages, create promotional materials, and place advertising where it will yield the best results. Requests for proposals outline the Office's needs and budget. The proposals submitted by advertising agencies include estimates of the cost to provide the requested services and portfolios of similar work to demonstrate their experience and persuade the decision makers.

Responses to RFPs must address each of the sections as thoroughly as possible while following any limitations on length, formatting, or content. RFPs include a point of contact (POC) who is responsible for answering questions about the organization and its needs. Use this service to understand the intent of the project and constraints that may limit options for solutions.

Components of Proposals

Although the content of proposals may be similar to reports, Richard Johnson-Sheehan identifies a different pattern of components.[16] The following categories may be used as headings to help readers find information quickly. The pattern is summarized in Table 9-2.

Introduction

The introduction is the most important part of the proposal because sometimes it is the only thing the audience will read. Introductions must capture their attention and keep

TABLE 9-2 ■ Proposal Sections
1. *Introduction:* State the purpose and provide background information.
2. *Current situation:* Define the problem, its causes, and its significance to the reader.
3. *Project plan:* Offer a solution, including implementation, timeline, and deliverables.
4. *Qualifications:* Describe the team and its relevant expertise.
5. *Costs:* Summarize the expenses and tally the total cost of the project.
6. *Conclusion:* Explain the benefits the reader can expect, describe next steps, and call for action on the plan.

them engaged through clear prose, concrete terms, examples, and metaphors and imagery that will help them understand new or difficult ideas. The purpose of the introduction is to give readers a cognitive framework to understand your project plan. The plan will be explained fully in a separate section, but you must summarize it in the opening. If you're writing a research proposal, include the hypothesis for a quantitative study or the research question for a qualitative study.

Conventional wisdom often advises writers to compose the introduction at the end of the writing process. This technique permits you to accurately introduce the main topics and forecast the organization of the proposal. Johnson-Sheehan suggests six components of effective introductions:[17]

1. State the subject of the proposal.

2. Identify the purpose of the proposal. Are you solving a problem, taking advantage of an opportunity, or managing change in some way?

3. State the main point that will be proven in the proposal. What is the expected outcome?

4. Explain the importance of the subject to the readers. Do not assume that readers will automatically agree that the subject is important.

5. Provide some background information on the subject. Your readers may be unaware of the problem, or they may not have realized its implications.

6. Forecast the organization of the proposal. List the sections or major topics of the proposal in the order in which they appear.

Current Situation

Research is a key ingredient in writing proposals. In order to develop a sound plan, you must thoroughly understand the problem and its causes and effects. The current situation, also called a needs assessment, demonstrates that you understand the situation and its impact on the reader. Describing the situation is a persuasive move because sometimes readers recognize that a problem exists, but they do not understand why or what to do about it.

The current situation reviews what is already known about the problem. It often includes secondary research from trade publications, news sources, or academic journals. Internal proposals often rely on internal data, but publicly available data may offer a look at broader issues or trends. Interviews with stakeholders or subject matter experts may provide insight into the background of the situation and its significance to the present moment.

When the topic is well understood, the current situation can often be organized using a cause-and-effect pattern. But if the topic is unfamiliar to readers, the project plan is an opportunity to tell a compelling story. In *Made to Stick*, Chip Heath and Dan Heath describe "sticky" messages using the mnemonic SUCCESs: simple, unexpected, concrete, credible, emotional stories.[18] For example, a proposal for a public service project to eradicate invasive buckthorn might tell a story about an ornamental shrub that was once valued as part of residential landscaping. But this plant, often used in privacy hedges, quickly spread into ravines, forests, and savannahs, choking out other helpful plants in the process.[19] Images of the plant and statistics about its pervasiveness in the wild would help readers understand why a buckthorn removal project is needed.

Project Plan

The project plan is the heart of the proposal. It explains the work to be done and how it will solve the problem or seize the opportunity that you described in the previous section. Although conciseness is always a goal, the plan must thoroughly describe your methods or procedures. It must also provide a timeline that defines the deadline and the work to be done in each major stage of the project.

An often-overlooked component of the project plan is its evaluation. How will your reader know that your plan was successful? The deliverables, outcomes, or impacts of interventions tell readers what to expect. Benchmarks and evaluation criteria are useful here.

The project plan is the promise you make to the decision maker. Analyze your audience to identify their concerns. Imagine the questions they are likely to ask and the reservations they may feel. Then compose your plan to put their minds at ease.

Qualifications

Proposals describe possibility, so decision makers must trust that you are capable of doing the work described in the plan. The qualifications statement should reassure readers that you and your organization are the right ones for the job. Be truthful and positive. Give readers a sense of who they would be working with on the project.

For external proposals, introduce your organization, its specialization, and the person or team who will be working on the project. Recommendations, testimonials, and portfolios of past work can bolster credibility.

Internal proposals should explain how your experience is relevant to the new project. You might need to pitch the creation of a new team to take advantage of varied expertise. When the team consists of only one or two people, you may not need a separate qualifications statement. A brief statement at the end of the project plan will often suffice.

Costs

Proposals are tools for solving problems, but solutions come at a cost. A proposal is considered a contract with the funding agency, so include an accurate tally of all the anticipated expenses. Budgets cannot be padded with a miscellaneous line item, and if items are not included in the budget, then you must identify another funding source or do without. For example, a nonprofit organization wrote a grant proposal to develop a new program. The budget focused on salaries, transportation, and recruiting activities. The grant was funded.

As the organization began to implement the plan, the staff wanted to buy new laptops and software to analyze the data. Because those items were not included in the proposal, they could not use grant money to purchase them. The staff realized that they had done a poor job of budgeting their project and were stuck with a contract that didn't cover all their needs.

When creating budgets, consider every expense that may be attributed to the project. Variable expenses like office supplies and fixed expenses like employee salary and benefits are commonly included in proposals. Some organizations require budgets to include indirect costs like office space, utilities, and shared administrative services. This category covers expenses that are not directly related to the work described in the proposal.

Readers must know what they committing to if they support the proposal. If the expenses are simple, costs may be explained in a sentence or two. For more than a few lines, create a table to organize the expenses. As you recall from Chapter 6, tables are easier to skim and allow readers to focus on specific items and mentally check your figures. If expenses are lengthy or complicated, summarize the total cost of work to be done in the body of the report and include an itemized budget as an appendix.

Conclusion

The persuasive nature of proposals is also evident in the way they conclude. The conclusion introduces new information, which is usually not advised in academic and business writing.

The first step is to describe the benefits of the plan. In the introduction, you described the importance of the problem in terms of the reader's interest. The conclusion describes the benefits readers can expect to see if they adopt your plan. Hard benefits are things readers can literally see or touch or count, such as product deliverables or income. Soft benefits are attributes that are difficult to measure, such as quality and satisfaction.

The proposal should close with a call to action. Begin by looking to the future. How will the situation be better once your plan is finished? What new information will be available that was unknown before? End the proposal by suggesting what the reader should do next to move ahead with the project. Ask to set a meeting, invite calls for more information, or schedule a visit to your office or theirs.

Like reports, informal proposals may be formatted as memos or letters. Formal proposals tend to be longer and more complex, with additional sections to guide the reader through the document. An executive summary provides an overview of the full proposal. A table of contents helps readers find specific sections quickly. Appendixes hold data and technical details about implementation of your solution.

Of course, if you are responding to an RFP, the organization and headings of your proposal must match those listed in the RFP. Nevertheless, the components listed here will be featured in your document.

CRITICAL THINKING QUESTIONS

1. If you want to recommend staff changes, how formal should your proposal be?

2. How would you describe the current situation to convince your supervisor that a problem exists?

3. How would you describe the benefits of the staffing change to the organization?

CRISIS COMMUNICATION

The rise of networked communications and social media has amplified and accelerated news about problems and accidents. When an event or information threatens an organization's operations or reputation, it is considered a crisis.[20] Although an organization's executive, legal, and public relations teams may take the lead on responding to a crisis, managers have a role in limiting the harm to the organization by communicating with internal and external audiences.

Crisis communication researcher W. Timothy Coombs says that three factors should guide a crisis communication response: timing, focusing on the victim, and countering misinformation.[21] Organizations should acknowledge a crisis as quickly as possible to "steal thunder" from critics. Social media channels can be effective tools for responding quickly and permitting stakeholders to engage in dialogue about the crisis. Although managers may hope that a wait-and-see approach will permit the crisis to blow over, it is far more likely that information will leak and the silence will be perceived as either ignorance or a cover-up. Being forthright may be uncomfortable, but it strengthens the organization's reputation as honest and responsible.

Reputational crises tend to be caused by personnel behavior, irresponsible messaging, or rumors. The victim is the organization. Operational crises, on the other hand, may be caused by natural disasters, accidents, product design flaws, management misconduct, or employee behavior. In these situations, victims are internal or external stakeholders who experience physical, psychological, or financial harm. Responses to an operational crisis must focus on safety. They must acknowledge the harm the victim endured, express sympathy, and offer support to help them recover.

Some crises are the result of rumors and inaccurate information. In those situations, the organization should quickly and aggressively deny the misinformation. But if the misinformation is ambiguous or incomplete, the manager would be better served by expressing sympathy but little more. Denying a rumor that is later proven to be true creates a secondary crisis.

In recent years, crises based on an organization's stance on moral issues have been on the rise. For example, Chick-fil-A was the focus of protests and boycotts for several years after the public learned that the organization donated to anti-LGBTQ charities and the founder, Dan Cathy, spoke out against gay marriage. In 2019, a spokesperson announced that the controversial charitable commitments had expired, and the organization would no longer support those causes.[22]

The democratizing effect of social media has increased the chances for crisis situations to occur. In addition to challenging behaviors and policies, stakeholders often turn to social media to complain about customer service or to vent about frustrations with the organization. If there is no specific damage, it may be better to monitor the comments without responding. But when the organization is at fault, managers should apologize and describe the actions being taken to rectify the situation. Although somewhat controversial, evidence suggests that apologies can defuse the situation.

CRITICAL THINKING QUESTIONS

Think about a controversy or crisis affecting an organization that you usually admire.

1. How long did it take the organization to respond?
2. How well was the response received by its stakeholders?
3. Did the response to the crisis appear to affect the organization's reputation in the short term? In the long term?
4. Have other organizations faced a similar crisis or controversy? How did their response compare?

Apologies

The United States has witnessed a remarkable rise in the number of public corporate apologies. In April 2017, for example, United Airlines was widely criticized for forcibly removing a customer from a flight when he refused to give up his seat for a crew member. CEO Oscar Munoz issued numerous profuse apologies. An open letter published in the *Houston Chronicle* on April 27, 2017, began, "We can never say we are sorry enough for the shameful way one of our customers was treated aboard United's flight 3411." A similar letter was published in United's inflight magazine, *Hemispheres*, the following month: "We broke that trust . . . we can never say we are sorry enough for what occurred."[23]

Apologies are a critical component of crisis communication, although their use can be controversial. Corporate attorneys have traditionally warned against apologizing because it implies responsibility for wrongdoing and even guilt, inviting legal action against the writer and organization. Public relations professionals agree that apologies can be interpreted as an admission of error or carelessness, damaging a company's image.[24]

Recently, however, the trend has been changing because of belief that an apology can help rather than hurt, in terms of both image and legal judgments. In the field of medicine, malpractice-reform advocates say an apology can help doctors avoid being sued and can reduce settlements. Consequently, 39 states in the United States have enacted apology laws. Apology laws facilitate apologies by making them inadmissible as evidence in malpractice trials.

This approach does not seem to be working. According to a Vanderbilt analysis of proprietary insurance data, apology laws do not have a substantial effect on the probability that a surgeon will face a claim or the average payment made to resolve a claim. Furthermore, for nonsurgeons, apology laws actually increase the probability of facing a lawsuit by 46 percent and increase the average payment made to resolve a claim.[25] The researchers conclude that apology laws alone are not enough to reduce malpractice litigation, but proper training on how to apologize and provide explanations could potentially be more effective.

If a manager makes the strategic decision to apologize, either individually or on behalf of the organization, what are some guidelines? A good apology is genuine and timely. It should consist of four parts:

- Acknowledge the mistake or wrongdoing and its effect on others
- Accept responsibility
- Express regret
- Promise that the offense will not be repeated[26]

Perhaps the most critical issue is acceptance of responsibility or fault.[27] A partial apology, where the manager expresses sympathy or regret without admitting guilt, softens the blow and may be wise when there is significant damage or injury. Partial apologies can also resolve disputes when the extent of fault is unclear or difficult to establish. In other circumstances, when a manager or company has clearly committed an egregious act, a more complete apology may be appropriate.

In either situation, the focus should be on the future and on making amends.[28] In the United Airlines case described previously, 2 weeks after the incident, the company announced sweeping policy changes, including increased compensation for voluntarily giving up seats (up to $10,000), reduced overbooking on certain flights, improved automatic check-in processes, and increased training for employees. These changes were designed to restore credibility and brand reputation, according to Rob Britton, professor of marketing at Georgetown University's McDonough School of Business.[29]

CRITICAL THINKING QUESTIONS

Think of a time when you were wronged.

1. How important was it for the perpetrator to apologize to you?

2. Did the apology contain all the components listed here? If not, what was missing?

3. If you did not receive an apology, what did you do?

4. Why is it difficult to apologize?

As with all other communications undertaken by managers, crisis communication messages should reflect decisions based on strategic analysis of the situation. Delayed or impersonal responses may be interpreted as being out of touch or lacking concern for others.

SUMMARY

Managers are called on to respond to a variety of special situations. In preparing to write a report, proposal, or crisis message, first define the problem to be addressed. Collect data to understand the situation, then compose a response or recommend a solution.

Reports are among an organization's most important communications and help managers plan, organize, execute, evaluate, and improve an organization. Managers write reports because they have been assigned to do so or because they see a need for one. Reports can address internal or external audiences and may be classified according to their level of formality or frequency.

All reports contain an introduction, a body, and a conclusion. The introduction describes the report's purpose and may preview conclusions and recommendations. The body of the report describes the background of the current situation, the methods used to analyze the topic, and the results of the any investigation. The writer uses headings, lists, charts, and infographics to guide the reader through the report body. The conclusion summarizes the findings and suggest what the reader should think about it all. It may suggest next steps or future actions that the reader should take. Formal reports may contain additional information as front or back matter.

The order of ideas chosen for a report is significant. Direct order is appropriate for good news, neutral information, and receptive audiences. It places the main conclusions and recommendations at the beginning of the report. Indirect order is best for bad news and resistant audiences. It puts the main points last. The material within the body may be organized by time, place, quantity, and other factors.

Proposals suggest solutions to problems. Readers may not be aware of the problem or may not understand its significance or cause, so the writer must explain the current situation in terms that are meaningful to the reader. The project plan describes the solution and its implementation, including a timeline, procedures, and deliverables. Because proposals form a contract, the cost assessment must be accurate and thorough. Describing the credentials of the implementation team reassures decision makers of an organization's expertise and credibility. Proposals conclude by stating the benefits the funding agency can expect to receive and issuing a call to action.

Crises are unexpected threats to an organization's operations or reputation. Managers should quickly acknowledge the crisis and display empathy by focusing on the victims. When the organization is at fault, a carefully worded apology that accepts responsibility and expresses regret may defuse the situation. Rumors and misinformation must be corrected to protect the organization's reputation.

CASES FOR ANALYSIS

Case 9-1

Boeing's 737 MAX Prepares to Fly Again

Boeing's 737 series of planes is the best-selling commercial jetliner in history, with more than 10,000 delivered worldwide over the past 50 years, and is the workhorse of dozens of airlines. In 2011, in response to increasing pressure from Airbus, its major competitor, Boeing announced a new addition to the series, the 737 MAX. Six years later, the MAX was put into service.

In October 2018, Indonesia's Lion Air Flight 610, a 737 MAX, crashed. Five months later, Ethiopian Airlines Flight 302, also a MAX, crashed. A total of 346 passengers and crew died in the two incidents. Subsequently, global aviation authorities grounded the 737 MAX.

Investigations indicate that there were several factors and failures that caused the tragic crashes. But the immediate cause was the model's flight-control feature, specifically, the software called Maneuvering Control Augmentation System (MCAS). In the instance of both fatal crashes, MCAS erroneously engaged, forcing the planes' noses to point down, and the pilots were unable to regain control of the aircraft.

There is evidence that Boeing knew of the MCAS problems early on. On October 17, 2019, Boeing revealed it had turned over text messages between two of the company's test pilots sent in 2016, one

of which described the MCAS's habit of engaging itself as "egregious." Later that month, as he appeared before two congressional committees, former CEO Dennis Muilenburg admitted Boeing knew of the test pilot concerns in early 2019.

Then on January 10, 2020, Boeing released a series of e-mails and instant messages to Congress in which Boeing employees discussed the 737 MAX. Some expressed regret for the company's actions in getting the aircraft certified, while others openly discussed the 737 MAX's flaws.

In May 2020, Boeing announced that production would begin again, with plans to build about 30 jets per month in 2021 and 57 per month in 2022. The company has a backlog of about 4,550 unfulfilled orders, signifying confidence within the airline industry that once the grounding is lifted, the plane will be reliable.

Southwest Airlines owns 34 of the grounded jets, more than any other airline, with orders for another 48 before 2022. "We're still wanting to get the MAX back into service," Southwest CEO Gary Kelly told shareholders at the company's annual meeting in May 2020. "The MAX airplane is superior to the [older versions of the] 737 that we're currently operating. It burns less fuel. It's an excellent airplane. And certainly in this environment, we would love to retire some of our older aircraft, avoid some expensive maintenance and a substitute with the newer airplanes."

Despite the fact that the COVID-19 pandemic had caused air travel to plummet worldwide, Boeing's May 2020 announcement triggered an immediate jump of 3.2 percent in the corporation's stock price. And in August, as Boeing approached the final steps to recertification, it scored its first orders for new 737 MAX jets of the year.[30]

Questions

The Federal Aviation Administration certified the 737 MAX as flight worthy in November 2020. Nevertheless, trust in its safety is slow to be restored. Consider the following:

1. What kinds of evidence or appeals will be most effective for the traveling public and airlines that are Boeing's customers?

2. What type of communication channels should Boeing use?

Case 9-2

Proposing a New Office Design

Cass Kline is a project manager in the information technology (IT) department of a medium-sized medical device manufacturer in the Midwest. Although the company had an airy, bright building, the IT department's space was cramped and dark. The center of the large room was dominated by a "cubicle farm" with 6-foot-tall walls. Some of the light fixtures had cardboard taped to the

covers to deflect the fluorescent lighting from the computer monitors below. The carpet was worn and loose on the main pathways, with folds rising up in places and loops of frayed threads visible at seams.

As Cass waited for a report to print, she looked around her workspace. The office did not inspire enthusiasm, and she wondered what effect it might have on employee morale. People tended to walk straight to their workspaces and communicate with each other mostly by e-mail. The carpet was unsightly, but more important, it could present a trip hazard. Cass wondered if her next project should be to renovate the bullpen to make it more collaborative and aesthetically pleasing.

Questions

1. What type of proposal would Cass need to write?

2. What information should she collect to develop her proposal?

3. What is the problem that needs to be solved?

4. What are some possible solutions?

5. How should Cass frame the problem and solution to maximize their persuasiveness to her boss?

6. What would be included in an outline of Cass's proposal?

EXERCISES

Exercise 9-1

Writing a Recommendation Report

You are a middle-level marketing manager in a large wholesale organization. This morning, your boss called you into her office and informed you that 126 cars in the company's sales fleet were ready for replacement. She asked you to do the research and write a report that would recommend a purchase to replace the cars about to be retired.

(Continued)

(Continued)

Pick four cars that are comparable—for example, the Ford Fusion, the Honda Accord, the Chevrolet Malibu, and the Toyota Camry. In selecting a particular type of car, you might want to make some assumptions about the products handled by your salespeople and whether they carry bulky samples. For the purposes of this report, we will assume you considered other, similar cars, but the four you chose are the top contenders.

Your next task is to identify the criteria to be used in selecting the car to be purchased. Remember that the quality of your research and report will hinge largely on how thoroughly you identify the relevant criteria to be weighed. Once you have identified the criteria to be used and all subfactors of those criteria, you are ready to begin your research. You will probably find *Consumer Reports* and websites such as cars.com to be invaluable sources of information, but do not overlook other, less obvious sources, such as dealerships.

After collecting and organizing your information, you will be ready to write your report. What format should that report take? Which strategic aspects ought to be considered in determining that format? If you choose to use a formal report format, which prefatory parts should you include? Which subsections should you include in the introduction? How should the body of the report be organized? What will the ending sections of the report proper contain?

Exercise Note

This type of report should use a direct, formal format because it is being written for superiors and contains neutral information. Prefatory parts must include a transmittal memo reflecting the authorization of the senior management official who originally assigned the writer responsibility for this report. The introduction should include the research method used, as well as the purpose and scope of the report. The report should be organized to include all of the automobiles considered and tables that report the necessary statistics on each auto to the deciding committee. Conclusions should be presented that will lead management to the same outcome outlined in the writer's report, as specified in the recommendation section.

Exercise 9-2

Writing an Informational Report

Develop a questionnaire containing at least 10 statements about typical ethical dilemmas faced by businesspeople. Use "strongly agree," "agree," "undecided," "disagree," and "strongly disagree" as response options. Possibilities might include "It is acceptable for a U.S. businessperson in a foreign country to bribe a public official if that practice is accepted and expected in that country." Another possibility might be "It is acceptable to give a poorly performing employee a good reference to get rid of him or her."

At the end of the questionnaire, ask for some demographic information that might make the analyses of your findings more interesting. You might ask for gender identity, employment status, age, marital status, years of work experience, educational level, and so on.

Next, circulate the questionnaire randomly on campus. Try to get at least 100 respondents. Remember that the larger your sample, the better your findings will be statistically. You might consider having a ballot-like box with you to ensure confidentiality.

After you have collected your data and analyzed your findings, you will be ready to put your information into a report to be presented to your instructor. What format will that report assume? What factors should you consider in determining that format? What parts will the report contain? Will you use the direct or indirect order? On what basis will the body of the report be organized?

An interesting twist on this report might be to circulate the questionnaire to businesspeople. If it were possible for you to circulate the questionnaire to people on campus *and* to businesspeople, you might then be able to compare the results overall.

Exercise Note

If you are addressing a business executive in this report, your results should be presented both informally and indirectly, because the findings and conclusions may not be welcomed.

SAMPLE DOCUMENTS

In the example of a planning proposal below, note the use of the direct strategy for organizing ideas. Also, note the use of design elements such as bullets and headings to make the message easy to read.

MEMORANDUM

To: Sanjay Gupta, Plant Superintendent

From: Max Holder, Manager

Date: June 20, 2021

Subject: Recommendation to Install Jetaire Hand Dryers

As you requested, this memo presents the results of my research about the relative cost effectiveness of installing hand dryers versus paper towel holders in the company restrooms. I recommend that we purchase Jetaire Hand Dryers.

Benefits

Wilson Manufacturing will gain three benefits by installing hand dryers:

- We will save $3,084 in 3 years, plus intangible costs.
- The restrooms will be more sanitary.
- The safety of our employees will be increased, because there will be less slipping on wet floors.

Analysis

During the preceding 3-year period, paper towels have cost us $3,168. The intangible costs are 50 percent of the 3-year cost, which is $1,584 (see Table 1). The intangible costs come from issuing purchase orders, storing extra towels, hiring plumbers to fix clogged pipes, and the disposal of towels. In total, Wilson Manufacturing has spent $4,752 to support the use of paper towels.

TABLE 1 ■ Cost of Paper Towels	
No. of employees	200
Towels avg.	2.5
Daily visits	4
Cost per towel	$0.002
Days per month	22
Monthly cost	$88
Three-year cost	$3,168
Intangible cost	$1,584
Total cost	$4,752

(Continued)

(Continued)

By comparison, installing Jetaire Hand Dryers will cost just $1,668 over 3 years (see Table 2), saving the company an estimated $3,084.

TABLE 2 ■ Cost of Jetaire Hand Dryers	
Three Jetaire units @ $120 × four restrooms	$1,440
Installation cost	$84
Electricity cost for 3 years	$144
Total cost for Jetaire	$1,668

Eliminating paper towels will have benefits beyond cost savings. For instance, the use of hand dryers will bring about a more sanitary environment. The toilets and sinks will not be as likely to overflow, thus reducing the need for repairs. This will make the workplace more enjoyable.

Another benefit is the reduction of safety hazards. Wet, slippery floors caused by clogged sinks and toilets could result in employee injuries. These issues will be reduced when paper towels are no longer used.

Action Item

Haworth, Inc., should be hired to install three Jetaire Hand units in each of the four restrooms. The machines can be installed in one afternoon, with no interruption to our operation.

In the example of an informal letter report below, note the use of the direct strategy for sharing good news. Also, note the use of design elements such as bullets to make the message easy to read and the table to organize data.

LAMAR CONSOLIDATED HIGH SCHOOL

4604 Mustang Avenue
Rosenberg, TX 77471
Main Phone: (832) 223-3000
Main Fax: (832) 223-3001

Mr. Alphonse Garcia
207 Pine Ridge Road
Rosenberg, TX 77471

Dear Mr. Garcia:

What a great privilege it is to report on Jennifer's progress in Algebra I this year. I know Jennifer's success in Algebra is important to you and Jennifer. Evidence suggests that the support systems at home and class must work together to facilitate learning for high school students.

The table below summarizes Jennifer's scores on her weekly quizzes, unit exams, and homework.

Month	Quizzes (20 pts)	Exams (100 pts)	Homework (10 pts)
September	20	100	10
	18	90	10
	15		10

Month	Quizzes (20 pts)	Exams (100 pts)	Homework (10 pts)
October	20	95	10
	17	100	10
	19	90	10
	20		10

As you can see, Jennifer is exceeding expectations across the board.

Finally, I would like to invite you to attend the annual Open House on Wednesday, November 15, so we can meet and discuss the rest of the semester. Here are the details:

- **Date:** Wednesday, November 15

- **Time:** 6:30 pm–8:30 pm (come-and-go event)

- **Location:** Lamar CHS cafeteria and classrooms

Additional information about the event can be found on the high school website at www.lchsisd.edu.

I am excited to partner with you this semester to help Jennifer learn and succeed in Algebra. Please contact me whenever you would like to discuss her work. I primarily rely on e-mail, but you can also phone me if you prefer. Conference Hours are Monday, Wednesday, and Friday between 3:30 and 4:30 pm, or by appointment. My phone number is (832) 223-3100. My email: mriggins@lchsisd.edu.

Sincerely,
Mark Riggins

Mark Riggins, MEd
Algebra and Mathematics Instructor

Source: Mark Riggins. Reprinted with permission.

Notes

1. Joanne Feierman, "The 7 Deadly Sins of Report Writing," *Journal of Government Financial Management* 61, no. 4 (Winter 2012): 50–52.

2. Barbara Shwom and Lisa Gueldenzoph Snyder, *Business Communication: Polishing Your Professional Presence*, 3rd ed. (Hoboken, NJ: Pearson Education, 2016), 332–33.

3. Dilip Kumar Sharma and A. K. Sharma, "Search Engine: A Backbone for Information Extraction in ICT Scenario," in *The Dark Web: Breakthroughs in Research and Practice*, ed. Information Resources Management Association (Hershey, PA: IGI Global, 2018).

4. Dorinda Clippinger, *Planning and Organizing Business Reports: Written, Oral, and Research-Based* (New York: Business Expert Press, 2016), 2.

5. Ibid.

6. Erin Frost, "So What's a Quad Chart, Exactly? Exercises in Genre," 2012, http://isuwriting.com/wp-content/uploads/2015/04/Frost_Erin_3.1_Quad_charts.pdf.

7. Karl Keller, Owner, Communication Partners, *Association for Business Communication Consulting SIG* (blog), November 7, 2013, http://www.businesscommunication.org.

8. David K. Farkas, "Toward a Better Understanding of PowerPoint Deck Design," *Information Design Journal + Document Design* 14, no. 2 (August 2006): 162–71.

9. F. Stanford Wayne and Jolene D. Scriven, "Problem and Purpose Statements: Are They Synonymous Terms in Writing Business Reports?" *Bulletin of the Association for Business Communication* 54, no. 1 (March 1991): 30–37.

10. "Elmore Leonard: 1925–2013—Prolific Novelist Rewrote the Crime Thriller," *New York Times*, August 21, 2013, A2.

11. Gerald J. Alred, Charles T. Brusaw, and Walter E. Oliu, *The Business Writer's Handbook*, 11th ed. (Boston: Bedford/St. Martin's Press, 2015), 191.

12. Michael A. Stelzner, *Writing White Papers: How to Capture Readers and Keep Them Engaged* (Poway, CA: WhitePaperSource Publishing, 2007).

13. Kim Sydow Campbell and Jefrey S. Naidoo, "Rhetorical Move Structure in High-Tech Marketing White Papers," *Journal of Business and Technical Communication* 31, no. 1 (January 2017): 94–118, doi: 10.1177/1050651916667532.

14. Bill and Melinda Gates Foundation, "What We Do," https://www.gatesfoundation.org/What-We-Do.

15. Louisiana Office of Tourism, https://crt.state.la.us/tourism.

16. Richard Johnson-Sheehan, *Writing Proposals*, 2nd ed. (New York: Pearson Education, 2008), 4.

17. Johnson-Sheehan, 118.

18. Chip Heath and Dan Heath, *Made to Stick: Why Some Ideas Survive and Others Die* (New York: Random House, 2008).

19. Friends of the Minnesota River, "Buckthorn: How Can a Shrub Be So Harmful?" December 1, 2019, https://fmr.org/conservation-updates/buckthorn-how-can-shrub-be-so-harmful.

20. W. Timothy Coombs, "State of Crisis Communication: Evidence and the Bleeding Edge," *Research Journal of the Institute for Public Relations* 1, no. 1 (2014): 1–12.

21. Coombs, "State of Crisis Communication."

22. Gaby Del Valle, "Chick-fil-A's Many Controversies, Explained," *Vox*, November 19, 2019, https://www.vox.com/the-goods/2019/5/29/18644354/chick-fil-a-anti-gay-donations-homophobia-dan-cathy.

23. Oscar Munoz, "Actions Speak Louder Than Words," *Houston Chronicle*, April 27, 2017, A16; Oscar Munoz, "A Message From Oscar Munoz," *Hemispheres* (May 2017): 10.

24. For a comprehensive overview of the philosophical issues behind corporate apologies and their applications to civil and criminal law, see Nick Smith, *I Was Wrong: The Meanings of Apologies* (New York: Cambridge University Press, 2008). See also Nick Smith, *Justice through Apologies: Remorse, Reform, and Punishment* (New York: Cambridge University Press, 2014).

25. Benjamin J. McMichael, R. Lawrence Van Horn, and W. Kip Viscusi, "'Sorry' Is Never Enough: How State Apology Laws Fail to Reduce Medical Malpractice Liability Risk," *Stanford Law Review* 71, no. 2 (2019): 341–404.

26. Peter W. Cardon, *Business Communication: Developing Leaders for a Networked World*, 2nd ed. (New York: McGraw-Hill Education, 2016), 268.

27. Roy J. Lewicki, Beth Polin, and Robert B. Lount, Jr., "An Exploration of the Structure of Effective Apologies," *Negotiation and Conflict Management Research* 9 (2016): 177–96, doi:10.1111/ncmr.12073.

28. Ameeta Patel and Lamar Reinsch, "Companies Can Apologize: Corporate Apologies and Legal Liability," *Business Communication Quarterly* 66, no. 1 (March 2003): 9–25.

29. Andrea Rumbaugh, "United Revamps Policies After Dragging Incident," *Houston Chronicle*, April 27, 2017, B1, B7.

30. "Boeing Going Wrong," *The Economist*, December 21, 2019, 89–90; Chris Isidore, "Boeing Is Building the 737 Max Again Even Though It Is Not Yet Approved to Fly," *CNN Business*, May 27, 2020, https://www.cnn.com/2020/05/27/business/boeing-building-737-max/index.html; Andy Pasztor, "Congressional Report Faults Boeing on MA Design, FAA for Lax Oversight," *Wall Street Journal*, March 6, 2020, http://www.wsj.com/articles/congressional-report-says-max-crashes-stemmed-from-boeings-design-failures-and-lax-faa-oversight-11583519145?; Andy Pasztor and Andrew Tangel, "Former Top Boeing 737 MAX Officials Defend Design Process," *Wall Street Journal*, September 12, 2020, http://www.wsj.com/articles/former-top-boeing-737-max-officials-defend-design-process-11599959139; Al Root, "Boeing Stock Rises on 737 MAX Production Announcement. That May Be Premature," *Barron's*, May 28, 2020, https://www.barrons.com/articles/boeing-stock-rises-on-737-max-production-announcement-that-may-be-premature-51590684069; Alison Sider, "Flight Attendants Question Safety of 737 MAX," *Wall Street Journal*, October 31, 2019, http://www.wsj.com/articles/flight-attendants-question-safety-of-max-737-11572563447?reflink=share_mobilewebshare; David Slotnick, "The 737 Max Will Be the Safest Plane in the Skies Once It Starts Flying Again," *Business Insider*, September 18, 2019, https://www.businessinsider.com/boeing-737-max-safe-boeing-analysis-2019-9.

UNDERSTANDING MESSAGES

10

LISTENING

UNDERSTANDING MESS

LEARNING OBJECTIVES

By the end of this chapter, you will be able to

- Describe the benefits of good listening skills for managers.

- Identify the barriers to good listening.

- List the steps to follow when preparing to listen.

- Demonstrate six specific techniques for active listening.

- Demonstrate three specific techniques for interactive listening.

- Explain the importance of listening to informal communication.

- Explain the importance of listening to the total environment.

- Plan steps to developing a micro and macro listening climate in the workplace.

During the past several decades, the essential role of listening in business and management has received increased attention. Nike is one major corporation that emphasizes listening. Former CEO Mark Parker told employees they needed to transform its culture from "a place where the loudest voices carry the conversation to a place where every voice is heard."[1] Business professionals typically spend half to two thirds of their time listening. More than 35 studies reveal that listening is the form of communication that is

- most important for entry-level positions,

- most critical in distinguishing effective from ineffective direct reports, and

- most critical for managerial competency.[2]

Yet many of these studies report that listening skills are seriously lacking in direct reports and managers. Seventy-five to 90 percent of what they hear is ignored, misunderstood, or forgotten.[3]

Communication is more than just talking and waiting to talk. Communication is a two-way process, an exchange of information, ideas, and feelings that requires participants to receive as well as send messages. Further, the process on the receiving side is often more difficult and complicated than on the sending side of the exchange.

Listening is more than just hearing, and effective managers differentiate between the two. Hearing is mechanical, an automatic sort of thing often difficult to avoid. A horn blaring, heavy construction equipment groaning, children shouting in a playground—all these sounds, plus others, may be heard even though they are not listened to actively. Hearing usually requires little special physical or mental effort.

By contrast, listening results from a concentrated effort; it requires both physical and mental effort. Listening requires a special effort because physical and psychological factors work against the process. In this chapter, we review those physical and psychological barriers to listening and then analyze techniques to reduce these barriers. But first we examine why listening well is worth the effort.

BENEFITS OF LISTENING

A number of essential managerial skills involve listening. First, many of the data necessary for decision making come through listening to employees, and poor listeners miss important information. One company that requires its managers to spend significant time listening to employees is Zappos, the online retailer of shoes, clothing, and accessories. In his best seller, *Delivering Happiness*, CEO Tony Hsieh wrote that he required his managers to spend 20 percent of their time away from their desks, informally interacting with their employees. The result, according to Hsieh, was a 20 to 100 percent increase in productivity that he attributed to the increased communication level.[4]

A second benefit is that listening makes a person more dependable. People who listen well follow directions better, make fewer errors, say foolish things less often, and generally become the kinds of people others will ask for advice or direction. Third, good listeners are more respected and liked by those they work with. Recent research conducted by Karen Huang and her team at Harvard found that people who listen actively and ask questions, particularly follow-up questions, are perceived as higher in responsiveness, understanding, validation, and care.[5] Managers who listen to their direct reports, even when receiving bad news, will learn what's really on their minds rather than just what the direct reports think that their managers want to hear.[6] This trait can lead to harmonious labor relations, because employees generally trust and support managers who show respect by listening rather than merely "hearing them out."[7] Fourth, better listening enables a manager to be better informed overall. We learn about the world around us by listening, not talking. Fifth, good listening spares a person many embarrassments. In many situations, people may miss a name because of poor listening, or they may need to have critical information repeated because of daydreaming. Worse yet, a direct question may be unanswered because of inept listening. Such embarrassing situations can quickly label a manager as unconcerned or even apathetic.

Ultimately, the major reason for developing effective listening is to build relationships between people. All people need to be heard for their own emotional well-being and to create understanding among others. Mutual understanding leads to trusting relationships, which are required for a productive work group.

Several successful organizations provide models for including listening in the list of key managerial skills. Harley-Davidson has survived and grown over the past 100 years to be one of the world's leading motorcycle manufacturers. Jeffrey Bleustein, a former CEO, attributes the company's success to respecting customers' wishes. "Other companies talk about customer loyalty, but we have a loyalty that goes beyond most businesses," he says. Further, Bleustein was known for listening to his employees. "He gets out and visits with his dealers and really promotes a strong team atmosphere in the company," according to one retailer.[8] Today, stakeholder engagement and customer loyalty continue to be values that drive the company.

Listening to customers can be especially crucial during a crisis. A recent example is the crash of an Ethiopian Airlines Boeing 737 MAX on March 10, 2019, which killed 157 passengers. In the aftermath of that tragedy, Boeing made a number of efforts to compensate the families of the victims, including direct payments to the grieving families and to communities affected by the crash, as well as building a permanent memorial at the crash site. Perhaps more important, executives from Boeing and Ethiopian Airlines spent hours in meetings with the families, listening to them as they described their loss and articulated their wishes. "Sometimes they're angry with us and that's OK, we accept that," said Jennifer Lowe, a Boeing executive who worked with the families.[9]

Another corporation that understands the power of managerial listening is Procter and Gamble. A profile in the *Harvard Business Review* described how the company developed an elaborate system for surveying employees, customers, and other stakeholders to gain new ideas for improving products, processes, and services.[10] Despite good intentions and recognition of the benefits, managers' listening success at work is affected by many factors, some of which are beyond their awareness. For instance, managerial listening can be limited simply by the fact that they have authority over their employees. Recent research indicates that the more powerful the listener, the more likely they are to judge or dismiss advice and ideas they hear.[11] Thus, managers might be listening from a concrete bunker of which they are not even conscious. On the other hand, there are a number of strategies that managers can adopt in an effort to improve their listening. This chapter takes closer looks at the most common barriers and offers strategies for overcoming them.

BARRIERS TO LISTENING

The term *barrier* may remind us of something mechanical rather than an interactive, dynamic process such as listening. As a result, the term *listening barrier* may misrepresent listening somewhat. The barriers to listening included here describe reasons why people may shift out of active listening to merely hearing someone speak. Because dynamic, interactive processes are easier to discuss when categorized, Table 10-1 presents the complete list of listening barriers.

One of the greatest barriers to listening arises from our own *physical limitations*. People speak approximately 25 percent as fast as they think. Thus, while most people in the United States speak at a rate of about 125 words per minute, they are able to think at least four times as fast. This barrier is known as the 25–75 problem.[12] As a result, instead of listening

TABLE 10-1 ■ Barriers to Listening
1. Physical limitations (the listening–speaking differential, or 25–75 problem)
2. Lack of motivation
3. Lack of willingness
4. Internal and external noise
5. Detouring
6. Debate
7. Time

carefully, some people think about other things and devote only a fraction of their capacity to taking in what is said. They become impatient with the slow rate of the spoken word and begin to think about topics other than the words being spoken; consequently, our inability to speak more rapidly becomes a physical barrier in listening situations. The listening–speaking differential, or the 25–75 problem, is listed first because our wandering attention partially causes many of the other listening barriers.

A *lack of motivation* is another barrier to listening. Many people find maintaining the continuous motivation required for listening to be a challenge. Managers who should be listening may be daydreaming, making private plans, or even focusing on an emotional problem. During that 75 percent void, many things can overpower the 25 percent listening.

Researchers have long known that motivation or incentive is a prevalent problem in the listening process. It's important that managers practice emotional control and remember that client trust and employee loyalty are developed most effectively by those who can be relied on to listen respectfully.[13] Because listening is hard work, we can expect greater effort when the goal is known and listeners can observe a positive outcome of the effort. This is why the listening goal discussed later is so important.

A barrier related to motivation is *lack of willingness*. A manager may not *want* to listen. Before listening is even required, the manager may have lost any desire to listen. Because we have already discussed motivation as a barrier to listening, we must differentiate willingness from motivation. These concepts are closely related, but for this discussion, assume that a lack of willingness develops *before* listening even begins. This is why it may supersede all other barriers. If a person consciously or unconsciously decides not to listen, listening skills are of no advantage. Manny Steil, who does extensive listening training for companies such as Honeywell, often refers to the LAW of listening—Listening equals Ability plus Willingness.

Why would a manager lack the willingness to listen? Several reasons explain this attitude. First, most people would rather talk than listen; even when they ask a question, they often interrupt the first sentence of the response. Second, the listener may quickly stereotype the speaker as one who has little to contribute and is not worth listening to. Third, a listener may lack willingness because they may not want to receive negative information. Defensive behavior works against listening. Some managers consider the slightest attack on one of their opinions as an attack on them personally; consequently, they will rise to the defense. This defense often involves verbal attacks that preclude the possibility for listening.

Psychological barriers and attitudinal biases are not easy to control because often they are subconscious.[14]

Internal noise that cannot be ignored is another barrier. Our autonomic nervous system involuntarily pays attention to certain events, such as a headache, sore feet, or an empty stomach. It is difficult to divide attention between these internal involuntary distractions and concentrated listening. *External, environmental noise* that may compete with the main topic of interest is also a barrier. It is hard to listen to a direct report who speaks softly in a noisy foundry or to a phone conversation mixed with static on the phone line. In these situations, separating the speaker's voice from all the surrounding noise can be exhausting.

Another barrier may be termed *detouring*. The listener may become distracted by a phrase or concept and detour toward the distraction. This distraction then stimulates thought on another subtopic more interesting than the central point of the message; consequently, thoughts detour to the more interesting topics. Detouring is closely related to bias. For instance, a listener's negative bias toward a mannerism can distract from the content of the message. If a speaker places their hands over their mouth while speaking, or continually plays with a pencil, or looks away from the listener, such mannerisms can distract and get in the way of messages.

The *debate* represents a sixth type of barrier. A listener may suddenly find themselves disagreeing with the speaker and begin to plan their rebuttal. As the listener plans the rebuttal, they block out the speaker and miss the message. For instance, a manager listening to complaints from another department might prepare a rebuttal as the other person explains the incident. As a result, the manager creates a defensive climate and misses the most important information.

Finally, *time*, an important factor in every manager's day, can also be a barrier to listening. "I just don't have time to listen to this" is a common reaction for managers. Time seems to drag when people have to listen to something in which they have no interest. When listening appears to take too much time, managers tend to stop listening. One way some terminate listening is by making a hasty conclusion. This time pressure may lead to the tendency to judge, evaluate, approve, or disapprove a person's statement too hastily. To achieve real communication, it is important to resist the temptation to form hasty conclusions.

The preceding review is only a summary of the many barriers to listening. All those personal factors mentioned in Chapter 2—knowledge, culture, status, attitudes, emotions, communication skills—can also create potential barriers to listening. Nevertheless, research indicates we can improve listening skills. When managers strategically analyze the critical components of communication and apply the techniques suggested in this chapter, their listening skills and effectiveness as managers will improve.[15]

CRITICAL THINKING QUESTIONS

1. Which of the listening barriers listed in Table 10-1 and described in this section can you relate to the most?

2. Under what circumstances do these listening barriers occur?

3. What are some benefits of overcoming these listening barriers?

PREPARING TO LISTEN

Let us first identify two different types of listening, so that we can select techniques that are appropriate for the situation: active and interactive.

For the purposes of this discussion, *active listening* occurs in situations in which a manager has little or no opportunity to directly respond to the speaker. People in a large audience use active listening, as do those listening to a recorded message or watching a podcast. People use *interactive listening* when they have the opportunity to interact verbally with the speaker by asking questions or summarizing. Interactive listening occurs when a manager is exchanging information or ideas with another individual or group.

Our commitment to listening is often determined by the relevance, the importance, or the significance of the information involved. Listening basically has three levels of intensity—casual, factual, and empathic. Table 10-2 shows examples of listening occasions for each intensity level. *Casual* or marginal listening is used when the specific or technical information being discussed is not critical. Because no goal for specific information is established, a manager need not be as alert as in other situations. For example, casual listening occurs in social conversations or when listening to music. Although it is not as intense as many types of listening, it is nonetheless important. Managers can indicate social support by simply listening to employees talk about special events in their lives. By listening, the manager is saying, "You are important as a person." A variation of casual listening is the recent practice of "social listening," usually wielded by companies attempting to follow consumer needs and trends through social media accounts. Reading customers' and clients' newsfeeds and Facebook posts, or following them on Twitter, can allow managers to network in an informal, noninvasive way. Jenni Fleck Jones, marketing manager of Belfint, Lyons and Schuman, a Delaware CPA and consulting firm, says, "We listen a lot online [to clients]."[16]

A note of caution is important here. What one person considers casual another may consider critical information. The importance of the information is not inherent in the information itself. Therefore, in the same situation, different people could be listening with different intensities.

The next level of intensity, *factual* listening, is necessary when specific information needs to be obtained. Probably the most common type of listening in business meetings and conferences, factual listening is the level that most people likely think of when they consider the topic of listening. At this level, the listener should ask questions and receive feedback to ensure effective communication.

TABLE 10-2 ■ Examples of Listening Situations		
	Active Situation	**Interactive Situation**
Casual	Podcast	Social conversation
Factual	Informative presentation	Conference
Empathic	Motivational speech	Employee counseling

A manager uses the *empathic* level of listening when she wants to understand another person from that person's internal frame of reference rather than from the manager's frame of reference. The empathic listener tries to get inside the speaker's thoughts and feelings. The listener expresses empathy when verbally and nonverbally communicating such messages as "I follow you," "I'm with you," or "I understand." The empathic level of listening is not easy to achieve because we naturally tend to advise, tell, agree, or disagree based on our own view. However, it is well worth the effort to become an empathic listener. A speaker who sees that a manager is really trying to understand his meaning will trust the manager and be more willing to talk and explore problems. Empathic listening can be such a powerful form of listening that even when it is only partially attained, the mere attempt can be enough to open communication.

To summarize, when preparing to listen, managers should first determine the level of listening they will need to achieve—casual, factual, or empathic. They can accomplish this by establishing a *listening goal*, a specific statement of the purpose for listening. In the give-and-take of most communications, the need to adjust one's listening goal arises as the interchange develops.

Adjusting the listening goal is not always easy. Walmart, the biggest retailer in the world, considers listening to be a key skill for its managers. The founder, Sam Walton, is quoted on Walmart's website as having said, "Listen to your associates. They're our best idea generators." To capture associates' ideas, suggestions, and concerns, Walmart developed a number of programs. One requires every area to create a "Grass Roots" action plan to make good on associates' ideas. Another, a policy called "Open Door," permits anyone to bring complaints to officers at the highest level of the company. A third program, "Associates Out in Front," is described in company documents as a way for Walmart to show workers "that we do appreciate you and that we have an ongoing commitment to listening to and addressing your concerns."[17] It requires every store manager to meet with 10 rank-and-file employees every week.

Given the cultural values of this corporation, consider the listening levels used by a typical regional manager. She visits a different Walmart store at least every week, where she wanders around talking to customers, stock clerks, and store managers. One minute she may be listening to someone describe the weather in Salem, Oregon, and the next minute she may be discussing the drop in sales of bedding items. Soon after that, she may be listening to a manager describe why he is so frustrated with his work. Within 5 minutes, each of the different types of listening intensities is required, so the regional manager must be quick to adjust.

CRITICAL THINKING QUESTIONS

1. What are some examples of casual, factual, and empathic listening in your day?

2. Which level of listening is the most difficult for you?

3. Which level of listening do you think is the most important? Why?

Once managers have established the level of listening, they need to prepare physically and psychologically to listen. The steps during the preparation stage are as follows:

1. Pick the best possible place. While it is not always possible to change the place, the manager should not overlook better facilities when available.

2. Pick the best possible time. As with place, it is not always possible to change the time. However, the astute manager must be careful not to eliminate more favorable opportunities.

3. Think about personal biases that may be present.

4. Review the listening objectives.

A brief review of these four steps shows why they are important in reducing the barriers to effective listening discussed earlier. First, selecting the best time and place helps one reduce internal and external noise. In addition, because time influences the psychological barriers of motivation, emotion, and willingness, the choice of time may significantly alter the outcome of the conversation.

Is it polite to tell another that you cannot listen at the moment? In a survey of more than 200 managers, respondents indicated they would not be offended if someone asked them to wait before discussing something for fear that important information might be missed. Of course, if time cannot be changed, it is important that the parties be aware of the barriers present and make a special effort to concentrate on the listening process.

Managers' personal biases may also have a drastic effect on the outcome of the communication. Managers who are unaware of personal bias may become selective and hear only what they want to hear. They may deal only with preconceived notions and even debate with the speaker on points of disagreement. To control this psychological barrier of bias, first be aware; then recognize the burden it places on the speaker–listener relationship.

Emotional words or phrases can also trigger listener bias. Such phrases as "it really isn't my job," "we tried that before, and it didn't work," or "you don't care about us" can lead to emotional responses. The danger in such phrases is that they cause a listener to attend (or not to attend) to different parts of a message. The listener should be aware of the possible emotional responses and not let them distract from the message.

Finally, it is important to review and be aware of the listening objective. Without the objective in mind, a manager may use casual listening when factual listening is required or factual listening when empathic listening would be more effective. The person who can state in one sentence the specific goal and the type of listening involved is well aware of the listening objective.

One typical situation when the speaker's and listener's objectives may be at odds is this: Chris approaches Pat, his supervisor, with a complaint; Pat assumes that Chris expects a solution to his problem, so Pat listens to determine the facts of the situation and identify alternative actions. If Chris resists these possible solutions by responding with "yes, but" statements, then the manager should probably rethink the listening objective. It may be that Chris is only seeking attention or "face time" with the boss or seeking a sympathetic ear. To check Chris's objective, Pat might ask, "Is this an action item?"

Thus far, we have examined some general strategies to use when preparing to listen. The manager who is physically and psychologically prepared to listen should use additional, more specific techniques during listening. Let us next look at techniques that are appropriate for active and interactive listening.

SPECIFIC TECHNIQUES FOR ACTIVE LISTENING

As explained in the previous section, a manager uses active listening in situations where direct response to a speaker is difficult or impossible. Because asking questions is not possible, the listener needs to have a clear and complete understanding of the message the first time. Effective active listeners will implement the following techniques.

Identify the Main and Supporting Points

A message usually has a single purpose with one, two, or three main points, each of which is supported by information (examples, figures, statistics, descriptions). One good clue to main points is the nonverbal techniques the speaker uses when giving them; the speaker might raise their voice, speak faster, repeat key words, or use gestures. Later, we will detail nonverbal aspects that can be invaluable when identifying the main and supporting points. In the following example of a president speaking at an annual meeting, note the emphasis on main and supporting points.

> The electronics division was pleased with the successful introduction of four new products [raised voice] in the past year. All four of these products sold at a better rate than projected. We were especially pleased with the temperature sensor that sold 14 percent above projections. This small sensor, which has many applications and is easy to install, should do as well or better next year.
>
> Besides introducing four new products [pause], we expanded the Western division's sales force by adding 16 high-quality salespeople. These salespeople were recruited from all over the United States, and we're confident of their ability to help us expand in the West. They all have a thorough understanding of the products and the changing nature of our industry.
>
> No immediate changes are seen in the home implement division [lowered voice]. It will be necessary to wait and see what happens with the entire housing industry. We're stable here since garage openers, intercom systems, and home security devices are all holding their own. One highlight is the new, simpler app for managing the burglar protection system remotely.

The three main points in this example are the new products, the expansion of the Western division's sales force, and a stable home implement market; the remainder of the message is supporting information. Separation of main and supporting points helps the listeners retain the critical information.

Organize the Message

Often, a speaker has some type of organizational pattern that a listener uses to understand the message. For instance, a speaker may organize the message by pros and cons, advantages and disadvantages, likes and dislikes, similarities and differences, chronological events, or functional duties. Just as it is easier to remember the basic structure of a chapter rather than every word in it, it is easier to recall the structure of a spoken message rather than all the specifics. A skilled listener will pay attention to the signs, markers, or transitions that speakers use to indicate structure. Numbering the points ("My second point is . . .") is one technique that speakers use, as described in Chapter 5. Another is the preview of points ("Today I'll discuss . . ."). A third strategy to listen for is the summary ("So today I talked about . . .").

Summarize the Message

Another active listening technique is the summary, which can take the form of a mental picture of the main points. The summary should not include lots of details; generalizations are usually sufficient. In essence, the listener synthesizes the highlights of the message to provide a focus. Furthermore, summarization does not have to wait until the end of the message; it may be more efficient at major transition points. The president's speech, shown earlier, could be summarized in three phrases: (1) four new products in electronics, (2) an expanded salesforce in the Western region, and (3) a stable home implement market.

Visualize the Message

A fourth specific technique for active listening, putting the message into a picture, will help keep the listener's mind on the message. The beauty of this technique is that it allows listeners to use some of that 75 percent of their mental capacity not required to keep up with the message. Consequently, managers can commit more effort to listening, thus reducing the possibility of missing a major part of the message. Finally, retention of the message improves because a picture can now be associated with it. In the annual meeting described earlier, a manager might imagine what the new products look like, which will help the manager remember one of the main points of the message.

Related to visualization is mnemonics. One mnemonic device is the acronym, a combination of letters, each of which is the first letter of a group of words essential to the message. For instance, suppose a person is presenting his main objection to taking additional training in computer programming. The objection may stem from the cost, the individual's ability, and the time involved. The mnemonic CAT—cost, ability, time—can be used to record these main ideas whenever the speaker refers to them. Mnemonics have practical use in the business sector. At one popular restaurant in Houston, Greek salads are prepared tableside. The servers remember the order of ingredients by recalling this mnemonic: "Very Fast Leopards Die Old." It translates to "first, add the Vegetables to the bowl, then the Feta, Lemon juice, Dressing, and Olives." Mnemonics in general and acronyms specifically may be considered a type of visualization because it is easy to see and recall the acronym. Other types of memory games, such as word association and riddles, are also beneficial tools for active listening and retention.

Personalize the Message

Effective listeners are those who search a message for information that has special meaning for the listener. A topic is naturally more interesting and easier to concentrate on if it personally relates to the listener. In fact, those who relate the message to personal experiences ensure that two key elements of listening—willingness and motivation—are present. At this point, the listener might also form a tentative interpretation about the speaker's feelings, desires, or meaning and attempt to find personal connections to that interpretation.[18] The managers listening to the president in the previous example may also personalize the message by asking questions of themselves: "How will these four products affect my job?" "Will continued expansion of the electronics group benefit me?" "Will those 16 new salespeople increase my workload for the Western region?" "How will the stable market in the home implement group affect our division?" In answering these questions, the managers find how the message personally relates to them. Then their incentive to listen to the message increases.

Take Notes

All these techniques are strengthened when the listener takes notes. College students understand the importance of notes, but they may lose this good habit once they leave the classroom. Listeners can easily make short notes to help organize, visualize, and personalize a message. Not only do notes provide a written record of the communication; they can also provide valuable feedback that tells the listeners just how well they are listening. If the notes are not well organized with main and supporting points, the listeners probably have not mentally organized the message. If a quick review indicates no notes have been taken for some time, the listeners may realize that their attention has been wandering.

Notes also benefit listeners by keeping them physically involved. Listening is a predominantly mental activity; consequently, people who are accustomed to being physically active get restless or impatient when listening for long periods.

Of course, note taking can be a problem for people who overdo it. One can concentrate on the notes to the extent that major components of the message are missed. Instead, managers should jot down just key words and phrases in outline form, using abbreviations when possible.

A final thought on notes: Listeners who take notes indicate a sincere interest in both the message and the speaker. Seeing the note taking, the speaker will have a greater degree of confidence that note-taking listeners are paying attention to the message. The fact that it is important to demonstrate effective listening is discussed in more detail later.

Each of these techniques—identifying the main points, organizing, summarizing, visualizing, personalizing, and note taking—is useful in both active and interactive listening. However, the techniques are especially critical in situations where the ability to ask questions and observe nonverbal messages is limited. When interaction is possible, the ideal is to ask questions of the speaker for clarity, in addition to the six techniques just discussed. The next section discusses situations in which it is easy to interact with the speaker. We refer to this as interactive listening.

CRITICAL THINKING QUESTIONS

Imagine that you are listening to a disgruntled customer on the phone. What is the customer's likely reaction if you say, "I'm taking notes on this. Will you spell the person's name for me?"

SPECIFIC TECHNIQUES FOR INTERACTIVE LISTENING

Table 10-3 summarizes techniques to use in active and interactive listening situations. When managers are engaged in two-way communication, they can improve their listening effectiveness by responding with paraphrases and questions.

TABLE 10-3 ■ Specific Techniques for Active and Interactive Listening	
Active Situation	**Interactive Situation**
Identify main and supporting points	Paraphrase
Organize the message	Ask open and closed questions
Summarize the message	Ask primary and secondary questions
Visualize the message	Ask neutral and directed questions
Personalize the message	
Take notes	

Paraphrasing

Paraphrasing is commonly thought of as simply repeating what a speaker has *said*. However, a true paraphrase does more than indicate awareness of the message; it reflects what the listener thinks the speaker *intended to say*. The listener uses different words to express the speaker's meaning, thereby checking understanding. Further, a paraphrase reflects the underlying attitudes or emotional tone of the message. While many people are reluctant to paraphrase for fear of sounding like a parrot, paraphrasing is an excellent listening technique for two reasons. When properly done, paraphrases allow the listener not only to be sure they have received the message as the speaker intended but also to strengthen the relationship between speaker and listener. When listeners paraphrase, they indicate effort, commitment, and good intentions, thereby increasing the likelihood that the speaker will respond in kind.

Knowing the important benefits of paraphrasing, you might wonder why we all do not do it more frequently when listening. It may be because we are afraid it will sound foolish. Consider a time when a team member returned from visiting a client's worksite and you asked, "How was your day?" If the answer was something like "I hate that place; don't ever send me back!" and you decided to paraphrase, you would not say, "So you hate that place, and you don't want to go back," because that response would probably trigger derision and a comment like "That's what I just said!" Instead, as a good listener, you would say, "Sounds like you had a tough day." Remember that a paraphrase should reflect the meaning of the message you think the speaker intended for you to receive, both verbally and nonverbally.

Questioning

The skillful use of questions adds immensely to a manager's ability to listen. Questions also help keep the focus on the speaker. While it's fine to show you can relate, it's important to avoid detouring the interaction to your own situation and feelings. This book recommends several situations when questioning techniques are appropriate: listening, interviewing, resolving conflict, and coaching.

Questions are important because they provide the two-way process of communication that Chapter 2 discusses. Without the use of questions, feedback and mutual understanding are severely curbed. Questions serve to request more information and/or clear up any confusion. Thus, in the example just described in the previous section on paraphrasing, a good listener should follow the paraphrase ("Sounds like you had a tough day") with a question like "What happened?"

In an interactive situation, when the meaning of a message is either unclear or incomplete, a listener should ask questions. Questions can benefit both the listener and the speaker. First, questions can help the speaker clarify and reanalyze their own intentions and meaning. Second, questions can help the listener clarify key words, phrases, or vague concepts and resolve inconsistencies and contradictions in the message. By asking questions, the listener signals that they have not just listened; they have heard. Jim Quigley, former CEO at Deloitte, set a goal in meetings to talk no more than 20 percent of the time. "One of my objectives is listening. Many times you can have bigger impact if you know what to ask, rather than knowing what to say," Quigley explained. As he increased his questions, Quigley gained a deeper understanding of his people's needs.[19] Managers should strategically determine the most appropriate questions for different situations. Three types of questions are appropriate to this discussion: open/closed, primary/secondary, and neutral/directed. Question types are also described in Chapter 15 in the context of interviewing.

Open and Closed Questions

The phrasing of an open question gives the respondent a wide choice of possible answers. At the other end of the spectrum is the closed question, which calls for a narrow range of possible answers. Here is an illustration of this point: Suppose a frustrated direct report describes to you a major problem with a new project. In their agitation, the employee jumps from one point to another while describing the problem. Naturally, this disorderly description makes it difficult to listen, so you ask questions for both clarity and completeness of information. The following list includes open and closed questions that you might ask the employee for clarification:

- What do you think are the major causes of the problem? (open)

- What more can you tell me about it? (open)

- Did you check the steam gauge? (closed)

- Where do you think we should go from here? (open)

- Would it be a good idea to wait until tomorrow? (closed)

Open questions not only ask for additional information; they also can guide the interaction from the problem-analysis phase toward the brainstorming-of-solutions phase ("What do you want to do about this?"). One risk of open questions is that they allow possible digression. By contrast, closed questions are more direct and help one focus on the problem or facts. Closed questions also call for commitment ("Will you . . . ?"). Managers must use strategic analysis to determine when to ask open and closed questions in each case.

CRITICAL THINKING QUESTIONS

Imagine that you are attending a company function and trying to start a conversation with a coworker you don't know well. You decide to ask a question.

1. What is a good open question to get your coworker to talk? (Hint: "How are you?" doesn't count as an open question, because the answer usually consists of one word.)

2. Considering your purpose, what is a good response if your coworker asks you a closed question?

Primary and Secondary Questions

The second category of questions that managers should consider asking is primary and secondary. A primary question is the first question about a topic. A secondary question is designed to obtain more specific information after the primary question has been answered. A secondary question is not merely an additional question; it also seeks to get at a deeper level of information than the primary question. Such probes call for clarification or elaboration. As discussed earlier in this chapter, a bonus for using secondary questions along with primary is a stronger emotional connection between speaker and listener.

The following dialogue shows the strategic use of primary and secondary questioning:

Manager: Do you think you'll be able to have the analysis done by Wednesday? (primary)

Employee: That shouldn't be any problem, if everything goes right for a change.

Manager: What might go wrong? (secondary)

Employee: The accounting information is hard to get sometimes.

Manager: What specific part is hard to get? (secondary)

Notice that each secondary question seeks further information on the preceding answer.

Neutral and Directed Questions

The third classification involves neutral versus directed questions. A neutral question seeks information without attempting to lead the speaker to answer in a certain way. The purpose is to try to understand what the speaker is trying to get across and to show interest. Simple variations of a neutral question are a filled pause ("uh huh") and statements such as "Tell me more" and "Then what happened?" On the other hand, a directed question leads the speaker to a response that the listener desires. A directed question or leading question opens with such phrases as "Doesn't it seem logical that . . . ?" or "Wouldn't you agree that . . . ?" or "Surely you won't . . . , will you?" Directed questions may be used to obtain confirmation or clarification on one specific point, whereas neutral questions can obtain an unintended response.

In summary, managers who use paraphrases and appropriate questions add clarity to communication because of the interactive process that develops. Interactive listening is clearly not a passive activity; rather, it requires managers' involvement through questions and paraphrases.

Responding to Negative Messages

Listening to negative messages from the boss, direct reports, customers, coworkers, or other stakeholders is especially difficult. While the techniques explained previously, chiefly paraphrasing and questioning, are the most appropriate responses when managers are listening to bad news, more typical responses are to defend, disagree, resist, retaliate, or deny. It's natural to react negatively to negative information, especially when feeling threatened. But managers who show empathy in bad news situations will go far to create and maintain open communication channels. Once empathy is established, managers can move on to an exploration of solutions. Sometimes speakers don't have solutions, but in a surprising number of situations, they do, and it's wise to listen to them.[20]

Culture can affect the exchange of feelings and ideas, problems, and solutions, as explored in Chapter 12. Various cultures view feedback differently. For example, in the United States and Western Europe, workers typically prefer direct communication and expect honest feedback. In Eastern cultures, on the other hand, workers typically prefer communicating more indirectly, and they may expect feedback to be subtle rather than blunt. In many Asian cultures, silence is respected. Silence rather than talk communicates. As a result, when working with people from many cultures, managers can benefit from using silence as a type of response.[21] Even if the manager is confident about what the speaker will say, it is important to be patient and let the speaker finish. Rather than assuming, an open attitude will help the manager see the other person's side of a situation and strengthen the working relationship.

To help us see how listening and paraphrasing work in a bad news situation, let us examine a hypothetical interview between the general manager (GM) of a manufacturing facility and the shop supervisor. The topic is the delivery deadline for a customer order. The manager begins the interview by reviewing the contract and asking the supervisor what has gone wrong. The supervisor turns their chair toward the GM, leans in and makes eye contact. The supervisor begins by paraphrasing the question, making it much simpler. "So you are asking about the likelihood that we will deliver the order on time? The answer is no."

The supervisor further clarifies that delays in equipment repairs on the line, caused by severe weather, prevented necessary parts from arriving the previous week. This break in the supply chain culminated in extended downtime and a reduction in product volume.

Rather than responding with anger or expressing frustration about the bad news, the GM, also maintaining eye contact, instead paraphrases the answer and proceeds to probe the supervisor by asking if the equipment is now repaired and working. The supervisor adds details, explaining that the repairs have been completed and the shop is now up and running. The GM summarizes and ends by saying, "So what is the new delivery date?" Both participants in the interview demonstrate good listening skills, including paraphrases, open and closed questions and probes, and nonverbal cues.

LISTENING TO INFORMAL COMMUNICATION

So far, this discussion of listening has emphasized times in which a formal speaking–listening situation is established. But informal, casual listening can also be extremely important—what began as casual listening can quickly become factual or empathic listening. A manager should always be aware of the rumors that circulate on the grapevine. At times, these rumors can provide important information; at other times, it may be important to attempt to alter the content of the rumor; and at still others, it may be best to ignore the rumors. But managers must stay tuned in.

The term *grapevine* has an interesting history. It arose during the Civil War when intelligence telegraph lines were strung loosely from tree to tree in the manner of a grapevine. Because the messages from the line often were incorrect or confusing, any rumor was said to be from the grapevine.

What causes rumors in modern organizations? To answer this question, the following formula is helpful:

Rumors = Ambiguity × Interest

Rumors are created when the available message is ambiguous. If all information were available and clear from the formal channels, no rumors would be created. When the message is ambiguous but interesting, rumors will result.

This relationship has an important implication for managerial communication. Managers can determine what is interesting to employees by listening to the rumors. For instance, a vice president recently resigned from a computer company. But the rumors on the grapevine did not address the replacement; rather, a new relationship between two employees was the major topic. This would imply that the employees were relatively secure about the management team and that one replacement would probably not rock the boat. Compare this to a company where the president suddenly retired. All that was discussed whenever people gathered was the latest rumor about the replacement. Obviously, this matter was of great concern to the employees.

Research indicates that information transmitted via the grapevine in organizations is 70 to 90 percent accurate. However, some amount of distortion always exists.[22] This core of truth, along with the degree of distortion, is often what makes a message on the grapevine believable, interesting, and durable.

As information proceeds from person to person on the grapevine, it tends to undergo three kinds of change. The first is *leveling*, the dropping of details and the simplifying of context and qualifications. This process is especially prevalent when the rumor is extremely complex. It is streamlined to make it easier to pass on to the next person. The second kind of change is *sharpening*, the preference for vivid and dramatic treatment of data. Employees work to make a story better and more entertaining as it is passed from one person to another. Third is *assimilating*, the tendency of people to adjust or modify rumors, to mold them to fit their personal needs. This makes the rumors more interesting to those on the grapevine.[23]

Effective managerial listening requires that managers critically assess informal communication to determine the extent to which leveling, sharpening, and assimilation have occurred. Inaccurate rumors can sometimes call for action. In one manufacturing plant, rumors maintained that a massive personnel layoff was about to occur because of the new machinery being installed. Management heard these incorrect rumors. Members of the management team met with employees to assure them no layoffs would occur. Listening to rumors helped prevent a loss of employee morale. As one manager once said, it is important to listen to "the talk on the street." Research shows that employees prefer to get their information from the formal channels, and they turn to informal channels when the formal ones have dried up because it's difficult to work in a vacuum. Managers concerned about rampant rumors should remember the relationship between formal and informal channels.

CRITICAL THINKING QUESTIONS

1. Why do employees prefer to receive their information through the formal channels?

2. When the formal channels dry up, such as when a company is in decline, why do employees turn to the grapevine for information?

3. How can managers minimize grapevine activity among their employees?

LISTENING TO THE TOTAL ENVIRONMENT

This chapter primarily discusses listening to the spoken word. Chapter 11 discusses nonverbal communication. Managers must listen to spoken and nonverbal messages both separately and jointly in formal and informal settings. Strategic managerial communication requires listening to messages that are not always obvious. Figure 10-1 graphically demonstrates the three possible aspects of a message: formal to informal, verbal to nonverbal, and obvious to hidden. The three possibilities are displayed in a triangle with equal sides because all three aspects should be considered equally.

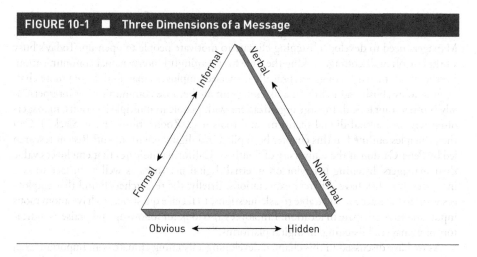

FIGURE 10-1 ■ Three Dimensions of a Message

This implies that it is necessary for managers to keep their eyes and ears open for all kinds of signals in their organization and its industry. When a person is aware of the signals of a forthcoming event, it is possible to take preemptive action—but first the manager must listen to be aware. An online magazine, *Madame Noire*, featured an article called "The Fourth Quarter Curse? How to Tell If a Layoff Is Coming."[24] The article discusses signals of potential restructuring, such as employees who voluntarily quit but are not replaced, increased debt, layoffs at other companies in the industry, rumors, unannounced meetings, and departures of top executives. It is possible that most employees could know about pending layoffs long before they were formally announced.

Of course, restructuring is a drastic action. It is important that managers listen to and analyze many other events in the company that can affect their careers. For example, which departments seem to be getting the best budgets? Employees in these groups will probably have the greatest opportunities for advancement. Although it is not always possible to determine budget allocations, it is possible to watch for the results of greater allocations. The hiring of additional support staff, the purchasing of newer and better equipment, the acquisition of new office furniture, and more frequent traveling to professional conferences can each signal a favored department.

The point is that managerial listening goes beyond listening to the words. It requires listening to nonverbal behaviors and the continuous signals that come from the environment. Recall our discussion of the strategic communication model in Chapter 2. The outer layer—culture and climate—is relevant here.

DEVELOPING A LISTENING CLIMATE

In addition to actually listening carefully, managers must also seem to be listening and establish a climate that demonstrates receptivity. You might recall that an organization's culture and climate were discussed in Chapter 2 and highlighted as the outer layer of the strategic communication model for developing a communication strategy.

While a manager is responsible for a tremendous amount of information and spends as much as 50 percent of the working day listening, one cannot listen if nobody is talking. Managers need to develop a listening climate to motivate people to open up. Today's busy workplace often discourages taking the time for meaningful interpersonal communication. Furthermore, managers of geographically dispersed employees may find it even more challenging to establish and maintain a listening climate because communicating interpersonally is often impractical. In large organizations with people in multiple locations, managers often rely on internal digital platforms and tools (e.g., Zoom, Blink, Fuze, Slack[25]). Can the principles outlined in this chapter be applied in a digital environment? Recent research led by Peter Cardon at the University of Southern California indicates that employees value their managers' listening behavior on internal digital networks as well as in face-to-face instances, but they have different expectations. Briefly, the researchers found that employees want to have access, to be able to ask questions, to receive questions, to have anonymous input, and to participate in ideation. Employees also look for follow-up and praise as indicators of managerial listening on digital platforms.[26]

As we have discussed in this chapter, developing a listening climate is an important goal for managers in any organization. The effort requires managers' attention on two levels. The first is the micro level, or the one-on-one situation. The second is the macro level, or the total climate. First, we will review the micro level.

The Micro Listening Climate

Clearly, successful interpersonal communication requires time—the listener needs to give undivided attention to the speaker, who usually does not want to be rushed to complete the message. This fact relates to the 25–75 rule discussed earlier. The listener's mind moves so much more rapidly than the spoken word that the listener's impatience may show as they attempt to complete the speaker's sentence. Even though the listener is paying attention, this impatience to complete the speaker's communication may develop a negative listening climate. The same is true when the listener works on something else while attempting to listen to a meeting, phone call, or videoconference. The speaker may soon get the feeling that the message being delivered is not perceived as very important.

Demonstrating a positive climate is most important when a manager is involved in empathic listening. As we have seen in this chapter, an empathic listener tries to understand the speaker's feelings. Stephen Covey, the noted business consultant, described empathic listening as listening with your ears, your eyes, and your heart.[27] Many people have a difficult time expressing their true thoughts to their boss, believing it is safer to tell the boss what they will want to hear. So an encouraging, supportive, receptive climate needs to be established. Managerial strategies include maintaining eye contact, leaning slightly toward the speaker, changing facial expression in relationship to the message, and taking notes. All these behaviors demonstrate a positive micro listening climate, which leads to a trusting work relationship and ultimately to greater productivity.

The Macro Listening Climate

Managers must take responsibility for ensuring that those who work around them are free to exchange information in a timely and accurate manner. They must develop a general atmosphere that promotes rather than hinders the opportunity to communicate. This macro level of listening is demonstrated by the manager's general demeanor and style.

One basic approach is managing by walking around. For example, when Ed Whitacre stepped in as CEO of General Motors (GM) in 2009, one of the first efforts was to make over GM's culture from an authoritarian, top-down environment to an open one. He preferred personal interaction to e-mail, making himself accessible to employees by using the employees' elevators, bathrooms, and dining rooms rather than those set aside for officers. He regularly stopped by workstations to ask how employees were helping sell more cars, and the employees grew to look forward to his visits.[28] When managers are physically available and not locked away behind closed office doors, they create an atmosphere that says "I am here to listen to you."

In his popular book *Thriving on Chaos*, Tom Peters presents a number of suggestions that create strong macro listening environments.[29] First, he suggests that opportunities to listen be built into managers' daily routines. This can be done by frequently visiting the cafeteria or break room.

A second technique is to have informal meetings; "huddles" or spontaneous gatherings of a few people to discuss a problem indicate that the manager wants and needs to listen to employees' ideas. In remote teams, regular check-in meetings can occur using videoconference or dedicated channels in digital collaboration software. An implication of this approach is the importance of ensuring that all employees can access and use the internal digital platform. Further, mechanisms must be in place for two-way communication on the digital platform so that employees feel that their voice is sought and heard.

Another technique is to keep official titles and symbols of authority to a minimum. People are more willing to talk when they do not feel inferior to another. In some contemporary organizations, job titles have disappeared not only from office doors but also from business cards. The implication is that everyone works together—communicates together—to get the job done. Transparency is a critical prerequisite for a macro listening climate.

Finally, it is important to understand that managers can develop a macro listening climate through informal as well as formal behaviors, as aptly demonstrated by Celeste, a first-line supervisor in a foundry. Her company was on the far south side of Chicago. Celeste was probably one of the most respected supervisors. Rather than stating that she had an "open-door policy," she simply remained available to the employees. For instance, one Saturday, the company rented a bus and arranged for employees to attend a Chicago White Sox baseball game. Celeste was one of the first to sign up. During the bus trip and at the game, she was part of the group, even though she was the only supervisor to attend. Such actions symbolized a positive listening climate.

In short, a number of elements influence employees' perceptions that managers are listening. Employees' work and personal backgrounds, the organizational culture, the employees' access to the organization's internal digital network, and the little symbolic behaviors of the manager all affect the macro listening climate. Managers would do well to take a periodic audit of their personal listening behavior and their environment to ensure that they have established a climate that says, "Yes, I am willing to listen."

SUMMARY

Managers need to work on their listening skills. The major benefit is improved understanding between people. Many of the data necessary for good decisions come through listening. Listening makes a person more dependable. Good listeners are more respected and liked by coworkers. Better listening enables a manager to be better informed overall.

Managers must exert an active, concentrated effort to overcome listening barriers. One of the primary barriers is that people think about four times faster than they can speak; consequently, the listener's mind tends to wander. Motivation and willingness are highly related barriers. Willingness develops before listening even begins, whereas poor motivation is largely caused by the 25–75 problem. Other barriers to listening include internal and external distractions, detouring, debate, and time.

Two main types of listening are active and interactive. Active listening occurs when a manager has little opportunity to respond directly to the speaker. Interactive listening occurs when the manager can verbally interact with the speaker by asking questions or summarizing.

Listening has three levels of intensity: casual, factual, and empathic. The level to use is determined by the importance and complexity of the message and occasion. Once the manager has determined the type and intensity level of listening called for, the manager must prepare physically and psychologically to listen.

Techniques for active listening include identifying the main and supporting points, organizing, summarizing, visualizing, personalizing the message, and taking notes. Techniques for interactive listening include paraphrasing and asking open/closed, primary/ secondary, and neutral/directed questions. When listening to informal communication, a manager should remember that information transmitted informally undergoes some distortion. Leveling, sharpening, and assimilating occur. A manager who is a good listener will listen to the total environment—both spoken and nonverbal messages are important.

Finally, a manager should work to develop a climate that demonstrates receptivity so that people are motivated to communicate. On a micro level, a manager should demonstrate good listening habits, such as paraphrasing and asking questions. On a macro level, a manager's general demeanor and style will indicate approachability.

CASES FOR ANALYSIS

Case 10-1

Listening and Technology

Veronica Sharpe, marketing manager for Diamond Communications, an outdoor advertising company, arrived in the boardroom for her teleconference with Brad Jones, a potential client. She was extremely busy that day and brought her smart tablet with her, checking e-mail along the way. She also brought her digital voice recorder so that she could record the conversation for reference later. She intentionally left the cameras off, opting to use only audio transmission. Brad called right on time, and they began to speak about Brad's plan for utilizing advertising space on the variety of electronic billboards along Interstate 45, a north–south route through Houston, Texas.

About 2 minutes into Brad's exposition of his plans, Veronica's smart tablet buzzed. It was an e-mail she had been waiting on for 2 hours, and time was of the essence—she had to reply quickly to settle a payment before the 4:00 p.m. deadline, 5:00 p.m. in the Eastern time zone from where the e-mail was being sent. She thought to herself, "I'm recording all this, so I can just review it later—I have to answer this e-mail now. Time to multitask."

About a minute later, in the middle of her e-mail response, she noticed a distinct pause in Brad's speech. "Veronica?" Brad asked. "Still there?"

"Oh, yes," Veronica answered, embarrassed. "Can you repeat that last thing?"

"I want to know if the plan is something that your firm can accomplish, or do I need to find another firm with electronic boards?" Brad asked.

Questions

1. What principles of effective listening was Veronica violating?

2. What do you think her best alternative was at this moment in time, given her lack of attention to Brad's proposal?

Case 10-2

Holgate's Listening Problems

John Holgate, a section manager in a chemical plant, has several engineers reporting to him. As part of his job, Holgate attends meetings during any given day with some of his junior engineers, as well as with people outside his immediate group. Occasionally, people higher up in the company (the technical director or vice president, for example) attend these review meetings.

The engineers who work for Holgate believe he often misrepresents them, and they also think Holgate does not listen to what is being said. He often interrupts the speakers and completes the sentence for them. Because the engineers do not want to disagree with their boss openly, they do not contradict him in front of higher management.

Naturally, this habit results in confusion, wasted time and effort, and poor morale. When members of higher management return for their next review, they usually find that the work they requested has not been done. In fact, they occasionally find that unrequested tasks have been carried out. As they listen to Holgate's project status review, management has lately been wondering what is going on. This doubt reflects not just on Holgate but on his direct reports as well. The direct reports' morale and productivity have been slipping.

Questions

1. Why does Holgate complete the speaker's sentences?

2. How can Holgate improve his listening skills?

3. Assuming you are Holgate's direct report, how could you help him improve?

Case 10-3

Pardon Me!

Bob Pierce is the president of ABC Construction Company. The company is considered the most progressive and innovative in highway, bridge, and dam construction in the area. Pierce has served in different functional areas of the company, is fairly well educated, and is oriented toward engineering.

Before becoming ABC's vice president of field operations, Wendy Horton was the chief engineer of a rival firm. She has a reputation for being a very good project manager and for knowing intimately the details of ABC field operations.

Pierce has just returned from sick leave. His bad cold is still slowing him down. It is now noon, and Pierce, who has finally caught up with the backlog of work, is preparing to go to lunch. Just then, Horton walks into his office. Horton has been trying to get in touch with Pierce the past few days for his decision about the construction plan for the new dam. Horton spreads her blueprints on the president's desk and starts her presentation.

After the presentation, the following conversation occurs:

Horton (somewhat absently):	Well, how do you feel about the plan?
Pierce:	Well, uh, pretty good . . .
Horton (a little too quickly):	Is there anything I haven't made clear?
Pierce:	Hmm . . . no . . .
Horton:	OK, good. Now I would like to present the plan to the board of directors and maybe—
Pierce:	Board of directors? Wait a minute. You're moving pretty fast.

(Continued)

(Continued)

Horton:	You agreed the plan's a good one, didn't you?
Pierce:	Well, yes.

Questions

1. What are the physical and psychological listening barriers Pierce faced during the presentation?

2. What assumptions is Horton making about Pierce's ability to grasp the situation?

3. What could Pierce have done to prevent the situation?

4. What are Horton's shortcomings as a communicator that would complicate the situation for anyone listening to her?

Case 10-4

Hearing but Not Listening

Cedar's Furniture and Appliance is a chain of five stores: two located in Youngstown, two in Akron, and one in Cleveland. Cedar's main office is in Akron.

Jane Pyle is the office manager at the main office. She supervises four administrative assistants. Three of Pyle's employees are efficient and

thorough. She tells them what she wants done once, and it is done. However, the fourth employee, Harriet Enders, seems to get little done right. She finishes her daily work, but she frequently has to redo it, thus putting an extra burden on the other three assistants. They have to make up the work Enders has no time for because she is redoing her original work. The other three employees are beginning to complain to Pyle about the problem.

Pyle does not want to terminate Enders because Pyle knows her direct report can be a hard worker. When she does follow directions, Enders is the first of the four assistants to finish. The office manager wonders why Enders does not understand directions, while the other three people always seem to. She is almost sure that although Enders is hearing, she is not listening. Enders's problem is preventing the office work from running smoothly.

Questions

1. Write the dialogue Pyle might use to open the discussion with Enders about this problem.

2. What environmental factors might be responsible for Enders's difficulty in listening?

EXERCISE FOR SMALL GROUPS

Exercise 10-1

This exercise offers practice in a disciplined approach to listening to others that provides focused support and clarity. It was developed by Dr. Mary Vielhaber at Eastern Michigan State University.

Prework Instructions

Please take some time to think about a communication problem that you face in your job. The

problem can be either a unique, unusual communication problem or a recurring communication problem that you continue to face in spite of several efforts to resolve the problem.

Select a problem that you are willing to share with your colleagues. Avoid problems with complicated technical details. You can disguise names and other facts so that people involved in the problem are not identified.

Briefly write down the problem in one or two paragraphs. Describe the context and key facts of the problem so that when you read your description, others will be able to quickly understand what you are facing.

Process

Divide into groups of three or four members. Each person either reads their description of their business problem or *briefly* explains the problem to the group. After all people in the group have presented their problem, select one problem for the group to focus on. Ask the person to read their written problem one more time to the group. Take a few minutes to jot down open questions you can ask the person about the problem.

Note: The questions you ask should be designed to help the person think through their difficult situation. You should not be trying to "solve" their problem. Instead, you are asking questions to help the person think through the issues involved.

Questioning Process

Ask open questions and probe for understanding the facts and the reasoning behind the person's assertions and conclusions. The presenter responds to the questions unless they do not have a response. In that case, the presenter may simply say, "I don't have an answer to that question." There should be no discussion among the group members or any statements hidden in the questions.

Post-Questioning Process

After approximately 10 minutes, the group stops to discuss the process used. The presenter is invited to describe their experience answering questions. Did the questions lead to a new insight? Did the presenter feel that the group was listening? A second or third round may continue if time permits.

Discussion Questions

1. What are the advantages of disciplined listening?

2. When can this technique be used in the workplace?

3. What are the barriers to disciplined listening?

Notes

1. Angelica LaVito, "Nike CEO Apologizes to Employees for Workplace Culture After Months of Turmoil," *CNBC*, May 4, 2018, https://www.cnbc.com/2018/05/04/nike-ceo-apologizes-to-employees-for-workplace-culture-after-months-of-turmoil.html.

2. Deborah Roebuck, *Communication Strategies for Today's Managerial Leader* (New York: Business Expert Press, 2012).

3. Mary Munter, *Guide to Managerial Communication: Effective Business Writing and Speaking*, 9th ed. (Upper Saddle River, NJ: Prentice Hall, 2012), 173–74.

4. Tony Hsieh, *Delivering Happiness: A Path to Profits, Passion, and Purpose* (New York: Business Plus, 2010).

5. Karen Huang et al., "It Doesn't Hurt to Ask: Question-Asking Increases Liking," *Journal of Personality and Social Psychology* 113, no. 3 (2017): 430–52.

6. I. M. Sixel, "Permission to Speak Freely to the Boss," *Houston Chronicle*, May 16, 2013, D1.

7. P. Senecal and E. Burke, "Learning to Listen," *Occupational Hazard* 1 (1992): 37–39.

8. Margot Denney, "CEO Drives Home Message," *Bryan-College Station Eagle*, April 10, 2003, 1A.

9. Alison Sider and Alexandra Wexler, "'Sometimes They're Angry With Us and That's OK': Boeing and 737 MAX Families Form Painful Partnership," *Wall Street Journal*, March 5, 2020, https://www.wsj.com/articles/a-year-after-the-ethiopian-737-max-crash-boeing-and-families-forge-a-painful-symbiosis-11583420085?shareToken=stfeaa087481fe40a1a516478f5b0e050d&ns=prod/accounts-wsj.

10. James R. Stengel, Andrea L. Dixon, and Chris T. Allen, "Best Practice: Listening Begins at Home," *Harvard Business Review*, November 2003, 106–16.

11. Kelly E. See et al., "The Detrimental Effects of Power on Confidence, Advice Taking, and Accuracy," *Organizational Behavior and Human Decision Processes Journal* 116, no. 2 (2011): 272–85.

12. Philip V. Lewis, *Organizational Communication: The Essence of Effective Management*, 3rd ed. (New York: Wiley & Sons, 1987), 146.

13. Joe Takash, "Motivation Needed Now More Than Ever: Four Steps That Work," *American Salesman* 60, no. 6 (June 2015): 3–7.

14. Cheryl Hamilton and Tony L. Kroll, *Communicating for Results: A Guide for Business and the Professions*, 11th ed. (Boston: Cengage Learning, 2018), 116–17.

15. A. N. Kluger and K. Zaidel, "Are Listeners Perceived as Leaders?" *The International Journal of Listening* 27 (2013): 73–84.

16. Danielle Lee, "Are You Listening?" *Accounting Today* 26, no. 8 (August 2012): 1, 50.

17. Michael Barbaro and Steven Greenhouse, "Wal-Mart Says Thank You to Workers," *New York Times*, December 4, 2006, http://www.nytimes.com/2006/12/04/business/04walmart.html?_r=0.

18. NCLEX Quiz, "Ten Skills for Active Listening," www.NCLEXQuiz.com/blog/10-Skills-for-Active-Listening.

19. Adam M. Grant, *Give and Take: A Revolutionary Approach to Success* (New York: Viking Press, 2013), 265.

20. Graham L. Bradley and Amanda C. Campbell, "Managing Difficult Workplace Conversations: Goals, Strategies, and Outcomes," *International Journal of Business Communication* 53, no. 4 (2016): 443–64, doi: 10.1177/2329488414525468.

21. William B. Gudykunst, *Bridging Differences: Effective Intergroup Communication*, 4th ed. (Thousand Oaks, CA: Sage, 2003), 173–74.

22. Ieva Zaumane, "The Internal Communication Crisis and Its Impact on an Organization's Performance," *Journal of Business Management*, no. 12 (2016): 24–33.

23. Geraldine E. Hynes, *Project Communication From Start to Finish: The Dynamics of Organizational Success* (New York: Business Expert Press, 2019), 86–87.

24. Tanvier Peart, "The Fourth Quarter Curse? How to Tell If a Layoff Is Coming," *Madame Noire*, November 24, 2013, http://madamenoire.com/325388/4th-quarter-curse-tell-layoff-coming.

25. "The Top 5 Business Communication Platforms," *DueDigital.com*, September 11, 2019, https://duedigital.com/insight/the-top-5-business-communication-platforms-1116390.

26. Peter W. Cardon, Yumi Huang, and Gerard Power, "Leadership Communication on Internal Digital Platforms, Emotional Capital, and Corporate Performance: The Case for Leader-Centric Listening," *International Journal of Business Communication* (February 2019), doi: 10.1177/2329488419828808.

27. Stephen R. Covey, *The Seven Habits of Highly Effective People* (New York: Simon & Schuster, 1989), 240–41.

28. Jason Buch, "His Repair Job: Texas Executive Ed Whitacre Steered GM at a Critical Time," *Houston Chronicle*, August 22, 2010, D1.

29. T. Peters, *Thriving on Chaos* (New York: Alfred A. Knopf, 1988).

COMMUNICATING NONVERBALLY

THE IMPORTANCE OF NONVERBAL COMMUNICATION

Understanding the importance of nonverbal communication is often difficult because it is a natural part of any interaction. Yet nonverbal factors bear studying independently. Without nonverbal communication as a source of information, most of the richness and much of the meaning in messages would be lost. In many cases, conversations would be muddled, and the time required for clarification would multiply enormously.

Nonverbal communication accompanies oral and, by logical extension, written messages, while consisting of the signals delivered through means other than verbal. In short, it includes *everything but the words*. Managers send, receive, and interpret nonverbal messages in the same way they send, receive, and interpret verbal ones. Let's say you are walking down the hall as a direct report approaches. You intend to send a message (recognition) and choose some nonverbal elements (a hand wave, eye contact, a smile, continued walking) to accompany a verbal message ("Good to see you. How's it going?"). Nonverbal communication may bear a clear meaning in itself (recognition), but often it serves as an adjunct to the spoken words, adding nuance in one place (power disparity) and clarity in another (too busy to stop and talk). At other times, nonverbal messages may even contradict the words being spoken.

Nonverbal communication is an important part of our daily managerial interactions.[1] Effective nonverbal communication improves the likelihood that others will comply with our requests.[2] While the extent of the nonverbal aspect varies from interaction to interaction, one set of oft-cited statistics shows that 55 percent of a message comes from the speaker's appearance, facial expression, and posture, while vocal aspects deliver 38 percent, and the actual words deliver only 7 percent.[3] This chapter provides an overview of nonverbal signals relevant to the managerial function. But first, three generalizations about nonverbal signals are stressed here.

CRITICAL THINKING QUESTIONS

1. If a nonverbal message contradicts the verbal, such as when a speaker's voice shakes and their facial expression is anxious, but they say, "I'm delighted to be here!" which do you believe?

2. To what extent has your choice in Question 1 proven to be accurate?

First, nonverbal signals rarely have one set meaning. (An exception is emblems, which are discussed later in this chapter.) For example, it is commonly assumed that our facial expression reveals our emotional state—smiling when happy, frowning when sad, and so on. Yet how people communicate anger, disgust, fear, happiness, sadness, and surprise varies substantially across situations, and even across people within a single situation. Furthermore, recent studies indicate that similar facial movements can express instances of more than one emotion category.[4]

Second, nonverbal signals vary from culture to culture and region to region in their meaning. Nonverbal signals derive from experiences within the communication environment (cultural, regional, or social) and are generally dispersed throughout it. It is not enough merely to translate the verbal language; the nonverbal must be expressed as well. The Japanese, for example, usually present a noncontroversial demeanor and are excessively polite by North American standards, which may cause confusion about meanings and intentions during meetings or negotiations.[5] Managers in cross-cultural situations should be sensitive to potential differences in interpretation of basic nonverbal signals—for example, bowing in South Korea—to minimize misunderstanding and communicate respect.[6]

Third, when nonverbal signals contradict verbal ones, the nonverbals are usually the ones we trust. When verbal and nonverbal disagree, credibility can suffer.[7] Law enforcement agents, trial attorneys, and insurance investigators are professionals who extensively study nonverbal behavior in order to improve their interrogation skills. They know that nonverbal signals can provide valuable clues to the truth of a message.

More specifically, the law enforcement community provides a contemporary example of nonverbal behavior's importance. When attempting to identify terrorists and criminals in public places, such as airports and subways, officials are trained to "read" suspects' body language. The technique is called behavior detection and is rooted in the notion that people convey emotions, such as fear, in subconscious gestures, facial expressions, and speech patterns.[8] Since the September 11, 2001, attack on the United States, behavior detection has been adopted by police, the Transportation Security Administration, and other authorities at most airports, universities, and mass transit systems.

THE FUNCTIONS OF NONVERBAL CUES

Nonverbal communication is a broader concept than just gestures and eye contact. A simple definition already offered is that in managerial interactions, nonverbal communication is everything but the words, but it is critical to appreciate the scope of that definition. Nonlinguistic signs are like any kind of sign in communication in that they are something tangible, capable of bearing meaning, just as linguistic signs are. They differ only in that they are nonverbal.

Burbinster identified six functions of nonverbal communication (see Table 11-1).[9]

Nonverbal signals that *complement* the verbal message repeat it. Typically, these signals occur simultaneously with the verbal message to reinforce or explain what is being said. For example, a technician explaining the varying gap widths in faulty components in a heating system might hold up her thumb and index finger and vary the gap between them as she discusses the problem.

Nonverbal signals that *accent* call our attention to a matter under discussion. A common example is a person pounding on a desk as she makes an important point. People may also use vocalics, the nonverbal aspects of the voice itself, to highlight a point. Someone differentiating between one choice and another might say "I want *this* one, not *that*."

The nonverbal signals that *contradict* are less obvious. These are usually sent unintentionally by the subconscious to say nonverbally the opposite of what is being said verbally. This complex interpretation of contradicting nonverbal signals will be discussed later in the chapter under the heading "Nonverbal Signs of Deception."

TABLE 11-1   ■   Functions of Nonverbal Behavior
Complement
Accent
Contradict
Repeat
Regulate
Substitute

Repeating occurs when we have already sent a message using one form of communication and wish to emphasize the point being made. It differs from complementing in that it is not done simultaneously with the verbal comment. For example, a demonstration following a verbal description of a tool's use is a nonverbal repetition.

Regulating, the fifth purpose Burbinster suggests, is a subtle and important one. Regulating occurs during conversations to signal to our partner to "slow," "stop," and even "wait your turn" and let the other person know when we are ready to listen or to speak. If you watch an ongoing conversation, you will quickly spot a variety of these cues. A speaker who is not finished but is being interrupted might speak louder or faster to keep their turn (thus using vocalics). Another might hold up their hand to say "not yet, let me finish." When a speaker looks directly at a listener, on the other hand, the listener's turn is imminent.

Substituting is a less common nonverbal signal than the others during face-to-face communication. When the environment prevents us from sending a message by speaking in words, we might choose to use nonverbal behaviors to get the point across. For example, a supervisor in a loud factory might use the thumbs-up sign to signal an employee instead of shouting.

In the case of written and electronic communication, we are seeing an explosive increase in the use of emoji and GIFs as nonverbal signs. Sometimes referred to as textual paralanguage, emoji are ubiquitous in electronic messages and have been called the body language of the digital age. Every day, 41.5 billion text messages are sent by one quarter of the world, using 6 million emoji.[10] Because body language and verbal tone do not translate in our text messages or e-mails, writers use emoji and reaction GIFs to convey nuanced meaning and emotion.

CRITICAL THINKING QUESTIONS

Which of Burbinster's functions is exemplified by the following gestures?

1. A woman dropping her voice to a hush as she conveys information

2. A candidate jiggling his leg during a job interview

3. A grandmother putting her finger to her lips as her 4-year-old grandson screams for candy

Emoji were developed in 1990 by Shigetaka Kurita, a Japanese telecom employee of NTT Docomo, the world's first major mobile Internet system.[11] Kurita's team created 176 icons to be used on mobile phones and pagers. The Unicode Consortium's Unicode Standard, Version 13.0 lists more than 3,000 emoji available in almost all social messaging apps, and while different apps have distinct emoji styles, emoji can translate across platforms. On Facebook Messenger, for instance, an average of 5 billion emoji are used daily.[12] Businesses have also adopted this hieroglyphic language, particularly for marketing. A study of thousands of social media posts from 22 corporate brands found that 20.6 percent of brand tweets, 19.1 percent of Facebook posts, and 31.3 percent of Instagram posts contained emoji as substitutes for words.[13]

Even color and how it is presented in the context of a message can serve as a nonlinguistic sign. Some studies have looked at the impact colors have on cognitive performance. Researchers at the University of British Columbia conducted tests with 600 people to determine the effects of the colors blue and red. Red groups did better on tests of recall and attention to detail. Participants in the blue groups tested better with skills requiring imagination and creativity.[14] So if your team is tasked with brainstorming for a new product or service, you may want to have them meet in a room with blue walls.

Depending on the culture, color is a nonlinguistic sign of certain emotions. For instance, Western brides generally wear white, but Eastern brides wear red. In China, white is a sign of bereavement and loss, just as black is in the United States.

A study of emotional responses to cell phone ads demonstrates how color creates different emotions in different cultures. Thirty-two people from six cultures (Finland, Sweden, Taiwan, India, China, and the United States) were asked to interpret a Nokia ad's external characteristics. The predominant blue and white colors, recognized by the Finnish respondents as their country's flag colors, provoked a positive impression. Further, the Finns found the colors "reliable," "natural," "trustworthy," and "comfortable." By contrast, the Chinese and Taiwanese respondents said that white is a funeral color for them, creating a negative impression. The Swedes recognized that blue and white are "Finnish colors" and rejected them as "boring" and "cold." The respondents from India thought the colors were warm and summery. The respondents from the United States were inconsistent about whether the blue and white colors were warm or cold, summery or wintery. Interestingly, several U.S. respondents connected the blue and white colors to "unlimited freedom" and "innovation," which no informants from other cultures mentioned.[15] These results show that nonverbal communication can result in frustratingly inexact interpretation. If placed in the proper perspective, however, it can be a valuable source of cues in communication situations.

From a theoretical perspective, Burbinster's six functions of nonverbal behavior (Table 11-1) all contribute to another important function: *communication redundancy*. This concept refers to the phenomena built into any language system that combat the effects of noise, whether in oral or written channels. It simply means that much of the meaning of a message can be deduced from other elements in the message that have already appeared. Think of the television game show *Wheel of Fortune*. The longest-running syndicated game show in the United States, the program has also gained a worldwide following with 60 international adaptations. Contestants try to predict the letters in a blank word puzzle; the game is an example of redundancy in that contestants can often guess the correct phrase before every word or letter is revealed on the game board.

More generally, communication redundancy is vitally important because it helps ensure that our message gets past the various barriers that environmental, organizational, or interpersonal elements erect. When a message is made more redundant—that is, when the information in it has been made more predictable to the receiver—the message has a greater chance of transferring the meaning the sender intends it to convey.

Every communication system is redundant. Verbal languages build in redundancy through a variety of means, including grammar and syntax. Most of the functions addressed by nonverbal communication described previously serve in some way as redundancy. Thus, as we discuss an issue with someone, we will use nonverbal signals to complement, accent, repeat, and substitute to get a point across. Even when a nonverbal signal contradicts the verbal, additional nonverbal signals are likely to follow to underscore the contradiction. Thus, a shake of the head denying a request is followed by a smile to indicate goodwill.

CRITICAL THINKING QUESTIONS

Consider a time when you had to handle a customer's or direct report's complaint.

1. In addition to the words, what nonverbal behaviors did the customer or direct report use?

2. Which of Burbinster's six functions were exemplified?

3. To what extent were these nonverbals redundant?

4. Why do you think the customer or direct report felt the need to use them?

Some nonverbal behaviors are *innate*, others are *learned* from the community around us, and some are *mixed*. For instance, eye-blinking patterns and blushing appear to be innate—universal, involuntary behaviors that occur in certain communication situations. Other cues such as the eyewink and the two-fingered "V" gesture are learned, and they signal different meanings in different cultures. The thumbs-up "Like" button on Facebook is an example: A raised thumb can mean "Number 1" in Germany, a noncommittal "this is nice" in the Netherlands, and an unprintable insult in Iran. A third group of nonverbal behaviors is a mix of innate and learned in that they occur in every culture, but they can be controlled, and their meanings can change. In some Asian cultures, for example, a small laugh may occur naturally, but a forced smile may convey discomfort and submission rather than affiliation and pleasure.

This chapter now explores several key types of nonverbal communication—movement, space, personal appearance, and voice—and explains how managers can use them to their advantage. It then examines how nonverbal indications of deception can be detected through careful observation.

MOVEMENT

Say "nonverbal communication" to most people, and they probably think of movement, which is technically kinesics. Nonverbal communication consists of far more than just one general category, but movement is the most studied of the categories. It includes gestures, posture, and stance, as well as bodily movement.

As summarized in Table 11-2, gestures may include *emblems*, *illustrators*, *regulators*, *affect displays*, and *adapters*.[16] While people usually use gestures without thinking, a conscious awareness of them can help a manager communicate more efficiently. An understanding of and training in effective signals can open up the possibility of our strategic, conscious use of them. The Walt Disney Company, a leader in customer service, understands the power of nonverbals. The Disney Institute, the company's consulting division, teaches employees at all its theme parks to give directions by pointing with two fingers rather than one because it seems more polite. Similarly, if a teacher calls on a student by extending an open palm rather than pointing a finger at the student, it seems more respectful and welcoming.

TABLE 11-2 ■ Types of Gestures
Emblems
Illustrators
Regulators
Affect displays
Adapters

Earlier, we noted that nonverbal signals usually suggest meaning; they do not give direct meaning. *Emblems* are an exception in that they actually stand for something else. The OK sign is one example; another is the time-out—one palm held at a right angle to the other.

Illustrators complement verbal communication by providing an example of or reinforcing what is being said. When a person is trying to explain an item that is not present, what is more natural than drawing it in the air?

Regulators are gestures that both subtly and obviously control what a speaker says. They arise from a variety of sources, including the hands—for example, when one holds up the hand palm outward to keep another from interrupting. Turning the palm toward you and wiggling the fingers is a beckoning gesture in the United States.

The *affect display* is more complex than most gestures and involves several parts of the body. For example, suppose you are talking to someone who has a scowl on their face as they sit up straight but turned slightly away from you. Their arms cross their chest, and you have little doubt this person does not like the idea under discussion. The affect display signals feelings and can show pleasure as well as anger, boredom as well as interest. Reading such nonverbal signals from others is rarely a problem. The challenge lies in controlling these within ourselves in situations when we do not want to show what we are feeling.

The *adapter* may be the least appreciated source of kinesic messages; however, it can be quite important. In many situations, when one behavior might be inappropriate, the body will adapt by sending signals that would provide a solution, if one could only implement it. For example, if you wish to leave but are unable to do so, you might start to move your crossed leg in imitation of walking. If you are conducting a disciplinary interview, you may begin to twist the paper clip you are holding as a socially acceptable substitute for what you would like to do with the person you are reprimanding. That employee being reprimanded may wrap their arms around themselves as a sort of substitute hug to provide the comfort they need at that moment.

While gestures may be the most obvious example of meaningful movement, other kinesic behaviors contribute significantly to message meaning as well. Take posture, for example. In the United States, slumping, leaning, standing with weight on one leg, and rounding the shoulders all connote weakness and lack of confidence. By contrast, standing at military attention (head up, shoulders back, chest forward, and weight evenly distributed on both feet) connotes power, alertness, and confidence. Managers who have mastered the elements of strong posture often are attended to even before they begin to speak.

Another example of kinesic communication is head movement. A listener often indicates attention by nodding and/or tilting their head. On the other hand, a speaker who nods or tilts while talking may be interpreted as unsure or even submissive.

Mimicry is a form of gesturing where two people mirror each other's movements. It is typically an unconscious and automatic behavior triggered by an abundance of mirroring neurons in the brain. Mimicry has been shown to positively influence the flow of conversation as well as mutual liking. The back-and-forth exchange of smiles, head nods, arm crossing, and hand movements creates this social circuit that leaves two people feeling better and better about the other person. Studies have proven this to be true in negotiations and job interviews, where ample mimicking correlated to strong feelings of trust and likeability.[17]

We also communicate meaning by the way we walk. Striding quickly to the platform makes a speaker seem energetic, bold, and in command of the situation. Credibility is enhanced by this nonverbal element. However, if a speaker walks around aimlessly or perhaps sways, rocks, or shifts their weight from foot to foot repeatedly, the impression is diminished.

To summarize, movement is a very important category of nonverbal communication. We pay attention to various parts of a communicator's body—head, trunk, arms, legs—as we watch and listen, drawing inferences from their movements. A list of common interpretations of kinesic cues appears in Table 11-3. But take note: As you will read in Chapter 12, our culture defines both verbal and nonverbal behavior, so keep in mind that the "meanings" of the kinesic cues in the table may change from culture to culture. For example, head nodding is a sign of affirmation in the United States, but it's a sign of disagreement in Greece, the South Slavic States, and Iran.[18] Managers in any culture must attend to kinesics when they communicate so that their body language contributes to rather than contradicts or detracts from the intended meaning.

TABLE 11-3 ■ Kinesic Cues		
Body Segment	**Movement**	**Interpretation**
Head	Gazing	Attentive; honest
	Shifting, darting eyes	Uncertain; lying
	Eyebrows up	Challenging; open
	Smiling mouth	Enjoyment; pleasure
	Nodding	Listening; agreeing
	Tilting head	Interested
	Head down	Defensive
Trunk and shoulders	Leaning toward	Interested; rapport
	Leaning away	Lack of interest; skeptical
	Posture slouched	Low self-esteem
	Expanded chest	Confident
	Shrunken chest	Threatened

Body Segment	Movement	Interpretation
Hands and arms	Buttoning jacket	Formal; leaving
	Touching others	Powerful
	Touching self	Nervous; anxious
	Repetitive movements	Lying; unsure of self
	Hand over mouth while speaking	Want to escape
	Arms crossed	Bored; closed to ideas
	Fingers steepled	Confident
	Hands on hips	Challenging; arrogant
	Hands in pockets	Secretive
	Palms showing	Trusting
	Pointing	Authoritative; aggressive
	Clenched hands; wringing hands; picking cuticle	Need reassurance

CRITICAL THINKING QUESTIONS

1. The next time you are dining with friends or family, deliberately take a sip of water, wipe your lips with your napkin, or lean away from the table. What happens next?

2. If, as predicted, everyone else at the table quickly mimics your nonverbal behavior, how can you apply that phenomenon to make your communication more effective?

SPATIAL MESSAGES

Proxemics refers to the space around us and how we and others relate to it. Space and distance can reveal much and merit careful attention. Most people hearing "proxemics" think only of personal space, the personal "bubble" surrounding a person. That is a good place to start, but the concept encompasses far more.

Spatial Zones

Our language suggests we all are aware of personal space to some degree. We talk about someone "keeping their distance," "invading our space" or "crowding us on this issue," when in fact what they are doing has little to do with geographic territory.

Edward Hall studied use of personal distances and determined that people in the United States have four arbitrarily established proxemic zones in which we interact, which are shown in Figure 11-1.[19] Strategic managers are aware of these zones and appreciate how they and others react when their spaces are invaded.

In the United States, businesspeople generally operate within four zones: intimate, personal, social, and public. In the discussion that follows, keep in mind that the figures are averages. They reflect the general culture, situational mandates, and the relationship between the parties. A number of factors enter into any interpersonal exchange. These can include personal appearance, culture, gender, and age. Thus, we may react differently to a tall person compared to a short person, and we may draw nearer to an attractive person than to another who is less attractive.[20] As discussed in the next chapter, meanings for nonverbal behaviors differ from culture to culture.

In the United States, the *intimate zone* ranges from physical contact to roughly 1.5 to 2 feet. It is reserved for those who are psychologically close. When others invade it, especially for more than a moment, a person usually feels uncomfortable and is likely to draw back or put up some sort of barrier, although often without consciously knowing why.

The *personal zone* extends from the edge of the intimate zone out to roughly 4 feet. People in the United States reserve it for close friends but permit others to enter it temporarily during introductions. Watch as two strangers come together for an introduction. As they shake hands, they will often stand with one leg forward and the other ready to

---

FIGURE 11-1   ■   Spatial Zones

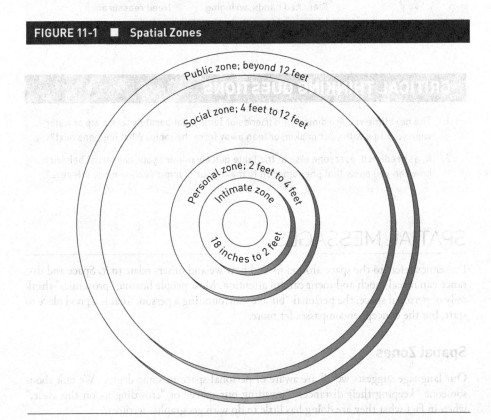

back up. Then, when the greeting is over, both will usually retreat into the next zone. Cooperating on a task or simultaneously studying a document may bring people into their personal space, but they typically compensate by not making eye contact.

The next area is the *social zone*. It extends from about 4 feet to 12 feet and is the space in which we would like to conduct much of our daily business. Relationships between managers and their employees might begin in this area and continue for a time. They will often move into the personal zone once trust has developed, but this takes time.

In the U.S. culture, the *public zone* extends beyond 12 feet and reflects the distance at which most would like to keep strangers. Little communication of a business nature takes place in this zone. Perhaps the only spoken communication that occurs is the public speech. We see the formal institutionalized reflection of this distance in the arrangement of public auditoriums or political rallies. Even if the latter is not too crowded, the audience will often keep its distance.

For managers, the value of understanding spatial zones is clear. An observant communicator can gauge the relative warmth that exists in a relationship by the distances individuals keep during interactions. As trust grows, distances generally diminish. Thus, allies sit next to each other in meetings. However, other factors determine spatial differences as well. Let us consider some of these.

Spatial Differences

As we have said, proxemic zones vary from culture to culture. For example, businesspeople in many South American and Arab countries typically interact with people at far closer ranges than do U.S. businesspeople.[21] Often, when people from the United States interact with individuals from these cultures, the varying proxemic zones expected by the groups create awkwardness until someone adapts to the needs of the others and either gives up some ground or extends the distance.

Naturally, circumstances may artificially affect our use of zones. The classic example of this is the crowded elevator, where people allow others to invade personal and intimate zones. Here, though, people will try to adapt by avoiding eye contact or blocking—by folding the arms across the chest or putting up their briefcases as a sort of shield. If someone accidentally touches another, apologies quickly follow.

CRITICAL THINKING QUESTIONS

The next time you are in a meeting, look around the table at the amount of space each person takes up, not just with their bodies but also with their belongings and artifacts.

1. Who spreads out and dominates the space?

2. Who does the opposite?

3. Do you see any consistencies across gender? Age? Power?

When traditional zones need to be ignored for an extended period, people will stake out their territory. One way is to create even spacing between participants, as when seated around a meeting table with movable seats. In other situations, people will erect some sort of barrier—piles of notebooks, jackets, coffee cups—on either side. Similarly, students in a class typically occupy the same seat throughout the term, claiming it as "their" space and setting their belongings all around them.

Permanent or "fixed" spaces, such as cubicles or large desks, are also perceived as barriers. It is considered rude to come behind another's desk or peek over the top of the cubicle. But semifixed spaces, such as conference tables, can connote cooperation and shared responsibility (see Figure 11-2), as the next section explains.

Strategic Use of Space

Recognizing the boundaries of both fixed and semifixed spaces communicates respect to the individual. Additionally, artifacts belonging to another individual should be regarded as personal. Rifling through a coworker's desk drawers, grabbing a file, or sitting on the edge of that person's desk can be interpreted as an invasion of spatial barriers.

Managers can use space to create an air of power and authority or an air of collegiality and respect. In some organizations, the amount of space allotted to another, the amount of privacy that space entails, and where in the building that space is located can speak volumes about organizational power. In addition, the closer people are to the organization's leaders, the more power they are perceived by others to enjoy.

On the other hand, managers who work in organizations that value open communication will try to work in proximity to their direct reports and coworkers, will minimize status-filled artifacts, and will discourage territoriality. Indeed, many contemporary organizations, in an effort to increase employees' proximity, visibility, and collaboration, have replaced private offices with open floor plans. Recently, Harvard researchers conducted field studies at two Fortune 500 multinational corporations and verified that workplace interaction is affected by office architecture, but in surprising ways. The researchers found that employees in open spaces actually reduced their face-to-face interaction, while increasing their use of text, e-mail, and IM.[22] The researchers suggest that a reason for this migration to digital communication in transparent workspaces may be related to a psychological need for privacy and quiet. Thus, the effects of workspace design on productivity, communication, comfort, and job satisfaction remain complex.[23]

FIGURE 11-2 ■ Fixed and Semifixed Space in the Same Office

Semifixed space
Conference table

Fixed space
Executive's desk

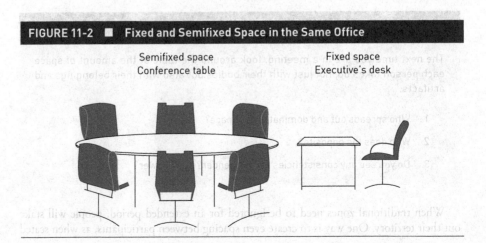

PERSONAL APPEARANCE

The old saying "beauty is only skin deep" may not be true in the business world. Recent studies have identified a connection between wages and appearance. Daniel Hamermesh, a University of Texas economist who has studied the beauty benefit for 20 years, determined that above-average-looking men earn 17 percent more than below-average-looking men, and above-average-looking women earn 12 percent more than below-average-looking women. Hamermesh translates those statistics into $230,000 more in earnings over a lifetime, on average.[24]

Further, there appears to be significant agreement about what is considered attractive. For one thing, height is a factor. In the United States, the average adult man is 5 feet 9 inches tall, yet men CEOs are on average 3 inches taller. Another aspect of appearance that equates with success is a strong chin. Among 42 CEOs from the top 50 *Fortune 500* companies, some 90 percent showed nonreceding-to-prominent chins, versus 40 percent of the U.S. population. Apparently, we equate such jawlines with business success and confidence.[25] Aspects of our appearance such as height, chin prominence, and physical beauty are not easily changed.

One might argue that appearance should not be a relevant factor for business success, anyway. Nevertheless, most businesspeople try to maximize the positive impact of their appearance, and one relatively simple way to reach that goal is with our choice of clothing. What we wear says much about who we are—or at least who we want to be perceived as. Consequently, managers should pay close attention to what they wear in order to send the right message to others. The next paragraphs focus on general principles for effective dress.

The key to dress is to fit in with the organization's culture, to show by your appearance that you have adopted the organization's values. Thus, most financial institutions expect employees to look conservative, assuring customers and clients of their stability. Ad agency employees are often expected to dress more fashion forward, indicating their flair, creativity, and contemporary style. High-tech organizations typically de-emphasize a formal, "corporate" appearance, to the extent that executives are dressed as casually as the lowest-level employee. Mark Zuckerberg, founder and CEO of Facebook, Inc., is one of the world's wealthiest and most influential business leaders and philanthropists. His typical style of dressing in a T-shirt, hooded sweatshirt, and jeans has become the norm for people in his industry.

Because workers' appearances also convey important messages about an organization and its culture, many companies have developed a detailed dress code or employee uniform. Legal issues can arise from dress policies, unless employers are careful to enforce dress codes on all employees, not just one group, to avoid accusations of discrimination. At Honda, one of the most successful multinational companies in the world, employees from executives to janitors wear white uniforms with the employee's first name above the right pocket, written in red. Above the left pocket is the word Honda, also in red. If the employee chooses to wear a hat, it is a green and white Honda baseball cap. Strict adherence to this uniform indicates parity and teamwork, two values of the corporation.[26]

Observers always assign meaning to details such as accessories, color, jewelry, and emblems worn on the jacket lapel or hat. IBM provides a prominent example of the symbolic nature of clothing. In *Who Says Elephants Can't Dance?* former CEO Lou Gerstner described how he revitalized the failing corporation.[27] One of his major efforts was culture change, and one of his methods was prescribing changes in employee dress. The famous "old" IBM look had been crisp white shirts, dark suits, and conservative ties. Originally, it had been adopted to match customer expectations. But when Gerstner took over, it seemed anachronistic, stuffy, and emblematic of the company's demise. The "new" IBM look was more casual and contemporary. In 2019, employees reported that business casual was the norm but without jeans or shorts.[28] Gerstner summarized workplace dress principles this way: "Dress according to the circumstances of your day and recognize who you will be with (customers, government leaders, or just your colleagues)."[29]

CRITICAL THINKING QUESTIONS

1. Look around your workplace. Is the old advice "dress for the job you want, not the job you have" still true?

2. To what extent is appearance a relevant factor in hiring and promotion decisions in your organization? What is the rationale for this criterion?

In summary, no matter whether the organization's culture is formal or casual, and no matter whether the occasion is special or ordinary, managers' appearance should reflect the expectations and values of their audience. By adhering to the principle of "fitting in," managers will enhance their credibility and improve their communication effectiveness.

VOICE

The final source of nonverbal signals this chapter will focus on is paralanguage, or vocal style. Nonverbal aspects of vocal delivery include the onset, pitch, rate, volume, tone, and duration of messages. Articulation and pacing are characteristics of voice that are regional in origin, such as the southern U.S. drawl and the northeastern U.S. clipped dialect. Vocal cues are among the least obvious to most listeners, with the likely exception of tone, yet they can be as important as or even more important than the words.[30]

Onset is the time that it takes between the beginning of a person's turn to speak and the beginning of their message. If we are asking someone about a serious issue and their responses come more quickly than expected, we might suspect they are not serious or have rehearsed the responses. Similarly, when someone takes far longer to answer a question than expected, we begin to wonder if all that is being said is true. And as the discussion in the upcoming section on nonverbal signs of deception shows, we even monitor pitch and can read meaning into changes of it.

Pitch is the relative highness or lowness of one's voice. Spoken English sentences follow certain pitch patterns, depending on their meaning. Declaratory sentences (statements) end with a dropped pitch, and interrogatory sentences (questions that ask for a response) end with a raised pitch. A common violation of these pitch patterns, known as "uptalk," occurs when speakers end their statements with a raised pitch, making them sound like questions. The listener, noticing the uptalk, often concludes that the speaker is unsure of the truth of their statements and is asking for validation. In a business meeting, when someone says, "Here's what I think the customer wants," with a raised pitch at the end, others may well conclude that the speaker in fact does not know what the customer wants.[31]

Speakers have a typical vocal style that distinguishes their voice from that of other speakers. They can vary their pitch, rate, and volume to emphasize their meaning and to communicate emotion. Failure to vary these vocal characteristics results in what is commonly known as a monotone vocal style. In the U.S. business culture, a monotone speaking style connotes lack of interest and even lack of authority. Managers may unintentionally undermine their message by the vocal style in which it is delivered. Chapter 5 described good vocal style in more detail, but these criteria apply to everyday speaking as well as to formal presentations.

The importance of vocal cues to managers is obvious in sending as well as receiving. It is important to monitor the signals being sent, particularly for tone, to ensure that the intended communication strategy is not being undermined by subtle nonverbal cues.

To summarize, in U.S. business, speaking in a clear, firm, low-pitched voice connotes confidence and results in more attentive listening. Nasal, shrill, quiet, breathy, or harsh voices are devalued. Excessive use of filled pauses ("uh," "well") gives an impression of uncertainty. Managers are wise to use their vocal qualities to maximize the message rather than detract from it, just as they are encouraged to use the preceding nonverbal categories.

APPLICATIONS OF NONVERBAL COMMUNICATION RESEARCH

Until recently, the impact of managers' nonverbal behavior was impossible to objectively measure. However, researchers at the Human Dynamics Group of the Massachusetts Institute of Technology (MIT) Media Lab have developed a range of small, wearable electronic devices that can easily and accurately gather data on tone of voice, proximity, and body language.[32] Their data about these nonverbal communication patterns can be applied to improving communication effectiveness in business settings.

Phone Sales and Service

In one case, the MIT researchers worked with a British call center outsourcing company, Vertex Data Science, to improve the effectiveness of call center operators. The MIT group used electronic sensors (or e-sensors) to measure the speech patterns of operators during calls with customers. The group did not measure the actual words used by the operators but focused on variations in tone and pitch, as well as the amount of time that the operators spent talking versus listening to the callers. The researchers concluded that successful operators spend more time listening than talking and use strong fluctuations in their voice amplitude and pitch to suggest interest and responsiveness to the customers' needs. After only a few seconds of measuring these factors, the researchers were able to accurately predict the eventual success or failure of a call the majority of the time.[33]

Teams and Meetings

The results of the MIT studies have implications for team communication. As discussed in Chapter 4, *groupthink* is a common problem in teams. Individuals often conform to the perceived group consensus despite their personal reservations. E-sensors measuring nonverbal communication behaviors could potentially help prevent groupthink by raising awareness of nonverbal communication patterns of individual team members. For example, one or two individuals in the team might be overbearing while not realizing that their nonverbal behaviors discourage others from voicing their opinions. The MIT group believes that they could eventually use e-sensors to select team members with complementary nonverbal communication styles so that the team would be "optimized" for communication effectiveness. Further, they believe they can create "smart environments" by using e-sensors to identify negative nonverbal behaviors in real time, thereby allowing them to prevent communication breakdowns.

The MIT research results can also be applied to formal meetings. Managers may inadvertently sabotage meetings by using inappropriate nonverbal communication or sending incongruent verbal and nonverbal messages. E-sensors can determine whether a manager is using enough vocal variation or body movement to convey the importance of a message. E-sensors also can show the manager what behaviors are confusing the meeting participants, eventually leading to more effective and efficient meeting management.

Body language can affect the outcome of negotiations during meetings. In a separate study, the MIT group simulated face-to-face salary negotiations and was able to accurately predict the "winner" of the negotiation with 87 percent accuracy after only 5 minutes of measuring body movement patterns.

Informal Communication

Informal coworker conversations are a common method of spreading messages throughout a company, and nonverbal communication is a part of how these messages are interpreted. E-sensors developed by the MIT researchers have been used to monitor nonverbal communication in informal settings; the data on proximity, body language, and vocal style allow more accurate sharing of information, with more people being on the same page.

In fact, in 2020, during the COVID-19 pandemic, Ford Motor Company experimented with wearable technology to monitor employee proximity. Employees wore smartwatches that vibrated when employees stood too closely together, discreetly reminding them to practice social distancing.[34]

These MIT studies affirm beliefs held in the Korean culture about the importance of attending to nonverbal cues. Koreans value social sensitivity to such an extent that they captured the concept in the term *nunchi*, which translates as "eye-measure." The concept signifies the ability to quickly observe others' moods and identify a group atmosphere by tuning into nonverbal cues. Further, *nunchi* helps one understand their status relative to the others in the room. Koreans apply *nunchi* in business settings to gauge how people are thinking and feeling in order to create connection, trust, and harmony.[35] Creating a harmonious environment is a key managerial strategy for improving interpersonal relationships, for influencing others, and even during negotiations, as discussed in Chapter 14.

CRITICAL THINKING QUESTIONS

1. What personality characteristics are most valued in your workplace?

2. What are some coworker behaviors that lead you to your response to Question 1?

3. To what extent do you attempt to emulate these behavioral norms? Why?

External Communication

Nonverbal communication has a powerful impact on business success. For example, research indicates that 60 to 70 percent of the interpersonal communication involved in effective sales is nonverbal.[36] Even a simple smile has been shown to affect customers' perceptions of a service provider's competence.[37]

Customer service is another area where data about nonverbal communication patterns can be used to benefit the company. Vertex Data Science's use of electronic monitoring of their call center operators (described previously) is one example. Sales teams and customer service personnel (e.g., hotel reservation clerks) could also receive valuable information from studies like the one conducted at Vertex. Again, the goal is to improve the level of service that customers receive, resulting in more business and an enhanced company reputation.

Nonverbal communication research can be applied to customer service in the tourism and hospitality industry. Following service failure, customers want their problems resolved as quickly as possible, and in doing so, they have certain expectations with respect to service providers' behavior. During this period of anxiety, customers are particularly vigilant about nonverbal cues in attempting to discern the service provider's intentions and attitudes. The display of inappropriate nonverbal behaviors, such as frowning, lack of eye contact, and closed body posture, is likely to create even more negative feelings.[38] The ability to objectively measure nonverbal communication with e-sensors and use that information to train customer service employees would greatly benefit the organization.

Another application of this type of research is with managers who operate in the global economy. As you will read in Chapter 12, acceptable nonverbal behavior varies from culture to culture and country to country. E-sensor data could be used to train business travelers in the most effective nonverbal communication patterns for the country and culture that they will be working in.

Finally, independent agencies (such as advertising firms) and/or individuals within a corporation who participate in business-to-business (B2B) relationships with other professionals could benefit from the use of e-sensors that measure nonverbal communication. These individuals regularly make formal presentations and give briefings to clients and other executives. E-sensor data would help them learn the most effective nonverbal communication patterns, such as conveying confidence, during presentations. Other applications include effectively using nonverbal communication to convey negative messages and strengthen client relationships.

CRITICAL THINKING QUESTIONS

1. What, if any, ethical issues surround the monitoring of employees' nonverbal behaviors?

2. Does asking employees to wear e-sensors violate their right to privacy?

3. Would you be willing to participate in similar studies/training programs at your organization?

4. To what extent is monitoring employees' nonverbal behaviors during workplace interactions similar to monitoring their computer usage?

NONVERBAL SIGNS OF DECEPTION

In many situations, managers must evaluate other employees to determine if the data they work with are accurate. While the data set out in a report can usually be tested objectively, information derived from interpersonal interactions, such as disciplinary and pre-employment screening interviews, frequently offers little opportunity for immediate objective verification. Often, managers assess the veracity of verbal statements by interpreting the accompanying nonverbal elements. As we have seen, nonverbal signals usually complement verbal ones and serve as needed reinforcement to reduce the uncertainty in communication. However, they may also unintentionally contradict the verbal ones they accompany.

General Motors' crisis over faulty ignition switches provides an interesting example of how nonverbal cues can signal deception at a macro level. In 2014, GM announced the recall of 3.2 million vehicles and paid $35 million in penalties after an 11-year history of accidents, injuries, and deaths related to a defect in ignition switches. An internal inquiry into the recall was conducted by Anton Valukas, a former U.S. attorney. His report notes that, notwithstanding a culture where safety was supposedly paramount, that message was routinely undermined in messages from top leadership at GM that focused instead on the need to control costs. Valukas's report includes CEO Mary Barra's description of the "GM nod" as "when everyone nods in agreement to a proposed plan of action, but then leaves the room with no intention to follow through, and the nod is an empty gesture."[39]

When contradictory nonverbal signals betray deception, they are called *leakage*. During deception, certain types of nonverbal signals often escape from the deceiver, despite attempts at control. The subconscious apparently betrays the speaker through this nonverbal leakage. People also often unconsciously read and interpret these signals. Managers can learn to spot nonverbal signs of deception.

Several patterns of nonverbal behavior crop up during deception. Because some sources of nonverbal signals can be controlled in deceptive situations better than others—for example, looking another in the eye while deceiving—we will focus on signals that are difficult to control consciously, such as movement, personal space, and voice.

Remember that nonverbal behavior usually *suggests* meaning rather than having a one-to-one correlation with a specific word or concept. The meaning of nonverbal signs might vary, particularly across cultures, and a gesture might be motivated by something besides what is suggested here.

To detect possible nonverbal signs of deception during interviews, it is important to be in the right place. The face, always likely to be visible, can be a poor source of deception cues (although hand-to-face contacts are valuable cues). When possible, seat the other person in an open chair facing you. Nonverbal signs from the hands, trunk, legs, or feet then will be more evident.[40]

Baseline

Deception signs are behaviors that differ from normal nonverbal interactions, so you also need to know what behavior is normal for the individual. Researchers have found that when observers see an individual giving honest answers before the person is seen lying, the observers' ability to detect dishonesty increases significantly over situations with no behavioral baseline. You detect dishonesty not by looking for the lie, according to psychologist Timothy Levine, but by identifying the change in behavior that suggests a person is nervous when they should not be.[41]

The individual's baseline is also invaluable because one person might behave differently from others in identical circumstances. A tragic example of the failure to establish a baseline when trying to detect truth or deception is the case of Amanda Knox, a U.S. student who was convicted in Italy of murdering her roommate and who spent 4 years in prison before her conviction was overturned. Despite the lack of physical evidence, investigators said they had been convinced of her guilt because she did not behave as they expected an innocent person should, according to Malcolm Gladwell in his book, *Talking to Strangers*. When interrogated, Knox gave "nervous, shifty, stammering, windy, convoluted explanations" and failed to make eye contact, all of which were interpreted as signs of guilt.[42] Gladwell concludes that we should "accept the limits of our ability to decipher strangers"[43] and be mindful of context when interpreting people's demeanor.

In the job interview, a baseline is relatively easy to establish. During the preliminary chat, the interviewer should ask nonthreatening questions. Begin with a review of the résumé before moving into the unknown, and watch the candidate for baseline nonverbal cues. An investigatory interrogation could use the same pattern. Small talk serves its traditional primary purpose of putting the other at ease and a secondary one of providing a behavioral baseline.

The following sections identify some typical signs of deception, as summarized in Table 11-4.

TABLE 11-4 ■ Nonverbal Signs of Deception
Unexpected movements and gestures
Changes in personal space
Artifacts
Vocal variations

Movement

Gestures and trunk movements, part of the broad category of kinesics, are probably the most valuable nonverbal signs of deception. Perhaps the most common deception-related gestures are hand-to-face movements, and the most common of these is the mouth cover. More subtle is the single finger to the mouth, the moustache stroke, or the nose rub. Other gestures suggesting deception are nail biting and lip biting. Hiding the hands by putting them in pockets or pulling sleeves down to the fingertips is a sign that the person is "hiding" something more than their hands.

Conversational gestures vary as well. Generally, when one is comfortable with honest responses, gestures are open and outward. During deception, people both limit their gestures and keep them closer to the body. And while smiling decreases and the frequency of gestures used to illustrate conversational points slows down in deception, the gestures suggesting deception increase. One of these is the hand shrug emblem. Researchers have found that deceptive speakers will *shrug their hands*—turning the palms up from palms down position—twice as frequently as in nondeceptive messages. This signal suggests a subconscious pleading for the listener to believe what is being said. Other telltale gestures involve clothing. An interviewee may suddenly close and button their jacket or begin to tug nervously at a pants leg or skirt hem. Other signals include straightening or tugging at the collar, smoothing the tie, picking at lint, and rubbing at a spot. Such subconscious gestures may betray a fear of having a deception revealed.

Some authorities also believe that an increase in leg and foot movements may indicate deception.[44] Foot tapping, leg rocking while the legs are crossed, and frequent shifts in leg posture are examples of this kind of activity. A rhythmic "walking" motion with one crossed leg has long been recognized as an intention gesture suggesting the person would like to walk away. But keep in mind the need to compare behavior with the baseline.

Signals of deception are not just confined to the body. They can also involve space and voice.

Personal Space

Proxemics, relating to the distance that one keeps from others as well as one's relation to the surrounding environment, may be a rich source of deception cues. An interviewee might shift the chair's position or might suddenly lean back on the chair's rear legs. Moving away from the interviewer may show a lack of cooperativeness or be a feeble attempt to put distance between the interviewee and interviewer by altering the environment. Often, when a person physically backs up, the other person comes closer. In formal conversations occurring while standing, an interviewee may lean back or step back during a deceptive response even while blocking by folding the arms across the chest.

An interviewee who has been relaxed may shift under pressure. For example, deception may leak out when the person suddenly crosses their arms and legs and leans back. The vulnerable forward posture is less comfortable when facing the fear of discovery. Conversely, an interviewee might "open up" during a response, suggesting openness and honesty. An interviewee may also try to erect "signal blunders" to hide behind. These may be such subtle activities as placing a handbag or briefcase in the lap as a barrier.

Artifacts

One's personal possessions in the office and the physical environment of the office itself offer cues, and they can be manipulated to create the intended perception. Some people will meticulously decorate their offices in an attempt to manage the impressions of their visitors. Although many of these decorations can reflect honest identity claims, some can be strategic and even deceptive.[45] How many times have you been lured back from the showroom to a salesperson's office to find an overabundance of religious symbols on display? How about cute kiddie photos? They seem to say, "You can trust me. I'm a man of faith, and a family man, and I would never give you a raw deal." Excessively showcasing awards, plaques, and framed certificates on a "brag wall" is another all-too-common attempt at self-promotion. Personal effects in the office should be used as clues toward the bigger picture of who the real person is, but the impression they give off needs to be interpreted carefully.

Voice

Voice is another rich source of cues. Most relevant in detecting deception are the voice's pitch, tone, and volume, as well as the response's onset and duration. Investigative authorities have long known that deceptive answers have a slower onset than honest ones.

In addition, deceptive answers are likely to be longer and less specific than honest ones. The deceiver may be attempting to fill in the gap with needless material. Some see length as an attempt to make a deceptive statement more elaborate and thus more convincing than the deceiver knows it is. A statement's length may also reflect the pauses, throat clearings, and hesitations needed as the speaker stumbles through the answer, according to innovative studies of CEO speech samples from their interactions with analysts and investors during earnings conference calls or video disclosures of corporate news and forecasts.[46]

Pitch is also a source of deception. Researchers have found that vocal pitch typically rises measurably in deceptive responses. While observers frequently could not say why they labeled such a response as deceptive, they believed it was, and research instruments could show the difference.[47]

In short, during managerial interactions, nonverbal elements are the source of most of the message. While not everything communicated nonverbally is done so consciously or intentionally, the unintentional signals may be as valid as the intentional ones and potentially more useful. Keep in mind, though, the suggestions about establishing a behavioral baseline for each person in specific situations. In addition, if deception is suspected, use that as an impetus for further investigation or at least caution, not as the final word.

SUMMARY

Everything but the words themselves is considered the domain of nonverbal communication. Every managerial interaction has nonverbal elements that add to or qualify the interaction. It is difficult to put precise meanings to nonverbal signals, and they vary from culture to culture; however, when nonverbal signals contradict verbal ones, the nonverbal signals are usually the ones to trust.

Nonverbal cues have six functions: complementing, accenting, contradicting, repeating, regulating, and substituting. In addition, nonverbal cues add redundancy to the verbal message and increase the probability that the verbal message will be understood as intended by the sender.

The study of movement includes gestures, posture, head movement, and style of walking. Gestures may include emblems, illustrators, affect displays, regulators, and adapters. The space around us and how we and others relate to it are also important. Four zones are presented and discussed in this chapter, but care must be taken in interpreting them because zones may differ among cultures. Inappropriate use of space may make a manager appear rude, while an accurate analysis of space indicates much about the importance of power in an organization.

Personal appearance is another integral part of the impression we give and often the key to credibility. Consequently, managers should pay close attention to their clothing, accessories, and grooming to be sure their appearance fits the expectations of the organization's culture and customers.

Voice is the final source of nonverbal signals discussed in the chapter. Vocal delivery includes the pitch, tone, onset, and duration of messages.

The first step to detecting deception is to establish a baseline. Once this has been accomplished, movement, space, artifacts, and voice can each be used to evaluate the potential for deception in an interaction. But in all managerial communication situations, it is important to remember that no dictionary exists for the meaning of nonverbal cues.

CASES FOR ANALYSIS

Case 11-1

Microsoft's Open Floor Plan

Over the past decades, workplace design has evolved from individual offices to cubicles to open floor plans to adaptable workspaces. These major changes in office geography have largely been driven by the goal to increase collaborating, idea sharing, and creative problem solving. Additional important considerations when redesigning workspaces are employee satisfaction and cost savings.

In 2010, Microsoft began replacing its software engineers' secluded offices with open designs. By 2014, it had completely renovated 10 buildings on its campus in Redmond, Washington, but the engineers complained that the open spaces were too noisy and distracting, which resulted in reduced levels of interpersonal communication. Microsoft listened and adapted. "You have to collaborate more; we absolutely have to change," said Michael Ford, Microsoft's general manager of global real estate.[48] By 2018, 20 percent of the workplaces were redone, and projections were that 80 percent would be finished within 5 years. Offices did not disappear entirely and are used for confidential conversations. Team areas hold only eight to 12 engineers, instead of 16 to 24. Walls are movable. Other new features include isolation rooms, as well as lounges with couches.

Questions

1. What are the major advantages of private offices? Major disadvantages?

2. What are the major advantages of open floor plans (no walls)? Major disadvantages?

3. Select a company in an industry of interest; analyze the needs of its workforce, including digital technology, and predict the workers' preferences for conditions such as sunlight, art, and greenspaces. Design a workplace for the company that incorporates optimal features and justify the projected costs according to the premise that space drives behavior.

4. In late 2020, as a response to the COVID-19 pandemic, Microsoft announced, "for most roles, we view working from home part of the time as now standard—assuming manager and team alignment."[49] Compare the efforts and expenses of creating ideal workspaces with the idea of people working from home. What are the advantages? Disadvantages?

Case 11-2

Nonverbal Cues and Videoconferencing

Faridah Khan was exhausted. As marketing manager for Green Dreams Landscaping, a lawn and garden center headquartered in Pittsburgh, Pennsylvania, her responsibilities as leader of a project team were taking up more time and energy than she had expected. The goal of the project was to determine ways to expand the business into new territories. The project had launched 4 months ago. Faridah, a veteran project leader, had quickly established specific goals, selected team members and clarified their roles, and created a reasonable timeline for delivering their recommendations to the board. The project was moving forward on schedule.

The members of her team worked at six locations across the state, making face-to-face meetings impractical, so the team relied on technology for communication. They used e-mail, text, group chat, and phone calls, but they chiefly relied on Zoom videoconferencing because it substitutes so well for human contact.

"Why do I feel anxious and drained after each video chat?" Faridah asked herself. Interacting with a grid of faces at close range, including her own, for extended periods should have been a benefit, she thought, because it allowed her to see and hear everyone's nonverbal behaviors. Yet she'd experienced some disadvantages to video chat, due to a lack of social conventions. For instance, there were awkward pauses when team members were unsure whose turn to talk it was. And sometimes she was distracted by people, noise, and objects in the team members' environments. Facial expressions seemed exaggerated; hand gestures were too large and close to the webcam; eye contact turned into stares;

variations in voice pitch and tone couldn't be ignored. Sometimes she wished she could just step back or walk around a bit during Zoom meetings.

Questions

1. Review the key points in this chapter and list some steps that Faridah should take to create a more normal, relaxed atmosphere during Zoom meetings with her project team.

2. Few of us can resist watching ourselves onscreen when videoconferencing. What are some ways to relieve overemphasis on nonverbal cues and reduce the feeling of being onstage?

3. When should managers use a communication technology that includes nonverbal cues, such as Zoom, over one that de-emphasizes nonverbals, such as e-mail? For instance, which is best when sharing information? When making decisions?

Case 11-3

Facing a Series of Interviews

Hanna Jenson recently applied for a position that involves supervising new-hire orientation in a large comprehensive insurance company. She has just received a letter notifying her to report for an interview for this position in 4 days. The letter indicates that Jenson will be required to attend a series of interviews, as follows:

> 9:00 a.m. Rodney Custer, Human Resources Director

> 10:00 a.m. Ahmad Syed, Training Department Manager

> 11:00 a.m. Bobbie Kent, Senior Trainer

If Jenson gets the job, she will receive a substantial raise in salary, as well as her first opportunity to gain supervisory experience. Therefore, she wants the job very badly and is concerned about how to prepare for each of the interviews.

Although she has never worked in this particular department, Jenson has worked for the company for several years. She knows Custer and Syed on a casual basis, but she has never met Kent. Custer is 38 years old, is meticulous in dress, and often points out his managerial accomplishments since becoming the HR director 2 years ago. Jenson's friends in HR have observed that Custer has hired only men in supervisory positions so far.

Syed is a seasoned manager who will be eligible for retirement in 2 years. He is somewhat unkempt in appearance, but his knowledge of employee training and education, as well as his skill in office politics, has earned him the respect of managers throughout the company.

Jenson is especially concerned about the interview with Kent. If she gets the job, she will be working directly under Kent, yet she knows nothing about her.

Questions

1. What positive and negative suggestions would you give Jenson about her choice of dress for these interviews?

2. What nonverbal cues given off by each interviewer should she pay attention to?

3. What nonverbal signals would you suggest Jenson send while speaking during each interview, given the profiles of Custer and Syed?

4. How could Jenson's strategy differ in each interview situation?

Case 11-4

Launching a Project Team Leader

Art Margulis is director of marketing research at a Fortune 500 consumer products company. He joined the firm 8 years ago after earning an MBA with a marketing emphasis. Because of his technical expertise, management skills, and outgoing personality, he was promoted to director of the 50-person department 2 years ago. His management style is

(Continued)

(Continued)

informal, and he frequently interacts with everyone in the department. Margulis has just formed a project team consisting of six persons from his department. The team's task is to solicit proposals for constructing a new marketing research outpost in a major suburban shopping mall, compare the bids, and compose a report recommending acceptance of the best proposal.

Margulis has appointed Maria Lopez to be the project team leader. Lopez has a PhD in applied statistics and has worked in the department for 6 months as a market analyst. She has quickly made several important contributions to the department and is considered a rising star. Because Lopez has no direct reports, Margulis decided that leading this project team will add to her skill set. Margulis will mentor her from the sidelines. Margulis has asked Lopez to meet with him and discuss team communication strategies before she calls the team together to launch the project. Margulis is now composing an agenda for this initial coaching session with Lopez.

Questions

Compose an agenda of topics for Margulis's coaching session to help Lopez accomplish the following goals:

1. Identify and apply nonverbal communication behaviors that will help establish her credibility as a competent project team leader.

2. Identify and apply nonverbal behaviors that will help Lopez establish rapport among the team members.

3. Identify and apply nonverbal communication behaviors that will help establish the team members' trust in Lopez.

4. Determine logistics of future team meetings (furniture arrangement, times, location, refreshments) that will expedite team effectiveness.

Notes

1. Judee K. Burgoon, Laura K. Guerrero, and Kory Floyd, *Nonverbal Communication: The Unspoken Dialogue* (Boston: Allyn & Bacon, 2010).

2. Malcolm Gladwell, *The Tipping Point: How Little Things Can Make a Big Difference* (Boston: Little, Brown and Company, 2002).

3. Albert Mehrabian, "Communicating Without Words," *Psychology Today*, September 1968, 53–55. See also Albert Mehrabian, *Nonverbal Communication* (London, UK: Routledge, 2007).

4. Lisa Feldman Barrett et al., "Emotional Expressions Reconsidered: Challenges to Inferring Emotion From Human Facial Movements," *Psychological Science in the Public Interest* 20, no. 1 (2019): 1–68. doi: 10.1177/152910061983293.

5. Haru Yamada, Orlando R. Kelm, and David A. Victor, *The Seven Keys to Communicating in Japan: An Intercultural Approach* (Washington, DC: Georgetown University Press, 2017).

6. Larry H. Hynson Jr., "Doing Business With South Korea—Park II: Business Practices and Culture," *East Asian Executive Reports* 13 (September 15, 1991): 18.

7. Sandra G. Garside and Brian H. Kleiner, "Effective One-to-One Communication Skills," *Industrial and Commercial Training* 23, no. 7 (July 1991): 27.

8. Paul Ekman, *Emotions Revealed: Recognizing Faces and Feelings to Improve Communication and Emotional Life* (New York: Henry Holt, 2004).

9. S. Burbinster, "Body Politics," *Associate & Management,* April 1987, 55–57.

10. Vyvyan Evans, *The Emoji Code: The Linguistics Behind Smiley Faces and Scaredy Cats* (New York: Picador, 2017).

11. Drake Baer, "A World-Renowned Harvard Linguist Thinks Emoji Fill a Gap in the English Language," *Business Insider,* August 12, 2015, http://www.businessinsider.com/why-steven-pinker-loves-emojis-2015-8.

12. Qiyu Bai et al., "A Systematic Review of Emoji: Current Research and Future Perspectives," *Frontiers in Psychology* 10, no. 2221 (October 15, 2019), doi: 10.3389/fpsyg.2019.02221.

13. Andrea Luangrath, Joann Peck, and Victor Barger, "Textual Paralanguage and Its Implications for Marketing Communications," *Journal of Consumer Psychology* 27, no. 1 (January 2017): 98–107, doi: 10.1016/j.jcps.2016.05.002.

14. Pam Belluck, "For a Creative Boost, Go Blue," *Houston Chronicle,* February 6, 2009.

15. Geraldine E. Hynes and Marius Janson, "Using Semiotic Analysis to Determine Effectiveness of Internet Marketing" (paper presented at the Annual International Convention of the Association for Business Communication, October 10–12, 2007), www.businesscommunication.org.

16. This classification system was developed by Paul Ekman and Wallace Friesen, "The Repertoire of Nonverbal Behavior," *Semiotica* 1 (1969): 49–98. For more recent categorizations, based on Ekman and Friesen's model, see Anthony Kong et al., "A Coding System With Independent Annotations of Gesture Forms and Functions During Verbal Communication: Development of a Database of Speech and Gesture," *Journal of Nonverbal Behavior* 39, no. 1 (March 2015): 93–111; and Susan M. Mather, "Ethnographic Research on the Use of Visually Based Regulators for Teachers and Interpreters," in *Attitudes, Innuendo, and Regulators,* eds. Melanie Metzger and Earl Fleetwood (Washington, DC: Gallaudet University Press, 2005), 136–61.

17. Alex (Sandy) Pentland, *Honest Signals: How They Shape Our World* (Boston: MIT Press, 2008), 10–40, 105.

18. "Importance of Interpreting Body Language," *Accredited Language Services International* (blog), August 13, 2013, https://www.alsintl.com/blog/interpreting-body-language.

19. Edward T. Hall, *The Hidden Dimension* (New York: Doubleday, 1966).

20. Mark L. Knapp, Judith A. Hall, and Terrence G. Horgan, *Nonverbal Communication in Human Interaction,* 8th ed. (Boston: Wadsworth, 2014).

21. Ibid., 133.

22. Ethan S. Bernstein and Stephen Turban, "The Impact of the 'Open' Workspace on Human Collaboration," *Philosophical Transactions R. Soc. B* 373, no. 20170239 (May 3, 2018), http://dx.doi.org/10.1098/rstb.2017.0239.

23. Craig Knight and S. Alexander Haslam, "The Relative Merits of Lean, Enriched, and Empowered Offices: An Experimental Examination of the Impact of Workspace Management Strategies on Well-Being and Productivity," *Journal of Experimental Psychology: Applied* 16, no. 2 (2010), 158–72.

24. Daniel Hamermesh, *Beauty Pays: Why Attractive People Are More Successful* (Princeton, NJ: Princeton University Press, 2011).

25. Kristie M. Engemann and Michael T. Owyang, "The Link Between Wages and Appearance," *The Regional Economist,* April 2005, http://research.stlouisfed.org/publications/regional/05/04/appearance.pdf.

26. Jeffrey Rothfeder, *Driving Honda: Inside the World's Most Innovative Car Company* (New York: Penguin Random House, 2014), 137.

27. Louis V. Gerstner Jr., *Who Says Elephants Can't Dance? Inside IBM's Historic Turnaround* (New York: HarperCollins, 2002).

28. "IBM: What Is the Dress Code in the Office?" Indeed, July 26, 2018, https://www.indeed.com/cmp/IBM/faq/what-is-the-dress-code-in-the-office?quid=1cjbe9k57brd99u0.

29. Gerstner, *Who Says*, 185.

30. Knapp et al., *Nonverbal Communication*, 323–55.

31. Jane Setter, *Your Voice Speaks Volumes: It's Not What You Say, but How You Say It* (London: Oxford University Press, 2020), 76–81.

32. Pentland, *Honest Signals*.

33. Mark Buchanan, "The Science of Subtle Signals," *Strategy + Business*, no. 48 (August 29, 2007), http://www.strategy-business.com/press/article/07307?pg=all.

34. Keith Naughton, "Ford Tests Buzzing Wristbands to Keep Employees at Safe Distances," *Bloomberg*, April 15, 2020, https://www.bloomberg.com/news/articles/2020-04-15/ford-tests-buzzing-distancing-wristbands-to-keep-workers-apart.

35. Euny Hong, *The Power of Nunchi: The Korean Secret to Happiness and Success* (New York: Penguin Books, 2019).

36. Chris Fill, *Marketing Communications: Frameworks, Theories, and Applications* (Upper Saddle River, NJ: Prentice Hall, 1995).

37. Susan A. Andrzejewski and Emily C. Mooney, "Service With a Smile: Does the Type of Smile Matter?" *Journal of Retailing and Consumer Services* 29 (2016): 135–41.

38. D. S. Sundaram and Cynthia Webster, "The Role of Nonverbal Communication in Service Encounters," in *Managing Employee Attitudes and Behaviors in the Tourism and Hospitality Industries,* ed. Salih Kusluvan (Hauppauge, NY: Nova Science, 2003), 208–21.

39. Anton R. Valukas, "Report to Board of Directors of General Motors Company Regarding Ignition Switch Recalls," 2014, 250.

40. Amit Kumar Kar and Ajit Kumar Kar, "How to Walk Your Talk: Effective Use of Body Language for Business Professionals," *The IUP Journal of Soft Skills* 11, no. 1 (2017): 16–28.

41. Timothy Levine et al., "Sender Demeanor: Individual Differences in Sender Believability Have a Powerful Impact on Deception Detection Judgments," *Human Communication Research*, 37 (2011): 377–403. See also Timothy Levine, *Duped: Truth-Default Theory and the Social Science of Lying and Deception* (Tuscaloosa: University of Alabama Press, 2019).

42. Malcolm Gladwell, *Talking to Strangers: What We Should Know About the People We Don't Know* (New York: Little, Brown and Company, 2019), 175.

43. Ibid., 343.

44. Mark L. Knapp and Mathew S. McGlone, *Lying + Deception in Human Interaction*, 2nd ed. (Dubuque, IA: Kendall Hunt, 2016).

45. Sam Gosling, *Snoop: What Your Stuff Says About You* (London: Profile Books, 2008), 13.

46. Alfredo Contreras, Aiyesha Dey, and Claire Hill, "'Tone at the Top' and the Communication of Corporate Values: Lost in Translation?" *Seattle University Law Review* 43, no. 2 (2020): 497–523.

47. Knapp and McGlone, *Lying + Deception in Human Interaction*.

48. Steve Lohr, "Don't Get Too Comfortable at That Desk," *New York Times*, October 6, 2017, https://www.nytimes.com/2017/10/06/business/the-office-gets-remade-again.html.

49. Kathleen Hogan, "Embracing a Flexible Workplace," *Official Microsoft Blog*, October 9, 2020, https://blogs.microsoft.com/blog/2020/10/9/emracing-a-flexible-workplace/.

12

COMMUNICATING ACROSS CULTURES

LEARNING OBJECTIVES

By the end of this chapter, you will be able to

- Define *culture* and provide a rationale for becoming familiar with intercultural business communication practices

- Identify several intercultural myths

- Explain six dimensions on which cultures differ

- Describe benefits of learning multiple languages

- Demonstrate awareness of nonverbal behaviors that differ across cultures

- Analyze the elements of intercultural communication sensitivity

- Compose a plan for developing interculturally sensitive managers in foreign and domestic environments

Do you see yourself as a candidate for an overseas assignment? Depending on the company you work for, the extent of its overseas operations, and the rules and regulations of the host country, people at various levels may be offered assignments abroad. Some companies with limited operations overseas prefer to send some of their newest people to staff those sites. This point will be addressed in greater detail later in this chapter. But whether or not you plan to work for a multinational corporation (MNC), cultural sensitivity is an important quality for managerial success.

RATIONALE

There are at least three reasons you should become familiar with intercultural business communication practices.

The Global Economy

First, the continuous increase in globalization as it relates to the U.S. economy is undeniable. According to the U.S. Department of Commerce, the total value of import/export trade in 2019 exceeded $5.6 trillion: more than $3.1 trillion in imports and almost $2.5 trillion in exports.[1] The top five trading partners of the United States are China, Mexico, Canada, Japan, and Germany. Economic forecasters predict that international trade and investment will continue to be strong through the 2020s, although the focus is shifting away from the superpowers and toward smaller nations, including Vietnam, Taiwan, the Netherlands, and Ireland.[2]

The United States has steadily become more "open" over the most recent decades, which significantly contributed to its rapid recovery from the economic collapse of 2008; that is, exports and imports have grown faster than GDP. But the United States is not the most globalized country, by far. For more than 45 years, the KOF Swiss Economic Institute annually has ranked 203 countries according to their degree of globalization, as measured by 24 economic, social, and political factors. Who is number one? Switzerland. In addition to high levels of trade in goods and services, Switzerland experiences the most foreign investment. Furthermore, the country is profoundly affected by ideas, information, and people from abroad. The Netherlands, Belgium, Sweden, and the United Kingdom round out the top five most globalized countries. The globalization index for the United States has been continuously increasing since the 1970s. The United States ranked 23rd in 2019, mostly because of economic activity rather than social and political globalization.[3]

Foreign Direct Investment

A second reason you should become familiar with best practices for intercultural business communication is that even if you do not conduct business internationally, you may find yourself working for an affiliate of a foreign-owned company. *Foreign direct investment* is an economic term used to describe when a company from one country builds facilities, purchases equipment, hires workers, and creates products and services in another country. When foreign direct investment happens in the United States, many of those products and services will be sold to U.S. consumers, while others will be exported to markets around the world. In the United States, 7.4 million workers are employed by majority foreign-owned firms in manufacturing, transportation, utilities, mining, finance, insurance, real estate, and banking. According to the Global Business Alliance, an organization of more than 200 MNCs, U.S. workers at international companies earn about 26 percent more than the average U.S. worker.[4]

You might be surprised by the following examples of businesses you may think are U.S.-owned but are in fact owned by companies headquartered in other countries: Anheuser-Busch is owned by Inbev, a Belgian company. Dannon Co., the yogurt maker, is owned by Danone Group, a French company. Henkel, a German corporation, owns the Dial Corporation, makers of Dial soap, Renuzit air fresheners, and Purex. A Mexican company,

Grupo Bimbo, owns Sara Lee, Entenmann's, and Mrs. Baird's, all makers of bakery products. An Italian conglomerate, Luxottica, owns LensCrafters, Pearle Vision, and Sunglass Hut. And Compass Bank is a wholly owned subsidiary of a Spanish company, BBVA.

CRITICAL THINKING QUESTIONS

1. If you own a car, in what country is the company's headquarters located? Where was your car assembled? Where were the parts manufactured?

2. What other items do you use that are products of international business and the global economy?

3. Can you find other examples of companies that you assumed were U.S.-owned but are actually owned by foreign-based companies?

Continuing our examination of global business connections, many products that you may think of as "foreign" may actually be made in the United States. For instance, Kraft Foods makes Grey Poupon mustard in the United States. Michelin tires are manufactured in South Carolina. And Evian water is distributed by Coca-Cola, which is headquartered in Atlanta, Georgia. These products are made by workers and bought by consumers in a global economy.

Culturally Diverse Workforces

A third reason to learn about intercultural business communication is the increasing likelihood that you will work with or for someone who is from a different culture than you. Immigrants make a big contribution to U.S. population growth, accounting for one third to nearly one half of population growth for decades. Over the last 10 years, immigration has been expanding the U.S. population at a rate of about 1 million people a year, which has had a significant impact on the size of the work force and, by extension, the productivity and growth of the economy.[5] As a result, U.S. managers will be leading a noticeably different workforce in the years ahead.

Furthermore, employees often bring their culturally based behaviors to work. For instance, one of the five pillars of Islam includes praying five times per day. Dell Inc. and Electrolux Home Products accommodate their Muslim workers in U.S. plants with a "tag-out" policy that allows a few employees at a time to step away for prayers. As the workforce becomes ever more diverse, such cultural differences in behavior will have a major impact on the likelihood of successful business–worker interaction. Here is an example of the extent to which a commitment to cultural sensitivity has become ingrained in the business environment: Legal Sea Foods, a chain of restaurants in the northeastern and southeastern United States, lists its corporate values on its paper place mats for customers to see. The company's first "pledge" is "to inspect and prepare the freshest, highest quality fish and shellfish." That is to be expected, right? The second pledge is "to assure you of a clean and comfortable environment." That is good but still unsurprising. Reading further down the place mat, you find the third pledge: "to promote diversity and respect for all human differences." Clearly, cultural sensitivity is a priority at Legal Sea Foods.

In summary, whether or not they deliberately choose to conduct business internationally, managers will need to be culturally sensitive communicators. Unfortunately, the quality of the training given to people headed for overseas assignments differs widely by company and by country. It has been estimated that 42 percent of U.S. managers perform inadequately abroad because they have not been sufficiently prepared for adjusting to the foreign culture. The most common methods of preparing employees for foreign assignments are giving an overview of cultural differences and providing language training (particularly in Europe, the Middle East, and Asia Pacific). Twenty-two percent of North American employers do virtually nothing. Companies in Japan and Australia, on the other hand, are noted for the high quality of training their workers are given before being sent abroad.[6]

CRITICAL THINKING QUESTIONS

1. What are some benefits of a culturally diverse workforce?

2. What are some challenges?

3. What can managers do to encourage interpersonal relationships among culturally diverse workers?

This chapter will not cover everything anyone ever needed to know about being an intercultural managerial communicator in all parts of the world. That ambitious goal is the subject of thousands of books and articles in any library and could not possibly be condensed into one chapter. Our goal instead will be to introduce the types of issues, concerns, and mores that managers need to study to become successful in intercultural business communication. Additionally, we will make a number of suggestions about what managers can do now and in the coming years to better prepare themselves to conduct global business.

WHAT IS CULTURE?

Before we review the many aspects of intercultural communication, we might want to get an idea of the meaning of the word *culture*. Though definitions of this term abound and vary widely in terms of their complexity, John Gould defines it in a clear and straightforward manner:

Culture is what we grow up in. Beginning in childhood, we learn the behaviors, habits, and attitudes that are acceptable to those around us. These are transmitted to us orally, nonverbally, and in writing. As time goes on, we gradually acquire the knowledge, beliefs, values, customs, and moral attitudes of the society in which we mature. A body of common understanding develops with which we feel comfortable. We know what to expect, and we know what is expected of us.[7]

Defined in such a way, culture includes the religious systems to which we are exposed, the educational system, the economic system, the political system, the recreational outlets, the mores governing dress and grooming, the standards of etiquette, the food and how it is prepared and served, the gift-giving customs, the morals, the legal system, the quality and quantity of communication among people, the greeting practices, the rituals performed, and the modes of travel available, as well as the many other aspects of people's lives that they come to take for granted.

Malcolm Gladwell explores the importance of culture in individual behaviors in his best seller *Outliers: The Story of Success*. He concludes that

> cultural legacies are powerful forces. They have deep roots and long lives. They persist, generation after generation, virtually intact, even as the economic and social and demographic conditions that spawned them have vanished, and they play such a role in directing attitudes and behavior that we cannot make sense of our world without them.[8]

Culture is all-encompassing and everlasting. When we recognize how pervasive a person's culture is and how much it can differ from country to country, we can then begin to appreciate more fully the difficult job facing a manager in an intercultural environment. The people in or from another country are quite comfortable with a culture that may seem strange to a U.S. businessperson. Yet it is we who will have to make the adjustments and live with the uncertainty and the unusual occurrences and practices. If we want to succeed in this highly competitive global marketplace, we will have to learn to see and accept things as others see and accept them.

INTERCULTURAL MYTHS

Before we examine the various aspects of intercultural business communication, we need to dispel a few myths. The global village concept, end of history view, and universality myth are three theories worth examining.

The *global village concept* was introduced by Marshall McLuhan in his 1967 book *The Medium Is the Message* and promoted more recently by Thomas Friedman in his book *The World Is Flat*. This concept proposes that advancements in communication and transportation technologies will ultimately shrink the world to a point where we will be one big, happy global village. Some believe the global village concept has been realized because we now know instantly of happenings in even the most remote parts of the world.

Others believe we are nowhere near fruition of the global village concept. They contend that the great advancements in communication and transportation technologies have only created a greater proximity among the various peoples of the world and that proximity has only enhanced the perceived differences among those peoples.[9]

In conjunction with the latter view, it has been suggested that you, today's students, are responsible for whether or not we ever do see the fruition of the global village concept. To be successful in the global marketplace, you will need to adjust to other cultures, and you will need to gain and maintain the trust of your intercultural partners. In other words, you will need to bridge the cultural gap. With each successful international business venture (successful for all parties involved), we move closer to the realization of the global village concept.

A second widely discussed theory is the *end of history view* advanced by Francis Fukuyama, a political economist at Stanford University. His assertion was that the end of the Cold War meant the end of the war of ideas. After the Berlin Wall crumbled in

1989, he predicted that one relatively harmonious world would unite in liberal democracy. Somewhat modeled after the global village concept, Fukuyama's theory included the idea that significant global conflicts would be a thing of the past as we blend into one.[10] Unfortunately, a quarter-century after Fukuyama published his vision of world peace, the world appears to be more like a clash of civilizations that threatens the forces of globalization, the basis for Fukuyama's more hopeful projections.[11]

The third myth of which we should be wary is the *universality myth*. This myth is often promoted by people who have spent a short time in a foreign country. Initially, they notice all the differences between their own culture and that of the host country. Then they start to note all the similarities. They come away from the experience concluding that we are all alike: brothers and sisters in the common family of humanity. Some promoters of this concept recommend the universal adoption of artificial languages, such as Esperanto, Unish, and Globish.[12]

Milton Bennett, an American sociologist and author of the developmental model of intercultural sensitivity, which is used internationally to assess intercultural competence, describes six stages of intercultural sensitivity.[13] He refers to the universality belief as *minimization*. He says that looking for similarities is a way to assuage our fears of difference and make us feel better about each other. A short visit does not provide people with the deeper insight into a culture that would have revealed major differences in beliefs, values, and mores. To illustrate, we might look at some of the results of a survey conducted in a number of countries. One of the questions asked of the respondents was "Do you agree or disagree with the statement: 'Most people can be trusted'?" The levels of agreement are listed in the following box:

United States:	55 percent
United Kingdom:	49 percent
Mexico:	30 percent
West Germany:	19 percent
Italy:	1 percent

One could argue that language differences might have been responsible for some of the variation. But even if we allow for some margin of error, we would still have a significant variation in a very basic belief.

Another example of differences in basic beliefs is the notion of constructive criticism. Many business professionals from individualistic cultures such as the United States typically perceive corrective feedback as an opportunity for performance improvement, and managers often deliver it openly to their direct reports. By contrast, people from more collectivist cultures may be extremely uncomfortable when receiving constructive criticism in the presence of their coworkers.[14] We differ appreciably, and those differences must be recognized, understood, and accepted if we are to do business with one another.

SOME OF THE WAYS IN WHICH WE DIFFER

One of the most extensive studies of cultural differences was conducted by Geert Hofstede in a very large U.S.-based MNC. He collected more than 116,000 questionnaires from this corporation's employees in 40 countries around the globe. A massive statistical analysis of his findings revealed six dimensions of national culture, as shown in Table 12-1: power distance, uncertainty avoidance, collectivism/individualism, masculinity/femininity, high/low context, and monochronic/polychronic time.[15] Hofstede's building of a cultural dimensional framework resulted in country clustering of shared cultural behaviors. His framework is still the Rosetta Stone for understanding major differences in cultural mindsets. The following sections describe each dimension and offer example countries.

TABLE 12-1 ■ Hofstede's Dimensions of Cultural Differences	
High power distance	Low power distance
High uncertainty avoidance	Low uncertainty avoidance
Collectivism	Individualism
Masculinity	Femininity
High context	Low context
Polychronic	Monochronic

Power Distance

Power distance indicates the extent to which a society accepts the fact that power in institutions and organizations is distributed unequally. It is reflected in the values of both the more powerful and the less powerful members of the society. According to Hofstede's research, the Philippines, Venezuela, Mexico, and the South Slavic States are countries with high power distances; Denmark, New Zealand, Austria, the United States, and Israel are a few of the countries with low power distances.[16]

A manager in a culture with high power distance is often seen as having dramatically more power than a direct report would have. This manager, who is usually addressed respectfully by title and surname, might favor a controlling strategy and behave like an autocrat. For instance, within the British Houses of Parliament, lawmakers can move to the head of the line at restaurants, restrooms, and elevators, whereas clerks, aides, and secretaries who work in Parliament must stand and wait. In a culture with a lower power distance, however, a manager is seen as having little more power than a direct report, is often addressed by first name, takes her place in line, and manages by using an equalitarian communication strategy.

A dramatic example of how power distance affects business is provided by the airline industry. Between 1988 and 1998, Korean Air's plane crash ratio was at alarming heights—4.79 per million departures. That figure was 17 times worse than the crash ratio for major U.S. commercial airlines in that time period.[17] Several investigations and studies were done to examine the cause of Korean Air's plane crashes. Finally, it occurred to someone to apply Hofstede's power distance theory. What they discovered was fascinating. The first officers in the cockpit were too paralyzed with fear to say anything that questioned the captain's ability. Afraid to speak up, they were trapped in subservient roles because of the high power distance ingrained in their culture. One Korean Air pilot revealed,

"The captain is in charge and does what he wants, when he wants, when he likes, how he likes, and everyone else sits quietly and does nothing." Fortunately, by understanding the underlying importance of culture and how it relates to the airline industry, dramatic improvements were made. The Korean Air flight crews were retrained and have enjoyed a spotless safety record since 1999.[18]

Uncertainty Avoidance

Uncertainty avoidance relates to the degree to which a society feels threatened by uncertainty and by ambiguous situations. It tries to avoid these uncertainties and ambiguous situations by providing greater career stability, establishing and following formal rules, not allowing odd ideas and behaviors, and believing in absolute truths and the attainment of expertise. According to Hofstede, Greece, Germany, England, Portugal, Belgium, and Japan have strong uncertainty avoidance, while Singapore, Hong Kong, Denmark, the United States, and Sweden have weak uncertainty avoidance.[19]

Belgium and Denmark are geographically close. However, when it comes to uncertainty avoidance, the two nations are far apart because of different histories, politics, religions, literature, and other cultural factors. Recall that earlier in this chapter Belgium was identified as the third most globalized of 158 countries. What do you think is the connection between that ranking and Belgians' avoidance of uncertainty, their respect for rules and plans, and their insistence on following procedures regardless of circumstances? Uncertainty avoidance is probably a major dimension for most intercultural managers to contend with. Most likely, they will be expected to challenge the status quo and implement change, and uncertainty avoidance is a significant obstacle to change. Such managers ought to remember that using an equalitarian communication strategy to get people involved and highlighting the benefits of change can greatly help reduce resistance.

Collectivism/Individualism

In the *individualism/collectivism* dimension, *individualism* suggests a loosely knit social framework in which people are expected to take care of themselves and their immediate families only. *Collectivism*, on the other hand, is evidenced by a tight social framework in which people distinguish between in-groups and out-groups. They generally expect their in-group (relatives, clan, organization) to take care of them, and because of that, they believe they owe absolute loyalty to it. The United States, Australia, and the United Kingdom are the most highly individualistic countries according to Hofstede's scale, while Guatemala, Pakistan, Colombia, Nigeria, Japan, and Venezuela are more collectivist countries.[20]

The huge social-psychological gap between collectivist and individualist cultures can be illustrated linguistically. In Chinese, for instance, there is no word for *individualism*. The closest one can come is the word for *selfishness*. In Japanese, the word *I*—meaning the unconditional, generalized self—is not often used in conversation. Instead, Japanese has many words for *I*, depending on audience and context. This reflects the Eastern conviction that one is a different person when interacting with different groups.[21] Managers from individualistic cultures and collectivist cultures typically conflict in many ways. In negotiations, for example, managers from collectivist cultures generally do not want to make decisions. They often collaborate first, to reach consensus. But managers from individualistic cultures often have difficulty collaborating, want to talk to a *decision maker*, and have difficulty understanding why the other group prefers to spend so much time in conference.

Masculinity/Femininity

Masculinity/femininity, as a dimension, expresses the extent to which the dominant values in the society are "masculine." This masculinity, according to Hofstede, would include assertiveness, the acquisition of money and things, and not caring about quality of life. These values are labeled masculine because within nearly all societies, men scored higher in these values. Japan, Austria, Venezuela, and Mexico were among the most masculine societies. Feminine cultures, by contrast, value family, children, and quality of life. Denmark, Sweden, and Norway are considered feminine cultures.[22]

Consider the following comparison. In the United States, men historically were judged on their ability to make a good salary. Frequently, this judgment precluded traditional U.S. feminine values of caring for children. In Helsinki, Finland, however, a man may be called away from a meeting to tend to the baby in the child care center in the next building, and no one considers this a wrong priority. Despite the passage of the Family and Medical Leave Act in 1993, far fewer working men than women take the full time they are eligible for when dealing with family and medical problems in the United States.

CRITICAL THINKING QUESTIONS

Think about a person you work with who comes from a different culture. How do Hofstede's dimensions of cultural differences help explain some of the differences you have experienced when communicating with that person?

High Context/Low Context

A fifth cultural difference an intercultural communicator needs to keep in mind is whether the culture is a high-context or low-context culture. These terms were first used by Edward T. Hall in 1977.[23] In a *high-context* culture, much information is either in the physical context or environment or internalized in the person. In such a culture, people look for meaning in what is not said—in the nonverbal communication or body language; in the silences, the facial expressions, and the gestures. Japan and Saudi Arabia are high-context countries, as are Chinese- and Spanish-speaking countries, according to Hofstede's research.[24]

In a *low-context* culture, most information is expected to be in explicit codes, such as words. In such a culture, communicators emphasize sending and receiving accurate messages directly, usually by being highly articulate. Canada and the United States are low-context cultures, according to Hofstede.[25] As one might suspect, negotiations between low-context and high-context cultures can be fraught with peril when the parties are not warned of the differences in approaches.[26] The value of contracts also varies widely between high- and low-context cultures. U.S. business-to-business transactions rely on documents, not handshakes or personal relationships.

A global approach to business has implications for companies' websites, which may be relied on for the sale of their products and services internationally. Website designers should consider the relevant business cultural values and conventions of the target countries, which numerous recent studies have identified. For example, one recent study compared the "About Us" feature of Western and Eastern companies' websites. The results demonstrate how low-context and high-context cultural values can manifest in subtle but important ways. The researchers found that Western companies projected a strong image in the About Us page of their websites by directly stating their achievements, status, industry rank, and profits. By contrast, high-context Eastern companies used indirect methods to promote themselves, such as describing their heritage and history, relationships with high-status others, and links to the home country.[27]

Monochronic/Polychronic

The sixth dimension of cultural differences, according to Hofstede, is *monochronic versus polychronic* time. In a monochronic culture, such as Germany, the United States, and most Westernized nations, we talk about saving time, wasting time, making time, and spending time. We measure time by the clock, often in nanoseconds. In hyper-punctual countries like Japan, pedestrians walk fast, and bank clocks are accurate. In Western businesses, we read quarterly returns and define "long-term" projections as those going out 3 to 5 years into the future. Time is linear.[28] That is, Westerners believe we continue to move forward in a linear fashion as the universe ages.

In polychronic cultures, such as Spain, Latin American nations, India, and most Asian countries, time just *is*. These cultures trace their roots back thousands of years. Time is measured by events, not the clock. It is, always and everywhere, circular. Universes come into and out of existence infinitely. Everything moves in a circular path, with no set points on which to anchor.[29] Thus, promptness diminishes in value, and being "late" is often a sign of status.

In polychronic countries, "long-term" thinking is over generations and even centuries. The moment does not matter, by comparison. People in polychronic cultures are more patient, less interested in time management or measurement, and more willing to wait for their rewards than those in monochronic cultures. To them, time is flexible, unfolding naturally. A culturally sensitive manager is wise to keep these perceptions in mind when determining "How late is late?" arrivals for a scheduled meeting.[30]

CRITICAL THINKING QUESTIONS

1. How does the concept of high- and low-context cultures explain an experience you have had at work when communicating with someone from another culture?

2. How does the concept of short-term and long-term orientation explain an experience you have had working with someone from another culture?

Given the globalization of today's marketplace and the increasing pace at which firms are becoming multinational, it has been suggested that organizations around the world will begin to look very much alike. One theory states that as the companies become more similar, the organizational culture might dominate or diminish the effects of the larger culture. Research thus far does not support the likelihood of these developments. Employees of different cultures generally maintain and even strengthen their cultural differences.[31] The implication is that we must accept, even value, our cultural differences for business success.

One way multinationals are demonstrating cultural sensitivity is in their hiring practices. PepsiCo, for instance, named Indra Nooyi as the company's CEO in 2006. Nooyi was born in India. She served as CEO for 12 years, during which time the company's sales grew by 80 percent. In 2017, she was ranked the second most powerful woman on the Forbes list of "The 19 Most Powerful Women in Business." Since 2001, half of all new hires at Pepsi have been either women or people of color. And managers earn their bonuses in part by how well they recruit and retain these new hires. Six of the company's top 12 executives are women or people of color. PepsiCo argues that a diverse leadership helps the company better understand the disparate tastes of new consumers globally.[32]

Having explored some of the fundamental dimensions on which the people of the world differ and how profound the differences are, we now turn our attention to more practical matters. The next sections present approaches to success as intercultural communicators. More specifically, the rest of this chapter discusses dealing with language differences, being nonverbally sensitive, being a good intercultural communicator, and preparing for assignments or careers in international business.

SHOULD YOU LEARN THE LANGUAGE?

The first decision facing an international business traveler is whether to learn the language spoken in the country to be visited. People who have learned a second language will testify that it can be a long, involved, and tedious task. Furthermore, the difficulty level varies with the language to be learned. Some have many subtle nuances that non-natives have a hard time capturing. And the many dialects that exist within a country complicate the process even more. According to the American Community Survey, the U.S. Census Bureau's primary source of language data, roughly 21 percent of U.S. citizens speak a language other than English at home.[33] In contrast, a 2019 study of people in the European Union nations found that more than two thirds of working-age adults know a language in addition to their mother tongue. Just over one fifth (21.0 percent) know two foreign languages, and almost one tenth (8.4 percent) know three or more foreign languages.[34]

Which languages are the most important to learn? According to the U.S. Department of Education, Chinese, Arabic, Farsi, Korean, Japanese, Russian, Hindi, and Urdu are the languages most vital to the future of the United States, although less than 1 percent of U.S. high school students are studying any of these. By contrast, in China, English is mandatory for students from third grade onward.[35]

For short stays in a country, perhaps just to set up a partnership or sign a contract, most people would agree that one need not learn the language. Because English is the recognized language of business throughout the world, the chances are good that the people one deals with will speak it. If they do not, one can always use an interpreter. Great care, however, should be exercised in selecting an interpreter, for they vary widely in ability and loyalty.

When trying to communicate in English with a group of people who have varying levels of fluency, managers should be receptive, adaptable, and alert to the possibility of misunderstanding. Dr. Jennifer Jenkins of the University of Southampton offers the following tips:

- Speak a bit more slowly than usual

- Enunciate carefully, especially during videoconferences and teleconferences

- Avoid slang and references specific to your own culture
- Use humor sparingly
- Keep it short, simple, and direct[36]

It is also important to be mindful of cultural style differences. "That's interesting" is considered an understatement, synonymous with "that's rubbish" among native speakers of British English, while most U.S. English speakers would take the word "interesting" at face value.

As the length of the stay increases, the need to learn and the wisdom of learning the language also increase. While occasional errors are inevitable and are often overlooked when tourists try to participate in conversations, the stakes increase with more formal and prolonged interactions, where the consequences of errors matter. Most authorities agree that an extended stay would justify the time and effort of learning the language of the land.

Literal translation errors can cause revenue loss in multinational companies. One company that takes care to avoid transliteration problems is IKEA, a Swedish retailer that has stores in 40 countries. IKEA is famous for using Scandinavian names to identify its sofas and beds. When IKEA prepared to launch a new superstore in Bangkok, Thailand, it hired a team of Thai speakers to go through the catalog, scrutinizing 9,000 Scandinavian terms to see how they sounded in Thai before transliterating them into Thailand's cursive, Sanskrit-influenced alphabet. "We've got to be careful," said Natthita Opaspipat, one of the team members. "Some of them can be, well, a little rude." For instance, "Redalen" is a bed sold by IKEA, named after a town in Norway, but the word has sexual connotations in Thailand. The team suggested a slight change to avoid offending shoppers.[37]

Furthermore, familiarity with the local language enables familiarity with the culture, values, traditions, and business practices. A deeply held belief in Japan is captured by the simple term *kaizen*, which literally means "to change to become good." This concept has been widely adopted in U.S. businesses that stress continuous quality improvement through reliance on team decision making and sophisticated, comprehensive communication networks. In addition, organizations following the kaizen philosophy value cleanliness and order. Walking through the workplace, one finds no litter on the floor and no tools out of place. Waste is minimized. As you can see, it takes many English words to describe this approach to business that is explained in Japanese by a single word.

To find other examples of how closely language is tied to the culture, we can examine some translation issues. Here is one: More than 47 million copies of the children's book *Diary of a Wimpy Kid*, by Jeff Kinney, are in print in the United States, and the book has been translated into 30 languages, including Spanish, Japanese, Greek, Hebrew, Thai, and German. But the German version is titled *I'm Surrounded by Idiots* because there is no German equivalent for *wimpy*. The closest German word is *ängstlich*, which translates into English as "uneasy, anxious."

Machine translators, such as Google Translate, should not be relied on because they do not account for many cultural factors, including slang usage, metaphors, and irony. Thus, the slogan for KFC, a chain of fast-food restaurants featuring chicken dishes, is "finger-lickin' good" in English, but in Chinese, this expression translates into "eat your fingers off." Ford had a backfire with translation of a truck model's name, the Fiera, which in Spanish means "ugly old woman."[38] Clearly, these literal translations are sure to hurt sales and damage the company's image. The more that managers understand about the culture, the more likely they are to be successful in that environment. Learning the local language leads to that end.

CRITICAL THINKING QUESTIONS

Think of an example of a slang expression in your native language that does not easily translate.

1. Where does slang come from?

2. To what extent does the origin of slang explain why it is culture-specific?

One last caution is advisable about language usage. Some people choose a middle-of-the-road approach and learn only specific statements that are common or are pertinent to a particular setting. Such people should remember that in some languages, particularly the Eastern languages, the same word can be used to mean many different things. The tone of the voice varies to indicate a specific meaning. Sometimes a little knowledge can be more damaging than no knowledge.

NONVERBAL SENSITIVITY

Whether or not traveling managers choose to learn the verbal language of the land, they should try to learn as much as they can about the nonverbal language common in that culture. Chapter 11 provided an overview of the range of nonverbal behaviors used in business settings to communicate meaning. Interpretations of greetings, dress, space, touch, posture, gestures, and rituals vary widely among cultures. Business deals have been lost over a seemingly harmless U.S. signal that was interpreted as a grave insult in another part of the world.

Greetings

From the start of any business contact, one should be aware that the form of greeting used may vary from culture to culture. Though the handshake is a fairly standard greeting in most parts of the world, the pressure used may differ. The high-pressure grip, which in the United States is supposed to suggest warmth and confidence, may be too aggressive where a lighter grasp is traditional.

In Japan, the bow is still practiced by older businesspeople. Sometimes the bow and handshake will both be used to signal respect for both cultures. Note, too, the different levels of bowing, each with significant meanings. In other parts of the world, a traditional greeting may be a hug, a nose rub, a kiss, or the placing of the hands in a praying position.[39]

On the subject of greetings, note also that business cards are treated differently in different parts of the world. In Japan, they are carefully offered to the recipient with both hands, with the information facing the receiver. Also, they are never put away hastily or scribbled on but studied at length and then arranged on the table during a business meeting. Finally, in any non-English-speaking country, printing the information on the reverse side of the business card in a second language is expected as a courteous practice.[40]

Dress

While the business suit is considered acceptable attire for a business meeting in most parts of the world, it may or may not be acceptable for an evening of entertainment. For men in tropical climates, a guayabera, or loose cotton shirt, worn over a pair of slacks is considered appropriate at even formal occasions. And in sunny Australia, men may often wear dress shirts and ties with shorts and knee socks to the office.

On the subject of dress, we should exercise caution even when we are not in business meetings or at official social functions. Standards of travel and entertainment dressing are much more conservative in some parts of the world than they are in the United States. Bare legs, arms, shoulders, or heads on the street or in holy buildings are considered offensive in many Arab and Eastern countries.

Space, Touch, and Posture

The space maintained, touching practiced, and postures assumed in business and social encounters vary appreciably across the globe. As discussed in Chapter 11, people in the United States are said to have a spatial bubble of up to 4 feet into which strangers should not encroach.[41] In Arab countries and Latin America, people typically speak almost face-to-face and nose-to-nose.

In some countries—Iran, Palestine, China, and Indonesia, for example—it is considered acceptable for two men to walk down the street holding hands as a sign of close friendship. However, in many of these same countries, it is not acceptable for a man and a woman to walk down the street hand in hand. This immodest public display of affection is frowned on.

Also on the subject of touching, managers should exercise some care about what is touched. In Thailand, the head is considered sacred. It should never be touched, and objects should never be passed above it. In Tonga, touching someone's head could get you the death penalty. Finally, in Muslim countries, it is considered insulting to show the sole of your shoe to someone else. Businesspeople are cautioned never to cross their legs with one ankle on the other knee and never to lean back in an office chair with their feet on the desk.

Gestures

In Bulgaria, Macedonia, Albania, Iran, and Sri Lanka, nodding the head up and down means "no." In Italy, Greece, and some African countries, the gesture that people in the United States use for "come here" means "goodbye." The thumbs-up gesture means "everything is good" in the United States, but to Australians it is an obscenity. The V-for-victory sign means something entirely different when reversed, with the palm facing the signer. In the United Kingdom, it then becomes an insult. In Ethiopia, pointing and the one-finger "come-here" gesture are used only with children and dogs.

As demonstrated by the preceding illustrations, the gestures we use in international encounters can be fairly dangerous. A friendly or innocuous gesture can turn out to be a vivid and/or profane insult. Something that very clearly means one thing in one country may mean the opposite in another country. To increase our level of success in the increasingly competitive global marketplace, we are going to have to become interculturally sensitive.

Food

Perhaps we become most aware of cultural diversity when we discuss food—what foods are used to celebrate special occasions, how the food is eaten, or even what is considered edible. Any traveler has tales of "exotic" meals, accompanied by value judgments.

Host nationals will want visitors to experience the culinary delights that bring so much pleasure to their taste buds, their national dining treasures. It can be hard for them to imagine or understand that these same treats might bring forth horror and revulsion in someone not experienced with them.

Thus, as the special guest at a banquet, one might be called on to try sheep's eyes in Saudi Arabia or Kazakhstan, shark's fin soup in China, or a live fish brought to the table and carved in Japan. While U.S. businesspeople may be reluctant to try such dishes, it would be supremely rude to refuse.

On the other hand, visitors to the United States are often critical of the daily consumption of processed foods and snacks, such as popcorn and Jell-O. Corn is animal food in most parts of the world. Further, the U.S. tendency to nibble throughout the day rather than sit through long meals is considered uncouth. In Italy and Japan, for instance, most people do not eat on the street or while standing.

The importance of sharing food when building intercultural relationships is exemplified by this Pakistani proverb: On the first cup of tea, you're a stranger. On the second, a guest. By the third cup, you're family.

Gifts

The Foreign Corrupt Practices Act (FCPA) of 1977 specifies that bribing someone during the conduct of business is illegal. A violator's company may be fined up to $2 million, and the participants in the bribe individually may be fined up to $100,000 each and jailed for up to 5 years. Despite these stiff penalties, MNCs continue to take risks. Why would U.S. corporations risk defying the FCPA? Anti-bribery laws are sometimes a source of competitive disadvantage when a company is trying to do business in a culture where gifts, fees, commissions, and "facilitation payments" to officials are normal practice and where other countries competing for lucrative contracts do not have anti-bribery restrictions. According to Transparency International, only seven of 44 major exporting countries actively enforce anti-bribery laws: Germany, Israel, Italy, the United States, Norway, Switzerland, and the United Kingdom.[42]

Gift-giving practices vary widely throughout the world. Common and expected in some countries, this practice is frowned on in others. For example, while gift giving is important in Japan, it is generally considered inappropriate in Germany, Belgium, or the United Kingdom.[43] Tipping for good service, a common practice in the United States, is not expected in China, Denmark, Italy, and France.

Even where it is practiced, the nature and the value of the gifts may differ greatly. Though flowers are often safe if one is invited to dinner in someone's home, chrysanthemums should be avoided in many European countries because of their funereal association. In Japan, white flowers carry the same message, as do purple ones in Brazil and Mexico. Remember, too, that numbers and shapes might have some significance. The number four is associated with bad luck in Japan and China, as is seven in Kenya—though seven is seen as lucky in the Czech Republic. The triangle is considered a negative shape in Hong Kong, Korea, and Taiwan.

Finally, investigate the interpretation of gifts bearing the company logo. While some people may interpret such gifts as a symbol of the business relationship being established or maintained, some might think the giver was simply too cheap to buy a gift on their own.

While not intended to be complete, the preceding discussion was designed to illustrate the very precarious world of the intercultural communicator. The dangers of nonverbal slippage are there whether or not a person chooses to learn the verbal language. In the end, the success of multinational firms will depend on how much effort their people expend toward being interculturally sensitive and thus sidestepping those dangers.

WHAT MAKES A GOOD INTERCULTURAL COMMUNICATOR?

Although it is not a comprehensive profile, the following description portrays some of the most important qualities and characteristics of a good intercultural communicator. You are a good intercultural communicator if you avoid the pitfalls described earlier and if you maintain harmonious relations with your intercultural partners.

First and foremost, you are a good intercultural communicator if you avoid *ethnocentrism*. As mentioned previously, Bennett designed a six-stage developmental model of cultural sensitivity (see Table 12-2). His model identifies three stages of ethnocentrism: *denial*, *defense*, and *minimization*. An ethnocentric person may acknowledge the existence of cultural differences but sees their own country as the best in the world and looks down on others as inferior because they are different. For whatever reasons, the ethnocentric person builds resentment rather than good relationships.

On the other hand, Bennett identified three stages of ethnorelativism: *acceptance*, *adaptation*, and *integration*. An ethnorelativistic manager recognizes and respects cultural differences and finds ways to make the workplace amenable to all.[44]

Second, you are a good intercultural communicator if you are *nondefensive* about your homeland. For example, when someone from another country criticizes the United States for problems such as the high divorce rate, drug abuse, gang warfare, child abuse, teen pregnancies, AIDS, racial discrimination, and corrupt politicians, people from the United States should not defensively deny the validity of these issues. While you may not be able to explain fully how these problems came to be, a straightforward discussion of the problems and what things are being done about them would be appropriate.

TABLE 12-2 ■ Bennett's Stages of Intercultural Sensitivity	
Ethnocentrism	**Ethnorelativism**
1. **Denial**—no perception of differences	4. **Acceptance**—differences are recognized and explored
2. **Defense**—hostility against other cultures	5. **Adaptation**—ability to empathize
3. **Minimization**—differences are real but superficial	6. **Integration**—differences are embraced

Third, you are a good intercultural communicator if you are *curious* about other parts of the world and *brave*. You must have a genuine interest in the people and the places that exist outside your national boundaries. Intercultural managers realize that the comforts of home are not always available throughout the world and are willing to try new foods and lifestyle behaviors before condemning them out of hand.

Fourth, you are a good intercultural communicator if you are *empathic, understanding*, and *nonjudgmental*. You are able to see the world through the eyes of your intercultural partners with some degree of objectivity. You understand that the initially strange behaviors and mores of others have locally very justifiable, long-standing reasons. You do not try to push your culture's ways on people for whom these ways may not work.

Fifth, you are a good intercultural communicator if you are *patient*. You learn to live with ambiguity; you come to expect the unexpected. Meetings will not always go as planned. Businesses will not always be open during the hours posted. Conveniences will not always be readily available. Though many of your coping behaviors will involve riding out the unexpected, you will also sometimes use your industriousness to come up with alternatives to what was expected. If one mode of transportation proves too unpredictable, you simply look for another. If one means of communication fails, you just find another.

CRITICAL THINKING QUESTIONS

1. Given that today's business environment is becoming more culturally diverse, what are the barriers to developing intercultural sensitivity?

2. What are some strategies you can apply to overcome the barriers?

Finally, you are a good intercultural communicator if you are *genuinely personable* to the people of the other country with whom you are dealing. A good intercultural communicator truly likes and respects those people. It cannot be faked.

DEVELOPING INTERCULTURALLY SENSITIVE MANAGERS

Interculturally sensitive managers will be the most successful, whether working abroad or in their home country.

Cultural Competence in Foreign Environments

At the time of writing, a global pandemic, along with isolationist government policies, has brought international travel to a standstill. Nevertheless, ambitious managers in MNCs should expect to work abroad sometime during their careers. Considering that relocating to another country is time-consuming and emotionally demanding for managers and their families, becoming an expatriate is often seen as a high-stakes career decision that leads to the executive suite.[45] In today's digital business world, why do managers and executives need to travel abroad in order to become fully informed citizens? Isn't online managerial communication sufficient? Probably not. The best way to get to know people who are different from ourselves, to understand and appreciate customs and beliefs that are unfamiliar, and to conduct business successfully is to immerse ourselves in that new environment. Mark Twain observed more than a century ago, "Travel is fatal to prejudice, bigotry, and narrow-mindedness."[46]

In addition, MNCs continue to practice global staffing, that is, recruiting talent from home-country, host-country, and other nations to fill key positions in their headquarters and subsidiary operations.[47] IBM, a major corporation, has two thirds of its workers abroad, both foreign nationals and U.S. citizens. "Thinking globally" is part of IBM's culture, values, and practices. IBM has integrated diversity and thinking globally into its onboarding, has a class called "Deeper Insight" for building competence in working internationally, and has other supports, such as diversity networks and a "Global Buddy" mentor program. "Talking global all the time" creates curiosity and savvy and drives inclusive behavior—getting people excited about what this means in terms of having a global advantage. The company offers expat and rotational assignments, language-learning programs for eight languages, and opportunities for team members to work on projects with a global reach.[48]

MNCs traditionally have sent their best employees on international assignments to grow new markets, maintain existing operations, or develop high-potential employees who can both contribute to the company strategy and craft a global view of the corporation's business. International business travel can offer managers diverse experiences that develop their professional networks and strengthen relationships with business contacts. Perhaps more important, international business travel helps managers develop cultural knowledge and skills, such as the ability to interact with other cultures and to adapt to foreign environments. Recent research indicates that quality interactions with foreign nationals during international business travel help employees develop a global mindset.[49]

You can do several things to prepare for a successful foreign assignment. As suggested earlier, you may want to learn another language. You should explore training and educational opportunities in multicultural communication at your organization, in your community, and at nearby universities. On the social side, you can befriend an international coworker. This experience will not only help them become acculturated to the host country; it will also provide you with insight into their culture. Finally, stay abreast of business, political, and economic developments throughout the world. Read newspapers with an international focus, such as the *Christian Science Monitor* or the *Financial Times*. In our increasingly global marketplace, your cross-cultural expertise will bring competitive advantage.

Cultural Competence in Domestic Environments

In the meantime, what can one do at home? Managers denied an overseas experience can still develop intercultural sensitivity. After all, managing diversity successfully brings high value to all contemporary organizations, not just multinational organizations. Research has found that people can control their bias and can become effective at bridging differences among their direct reports. Howard Ross, the founder of Cook Ross, an international diversity consulting company and author of *Everyday Bias* and *Reinventing Diversity*, suggests four strategies for developing cultural competence in domestic environments:

1. Recognize and accept that you have biases. Bias is a normal psychological phenomenon. Rather than feel guilty about your biases, take responsibility for them. Once you accept them, you can begin to limit their impact.

2. Practice "constructive uncertainty." Slow down decision making, especially when it affects other people.

3. Try to interact regularly with and learn about people you feel biased against. Exposing yourself to positive role models will reduce the risk of discrimination.

4. Look at how you make decisions. Consider the impact of environmental factors, time of day, and your physical and emotional state in order to identify barriers to perception.[50]

Let's apply Ross's four strategies. If you are conducting a job interview and your first impression of the candidate is negative because you perceived their outward characteristics (age, appearance, race, gender, voice, handshake, etc.) to be different from yours, what should you do? First, recognize your bias and the possibility of premature judgment. Next, deliberately decide that you won't jump to conclusions. Ask questions and listen closely to the interviewee's responses. Try to penetrate well below the surface so that you can exchange information more accurately. You might even bring in another interviewer whose opinions you respect and then compare impressions afterward.

While it's true that similarities make it easy to build relationships at work, diversity of traits and outlooks will give your team balance, opportunities for growth, and possibilities for learning new ways of thinking. Furthermore, developing cultural competence will help you make better decisions.

Clearly, cultural competence has taken on great significance, both in recruitment and retention of multicultural workers and in reaching the multicultural consumer market. Managing diversity is every manager's challenge. The strategies described in this book will help develop a welcoming culture that values individuals regardless of culture, intellect, talents, gender, or age. Strong communication skills will help managers connect with others in a deep and direct way and develop relationships that will bridge differences.

SUMMARY

Given the changes occurring in the world marketplace and the increasingly competitive nature of markets both at home and abroad, firms must become more active internationally to survive and prosper. These trends and developments all suggest that today's students have a noteworthy chance of becoming tomorrow's international business professionals. To be successful international businesspeople, they will have to be successful intercultural communicators.

A person's culture is pervasive, a body of common understanding with which they feel comfortable. But cultures differ appreciably, and those differences must be understood and accepted if cross-cultural business ventures are to succeed. The world has not yet become one big global village, and people are not all alike. In fact, the opposite is true—as we become globalized, we hold onto aspects of our cultural uniqueness. International businesspeople must still work to bridge the cultural gaps that exist among the peoples of the world.

For short business trips to another country, it is probably not necessary to learn the language of that country. For longer stays, it might be a good idea to do so. Learning the language frees the businessperson from having to rely on interpreters. It also lessens the chances of encountering the interpretational disasters some companies have experienced in their advertising and product labeling. Most important, it offers insights into the local culture.

Regardless of whether or not the language of the host country is learned, international businesspeople need to become nonverbally sensitive, tuning in to different greeting rituals and standards of dress, as well as the way in which space, touch, gestures, and posture are dealt with. They need to accept patiently others' interpretations of time, to be open to culinary adventures, and to be familiar with gift-giving rituals and bribery laws.

Good intercultural communicators are not ethnocentric, are nondefensive about their homeland in the face of questions about its problems, are curious about other people and brave with regard to the conditions they might have to confront, are empathic and understanding and nonjudgmental of intercultural partners, are patient in living with ambiguity and expecting the unexpected, and are genuinely personable to the people of the culture with whom they are conducting business.

Finally, managers who accept the possibility of an international assignment or career should seize whatever opportunities are available to prepare themselves. They might consider learning the local language. They should investigate the social and academic development programs available. Additionally, they need to stay abreast of business, economic, and political developments throughout the world and the opportunities that arise from them. Managers who are denied an international experience can still develop cultural sensitivity. By doing so, they ensure that their employees perceive the workplace as just, respectful of differences, and fair.

CASES FOR ANALYSIS

Case 12-1

Coming to Terms With Age

In the aftermath of the Vietnam War, Oanh Ngo Usadi and her family were exiled from Saigon to the Mekong Delta and ultimately escaped to Port Arthur, a small town in Texas, in the United States. Usadi wrote a memoir describing these traumatic transitions as she and her family adapted to new environments and cultures. In her book, *Of Monkey Bridges and Bánh Mì Sandwiches: From Sài Gòn to Texas*, she explains that the Vietnamese language has countless words for "I" and "you" based largely on age.[51] Speakers select a form of address to show the appropriate level of respect, especially to someone older. So, for instance, she was called "child" or "younger sister" during her early years. Then she became "older sister" to little kids and gradually shifted into "younger aunt" in her 20s, though she remained "child" to anyone older than she.

Living in Texas, Usadi was called only "miss" as a child, then suddenly as an adult in her 30s,

someone addressed her as "ma'am." She writes in her memoir that she felt proud, with a deep sense of something gained. But 20 years later, the term "ma'am" made her feel old, with a vague sense of something lost. Ultimately she came to realize how culture and experience affect our interpretation of language. "Where I once embraced each age distinction as a promotion, I now just want to stay put. I . . . am very glad that English has no designations after 'ma'am' despite all the respect that other titles in Vietnamese might confer."[52]

Questions

1. To what extent does the English language tie one's identity to others? Or is "I" always how English speakers refer to themselves and "you" always how they refer to others despite age and status differences? How does this fact about the English language reflect a cultural value?

2. Why do you think Oanh Ngo Usadi felt proud the first time she was called "ma'am"? Describe a time when you had a similar experience, such as the first time someone addressed you as "boss." What revelations did you have from this event concerning your relationship with others in your environment?

3. Which of Hofstede's dimensions of cultural differences, as described in this chapter, are relevant to this case?

Case 12-2

Intercultural Business Communication and Technology

Bryan Kilter opened the e-mail from his Chinese supplier. It seemed to be a request to alter some of the garment patterns currently in Kilter Fashions' standard inventory items. Bryan was beginning to become overwhelmed with his relationship with the Chinese garment manufacturer. He did not speak Chinese, and the supplier did not speak English, so they both depended on software translation when they exchanged messages. This particular e-mail read, "Sweetheart Bryan, The dress have cheap wide contraction joints in the seams, if you get the goods to wear inappropriate, you can own in a local sewing shop click on it. The Costs need to accept yourself, Hope you can understanding us. Approve changes please don't correspond by click here."

The e-mail had just come in, so Bryan quickly replied: "Hello, Chin Lee. Are you saying that the new design will have an elastic panel in the sides, so that it will be easier to fit without alterations? I think I understand that the dress will cost $0.70 more now. Please let me know if I understand you correctly. Thanks."

Bryan went back to work on the end-of-month inventory. Before 5 minutes had gone by, he received a reply from Chin Lee: "Sweetheart Bryan, The seams wear inappropriate for contraction joints, why not question your meaning.

Your own construction technician able to do construct. OK?"

Bryan scratched his head in bewilderment.

Questions

1. What challenges in conducting business across cultural divides does this case demonstrate?

2. What specifically would you suggest to Bryan as the next step?

Case 12-3

Preparing for Sonora

You are a human resources training specialist working for a large automaker. Your company will soon complete construction of a plant in Sonora, Mexico. This plant will specialize in the production of your very popular subcompact, the Chaperone.

Initially, all the new plant's management will be transferred from various locations in the United States. Later, supervisors will be promoted from the ranks of the Mexican nationals hired to work on the production line. It is hoped that many of these supervisors will eventually rise to the ranks of at least middle management.

The company now faces a twofold problem, however. First, it needs to identify the criteria used to select the managers who are going to be transferred from the United States to the Sonora plant. Second, it needs to train them to function in a different culture.

Because you earned an international business certificate along with your degree in human resources management, your boss has decided that this job is right for you. She believes this to be true even though your familiarity with Mexico is limited to two coastal vacations there 3 and 4 years ago.

She wants a three-page proposal, in memo form, on her desk in 2 days. The first page should cover the criteria to be used in selecting the managers to be sent to Sonora. She notes that you

(Continued)

(Continued)

need not bother with their technical expertise. Others will screen the candidates on that basis. You should instead focus on the qualifications they should have to be good intercultural managers and communicators and how the company should assess those qualifications.

The remaining two pages of the memo should outline the training program through which the transferees would go. This program will have to cover, at a minimum, language training, the larger cultural variations, nonverbal sensitivity, managerial philosophies, and organizational cultures in the two countries.

Project

Write a memo that will establish the foundation for success in this international venture. Your selection criteria should single out the candidates with the greatest potential for success. Your training program should then ensure that they will achieve that success.

Case 12-4

Tsunami Relief

A $245 million stretch of blacktop intended to be the signature goodwill gesture from the U.S. people to the Indonesian survivors of the 2004 tsunami instead became a parable of the problems of Aceh Province's recovery.

Construction of the 150-mile road along the devastated coast never started, stalled by a host of obstacles like acquiring rights of way through residential areas and farmland and, particularly, through several hundred graves of mystical and religious significance.

Though some villagers welcomed the idea, some had reservations about a U.S.-style thoroughfare with a wide shoulder on either side that would replace the existing ribbon of mostly churned dirt and mud. Villagers said they feared speeding traffic—they threw rocks at fast-traveling cars of foreign aid workers—and wanted to be able to sell snacks and tea from stalls snug by the roadside, as they had always done.

A demonstration outside the main Indonesian reconstruction agency turned violent when protesters complained that they still lacked basic services and demanded more financing for education.

The patience of U.S. officials wore thin, too. They complained that the government had been too slow in buying up the land and resolving the issue of graves. Finally, the U.S. officials had become so disconcerted about delays that they had tried to pry more action from the Indonesians by suggesting that the money for the road would be diverted to the reconstruction efforts in Lebanon.

"It was threatened they would take the money away," said Kuntoro Mangk Usubroto, the director of the Indonesian rehabilitation and reconstruction agency in Aceh. "That's standard."

The Indonesians said the United States was imposing first-world standards of efficiency on a poor region that was pounded by civil war and then swamped by the tsunami, which killed more than 100,000. Records of land titles were washed away, and questions of inheritance among devastated families take a while to decide what they say.

The idea for the road evolved soon after the tsunami when the Bush administration wanted to show that the United States cared about Indonesia, the world's most populous Muslim country, in its moment of need.

It was decided early on to finance one substantial project rather than a number of smaller ones. At first, rebuilding a significant portion of the provincial capital, Banda Aceh, into a kind of "signature city" was discussed. Instead, a well-engineered road from the capital to Meulaboh, the southernmost coastal town, which was nearly completely wiped out, was considered a more fruitful project that played to the U.S. strength of fast and modern construction. The new road would connect the poor fishing communities of the wasted west coast of Aceh to the outside world.

Questions

1. Identify the cultural values that are clashing in this case.

2. Which dimensions of cultural differences in Hofstede's model are relevant to this case?

EXERCISE

Exercise 12-1

In groups, share stories about your experiences with cultural differences regarding each of the following nonverbal elements. In particular, talk about a time when you misinterpreted the nonverbal signals and what happened as a result. Select the best story in your group and be prepared to share it with the rest of the class.

- Facial expressions and eye contact
- Body movements and gestures
- Clothing and personal appearance
- Distance and personal space
- Physical environment
- Time

Notes

1. U.S. Department of Commerce, International Trade Administration, "Top U.S. Trade Partners," https://legacy.trade.gov/mas/ian/build/groups/public/@tg_ian/documents/webcontent/tg_ian_003364.pdf.

2. Ruchir Sharma, "Small Is the New Big Thing," *New York Times,* December 29, 2019, SR3.

3. KOF Swiss Economic Institute, "KOF Globalisation Index 2019," https://kof.ethz.ch/en/forecasts-and-indicators/indicators/kof-globalisation-index.html.

4. Global Business Alliance, "Foreign Direct Investment," https://globalbusiness.org/about-us/foreign-direct-investment/foreign-direct-investment.

5. Ruchir Sharma, "To Be Great Again, America Needs Immigrants," *New York Times,* May 7, 2017, SR7.

6. Roy Maurer, "Survey: Companies Fail to Train Managers for Overseas Assignments," Society for Human Resource Management, July 8, 2013, https://www.shrm.org/resourcesandtools/hr-topics/global-hr/pages/fail-train-managers-overseas-assignments.aspx.

7. John W. Gould, as cited in Norman B. Sigband and Arthur H. Bell, *Communication for Management and Business,* 4th ed. (Glenview, IL: Scott Foresman, 1986), 69–70.

8. Malcolm Gladwell, *Outliers: The Story of Success* (New York: Little, Brown and Company, 2008), 175.

9. For a review of the different worldviews captured by the concepts of "Gemeinschaft" (village, community) and "Gesellschaft" (anonymous large city), see Val Larsen and Sweta Chaturvedi Thota, "Truth and Consequences in the Global Village," *Academy of Marketing Studies Journal* 18, no. 1 (2014): 217–34.

10. Francis Fukuyama, *The End of History and the Last Man* (New York: Free Press, 1992).

11. Matthew Taylor, "Scenes of Distress: Reflections on Francis Fukuyama's 'End of History,'" *Anthropoetics: The Journal of Generative Anthropology* 22, no. 2 (Spring 2017): 1–18.

12. Esther Schor, *Bridge of Words: Esperanto and the Dream of a Universal Language* (New York: Metropolitan Books, 2016). See also Joan Acocella, "A Language to Unite Humankind," *New Yorker,* October 31, 2016, http://www.newyorker.com/magazine/2016/10/31/a-language-to-unite-humankind.

13. Milton J. Bennett, "A Developmental Approach to Training for Intercultural Sensitivity,"

International Journal of Intercultural Relations 10 (1986): 179–96.

14. Ginka Toegel and Jean-Louis Barsoux, "3 Situations Where Cross-Cultural Communication Breaks Down," *Harvard Business Review*, June 2016, https://hbr.org/2016/06/3-situations-where-cross-cultural-communication-breaks-down.

15. Geert Hofstede, "Motivation, Leadership and Organization: Do American Theories Apply Abroad?" *Organizational Dynamics*, Summer 1980, 42–63. For a summary of recent Hofstede-based research in international business, see Sjoerd Beugelsdijk, Tatiana Kostova, and Kendall Roth, "An Overview of Hofstede-Inspired Country-Level Culture Research in International Business Since 2006," *Journal of International Business Studies* 48, no. 1 (January 2017): 30–47.

16. Hofstede, "Motivation, Leadership and Organization," 51.

17. Gladwell, *Outliers*, 177–223.

18. Ibid.

19. Hofstede, "Motivation, Leadership and Organization," 51.

20. Ibid.

21. Richard Conrad, *Culture Hacks: Deciphering Differences in American, Chinese, and Japanese Thinking* (Lioncrest Publishing, 2019), 12–22. See also Richard E. Nisbett, *The Geography of Thought: How Asians and Westerners Think Differently . . . and Why* (New York: Free Press, 2003), 51–56.

22. Geert Hofstede and Associates, *Masculinity and Femininity: The Taboo Dimension of National Cultures* (Thousand Oaks, CA: Sage, 1998), 37.

23. Edward T. Hall, *Beyond Culture* (Garden City, NY: Anchor Press/Doubleday, 1977).

24. Hofstede, "Motivation, Leadership and Organization," 52.

25. Ibid.

26. Robyn Walker, *Strategic Management Communication for Leaders*, 3rd ed. (Stamford, CT: Cengage Learning, 2015), 91–92.

27. Yong-Kang Wei, "Projecting Ethos Through 'About Us': A Comparative Study of American and Chinese Corporations' Websites" (unpublished paper presented at the First Annual General Business Conference, Sam Houston State University, April 18, 2009). See also Pinfan Zhu, "Impact of Business Cultural Values on Web Homepage Design That May Hinder International Business," *Journal of Technical Writing and Communication* 46, no. 1 (2016): 105–24.

28. Erin Meyer, *The Culture Map: Breaking Through the Invisible Boundaries of Global Business* (New York: Public Affairs, 2015), 219–42.

29. Conrad, *Culture Hacks*, 14.

30. Meyer, *The Culture Map*, 219.

31. Barbara Parker, *Introduction to Globalization and Business: Relationships and Responsibilities* (Thousand Oaks, CA: Sage, 2005): 412–19.

32. John Hilton, "How PepsiCo Is Supporting Gender Diversity," *HRD Magazine*, April 23, 2018, https://www.hcamag.com/au/specialisation/corporate-wellness/how-pepsico-is-supporting-gender-diversity/152193.

33. Camille Ryan, *Language Use in the United States: 2011* (Washington, DC: U.S. Census Bureau, August 2013), https://www.census.gov/prod/2013pubs/acs-22.pdf.

34. Eurostat, "Foreign Language Skills Statistics," *Statistics Explained*, April 2019, https://ec.europa.eu/eurostat/statistics-explained/index.php/Foreign_language_skills_statistics#Number_of_foreign_languages_known.

35. Nisbett, *The Geography of Thought*.

36. Lennox Morrison, "Native English Speakers Are the World's Worst Communicators," *BBC*

Capital, October 31, 2016, http://www.bbc.com/capital/story/20161028-native-english-speakers-are-the-worlds-worst-communicators.

37. James Hookway, "IKEA's Products Make Shoppers Blush in Thailand," *Wall Street Journal*, June 5, 2012, https://www.wsj.com/articles/SB10001424052702304707604577422073271517262.

38. Elizabeth Martin, *Marketing Identities through Language: English and Global Imagery in French Advertising* (London, UK: Palgrave Macmillan, 2005), 39.

39. Jeanette S. Martin and Lillian H. Chaney, *Global Business Etiquette: A Guide to International Communication and Customs*, 2nd ed. (Santa Barbara, CA: Praeger, 2012), 23–32.

40. Ibid.

41. Mark L. Knapp, Judith A. Hall, and Terrence G. Horgan, *Nonverbal Communication in Human Interaction*, 8th ed. (Boston: Wadsworth, 2014).

42. Transparency International, "Foreign Bribery Rages Unchecked in Over Half of Global Trade," September 12, 2018, https://www.transparency.org/en/news/exporting-corruption-2018.

43. Martin and Chaney, *Global Business Etiquette*, 38–40.

44. Bennett, "A Developmental Approach to Training," 184–86.

45. R. Krishnaveni and R. Arthi, "An Overview of Multidimensional Factors Influencing Effective Performance of Expatriates," *Management: Journal of Contemporary Management Issues* 20, no. 2 (December 1, 2015): 135–47.

46. Mark Twain, *The Innocents Abroad, or The New Pilgrims Progress* (Hartford, CT: American Publishing Company, 1869).

47. David G. Collings and Michael Isichei, "The Shifting Boundaries of Global Staffing: Integrating Global Talent Management, Alternative Forms of International Assignments and Non-Employees Into the Discussion," *The International Journal of Human Resource Management* 29, no. 1 (2018): 165–87, https://doi.org/10.1080/09585192.2017.1380064.

48. Kara Laverde and Cory Bouck, "A Collaborative Approach Advances Global Mindset as a Competency," *TD: Talent Development* 68, no. 9 (September 2014): 48–52. See also Tsedal Neeley and Robert S. Kaplan, "What's Your Language Strategy?" *Harvard Business Review*, September 2014, 70–76.

49. Mihaela Dimitrova et al., "Forgotten Travelers: Adjustment and Career Implications of International Business Travel for Expatriates," *Journal of International Management* 26, no. 1 (March 2020), https://doi.org/10.1016/j.intman.2019.100707.

50. Howard J. Ross, *Reinventing Diversity: Transforming Organizational Community to Strengthen People, Purpose, and Performance* (Lanham, MD: Rowman & Littlefield, 2013).

51. Oanh Ngo Usadi, *Of Monkey Bridges and Bánh Mì Sandwiches: From Sài Gòn to Texas* (New Jersey: O&O Press, 2018).

52. Oanh Ngo Usadi, "An Age-Old Query: Coming to Terms With the Years," *Houston Chronicle*, April 14, 2019, A29.

COMMUNICATING INTERPERSONALLY

COMMUNICATING
INTERPERSONALLY

13

MANAGING CONFLICT

The world seems to be full of conflict. Conflict is also pervasive at the corporate level, as demonstrated by the frequency of mergers, acquisitions, and unfriendly takeovers.

Within companies, tensions can also run high. A recent study indicates that nearly 15 percent of U.S. employees do not feel safe at work, and one third do not know what to do if they witness or experience workplace violence.[1] Workplace violence is physical violence, harassment, intimidation, or other threatening behavior that disrupts the workplace.[2] Threats and violent behavior may come from colleagues or customers. Managers must protect workers from violence by developing intervention efforts, including training in conflict resolution.

According to a survey of executives by the staffing firm Accountemps, managers spend about 15 percent of their time dealing with conflict, a number that has not changed much in the past 30 years.[3] Conflict may occur as a simple disagreement over the meaning of a work procedure, or it may be an argument over priorities and involve deciding which of two projects should draw from the limited funds available for project development. Personality differences, real or perceived inequities of resources, incomplete information and uncertainty, and poor communication are all common causes of conflict at work.[4]

Managers were asked to describe the type of conflicts in which they became involved. One manager described a situation in which four computer programmers wanted to go to a training seminar, but funds were available for only one. Another manager described how both she and a colleague wanted to take their vacations at the same time. Their manager said they could not do that and told them to work out the schedule between them. In both these situations, conflicts had to be resolved.

Organizational conflict is a natural part of the traditional organizational structure because a built-in opposition between units often exists. The causes of workplace conflict are complicated and situational, but factors correlated with conflict include

- unclear business goals, ambiguous roles, time pressure, and uncomfortable work environments;

- an organizational culture that permits bullying and discourages open communication;

- autocratic and laissez-faire leadership styles;

- office politics and performance-based reward systems that favor bullying behavior to get work done; and

- organizational change, including changes in management, staffing, and budget.[5]

In fact, organizational conflict is so pervasive that more than 75 university-affiliated centers, institutes, associations, and consortia are dedicated to research on this subject. One such organization, the Association for Conflict Resolution (ACR), has more than 6,000 members: mediators, arbitrators, facilitators, educators, and others involved in the field of conflict resolution and collaborative decision making. The ACR has chapters in nine U.S. states.

An increasing number of companies are also creating programs that help employees resolve their problems quickly and without external intervention. The policies are integrated into the corporate culture and use a variety of approaches, including hotlines, peer-review panels, mediation, and arbitration, to resolve conflicts.

BENEFITS OF CONFLICT

Conflict generally has a negative connotation; however, conflict is a positive occurrence if managed properly. Conflict requires managers to analyze their goals, creates dialogue among employees, and fosters creative solutions. Without conflict, employees and organizations would stagnate.

Generational conflict in the workplace is one example of how conflict can have positive effects. For the first time in U.S. history, five generations are working together. Possibilities for conflict run high because of differences in work style and philosophy. Tammy Erickson, author of *Plugged In: The Generation Y Guide to Thriving at Work*, compared generational preferences for communicating in team environments. She described Boomers and Generation Xers as "planners and schedulers," while Millennials are "coordinators" who prefer to get together only as needed and who find the extent of scheduling that goes on in most workplaces to be inefficient. Team leaders working with colleagues from other generations need to avoid forming negative conclusions, to bring team members' diverse communication preferences out in the open, and to help the team legitimize each person's view. Teams can decide together which norms will work best for the team and for the work that must be accomplished.[6]

Conflict also may foster creativity. Research suggests that moderate conflict yields higher-quality decisions than little or no conflict.[7] Task conflict helps overcome individual psychological distortions and biases by forcing people out of their traditional modes of thinking. In this way, conflict promotes the unstructured thinking that some see as required for developing good, novel alternatives to difficult problems.[8] The conflict is particularly useful in the early stages of teamwork, when the group is establishing goals and tasks, and less useful near the end of the project.[9]

CRITICAL THINKING QUESTIONS

1. To what extent do age, culture, or value differences among employees at your workplace cause conflicts?

2. How can these differences be beneficial to productivity?

Thus, managers who pride themselves on running a smooth ship may not be as effective as they think. The smooth ship may reflect suppressed conflict that could have potential benefit if allowed free play. In fact, the conflict might not be as harmful as its suppression.

What causes conflict? When is it functional, and when is it not? What methods can be used to resolve conflict? Is any one method best? The following discussion answers these questions, but first we review the relationship between communication and conflict.

THE RELATIONSHIP BETWEEN COMMUNICATION AND CONFLICT

As is true with many other terms, *conflict* has both a colloquial meaning and a long list of specific definitions. However, a quick review of these definitions will help describe the nature of conflict. Daniel Katz and Robert Kahn state that two systems—which could include persons, groups, organizations, or nations—are in conflict when they interact directly in such a way that the actions of one tend to prevent or compel some outcome against the resistance of the other.[10] Another author states that conflict characterizes a situation in which the conditions, practices, or goals of individuals are inherently incompatible.[11] A third definition presents conflict as a struggle over values or claims to scarce resources, power, or status. In this struggle, opponents aim to neutralize, injure, or eliminate their rivals.[12]

These three definitions help define the nature of conflict and indicate the role of communication in conflict. The first definition uses the word *interact*, implying a communication interaction of some kind. The second definition uses the phrase *inherently incompatible*, and the third definition includes *a struggle over values*. Communication is the method by which managers determine whether something is inherently incompatible, and the struggle over values is carried out through communication behaviors. Thus, the ability to communicate effectively may eliminate conflict immediately; however, ineffective communication may cause a situation to appear inherently incompatible; thus, a struggle over values may ensue. The conclusion is that communicative behavior may cause as well as resolve conflict.

Let us examine the specific characteristics of conflict and the corresponding implications for communication. The following four axioms are particularly relevant to communication.[13] These axioms are reviewed to demonstrate how effective communication can make conflict a constructive, positive process.

1. *Conflict involves at least two parties.* Because conflict involves at least two parties, communication is an integral component. Conflict can be generated or resolved only through communication. Consequently, managers must understand the types of communication interactions that can cause conflict and the communication patterns that are most functional after conflict has developed. In fact, a good communicator can bring conflict to the surface and make it a productive process.

2. *Conflict develops from perceived mutually exclusive goals.* Mutually exclusive goals may exist as a result of objective facts or an individual's values and perceptions. However, the key factor is that the parties involved perceive the objectives as mutually exclusive. But only through communication can the parties in conflict determine the existence of a superordinate goal that may meet both parties' goals. Again, the positive nature of conflict is evident because without conflict the parties may not know about the superordinate goal.

3. *Conflict involves parties who may have different values or perceptions.* To illustrate how conflictive parties may have different value systems, consider how a first-level supervisor who was once a member of a trade union would have values much different from those of a college-educated engineer. This value difference may result in a potential conflict when the two employees consider implementing a computerized production control system. The supervisor could perceive the computerized system as too difficult to learn and as a threat to employees' job security. However, the engineer might perceive it solely as an engineering challenge. In this case, values affect perception.

   The selective-attention principle says that we tend to perceive what is important and pleasing to us and avoid what is not. The following example shows how differences in perception led to a major conflict.[14] A textile mill allowed a conflict to develop that resulted in a big labor turnover. The mill had informed employees when they were hired that it gave automatic raises each year and merit raises for deserving employees after 9 and 18 months. The employees, however, understood this to mean they would receive an automatic raise at *all three* of these periods—9, 12, and 18 months. When they did not obtain their raises, many of them quit because they thought the employer had not maintained the original promise to grant wage increases. In this case, the differences between employee and employer perception led to conflicting views.

   When conflicting parties have different values or perceptions, communication is important in two ways. First, exposure and communication between two individuals will likely result in the individuals eventually sharing values and becoming friendlier toward each other.[15] Second, as more accurate communication develops between two managers, the perceptual differences will subside; hence, the probability of conflict will be reduced.

Chapter 1 indicated that diversity is increasing in organizations. This diversity will create conflict, but it will be exciting and productive because diverse viewpoints, when managed appropriately, will result in more creative outcomes.

4. *Conflict terminates only when each side is satisfied that it has won or lost.* Win–lose situations seem to dominate U.S. culture—for instance, law courts use the adversary system, and political parties strive to win elections. Competition to win in sports is so keen that fights among spectators are not uncommon. The pervasive win–lose attitude in U.S. culture has made it difficult to imagine that both parties may "win" in any situation labeled a conflict. This problem recalls the second axiom, which states that conflict develops from mutually exclusive goals. However, accurate communication may reveal that a win or a loss is not the only alternative.

SOURCES OF CONFLICT

When managers perceive conflict in the workplace, they may assume it is due to incompatible personalities. "Why can't everyone just get along with each other?" they plead. But managers need to understand that the sources of conflict are often deeper than individual personality. Then they will be better able to select the appropriate communication strategy. The underlying causes or sources of conflict situations often are built into the organization's hierarchy and ways of doing business.

The lines of authority in an organization can encourage conflict. For example, the lending and the savings departments are interdependent in all banks. The lending department cannot lend funds until the savings department has collected funds. By the same token, the savings department would be hard pressed if the lending department had no customers. These two areas have common goals within the bank (profit and continued operation of the bank), but their interdependence can lead to conflict over their respective authority. While the savings department would like to give high interest rates to please its customers, the lending department wants to provide low interest rates to please its customers. When the interdependence of these departments becomes a central issue, conflict will arise over whose authority takes precedence or whose responsibility for the bank's profit goal is more relevant.

CRITICAL THINKING QUESTIONS

1. In your work experience, which departments were in conflict most often?

2. How could these conflicts be resolved?

The distribution of the limited resources available in an organization is another source of conflict. If resources were unlimited, few conflicts would arise, but this condition seldom exists. When resources are limited and more than one person or group wants a share, conflict develops. The most obvious conflict occurs during the annual budget review.

With funds traditionally limited, it is necessary to decide which department will get what amount. Because each department manager's goal appears most important from their own perspective, the funds allocated to one department may appear to be funds taken from another. The interdependency of the various departments vying for budget allocations thus can become a major source of conflict.

Diverse goals are a third source of organizational conflict. For instance, clashes may occur between quality-assurance managers and production managers in a manufacturing environment. The goal of the quality people is zero defects, while the goal of production is filling the customer's order on time. Conflicting goals and roles can also explain why a company's salespeople routinely ignore the accounting staff's requests for expense forms and receipts or why a shift foreman refuses to let his workers attend an employee development session offered by human resources. To alleviate such traditional conflicts between functional units, senior executives should remind their managers of the overarching goals, mission, and vision.

Conflict and Perception

The relationship between conflict and perception has already been briefly discussed. Perceived conflict is present when the parties misunderstand one another's true position.

Clearly, identifying potentially conflictive situations may prevent conflicts from developing immediately. More often, though, the inaccurate or illogical perception of a situation causes unnecessary conflict. An example of inaccurate perception is the case of manager praise. A poll by Maritz Incentives found wide-ranging opinions on appreciation in the workplace: 55 percent of employees said their bosses never or rarely thank them for their efforts. On the other hand, only 6 percent of supervisors said they never praise their direct reports; 34 percent said they praise their direct reports daily, and 45 percent said they do so weekly or monthly.[16] It is easy to see how this discrepancy of perceptions can lead to conflict.

The grid in Figure 13-1 shows why inaccurate perceptions create conflict in the managerial process. Assume two managers are discussing an issue. Two possibilities exist for each manager: Each correctly perceives the existence of a potential conflict or incorrectly perceives it. This results in the four possibilities diagrammed. The grid shows that an accurate mutual perception could possibly exist in only one of four occurrences. Of course, this is not always the case, but numerous conflicts not warranted by the actual situation may develop.

FIGURE 13-1 ■ Accuracy of Perceptions and Conflict

		Manager 2	
		Accurate	Inaccurate
Manager 1	Accurate	Accurate mutual perception	Inaccurate mutual perception
	Inaccurate	Inaccurate mutual perception	Inaccurate mutual perception

Further, two managers may be aware of serious disagreement over a policy, but it may not create any anxiety or affect their feelings toward one another. Competition for budget allocations, for example, do not need to be personalized.

Personally felt conflict may find expression in fear, threat, mistrust, and hostility. Consider the bank teller who called in a bomb threat on the day he was fired, so that he could meet his former coworkers for drinks. No one knows the financial costs of such workplace revenge behaviors, but everyone agrees that a lack of communication causes most employee sabotage. "Getting back is the way of communicating when you can't, or when you're afraid to speak up for yourself," explains William Lundin, a workplace relations specialist.[17] Employees often retaliate by decreasing their effort, time spent at work, and quality of work.[18] Other forms of sabotage by disgruntled employees include deleting data, copying data, and blocking user access to systems.[19] The worst-case scenario is an incident of workplace violence. According to the U.S. Department of Labor, there were 500 workplace homicides in 2016.[20] And just as we prepare for natural disasters, we need to prepare for workplace violence.

What can managers do to prevent violence and acts of hostility? It is important to maintain a communication program that allows employees to understand the manager's expectations and how their performance level is being evaluated. If employees are issued an official warning or reprimand, it must explain the consequences of changing (and not changing) their behavior and offer an opportunity to discuss their problems.

De-escalation Strategies

If a conversation becomes hostile or an employee demonstrates aggressive behavior, the following steps may help you defuse anger:

1. Keep everyone safe, including yourself. If the employee's words or behavior suggest violence to themselves or others, call security. If the exit is clear, escort others from the room.

2. Do not respond in anger. Manage your emotions by breathing deeply and pausing to collect your thoughts.

3. Find out why they are angry. Don't interrupt. Be empathetic, acknowledge their feelings, and reflect back what they are saying to ensure you understand. Asking, "What else could this mean?" can help you empathize with the person. Fear, grief, stress, fatigue, and even normal hunger can cause people to respond in anger.

4. Monitor your nonverbal behaviors. Speak calmly and use nonthreatening gestures. Do not cross your arms or put your hands on your hips. Stand at a 45-degree angle rather than confronting the other person directly.

5. Try to find a solution by focusing on what can be done rather than what cannot. Choose positive wording and plain language for your responses. Use "I" and "we" statements rather than "you" statements to avoid putting the other person on the defensive. Do not threaten or argue. Remind them of shared goals and values.

The venting of hostility can be therapeutic rather than detrimental, if managed properly. Group discussions can act as a safety valve for this hostility, as can periodic meetings between supervisors and direct reports. Effective managers do not become defensive even when they are the focus of the hostile communication. Nondefensive communication is the key to managing personally felt conflict.

CRITICAL THINKING QUESTIONS

1. Think about a recent disagreement that became heated. What did you do to defuse the situation?

2. What shared goals and values could you have used as the focus of a resolution?

The observable behavior of the manager, based on conditions, perceptions, and feelings, may be seen as either conflict or an attempt to establish mutual goals. The most obvious manifestations of conflict are open aggression or violence at one end of a continuum and integrative problem solving at the other end, as depicted in Figure 13-2. A continuum is used because generally neither totally open aggression nor completely satisfactory problem solving is manifest. However, the goal is to move as close as possible to integrative problem solving. As the remainder of this discussion shows, managers have numerous ways to manage conflict along this continuum as they attempt to resolve it.

FIGURE 13-2   ■   Ways to Manifest Conflict

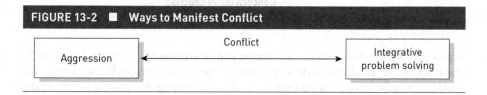

STRATEGIES FOR CONFLICT RESOLUTION

Now that we have looked at the relationship of conflict to managerial communication, discussed constructive conflict, and reviewed the sources of conflict, we can identify strategies for conflict resolution. Managerial communication strategies for managing conflict could be put into many categories. For our discussion, we use the system presented in Figure 13-3. This figure demonstrates that during a conflict, managers may emphasize interpersonal relations, task production, or a combination thereof. Five possible strategies are presented: avoiding, accommodating, forcing, compromising, and problem solving.[21]

While reviewing these strategies, the contingency approach to managerial communication should be kept in mind. Various conflict situations require different strategies, so effective communication requires that managers match the strategy to the situation.

Avoiding

The avoidance or withdrawal strategy combines a low concern for production with a low concern for people. The person using this style often sees conflict as a hopeless, useless

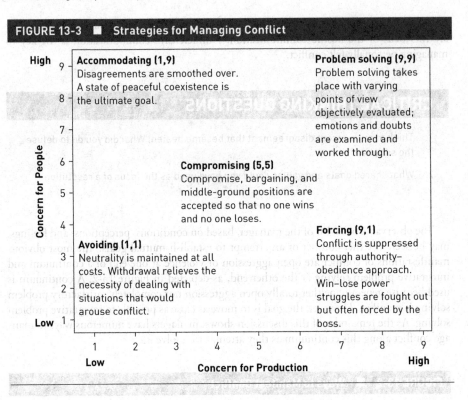

FIGURE 13-3 ■ Strategies for Managing Conflict

experience. Rather than undergo the tension and frustration of conflict, managers using the avoidance or withdrawal style simply remove themselves from conflict situations. This avoidance may be physical or psychological. The person using this strategy will avoid disagreement and tension, will not openly take sides in a disagreement between others, and will feel little commitment to any decisions reached.

This strategy is frequently used in large bureaucracies that have an overabundance of policies. Rather than attempt to resolve the conflict, managers simply blame it on *policy*. Managers who lack self-confidence in their communication abilities may hope the problem just disappears. However, this usually does not work. In fact, withdrawal from conflict has been negatively correlated with constructive conflict resolution. Withdrawal has been further negatively correlated with knowledge of the supervisor's feelings and attitudes; open, upward communication; helpfulness of the supervisor; and adequacy of the planning relationship. Thus, managers who avoid conflict do not operate effectively in these critical managerial areas.[22]

This avoidance strategy is associated with the laissez-faire leadership style.[23] Managers may use avoidance when situations contain too much uncertainty to make decisions. It can also be useful to help managers pick their battles, saving energy and social capital for more pressing concerns.

Avoidance need not be dramatic. Many managers avoid by ignoring a comment or quickly changing the subject when conversation begins to threaten. Another way to avoid is to place the responsibility for an issue on a higher manager. A third way to withdraw is to use a simple response of "I'm looking into the matter." The avoidance strategy can give the parties involved time to cool off before the conflict becomes too intense. It can also give them time to think about the source of the conflict, research the situation, and plan a new strategy.

Accommodating

In accommodating, the second type of conflict resolution, managers try to deal with conflict by making everyone happy. This approach emphasizes maintaining relationships with fellow employees and de-emphasizes achieving productive goals. When managers want others' acceptance or to be the peacemaker in tense situations, they will give in to others' desires in areas that conflict with their own. Managers using this style often believe confrontation is destructive. Constructive uses of the accommodating strategy are when the manager has a lower investment in the outcome than the other party, when the situation is flexible and other topics require a firm stance, and when the manager needs to be a "good soldier" and follow directions from above. But long-term use of this strategy can lead to burnout and low trust.[24]

Typical attempts to accommodate may include such things as calling for a coffee break at a tense moment, breaking tension with humor, changing the topic, or engaging in some ritual show of togetherness, such as an office birthday party. Because these efforts are likely to reduce felt conflict, they are more beneficial than simple avoidance. This reduction of felt conflict will probably have short-range effects and may even have some long-range benefit. However, just because someone does not experience a hostile or negative feeling does not mean the real cause of the conflict is resolved. In fact, accommodating is a camouflage approach that can break down at any time and create barriers to progress. Thus, research has found that it is used more in low- or medium-performance organizations than in high-performance organizations. In addition, accommodating style decreases as managers move up in an organization.[25]

Forcing

Forcing, the third conflict management strategy, is used by the manager who attempts to meet production goals at all costs, without concern for the needs or acceptance of others. For such a manager, losing is destructive because it is viewed as reduced status, weakness, and the loss of self-image. Winning must be achieved at any cost and gives this manager a sense of excitement and achievement. Not surprisingly, forcing is commonly used by managers who use an autocratic leadership style or focus on performance goals.[26] A situation characterized by the forcing strategy will probably cause later conflicts. The language managers use to describe conflict situations in their organizations often reflects the negative effect this style may have: *opposition, battle, fight, conquest, head-to-head, coercion,* and *smash*. Such language and imagery can result in long-lasting emotional wounds.[27] While force can resolve immediate disputes, the long-term effects will probably include a loss of productivity. Forcing in conflict situations negatively correlates with team development and may even trigger retaliation.[28] The major difficulty of a forcing strategy is that employees are reluctant to plan or carry out plans when they perceive that the ultimate resolution of the conflict will put them on the losing side of a win–lose position.

Interestingly, while little doubt exists that forcing has limited use, managers consider forcing to be their favorite backup strategy for dealing with conflict.[29] Immediate compliance is misperceived as a long-term solution in these cases.

The forcing strategy has limited constructive uses. It can defend the mission of the organization. It can permit managers to move quickly in times of crisis and respond decisively when violations of organizational values or community morals occur. It can also bring organizations into compliance with legal or policy constraints. But its heavy-handedness makes this a strategy of last resort.

Compromising

Compromise, the fourth strategy for conflict resolution, assumes that half a loaf is better than none. This approach falls somewhere between forcing and accommodating. Because compromise provides some gain for both sides rather than a unilateral victory, many participants judge this approach as better than the other strategies just discussed.

Compromise is used when one of three conditions exists: (1) Neither party involved believes they have the power to "force" the issue on the other party; (2) one or both of the parties believe winning may not be worth the cost in money, time, or energy; or (3) the situation is high-stakes and time-sensitive. Compromise is often highly related to negotiating, which is the topic of the next chapter; however, several important points are pertinent here. First, compromise may lead to both parties' perceiving themselves as winners, but they may also both feel like losers. A negative overtone may develop in the working relationship between the employees involved, and any sense of trust may break down. While both parties involved probably entered the negotiations with a cooperative attitude, a sense of competition may be the result of compromise.

A second concern with compromise is that the party with the most information has the better position. This power of information may restrict open communication among employees. This situation in turn often results in a lopsided compromise. A third factor is the principle of the least interested party: The party that has the least interest in the outcome is in the more powerful position in the negotiations. As a result, an employee who has little concern about the welfare of the company may have an inordinate amount of influence in a compromise.

Like the accommodating strategy, compromise works well if the goal is to maintain relationships and each party can easily prioritize their interests. But both sides must be able to give up some of their terms, and they must be able to live with only a partial win.

PROBLEM SOLVING: THE WIN–WIN STRATEGY

Thus far, it may seem that no totally acceptable, productive strategy exists to manage conflict. Fortunately, this is not the case. Problem solving, the fifth strategy to be discussed, is a win–win strategy for conflict. This complex and highly effective style requires skillful, strategic managerial communication, but it reaps a big dividend; thus, the remainder of our discussion centers on this strategy. Let us first describe the win–win strategy and then examine specific techniques for implementation.

Description of the Strategy

The key to this strategy is that it follows a mutual problem-solving approach rather than a combative one. In contrast to managers who use a forcing or avoiding strategy, managers engaged in problem solving assume that a high-quality, mutually acceptable solution is possible. The parties direct their energies toward defeating the problem and not each other.

The following example presents a clear description of the problem-solving approach to conflict resolution. It details a meeting in Wisconsin that set out to explore possible prison reforms.[30]

Nine of the state's top prison officials met to design an ideal correctional institution. In the course of the discussion, one group member proposed that uniforms traditionally worn by prison guards be eliminated. The group then began a lengthy argument about whether or not uniforms should be worn. One group member suggested that the issue be resolved democratically by vote. As a result, six people voted against uniforms, and three voted in favor of them. The winning members looked pleased, while the losing members either got angry or withdrew from further discussion.

A group consultant present at the time suggested that the members take another look at the situation. Then he asked those in favor of uniforms what they hoped to accomplish (establishing goals). Those officials stated that part of the rehabilitative process in correctional institutions is teaching people to deal constructively with authority, and they saw uniforms as a means for achieving the goal. When asked why they opposed uniforms (analyzing the problem), the other group members said that uniforms created such a stigma that guards had an additional difficulty laying to rest the stereotypes held by inmates before they could deal with them on a one-on-one basis. The group consultant then asked the group what ways might be appropriate to meet the combined goals, namely, teaching people to deal with authority and avoiding the difficulty of stereotypes held about traditional uniforms (generating solutions). While working on the problem, the group identified 10 possible solutions, including prison personnel using name tags, color-coded casual dress, or uniforms for guard supervisors but not for guards in constant contact with prisoners. After discussing the various alternatives, the group decided on the third solution (selecting the best solution).

In its first discussion, the group engaged in clear conflict that was only partially resolved by vote. In the discussion led by the consultant, the group turned to problem solving, eventually reaching consensus and a win–win solution.

Beliefs Necessary to Implement the Strategy

We are suggesting that the problem-solving strategy is the most desirable; however, a manager wanting to effectively use this approach must hold a series of beliefs.

Belief 1: Cooperation Is Better Than Competition

The manager must first believe cooperation is better than competition. U.S. management seems to be based on competition, so it is difficult to envision cooperation as a viable possibility at times.[31] This competition may develop out of Darwin's concept of survival of the fittest: A manager who has a self-image of weakness may fear extinction. Lacking confidence, this person feels a sense of competitiveness with others in the company.

CRITICAL THINKING QUESTIONS

1. In today's team-based work environment, why do employees continue to be evaluated on the basis of their individual achievements?

2. What would be the effect of rewarding employees on the basis of their team's achievements?

Competition also has an important role in stimulating employees to achieve more. However, as technology becomes more complex and employees more specialized, interdependence is required. Few tasks can be completed without the cooperation of many employees. The group as a whole becomes greater than the sum of all the individuals, so cooperation is required. This is not to say that differences of opinion should be prevented.

Different opinions can lead to new insights and creativity, as long as the opinions do not disrupt the group process. A manager must enter the conflict situation believing others' opinions are beneficial. The manager must be willing to listen. The emphasis on teamwork in today's work environment makes cooperation mandatory.

Belief 2: Parties Can Be Trusted

The second belief is that the other parties involved in the conflict can be trusted. Managers who are trusting will not conceal or distort relevant information, nor will they fear stating facts, ideas, conclusions, and feelings that would make them vulnerable.

In a study of group problem solving, half the groups were directed to trust other people, to express their views openly, to share information freely, and to aim at a high level of mutual confidence. The other groups were directed to behave in opposite ways. The researchers found that problem-solving groups with high trust will

- exchange relevant ideas and feelings more openly,

- develop greater clarification of goals and problems,

- search more extensively for alternative courses of action,

- have greater influence on solutions,

- be more satisfied with their problem-solving efforts,

- have greater motivation to implement conclusions,

- see themselves as closer and more of a team, and

- have less desire to leave their group to join another.[32]

Trusting behavior causes reciprocity. Trusting cues will likely evoke trusting behavior from others. Conversely, when a manager does not trust others, the cues to mistrust will evoke mistrustful behavior on the other's part. So it is best to assume a person can be trusted and to change that view only with evidence to the contrary.

Belief 3: Status Differences Can Be Minimized

The third belief that managers must possess is that status differences between parties can be minimized in a conflict situation. Differences in power or status that separate two individuals into a we–they orientation inhibit conflict resolution. A manager who is in a higher power position may yield to the temptation to use the power inherent in the position as the rationale for forcing the solution. If that happens, the participants, rather than confronting the problem and treating each other as equals, will regress into a win–lose style, and the result is much less productive. Managers who do not rely on status will spend time listening to everyone involved. The section in Chapter 10 on developing a listening climate provides ideas for managers who want to minimize their perceived power and encourage communication both upward and laterally.

Belief 4: Mutually Acceptable Solutions Can Be Found

The final belief managers must hold is that a mutually acceptable and desirable solution exists and can be found. Unless both parties believe this is possible, a win–lose strategy will result. Conflict resolution can be extremely frustrating and time-consuming unless both parties remain optimistic about finding a mutually acceptable answer. This is not to say that both parties are meeting the same goal. Rather, both parties can reach their different goals in an acceptable manner.

Each of these four beliefs—cooperation, trust, equal status, and mutually acceptable goals—is important. A manager must believe in these concepts to implement an effective win–win conflict resolution strategy. But belief in these concepts is not enough; managers must also use the appropriate communication skills in a strategic manner. The next part of this discussion describes these skills and the appropriate method for implementing them.

Implementing the Strategy

Specific steps should be followed to achieve the problem-solving strategy. However, before these steps are reviewed, key communication principles must be applied:

1. Use neutral rather than emotional terms. "I still tend to prefer my approach" is better than "Your idea is not functional."

2. Avoid absolute statements that leave no room for modification. "I think this is the way . . ." is better than "This is the *only* way."

3. Ask open-ended questions.

4. Avoid leading questions. This rule is especially important when status differences are present.

5. Repeat key phrases to make sure all parties are communicating on the same wavelength.

6. Use terms that all parties clearly understand.

7. Allow the other person to complete statements. Do not interrupt.

8. Use effective listening skills, especially paraphrasing, to ensure the other person's ideas are fully understood.

9. Be aware of the importance of physical arrangements. For instance, sitting in front of a big desk may cause a person to feel defensive.

When managers use the communication principles just presented as they follow the sequence given next, they should be able to resolve conflicts successfully.

The first step in implementing the problem-solving strategy is to maximize environmental conditions, as summarized in Table 13-1 and discussed as follows.

- *Review and adjust conflict conditions.* Earlier, we identified sources of conflict inherent in the organization, including goals and resources. When a manager can identify these conditions, it is sometimes possible to adjust them to promote cooperation.

- *Review and adjust perceptions.* Managers should adjust and correct their perceptions through reality testing: "Am I viewing the situation or the behavior as it actually exists?" Perceptions become more accurate as an individual learns more facts about the condition and has resulting impressions confirmed by others' perceptions.

- *Review and adjust attitudes.* Because an optimal outcome depends on trust, mutuality, and cooperation, little success will result if the parties are distrustful, hostile, and competitive. Accordingly, one should identify the attitudes and feelings of the parties engaged in the conflict as far as possible. Often, the best strategy is to start with the easily solved problems. Once the easier problems are solved, a more positive attitude develops for the more complex conflict situation. The trust that results may make cooperative communication easier.

Once environmental conditions and perceptions have been identified and perhaps adjusted, you are ready to begin the actual problem-solving strategy. John Dewey, a U.S. educator who lived and wrote in the early part of the 20th century, first articulated this process in one of his books, *How We Think.* More than 100 years later, this rational problem-solving process is still frequently and successfully used in contemporary businesses. The reason for the popularity of this process is that it really does conform to human thought; it is how we think. In Chapter 4, you learned Dewey's problem-solving process and how to apply it in meetings and team projects. Let us now review the six steps in the problem-solving process (summarized in Table 13-2) and see how they apply to conflict resolution.

TABLE 13-1 ■ Maximizing Environmental Conditions
Review and adjust conflict conditions
Review and adjust perceptions
Review and adjust attitudes

TABLE 13-2 ■ Dewey's Problem-Solving Process
1. Define the problem
2. Analyze the problem
3. Brainstorm alternatives
4. Develop criteria for a good solution
5. Evaluate the brainstormed alternatives using the criteria for a good solution
6. Implement the solution

1. *Define the problem.* A statement of the problem in a conflict situation is usually much more difficult than it seems. People tend to discuss solutions before they clearly define the problem. Because of this, our inclination is to state the problem as a lack of a given solution rather than as a goal. This results in ambiguous communication and mismatched goals. The outcome may be increased conflict. Second, managers must state the problem in the form of group goals rather than individual priorities. Third, the problem definition must be specific. One helpful strategy is to clearly write out the problem statement so that everyone can see it and agree on it. Stating the problem in a question format can help the group evaluate the solution as an acceptable answer.

2. *Analyze the problem.* Again, managers tend to want to skip this step. After all, they may argue, they live with the problem. What is the point of spending more time wallowing in it? Dewey's answer is that by exploring the depths of the problem, by looking at its history, causes, effects, and extent, one can later come up with a solution that addresses more than symptoms and that is more than a bandage. It will address the root cause of the problem, thus improving its chances of being successful.

3. *Brainstorm alternatives.* All parties should offer potential solutions. One idea may stimulate other ideas. The more employees communicate in an open, trusting environment, the greater the potential for generating effective solutions. Trust, of course, evaporates when an idea is criticized during a brainstorming session. As soon as someone says, "That's a terrible idea. It'll never work," who would be willing to take the risk of offering another idea? Managers must ensure that premature judging of solutions is avoided during this step.

4. *Develop criteria for a good solution.* These criteria or standards may already be in place and available. Other times, the organization's executives will specify to the problem-solving managers what a good solution must look like. Occasionally, the managers are expected to develop their own criteria. Common criteria for an optimal solution include the following: It must be cost-effective, it must be easily or quickly implemented, it must use only resources that are currently available, it must be legal, and it must be consistent with the organization's mission or values.

5. *Evaluate the brainstormed alternatives using the independently developed criteria for a good solution.* This is really the easiest step. By this time, attention to the problem is unified, and an open communication environment has been achieved with active participation by all the parties involved. The best solution appears automatically as the brainstormed alternative that matches your list of criteria.

6. *Implement the solution.* The analysis and discussion in the previous steps should result in commitment to the solution and confidence in its success. After the organization has adopted the solution, routine monitoring will help the group evaluate how well their decision is working and make suggestions for adjustments.

CONFLICT AND MANAGEMENT SUCCESS

The basic nature of organizational dynamics creates conflict.[33] As discussed earlier in this chapter, lines of authority, especially the supervisor–direct report relationship, often engender conflict. A typical example is when the supervisor provides corrective feedback and the direct report interprets it as aggressive, threatening, disrespectful, or offensive. Such negative emotions can escalate conflict and even prompt retaliation.[34] As a consequence, the professional relationship suffers, and employee morale and productivity decline. To minimize the damage triggered by poorly communicated feedback, managers must understand and learn to manage conflict (see Table 13-3).

This chapter proposes that communication is at the foundation of conflict management. Because conflict is a pervasive, vital, but often troublesome aspect of organizational life, effective conflict management has become a major focus for business and industry training programs.[35] Recent studies indicate that employee training that develops social and

TABLE 13-3 ■ When to Choose Each Conflict-Resolution Approach	
Conflict-Resolution Approach	**Context of Conflict**
Avoiding works best when	• There's little chance you'll get your way • The potential damage of addressing the conflict outweighs the benefits of resolution • People need a chance to cool down • Others are in a better position to resolve the conflict • The problem will go away by itself
Accommodating works best when	• Preserving harmony is important • Personal antagonism is the major source of conflict • The issue itself is unsolvable • You care more about the other person than getting your way
Forcing works best when	• Quick, decisive action is needed • A rule has to be enforced • You know you're right • You must protect yourself or the company
Compromising works best when	• Two opponents are equal in power • Temporary settlements on complex issues are needed • Opponents do not share goals • There is latitude about acceptable solutions • A deadline is looming • Forcing or problem solving won't work
Problem solving works best when	• Both sets of concerns are too important to be compromised • It is important to work through hard feelings • Commitment to the resolution is important • A permanent solution is desired

emotional competency (popularly known as emotional intelligence, or EI) is a better predictor of professional success than cognitive intelligence or specialized knowledge.[36] Daniel Goleman's landmark book about EI listed six noncognitive competencies that help people cope with workplace pressures and the resulting conflict. These competencies are generally accepted as the starting point for employee training in emotion management:

- Become self-aware in managing emotions and controlling impulses

- Set goals and perform well

- Be motivated and creative

- Empathize with others

- Handle relationships effectively

- Develop appropriate social skills[37]

Mastery of these competencies greatly affects the way employees interact with their coworkers, direct reports, and managers. Clearly, whether one is a college student anticipating a career in management or a practicing manager with years of experience, it is necessary to continually hone constructive communication strategies for conflict management.

SUMMARY

Managers are likely to spend at least 15 percent of their time dealing with some kind of conflict, so it is important to understand the causes of conflict and productive methods for resolution. Because miscommunication is an integral element behind conflict, effective managerial communication is one key to resolution.

Conflict can be constructive as well as destructive. The nature of the word *conflict* implies opposing positions with negative results; however, when properly managed, conflict may be a positive force. An important managerial role is to be able to identify the difference between destructive and constructive conflict.

Managers can use one of five strategies to resolve conflict: avoiding, accommodating, forcing, compromising, or problem solving. The first four strategies are termed win–lose or lose–lose because one or both parties in the conflict will lose. Although each may be appropriate for specific situations, none yield fully satisfying solutions. However, the fifth strategy is termed a win–win approach because both parties in the conflict are potential winners; consequently, the effective manager should strive for the win–win style.

The problem-solving strategy can be achieved when the manager believes in cooperation, trusts the other party, minimizes status differences, and believes a mutually acceptable and desirable solution is available. These beliefs are a prerequisite to success, but satisfactory results cannot be obtained unless sound communication principles are used to put the beliefs into action. A sequence of steps should be followed when implementing the win–win strategy: review and adjust conflict conditions, perceptions, and attitudes; develop a problem definition; analyze the problem; brainstorm alternatives; evaluate alternatives according to criteria and identify the best solution; and implement the solution.

When a manager uses strategic communication skills, believes in the win–win approach to conflict resolution, and follows the correct sequence of activities, a constructive approach to conflict resolution can result.

CASES FOR ANALYSIS

Case 13-1

A Fallen Unicorn: Theranos Leader Quashed Constructive Conflict

What if a wide range of laboratory tests could be performed from a single drop of blood? That is the premise on which Theranos, a Silicon Valley startup, was based. Theranos's founder and CEO, Elizabeth Holmes, claimed she had developed technology that would make blood tests not only convenient but more accurate, faster, and cheaper. Long waits for crucial test results, misdiagnoses, and unnecessary treatments would be eliminated. At its height in 2015, Theranos's valuation was $10 billion. A *Fortune* cover story compared Holmes to Bill Gates and Steve Jobs, other Silicon Valley entrepreneurs. Unfortunately, the blood testing devices didn't work.

Holmes was a college dropout with no medical or scientific training, yet her energetic, confident speaking style inspired others to adopt her vision. She easily convinced wealthy venture capitalists to invest in her company, presenting what turned out to be false claims about the system. Internally, however, her management style was very different—stiff and aloof. When employees raised doubts about the technology's efficacy, she quickly squashed the objections, firing even high-level executives. As early as 2006, she fired her CFO, Henry Mosely, for questioning the prototype's faked demonstrations. "We've been fooling investors," he said. "We can't keep doing that." Holmes replied, "Henry, you're not a team player. I think you should leave right now."[38]

Rapid turnover created a chaotic work environment, and employees quickly learned not to challenge anyone. When Diana Dupuy, a state-certified lab technologist, reported procedural violations to her supervisor, she was summarily fired. In an angry e-mail to Holmes, she argued, "You have created a work environment where people hide things from you out of fear. You cannot run a company through fear and intimidation . . . it will only work for a period of time before it collapses."[39]

As predicted, Theranos was dissolved in 2018. Elizabeth Holmes was indicted on two counts of conspiracy to commit wire fraud and nine counts of wire fraud, charges to which she has pleaded not guilty. The trial was scheduled to begin in March 2021. If convicted, Holmes faces a prison sentence of up to 20 years and fines of almost $3 million.[40]

Questions

1. Which of the five conflict management styles described in this chapter did Elizabeth Holmes exemplify? What are its strengths?

2. As a business communication consultant, which conflict management strategy would you recommend that Holmes adopt to handle employees' dissent? How could you convince Holmes to change her style?

3. What are some policies and procedures you would introduce to help change the company's reaction to conflict?

Case 13-2

Conflict and Technology

Janna White sat in her office, perplexed. Two days previously, she had been given responsibility to lead a team on a project that would have a significant impact on the investment decision under consideration at PlexiWarm Corporation. The decision involved an expansion of the firm's product lines to include high-density spray foam insulation (the firm currently produces rigid foam insulation panels). Janna had scheduled the first team meeting for this afternoon and was looking forward to working on such a significant project. She had just opened her e-mail to find a stream of confusing communications from two team members. Apparently, the two had been exchanging e-mail and text messages in such rapid succession that the replies had become very disjointed. The final messages had come about an hour earlier; both parties had basically concluded that they simply could not work together because of the poor communication of the other person!

Janna had the record only of the e-mail messages—the text messages had been sent between each person's individual cell phones. Without a complete record of the communication, Janna did not have a clue about how to try to resolve the conflict. She e-mailed each person, asking whether they had kept a record of the "text thread." She quickly got responses that neither had kept the stream of messages and that each now refused to work with the other.

Questions

1. What could Janna have done in advance to try to prevent the conflict?

2. Now that the conflict has occurred, and considering that this significant project still must be carried out, how should Janna manage the conflict?

3. Looking ahead, what is the likely effect of the conflict on team productivity?

Case 13-3

Conflict Over Job Duties

Linda Sims is the manager of the accounting department for a production company, and Jose Martinez is the manager of the credit department. This is a fast-growing firm, and the staff of the accounting department (11 employees) are often overwhelmed with work.

Because the accounting department is located immediately next to the credit department, Ruth Rankin, the administrative assistant in credit, sometimes works on journal entries assigned to her by Sims.

The company has experienced especially rapid growth over the past 6 months, which has caused everyone to be busier than usual. With the increase in sales volume, the credit office is under pressure to process applications more quickly, and Rankin is available to help Sims out with accounting overflow less often.

Sims complains to Martinez that she needs Rankin to work in accounting more than he needs her in credit. Martinez's responds, "If I can't move the credit applications through the pipeline in a timely manner, soon there'll be no need for an accounting department, because this company will be out of business."

Questions

1. What is the cause of this conflict?

2. Write a problem statement for this situation.

3. If you were Sims, how would you approach Martinez in this situation?

4. What style did Sims initially use?

5. What could Sims do to gain Martinez's cooperation rather than make him defensive?

Case 13-4

Conflict Among Team Members

Rod Edwards, the advertising manager for Waterlite Advertising and Associates, has two assistants. One is Gina Reese, an account executive who gets clients for the company. Edwards's second assistant is Mina Patel, a copywriter. She does the actual writing and designing of the ads for the clients.

Reese and Patel usually have a close working relationship because they work as a team on all clients' accounts. Reese meets the clients and discusses their needs with them. Afterward, she tells Patel about the conversation and the clients' needs, so that Patel can design the right ad. Once Patel finishes the ad, Reese presents it to the client. If the ad is a success, it is usually Reese who gets the praise and recognition because she is the one who interfaces with the client.

In the past, Patel was not bothered by the recognition Reese got because she always knew she was the one who designed the ad. But the last ad Patel designed brought in a $1 million contract to the firm. Edwards immediately gave Reese a raise

(Continued)

(Continued)

for bringing in the client but did not give Patel any recognition.

Naturally, this caused friction between Reese and Patel, and their relationship began to deteriorate. Four days after Reese got the raise, their conflict reached a climax. Reese borrowed Patel's stapler (a trivial occurrence) and forgot to return it. Patel caused a scene and refused to talk to Reese for the next few days.

The problem was brought to Edwards's attention because his department's productivity was declining. For the ads to be developed, the assistants had to work as a team.

Edwards called both employees into his office and immediately started lecturing them. He insisted they get along and begin working on the next ad. He told them he expected an ad finished by noon the following day. Reese and Patel walked out of Edwards's office without resolving the problem. They did get some work done the next day, but their close relationship never resumed.

Questions

1. What kind of conflict-resolution strategy did Edwards use? What kind should he have used?

2. This is an example of destructive conflict. Could it develop as a constructive situation?

3. What steps should Edwards have followed to develop a win–win strategy?

EXERCISE

Exercise 13-1

Conflict-Resolution Survey

For each of the 30 statements listed below, indicate how frequently you typically behave as described when you come into conflict with another person. (Rather than responding to these statements generally, you may wish to relate the statements to a particular person or setting familiar to you.) Use the following scale:

2 = Most of the time

1 = Some of the time

0 = Rarely

_1_ 1. I ask for help in resolving the conflict from someone outside our relationship.

_2_ 2. I try to stress those things on which we both agree rather than focus on our disagreement.

_2_ 3. I suggest we search for a compromise solution acceptable to both of us.

_1_ 4. I attempt to bring out all the concerns of the other person.

_1_ 5. I am firm in pursuing my goals.

_2_ 6. I strive to preserve our relationship.

_0_ 7. I seek to split the difference in our positions where possible.

_2_ 8. I work toward a solution that meets *both* our needs.

_1_ 9. I avoid the discussion of emotionally charged issues.

_2_ 10. I try to impose my solution on the other person.

_1_ 11. I emphasize whatever similarity I see in our positions.

_1_ 12. I try to postpone any discussion until I have had time to think it over.

_2_ 13. I propose a middle ground to the other person.

_0_ 14. I use whatever power I have to get my wishes.

_2_ 15. I attempt to get all our points immediately out in the open.

_0_ 16. I give up one point in order to gain another.

_2_ 17. I encourage the other person to offer a full explanation of their ideas to me.

_2_ 18. I try to get the other person to see things my way.

_2_ 19. I treat the other person as considerately as possible.

_0_ 20. I suggest we think our concerns over individually before we meet in the hope that the anger will cool down.

_2_ 21. I press to get my points made.

_2_ 22. I support a direct and frank discussion of the problem.

_2_ 23. I try to find a fair combination of gains and losses for both of us.

_2_ 24. I try not to allow the other person's feelings to become hurt.

_1_ 25. I avoid taking positions that would create controversy.

_2_ 26. I suggest we each give in on some of our needs to find a solution we can both live with.

_2_ 27. I listen carefully in order to understand the other person as well as possible.

_1_ 28. I soothe the other person's feelings if emotions are running high.

_1_ 29. I assert my position strongly.

_1_ 30. I shrink from expressions of hostility.

Scoring the Conflict-Resolution Survey

Fill in the blanks below with the same scale scores you entered on the survey. Then total your scores for each conflict-resolution approach. Note that the blanks to be filled in do not always appear in the same order as the items on the survey.

Scale Score	Item No.	Scale Score	Item No.	Scale Score	Item No.	Scale Score	Item No.	Scale Score	Item No.
1	1	2	2	1	5	2	3	1	4
1	9	2	6	1	10	0	7	2	8
1	12	1	11	0	14	2	13	2	15
0	20	2	19	2	18	0	16	2	17
1	25	2	24	2	21	2	23	2	22
1	30	1	28	1	29	2	26	2	27
Avoiding 5		Accommodating 10		Forcing 7		Compromising 8		Problem Solving 11	

This is your conflict-resolution profile. Note that your score for each approach can range from a low of 0 to a high of 12. The approach with the highest score is your preferred approach to conflict. The second highest is the one you tend to use under pressure.

Notes

1. Society for Human Resource Management, "With Workplace Violence on the Rise, 1 out of 7 People Don't Feel Safe at Work," March 19, 2019, https://www.shrm.org/about-shrm/press-room/press-releases/pages/2019-workplace-violence-research-report.aspx.

2. Occupational Safety and Health Administration, "Workplace Violence," accessed June 15, 2020, https://www.osha.gov/SLTC/workplaceviolence.

3. Accountemps, "Clash of the Coworkers," March 9, 2017, http://accountemps.rhi.mediaroom.com/2017-03-09-Clash-Of-The-Coworkers.

4. Society for Human Resource Management, "Managing Workplace Conflict," accessed June 15, 2020, https://www.shrm.org/resourcesandtools/tools-and-samples/toolkits/pages/managingworkplaceconflict.aspx.

5. Denise Salin and Helge Hoel, "Organisational Causes of Workplace Bullying," in *Bullying and Harassment in the Workplace: Developments in Theory, Research, and Practice,* 2nd ed., ed. Ståle Einarsen et al. (Boca Raton, FL: CRC, 2011), 227–43.

6. Tammy Erickson, "The Four Biggest Reasons for Generational Conflict in Teams," *HBR Blog Network* (blog), Harvard Business Publishing—for Managers, February 16, 2009, http://blogs.harvardbusiness.org/erickson/2009.

7. L. R. Hoffman, E. Harburg, and N. R. F. Meier, "Differences and Disagreements as Factors in Creative Problem-Solving," *Journal of Abnormal and Social Psychology* 64, no. 2 (1962): 206–24.

8. L. Putnam and S. Wilson, "Argumentation and Bargaining Strategies as Discriminators of Integrative and Distributive Outcomes," in *Managing Conflict: An Interdisciplinary Approach,* ed. A. Rahim (New York: Praeger, 1988).

9. Jiing-Lih Farh, Cynthia Lee, and Crystal I. C. Farh, "Task Conflict and Team Creativity: A Question of How Much and When," *Journal of Applied Psychology* 95, no. 6 (2010): 1173–80, doi: 10.1037/a0020015.

10. Daniel Katz and Robert L. Kahn, *The Social Psychology of Organizations,* 2nd ed. (New York: Wiley & Sons, 1978), 613.

11. Clagett G. Smith, "A Comparative Analysis of Some Conditions and Consequences of Intra-Organizational Conflict," *Administrative Science Quarterly* 10, no. 3 (1965–66): 504–29.

12. K. W. Thomas, "Conflict," in *Organizational Behavior,* ed. S. Kerr (Columbus, OH: Grid, 1979), 151–81.

13. Charles E. Watkins, "An Analytical Model of Conflict: How Differences in Perception Cause Differences of Opinion," *Supervisory Management* 41, no. 3 (March 1974): 1–5; and J. L. Hocker and W. W. Wilmot, *Interpersonal Conflict,* 2nd ed. (Dubuque, IA: Wm C. Brown, 1985).

14. Lewis Benton, "The Many Faces of Conflict: How Differences in Perception Cause Differences of Opinion," *Supervisory Management* 15, no. 3 (March 1970): 7–12.

15. Robert Zajonc, "Attitudinal Effects of Mere Exposure," *Journal of Personality and Social Psychology Monograph Supplement* 9, no. 2 (June 1968), 1–27.

16. "Does the Boss Say Thanks?" *St. Louis Post-Dispatch,* September 19, 2003, C9.

17. Carol Vinzant, "On the Job: Messing With the Boss's Head," *Fortune,* May 1, 2000, 329.

18. Christine Porath and Christine Pearson, "The Price of Incivility," *Harvard Business Review* 91, no. 1/2 (2013): 114–21.

19. CERT Insider Threat Center, "Handling Threats from Disgruntled Employees," Carnegie Mellon University Software Engineering Institute, July 15, 2015, https://insights.sei.cmu.edu/insider-threat/2015/07/handling-threats-from-disgruntled-employees.html.

20. U.S. Department of Labor, Bureau of Labor Statistics, "There Were 500 Workplace Homicides in the United States in 2016," *TED: The Economics Daily*, January 23, 2018, https://www.bls.gov/opub/ted/2018/there-were-500-workplace-homicides-in-the-united-states-in-2016.htm.

21. This diagram is based on the works of R. R. Blake and J. S. Mouton, "The Fifth Achievement," *Journal of Applied Behavioral Science* 6, no. 4 (1970): 413–26; J. Hall, *How to Interpret Your Scores From the Conflict Management Survey* (Conroe, TX: Teleometrics, 1986); R. W. Thomas, "Conflict and Negotiation Processes in Organizations," in *The Handbook of Industrial and Organizational Psychology*, 2nd ed., ed. M. D. Dunnette and L. Hough (Palo Alto, CA: Consulting Psychologists Press, 1992), 651–718; and K. W. Thomas and R. H. Kilman, *The Thomas-Kilman Conflict Mode Instrument* (Tuxedo, NY: Xicom, 1974).

22. W. A. Donohue, M. E. Diez, and R. B. Stahl, "New Directions in Negotiations Research," in *Communication Yearbook 7*, ed. R. N. Bostrom (Beverly Hills, CA: Sage, 1983), 249–79.

23. Tahir Saeed et al., "Leadership Styles: Relationship With Conflict Management Styles, *International Journal of Conflict Management* 25, no. 3 (2014): 214–25.

24. Todd Thorsgarrd, "The Art of Supervision" (program presentation, Minnesota State Colleges and Universities, January 22–24, 2020).

25. Kenneth Thomas, Gail Fann Thomas, and Nancy Schaubhut, "Conflict Styles of Men and Women at Six Organization Levels," *International Journal of Conflict Management* 19, no. 2 (2008): 148–66, doi: 10.1108/10444060810856085.

26. Tal G. Zarankin, "A New Look at Conflict Styles: Goal Orientation and Outcome Preferences," *International Journal of Conflict Management* 19, no. 2 (2008): 167–84.

27. Gareth Morgan, *Images of Organization* (Newbury Park, CA: Sage, 1986).

28. Paul Sanghera, *Ninety Days to Success as a Project Manager* (Boston: Cengage Learning, 2009), 259.

29. Jay W. Lorsch and Paul R. Lawrence, eds., *Studies in Organizational Design* (Homewood, IL: Irwin-Dorsey, 1970), 1.

30. Alan C. Filey, *Interpersonal Conflict Resolution* (Glenview, IL: Scott Foresman, 1975), 33.

31. N. J. Adler, *International Dimensions of Organizational Behavior* (Boston: Kent, 1986).

32. D. E. Zand, "Trust and Managerial Problem Solving," *Administrative Science Quarterly* 17, no. 1 (1972): 229–39.

33. Daniel Robey, *Designing Organizations* (Homewood, IL: Richard D. Irwin, 1986), 176–201.

34. Tab W. Cooper and Lucia Stretcher Sigmar, "Constructive Supervisory Confrontation: What Employees Want," *International Journal of Management & Information Systems* 16, no. 3 (2012): 255–64.

35. Linda L. Putnam, "Communication and Interpersonal Conflict," *Management Communication Quarterly* 1, no. 3 (February 1988): 293–301.

36. Lucia Stretcher Sigmar, Geraldine E. Hynes, and Kathy L. Hill, "Strategies for Teaching Social and Emotional Intelligence in Business Communication," *Business Communication Quarterly* 75, no. 3 (2012): 301–17.

37. Daniel Goleman, *Emotional Intelligence* (New York: Bantam, 1995).

38. John Carreyrou, *Bad Blood: Secrets and Lies in a Silicon Valley Startup* (New York: Vintage Books, 2020), 8.

39. Ibid., 116.

40. U.S. Department of Justice, U.S. Attorney's Office, Northern District of California, "Public Notification: *U.S. v. Elizabeth Holmes, et al.*," August 17, 2020, justice.gov/usao-ndca/us-v-elizabeth-holmes-et-al.

NEGOTIATING

LEARNING OBJECTIVES

By the end of this chapter, you will be able to

- Describe the relationship between negotiating and networking.

- Compare and contrast negotiation and conflict.

- Explain how culture and organizational climate affect negotiations.

- Identify negotiation strategies that are adapted to the sender, receiver, and purpose.

- Identify negotiation strategies that are adapted to the time, environment, content, and channel.

- Describe and demonstrate six core negotiation strategies.

Negotiation is an integral aspect of management. Successful managers negotiate for increased budget allocations, better purchasing prices, higher salaries for themselves and their direct reports, increased time to finish important assignments, more favorable annual objectives, or even better salary offers when starting with a new company. Many managers, however, shy away from negotiation. They do not feel comfortable doing it because either they have not succeeded in previous negotiations or they have not learned the process of dynamic negotiation.

By building their skills, managers will avoid ineffective negotiations in the workplace, which can reduce organizational productivity, demoralize those involved, and generate hostile feelings among other parties.[1]

Furthermore, recent research shows gender differences in the use of negotiation. In general, men initiate negotiation four times more often than women do.[2] This tendency has important consequences in business, particularly concerning pay, promotion, and recognition. Linda Babcock and Sara Laschever report in their book *Women Don't Ask* that only 7 percent of women MBAs graduating from Carnegie Mellon University negotiated for a higher salary than the one initially offered by a potential employer, while 57 percent of men MBAs did. On average, those who negotiated raised the initial offer by $4,053. The starting salaries for men were more than 7 percent higher than those for women overall.[3] Babcock and Laschever conclude that a different negotiating style explains at least some of the gap in women's starting pay, while acknowledging the complexity of the issue.

This gap explains a large part of the persistent pay differential between men and women throughout their careers. A recent study by the U.S. Government Accountability Office found that women still make 81 cents for every dollar a man makes in a similar job, despite the fact that women make up 50 percent of the workforce, 51.4 percent of managerial and professional jobs, and 43 percent of MBAs.[4] Controlling for a number of variables like tenure, age, company size, and market capitalization, a 2012 study of chief financial officers (CFOs) working in 3,000 U.S. companies found that gender is a strong predictor of CFO compensation; men earn 16 percent more than women on average.[5] Learning how to negotiate may eventually have an impact on this disparity.

NEGOTIATION AND NETWORKING

Negotiation can have a broader application than as a means to an end, or a tool for creating a desired outcome. Negotiation is a relational process. Each party in the negotiation is not merely acting as a self-interested individual but is interacting and engaging with another party. So negotiation can be thought of as standing one's own ground while being open to the interests of the other. As such, the outcomes of negotiation include not only solutions but relationships.[6]

Networking skills are relevant to managerial negotiation skills. Because negotiating is a process, not an event or a one-shot deal in most business situations, it is important to foster relationships while negotiating. Negotiating strategically means thinking long-term and building our networks. It means balancing relationships and results, cooperation and competition. It also means using our networks to help us negotiate successfully.

Again, research has identified gender differences in the ways managers use their networks during negotiations. When asking for a pay raise or promotion, women are more likely to rely on their job performance alone. Conversely, men are predisposed to ask for a raise when they feel it is warranted by comparison to others' performance. Men tend to use their networking abilities and relationships as leverage for their personal goals, while women tend to be less outcome oriented and more concerned with preserving goodwill. Often, women are also inclined to wait for someone else to sing their praises. These tendencies can be a detriment at the negotiation table.[7]

CRITICAL THINKING QUESTIONS

1. What are some of the cultural values that might explain these gender differences in the way men and women network?

2. Under what circumstances is each approach the most effective? Should negotiators learn to use both approaches?

When negotiating, a manager has to strike a balance between what is good for a business relationship and what is good for the manager and the organization. It is also important in a management position to network with other managers, so that you can ensure you are on par with industry and company standards when negotiating.

NEGOTIATION AND CONFLICT

Before discussing the dynamic process of negotiation, we should first specify exactly what the term means. Chapter 13 dealt with conflict resolution in terms of win–lose, lose–lose, and win–win strategies. That discussion urged that a win–win solution to conflict is best, and it reviewed the beliefs necessary to implement this approach successfully. However, such an outcome is not always appropriate. When one or both parties see a situation as that in which one party will lose or gain something in exchange for the other party's loss or gain, a negotiation strategy is best. In this situation, one party cannot easily determine the needs or desired outcome of the other party, and one of the parties may not fully trust the other.

Win–lose situations occur every day in a manager's life. When managers consider the term *negotiation*, they may often think of special, formal situations, such as collective bargaining between labor and management or a sports agent negotiating on behalf of an athlete. These examples are generally termed *third-party negotiations*. Research indicates that managers are more frequently becoming involved in third-party negotiations and even mediating to resolve disputes with customers.[8] However, the discussion in this chapter emphasizes the type of everyday negotiation situations any manager may face, such as obtaining additional resources for their team, winning a budget increase, or securing additional support from another department. Effective managers win more than they lose.

CRITICAL THINKING QUESTIONS

1. What are some of the key differences between negotiating to reach a compromise and negotiating to reach a consensus?

2. What are some of the key similarities?

3. Which type of negotiation strategy—compromise or consensus—do you think works best for most manager–direct report interactions? Why?

Every negotiator has two universal concerns. The parties must balance their concern for the outcome of the negotiation with the relationship needs between the parties.[9] However, the degree of these concerns varies from one situation to another. In some situations, winning is all that matters, but in other situations, the value of the relationship may outweigh the need to win. In between these opposite extremes is the risk of obtaining a winning outcome while damaging the relationship, which affects the losing party's willingness to fulfill the agreement. A manager may need to work with this party in the future, and if the relationship is damaged, future transactions could be controversial. For example, when a direct report requests a salary increase, the manager must weigh the need to manage the budget at the lowest cost with the need to maintain a positive relationship with the direct report. If the direct report's work performance is highly valued, the manager may want to make concessions to ensure continued good work.

A manager's approach to the negotiation process may be served by referring to the negotiation styles that balance these universal concerns, as demonstrated in Chapter 13 (Figure 13-3), where a manager's concern for production is balanced against the concern for people. Knowing the appropriate negotiation strategy can help a manager reach success.

A STRATEGIC MODEL FOR NEGOTIATIONS

The best way to approach the negotiation process is through the strategic analysis of managerial communication illustrated in Chapter 2.

The basic model of strategic managerial communication presented in Chapter 2 is shown here again in Figure 14-1. We must consider the factors in each layer of the model in order to arrive at a strategy for the message. Our discussion first focuses on the contextual factors—the communication climate, culture and values, and stakeholder concerns (Layer 1).

Next, factors related to the communication situation are explored: the sender (manager), the receiver's (the adversary's) style, and the purpose or goal of the negotiations (Layer 2). To develop a negotiation strategy systematically, one must also analyze the content, channel, physical environment, and time of the message (Layer 3). Although the following discussion treats these topics independently, managers must consider all the layers simultaneously when developing a negotiation strategy because they all affect each other. This chapter concludes with a description of six negotiation strategies that align with our strategic communication model.

FIGURE 14-1 ■ Strategic Managerial Communication Model

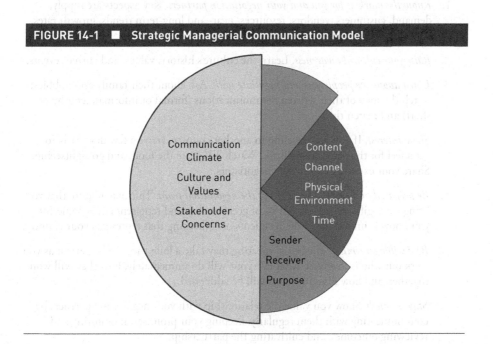

Layer 1: Contextual Factors

As mentioned throughout this book, culture is a primary concern in any communication situation. "First seek to understand, then to be understood" is Stephen Covey's fifth habit described in the *7 Habits of Highly Effective People*.[10] Managers must review and analyze the situation that initiates the need to negotiate and the culture/climate that surrounds each negotiation scenario. Then the manager can begin to identify alternative ways to resolve the need for the negotiation process. True understanding requires both talking and listening. The manager does not have to agree with the other party but does need to understand the other party's position. In addition, the manager can show empathy without feeling sympathy and evaluate the difference between fact and emotion that may derive from the nature of the culture or climate.

Both national and organizational culture must be considered when negotiating. Some cultures support an assertive, almost demanding negotiation style, whereas in other cultures, a more passive approach is expected. One culture may encourage long negotiation sessions that require patience, whereas another supports quick resolution. Some cultures encourage initial offers close to an expected settlement, while in other cultures, the initial offer is nowhere near an expected outcome. In some cultures, it is important to develop a personal relationship before negotiating, but in others, only a superficial knowledge of the other persons involved is required. Managers must be thoroughly aware of the other party's national culture to negotiate successfully.[11]

Eliane Karsaklian, director of the Master's Program in International Negotiation at Université Sorbonne, Paris, calls this approach "sustainable negotiation" and argues that it is the path to better relationships, greater innovation, and higher growth and profits. She offers the following guidelines:

1. *Know the markets for you and your negotiation partners.* Key aspects are supply, demand, customers, vendors, resources, near- and long-term trends, growth rates, barriers to entry and exit, and competitors.

2. *Raise your cultural awareness.* Learn the culture's history, values, and current events.

3. *Learn about the people you will negotiate with.* Ask about their family and hobbies; watch the tone of their written communications (formal or informal, lengthy or short) and match this.

4. *Show interest.* If you are traveling to another country, arrive a few days early to get a feel for the place and culture. Watch TV, taste the food, and go sightseeing. Share your experiences with the negotiators.

5. *Be prepared to meet new members of the negotiation team.* This may require that you bring extra gifts, which should be of good quality and represent either something you know is important to the recipients or something that represents your country.

6. *Be flexible on timing.* The initial meeting may take a long time, so be patient as you work out who is involved, what everyone will do immediately, how they will work together, and how disagreements will be addressed.

7. *Stay in touch.* Show you value the relationship with your negotiating partners by communicating with them regularly, keeping your promises, monitoring and reviewing outcomes, and cultivating the partnership.

8. *Find new solutions.* Consider this a never-ending relationship, despite changes in markets, situations, people, and even in the approach for handling these issues.[12]

Organizational culture largely determines who has the power within an organization and the extent to which a person can make decisions. There is no reason to negotiate with someone if that person cannot make decisions, and this is often the case where power is centralized. Also, in bureaucratic organizations, numerous policies and procedures may preclude flexibility, so there is little that can be negotiated. But most organizations are not so highly centralized and bureaucratic that negotiation is of no value. The manager's challenge is to determine what can be negotiated and with whom. This challenge is a result of the organizational culture and communication climate as well as the political structure within the organization. In short, negotiators should adopt the characteristics of cultural intelligence as described in Chapter 12.

Layer 2: Situational Factors

We next examine elements in the second layer of the strategic communication model (Figure 14-1)—the negotiator's personal style and purpose.

Manager's Style

Just as some people are outgoing and talkative and others are withdrawn and quiet, some managers enter a negotiation with confidence and a positive attitude, whereas others see defeat from the outset, believing they do not have a chance. Before negotiators can succeed, they must believe in themselves. A manager can gain confidence by becoming aware of the negotiation process and properly preparing for the interaction. In addition, practice in negotiation, if done properly, leads to greater confidence because of the positive results.

A manager creates power in negotiations when confident. Being confident, however, is not enough; during negotiations, you must also act and look confident. To begin, do not look as if you are expecting a long fight. One of the poorest practices is to appear to be settling in for an extended session. In addition, take care not to project a tired, listless image. In negotiation, appearance is an important source of communication; during face-to-face discussions, negotiators watch one another closely. You can promote success with a neat appearance that suggests you are well organized and a person who cannot easily be exploited. As described in Chapter 11, nonverbal signals such as tapping a finger on the desk or playing with a pencil can project a nervous, vulnerable image.

Negotiating through technological media may restrict managers' ability to read body language. A study of online negotiation found that when participants could not see their counterparts, they were less able to perceive clues to their style and consequently could not modify their behavior and attitudes accordingly.[13] Tactics for overcoming the disadvantages of e-negotiating are offered later in this chapter.

Purpose

The purpose of the negotiation process is simple: to maximize your advantage. Initially, that purpose is one of the most critical elements to consider when developing a negotiation strategy. The purpose of the negotiation may translate to "know what you want" or, more appropriately, "know what is reasonable to expect." Obviously, wants and expectations are vastly different, but unless you have clearly differentiated between the two, confusion and failure can result.

Negotiation is useless in certain situations. Consider, for example, a production manager who has successfully negotiated personal salary increases in the past. Unfortunately, poor market conditions have affected the company, and nobody is receiving a salary increase. If the manager tries to negotiate now, they will not only fail to get an increase but also might create resentment because they are making demands during hard times.

If the time is ripe and the other party is committed to the negotiation, then the manager can establish the negotiation goal. The following discussion presents three strategies: determining the maximum supportable outcome (MSO), the least acceptable outcome (LAO), and the best alternative to a negotiated agreement (BATNA).

Defining the Maximum Supportable and Least Acceptable Outcomes. The MSO is the absolute most one can ask for in the opening position within reason. A negotiation can be quickly terminated if the MSO is beyond reason.

The LAO is the least acceptable result you will accept from the negotiation. If the outcome of the negotiation is anything less than your LAO, it would be better to terminate the negotiation. Planning is important so that the LAO is established before the negotiation.

Of course, both the LAO and the MSO also reflect primary, secondary, short-term, and long-term considerations. An outcome frequently is complex and includes more than one aspect.

Because the LAO and the MSO are the guideposts for negotiation, their terms must be clear before you enter any negotiation. And it is a critical error (and possibly the most common) for a person to modify either of these two points after the negotiation has begun. Doing so suggests the adversary has undue influence.

You should keep in mind throughout our discussion of LAO and MSO that the terms are reversed for the adversary in the negotiation. Consider the example of a sales manager for a clothing distributor who is negotiating the price of 100 new suits with the purchasing manager of a clothing store. Table 14-1 demonstrates how the two see the terms differently.

It is important to keep this *reversal of terms* in mind when studying the following material. One outcome may be desirable to one person but undesirable to another. In negotiation, as with other aspects of communication, individual perception and frame of reference are important to remember.

Finding the LAO and MSO. Because the guidelines provided by the LAO and the MSO are so critical, managers should give careful thought to finding these outcomes. The LAO is probably easiest to establish. This is the point below which nothing could be accepted because of the potential loss. In effect, when a negotiator commits to this point, loss is unlikely.

The LAO is both objective and subjective, a combination of the facts surrounding the situation and the value placed on them. Because it is subjective, no magical formula

TABLE 14-1 ■ Reversed Terms		
Sales Manager		**Purchasing Manager**
Maximum supportable outcome (MSO)	$25,000	Least acceptable outcome (LAO)
Least acceptable outcome (LAO)	$21,500	Maximum supportable outcome (MSO)

determines the LAO. Thus, managers should make every effort to separate what is acceptable from what is wanted.

In determining exactly what an LAO is, it is worthwhile to develop some kind of decision worksheet to ensure a systematic and objective process. Table 14-2 presents an example of determining the LAO of a job offer.

Any format that helps managers think through the process is of value. Of course, we would all prefer to be at the other extreme of the range, the MSO. The MSO is the furthest point from the LAO that the negotiator can reasonably justify.

That area between the MSO and the LAO is the settlement range.[14] Both parties in the negotiation will have a conscious (or unconscious) settlement range. To help achieve success, the negotiator must be able to justify the MSO convincingly. Otherwise, the MSO may be set at a point that is beyond the opponent's LAO. Even though the negotiator might be willing to settle for much less, this possibility may be obviated because the opponent will see no reason to continue the discussion. But the reciprocal of this is also true; the maximum should not be too low, because once the MSO is out, one cannot readjust it. Negotiation will surely cease at that point.

The establishment of the MSO reflects the one-trip-to-the-well principle. The negotiator gets to state the opening position only once, and it is vital to make the most of it. It is almost impossible to reverse directions and ask for more when, after looking more closely at the situation, one belatedly realizes that the MSO was set too low.

But what is maximum? It is whatever one can support, and this justification may require some creativity. In developing the MSO, a manager should look for unique attributes to include. Do not become so fixed on one or two items that other possible combinations are not considered. For example, a marketing manager is negotiating with the vice president for an additional employee position in the marketing department. The additional position may not be as big an obstacle to overcome as the salary requested for the position. How can the manager justify a salary of $180,000 for the position? It may be possible to divert attention to something positive, like increased sales, to distract the vice president from the salary. The manager should make a reference list that outlines the benefits to upper management of agreeing to the salary request as well as an undisclosed list of possible responses that could negatively affect the negotiating position. By establishing such lists, the manager can prepare possible responses to overcome criticism regarding the salary request.

TABLE 14-2 ■ Establishing the Least Acceptable Outcome		
Item	Relative Importance	LAO
Salary	4	$68,000
Location	3	Within 500 miles of hometown and near a lake
Company size	1	Member of Fortune 500
Job duties	5	At least 20 percent of the job involving use of Excel spreadsheets
Social climate	2	Several people with interests similar to mine in the department

Defining the BATNA. So far, we have seen that to achieve a negotiation's purpose, the manager must determine the LAO and MSO. But sometimes negotiating with a bottom line is less effective and beneficial than developing a solid BATNA, or best alternative to a negotiated agreement. The BATNA was the brainchild of Roger Fisher and Bill Ury of Harvard Law School, first described in their series of books on principled negotiation that started with *Getting to Yes*.[15] The basic idea is that each party in a negotiation needs to identify what, if any, options are available if there is a stalemate. If there is no alternative, the negotiator will walk away from the table empty-handed. The BATNA must be decided prior to the start of negotiations.

An example is an offer from a dealer to buy your old car for $10,000. You decide to advertise your car on a Facebook buy-and-sell page for $12,000 (the MSO). Your BATNA is now $10,000, because you know you can fall back on that dealer's offer if no individual sale is successful. But wait. Other offers that you might consider include selling your car to your younger sister for $7,500. This might or might not be a better alternative than the dealer's offer, because of your relationship value. Thus, finding the BATNA requires weighing a broad range of factors.

The BATNA prevents a negotiator from accepting terms that are too unfavorable and from rejecting terms that should be accepted. If the proposed solution is better than the BATNA, then it is the MSO, and the negotiator should take it. If the agreement is not better than the BATNA, then the negotiator should reopen negotiations. But the BATNA is not the same as the LAO, the least acceptable offer. Instead, it is where the negotiator will go if the LAO is unreachable. When the parties have similar BATNAs, then the negotiation is ripe for agreement. Much time and money can be saved by "settling" for a BATNA rather than continuing a dispute. In the United States, about 90 percent of lawsuits settle out of court because the lawyers understand the strength of each side's case and how likely each is to prevail in court. Thus, when negotiations threaten to break down, parties should reveal their BATNAs to see if they are similar.

Layer 3: Message Factors

After examining the factors in the first two layers of our strategic communication model (Figure 14-1), we come to the third layer, which has four new and more specific strategic considerations. The first one we describe is time.

Time

Time is a vital component of strategy. Two issues should be addressed when considering time factors: (1) when to negotiate and (2) how to best use the time within the negotiation. The answer to the second question also provides insights for the best time to make an offer or counteroffer. First, let us look at when to negotiate.

To optimize energy and prevent major setbacks, try to conduct a negotiating session when the manager feels healthy and rested. Many individual idiosyncrasies exist, but the consensus seems to be that most people are at peak efficiency at about 11:00 a.m.[16] Although the ideal is to select the best time to negotiate, it is not always practical. Thus, the savvy negotiator is always fully prepared and never loses an opportunity to negotiate. A quick meeting in the cafeteria, a chance encounter in the elevator, or an apparently spontaneous telephone call can represent opportunities for negotiation. To quote John Ilich, author of several best sellers on power negotiation, including *The Complete Idiot's Guide to Winning through Negotiation,* "Never lose an opportunity to negotiate, but never negotiate until you are certain it's an opportunity."[17]

In any negotiation, the main question to ask is "When do I have the most power, and when is my adversary the weakest?" Naturally, the answer changes. Assume a manager wanted to adopt a flextime policy for their staff. The best time to negotiate this with upper management is probably just after some major accomplishment or even when another department has changed its work schedule. Strategic timing can add significantly to a person's power in negotiation.

A second question is how to best use time within the negotiation. Generally, one expects most significant concession behavior and settlement action to occur close to the deadline.[18] An approaching deadline puts pressure on the parties to state their true positions and thus does much to squeeze any elements of bluff out of the latter steps of negotiation. A number of major studies verify the power of time limits on the negotiation.[19]

Because of the significance of deadlines, note the following guidelines:

1. *Do not reveal the true deadline.* When an adversary knows the other person's deadlines, negotiations stall until the deadline acts as a pressure for concession. When a person has an extremely tight deadline, she may be wise to extend the deadline rather than to enter the negotiations at a disadvantage.

2. *Be patient.* Negotiators should take time to answer questions, provide information, and make decisions. This includes keeping defensive reactions under control, as well as avoiding the tendency to take an offensive posture when being verbally attacked. The time provided through patience allows the opportunity to organize, understand issues, test the opponent's strengths and weaknesses, and weigh risks. Also, it creates a sense of pressure in the opponent, especially when the deadline approaches.

3. *Use the clock.* Because most people in the United States are so conscious of time, seek concessions or even provide minor concessions toward the end of a time period. Thus, a negotiator might elicit action on the part of the opponent immediately before lunch or dinner because people like to have a sense of accomplishment when taking a break. And a flurry of action can be used to the negotiator's advantage if taken at the right time.

Environment

In addition to time and timing, the physical environment is strategically important. This section explores two aspects of the physical environment: site and physical arrangement.

Site selection is often important because it bears directly on the amount of control each party may exercise over the physical arrangements at that site, as well as the psychological climate in which the exchange occurs. In negotiations conducted in one's home territory, the host has a legitimate right to assume responsibility for arranging the physical space. This is similar to the home-field advantage in sports; the home team is more likely to come out as the winner in both situations.[20]

What is the best way to arrange a conference room or office for negotiations? First, prevent distractions and ensure privacy. Second, avoid sitting in a position that suggests subordination or even equality. If in a conference room, sit at the head of the table. If in your office, sit behind the desk to maximize the implication of power or authority. Prominent placement of status artifacts in the room (awards, photos of celebrities) can add to an environment where the visitor feels at a competitive disadvantage. On the other hand, if the importance of the relationship of the negotiating parties is primary, power arrangements may be less important. Sitting at a round table and showing mutual respect may provide the manager with more power because the manager has chosen an environment that indicates empathy for the other. This strategy may actually elicit more concessions based on the trust established between the two parties.

Observing the furniture arrangements of a room and physical position that an opponent takes in a negotiation provides valuable information. Figure 14-2 illustrates several possibilities. For example, a researcher conducted observation and questionnaire studies of seating preferences in several social contexts and found that people in the United States engaging in casual conversation normally prefer to sit at right angles to each other (if seated at square or rectangular tables) or beside one another when seated at circular tables. The study also found that side-by-side seating typically occurred in cooperative relationships. However, face-to-face seating was the most typical configuration in competitive relationships, such as negotiations, with a moderately wide space separating the parties. Results indicated less conversation when people were seated far apart than when they were side by side or opposite one another.[21]

If you cannot use home ground for negotiation, try for neutral territory. Thus, in a negotiation with a high-level manager, it might be inappropriate to ask the senior member to come to a lower-level manager's office. However, one could suggest that both parties meet in a conference room to avoid interruptions.

When you have no alternative to meeting in the adversary's office, you do not need to assume a subordinate role immediately. If the adversary is at a desk and you are in a side chair or, worse, in a low-slung occasional chair, you can quickly offset the disadvantage merely by standing up and moving around while speaking. With this little nonverbal technique, it is now possible to look down on the adversary.

FIGURE 14-2 ■ Seating Arrangements

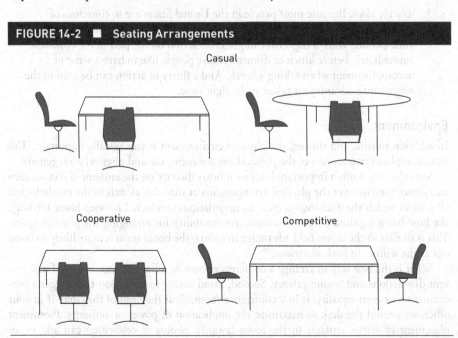

Casual

Cooperative   Competitive

Message Content

Sender, receiver, purpose, time, and environment all help set the stage for what is really the essence of the negotiation: the message itself. Negotiation revolves around the amount of information that each party decides to relate (or not to relate) about true motives and preferences. Negotiators base such a decision not only on their own standards but also equally on their opponents' behavior, openness, and honesty before and during the exchange.

Although nonverbal messages are important, the spoken word is the predominant form of communication in negotiation. The major types of verbal messages appropriate for discussion here are making concessions and responding to and presenting questions. But first, we will consider the opening messages.

Opening Messages. Should the negotiations begin with an immediate discussion of key issues, or is it best to begin with a friendly, neutral conversation? The answer depends on the total time allowed for the negotiations, the type of previous relationship with the parties involved, and whether the general atmosphere is friendly or hostile.

In the United States, the accepted practice is to begin with a general conversation on neutral topics. But the conversation moves rather quickly toward the issues. The same pattern is true with many Western Europeans; however, in Mexico, the Arab world, and most Asian countries, the initial neutral conversations are generally much longer.[22]

Concessions. We have mentioned that it is important to establish the LAO and MSO before negotiating. But it is not advisable to state these early in the negotiation. Rather, it is best to determine the other person's LAO. You then begin to move away from your MSO toward your LAO and toward the other person's MSO. This is generally accomplished through a series of concessions.

When and how to make concessions is determined by information obtained from questions—our next topic. However, principles of the equality rule can serve as a guideline for making concessions. The first equality principle suggests that negotiators generally expect one another to make an equal *number* of concessions from their initial starting point. The second principle is that of an equal sacrifice. By this rule, "equality" is judged by *how much* an individual concedes relative to his aspirations—in other words, who makes the bigger sacrifice.

Imagine a situation in which two managers are negotiating a reorganization among several departments. A third manager has left and has not been replaced; consequently, the duties of that manager's department will be assigned to the two remaining departments. During this negotiation, the two managers must perceive that each has made an equal *number* of concessions as well as an equal *amount* of concession. But numbers and amounts are difficult to quantify when negotiating such items as job duties, reporting relationships, and budgets. Consequently, the manner in which these concessions are made is important. An effective negotiator uses positive language to ensure concessions appear frequent and large.

CRITICAL THINKING QUESTIONS

1. When you begin moving from your MSO (maximum supportable outcome) toward your LAO (least acceptable outcome), should you make relatively small concessions or big concessions? Why?

2. Later in the negotiations, should your concessions become bigger or smaller?

Questions. Making concessions is closely related to asking and responding to questions. Dorothy Leads discusses the power of questions in her book *Smart Questions.*[23] Leads points out that individuals pay more attention to a question than to a statement, because they know that they will be expected to respond to a question. When they hear a statement, on the other hand, they may not be expected to respond at all. While closed questions are appropriate for, say, ensuring commitment, open-ended questions often gather more valuable information that can be used in the negotiation process. It is through these questions that an effective negotiator determines when and how much of a concession to offer.

A negotiator may unintentionally strike an emotional chord with a question and arouse antagonism; consequently, it may be necessary to prepare the ground before asking questions. One way to accomplish this is by explaining the reason or reasons for asking a question if the potential exists for embarrassment.

Questions serve five purposes:

1. *To arouse attention:* "When did that change?" or "Did you know about . . . ?"

2. *To obtain information:* "What is the difference between the two items?" or "What's the value of that point?"

3. *To clarify:* "I still am confused about your motive here. What else is key to you?" or "What are the terms we've settled on so far?"

4. *To stimulate thinking:* "Could you give me your reaction to the second item?" or "What are some other alternatives?"

5. *To bring to a conclusion or summary:* "Will you summarize your proposal?" or "Are we ready to act?" or "Have we got a deal?"

If you want a particular answer, ask a *leading question.* A leading question directs the person who is answering from statement to statement until the logic of the questioner's argument is made. Here is a series of leading questions:

Is research included in your cost? Where? How is it prorated between jobs? Exactly why do you include it in our charges when you just said that this job requires no research?

In this example, the questioner may or may not know the answers, but the questions lead opponents to a planned conclusion.

When no need exists to lead the opponent in a particular direction, use *open-ended questions*—questions that usually begin with how, why, or what. For example, "How would you recommend we close the gap?" "Why is Plan A preferable to Plan B?" "What is the proposal?" Open questions invite people to express their thinking freely. These are the types of questions that Leads refers to as *smart questions.*

Another type of question, the *rhetorical question,* is one that is asked not to get an answer but for effect. Rather than seeking an answer, this type of question attempts to draw attention to a particular item. Examples of rhetorical questions include "What do you think the vice president would say to something like that?" or "Do you really want us to believe that?"

In general, avoid *bipolar, either-or,* or *shotgun* questions. Such a question as "Would you prefer a corner office with a computer, or would you rather have a larger desk and no extra chair?" needs to be divided into two questions. As the question is presently stated, confusion will result, or the opponent may even ask for both. Similarly, forced-choice questions will make your opponent feel cornered and may end the negotiations. Also, a wise negotiator avoids a rapid-fire questioning approach. An opponent needs time to respond, and the questioner needs to listen to the responses.

A final effective use of questions is to get negotiations back on track when an opponent has created a roadblock. Stuart Diamond, a professor at Wharton School of Business and a prominent expert in negotiation, emphasizes the importance of questions to pursue the goal. For instance, when an opponent states, "I can't possibly do that for you at this time," a closely listening negotiator might respond, "When can you do it?" or "Who else can?"[24] By responding with questions, the negotiator continues the process.

To summarize, keep the purpose of your question in mind, listen for the right time, and then phrase the question to meet the prevailing needs. Table 14-3 summarizes various question types and their purposes in negotiations.

Answering Questions. Negotiation is a game of asking and answering questions. The preparation and mental alertness required to ask purposeful questions are just as essential for answering them. Perhaps the most important preparation is to brainstorm and write down in advance questions most likely to arise. Ask an associate to act as devil's advocate and raise a host of hard questions before negotiation. The more you prepare possible answers, the better those answers will be.

Keep two universal guidelines in mind when answering questions: (1) Never answer until the question is fully understood, and (2) take time to think through your answer. Besides applying these two guidelines, you can exercise two options in answering. First, you may answer the question accurately and completely. However, such openness may be inadvisable, especially when dealing with a party you mistrust. The second option is to be less direct when answering.[25] For instance, when negotiating for the salary to go with a new position, it is not wise to directly answer the question "What is the salary you are looking for?" It is probably best to respond with a comment like "Do you agree that I qualify for the

TABLE 14-3 ■ Questions to Ask When Negotiating	
Question Type	**Purpose**
Closed	Arouses attention
	Gets commitment
	Clarifies
	Redirects
Open	Obtains information
	Stimulates thinking
Leading	Directs the answer
Rhetorical	Draws attention
	Creates an effect

top of the pay range?" If your MSO and BATNA are below the other party's lower limits, you will not have revealed your limits too soon.

When you do not wish to give an answer, several alternatives are available. First, you may choose to answer only part of the question. For instance, a question may be "What is required to have this project completed by May 1?" You respond by listing all that is required to have the job done without relating to the date. By receiving complete and detailed information, the interrogator thinks the question has been answered. Meanwhile, you can stay away from potentially damaging information.

Another possibility is to ask for clarification even when the question is fairly clear. Often when people are clarifying a question, they intentionally or unintentionally change the question substantially or provide additional insight into the type of answer sought. Also, the time it takes to restate the question provides additional maneuvering time for you to consider possible answers. A variation is to ask for clarification for part of the question, thus diverting attention away from the remainder of the question—as a result, you may end up having to answer only part of the question.

CRITICAL THINKING QUESTIONS

1. What are some of the advantages of answering a question with another question?

2. What are some of the pitfalls?

A third possibility is to answer a different question. In such a ploy, the question being answered is so similar to the one asked that the interrogator actually considers the answer satisfactory. For instance, when asked which budget item would be the best to drop from next year's request, you might answer that inflation is affecting all areas of the budget and then provide a specific example of inflation effects. This, in turn, could be followed by the next alternative: answering the question with a question—for example, "Where do you think the new acquisition has had the greatest impact on the company?" This tactic may or may not divert attention away from the initial question but is often better than giving a direct answer.

A fourth alternative is to answer a negative question with a positive response. When negotiating for a promotion, a typical scenario has the opponent asking, "What do you consider to be the biggest weakness you'll bring to this job?" Naturally, a thorough and accurate answer would put you at a disadvantage. A positive, strategic answer might be "Well, sometimes I get too caught up in my work, and I'll stay until late at night. This really isn't fair to my family, so I have to learn to balance my time between family and work." This answer takes the advantage away from the opponent because it is difficult to fault a hard worker who is also a family person.

The real key to answering questions, then, is the ability to think on your feet. This task becomes easier with experience, but no substitute exists for rehearsing the possible questions and being prepared.

Channel

Face-to-face (F2F) is the richest channel for negotiations, meaning that negotiators can observe and interpret their opponents' nonverbal behaviors. As discussed in Chapter 11, numerous subtle behaviors can indicate what the other party may be thinking. For example, a quick flinch or pained expression may indicate that an offer is completely unacceptable. Alternatively, a negotiator may feign a flinch in order to manipulate the other party into a better offer. Research also reveals that the raising of both eyebrows or the widening of eyes is evidence of surprise. This may occur because an offer or concession is more charitable than expected or because unexpected information has been disclosed. If negotiators detect signs of surprise, they may need to consider the possibility of having made strategic errors.

While face-to-face used to be considered the only viable channel for successful negotiation, there are others. Negotiators today should consider the advantages of several communication channels when developing their negotiation strategy.

Negotiations in Writing. The letter of intent is a common tool employed either before or after negotiation that can serve to express an agreement of interests.[26] A person's memory is always much better 5 minutes after a conversation than 5 days later. The letter or memo of intent ensures that all the critical items are mutually agreed on. The person who writes the memo or letter has the advantage, for this person interprets meanings and shapes words to reflect their understanding of the discussion. The question is not one of exploiting the party or catching the opponent in some trap. It is simply setting out the area of agreement in your own way rather than leaving it to the opponent.

Of course, the negotiator should not write the letter in such a tone that it sounds as if the opponent cannot be trusted. It's easy to achieve such tact. In one situation, a manager hosted several employees from an out-of-town office. She submitted an expense voucher for $600, but the next paycheck did not cover the expenses. A discussion with her supervisor followed, and after a long negotiation, he agreed to pay $450 of the $600. After the negotiation, the manager sent the following short e-mail:

DATE:	March 11
TO:	Chris Averson
FROM:	Pat Harolds
SUBJECT:	Expense Voucher

Thanks for taking the time to sit down with me and discuss the expenses incurred while hosting the engineers from St. Paul. I'll be looking forward to receiving the $450 with the next paycheck.

This quick e-mail not only confirms the result of the negotiation but also establishes goodwill.

Managers can also use written correspondence to de-emphasize an issue or soothe a highly emotional situation. Correspondence brings an issue back into perspective merely by tactfully showing that a matter is not of great importance. Often, the printed word can lend credibility that face-to-face communication lacks because some people are more apt to take seriously what they see than what they hear. Also, a carefully written document tends to be less emotional than a face-to-face interaction. The section of Chapter 8 that describes the political uses of written messages in business is relevant here.

Finally, managers can use written correspondence to present a position when a complex explanation is required. It is difficult to present a complex argument that includes cost figures and diagrams with only an oral presentation. A written statement or even a chart can be helpful when presenting such an argument. In addition, if the opponent has no such aids, counterarguments might be harder to formulate.

E-negotiations. Negotiations conducted through technological channels are becoming more common as business-to-business interactions take place in the global economy. Recent studies that focus on architectural, construction, engineering, and consulting companies indicate that e-negotiations are the norm and that negotiation tactics that work in traditional interfaces (e.g., F2F, phone) often fail in virtual settings, as managers struggle to assess the client's mindset in e-communications.[27]

Some best practices for e-negotiations are emerging. For instance, a study of sales professionals found that the concurrent use of assertiveness and promise tactics during

TABLE 14-4 ■ Advantages and Disadvantages of Online Negotiation	
Online Communication Mode: Synchronous	
Advantages	**Disadvantages**
The setting allows for more persuasive behavior and less exchange of private information.	The setting can cause spontaneous, unhelpful emotional behavior.
The setting allows a richer information exchange in terms of signals.	Less time is available to consider alternatives and to analyze the actual situation.
Time pressure forces negotiators to prepare better.	The negotiators are more susceptible to mistakes.
Aggressiveness as a tactic might impose solutions on the less experienced/weaker side.	Information quality and depth are not very rich.
Online Communication Mode: Asynchronous	
Advantages	**Disadvantages**
Emerging emotions can be reflected and positively impact behavior.	It is difficult to corner the adversary.
More quality information might be exchanged because negotiators have time to formulate responses.	The format allows the adversary to reflect and develop a more efficient strategy.
More alternatives might be presented and considered.	It is difficult to deduce the experience level or the depth of situational knowledge of the adversary.
Time allows for simulation and formal analysis of the positions.	Statements can be taken out of context and used in future communications against the adversary.

e-negotiations boosts buyer attention, as does the concurrent use of information sharing and recommendation tactics.[28] Negotiating online eliminates the benefit of incoming nonverbal information like eye contact and handshakes that act as warm-ups for civilized exchanges. This lack of communication signals can affect trust, leading everyone to be extra cautious and reserved in their commitments and promises. To rebuild trust between the parties, negotiators can focus on each other's reputation. In addition, it's wise to create ground rules to build trust in both the process and the parties.[29]

If you have the option of selecting a channel in which to conduct your negotiation, either face-to-face or online, think strategically. The major advantages and disadvantages of using technology for negotiations are summarized in Table 14-4. Both synchronous and asynchronous modes are included in the table.[30]

CORE NEGOTIATION STRATEGIES

We have arrived at the core of our strategic managerial communication model. How a manager acts and looks, communicates the maximum supportable outcome, reacts to the adversary's style, uses time, establishes the environmental conditions, and asks and answers questions all contribute to the negotiation strategy. Managers combine these communication variables either by design or by accident to develop a core strategy for negotiating. Six general strategies reviewed in the following paragraphs can assist you in combining the different aspects of communication systematically. No particular approach is recommended over another; rather, these six approaches represent possibilities that may best fit a particular situation.[31]

Surprise

The surprise strategy involves unexpectedly introducing a goal or concession into a negotiation. For instance, a manager negotiating budget items with a vice president might suddenly request a new title. The total surprise may catch the VP off guard, so the additional request is approved, especially considering that it does not add additional expense.

A quick concession on a nonessential item is another form of surprise. Once again, this concession may be on an item unrelated to the main focus of the negotiation in hopes that the concession will foster a reciprocal concession by the adversary. Surprise may be particularly valuable with an adversary who is under time pressure, because it may stimulate some quick concessions.

Bluff

In poker, a player may bluff by placing a large bet even though there is no strong hand to back it up. By bluffing, the player hopes to mislead the other players. This tactic is also occasionally appropriate in managerial negotiation. Bluffing, the act of creating illusions without the use of lies or outright misrepresentations, is fair play in negotiations because each side is attempting to maximize its own benefit. A difference exists between withholding information and presenting wrong data. For instance, when a person is negotiating to buy an office desk, it is not the same thing to say "I would like to pay no more than $900" as it is to say "I have only $900 to spend." A person may want to spend no more than $900 but has additional funds if they are needed.

Stacking

The stacking strategy is used when one idea is attached to another. For instance, a public relations manager might use this approach when negotiating a new strategy with the administrative vice president: "I was just reading in *Fortune* that ABC International has changed its approach for its stockholders' meeting. ABC used an approach similar to what I'm suggesting." This manager is stacking the negotiation purpose on top of ABC's to build credibility.

Legislators also use a form of stacking when presenting bills by attaching a controversial item as a "rider" onto something that has wide support. Managers use this tactic in negotiations when they stack an undesirable characteristic onto a desirable one. For instance, a person may be asked to take a transfer (undesirable) in combination with a promotion (desirable).

Fait Accompli

The *fait accompli* is a type of bluff that says, in effect, "Here it is; it is a done deal." The negotiator states the terms of an offer and acts as if the terms are acceptable to the adversary. The expectation is that when an issue is phrased as if it were a negotiated final settlement, the adversary will accept it with little or no protest. Assume an item has been discussed for some time, but no solid agreement has been reached. You may write a letter of intent regarding the negotiation and state the issue as settled. Using this approach, real estate agents will occasionally push stubborn buyers into action by writing the buyer's tentative terms onto a contract. Once the details are down, the buyer is asked to sign and often does.

Take It or Leave It

The take-it-or-leave-it position lets an adversary know this offer is your best one; it represents the maximum goal adjustments a person is willing to make. In making a take-it-or-leave-it offer (which is, in fact, an ultimatum), you take the risk that the offer will be rejected, so there may be no chance to improve it or even revive the negotiations. The negotiator could follow with a different offer if the initial take-it-or-leave-it proposal was rejected; however, credibility would be lost. This strategy should be used only once.

Screen

In negotiation, a screen is a third party used by the negotiator as part of the process, as a screen between the opponent and the final decision maker. For instance, assume you are negotiating with an outside contractor. You can say that certain conditions proposed by the contractor need to be approved by others in the company. When these conditions are not approved, the adversary may find it necessary to grant concessions to keep the deal going. The third party may actually be a phantom person in the background, but this procedure generates thinking time and may take away some of the opponent's offensive advantage. Instead of negotiating one on one, the opponent has two adversaries, and it is difficult to negotiate through a "barrier" or screen.

The screen has a serious drawback: It gives the impression of limited power. A manager should use this procedure sparingly when negotiating salaries and budgets with direct reports because it will soon appear that the manager has little decision-making authority; thus, both respect and influence are weakened.

If possible, do not let an adversary use the third-party technique. Instead, try to get directly to the decision maker. The screen filters out the communications, so much of the strategy used on the adversary is weakened.

These six strategies are only suggestions. Combinations of these or even other strategies are possible. Every strategy has potential drawbacks, strengths, and risks, depending on the variables discussed in this chapter and summarized in the strategic communication model (Figure 14-1). Formulating the appropriate strategy is not an easy task. Good negotiation strategy requires analytical ability, an understanding of communication, a refined set of skills, and creativity. However, after studying this chapter, you should be able to enter a negotiation confidently.

SUMMARY

Negotiation is an appropriate tool for compromise in conflict-resolution situations. Before negotiating, the manager should establish the maximum supportable outcome (MSO) and least acceptable outcome (LAO) to know the negotiation range. Both limits must be carefully thought out so that managers can protect their best interests while negotiating in a credible manner. The MSO must be one the manager can support convincingly, and the LAO must be one the manager can live with. It is also wise to define the BATNA, the best alternative to a negotiated agreement, to prevent a stalemate.

Negotiators need to consider when to negotiate, how long to continue, and when to make a counteroffer. Because negotiation is liable to be most fruitful when close to an opponent's deadlines, several suggestions about deadlines are appropriate: (a) Do not reveal the true deadlines, if possible; (b) be patient; and (c) use the clock. Strategic negotiators should also seek an optimum physical environment that benefits them without giving advantage to the opposition.

Another consideration is language used during the negotiation. Negotiators should use common, basic language; should strive for clarity; should be specific; and should not be apologetic. Questions asked during negotiations have five purposes: to create attention, to obtain information, to clarify, to stimulate thinking, and to conclude or summarize. In phrasing questions, strategy dictates whether to use open-ended, leading, or closed questions. In answering questions, negotiators must protect their interests by taking time to think through the answer and respond only when the question is fully understood. The chapter suggests strategies for adapting answers to suit one's interests.

The channel chosen for negotiation is important. Which channel is chosen depends on the circumstances. The letter or memo of intent that follows many negotiations requires care in preparation and can work to the advantage of the person preparing it. E-negotiations are becoming common; negotiators should consider the advantages and disadvantages of technological channels.

Six core strategies that can be applied in negotiations are surprise, bluff, stacking, *fait accompli*, take it or leave it, and the screen.

CASES FOR ANALYSIS

Case 14-1

Salary Negotiation Is Transparent at The Riveter

The Riveter is a for-profit company headquartered in Seattle, Washington, in the United States, focused on supporting women in the workplace. It engages in political advocacy, provides office and work space, hosts events, and publishes content. It was named after Rosie the Riveter, a symbol for working women during World War II. As of late 2019, locations have expanded to six states— Washington, Texas, Minnesota, Colorado, Oregon, and California. The founder and CEO of The Riveter is former attorney Amy Nelson.

According to its website, The Riveter is "working to champion and elevate the conversation about diversity, equity and inclusion in work and in business." The Riveter primarily offers "community spaces for work and activation designed with the needs of women in mind." In addition, the company sponsors content, live events, and programming from "the leading minds of the day." Members, 75 percent of whom are women, also benefit from fitness tips, discounts, career advice, networking opportunities, and other resources. "At The Riveter, we think of ourselves as a modern union for working women. Our spaces are there for work, for meetings, for collective action. . . . We also offer a lot of access points."

In early 2019, an employee who had been hired only a few months earlier approached The Riveter's chief marketing officer, Kerry Murphy, asking to renegotiate her salary. The new hire had just learned that a coworker in a similar position was earning more, and she felt an adjustment was appropriate. Murphy reported this situation to the CEO, Nelson, who was surprised that employees were openly comparing pay. During her years as a corporate lawyer, salary was not considered a topic for discussion. "I was taught you didn't talk about money," Nelson said. "It wasn't polite. It was tacky."

Nelson decided to make two major changes as a response to the employee's complaint of pay inequity. First, she created pay bands for various positions. Next, she made the salary ranges accessible to her workforce as well as to the public by posting them on the company's website. For full-time positions, for example, "level 1" is $16 to $22 per hour, while "level 6" is $175,000-plus per year.

Transparency in employee compensation may trigger salary negotiations. Furthermore, it is controversial because research has found that employee morale and even turnover can be negatively affected by perceived pay inequities. Employees at a Canadian engineering company reported to researchers that they lost trust in management after the formula used to calculate bonuses was publicized. And a study conducted at Princeton and the University of California–Berkeley found that employee job satisfaction declined when pay scales were made transparent.[32]

Questions

1. From an employer's perspective, what are the major advantages of transparency in compensation? What are the major disadvantages?

2. From an employee's perspective, what are the major advantages of transparency in compensation? What are the major disadvantages?

3. As a prospective new hire, what strategies do you think would be most effective when negotiating your salary?

Case 14-2

Negotiation and Technology

Jessie had just taken his second test-drive in the new three-quarter-ton pickup truck he was considering purchasing. The sales associate had been friendly and welcoming, warmly introducing Jessie to other managers at the dealership, offering free soft drinks, curb service with two vehicles he had test-driven, and assurances that the salesperson was "working for Jessie" and wanted to "earn Jessie's business." The salesperson asked Jessie about his personal life and baited him with "Truck Month," "special deals," and "incentives for a short time only." The salesperson had figured out Jessie's payment schedule for him, an amazingly low payment per month. Then Jessie said, "I have to be somewhere in 20 minutes, but I might come back tomorrow—when do you open in the morning?"

The next day, Jessie returned to the dealer with estimates of his trade-in value from three used-car websites, a loan preapproval from his credit union, and a summary of the dealership's actual cost of the truck he was interested in from another website. He greeted the sales associate and made an offer for the truck. "We just can't do that, Jess," was the response. "That's below what we have to pay for the truck."

"Well, first, you have added charged items that aren't even done yet, like the sprayed-in bed liner for $670 that I can have done for $230 from the same place you guys have it done. So I deducted that, and the special sealant extra charges that are included if a vehicle is painted, and all of them are (painted). . . . Here are some other items that are similar, and they come to $1,945. I deducted half of your destination charge, and then I deducted half of your holdback to arrive at this number." The shocked sales associate took the information to her manager, who returned with another two managers to try to convince Jessie that his offer was not possible. The hard sell continued into a discussion of Jessie's trade-in, and finally, Jessie told them he might find a deal at another dealer or even with a different truck brand and that if they were interested in trying to meet his offer, they should e-mail him. And then he left.

The next day, Jessie received an e-mail from the sales manager, saying they had agreed to his offer. When Jessie arrived, the truck had been cleaned, had a large Sold sign in the window, and was parked at the front door. The manager had agreed to Jessie's offer on the new truck but had priced his trade-in at $8,000 less than the trade-in value Jessie had found online. After another

30 minutes of hard-sell tactics, Jessie left the dealership for the third time.

That afternoon, the used-car manager called Jessie to talk him down from his expected trade-in value. That evening, the sales manager called Jessie to say that he could come within $450 of Jessie's offer and that if Jessie would come back to the dealership, the deal would be made. Jessie agreed and returned to the dealership the next day.

The deal was indeed done and written up, and the official "offer" reflected all of Jessie's requirements. But it was exactly $450 more than the deal Jessie had proposed. To a chorus of how much money the dealership was losing, he was hustled into the finance manager's office, where Jessie was offered credit, life insurance, gap insurance, extended warranties—and special deals on all four after he refused them all; he also refused the special deals on the discounted items. Jessie stood his ground, and the papers were finally signed.

That night, Jessie summed up the total additional costs the dealer tried to talk him into accepting. His truck would have cost $72,360. The additional costs he could have incurred if he had given in to the hard sell totaled $19,763.

Jessie later acquired an extended warranty for 30 percent of the cost of the dealer warranty, and he had some custom touches added for a fraction of the cost the dealer had wanted to charge.

Questions

1. What negotiation strategies described in this chapter are exemplified in this case by both parties? How effective was each?

2. What role did technology play in the negotiation? At what stages was F2F interaction key?

3. How important is it to be well informed about a negotiation before beginning the negotiation? Where would you go for guidance in establishing your MSO and LAO?

(Continued)

(Continued)

4. There was a material cost of failing to negotiate effectively in this case. How could Jessie have reduced his costs further?

Case 14-3

Purchasing and Accounts Payable

Saul and Latisha are both managers in a machine tool company. Latisha is the director of purchasing and has four purchasing agents and an administrative assistant reporting to her. Saul is the director of accounts payable and has two people reporting to him. The administrative assistant for the accounts payable group also works for the accounts receivable group, so in effect, the accounts payable group has only a part-time admin.

Saul and Latisha both have business degrees and graduated from college 3 and 5 years ago, respectively. They are both ambitious, and there is a high level of competition between them. The following discussion occurs in Latisha's cluttered, cramped cubicle. It is about 45 minutes before the normal quitting time, but it looks as if Latisha may not be able to get away soon because she has a number of end-of-month tasks to finish.

Saul: Latisha, could I use your admin for a few hours tomorrow? We are really behind, and I've noticed that she doesn't seem to be too busy.

Latisha: What do you mean "too busy"? We all have work backing up on us.

Saul: Well, you have one admin, but we have to share time with accounts receivable.

Latisha: Well, I'm sorry, we're just too busy.

Saul: How about asking her to work some overtime but charge it to our department? Does she like to work overtime?

Latisha: She might want to do that. You can ask.

Saul: Would you please ask? That might be better because you're her supervisor.

Latisha: No, you go ahead and talk to her. Also, remember you will have to pay the time-and-a-half for overtime.

Saul: I really think you should talk to her.

As Saul says this, the telephone rings, and he walks out of the office.

Questions

1. What could be done to improve the effectiveness of this interaction?

2. Return to Figure 14-1. What are the major variables presented in the figure that influence the communication presented in this case?

EXERCISE

Exercise 14-1

Negotiating an Employment Agreement

Background: Managers seeking new positions may find there is far more to agree to than just pay, benefits, and job responsibilities. Today, companies want to protect their trade secrets, inventions, and clients. To do so, they ask new executives and managers to sign employment agreements that safeguard their interests.

Instructions: In pairs, students should negotiate the conditions for employment in the following scenario. One student is the candidate; the other is the hiring agent. The negotiators should determine the MSO, LAO, and BATNA for each topic to be negotiated.

Company: Bio-Analytics, Inc., a scientific software development company. The organization's chief clients are pharmaceutical companies, research and development laboratories, and universities. Products are software programs that support scientific research.

Position: Director of Marketing.

Responsibilities: Manage the Marketing Department, which is responsible for finding clients, selling Bio-Analytics products, and servicing the accounts.

Topics for Negotiation

1. *Noncompete clause:* When the director leaves, they cannot work for similar types of companies for a specified period of time or in a defined geographical area. They also cannot work for a competitor while employed in the current job.

2. *Invention clause:* The company, not the employee, owns whatever the employee developed or invented while working for the firm.

3. *Nonsolicitation of clients:* When the director leaves, they cannot seek business from former clients for a specified time.

4. *Nonsolicitation of employees:* When the director leaves, they cannot try to attract former colleagues to the new firm for a specified time.

5. *Confidentiality agreement:* When the director leaves, they may not disclose to outsiders the company's private business and technical data, such as products in development, formulas, test results, and sales strategies.

Negotiation Tips for the Candidate

- With noncompete clauses, try to limit the time you can't work for a competing company. As a bargaining chip, point out that your useful knowledge about a company lasts only a limited time, such as a few months after you leave the company.

- With clients, ask to be allowed to identify which clients you can and can't contact after you leave the company.

- Focus the negotiation on conditions worth fighting for. For instance, the duration of noncompete and nonsolicitation provisions can limit your future ability to earn a living.

Notes

1. Dean G. Pruitt and Peter Warr, *Negotiation Behavior* (Burlington, MA: Elsevier Science, 2013).

2. Stuart Diamond, *Getting More: How You Can Negotiate to Succeed in Work and Life* (New York: Three Rivers Press, 2010).

3. Linda Babcock and Sara Laschever, *Women Don't Ask: Negotiation and the Gender Divide* (Princeton, NJ: Princeton University Press, 2003).

4. Susan Chira, "Why Women Aren't C.E.O.s, According to Women Who Almost Were," *New York Times*, July 23, 2017, 1SR, 6SR.

5. Tom White and Kimberly Gladman, "Female Chief Financial Officers and the Glass Ceiling," *GMI Ratings*, March 29, 2012, http://www.gmiratings.com.

6. Cynthia L. King, "Beyond Persuasion: The Rhetoric of Negotiation in Business Communication," *Journal of Business Communication* 47, no. 1 (January 2010): 69–78.

7. Barbara Safani, "Nuances of Negotiation," *Insider's Guide to Job Search* (Career Hub blog, 2006), https://www.uis.edu/career/wp-content/uploads/sites/114/2013/04/careerhub_guide_to_job_search.pdf.

8. Jessica Nagle and Cynthia Pasciuto, "Utilizing ADR in Medical Billing Disputes," *Proceedings of the Northeast Business & Economics Association* (2013), 189–92.

9. Roger Fisher, William Ury, and Bruce Patton, *Getting to Yes: Negotiating Agreement Without Giving In,* 2nd ed. (Boston: Houghton Mifflin, 1992). See also William Ury, *Getting Past No: Negotiating in Difficult Situations* (New York: Bantam Books, 1993).

10. Stephen R. Covey, *The 7 Habits of Highly Effective People: 25th Anniversary Edition* (New York: Simon & Schuster, 2013).

11. Andrew Rosenbaum, "How to Steer Clear of Pitfalls in Cross-Cultural Negotiation," in *Winning Negotiations That Preserve Relationships,* The Results-Driven Manager Series (Boston: Harvard Business School Press, 2004), 154–60.

12. Eliane Karsaklian, *Sustainable Negotiation: What Physics Can Teach Us About International Negotiation* (Bingley, UK: Emerald Publishing Limited, 2017), 134–39.

13. Sabine Koeszegi, Rudolf Vetschera, and Gregory Kersten, "National Cultural Differences in the Use and Perception of Internet-Based NSS: Does High or Low Context Matter?" *International Negotiation* 9 (2004): 79–109.

14. *Winning Negotiations That Preserve Relationships,* The Results-Driven Manager Series (Boston: Harvard Business School Press, 2004).

15. Fisher et al., *Getting to Yes.*

16. Sue Shellenbarger, "The Peak Time for Everything," *Wall Street Journal,* September 26, 2012, https://www.wsj.com/articles/SB10000872396390444180004578018294057070544.

17. John Ilich, *The Art and Skill of Successful Negotiation* (Englewood Cliffs, NJ: Prentice Hall, 1983), 22. See also John Ilich, *The Complete Idiot's Guide to Winning Through Negotiation* (New York: Alpha Books, 1996).

18. Francesca Gino and Don Moore, "Using Final Deadlines Strategically in Negotiation," *Negotiation and Conflict Management Research* 1, no. 4 (2008): 371–88, doi: 10.1111/j.1750-4716.2008.00022.x.

19. Al K. C. Au and Ivy Yee-Man Lau, "Myopic Perception of Having a Deadline in Negotiations: An Anchoring Effect Due to Question Order," *Asian Journal of Social Psychology* 18, no. 3 (2015): 209–15, doi: 10.1111/ajsp.12084.

20. Markus Baer and Graham Brown, "Location in Negotiation: Is There a Home Field Advantage?" *Organizational Behavior and Human Decision Processes* 114, no. 2 (March 2011): 190–200.

21. Michael Benoliel, *Negotiation Excellence: Successful Deal Making,* 2nd ed. (Hackensack, NJ: World Scientific, 2014), 30.

22. Rosenbaum, "How to Steer Clear."

23. Dorothy Leads, *Smart Questions: A New Strategy for Successful Managers* (New York: McGraw-Hill, 1987).

24. Stuart Diamond, *Getting More: How to Negotiate to Achieve Your Goals in the Real World* (New York: Three Rivers Press, 2010).

25. Almut Koester, "'We'd Be Prepared to Do Something, Like If You Say . . .': Hypothetical Reported Speech in Business Negotiation," *English for Specific Purposes* 36 (2014): 35–36, doi: 10.1016/j.esp.2014.03.005.

26. G. G. Gosfield, "The Structure and Use of Letters of Intent as Prenegotiation Contracts for Prospective Real Estate Transactions," *Real Property, Probate & Trust Journal* 38, no. 1 (2003): 99–168.

27. David Pearl, "Does Virtual Negotiation Work?" *Commitment Matters,* May 12, 2014,

https://commitmentmatters.com/2014/05/12/does-virtual-negotiation-work.

28. Sunil K. Singh, Detelina Marinova, and Jagdip Singh, "Business-to-Business E-Negotiations and Influence Tactics," *Journal of Marketing* 84, no. 2 (2020): 47–68. doi: 10.1177/0022242919899381.

29. Nicholas Harkiolakis, Daphne Halkias, and Sam Abadir, *e-Negotiations, Networking, and Cross-Cultural Business Transactions* (New York: Routledge, 2016), 113.

30. Ibid., 114–15 (adapted).

31. These strategies are partially drawn from Roy J. Lewicki, *Mastering Business Negotiation: A Working Guide to Making Deals and Resolving Conflict* (Hoboken, NJ: Wiley, 2006).

32. Amy Shoenthal, "How The Riveter's Amy Nelson Built a More Inclusive Women's Coworking Space While Changing the Motherhood Narrative," *Forbes,* September 20, 2019, https://www.forbes.com/sites/amyschoenberger/2019/09/20/riveter-amy-nelson/#41a9f54b6993. See also Susan Dominus, "The Last Taboo: Transparency about Salaries Can Make Workplaces More Equitable, Especially for Women and People of Color," *New York Times Magazine,* February 23, 2020, 52–56. See also https://theriveter.co/about-us.

15

CONDUCTING INTERVIEWS

LEARNING OUTCOMES

By the end of this chapter, you will be able to

- Recognize and avoid several barriers to effective interviews.

- Analyze the situation to strategically plan interviews.

- Compose interview questions that will yield the type of information you need to make decisions.

- Prepare for three special interview situations: employment interviews, performance interviews, and professional networking.

A manager conducts many different kinds of interviews: performance, employment, persuasive, grievance, exit, problem-solving, and informational. No matter what the situation, the process is an intensive communication transaction designed to obtain or share certain predetermined kinds of information. But successful managers must learn to avoid the special communication barriers that accompany the process. Accordingly, this chapter examines interviews from the perspective of the interviewer, suggests ways to overcome the special barriers, and offers guidelines for conducting the most common kinds of interviews.

BARRIERS TO EFFECTIVE INTERVIEWS

All the communication dynamics discussed in Chapter 2 are present in the interview, but six barriers are particularly relevant: (1) differing intentions of the people involved, (2) bias, (3) confusing facts with inferences, (4) nonverbal communication, (5) effects of first impressions, and (6) organizational status.

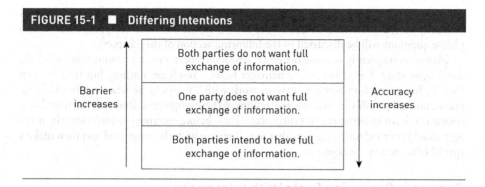

FIGURE 15-1 ■ Differing Intentions

Barrier 1: Differing Intentions

Managers cannot always assume all participants agree on the information that should be exchanged in an interview. In fact, rarely do both the interviewer and interviewee agree. One obvious instance is the employment interview. While the interviewer wants to know all the strengths and weaknesses of the applicant, the applicant (interviewee) wants to reveal only strengths to the interviewer.

The intentions of each party may align or conflict. In some situations, both parties consciously may intend to have a clear and accurate exchange of information. Examples of aligned intentions include performance appraisal interviews and informational interviews at networking events. In other situations, one of the parties does not intend to disclose certain relevant information. This often occurs in exit interviews, when the employee does not reveal the real reason for leaving. Occasionally, neither party intends to disclose certain relevant information. This may happen when an employee interviewed for a promotion discusses the potential salary. The employee will probably not reveal the lowest acceptable salary, and the interviewer does not indicate the highest possible salary. Figure 15-1 depicts these three levels of intentions.

Skillful questioning, which is reviewed in the next section of this chapter, helps overcome this barrier. Listening to the other person and understanding their point of view also help reduce this barrier. However, the key is to remember that the other person's goal may not always be the same as the manager's in the interview process.

Barrier 2: Bias

Bias is a barrier because it filters people's perceptions, so they tend to see and hear only what they want to see and hear. The most prevalent type of bias is the *halo effect*. Managers may unwittingly allow one aspect of the job to affect their impression of the employee in other areas.[1] If an employee has a tendency to be late, for instance, the manager could let this shortcoming influence their impression of the employee on other, unrelated characteristics, such as technical skills. The bias can create problems in employment and performance evaluation interviews in particular, as discussed later in this chapter. Another type of bias is the *recency effect*. This occurs when the latest information is weighed more heavily than earlier information. Bias is a barrier when irrelevant factors strongly influence managers' decisions.

Questions can also subtly bias an interview. For instance, one manager asked this loaded question: "Should the consumer group continue its generous support of the marketing research department when the research has proved to be of little value?" The question is obviously biased and would be difficult to answer in the affirmative. Appropriate ways to phrase questions will be discussed in the following section of this chapter.

Managers frequently become biased by coworkers' opinions, a phenomenon called the *bandwagon effect*. For instance, if a manager hears, "You'll get nothing but trouble from Patrick, but you'll find Semkins easy to work with," it would be wise to resist forming premature and possibly inaccurate impressions of these employees. Research has found that people can learn to better control their bias.[2] Thus, before entering the interview, the manager should try to identify any bias that may interfere with the main goal and then make a special effort to remain objective.

Barrier 3: Confusing Facts With Inferences

Managers actually deal with very few facts in an interview. Rather, they must make inferences based on the words and actions of the interviewee. Sometimes, managers can be "almost certain" about their conclusions from an interview, but other times they are not too sure.[3] When they are not sure, however, problems can arise. Table 15-1 reveals some problems caused by discrepancies among words, facts, and inferences.

Managers need to be on the alert to determine when they are making plausible inferences and when they are jumping to unfounded conclusions. Many of the techniques discussed later in the chapter help overcome this barrier. The simplest method for avoiding this confusion is to remember that a fact can be measured and proven, while an inference is an opinion or judgment and by definition subjective. Rereading the section in Chapter 2 about the assumption–observation error in communication may add to your understanding of this barrier.

TABLE 15-1 ■ Facts and Inferences		
Words	**Facts**	**Possible Inference**
"I like selling office equipment."	The record shows that the person has been selling for 2 years but before that was unemployed for 6 months.	This is the only work the person is able to get.
"I did well in college and was involved in some extracurricular activities" (when asked to fully describe college experiences).	The person tends to avoid discussion on these activities and changes the subject when asked specifically about grades.	The person did not do well in academic work in college and wasted time in extracurricular activities.
"I did not care for the atmosphere in that department" (said by an applicant for a job transfer).	The person received a poor performance review.	The applicant is a troublemaker.

Barrier 4: Nonverbal Communication

A quizzical look, a frown, a shrug, and a look of indifference are all important nonverbal messages, but those reading them must exercise caution before interpreting them. Nonverbal information can be a problem in an interview because interviews are generally short and intensive. If a person slouches in a chair for a few minutes during a 20-minute interview, this behavior is more noticeable than slouching for a few minutes during a 4-hour meeting. Because of the compact time span, nonverbal signals have a greater impact.

Accurately reading nonverbal signals during a compact time span is complicated by the *primary effect*—one piece of information overpowering all others. In a short period, one nonverbal cue can more easily overpower the others. This is especially the case when one has no baseline of nonverbal signs for judging the candidate. The careful interviewer also uses nonverbal signs from the interviewee to judge the honesty of responses. Research has indicated that through training and practice, managers can improve their ability to detect nonverbal deception.[4] This is further elaborated in the discussion of nonverbal leakage in Chapter 11.

Barrier 5: Effects of First Impressions

Managers may form a quick first impression that colors what they see during the rest of the interview. If the interview is short, this strong first view may affect their overall impression because they do not have the time to find data to the contrary. Further, research indicates that interviewers are influenced more by unfavorable than by favorable information, and the earlier in the interview the unfavorable information, the greater its negative effect.[5] In addition, it is more likely that the interviewer's impression will change from favorable to unfavorable than the opposite.[6]

This barrier may also be referred to as *hypothesis testing*, meaning that the interviewer establishes a hypothesis early and then seeks information that supports it. The fear is that any information that does not support the hypothesis will be ignored.[7]

Because this barrier is so pervasive, managers must act to limit its impact. Part of the solution is simple: Be cautious about making value judgments until evidence other than that available from first impressions has been considered. Then, too, be aware that short interviews encourage managers to make decisions prematurely.

CRITICAL THINKING QUESTIONS

1. When you are forming a first impression of someone, how important are that person's nonverbal behaviors (eye contact, body language, appearance) compared to what they say?

2. How can you avoid the hypothesis effect when conducting interviews?

3. What are the implications for your strategic processes as an interviewee?

Barrier 6: Organizational Status

Perhaps the most pervasive communication barrier results from hierarchical rank. In any workplace interview situation, the parties involved know who holds the balance of power.[8] While a higher-ranking person may encourage candor, the lower-level person may fear the consequences of such openness. It is only human to worry about the reactions of people in powerful positions, so candor frequently suffers.

Several suggestions can prevent it. For one thing, managers should recognize that employees almost always want to make the best impression when communicating with the boss. An effective manager should try to create an open, supportive communication climate that minimizes power differences. Details about communication strategies that will lead to supportive climates are provided later in this chapter. And when a manager hears something unpleasant, harsh, or unwarranted from a direct report, the manager should check any defensive reactions and try to remain open-minded and fair.

STRATEGIES FOR EFFECTIVE INTERVIEWS

Thorough analysis and planning are required for effective interviews. We believe the numerous contingencies can best be managed by addressing the following seven questions.

Strategy 1: What Is the Interview Objective?

First, consider the interview objective. Are you trying to obtain general information, gather specific data, or persuade someone to accept an idea? The interview objective indicates the format. However, the objective is not always clear, or the interview may have more than one objective. Consider the employment interview, in which a manager is simultaneously trying to gather general information about the applicant and specific information about the applicant's skill set in order to determine whether they fit the requirements. All the while, the manager is trying to sell the applicant on the benefits of joining the company. Because several goals may apply at one time, it is important to clarify the purpose of the interview and set priorities.

Strategy 2: Where Is the Best Place to Conduct the Interview?

Time and place have an impact on the success of an interview. Managers should select a time that is mutually convenient. Managers should also allow adequate time so that neither party in the interview feels rushed. Finally, managers should be aware of the primacy–recency effect when scheduling a series of interviews. People tend to recall most favorably the first and the last of a series of events. This psychological phenomenon can affect hiring decisions in particular.

Privacy is also a primary concern. It ensures confidentiality, reduces anxiety, and minimizes interferences. Many managers find they can best eliminate distractions by conducting the interview in a place other than their work area or office. Remember that a neutral setting also reduces the status barrier present in many interviews.

Strategy 3: What Is the Best Way to Begin the Interview?

This question and the next are closely related. The opening statements lay the foundation for the questioning to follow. The opening of an interview generally serves two purposes: (1) It establishes the communication climate, and (2) it explains the purpose of the interview.

The interview climate is established as soon as the manager meets the interviewee. At that point, nonverbal communication plays a crucial role. A friendly greeting, handshake, or smile will break the ice and help put the interviewee at ease. Friendly conversation about a neutral topic also puts everyone at ease. In her book *The Art of Civilized Conversation*, Margaret Shepherd suggests avoiding clichéd topics such as the weather and instead beginning by asking about the journey ("Did you have any trouble finding us?"), the situation ("What did you think of that speech?"), or the recent past ("How was your summer vacation?").[9] One to 4 minutes of small talk should be sufficient. No matter what the purpose of the interview is, managers should always begin by establishing rapport. This makes the interviewee feel safe and ensures two-way communication.

Next, the manager should affirm the interview's purpose. Typical starters are

- summarizing the problem or task at hand,

- requesting advice or assistance,

- mentioning an incentive or reward for taking part in the interview, or

- requesting a specific time commitment for the interview.

In addition to stating the purpose of the interview, the manager should check to be sure that the interviewee agrees. This encourages a participatory attitude and may stimulate the other person's involvement in the interview. Thus, the opening, which may take the least time of all the segments in the interview process, is a crucial part and sets the stage.

Strategy 4: What Is the Best Questioning Strategy?

Developing a questioning strategy before the interview helps a manager reach the interview's goal (see Table 15-2). One strategy is the *structured interview*, in which the interviewer writes out preliminary questions in sequence. This technique is effective for ensuring

TABLE 15-2 ■ Interview Questioning Strategies	
Strategy	**When to Use It**
Structured	Inexperienced interviewer
	To compare interviewees' responses to the same questions
Semi-structured	Experienced interviewer
	When the flexibility of the question sequence may bring unexpected information to the surface
Unstructured	When the interviewee should set the direction of the interview

consistency across multiple interviewees, especially in job interviews.[10] A rigid structure also supports inexperienced interviewers. In these situations, the interviewer knows exactly what information they are trying to elicit.

In unique or developing situations, interviewers may need to use an exploratory technique. An *unstructured interview* permits flexibility for the interviewer to adapt the questions as the situation evolves. Here, the interviewer has a clear objective but has prepared no specific questions in advance. With an unstructured format, the interviewer initiates the discussion, letting the initial responses lead into the next question. This type of interview is particularly valuable when it is important that the interviewee helps set the direction—as in some performance interviews or certain counseling sessions. Also, this type of interview facilitates the communication flow in informational interviews at networking activities.

A compromise between the structured and unstructured interview is the *semi-structured interview*. In this format, the interviewer prepares a list of critical questions that will cover all important points by the close of the interview. Meanwhile, the interviewer maintains flexibility because the sequence of the questioning is not completely planned. Many consider this the most appropriate format for most situations faced by experienced managers.

Strategy 5: What Is the Best Sequence for the Questions?

For a semi-structured interview, a funnel or inverted funnel question sequence is recommended. The funnel sequence opens with broad, open-ended questions and proceeds with increasingly restricted questions. The inverted funnel sequence begins with closed questions and gradually proceeds toward open-ended ones. Figure 15-2 shows these two sequences.

The appropriate strategy depends on the situation. The funnel sequence works best when the interviewee is able and willing to talk freely, such as in an employment interview. The inverted funnel works best when the interviewee is reluctant to participate or is hostile

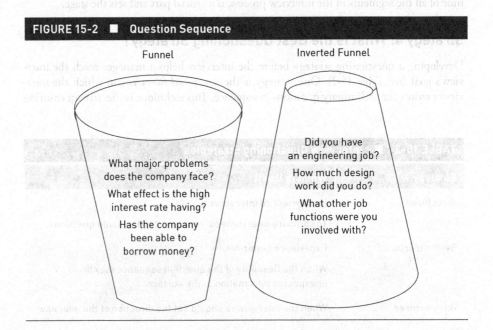

FIGURE 15-2 ■ Question Sequence

Funnel

What major problems does the company face?

What effect is the high interest rate having?

Has the company been able to borrow money?

Inverted Funnel

Did you have an engineering job?

How much design work did you do?

What other job functions were you involved with?

toward the manager. Thus, for example, during an exit interview, the manager might begin with specific, factual questions and move gradually toward general questions about changes the interviewee feels are needed in the workplace.

Strategy 6: What Are the Best Types of Questions?

Interview questions fall into three wording categories: open/closed, primary/secondary, and neutral/directed. The various types of questions were discussed in Chapter 10 and are summarized here.

An *open* question has virtually no restriction on the type of response that is received. At the other extreme is the *closed* question, which calls for specific, short responses. Table 15-3 compares examples of open and closed questions.

TABLE 15-3 ■ Open Versus Closed Questions	
Open Questions	**Closed Questions**
1. How was your last job?	1. What part of your last job did you dislike?
2. Tell me more about the Niles project.	2. What percentage of the Niles project is completed?
3. How is everything in the Denver Division?	3. Did you complete the quarterly report for the Denver Division?
4. Tell me about yourself.	4. Have you ever toured our Los Angeles facility?

Managers sometimes ask closed questions when they should be asking open questions. Managers need to decide if they are looking for a general response or a specific answer. Are they trying to solicit information (open), trying to make the interviewee comfortable (open), or trying to get to a specific point or commitment as quickly as possible (closed)? The answers to these strategic questions help one select open or closed question formats.

The second category of questions is *primary* and *secondary*. A primary question introduces a topic in an interview, while a secondary question follows up, probing further into the response to the primary question. A secondary question is most valuable when the primary question did not elicit all the desired information.

The following dialogue gives an example of the use of primary and secondary questions:

Interviewer:	What was your most recent job? (primary)
Interviewee:	I supervised the AR Department.
Interviewer:	What is the AR Department? (secondary)
Interviewee:	That's the accounts receivable group that does all the. . . .

In this example, the secondary question elicited additional information for the interviewer.

A subtle form of secondary question is a probe. Table 15-4 presents seven types of probes. Again, notice that in an informal interview, although these probes obtain additional information, they may not appear to be questions but rather may seem to be part of the conversation. They are subtle but effective.

TABLE 15-4 ■ Seven Probes		
Probe	**Definition of Probe**	**Illustration of Probe**
1. Brief assertion of understanding	B indicates interest and understanding, thus encouraging A to continue.	"So first I said to him, how'd you like a cup of coffee?" *"You thought it would break the ice."*
2. Neutral phrase	B elicits more information from A without affecting (biasing) the information.	"I don't know . . . kids today seem to be getting away with murder." *"Huh."*
3. Silence	B does not speak and looks attentively at A. The pause is under 10 seconds.	"Wow . . . what a day I've had." *Silence—2 seconds.* "I mean, I didn't have a minute to myself the way they kept me working."
4. Echo	B converts the last portion of what A says into a question . . . generally with almost the same words.	"I'm not sure that I can take any more. . . . I'm at the end of my rope." *"At the end of your rope?"*
5. Clarification	B tries to get a definition or further explanation from A that is not understood.	"I'll tell you, shortening our lunch breaks isn't right." *"Oh . . . how so?"* "Well, for one thing, it prevents me from running errands."
6. Elaboration	B requests new information that is directly related to something A already said.	"Bob, I'm really worried about the parade tomorrow." *"Why are you worried?"* "Well, I think we might be in for some trouble." *"Oh . . . what makes you think that we might have trouble?"*
7. Summary	B tries to pull together the main points A made during the past few minutes.	"And finally, Boss, we just don't get paid enough for the work we do." *"Let me see if I have it straight. First, you say the work is dirty, not carefully scheduled, and finally, you're underpaid, correct?"*

Secondary questions help gain complete and accurate information, but they also establish a positive communication climate in the interview. The effective use of secondary questions and probes can demonstrate that the manager is interested in listening. Initially, the interviewee may not know how much information is wanted or whether the manager is really interested in their comments; however, the use of secondary questions and probes helps establish a willing and open atmosphere.

A *neutral* question does not lead the interviewee to answer in one particular way. A *directed* question, on the other hand, leads the interviewee to give a particular answer. The classic example of a directed question is the courtroom ploy "Isn't it true that . . . ?" In reality, this type of extreme directed question may be considered a plea for agreement rather than a true question, even when an interrogative tone is used.[11] Table 15-5 compares examples of neutral and directed questions.

TABLE 15-5 ■ Neutral Versus Directed Questions

Neutral Questions	Directed Questions
1. What kind of car do you prefer?	1. Don't you think that foreign cars are superior to American cars?
2. What is your reaction to decentralization?	2. You are opposed to decentralization, aren't you?
3. What do you think of unionization?	3. Naturally, you are opposed to any kind of unions, right?
4. Do you feel we should hire more employees?	4. I don't think we should hire any more employees. Do you?

The skillful use of directed questions can be valuable because such questions can help keep the interview on track and can be used effectively for persuasion. In persuasion, they point the interviewee in a particular direction and help them think about the benefit of some concept.

Strategy 7: What Is the Best Way to Close the Interview?

When it is time to close the interview, as with many other communications, it is important to summarize the main information and ensure understanding. The close also provides the opportunity to arrange for any follow-up activity and to express appreciation. Goodwill is always appropriate, whether the interviewee is a job applicant, a disgruntled customer, a networking associate, or a long-term, loyal employee. End with agreement, a statement of appreciation, and a handshake.

So far, this chapter has described the barriers to interviews, as well as the strategies managers should use in any type of workplace interview. Next, we will focus on three specific interview situations that managers experience, as well as the appropriate strategies for each: employment interviews, performance interviews, and networking.

EMPLOYMENT INTERVIEWS

Selecting the most qualified people available for a position is a major managerial responsibility. Many screening tools are used in employee selection, including application forms and aptitude and personality tests, but the most common is the interview.

While a member of the human resources department often screens applicants, the applicant's future manager generally makes the final decision. The ability to match competent applicants with the correct job leads to the success of an organization. Making good hiring decisions also reduces the cost of turnover, which can be significant. According to a study by the Society for Human Resource Management, employers will need to spend the equivalent of 6 to 9 months of an employee's salary in order to find and train their replacement.[12] More than 75 percent of turnover can be traced back to poor interviewing and hiring practices, according to a Harvard Business School study.[13] Managers have a responsibility to both the organization and the applicant to see that an applicant–job match exists.

CRITICAL THINKING QUESTIONS

1. If a job applicant's résumé indicates they have the skill set required to do a certain job, why should you conduct a pre-employment interview before making an offer?

2. What are some qualifications that can be determined only by an interview?

Yet employment interviews are typically not used to their best advantage. While research shows that an unstructured interview, where a manager attempts to "get to know" an applicant, is low in both reliability and validity,[14] a well-planned structured interview gives managers the chance to personally evaluate candidates and to gather useful information that résumés and personality tests cannot provide.

Planning

The employment interview, like all communication situations, requires planning but in a more specific way. Managers should list the position's requirements, recall the organization's culture, and review the applicant's documentation before heading into an interview. A manager's first step is to ensure a clear understanding of the job requirements. This effort helps avoid putting too much weight on irrelevant information. An interviewer familiar with extensive details about the job to be filled (such as that provided by detailed job descriptions and job titles) enhances the reliability of employment selection decisions. When no comprehensive job description is available, it may be necessary for the interviewer to complete a job analysis.

When reviewing the nature of the job, be careful not to compare the last *person* holding the job with present candidates. Doing so can inaccurately affect your impressions of a candidate. Also, many job incumbents change the nature of a position slightly to match their personal capabilities and interests. A good time to analyze the present and future qualifications required for performance on a job is when personnel changes are made.

Another consideration for managers who are preparing to conduct a job interview is the organization's culture, mission, and vision. C-level executives (CEO, CFO, chief information officer [CIO], chief operating officer [COO], etc.) in particular are likely to ask questions that will determine whether a candidate's values align with the organization's philosophy.[15] For instance, Barry Salzberg, CEO of Deloitte LLP, says that he looks for an applicant's speaking and writing skills, values, and "worldly experiences," including traveling and working for nonprofits. If he could ask only a couple of questions in an interview, they would be "What are the values that are most important to you? How have you demonstrated your commitment to those values in the last two years?"[16] As a list of requirements develops, the interviewer should prepare questions that will determine whether an applicant can meet them. For example, if the job requires extensive teamwork, a poor question is "Are you a team player?" because it is closed and because a yes response tells the interviewer nothing useful. A better question is "Can you describe the advantages and disadvantages of working on a team?" because it is open and will reveal the applicant's experiences, beliefs, and behaviors.

Finally, interviewers should review the application packet before the interview to plan specific questions. Remember that the interview objective is to get information that documents cannot easily reveal, including motivation and personality characteristics. Clearly, time is wasted if the interview covers the same material that appears in the documents. But managers can also use the interview to clarify inconsistencies or fill in gaps. In short, use the documents as a springboard for the interview topics.

Legal Concerns

By now, almost all managers are familiar with the Americans with Disabilities Act of 1990 and the Civil Rights Act of 1964, which was amended by the Equal Employment Opportunity (EEO) Act of 1972. Unfortunately, knowledge of the legal restrictions of employment interviewing is too often misapplied. Managers may become too cautious in their questioning out of fear of the law and miss valuable information, or they may ignore the legal restrictions. Although the following paragraphs do not constitute a comprehensive discussion of the legal components of employment, several suggestions may help you in your employment interviews.

Probably the first thing that comes to managers' minds when discussing EEO is what constitutes a lawful or unlawful question. To answer this, one needs to be aware of the concept of bona fide occupational qualification (BFOQ), which is *any characteristic that is a valid criterion of job performance*. Race, age, national origin, general health, religion, gender, ethnic background, number of children, and marital status are generally not bases on which people's ability to do a job should be judged.

Generally, education, experience, abilities, and skills are the basic elements of BFOQs, although each job must be analyzed. In most situations, managers can follow guidelines that ensure no condition of the Equal Employment Opportunity Act is being ignored. The best advice is to ask only questions that are related to BFOQs or directly related to making an objective employment decision.

Keep in mind, too, that casual conversations with job applicants should respect the guidelines set out here. For example, suppose a job applicant is being treated to lunch. Do not confuse this with a truly social situation and make small talk about family, personal finances, or religion. These could be misconstrued by the candidates as irrelevant, non-BFOQ questions and represent grounds for later disputes should a job offer not materialize.

CRITICAL THINKING QUESTIONS

When, if ever, are these job interview questions lawful?

1. Can you drive?
2. Can you work on Sundays?
3. Is English your first language?
4. Do you own your own home?
5. Are you willing to relocate for the job?

Table 15-6 presents guidelines regarding lawful and unlawful questions during the employment interview. These same considerations also apply to application forms. Discrimination occurs when an individual who has an equal probability of being successful in a job does not have an equal probability of getting the job.[17] A manager is responsible for seeing that discrimination does not occur.

TABLE 15-6 ■ Question Guidelines for Employment Interviews		
Focus of Question	**Nondiscriminatory**	**Possibly Discriminatory**
Name	Have you ever used a different name in other jobs?	What was your name before you changed it?
Birthplace and residence	Which state do you presently live in? How long have you lived in Cedar Falls (or a given state)? Are you over 18 years of age?	Where were you born? In which country were your parents born? How old are you?
Physical characteristics, including race	Do you have any distinguishing marks or scars?	Are you Asian?
National origin or ancestry	If hired, can you verify that you can legally work in the United States?	You're from Germany, aren't you? Are you related to the Manuels from Hermosa?
Family status	(No nondiscriminatory options.)	How many children do you have? Are you married? Pregnant?
Religion	Here are the regular days, hours, or shifts to be worked: . . .	Are you Jewish? Do you pray? What religious holidays will you be taking off if we hire you?
Citizenship	Are you legally able to work in the United States?	Are you Canadian?
Affiliations	Do you belong to any professional-related organizations?	Are you in the Daughters of the American Revolution (DAR)? Were you a member of the Catholic Students Club?
Arrest record and convictions	(No nondiscriminatory options. May be illegal to ask in some areas.[18])	How often have you been arrested and for what?
Physical abilities or limitations	This job requires lifting and carrying; do you see any problems with that?	How severe is your arthritis?
Financial status	(No nondiscriminatory options.)	Have you ever had your wages garnished? What is your approximate net worth? How much is your mortgage?

The Employment Interview Process

During the employment interview, managers try to find out as much as possible about a candidate that relates to potential job success. The following guidelines assist managers in their efforts to increase the reliability and validity of the interview.

Use an Appropriate Questioning Strategy

Research indicates that the form and sequence of questions profoundly influence the outcome of the interview.[19] Most interviews open positively, with the manager attempting to put the interviewee at ease. The résumé can be a useful guide for selecting some strong point from the candidate's background to help make the interviewee comfortable in the beginning.[20] The interviewer next proceeds to gather information, generally using a semi-structured format that not only ensures a definite direction is taken but also allows the opportunity for additional questions based on the applicant's responses. Toward the end, the interviewer invites the applicant to ask questions, the choice of which might also reveal the applicant's interests and motivations. At the close, the interviewer should summarize and explain the next step. Table 15-7 lists appropriate questions for each part of the interview.

When designing the questions for the interview, remember the difference between open and closed, primary and secondary, and neutral and directed questions. Know the benefits and shortcomings of each of these types of questions so that you can implement an effective questioning strategy. An employment interview generally uses open questions, but it can also probe with closed and directed questions.

A special type of question that is successfully used in employment interviews is the *behavioral question*. Based on the premise that past behavior predicts future behavior, these questions ask about specific instances of a particular action. Managers can use behavioral questions to probe for more information behind empty generalizations, such as "I'm a people person" and "I'm a hard worker." Typically, behavioral questions begin with "Tell me about a time when you . . ." and follow with situations or qualities relevant to the position, thus requiring evidence to "prove" the applicant's claims. Behaviors demonstrating leadership, conflict management, handling difficult customers, goal setting, teamwork, attention to detail, and the like can be effectively explored using behavioral questions. For example, if a manager of a diverse workforce is looking for someone who fits in with people with different values, cultures, or backgrounds, an appropriate behavioral question is "Describe a time when you adapted your behavior around another person's style," or "Describe something you did to optimize the benefits of diversity at work."

Another special type of question that is becoming popular in certain employment interviews is the *problem-solving question*. Its purpose is to seek out creative talent, a necessity for companies where competitive advantage is gained through its people. Microsoft, Boeing, IBM, Southwest Airlines, and Weyerhaeuser are among the 20 to 30 percent of companies using situational or problem-solving questions, according to Professor Vandra Huber of the University of Washington.[21] The following are some sample problem-solving questions that have been used during Microsoft interviews:

- Estimate the number of gas stations in the United States.

- If you could remove any of the 50 states, which would it be, and why?

- Design a bathroom for me.

- If you have a fishbowl with 200 fish and 99 percent are guppies, how many guppies do you need to remove to get to the point where 98 percent of the remaining fish are guppies?[22]

Clearly, the answers to such questions are not as important as the process the candidate uses to (a) determine the problem and (b) develop solutions. A description of the steps in the rational problem-solving process can be found in Chapters 4 and 13.

TABLE 15-7 ■ Interviewer Question Options

Opening
How was the trip over here?
I see from your résumé that you were a college athlete. Tell me how that helped you prepare for the workplace.

Body—Determining Motivation
Why do you want to change jobs?
What led you to enter this profession?
Where would you like to be in your career 5 years from now? Ten years?
What do you see as the perfect job for you?

Body—Determining Experience
What did you do while you were in the military that would be relevant to this position?
How would you go about improving our operations?
What aspects of your last job did you like best/least? Why?
What are your greatest strengths/weaknesses for this position?
How do you like to be managed?
What are your greatest achievements to date?
What equipment/software are you familiar with?
May I see examples of your work?

Body—Evaluating Educational Background
Why did you choose your college major?
What extracurricular activities did you participate in that helped you prepare for your profession?
What honors did you earn?
To what extent do your grades reflect your full ability?
What special training have you had for this position?

Closing
What questions do you have for me?
Is there anything else you want us to know as we consider your application?

Do Not Do Most of the Talking

In employment interviews, some interviewers make the mistake of talking more than listening, which risks gathering inadequate information about the interviewee.[23] Active listening is essential during the interview process, as it allows for more information about the applicant to be gained and better decisions to be made. A guideline is that the manager should talk only 30 percent of the time during an employment interview.

Keep Records

Given all the information revealed during an interview, it is unrealistic to expect that it can be remembered accurately for any length of time. One study showed that half the interviewers could not accurately recall the most critical information produced in a 20-minute interview.[24] Thus, managers should record a summary of the interview immediately after its completion. One option is to use a rating system. This minimizes the possibility of erroneously making an early decision or letting one or two negative characteristics predominate. Another option is to have a routine form that reports on the same areas for each candidate interviewed or records answers to the same questions. A formal evaluation procedure guards against bias and unwarranted impressions, as described earlier in this chapter.

Be Cautious About Virtual Interviews

Virtual interviews are increasingly popular, particularly at the screening phase of employment interviews. Interviewing by phone, videoconference, or computer permits an organization to broaden its pool of applicants beyond its normal geographic borders while keeping costs low. However, as discussed in Chapter 3, computer-mediated communication removes many nonverbal cues that managers rely on to evaluate candidates' interpersonal skills. For example, in a videoconference interview, camera angles can prohibit eye contact, which is often considered a marker of honesty. In a phone interview, the parties may accidentally interrupt each other, which can seem rude, and then overcompensate with long pauses between responses, which can seem timid. Digital interviews, in which applicants record short video answers to structured prompts, often feel impersonal and even creepy.[25]

The awkwardness of virtual interviews interferes with impression management, a candidate's attempt to influence how interviewers perceive them.[26] They may struggle to accurately gauge the response to their answers and feel they did not get an adequate chance to demonstrate their knowledge and skills to the interviewers. At best, their confidence may be weakened; at worst, candidates may feel frustrated and leave with a negative impression of the organization.[27]

To alleviate some of the reservations toward virtual interviews, managers should explain the rationale for their use. In addition to lowering the costs of interviewing for both parties, the structured nature of virtual interviews offers greater reliability and may remove some bias, particularly the primacy bias mentioned earlier.[28] For interviewers, virtual interviews consume less time than traditional interviews. For interviewees, they create opportunities to meet with a greater range of organizations and remove the inconvenience of travel in early stages of the job application.

PERFORMANCE INTERVIEWS

Periodically, managers are called on to conduct performance interviews. In addition to fairly and accurately assessing an employee's past performance, effective managers use interviews to accomplish a number of other goals. More than 20 purposes have emerged from a robust body of research on performance interviews, which can be categorized into four factors:[29]

- *Administrative:* recognizing individual performance for salary, promotion, retention, and termination

- *Developmental:* identifying training needs, determining assignments, and identifying strengths and weaknesses

- *Strategic:* setting goals, evaluating goal achievement, and aligning performance with goals

- *Role definition:* reinforcing authority structure and clarifying organizational processes

While the potential benefits of the performance interview seem evident, its infrequent and ineffective use in organizations is widely recognized. Samuel Culbert, a professor of management at the University of California, Los Angeles, and author of *Get Rid of the Performance Review!*, calls it "the most ridiculous practice in the world [because] it's . . . fraudulent, dishonest at its core, and reflects . . . cowardly management." Culbert sees performance reviews as a way to intimidate employees and concludes that they do more harm than good.[30]

CRITICAL THINKING QUESTIONS

1. Refer to the discussion of feedback in Chapter 2. How can a performance interview help a manager improve, as well as an employee?

2. What types of questions should a manager ask when eliciting feedback from an employee about the manager's performance?

This contradiction exists for several reasons, including that managers do not like to be put into the role of evaluator. Some managers may fear that their working relationship with direct reports will be destroyed because of the discomfort created by a poorly conducted performance interview.[31] Another reason may be that managers often are not adequately trained in conducting these interviews.[32] Knowledge of the following information should encourage managers to conduct performance interviews that reach their intended purposes.

Types

In general, performance interviews either focus on evaluating the worker's past performance or focus on future activities and set goals that will lead to increased employee performance. A critical question is relevant here: Does a manager discuss goals, performance improvement, and personal development in the same interview as salary increases? Extensive review of the available research on this question makes it clear that one should not combine specific developmental topics and salary discussions in one interview. The importance of the salary review typically dominates the interview, so neither the manager nor the employee is in the proper frame of mind to discuss plans for improvement in a positive manner.[33] Instead, two separate interviews would be more appropriate: a *performance review* that can occur any time, such as weekly or quarterly, as part of an ongoing feedback loop; and a *performance appraisal* that is part of a formal process linked to decisions about compensation, promotion, and job assignment. This requires more time but generally yields more positive outcomes.

Goals of performance interviews can vary according to the nature of the job and the employees[34] (see Table 15-8). *Developmental* interviews are used for high-performing, high-potential employees who have discretionary jobs giving them the opportunity to implement performance improvement.

The *maintenance* interview is used for those who have performed at a steady, satisfactory level for some time and are not likely to improve because of constraints of ability, motivation, or the nature of their jobs. In this situation, the interviewee focuses on maintaining performance at the currently acceptable levels.

The *remedial* interview is used for low-performing or marginal employees in an attempt to raise performance to acceptable levels. This category involves two processes: evaluation and development. First, evaluate the present and past performances and then determine how they can be improved.

Each interview calls for a different degree of evaluation and development. More development is emphasized in the developmental and remedial interviews and more evaluation in the maintenance interview. A performance interview does not always meet the same purpose; consequently, different communication strategies must be implemented to meet the established goals of either evaluation or development. In implementing the appropriate strategy, planning is required, just as it is in other interview formats.

Planning

Recall the strategic managerial communication model presented in Chapter 2. The third layer of the model shows the three main factors that managers should consider when planning the performance interview: the timing, the environment, and the message content— that is, when, where, and what.

TABLE 15-8 ■ Goals of Performance Interviews	
Goal	**When to Use**
Developmental	High-performing employees
	High-potential employees
Maintenance	Steady, satisfactory employees
	Long-term employees
Remedial	Low-performing employees
	Marginal employees

Timing

Formal appraisals are usually conducted on an annual basis, but coaching and informal feedback should be provided to employees throughout the year. There should never be surprises during a formal appraisal because it should be a summary of all the prior conversations between managers and their employees about positive feedback, corrective feedback, career path, and compensation.

Why perform a formal appraisal once a year when more frequent feedback is provided? For one thing, an annual appraisal helps overcome the critical communication errors discussed in Chapter 2. A formal appraisal also provides the opportunity to systematically review the possibility that different assumptions have developed between employees and managers. Periodic "course correction" makes sense for even very satisfactory employees. It can be used to update the position descriptions to reflect current needs or identify gaps that need to be addressed or reassigned to someone else. Also, certain situations, such as the completion of a major project or unusually poor performance, require formal feedback. Consider the entire situation when determining the best time for a performance appraisal.

Once the time is selected, inform the employee of the interview well in advance. The lead time required may vary from several hours to several weeks, depending on the employee and the type of job involved. In any event, avoid the "stop by my office as soon as you get a chance" type of preparation, which deprives the employee of the opportunity to prepare psychologically for the interview.

Environment

Once the necessary time and timing are determined, consider the best place for the interview. Managers tend to schedule the performance appraisal in their own offices without realizing how potentially threatening this environment may be, especially when the employee is not accustomed to spending much time in the manager's office. Often, the best place for the interview is in a neutral, safe, private location to maximize two-way interaction.

Message Content

Once the time and place of the interview are established, focus on the content of the session. Regardless of the specific interview purpose, review expectations and goals. To appreciate these fully, review the position description and other dimensions of the employee's job. Research suggests that employees are more satisfied by performance interviews that focus on role definitions and connect their work to organizational goals.[35] In addition, review the previous performance appraisal, notes from informal meetings or correspondence with the employee, and recent job performance items. You may even want to solicit information from customers or other managers who have observed the employee's performance. All these procedures allow a manager the opportunity to list specific items that must be discussed in the interview.

To give employees the opportunity to prepare for the interview, they might complete a self-evaluation form before the interview. Managers often use standardized performance evaluation forms or a separate form similar to that shown in Table 15-9.

The more opportunity an employee has to participate in the process, the greater the possibility that open and valuable communication will result. Studies show that performance appraisal discussions based on a self-review of performance are more satisfying than are those based strictly on manager-prepared appraisals.[36] For the performance appraisal to provide feedback to an employee and to establish goals, a trusting environment must be established.

The next section describes the process that will lead to a trusting environment.

TABLE 15-9 ■ Employee Self-Appraisal Checklist

The purpose of this form is to help you prepare for your performance appraisal.

Be ready to discuss any of your specific accomplishments or problems that have occurred since the last performance appraisal.

Set aside some time and review your job since the last appraisal, so that you can answer the following questions:

1. How would you evaluate your communication and interpersonal skills? Examples include communicating effectively, developing and maintaining positive working relationships with others, and demonstrating cultural competence and sensitivity to diversity.

2. How would you evaluate your planning and effectiveness? Examples include planning projects appropriately, completing tasks thoroughly and in a timely manner, managing multiple responsibilities, delegating when appropriate, and being flexible and dependable.

3. How would you evaluate your decision making and problem solving? Examples include identifying and evaluating problems objectively, formulating sound decisions and recommendations, encouraging participation in decision making, demonstrating resourcefulness in problem solving, dealing effectively with changing situations, and working effectively under pressure.

4. How have you demonstrated leadership? Examples include modeling integrity and ethical behaviors, providing initiative and direction for your unit, building positive relationships internally and externally, modeling good judgment, and providing effective supervision.

5. How would you evaluate your overall contribution to the organization? Examples include understanding and contributing to achieving the strategic goals, representing the organization competently to external constituencies, contributing to positive morale, demonstrating interest and involvement in organizational activities, and promoting positive public relations.

6. What are some unusually difficult problems you have solved?

7. Describe any special assignments that you carried out with distinction or any emergencies that you handled skillfully.

8. Determine one or two areas where you think you could improve something if you had the right support from your manager.

Source: Adapted from "Performance Evaluations" in the Minnesota State University, Mankato *Supervisor's Toolkit,* http://www.mnsu.edu/hr/supertool/performance2.html.

The Performance Interview Process

Although the parties involved already know each other and the purpose of the meeting is established in advance, it is still necessary to begin in a friendly, warm manner. It is a good practice to establish rapport, then quickly restate the purpose of the session to ensure mutual agreement and to open the communication channels.

Once the climate is established, the manager reviews past performance with the employee. This step includes the element of listening. As Chapter 10 emphasizes, listening is the key skill to learning. Thus, an early question might be "What is the accomplishment you are most proud of during the period since your last performance interview?" After listening to the answer, the manager can agree and expand and possibly note other achievements.

The logical next topic might be introduced with the question "During this period, what do you think you should have done differently?" This question not only allows the manager to learn what mistakes the employee self-identifies but also moves the discussion quickly away from blame and toward solutions. Thus, the body of the interview does not consist solely of the manager telling the employee what was observed regarding their performance; the manager also elicits the employee's perceptions, both positive and negative, and listens to the reasons they give for their performance, whether it was satisfactory or unsatisfactory. The employee may even indicate the causes behind the behaviors, which the manager may then reinforce or redirect. In addition, research shows that when managers work together with employees to make judgments about employee performance, perceptions of procedural and interactional justice in the process have a positive impact on organizational commitment.[37]

The closing of the interview should focus on the future, identifying concrete action plans for both the employee and the manager. This problem-solving approach is based on the premise that two-way communication leads to a mutually acceptable plan for performance improvement. This approach allows employees a measure of freedom and responsibility to participate in goal setting; however, the climate must be right for employees to express themselves.

Supportive Communication Climate

Two researchers at an Australian university recently studied difficult conversations in three work situations. Their purpose was to discover why these conversations are difficult and what can be done to make them less so. They concluded that difficulties arise when participants feel criticized, threatened, and defensive; managers who can minimize such negative emotions by creating a supportive communication environment are able to maximize positive outcomes such as behavior change.[38]

The researchers' findings about the importance of supportive communication provide empirical evidence for the iconic model of supportive climates that was developed by Jack Gibb more than 50 years ago. Table 15-10 draws on Gibb's classic work to differentiate the communication process that leads to a supportive rather than a defensive environment.[39] Examples of statements from each of these categories are shown in Tables 15-11 to 15-15; comparing the paired examples may help you develop an effective communication strategy for the performance interview.

TABLE 15-10 ■ Supportive and Defensive Climates	
Defensive Climate	**Supportive Climate**
Evaluative	Descriptive
Control	Problem orientation
Neutrality	Empathy
Superiority	Equality
Certainty	Provisionalism

TABLE 15-11 ■ Examples of Evaluative Versus Descriptive Statements	
Evaluative	**Descriptive**
You simply have to stop making so many silly mistakes.	We're still getting more than three errors per run with the new system.
Bob, you're tactless and rude.	Bob, some people say they are offended by your humor.
The delay was definitely your fault because you didn't follow instructions.	There seems to be some confusion about the instructions.

TABLE 15-12 ■ Examples of Statements Reflecting Control Versus Problem Orientation	
Control	**Problem Orientation**
Here is what you can do to reduce errors.	What do you think could be done to reduce errors?
You definitely have a problem with that project.	We've got a problem with this project. What's our best move?
Stop being so negative around here.	How do you think we could develop a more positive approach?

TABLE 15-13 ■ Examples of Statements Reflecting Neutrality Versus Empathy	
Neutrality	**Empathy**
That really isn't much of a problem.	Sounds like you're really concerned about it. Tell me more about the situation.
Everybody has to face that at one time or another.	That can be a tough situation. I'll tell you how I've seen it handled before, and then you can give me your reaction.
Well, everyone is entitled to an opinion.	I think we disagree. Let's discuss this further and compare viewpoints.

TABLE 15-14 ■ Examples of Statements Reflecting Superiority Versus Equality	
Superiority	**Equality**
After working on this kind of problem for 10 years, I know how to handle it.	This solution has worked before, so it should work here, too.
I'm getting paid more than you, so it is my responsibility to make this kind of decision.	It's my ultimate responsibility to make the decision, but I want your recommendations.
The type of problems I face shouldn't be of interest to people at your level.	I want to share with you the type of situations I'm involved with.

TABLE 15-15 ■ Examples of Statements Reflecting Certainty Versus Provisionalism	
Certainty	**Provisionalism**
I know what the problem is, so there isn't much reason to talk about it.	I have some ideas, but it would be good to talk about it.
This is the way it's going to be done.	Let's try it this way for a while and see what happens.
I want it to be completed by June 1.	What needs to be done to ensure that it's completed by June 1?

Evaluative Versus Descriptive

Communication that blames a direct report naturally leads to a defensive climate. Avoid statements that make moral assessments of another or that question an individual's values and motives. Descriptive communication provides specific feedback and does not judge the receiver. The examples in Table 15-11 show the difference that might occur during a performance interview.

Notice that the evaluative examples typically are less specific and make inferences about the receiver's personality. These types of comments lead to defensiveness.

Control Versus Problem Orientation

Problem-oriented communication defines a mutual problem and seeks a solution. Controlling communication tries to do "something" to another person, such as forcing a change in a behavior or an attitude. The problem orientation conveys respect for the employee's ability to work on a problem and to formulate meaningful answers to the problem. Table 15-12 shows some examples of control and problem-oriented communication. The problem-oriented comments develop more opportunities for two-way communication by using open questions and indicating a concern for solving the problem in a cooperative manner. Listening is also a productive by-product of the problem-solving approach.

Neutrality Versus Empathy

Neutrality expresses a lack of concern for the well-being of the employee, whereas empathy shows that the manager identifies with the employee's problem, shares their feelings, and accepts the emotional values involved. Compare the examples in Table 15-13.

Managers show empathy in the performance interview when they are willing to listen, when they inquire how the employee feels about something, and when they attempt to understand and accept the employee's feelings. Empathy cannot be developed when a person is hastily cut off from communicating any further or the listener demonstrates a lack of interest in the message.

Superiority Versus Equality

The smaller the psychological distance between the manager and the employee, the greater the probability of a productive performance interview. Managers often inhibit employees by subtly indicating both verbally and nonverbally their superiority in position, wealth, power, intellectual ability, or even physical characteristics. Table 15-14 contains examples of verbal communication demonstrating superiority and equality.

Managers demonstrate superiority or equality with nonverbal as well as verbal communication patterns. Sitting behind a big desk, putting your feet on the desk, looking uninterested, and checking your phone are all signs of superiority. Showing superiority can only add to defensiveness and reduce two-way communication.

Certainty Versus Provisionalism

Managers who emphasize certainty often phrase what they say as if the decision cannot be changed. This dogmatic approach makes the employee feel that offering new ideas or a different solution is futile. Provisionalism demonstrates that a manager is willing to be challenged to arrive at the best possible solution. Provisionalism promotes enthusiasm and provides a challenge to employees, as the examples in Table 15-15 demonstrate.

These five elements of an effective communication strategy—description, problem orientation, empathy, equality, and provisionalism—are major factors in establishing a supportive climate, reducing defensiveness, and developing trust. Once trust has been developed, managers can provide effective feedback to employees.

Providing Performance Feedback

A recent survey of U.S. corporate managers showed that one third hesitate to dispense critical feedback because they are concerned about being seen as "mean or hurtful" or don't want to be disliked.[40] But employees will see performance feedback as constructive criticism rather than as negative criticism if managers keep in mind the following strategies:

1. *Identify concrete behavior.* Statements that identify specific, concrete behaviors are easier to accept than ambiguous, abstract statements.

2. *Avoid inferences.* Resist jumping to conclusions about motives, intents, and feelings unless you can cite specific behaviors to support these inferences.

3. *Focus feedback on a limited number of observable behaviors.* Employees can act on only a few feedback statements at a time. If one must deal with a large number of items, it is probably better to schedule several sessions.

4. *Time feedback to follow closely the behavior being discussed.* Immediate feedback almost always has more impact on the receiver than does delayed feedback.

5. *Give feedback to help the employees rather than to make you feel better.* Avoid giving feedback when feelings are not under control.

Managers who experience difficult situations may ask, "What about the employee who receives extensive negative feedback? How can I continue to administer it in a positive environment?" Once again, the manner in which the feedback message is structured is important. Another factor to consider is that no matter how much negative feedback the situation calls for, positive comments can usually also be used; however, the old "sandwich" approach is not recommended.

In the sandwich approach, a manager places a negative statement between two positive comments. However, most employees quickly recognize the manager's attempt to manipulate the situation; consequently, the strategy usually falls short of its intended purpose. A more effective procedure is to dispense supportive feedback almost exclusively at the beginning of the interview. This tactic helps establish an initial positive climate, and once the employee is aware that the manager duly appreciates past success, the employee becomes more receptive to a thorough analysis of those areas where a need for improvement exists.[41]

Goal setting is a valuable process when structuring feedback in a positive manner. The following discussion points out several implications that need to be considered when establishing goals that help build a positive climate.

Establishing Goals

Performance goals help keep the focus on the future. Managers clearly state objectives when they include the elements of *time*, *quality*, *quantity*, and *priority*. Consider the following example:

> During the next 60 days, you will set aside 20 minutes each day to meet with your crew and state what is expected in terms of their production and work schedules. You will counsel, on a daily basis, direct reports whose work schedules are not up to standard. If your turnover rate continues to be the same and you fail to counsel your employees, we will change your supervisory responsibilities.

Notice that this activity is clearly stated. The time period is stated; quality is stated in terms of production and work schedules; quantity is established in terms of turnover and the frequency of the meetings. These are presented as important priorities for the supervisor, because if the conditions are not met, the supervisor could be demoted.

To ensure that the objectives or action plans are clear, it is wise to write down the agreed-on activity. This allows both parties to review the statements and ensure that all the meanings are mutually clear. Action plans guide employees' future activities to achieve established goals. Clearly stated expectations can reduce risk exposure from litigation if personnel or responsibilities change because of unmet objectives.

A Change in Performance Interviews

While annual performance interviews are standard at many organizations, others are turning to more frequent coaching. In addition to the time involved, traditional reviews look backward. The information may come too late (and too seldom) to provoke real improvement in employee performance. Companies like Gap, Kelly Services, and GE have found that short-term projects, changing environments, rapid innovation, and teamwork require specific feedback for employees throughout the year, especially at project milestones, rather than year-end appraisals.[42]

Some companies use a mid-year "stay interview" to check in with employees about relationships and satisfaction. Susan Seip, a human resources manager for Geocent, a Louisiana technology company, explains that stay interviews ask, "What's your relationship to the company, the project team, and your manager, and what is within your purview to make those better?"[43] By focusing on employee experience as well as performance, stay interviews may reduce turnover.

Managers are responsible for overseeing the performance interview process. They are challenged with balancing the needs of the organization and the needs of their employees. Managers who approach performance interviews fairly and free of bias can achieve their objectives and limit their organizations' risk exposure. Managers can acquire valuable information to improve their techniques for delivery of performance interviews and other duties through networking channels.

NETWORKING

Our discussion of managerial interviewing strategies warrants attention to a third application: networking. Social and professional networking provides excellent resources for intellectual and career management, as pointed out in Chapter 14. Managers are very aware that knowledge is power and that shared knowledge fosters beneficial relationships. Networking involves time and energy commitment to maximize managers' potential rewards. A clear understanding of purpose, mode, and potential outcomes enhances networking efforts.

Purpose

The main purpose of networking is to build relationships through informational interviews. There are numerous payoffs. First, a strong network of professional relationships will enhance a manager's own career path. According to a study by Pepperdine University's Graziadio School of Business and Management, successful professionals with annual incomes in excess of $200,000 cite networking as a critical factor in career advancement.[44] As we saw in the previous chapter, networking skills can be very useful during salary and promotion negotiations. While promotion decisions are based on a number of factors, such as performance, image, and style, studies suggest that 60 percent of promotion decisions are based on networking activities within the organization.[45] But managers will fail at networking activities if their goals are exclusively self-centered.

A second payoff is that managers can help their companies by using their networks to identify potential customers and employees. If a referred applicant is trusted and well qualified, this can save the company crucial overhead dollars and time spent in the search process. In fact, a 2006 study found that up to half of U.S. jobs are found through families, friends, or acquaintances.[46] According to *Bloomberg BusinessWeek* contributor Stephen Baker, the increasing popularity of social and professional networking sites such as LinkedIn and Facebook is making networking easier than ever before.[47] An online network of friends is an important source for both recruiters and job seekers inside and outside of companies.

A third purpose of networking is altruistic. Managers can assist others by sharing their own expertise, referring expert contacts, or simply forwarding information on relevant events and articles. By helping others, a manager gains a reputation for generosity and becomes a contact worth keeping. These actions reinforce professional ties that may lead to reciprocity down the road.

In short, effective networking involves developing mutually beneficial, long-lasting, meaningful relationships. This rapport depends on trust.

How to Network

The number of networking associations and activities is endless. The most frequently used channels to exchange information for networking activities include electronic media, such as Facebook and LinkedIn, as well as face-to-face interactions. Networking occurs in formal and informal settings, and applying appropriate networking etiquette improves communication.

Managers can acquire valuable knowledge specific to their occupation, firm, and industry through a diverse group of professional contacts. Influential contacts within the company include mentors, colleagues, and other professionals. External network groups include professional associations, as well as specialized groups for people of color, women, and executives. Internet searches reveal numerous sites to acquire specific activities for individual groups. Social networking through university alumni, former supervisors, previous colleagues, and casual gatherings increases one's pool of resources. Successful networking requires planning, setting goals, and tracking results.

Basic steps for successful networking include these actions:

- Identify networking groups that foster mutually beneficial interaction.
- Join professional associations and attend local and national meetings.
- Volunteer as a speaker, committee member, and/or officer.
- Know and promote your strengths, not your title.
- Display an attitude of enthusiasm, confidence, and sincerity.
- Listen carefully to identify opportunities to contribute to others.
- Mingle and meet several new contacts at every event.
- Ensure that business cards are readily available.
- Follow up with former and new contacts.

Frequently, important relationships are created and maintained outside the work environment. It is important to recognize that every conversation and social activity creates networking opportunities and career advancement.[48] First impressions are permanently embedded, so appearance and demeanor are always important. The rules of body language are as critical here as in other interview settings. Networking groups have a set of acceptable standards and expectations of group members.

Networking etiquette is founded on the golden rule that members are expected to reciprocate. It is equally important to recognize that the group's purpose is to share information. These are other networking etiquette guidelines:

- Never ask for a job.
- Return calls and e-mails promptly.
- Always respond as promised.
- Recognize participants' time constraints.
- Treat all participants as equals.

- Be knowledgeable about current events.

- Be helpful and grateful.

- Maintain participants' confidentiality.

These and other factors create mutually beneficial relationships. Networking also calls for the participants to be open-minded, prepared, persistent, and patient. These characteristics combined with clear goals lead to successful outcomes.[49] Managers who build strong relationships with key people through effective interviews are on the road to success.

SUMMARY

This chapter presents general principles for conducting interviews and then applies them to special situations. The term *interview* includes many daily interactions that have a time limit and an identifiable purpose. The interview is an opportunity to gain and share information, but it is important to be aware of special communication barriers that make this difficult. First, the interviewer and interviewee might have different intentions. Second, personal bias results when people hear and see what they want to hear and see. The third barrier is confusing facts with inferences. Nonverbal communication, the fourth barrier, presents problems because the interview is generally a short, intensive communication interaction where one nonverbal behavior may result in faulty conclusions. The last two barriers are the powerful effects of first impressions and organizational status.

To help overcome these barriers, managers should consider seven strategies. A semi-structured format is recommended for most interviews. This means some of the questions should be established before the interview, but others will depend on how the interview develops. Either the funnel or inverted funnel sequence of questions may be used. Three categories of questions are reviewed when discussing the phrasing of questions—open/closed, primary/secondary, and neutral/directed. Each may be appropriate at the correct time. Seven types of probes also are presented. Strategic analysis is required to use the appropriate questions in different situations.

Finally, consideration is given to ending the interview. Both the manager and the interviewee must be clear on the main points and future action and close with goodwill.

All managers conduct employment and performance interviews during their careers; consequently, they need to be aware of several aspects of each of these interviews. The employment interview requires planning to ensure that the manager clearly understands the job opening. Legal concerns are unique during the employment interview, so it is necessary to be aware of the general guidelines for lawful questions.

An appropriate questioning strategy is important, and the manager can draw on a large number of potential questions to evaluate the applicant's motivation, education, experience, and fit. Each type of question has a specific purpose. The most common errors to avoid in the employment interview are talking too much rather than listening and keeping inadequate records.

Performance interviews are critical for a number of reasons; unfortunately, they are often avoided or are ineffective. The effectiveness can be increased by scheduling the interview at the appropriate time, conducting it in the correct place, and discussing relevant topics. Performance interviews should be fair, consistent, objective, and unbiased.

Strategic communication is essential when discussing performance; otherwise, defensive behavior may be aroused by critical feedback. Strategic communication allows the manager to develop a supportive environment that encourages a problem-solving approach. This communication should contain messages that are descriptive, problem-oriented, empathetic, equal, and provisional. These characteristics should be present when giving feedback and setting goals.

Networking is founded on informational interviews. The main purpose of networking is to share information through mutually beneficial relationships developed through social and professional network channels. Following basic steps and etiquette for networking improves successful outcomes that can accelerate career advancement and benefit the employer company.

CASES FOR ANALYSIS

Case 15-1

Ethel's Club Creates a Space for People of Color

The 2018 congressional election was lauded as a sign of change when 117 women were elected. Among them were Alexandria Ocasio-Cortez and Abby Finkenauer, the youngest women ever elected to Congress; Deb Haaland and Sharice Davids, the first Native American women elected to Congress; and Rashida Tlaib and Ilhan Omar, the first Muslim women elected to Congress. And for the first time, Black and Native American representation in the House of Representatives matched the U.S. general population (12 percent and 1 percent, respectively).[50]

The election was a remarkable achievement, in part because many of these women lacked role models to emulate. Professional networks of seasoned professionals offer roadmaps for career paths and offer advice to managers and other professionals when making crucial decisions. But a Catalyst report notes that professional networking is particularly difficult for women of color. Without mentors and sponsors to point out opportunities and advocate on their behalf, these women are often overlooked when high-visibility work assignments are made.[51] Without visibility, these women often find that their careers stagnate, they lose access to funding, and they miss out on innovative projects.

One recent project intended to create opportunities for networking is Ethel's Club, a co-working space and social and wellness club for people of color. Founder and CEO Naj Austin explained that she created the space to give people of color a safe space to connect:

There is both power and safety in shared, collective experience. People of color deserve a space where they can show up and not fear being excluded, considered, or discriminated against. The creative, professional, and social potential that comes with being able to bring your full self to the table is what we hope our members can access and achieve through a people-of-color-centered space.[52]

Questions

1. What are your own personal and professional networks?

2. How might you use those networks to advance your own projects or career?

3. How might you be a resource for others within those networks?

4. What kinds of professional networks exist in your industry or community?

5. What benefits might occur from connecting with people who are different from yourself?

Case 15-2

Conducting Interviews and Technology

Stacy Rollins was pensive as she waited for her interview with an investment banking firm. She felt well prepared because she had summarized all her critical information into her résumé, which had been reviewed by her business communication professor prior to sending it to the recruiter. She felt well qualified for the position and wanted to make a good impression. She had been through three other interviews for different positions and had developed the ability to respond to questions that all the recruiters seemed to have in common. Unlike the first three, however, this interview was going to be conducted as a teleconference. The recruiter placed the phone call, introduced herself, and added that she was placing Stacy on speakerphone, although she did not describe who else was in the room listening in.

The recruiter began the interview by saying, "Stacy, we have the résumé you e-mailed yesterday. It looks good. You are familiar with the job requirements, I suppose. We are seeking a candidate with superb analytical skills, demonstrated ability to work in team settings, and the ability to communicate and to manage communication effectively."

"Oh, yes!" Stacy replied. "I think I am a good match for your criteria."

The recruiter was silent for a moment. "So . . ." she said finally. A prolonged pause ensued. The recruiter said nothing further, though the phone line was apparently still open. Stacy was perplexed. She had not experienced this in other interviews. She did not know what to do.

Questions

1. Place yourself in Stacy's shoes; knowing what you do about interviews, what would you do at this point?

2. What could the recruiter's objective be for posing the non-question and then saying nothing further?

3. What advantages and disadvantages of conducting interviews by teleconference does this case demonstrate?

Case 15-3

Kern and the Quiet Nurse

Kay Kern is the director of the Corporate Safety Department for a large, multiplant manufacturing company in the Midwest. The company has six major manufacturing plants, and each has its own industrial nurses.

Twice a year, Kern has individual formal interviews with the nurses to find out if they have any major concerns or if Kern can help in any way. Because these nurses report to the personnel manager of each plant and not to Kern, this is not a performance review. Kern gets a lot of valuable information from the nurses through the interviews and seems to have developed a positive relationship with them. There is only one nurse, Joe James, who does not really open up to Kern and say much. On several occasions, Kern has tried to get information from James, but generally when Kern asks a question, all she gets is a one-word or superficial response. For instance, several months ago, all the plants instituted a new program for monitoring the number and types of visits to the nurses' offices. Kern asked James if everything was all right with the new program. James merely shrugged and said, "Yes."

This worries Kern because James is a young nurse with only 2 years of experience, and he probably has questions and could use some help. Kern has even asked some of the other employees in the plant if James was naturally quiet, but everyone said he was rather outgoing and easy to get to know. Kern is getting frustrated, because in her 25 years of experience, she has never had this much trouble getting someone to open up.

Questions

1. What are some possible incorrect interview strategies that Kern may be using?

2. What would you recommend to Kern?

(Continued)

(Continued)

Case 15-4

Motivation and the Performance Appraisal

Samuel Jones has worked diligently for his supervisor, Eric Donnell, during the past 3 years in the accounting department of a local bank. During that period, he has never been reprimanded for any of the work he has done. In fact, only recently, he received his first, supposedly annual, performance appraisal. Although he received a raise in each of the two prior years, this was the first time he was formally evaluated. The first year, he received a memo from Donnell stating the amount of his raise. The next year, Donnell did not even inform him of a raise. Rather, Jones had to figure it out for himself from his paycheck stub.

After sitting through his first formal evaluation, Jones is stunned. Donnell informed Jones that his work effort is just average and that he does not always show enough motivation in the tasks he undertakes. This is the most Donnell has said to Jones concerning his work since Jones began working there more than 3 years ago.

Donnell works on important matters alone in his office and shuts himself off from his employees' activities. Some of Jones's fellow workers see this as a sign the boss has faith in them to get the job done and to accept responsibilities on their own. But Jones believes Donnell is just avoiding responsibility and is not interested in involving himself with his employees. Jones believes his boss thinks, "I've got my own problems, so don't come to me with yours."

Jones has healthy working relationships with several other supervisors in the bank, and they all have told him more than once that his performance is above average. Because of this, Jones feels hurt that Donnell called him *average*. As far as motivation goes, Jones does not see what there is to be motivated about. He never receives rewards, verbal or otherwise, at times when he does good work. Consequently, he is confused about what levels of effort and performance will lead to the recognition he feels he deserves.

Questions

1. What should Donnell do differently if he wants Jones to increase his work effort?

2. List some elements of job performance that Donnell must make sure are present to get better performance from his employee.

3. What can Donnell do to get the most out of his performance evaluations?

4. What, if anything, can Jones do to increase the flow of feedback from his supervisor?

EXERCISE

Exercise 15-1

Create a list of behavioral questions you should ask when interviewing applicants for a faculty position at your university. The professor you hire would teach business communication.

Notes

1. Elisha Babad, Eyal Peer, and Yehonatan Benayoun, "Can Multiple Biases Occur in a Single Situation? Evidence From Media Bias Research," *Journal of Applied Social Psychology*

42, no. 6 (June 2012): 1486–504, doi: 10.1111/j.1559-1816.2012.00909.

2. Ben Kirshner, Kristen Pozzoboni, and Hannah Jones, "Learning How to Manage Bias: A Case Study of Youth Participatory Action Research," *Applied Developmental Science* 15, no. 3 (2011): 140–55, doi: 10.1080/10888691.2011.587720.

3. James P. Walsh, "Selectivity and Selective Perception: An Investigation of Managers' Belief Structures and Information Processing," *Academy of Management Journal* (December 1988), 873–96.

4. Mark L. Knapp and Mathew S. McGlone, *Lying + Deception in Human Interaction*, 2nd ed. (Dubuque, IA: Kendall Hunt, 2016).

5. Loren Falkenberg, "Improving the Accuracy of Stereotypes Within the Workplace," *Journal of Management* 16, no. 1 (March 1990): 107–18.

6. K. J. Williams et al., "Initial Decisions and Subsequent Performance Ratings," *Journal of Applied Psychology* 71, no. 2 (1986): 189–95.

7. M. Snyder and B. H. Campbell, "Testing Hypothesis About Other People: The Role of the Hypothesis," *Personality and Social Psychology Bulletin*, 1980, 421–26.

8. G. Dobrijevic, M. Stanisic, and B. Masic, "Sources of Negotiation Power: An Exploratory Study," *South African Journal of Business Management* 42, no. 2 (2011): 35–41.

9. Margaret Shepherd, *The Art of Civilized Conversation: A Guide to Expressing Yourself With Style and Grace* (New York: Broadway Books, 2007).

10. Jason Dana, "Against Job Interviews," *New York Times*, April 9, 2017, 6SR.

11. Thomas Diamante, *Effective Interviewing and Information Gathering: Proven Tactics to Improve Your Questioning Skills* (New York: Business Expert Press, 2013).

12. Julie Kantor, "High Turnover Costs Way More Than You Think," *Huffington Post*, February 11, 2017, http://www.huffingtonpost.com/julie-kantor/high-turnover-costs-way-more-than-you-think_b_9197238.html.

13. S. Highhouse, "Stubborn Reliance on Intuition and Subjectivity in Employee Selection," *Industrial and Organizational Psychology: Perspectives on Science and Practice* 1 (2008): 333–42.

14. Jason Dana, Robyn Dawes, and Nathanial Peterson, "Belief in the Unstructured Interview: The Persistence of an Illusion," *Judgment and Decision Making* 8, no. 5 (September 2013): 512–20.

15. CareerBuilder, Survey of 2,775 hiring managers and 5,518 job seekers conducted in the United States and Canada, July 2013, http://www.careerbuilder.com.

16. Adam Bryant, "Corner Office: Barry Salzberg," *New York Times,* May 22, 2011, 2.

17. U.S. Equal Employment Opportunity Commission, https://www.eeoc.gov/laws/types.

18. U.S. Equal Employment Opportunity Commission, "Pre-Employment Inquiries and Arrest & Conviction," https://www.eeoc.gov/pre-employment-inquiries-and-arrest-conviction.

19. Diamante, *Effective Interviewing and Information Gathering.*

20. Fredrick M. Jablin and Vernon D. Miller, "Interviewer and Applicant Questioning Behavior in Employment Interviews," *Management Communication Quarterly* 4, no. 1 (1990): 51–86.

21. Wendy Kaufman, "Job Interviews Get Creative," *All Things Considered,* National Public Radio, August 22, 2003, http://www.npr.org/display_pages/features/feature_1405340.html.

22. William Poundstone, *How Would You Move Mount Fuji? Microsoft's Cult of the Puzzle* (New York: Little, Brown and Company, 2003).

23. Diamante, *Effective Interviewing and Information Gathering*, 75–76.

24. Catherine H. Middendorf and Therese H. Macan, "Note-Taking in the Employment

Interview: Effects on Recall and Judgments," *Journal of Applied Psychology* 87, no. 2 (2002): 293–303.

25. Markus Langer, Cornelius J. König, and Kevin Krause, "Examining Digital Interviews for Personnel Selection: Applicant Reactions and Interviewer Ratings," *International Journal of Selection and Assessment 25* (2017): 371–82, doi: 10.1111/ijsa.12191.

26. Nikki Blacksmith, Jon C. Willford, and Tara Behrend, "Technology in the Employment Interview: A Meta-Analysis and Future Research Agenda," *Personnel Assessment and Decisions* 2, no. 1 (2016), doi: 10.25035/pad.2016.002.

27. Johannes M. Basch et al., "Smile for the Camera! The Role of Social Presence and Impression Management in Perceptions of Technology-Mediated Interviews," *Journal of Managerial Psychology* 35, no. 4 (2020): 285–99, https://doi.org/10.1108/JMP-09-2018-0398.

28. Hung-Yue Suen, Mavis Yi-Ching Chen, and Shih-Hao Lu, "Does the Use of Synchrony and Artificial Intelligence in Video Interviews Affect Interview Ratings and Applicant Attitudes?" *Computers in Human Behavior* 98 (September 2019): 93–101. https://doi.org/10.1016/j.chb.2019.04.012.

29. Muhammed Zahid Iqbal, Saeed Akbar, and Pawan Budhwar, "Effectiveness of Performance Appraisal: An Integrated Framework," *International Journal of Management Reviews* 17, no. 4 (2015): 510–33, doi: 10.1111/ijmr.12050.

30. Samuel A. Culbert, *Get Rid of the Performance Review! How Companies Can Stop Intimidating, Start Managing, and Focus on What Really Matters* (New York: Hachette Book Group, 2010).

31. R. M. Glen, "Performance Appraisal: An Unnerving yet Useful Process," *Public Personnel Management* 19, no. 1 (1990): 1–10.

32. Tanya du Plessis and Annelize van Niekerk, "Factors Influencing Managers' Attitudes Towards Performance Appraisal," *SA Journal of* *Human Resource Management* 15, no. 1 (2017): 1–10, doi: 10.4102/sajhrm.v15i0.880.

33. Iqbal et al., "Effectiveness of Performance Appraisal."

34. L. L. Cummings and C. P. Schwab, "Designing Appraisal Systems for Information Yield," *California Management Review* 20, no. 1 (1978): 18–25.

35. Muhammad Zahid Iqbal et al., "Effectiveness of Performance Appraisal: Evidence on the Utilization Criteria," *Journal of Business Research* 101 (August 2019): 285–99, https://doi.org/10.1016/j.jbusres.2019.04.035.

36. Paul Falcone, "Three Questions: Incorporate Self-Review Into Your Appraisal Process," *HR Weekly* 5, no. 17 (April 24, 2017): 7.

37. Elaine Farndale and Clare Kelliher, "Implementing Performance Appraisal: Exploring the Employee Experience," *Human Resource Management* 52, no. 6 (November/December 2013): 879–97.

38. Graham L. Bradley and Amanda C. Campbell, "Managing Difficult Workplace Conversations: Goals, Strategies, and Outcomes," *International Journal of Business Communication* 53, no. 4 (2016): 443–64.

39. Jack R. Gibb, "Defensive Communication," *Journal of Communication* (September 1961), 141–48.

40. Lean In and McKinsey & Company, *Women in the Workplace 2016*, https://www.calpers.ca.gov/docs/diversity-forum/2017/women-in-the-workplace-report-2016.pdf.

41. Douglas Cederblom, "The Performance Appraisal Interview: A Review, Implications, and Suggestions," in *Readings in Organizational Communication*, ed. Kevin L. Hutchinson (Dubuque, IA: Wm. C. Brown, 1992), 310–21.

42. Peter Cappelli and Anna Travis, "The Performance Management Revolution," *Harvard Business Review*, October 2016, https://hbr

.org/2016/10/the-performance-management-revolution.

43. Monster.com, "Using Stay Interviews to Improve Retention," https://hiring.monster.com/employer-resources/recruiting-strategies/interviewing-candidates/stay-interviews.

44. Paula Ketter, "Social Net What?" *T + D* 63, no. 2 (March 2009): 22.

45. "Need to Know Networking," *Personnel Today*, March 24, 2009, 19.

46. Linda D. Loury, "Some Contacts Are More Equal Than Others: Informal Networks, Job Tenure, and Wages," *Journal of Labor Economics* 24, no. 2 (April 2006): 299–318.

47. Stephen Baker, "What's a Friend Worth?" *Bloomberg BusinessWeek*, June 1, 2009, 32–36.

48. Judy Estrin, "Networking: It's the Way to Grow," *T+D* 62, no. 10 (October 2008): 100–101.

49. "Networking and Professional Etiquette," accessed June 1, 2009, http://www.career

.caltech.edu/resources/handouts/Networking%20Handouts.pdf.

50. Kristin Bailik, "For the Fifth Time in a Row, the New Congress Is the Most Racially and Ethnically Diverse Ever," Pew Research Center, February 8, 2019, https://www.pewresearch.org/fact-tank/2019/02/08/for-the-fifth-time-in-a-row-the-new-congress-is-the-most-racially-and-ethnically-diverse-ever.

51. Catalyst, "Connections That Count: The Informal Networks of Women of Color in the United States," 2006, https://www.catalyst.org/wp-content/uploads/2019/01/Connections_that_Count_The_Informal_Networks_of_Women_of_Color_in_the_United_States.pdf.

52. Amari D. Pollard, "Ethel's Club's Naj Austin on the Power of Wellness Spaces Made for People of Color," *MindBodyGreen*, February 3, 2020, https://www.mindbodygreen.com/articles/why-naj-austin-created-ethels-club-wellness-space-for-people-of-color.

INDEX

ABC Construction Company, 285–286
Accenture, 240
Accommodating strategy, 351–352
Accountemps, 342
Active listening, 269, 272, 274, 275 (table), 284, 407
  main/supporting points, 272
  message, organizing, 273
  message, summarize, 273
  personalizing message, 274
  taking notes, 274
  visualizing message, 273
  See also Interactive listening
Adelphia, 11
Adidas, 73
Administrative theory, 5–7
Adobe Connect, 63, 100
Age, 334
  affecting communication contingencies, 15
  body language of digital, 292
  diversity, 15
  retirement (United States), 15
  social media, use of, 63
Alexander the Great, 5
Alignment, 145, 168
Alley, Michael, 128
Allness error, 42–43, 44, 244
Amazon Echo, 70
American Management Association, 19, 82
American Psychological
  Association (APA), 246
American Psychological Association (APA) style, 246
Americans with Disabilities Act of 1990, 403
Amplification, 21
Analogous color schemes, 149
Anheuser-Busch, 316
Apollo 11 spacecraft, 48
Apple Keynote, 127
Applications, nonverbal communication
  external communication, 305
  informal communication, 304

phone sales and service, 303
  teams and meetings, 303–304
Aristotle, 29, 56, 123
The Art of Civilized Conversation (Shepherd), 397
Arthur Andersen, 17
Artificial intelligence, 69, 73
Assertion–evidence (AE) design, 128
"Associates Out in Front" program, 270
Association for Conflict Resolution (ACR), 343
Assumption–observation error, 40–41, 43–44, 394
Audience adaptation
  anticipating questions, 211
  attitude, basis of, 211
  avoiding negatives, 212
  diction, 212
  nonverbal elements and
    attitude, 212–213
  stressing reader benefits, 211
Audience Analysis Worksheet, 138
Audiences, 33, 113–115, 120, 124–125,
  148, 150–153, 159, 228
  analysis, 116, 120–121, 251
  attention of business, strategies, 117
  data displays, 154, 174
  screen-reader software, 168
  using social media, 63–64
  visual learners, 122
Austen, J. L., 9
Austin, Naj, 420
Australia
  collectivism, 322
  culturally diverse workforces, 318
  dress, 328
  plain-language, 184
Austria
  masculinity, 323
  power distances, 321
Authority, 90, 104, 125, 180, 241, 346, 375
Autocratic approach, 7, 11, 351
Avoidance strategy, 350